Endorsements for *Private Ryan an...*

Thomas Keneally, eminent Australian novelist and historian, author of *...Eureka to the Diggers* (2011)

> "An arresting story about an Australian boy who believed that just because he became a Digger, it did not mean he gave up the high office of being a free citizen. I hope the spirit and ethos of Private Ryan still resonates in modern Australia, for no one believed in the dignity of the individual more passionately than he."

Joan Beaumont, Professor Emerita, Australian National University, author of *Broken Nation: Australians in the Great War* (2013)

> "Two interwoven and shocking narratives of World War I — one explores the acquisitive war aims of the Allied Powers that made peace impossible; the other, the soldier from Broken Hill who, realising this, chose to protest and even to endure prison rather than fight."

Frank Bongiorno, Professor of History, The Australian National University, author of *The Eighties* (2015)

> "In this remarkable history, Douglas Newton reveals that one Australian working-class soldier's rebellion against the First World War was joined to the revolt of millions across the world against the slaughter and in favour of peace. Private Ryan's fascinating story is a reminder that the 'big' politics of strategy, diplomacy and treaties makes little sense if we lose sight of the ordinary people whose lives are the currency in the amoral haggling of their rulers. A profoundly moving and timely reflection on one war and all war."

Paul Daley, historian and journalist at *The Guardian*, author of *Beersheba* (2017)

> "A compelling counterfactual to the Anzac narrative of Australia and the Great War that narrates the courageous dissent of Private Ted Ryan against the war machine in which he was a cog, upon a stage of opaque international diplomacy that unnecessarily prolonged the industrialised slaughter."

Justin Fleming, eminent Australian playwright and librettist

"I found this a most compelling narrative, exquisitely written – an account everyone should read of a courageous, passionate, defiant lad from Broken Hill, who takes on the very top of the wartime establishment when its brutal suppression of peace initiatives drives him to a breathtaking act of rebellion."

Michael McKernan, Australian historian, author of *When This Thing Happened* (2015)

"Beautifully written by an eminent Australian historian, this comprehensive account of one man's desire for peace and an end to war will resonate with readers seeking an insight into the minds of Australia's soldiers. Court-martialled four times, once sentenced to death, Ted Ryan, from Broken Hill, showed great courage in holding to his beliefs. Douglas Newton asks what is courage in war?"

Ross McMullin, Australian historian, author of *Farewell, Dear People* (2012)

"Prodigiously researched, written with verve and fervour, this is an illuminating and compelling successor to his brilliant *Hell-bent: Australia's Leap into the Great War* (2014)."

Henry Reynolds, Honorary Research Professor at the University of Tasmania, author of *Unnecessary Wars* (2016)

"*Private Ryan and the Lost Peace* is an engaging and challenging addition to Australian literature about the First World War. Newton skilfully weaves together the story of Ted Ryan's war and the great forces that determined the course of the conflict. But above all this is a book which challenges what he calls the 'fixed gaze that has been offered to the Australian people' during the recent carnival of commemoration. It is essential reading for anyone wishing to broaden their understanding of the great catastrophe with 'the nationalist blinkers' removed."

Peter Stanley, Research Professor, University of New South Wales Canberra, author of *Bad Characters: Sex, Crime, Mutiny, Murder and the AIF* (2010)

"Douglas Newton offers a vigorous and vivid corrective to the nationalist boasting of the Anzac legend – but also an inspiring story of a hitherto unknown Australian soldier of the Great War who bravely stood up against the mindless militarism which condemned him and millions like him to a hellish war. This is an Anzac story of a different kind, one that needs to be told and known."

PRIVATE RYAN AND THE LOST PEACE

A Defiant Soldier and the Struggle Against the Great War

Douglas Newton

LONGUEVILLE
MEDIA

LONGUEVILLE
MEDIA

First published 2021 for Douglas Joseph Newton
by
Longueville Media Pty Ltd
PO Box 205 Haberfield
NSW 2045 Australia
www.longmedia.com.au
info@longmedia.com.au

Copyright © 2021 Douglas Joseph Newton

Except as permitted under the *Copyright Act 1968* (Cth) Australia, no part of this publication may be reproduced, stored in a retrieval system, or transmitted in any form or by any means without prior written permission of the copyright owner, Douglas Joseph Newton.

ISBN Print: 978-0-6489736-3-8
ISBN eBook: 978-0-6451742-0-5
ISBN POD: 978-0-6451742-2-9

 A catalogue record for this book is available from the National Library of Australia

In memory of Beth Sutton (née Ryan), 1927-2019,
daughter of Private Edward James Ryan,
who kept her father's faith

And for the children of the rising generation,
Keira Grace Newton and James Theodore Newton

I met a wounded Australian soldier, and as we talked he gave me some of his experiences... Of the horrors he had been through, what was most deeply fixed in his mind was that several times in the advance he had slipped while up to his shoulders in liquid mud, and been for a time below the surface and drowning. ... In these soldiers all the civilian passions of national pride and hatred of the enemy are gone. If there is bitterness, it has another target. As my simple Australian said to me, 'I wish the Kaiser and King George could be stuck in the trenches.'[1]

— Charles Trevelyan MP, December 1917

Private Edward James Ryan, full-length portrait, probably Egypt, 1916 – cropped, but originally endorsed 'best wishes, Ted' (courtesy of the late Beth Sutton).

CONTENTS

Acknowledgements — ix
List of Illustrations — xiv
Introduction — xvii

1 Private Ryan's Defiance – Perham Down, October 1916 — 1
2 Brothers In Arms – Rosebery Park and Perth, 1914 and 1915 — 9
3 Solidarity – Broken Hill, 1900 to 1914 — 19
4 Choosing War – London, Melbourne, Broken Hill, Perth, 1914-1915 — 33
5 'Wider Still and Wider' – Cairo and London, March 1915 — 45
6 Gallipoli – Cairo, Anzac Cove, London, April 1915 — 55
7 Bayonet Sticking – Subiaco to Blackboy Hill, September 1915 to February 1916 — 65
8 Sailing – Fremantle to Suez, February to March 1916 — 73
9 Sandbox – Heliopolis to Habieta, March to May 1916 — 87
10 To the Shambles – Marseille, Paris, Fleurbaix, June 1916 — 99
11 Carnage – Fleurbaix to Étaples, June to August 1916 — 105
12 Shell Shock – 4th London General Hospital, Camberwell, August 1916 — 119
13 Broken Dolls – Byfleet, Edinburgh, London, September 1916 — 125
14 Rage – Perham Down to Westminster, October 1916 — 137
15 A Winter Peace – Perham Down, December 1916-January 1917 — 151
16 Escapade – Perham Down to Arbroath, January-April 1917 — 165
17 Resistance – Perham Down, May-June 1917 — 179
18 Freedom – Ypres to Le Havre, July-August 1917 — 187
19 Defiance – and Death Sentence – Château de Bomy, September 1917 — 199
20 Confinement – Caëstre, September to December 1917 — 219
21 Darkness – Dunkirk and Calais, December 1917 to August 1918 — 225

22 Sentence Suspended – Calais to Amiens, August 1918	237
23 On Strike – Rivery to Bovelles, September-October 1918	249
24 Field Punishment – Flixecourt, October to November 1918	257
25 Return – From Belgium to Broken Hill, 1919	263
26 After the Deluge – From Broken Hill to Wahroonga, 1919 to 1943	275
27 A Vindication	281

Appendices	295
1 Private E.J. Ryan's letter to Ramsay MacDonald MP, 18 October 1916	297
2 Private E.J. Ryan's statement to his court martial, 12 September 1917	300
3 Private Edward James RYAN, 4635, Service Summary	301
4 War Aims and Secret Treaties of Britain and the Entente Powers, 1914-1918	304
5 Lost Opportunities for a Negotiated Peace, 1914-1918	306
6 The Straits and Persia Agreement of March 1915	308
7 Lewis Harcourt's Cabinet document, 'The Spoils', 25 March 1915	311
8 The Secret Treaty of London, 26 April 1915	314
9 Lord Lansdowne's secret Memorandum to the Cabinet, 13 November 1916	323
10 Lord Lansdowne's letter to the *Daily Telegraph* [London], 29 November 1917	327

Abbreviations	330
Notes	331
Index	367

THE AUTHOR

Douglas Newton was Associate Professor of History at Western Sydney University, and has also taught history at Macquarie University and the Victoria University of Wellington. He is the author of: *The Darkest Days* (Verso); *Hell-Bent* (SCRIBE); *British Policy and the Weimar Republic 1918–19* (OUP); *Germany 1918-1945: From Days of Hope to Years of Horror* (Pearson); and *British Labour, European Socialism and the Struggle for Peace 1889–1914* (OUP). He lives in Australia.

Hell-bent: 'an instant classic of Australian historical literature.' – Professor Henry Reynolds

The Darkest Days: 'compellingly written, tightly argued, deeply researched and bracingly revisionist.' – Professor Sir Christopher Clark, Regius Professor of History, The University of Cambridge.

ACKNOWLEDGEMENTS

This book came about by a happy accident. For many years I have been teaching and researching aspects of the First World War, with a special interest in the political and diplomatic history rather than the military history of that conflict. My project over the last decade has been to write a history of the peace movement in Britain during that war. My research in this field led to an invitation to work on the private papers of Arthur Ponsonby, a British parliamentarian who was an especially tenacious peace activist during the First World War. Ponsonby's papers are still in the care of his grand-daughter Kate Russell and her husband Ian at the family home, the beautiful and historic Shulbrede Priory, near Haslemere, in Surrey. There my generous hosts, the Russells, suggested I get in touch with another enthusiastic researcher whom they had also welcomed to Shulbrede, Duncan Marlor, from Derbyshire.

I exchanged emails with Duncan in 2014. It was in sharing our research that a discovery emerged. In Duncan's draft history of parliamentary resistance to war and conscription, under the alluring sub-heading 'No Saving Private Ryan', I first read of a wonderful letter from an Australian soldier dating from October 1916, a letter urging a compromise diplomatic settlement to end the war. Duncan had found it in the files of the leading British Labour personality Ramsay MacDonald at The National Archives in Kew, London. I had worked on those same MacDonald papers some years before, but somehow I had missed this letter in his 'General Correspondence' file for 1916. Duncan kindly volunteered to send me a typescript copy of the complete letter. Here were the defiant words of one humble soldier, Private Edward James Ryan of the Australian Imperial Force, condemning the mechanised killing on the Western Front as akin to that of an 'abattoir'. The letter proved to be not only a fiery denunciation of the slaughter that Ryan had witnessed in France in the summer of 1916, but also an eloquent plea to the men in the parliaments and cabinet rooms to put aside their pride and mount a determined effort to end the war by diplomatic means, using the United States as a neutral mediator.

This letter sparked my imagination. Who was this soldier with principled objections to the war? And what became of him? Here was a chance to get beyond the politicians, the diplomats, the generals, the press barons, the journalists, and the civilian activists shouting their slogans for and against war, and to explore instead the insights of a common soldier with a commitment to an early peace. Fortunately, all the service records of Australian soldiers from the First World War have been preserved and recently digitized, so that I was soon able to discover a good deal about Private Edward

James Ryan's service, and his childhood home – Broken Hill. His next of kin was also listed, his uncle, a 'James Ramsay Mudie', and an address in Broken Hill.

Might there be descendants? The historic mining city, deep in western New South Wales, is not large, and the name Mudie is not so very common. Soon the telephone directory for Broken Hill helped me locate a handful of the surviving members of the Mudie family. Two phone calls later I was speaking on the phone with a keen and very helpful man, Don Mudie, a grandson of Ryan's uncle still living in that city. He knew well that his grandfather James and grandmother Margaret Mudie had generously agreed to take in a young Eddy (or Ted) Ryan, and his two brothers Tom and Harry, about 1900, after the death of their mother and the disappearance of their father. It was Don who alerted me to the fact that Private Edward James Ryan's daughter Elizabeth (Beth) Sutton (née Ryan), born in 1927, was still alive and had visited Broken Hill as a tourist a decade before. By pure chance, Don and Beth's linkages had emerged in a conversation at the GeoCentre, the city's minerals and mining museum, where Don served as a volunteer. Don had a contact number for Beth. She was living in Newcastle, New South Wales, not far from my home in Sydney. I was quickly in touch with her, and we met in Newcastle. She was vivid in her recollections of the past, absolutely loyal to her father's rebellious stand for peace during the Great War, and keen to help put his story together, in context.

Thus, in the thoughtfulness of Kate and Ian Russell of Shulbrede Priory, in the generosity of Duncan Marlor who so willingly shared his research, in Don Mudie's knowledge of his family's history in the city of Broken Hill, and in the memories of Beth Sutton are to be found the origins of this book.

I am indebted to many. Most importantly, I want to acknowledge the late Beth Sutton. Sadly, she passed away in February 2019, but she did see the bulk of this book in typescript. She welcomed my wife Julie and me into her home in Maryville, Newcastle, just north of Sydney, in 2016 and 2017, and she paid us return visits to Sydney. Beth entertained us with many tales, and shared with us her father's very few surviving papers and precious photographs. Beth helped resolve certain mysteries concerning our Private Ryan. Her much loved father and mother, Ted and Marie, her uncles Tom and Harry, and their children, who were part of Beth's childhood from the 1930s to the 1970s, lived in her memory, and she met them in her dreams. She brought them alive for us. She inspired me to create the book, in the hope that more Australians could learn from her father's experience. This book is dedicated to her memory.

A number of generous people have helped me in different ways. Beth Sutton's children, Avril and David, have encouraged and assisted me in crucial ways, kindly putting me in touch with their late mother. When Julie and I visited Broken Hill, Don Mudie of Broken Hill was a reliable guide to the Silver City. He knew a great deal about the world of the Ryan brothers from the 1890s to 1914 through his knowledge of James Ramsay Mudie and Margaret Nicholas Mudie, his grandparents, and their children –

his aunts and uncles. Don kindly read the entire manuscript and offered many crucial corrections. Other friends from Broken Hill, the late Maxine Matthews, Doug Jones, Jenny Camilleri, the staff of the *Barrier Daily Truth*, and Paul and Valerie Mudie of Adelaide were enthusiastic about the story of Private Ryan and helped me piece together various aspects of this tale. I thank Paul Mudie for permission to reproduce some family photographs.

As always, I have profited from the suggestions of my family, my late mother Pamela, Ethel Mulder, Michael Newton, Mary Ann and Bill Anastasiadis, Robert Newton, Richard Newton, and Pamela Newton. My brother Robert also read an early version of the manuscript and offered perceptive advice and encouragement.

Beyond family, I want to record my very special thanks to my friend and colleague Duncan Marlor. His own research into the peace movement in Britain makes him an adviser without peer. He provided the crucial discovery from the National Archives in Britain that was the spark for this project: the remarkable letter from Private Edward James Ryan to Ramsay MacDonald written in October 1916.

I thank Gregory Bateman who kindly read my manuscript and offered both advice and constructive criticism. I adopted a number of his helpful suggestions. At his insistence, my acknowledgement and thanks are limited to just these words.

Greg Lockhart, a former Australian military officer and historian, also read every page of various early drafts. He offered invaluable advice on the very best structure to adopt in order to blend narrative and context. He also provided insights into the military side of the story that only a man of his military experience could offer. My warm thanks goes to Greg.

Various other scholars, teachers, and friends have provided assistance and ideas in discussion along the way. Among those scholars who have introduced me to peace studies and continued to encourage me to pursue work in this field I must mention Nicholas Jacobs, Joy Melhuish, Kenneth O. Morgan, Tom Reifer, Andreas Rose, and the late Keith Wilson. Most especially, I thank my friend from Macquarie University, Rod Miller, who read and responded to the manuscript more than once. I should acknowledge my debt to Paul Robert Adams and his path-breaking work on the labour movement in Broken Hill. Similarly, I have profited also from the research of Kevin Fewster on wartime censorship, and the brilliant statistical analyses of Edward Garstang and Richard Glenister on crime and discipline in the AIF.

I am grateful also for support along the way from Michael Barnes, Brian Brennan, Peter Butt, Fran Byrnes, Beverly Firth, Gerhard Fischer, Judy and Ian Higson, Justin Fleming, Peter Lowry, Daryl Le Cornu, Adrienne McClymont, Megan and Bill McDonald, Colin Milner, Carmen Miller, Andrew Moore, Melanie Oppenheimer, Paul O'Sullivan, Ros Pesman, Suzanne Rickard, Alan Roberts, Helen Roberts, Geoff Sherington, Youssef Taouk, and Sue Wareham.

I must single out Claire Greer from Perth, who was extremely generous in sharing her research on the period Edward and Thomas Ryan spent in Perth in 1914 and 1915 before enlisting. I must also offer warm thanks to Peter Henderson for his expertise and advice on the photographs produced for this book. Thank you all.

At a late stage in my writing, Peter Cochrane generously read the whole manuscript. He provided a dozen essential insights, and much-needed encouragement for me to move forward toward publication. Thanks so much, Peter.

I am also very grateful to my friend Reingard Porges for enabling me to bring various German perspectives to this study, widening its focus. Reingard, an historical expert in her own right on dissident Germans in this period, provided superb English translations of a series of landmark German studies of peace diplomacy and war aims during the First World War.

The assistance of the staff of the Mitchell Library in Sydney, the Australian War Memorial, and the National Archives of Australia, has been at every stage indispensable. I want to thank especially Elise Edmonds and her staff and volunteers at the Mitchell Library for their work on the library's splendid collection of World War 1 diaries and letters. I am grateful also to Emma White and Jennifer Selby in the Sound Section at the Australian War Memorial for providing transcripts of veterans' interviews. The digital search tools created and maintained by the many archivists and librarians at these institutions, especially the tools 'Trove' for historic newspapers and 'Historic Hansard' for parliament, have greatly facilitated my research.

I must acknowledge the assistance of the following in granting me permission to quote from interviews with veterans of the First World War held at the Australian War Memorial: Emma White for extracts from recorded interviews with Harry Percival Sennett, Alfred George Hayden, Bill Richardson, and Eric Kingsley Abraham; Paul Cobb for extracts from his interview with Arthur Cyril Ebdon; and Alistair Thomson for extracts from his interviews with Ernest Morton, Jack Flannery, and Albert Charles Linton. I profited immensely from Peter Rubinstein's hard work in assembling so many recorded interviews with Australian veterans of the war; I thank Peter warmly for permission to quote extracts from his interviews with Jesse Palmer, Frederick John Kelly, Harold Lionel Angel, Thomas Lawrence Talty, Jack Lockett, and Charlie Mance.

I would like to thank Kus Pandey for extending the permission of the Australians at War Film Archive at the University of New South Wales to quote from recorded interviews with Eric Abraham, Marcel Caux, Jack Lockett, and Ted Smout.

I would like to acknowledge the Mitchell Library, State Library of New South Wales, for permission to quote from these diaries and letters in the World War I collections over which the library holds copyright: Sydney James Dacres Stutley, Thomas H. Alcock, George B. King, Walter Edward Gillett, Norman Gilroy, Benjamin Alfred Cohen, Archie Barwick, Geoffrey Bell Hughes, Frank H. Molony, Richard Blundell, Charles Rosenthal, Edward Luders, Aubrey Roy Liddon Wiltshire, H.E. Gissing, Clifford Mervyn Geddes,

Robert Saunderson Hamilton, Thomas Alexander White, and W.J.A. Allsop. I thank the family of Ramsay MacDonald for permission to reproduce Ted Ryan's letter to Ramsay MacDonald from October 1916 held at The National Archives, Kew.

I have been unable to find individual copyright holders for the following collections at the Mitchell Library: Jabez Leonard Lawry Waterhouse, Eric Dark, and Sir David Gilbert Ferguson. Extracts from these collections are quoted by courtesy of the Mitchell Library.

I thank Kate Eckersley at the State Library of Western Australia for her assistance with copyright. Extracts from interviews with George Baron Hay and William James Purvis are sourced from the collections of the State Library of Western Australia and reproduced with the permission of the Library Board of Western Australia.

I thank Graeme and Trish Sawyer for permission to reproduce short extracts from the letters of their relative, the soldier John George Tarrant, in their keeping.

I extend my warmest thanks to David Longfield and his staff at Longueville Media for their advice and never-failing professionalism in seeing this book through to production. I thank especially Philippa Findlay, whose keen eye and sharp mind at the editing stage was of very great assistance.

Finally, Julie Anne Newton, David Keir Newton, Juliette Kim Warren, Keira Grace Newton and James Theodore Newton, have provided the stimulus I needed to go on researching and writing about all those who share with me both a passion for peace and a detestation of war.

Douglas Newton

LIST OF ILLUSTRATIONS

Page	Item
v	Private Edward James Ryan, full-length portrait, probably Egypt, 1916 – cropped, but originally endorsed 'best wishes, Ted' (courtesy of the late Beth Sutton).
xx	Private Edward James Ryan, Service Number 4635, close-up portrait, 51st Battalion, AIF, probably Egypt, 1916 – endorsed 'Your loving nephew, Ted' (courtesy of Paul Mudie)
4	Ramsay MacDonald (Library of Congress, LC-DIG-ggbain-37952)
5	David Lloyd George (Library of Congress, LC-USZ62-8054)
7	William Morris Hughes (National Archives of Australia, NAA: A1200, L11181B)
10	Alderman Edward James Ryan, Alderman on the Broken Hill District Municipal Council, 1888-1891 (courtesy of Don Mudie).
11	Margaret Nicholas Couch (L) and Elizabeth Martin Couch (R), the mother of the future Private Edward James Ryan, probably taken in Moonta Mines, South Australia, in the mid-1880s (courtesy of Don Mudie).
16	Private Henry ('Harry') Martin Ryan, (who falsely enlisted as 'Edward James Ryan', Service Number 672), probably Egypt, 1915 (courtesy of the late Beth Sutton).
18	The three Ryan brothers, (L to R) Harry, Eddy (Ted), Tom, Broken Hill c. 1901-02 (courtesy of the late Beth Sutton).
20	James Ramsay Mudie and Margaret Nicholas Mudie, with their first two children, Beatrice and Ruby, c. 1896 (courtesy of Paul Mudie)
21	Eddy Ryan and the Mudie children, probably taken in Broken Hill, c. 1906. Back row: Edward James 'Eddy' Ryan, Beatrice Mudie, Alma Mudie, Ruby Mudie. Front row: Jim Mudie, Charlie Mudie, Elizabeth 'Betty' Mudie (courtesy of Paul Mudie).
28	Keir Hardie (National Portrait Gallery, London, NPG x13172)
30	Herbert Henry Asquith (National Portrait Gallery, London, NPG x12638)
38	Andrew Fisher (L) with Keir Hardie, 14 December 1907
43	Leon Trotsky (Library of Congress, LC-DIG-ggbain-28899)
44.	Amalgamated Miners' Association Band on a visit to Sydney, 1913
48	Lord Hardinge (Library of Congress, LC-DIG-ggbain-07439)
50	Count Alexander Benckendorff (Library of Congress, LC-DIG-ggbain-19063)
51	Sergei Sazonov (Nikolaï Aleksandrovich Bazili papers, Box 30, Folder G, Hoover Institution Library & Archives)

53	Lewis Harcourt (National Portrait Gallery, London, NPG x168115)
58	Pope Benedict XV (Library of Congress, LC-DIG-ggbain-17666)
62	Andrew Bonar Law (Library of Congress, LC-DIG-ggbain-35667)
71	Lord Northcliffe (Library of Congress, LC-DIG-ggbain-19626)
76	Jane Addams (Library of Congress, LC-USZ62-13484)
77	American delegates depart from New York for the International Congress of Women at The Hague, April 1915 (Library of Congress, LC-DIG-ggbain-18848)
77	The US delegation at the International Congress of Women at The Hague, April 1915, showing Jane Addams, 2nd from the left in the front row (scpcPhoto55, Women's International League for Peace and Freedom, Records, Swarthmore College Peace Collection)
78	The International Congress of Women in session in a large hall, the Dierentuin, in the Zoological Gardens at The Hague, April 1915 (scpcPhoto57, Women's International League for Peace and Freedom, Records, Swarthmore College Peace Collection)
79	Albert Einstein (Library of Congress, LC-DIG-hec-31012)
80	Charles Trevelyan (Library of Congress, LC-DIG- ggbain-37098); Arthur Ponsonby (National Portrait Gallery, London, NPG x198588)
81	Delegates of the unofficial Neutral Conference for Continuous Mediation, Stockholm, February 1916 (Library of Congress, LC-DIG-ggbain-21257)
84	Colonel House (Library of Congress LC-DIG-ggbain-20684) and Woodrow Wilson, 1912 (Library of Congress LC-USZ62-13028)
85	Arthur Balfour (Library of Congress, LC-DIG-ggbain-19445)
97	Private Edward James Ryan, full-length portrait, probably Egypt, 1916 – cropped, but originally endorsed 'best wishes, Ted' (courtesy of the late Beth Sutton).
104	Sir Edward Grey (Library of Congress, LC-DIG-ggbain-29474)
108	Emily Hobhouse (National Portrait Gallery, London, NPG x15582)
109	Gottlieb von Jagow (Library of Congress, LC-DIG-ggbain-21135)
110	German Chancellor, Theobald von Bethmann Hollweg (Library of Congress, LC-DIG-hec-04728)
115	General Sir Douglas Haig (Library of Congress, LC-DIG-ggbain-07439)
117	Margaret Mudie and James Ramsay Mudie, Broken Hill, c. 1916 (courtesy of Don Mudie).
132	Michael Considine (National Library of Australia, NLA.obj-136740440)
133	Percy Brookfield (portrait by C. H. Conlon, State Library of Victoria, H29011)
134	The postcard entitled 'Australians Parading for the Trenches', sold as *Daily Mail* War Picture, No. 40. This was the photograph featured in the *Daily Mail* and criticised by Private Edward Ryan. The caption on the reverse side read: 'These are the men who shortly after midnight of Sunday, July 23, 1916, took Pozières by a splendidly dashing advance through shrapnel, shell, and machine-gun fire.

135	The original photograph on which the *Daily Mail* War Picture, No. 40, was based. In fact, the men photographed had not yet faced action in France and had only just received their steel helmets. The original caption at the Australian War Memorial reads: 'Outdoors group portrait of a battalion of the 6th Brigade that was newly arrived in Flanders from Egypt. The men are balancing their newly issued steel helmets on the ends of their rifles.' (Australian War Memorial photograph, AWM EZ0003).
139	The first page of Ted Ryan's letter to Ramsay MacDonald, 18 October 1916 (The National Archives, Kew, TNA: PRO/30/69/1160 f. 108, reproduced with the permission of the MacDonald family).
148	Lord Lansdowne (National Portrait Gallery, London, NPG x24072)
155	The scene in the Reichstag on 12 December 1916 as Chancellor Bethmann Hollweg announces the sending of the German Peace Note (Library of Congress, LC-DIG-ggbain-23314)
156	Sidney Sonnino (Library of Congress, LC-DIG-ggbain-28372)
158	Lord Milner (Library of Congress, LC-DIG-ggbain-31907)
169	Aristide Briand (Library of Congress, LC-DIG-ggbain-19305)
171	Tsar Nicholas II of Russia (Library of Congress, LC-DIG-hec-04921)
190	Matthias Erzberger (Deutsches Historisches Museum, Inv.-Nr. Pk 96/185)
198	The Château de Bomy, scene of Private Ryan's first Field General Court Martial, 12 September 1917, at which he was sentenced to death (Wikimedia Commons).
202	The first page of Ted Ryan's statement to his court martial, 12 September 1917
216	Richard von Kühlmann (Library of Congress, LC-USZ62-85667)
217	Alexander Ribot (Library of Congress, LC-DIG-ggbain-18205)
232	Emperor Karl of Austria (Library of Congress, LC-DIG-ggbain-16767)
247	The Château de Bovelles, scene of Private Ryan's second Field General Court Martial, 15 October 1918 (Wikimedia Commons)
267	Lloyd George, Vittorio Orlando, Georges Clemenceau, and Woodrow Wilson, Paris, 1919 (Library of Congress, LC-DIG-ggbain-29038)
271	Georges Clemenceau, Woodrow Wilson, and David Lloyd George, leave the palace of Versailles after the signing of the treaty, 28 June 1919 (Library of Congress, LC-DIG-stereo-1s04279)
285	Lord Curzon (Library of Congress, LC-DIG-ggbain-35223)

INTRODUCTION

I enlisted to fight for a Peace without conquerors or conquered, as a Peace under those conditions [does] nothing to justify another war.

— Private Edward James Ryan to his court martial,
12 September 1917

The First World War was a vultures' frenzy. All those nations that fought over the spreading carcass of spoils were degraded by it. All preached high ideals, but all plotted for conquest. All thwarted promising opportunities to end the war by any means short of the military triumph that they all claimed was indispensable and achievable. And so the long war remains a great scar upon our civilisation – a catastrophe unredeemed by victory.

But one feature of the story can uplift our hearts – the persistence of dissent. Across the world, even among those soldiers caught up in the clanking kill-chain of mechanised warfare, there were men and women of principle who were so revolted by what they saw that they passionately denounced the war, even while tethered to the war machine. And many pointed to the alternative: a peace negotiated by diplomatic means.

This is the story of one such man – a very rebellious Australian soldier, Private Edward James Ryan, who was always known to his family and friends as 'Ted'. In condemning the ongoing war, Ted Ryan claimed to speak for many fellow soldiers, and undoubtedly he did. In the aftermath of the bloody battles of 1916, he was convinced he must take some action to oppose the war. He had come to the view that the war was wrong, that it was being unnecessarily prolonged, and that he must stand up against it. He had developed his own principled political objections to the machine-made mass murder he had witnessed in France. He wrote them down and despatched them in a letter to a leading anti-war figure in the British Parliament at Westminster. In this letter, Ted Ryan argued that the war he was fighting in was no longer the war for which he had enlisted. He had volunteered to fight for right, to defend the innocent, to wage war in order to help the people of Belgium and France to drive out the German invader. But the conflict had exploded far beyond these initial aims; it had grown into a gigantic imperial struggle. It was no longer a just war of self-defence on the part of the 'Entente Powers' as they were known, Britain and her principal allies – France, Russia, and Italy. The war machines of all the nations were grinding on and on, Ryan loudly complained, because the war-makers were secretly escalating war aims, and recklessly – and again secretly – snuffing out the chances of ending the war by diplomatic negotiations. This was the 'secret war' that infuriated him. He decided to defy it.

The defiant Anzac soldier whose story is told here, Private Ted Ryan, before the war was a mineworker and trade unionist from Broken Hill, and then a soldier of the 51st Battalion of the Australian Imperial Force (AIF). For various acts of defiance, he would eventually face trial before four courts martial, where he was twice accused of being absent without leave and twice accused of a much more serious crime – desertion. Found guilty by every court martial, he would eventually spend more than a year in various detention barracks and prisons.

From Peephole to Panorama

But this book is about more than one soldier's experience. To understand the sprawling tragedy of this war, and Ryan's protest against it, we need more than a mere peephole into it. A fixed gaze on Australian military experience and achievement will not suffice. In countless books, documentaries, and memorial addresses about the Great War, especially during the recent 'Centenary of Anzac', that is the fixed gaze that has been offered to the Australian people. We need to lift our eyes from that mere peephole to the panorama beyond. We need to see the big forces at work behind the tragedy, in the so-called 'war behind the war'. Our narrative must zoom out, to include the diplomatic front, where handfuls of men bargained over the war aims that defined the purposes of the war, extended the battle lines, and throttled the chances of peace. It must zoom out to include the domestic political front, where dissenting politicians, activists, and masses of ordinary men and women were locked in fierce debates that spilled over into strikes and street battles, over the justice – or injustice – of the war.

Therefore, in order to see Private Ted Ryan's protests against the war in context, this book aims to braid together two narratives, the personal and the political. To achieve this, the narrative will take brief excursions away from Ted Ryan's training camps, trenches, hospitals, and the prisons that held him, to explore the questions he posed. Was it a morally tainted war – a war for conquest, on every side, including our own? Was it a war that was needlessly prolonged? Answering these questions will involve weaving into the narrative an analysis of the 'secret war' that provoked Ryan's rebellion – in particular, as Ryan alleged, the war-makers' constant escalation of war aims, and their callous neglect of peace opportunities.

In short, we need to explore a host of uncomfortable questions. On the one hand, what were the wider purposes of this war, to be glimpsed in the mainly secret diplomatic deals that bound the warring coalitions together and kept the war going? On the other hand, with military stalemate so clear for so long, why did peace talks not begin? For the men who were swept into the maelstrom of industrialised killing that was the Great War – and for us a century later – these were, and should be, the crucial questions.

Private Ted Ryan in a sense was simply the 'everyman' at the front – a working-class man of the lowest rank, in uniform. But for Australians, he is more intimately 'one of us'. True respect for the troops of Anzac should mean more than finding stories that stoke 'our pride' in 'their spirit', as the slogan goes. We do not have to choose between pride and shame. We should simply be open to all the truths that the records show.

Therefore, this book urges readers to think critically about that catastrophically long First World War, to refuse to take it for granted, and refuse to insist that it must be yet another stand-tall moment in our national story. This book takes readers into unfamiliar places – the world of dissidents, rebels, renegades and insightful humanitarians, waging an international 'war against war' in many countries during the First World War. These were the men and women who, just like Private Ryan, refused to accept that there was no alternative to slaughter, refused to make rational what was irrational, and refused to make holy what was hideous.

This book joins with those who plead for a more realistic assessment of our role in the common European tragedy that was the Great War – free of 'big-noting' our military effort, and free of the simple-minded assumption that our forces were fighting for purely defensive purposes and democratic goals. It seeks to shake off the nationalist blinkers that prevent our seeing the murky realities behind this gigantic imperial struggle to decide the mastery of Europe, the division of the Ottoman Empire, and the repartition of great stretches of the colonial world. Importantly, this story seeks to escape the nationalist froth that masquerades as red-poppy respect for the troops. Instead, this book maintains the essential distinction we should all keep in mind in discussing the Great War: we must respect the warrior; we may disrespect the war. We do not forget – nor should we forgive.

Finally, it is important to stress that the defiant Private Ted Ryan depicted here cannot be lightly dismissed as an isolated troublemaker. In his disenchantment and in his defiance, as we shall see, he was not one of a mere handful of rebels in the ranks. His opinions were not those of a mere remnant of underground 'pacifist' opinion. As the carnage grew wider, in space and time, bringing with it unprecedented hardship, violence and bloodshed, the war aroused bitter controversy, unleashed wild expectations, and provoked passionate protests in numberless places tormented by the war. Like-minded dissenters would gather before palaces, parliaments, factory gates, and in the barracks – and indeed even in the trenches – to share their fury and plan for their freedom. Eventually, empires would shake, and fall, as the rebels against war reached for power. If we keep the wider reality of this tragedy in view, then in Ted Ryan's protests against the war we may catch the voices of millions.

Private Edward James Ryan, Service Number 4635.
Close-up portrait, 51st Battalion, AIF, probably Egypt, 1916 – endorsed
'Your loving nephew, Ted' (courtesy of Paul Mudie).

Chapter 1

PRIVATE RYAN'S DEFIANCE

– Perham Down, October 1916 –

Every man I have spoken to is absolutely sick of the whole business.[2]

— Private Edward James Ryan to Ramsay MacDonald MP,
18 October 1916

In October 1916, a young Australian soldier from the 51st Battalion of the Australian Imperial Force (AIF) was recovering in England from wounds and shell shock.[3] He was Private Edward James Ryan, Service Number 4635, originally from Broken Hill. In June that year, he had suffered burns and abrasions to his face when an artillery shell exploded very close to his trench. He was fighting near Fleurbaix, just south of Armentières, in France. He spent some weeks in hospitals on the French coast. After returning to the front, he was injured again in August, his left hand crushed. This second time he was transferred to hospitals in England. On top of his physical wounds, the doctors assessed him as a shell-shock case. He spent weeks convalescing. Finally, at the end of September 1916, he was ordered to return to service with the AIF in England, at a large army camp known as the 'No. 1 Australian Command Depot'. It was located in open country at Perham Down, close to the Wiltshire-Hampshire border, and near the edge of the British Army's desolate training grounds of Salisbury Plain.

Private Ted Ryan was housed at No. 3 Camp inside the military complex at Perham Down. The Australian soldiers usually called it by the plural form, 'Perham Downs'. Perhaps this was more in line with the Australians' expectations of what a little piece of rural England should be called, with the word 'Downs' suggesting the soft, green, pastureland of their imaginations – a restorative place, that might soothe those wounded in body and soul. In fact, no solace was to be found there. The area was a sombre network of parade grounds fringed by 'long greyish coloured huts', all cheaply built, and often very chilly.[4] More than five thousand soldiers could be crammed into this facility at any one time, with thirty men per wooden hut. There was also a smattering of tents for any overflow of soldiers, and for those temporarily shifted out of the huts during their periodic disinfections to kill lice and fleas.

The camp, formerly a British facility, had been allocated to the Australians in mid-1916. It was set up in the expectation that soldiers wounded in the first battles to be fought by the Australian divisions in France, during the coming summer offensive, would be sent here to recover and retrain. Thousands came. Many were survivors from the horrific battles around the River Somme, Fromelles, Pozières, and Mouquet Farm, or 'Mucky Farm' in the troops' dialect. After a stint in hospitals scattered across Britain, those soldiers who could be restored to some degree of strength were despatched to Perham Down.

The camp was officially designated a 'Hardening and Drafting Depot'. The Australians' commanders sent the men here to be toughened up in preparation for their return to the front. After assessment, some would be funnelled to other Australian depots in England for still more training. Others, once 'hardened', would be 'drafted' directly from Perham Down back to their units in France.

Surrounding the camp were firing ranges for rifles, machine guns and mortars. The ranges were backed up against several small hills near the camp, with banks of earth added, providing safe backstops. There was also an extensive network of practice trenches in fields about two kilometres away, near the tiny village of Shipton Bellinger. These trenches had been initially dug into the chalk by British units in 1915, for the training of the volunteers in Kitchener's New Army who would eventually fight at The Somme in July 1916. The Australians had inherited these practice trenches. They included front-line trenches with fire-steps, support and communication trenches, dugouts, shelters, latrines, aid posts, machine-gun emplacements, and even 'German' trenches, known as 'Bedlam trenches'. The trenches came complete with screw-pickets laced with barbed wire. Thus, a replica of a part of the Western Front was created on Salisbury Plain, where troops could rehearse storming German trenches. All these diggings honeycombed more than a hundred hectares of the countryside around Perham Down, scarring the landscape.[5] Here in the autumn of 1916 Australia's wounded and damaged from the Somme battle fronts were schooled again in trench warfare. No doubt, with outbreaks of rifle and machine-gun fire, and with Mills bombs erupting regularly, many men were violently flung back in their minds, by the sounds and sights and smells of mechanised warfare, to the haunting scenes of devastation that they had witnessed in France.

During the English autumn of 1916, Perham Down was a bleak camp, earning its colloquial nickname among the troops as 'Perishing Downs'.[6] 'The rottenest hole on earth', was one soldier's blunt description after arriving there in October 1916, the same month as Ted Ryan. 'No mattresses to sleep on. Bare boards.'[7]

The statistics generated at the camp make grim reading. At the end of October 1916, the No. 1 Command Depot's war diary recorded that 5,311 men were 'on strength' at the camp. Some 3,266 men had arrived during the month, and altogether 8,577 men had been 'handled', with many sent on to other camps. Only 79 soldiers at Perham Down had been deemed fit to return directly to France that month.

Sagging discipline at Perham Down began to worry the officers. The depot's war diary for October 1916 tried to look on the bright side, asserting that discipline was generally 'good', given the large numbers of men and 'the many indifferent characters' moving through the camp. But this was wishful thinking. Figures showed that there were in fact 440 cases of 'absence without leave', 45 remands for a District Court Martial, and a total of 766 incidents requiring punishment during the month of October. The lure of London, and even nearby Stonehenge, was too much for many soldiers. Perhaps most distressingly, the war diary also recorded some cases of men 'taking fits'. It offered a matter-of-fact explanation: the nervous fits endured by many men during training 'appear to be due to the nearness of the depot to the Trench Mortar Range. The noise, when practice is going on, affects the Shell Shock cases sent here for short convalescence.'[8] And there was a lot of noise.

A Letter from the Killing Floor

After almost three weeks at Perham Down, Private Ted Ryan, one of those unfortunate victims of shell shock, resolved upon a risky course of action: he would denounce the war. Something irresistible arose in his blood: he felt he must record his own protest against the chaotic mass killing that he had seen in France, the mass killing that politicians in Britain, and in Australia, were apparently quite willing to see prolonged. He resolved to tell the truth about the horrors he had seen.

On 18 October 1916, Ted Ryan found a quiet place in the camp to sit down and compose an angry letter condemning the war and roasting those behind it. Soldiers wanting to write often found the huts at Perham Down too noisy, but it was possible, as one put it, to 'sneak away into a quiet corner of the YMCA [Young Men's Christian Association] to write romantic letters to the folks at home'.[9] The YMCA, or 'the Y', was just one of a number of church-run organisations in the camp. It provided free writing paper.[10]

Ted Ryan planned to send a very unromantic letter. He addressed it to the man the pro-war newspapers depicted as the best-hated and most dangerous man in Britain, the anti-war Labour politician Ramsay MacDonald MP. The notorious Scot was a veteran socialist and former chairman of the British Labour Party at Westminster. In August 1914 he had resigned from that party leadership position in protest against Britain's decision to rush into war or, more accurately, against his own party's failure even to register its dissent by abstaining on the parliamentary vote to fund the war from a 'War Credit'. Immediately engulfed in controversy, MacDonald nevertheless held firm to his dissenting position, while being monstered in the press as no better than an 'agent of Germany', a 'pro-German', a 'traitor'.[11]

Ramsay MacDonald

Ryan's letter to MacDonald glowed with the white heat of passion. Importantly, he claimed to speak for most Australian soldiers. And he had big truths to tell. The surviving Australian soldiers from the bloodshed in France, Ryan insisted, hated the war. They called the battlefield 'The Abattoirs'. Indeed, under shellfire every trench was potentially a kill-box. He seized his chance to put down on paper the real opinions of those Australian troops, because the British press was hyperventilating about how much the brave Australians 'relish the glories of war'. For instance, Ryan wrote, two men fresh from the battlefront had just told him that they 'would rather be shot than face another bombardment like we received at Pozières'. So, Ryan complained, the blood-and-thunder newspapers were lying about the Australians! Ryan railed at one newspaper in particular for depicting the Anzacs as 'bright & cheering, hooraying' as they came away from the Somme battlefield. The truth was, wrote Ryan, that the 'frightfulness' of the bombardments at the front was 'beyond their imagination'. Every soldier he had talked to was 'absolutely sick of the whole business'.

Ryan clearly knew not only of MacDonald but also the leading pro-war politicians. He heaped praise upon MacDonald for his consistent anti-war stand – for refusing, as Ryan put it, to hide behind 'the veil of Patriotism' like so many stay-at-homes, safely spouting their determination to fight on to the 'bitter end' while too old for military service. In this spirit, Ryan turned his fury on Herbert Henry Asquith, the British Prime Minister, and David Lloyd George, his Minister of War. These two were contemptible and cruel, Ryan argued, for vowing to fight on, at any cost, until military victory was achieved. Did Lloyd George, in his 'nice spring bed', even think of those in the trenches with their 'nerves shattered to the uttermost'? Why did both Asquith and Lloyd George say 'we are out to crush Germany'? Waging war until Britain could impose her peace terms upon Germany would 'make thousands face this hell'.

David Lloyd George

Ryan's letter also showed he was in touch with the latest sensations in British politics. Only a month before, in late September 1916, Lloyd George had slapped down the President of the United States, Woodrow Wilson. America was still neutral at this stage of the war, and Wilson had repeatedly urged negotiations. Lloyd George chose to block him. In a newspaper interview given to an American journalist, to be published across the world, Lloyd George stubbornly insisted that Britain could not discuss peace terms and must refuse Wilson's offers – or any offers – to mediate. This enraged Ryan. He piled on the rhetorical questions. By what right, he asked, did Lloyd George shout 'Hands off Neutrals'? 'Now, Mr MacDonald, why shouldn't we know what terms of Peace we are fighting for, why shouldn't we discuss what terms we are supposed to accept?' For Ryan, Britain's lust for imperial conquest was the real stumbling block. Britain was committed to 'her old ideal' – to 'Conquer'. Britain had no real commitment to the 'supposed new ideal', the ideal of 'Peace'. The 'horrors of war' in France were mind-numbing. What could Britain possibly gain that would be worth 'such a human sacrifice?'

Fear and loathing at 'Perishing Downs'

What had prompted this outburst from Australia's Private Ryan? Political controversies erupting across the mess tables at Perham Down had a lot to do with it. A referendum on military conscription was due to be held in Australia at the end of October 1916. Australian troops deployed overseas were given the chance to vote early. This was to ensure that the soldiers' votes could be counted in the final tallies. Noticeboards at Perham Down explained to the troops that they would cast their ballots on 19 October – the day after Ryan penned his angry letter to Ramsay MacDonald.

Those supporting conscription in Australia had high hopes that the Anzac troops would lead the way, and give a resounding 'Yes' in favour. General Sir William Birdwood, the British Commander of the AIF, and Labor Prime Minister William 'Billy' Morris Hughes, had blitzed Perham Down with 'patriotic circulars' pleading the 'Yes' case. Birdwood argued that 'no sacrifice can be too great'. Moreover, conscription would catch that loathed being, 'THE SHIRKER'. Hughes's accompanying 'Manifesto' pleaded that Australia must double the number of men that had been sent abroad so far, up to a total of 500,000 soldiers. There could be no peace, Hughes vowed, until Germany was 'decisively beaten on her own soil'. As in much of his wartime speechmaking, Hughes incited dread. He warned that a 'No' vote would be a catastrophe that would only 'encourage the enemy'. Indeed, he claimed that 'No' voters would bring 'eternal shame' to Australia, and 'the glorious name Anzac' would be left 'a tarnished and dishonoured thing'.[12]

In his letter to MacDonald, Ryan referred directly to this imminent referendum. He was scathing of Hughes. He attacked especially his insinuation that the demand for peace was all a German plot. The AIF soldiers overwhelmingly opposed conscription, he asserted. Only those freshly arrived Australian troops who 'have not yet been out to face the "music"' would be voting 'Yes'. He told MacDonald that he, as a serving soldier, had all the patriotic credentials he needed to urge peace: in fact, all three young Ryan boys, he and his two brothers, had joined the AIF. All had fought – and all had been wounded. Hughes's tired old taunt of 'pro-German!' was contemptible.

William Morris Hughes

Finally, Ryan encouraged MacDonald and his followers 'to do everything possible in your power to bring about a Peace and save this slaughter of Human Lives'.[13]

Ryan had distilled his passionate anti-war arguments into five pages of handwritten script. The letter was littered with underlined and randomly capitalised words. There were meandering sentences and errors in spelling, all testifying to raw emotion and heartfelt conviction. The letter shouted out its own authenticity. Ryan ended it emphatically, too. There was no attempt to hide behind anonymity. He wrote out his name, service number, and full contact details, and extended an invitation to MacDonald to use the letter, just as he wished.

Speaking Truth – to Parliament

Private Ted Ryan enclosed his letter in an envelope addressed to Ramsay MacDonald at the House of Commons in London – ready for posting.

In fact, troops were forbidden to use the civilian post, because this involved deliberately evading the officers' censorship of their mail at the camp.[14] In doing so, Ted Ryan risked punishment under various vindictive interpretations of the *Army Act 1881* (UK) – the all-encompassing British legislation on military discipline, which applied to Australian troops.[15] For example, he might have been court-martialled for spreading 'reports calculated to create unnecessary alarm or despondency', for which the maximum penalty was 'penal servitude' – jail for five years.[16] Similarly, he might have been skewered under certain paragraphs in the *Kings' Regulations and Orders for the Army* (1912), or in the *Manual of Military Law* (1914), tomes of military law readily available to most officers. His letter might have been construed as an attempted illegal communication with the press, as an effort to evade the prescribed army channels for the redress of grievances, or even as an attempt to stir up mutiny.[17] He might have been charged with conduct 'to the prejudice of good order and military discipline'.[18] Worst of all, he might have been caught up under the sweeping regulations proclaimed under the British state's war-emergency legislation, the *Defence of the Realm Act 1914* (UK), known as 'DORA', which prohibited any person from spreading 'reports likely to cause disaffection or alarm among any of His Majesty's forces or among the civilian population'. Under DORA, civilians or soldiers igniting such 'disaffection' and 'alarm' risked a court martial that might impose the penalty of 'penal servitude for life or any less punishment'.[19] Thus, in sending a letter of outrage to a prominent MP and inviting him to shout its contents from the rooftops, Ryan was risking a long stretch of imprisonment.

How did he get it to MacDonald? Possibly Ryan went to the nearest village, Ludgershall, or to one of the towns in the vicinity, such as Tidworth, Bulford or Andover, to post his letter. These were common destinations for outings and route marches for the troops.[20] But mail posted in such garrison towns was no doubt easily intercepted and inspected. More likely, in order to be sure of evading the officer-censors, Ryan resorted to a popular ruse: he gave his letter to a soldier, a trusted friend, who was either on leave or being invalided home from Perham Down, to post in London or any one of the bigger towns beyond the military areas.[21]

By whatever means, Ryan's letter made it to Westminster. Thus, he had despatched his 'truth bomb' to the heart of the Empire, to the Parliament of Britain.

Chapter 2

BROTHERS IN ARMS

– Rosebery Park and Perth, 1914 to 1915 –

> Our family consists of three boys & the three of us are on Active Service. One Brother is in the 13th battalion & was wounded once, (in Gallipoli). The other Brother was in the first reinforcements of the 11th Battalion & has been wounded twice. I have been slightly wounded twice. My Mother & Father are both dead, so I don't think our family has done much for Germany ...[22]
>
> — Private Edward James Ryan to Ramsay MacDonald MP, 18 October 1916

Who was this defiant Australian soldier?

Edward James Ryan was one of three brothers from the Ryan family then serving with the Australian Imperial Force.

Firebrand Father, Methodist Mother – and Lives of Scarcity

Where did they come from, these Ryans? The three boys had grown up in the 1890s, a depression decade, in Broken Hill, a dusty and big-skied Australian mining town located in the hot and dry far west of New South Wales. A giant ore body, rich in silver, lead, and zinc, had been discovered there in the early 1880s. Within ten years, the frontier town's population had blossomed, and was variously estimated at between 12,000 and 20,000 people.[23]

The father of the three Ryan brothers was Edward James Ryan senior, a Catholic Irish immigrant, born in Cork in about 1848 – and so a child of the famine years. In Broken Hill, he worked as an engine driver in the mines. He was powerfully built and sported a luxuriant, baby-frightening beard. He was flamboyant in style and speech. Public life beckoned. Edward Ryan was elected to the very first Broken Hill District Municipal Council in November 1888. Serving only one term, he played the role of the people's firebrand and loveable rogue on the council, crusading noisily on the periodic 'water famines' facing the city, demanding public supplies, and denouncing the rich monopolists who were 'conspiring to prevent the little ones in Broken Hill from getting a drink of water in the summer'.[24]

Alderman Edward James Ryan,
Alderman on the Broken Hill District Municipal Council, 1888-1891 (courtesy of Don Mudie).

His egalitarian instinct was visceral. In February 1890, when the council decided to invite Sir Henry Parkes, the Premier of New South Wales, to lay the foundation stone of a projected Town Hall, Edward Ryan stood alone in opposition. He protested that 'he did not care two sprats' who cemented in the stone, but he 'did not see why they should toady to Sir Henry'.[25] On another occasion he was fined by the local Police Court for cursing the mayor, Zebina Lane, a wealthy mine manager, and Ryan was briefly imprisoned for refusing to pay.[26] He was prominent also in his trade union, the Engine Drivers and Firemen's Association, but a whiff of drink about him injured his reputation in these circles.[27]

In June 1890, the forty-one-year-old Ryan married Elizabeth Martin Riter (née Couch), aged twenty-two. It was Elizabeth's second marriage. Her young life had already been very tough, and her first marriage marred by tragedy.

Born in October 1867, Elizabeth had grown up in the isolated copper-mining town of Moonta Mines on the Yorke Peninsula of South Australia. A miners' strike against wage cuts there in April 1874 was a foundational moment for the South Australian labour movement. Elizabeth was the eldest surviving child of seven born to James Couch, a miner, and Jane (née Pearce). In Moonta, the family was devoutly loyal to the local Primitive Methodist Church. This was a mainstream religion at this time, particularly strong in South Australia and in Broken Hill, with a strong commitment to the social gospel.[28] But few blessings came the way of the Couch family. In 1867, their first child, George, was accidentally drowned at age two.[29] In 1883, a sixth child, also named George, died at age six. This second death apparently threw James into a deep depression. The following year Jane tried, unsuccessfully, to have him committed to an asylum as a 'lunatic', but a doctor diagnosed 'melancholia' and he remained at home.[30]

Margaret Nicholas Couch (L) and Elizabeth Martin Couch (R), the mother of the future Private Edward James Ryan, probably taken in Moonta Mines, South Australia, in the mid-1880s (courtesy of Don Mudie).

In August 1886, at age eighteen, Elizabeth left this troubled household to marry a young Englishman, Fredrick Riter, a baker from London, and a fellow Primitive Methodist. Their first child, Beatrice ('Beatie') Mary, was born at Moonta in June 1887. Fred Riter evidently struggled to find work as a baker. In December 1887, in spite of reports of typhoid fever in Broken Hill, Fred travelled there, alone, in pursuit of work.

Many miners from the South Australian mining towns of Burra and Moonta had made that same journey almost 500 kilometres across the border of New South Wales to Broken Hill. But after just a few weeks in the town, Frederick Riter died of typhoid fever in January 1888. 'No friends at Broken Hill', the death certificate recorded pathetically. Elizabeth evidently had been staying with her seven-month-old baby Beatrice at Moonta. At age twenty she was suddenly a widow.[31]

Soon after, Elizabeth appears to have moved to Broken Hill, possibly to be with her younger sister Margaret, and she found work as a domestic servant. Here she met the burly alderman Edward Ryan and a second chance at marriage beckoned. The ceremony for Elizabeth and Edward took place in June 1890 at the Manse of the Primitive Methodist Church in Broken Hill – her church – with Elizabeth's younger brother Henry Couch witnessing the event.[32] In marrying 'outside the church', Ryan displayed an independent spirit, for he was defying the expectations of his Irish Catholic upbringing. Elizabeth acted unexpectedly also. At some point now impossible to fix, she decided it was best to leave her first-born child, Beatrice Mary, in Moonta, first in the care of her parents, and later with her brother Thomas. Life began afresh. The newly-married Ryans lived at a number of addresses, but eventually settled in a humble tin-walled house on the corner of Brown and Zebina Streets, at the northern edge of Broken Hill. Nothing remains of the house on the site today.

Edward and Elizabeth's first-born child, Edward James Ryan junior, the future Private Ted Ryan, was born on 29 July 1891, at Moonta Mines, South Australia, while Elizabeth was making a return visit to her family for her confinement, and presumably to see Beatrice.[33] As a boy he would be known as 'Eddy'. Two more boys were born to Elizabeth at home in Broken Hill, Thomas Pearce Couch Ryan (known as Tom) in September 1893 and Henry Martin Ryan (known as Harry) in December 1895.[34]

Early in the marriage there were signs of trouble. Alderman Ryan pulled out of the second council elections at the very last moment in February 1891.[35] In June, Ryan and another man quarrelled over a land transfer. Fisticuffs landed the two in the Police Court.[36] The dispute rumbled on into the Small Debts Court.[37] Another dispute in August saw Elizabeth Ryan in the Warden's Court, defending her furniture from seizure to settle her husband's debts. The court heard that Edward had left Broken Hill for a new silver mining venture at Black Mountain, 100 miles away. Perhaps he had temporarily abandoned the family.[38] Two years later he was listed as bankrupt.[39] But by 1897 he was back driving a steam-winch at one of Broken Hill's large open-cut mines.[40]

It soon became obvious that the Ryan family was fracturing. The father of the three boys may well be the 'Edward Ryan' who appeared repeatedly at the Broken Hill Police Court, facing fines for drunkenness.[41]

At the end of the decade, the Ryan family was suddenly wrecked. Elizabeth Ryan died at home on Wednesday 6 December 1899.[42] She was only thirty-two. A doctor had treated her for 'hysteria' a fortnight before her death. Another doctor, summoned on 6

December, found her dead. Initially both doctors 'refused to give a certificate of death', perhaps an indication that they believed Edward had done too little to save his wife. The local Primitive Methodist Minister interred Elizabeth's remains into the earth at the General Cemetery on the morning of Friday 8 December. On the afternoon of that same day, a magistrate's inquest was held at a local hotel. Ryan explained that his wife had suffered from Bright's disease, an extremely painful kidney ailment. The magistrate concluded that Elizabeth had died of 'Enteritis following on Influenza'. The ruling was 'death from natural causes'.[43]

Elizabeth's relations in Broken Hill, chiefly her sister Margaret Mudie (pronounced 'Moody'), and her brother Henry Couch, who had married there in 1899, had a decision to make about the boys' future. What guided their decision? We can only speculate. Perhaps the magistrate's inquiry fuelled their suspicions that Edward Ryan senior had neglected Elizabeth, because he was drifting into alcoholism and poverty. Or perhaps the Methodist Couch and Mudie families felt a lingering prejudice against him as a Catholic. For whatever reason, Margaret, and her husband James Ramsay Mudie, stepped forward to give a home in Broken Hill to the three motherless Ryan boys – Harry, aged three, Tom, aged six, and Eddy, aged eight.

The father of the Ryan brothers soon slipped out of their young lives. In the decade after his wife's death, Edward Ryan senior appears to have descended deeply into a cycle of drunkenness, arrests, debts and fines – and finally disappeared.[44] His ultimate fate is not clear. But none of the Ryan brothers was to cite his father as next of kin in his enlistment papers. Edward Ryan was dead – or dead to the boys – by 1914.

As working-class boys growing up in Broken Hill, they must have been acutely conscious of the tragedy that had taken their mother from them, and perhaps their father too. Very probably they heard stories also of the sad and sudden end of their mother's first marriage, and the losses that had been suffered by the Couch family back in Moonta when she was a girl. The boys evidently knew of 'Beatie', their older half-sister, but she remained in Moonta with the Couch family. No doubt the three Ryan boys learned from those who raised them that life was always going to be something like warfare.

'SO HELP ME, GOD'

When Ted Ryan wrote to Ramsay MacDonald in October 1916, it was just over a year since he had volunteered to join the Australian Imperial Force, on Tuesday 21 September 1915. He had joined up in Perth, Western Australia, having moved from Broken Hill with his brother Tom, very likely in search of work, in the early months of the war. He presented himself at the recruiting centre, an old Drill Hall within the Swan Barracks, on Francis Street, Perth.

Ted Ryan fronted up to the recruiting officer, the fifty-seven-year-old 'Honorary Lieutenant' Charles Weaver. He was a former Warrant Officer with the volunteer forces. Promoted to the position of 'Honorary Lieutenant' in early 1915, he was from that moment a fixture at the Drill Hall in Perth, the enlistment centre.[45] Weaver was notorious: on one occasion he told a short man to 'Go home and grow'; on another occasion he refused a poor man's application to enlist because he judged him to be a vagrant; and on another 'slack day' he strode out to exhort twenty men standing idly near the Drill Hall to 'step inside' before he 'ordered them away from the barracks'.[46] Weaver's eagerness was legendary. He worked 'double shifts' at the Drill Hall.[47] Later, when open-air recruiting events took place in Perth, there was 'no more enthusiastic official than Lieutenant Weaver'.[48] Thousands of young men would pass through Weaver's hands during the Great War – and he would make old bones, dying in 1945 at the age of 86.

Thirty-three men walked in to the Drill Hall to be given the once-over by Weaver on the day Ted Ryan enlisted in September 1915. Ryan was among the twenty-three men passed as fit that day.[49]

First, Ted Ryan had paperwork to complete: a document entitled, 'Australian Imperial Force – Attestation Paper of Persons Enlisted for Service Abroad'. A clerk recorded his details. Ryan reported that he was a 'natural born British subject', aged twenty-four years and two months old. His complexion was 'Dark', his hair 'Fair', and his eyes 'Blue'. He was taller than many soldiers at just over 175 centimetres (5 feet and 9 inches). He was slender, at 74 kilograms (156 pounds). He was unmarried. Being young and single, he was like the vast majority of men enlisting in the AIF.[50]

And in common with most, he was of the working class. 'What is your trade or calling?' Ryan answered 'Labourer'. It was the most common occupation given by the thousands of enlisting men, the great majority of whom were workers.[51] Indeed, the largest proportion of enlisting men coming from any one organisation in Australia during the first year of warfare came from the Australian Workers Union (AWU). The leaders at the annual convention of the AWU in February 1916 reported proudly that 20,000 of the union's members had already enlisted, that is 'about 25 per cent of the membership'.[52]

'Next of kin'? Because both his mother and father were dead, Ryan listed 'Uncle, James Mudie', residing at 'Argent Street, Broken Hill, NSW'.

'Religious Denomination'? 'Methodist'. It had indeed been Ted's late mother's religion, and the religion of the chapel-going Mudie family.

Ryan was then medically examined: he stripped to the waist, had his measurements taken, his eyesight tested, and was required to perform 'a succession of acrobatic feats' in front of the medical officer.[53] He passed everything.

Finally, Ryan was required to swear an oath. He stood, with his right hand raised, and, while holding the Bible in his left, solemnly read the formal words. He swore that he would 'truly serve our Sovereign Lord the King' and 'resist His Majesty's enemies' for the duration of the war, and for 'four months thereafter', ending with 'SO HELP ME, GOD'. He then signed the paper.

In fact, Ryan signed, as they all did, in two places. For he was acknowledging not only his oath to serve the King Emperor, but also a declaration that he was 'willing and hereby voluntarily agree to serve in the Military Forces of the Commonwealth of Australia within *or beyond* the limits of the Commonwealth'.[54] In this way, the letter – if not the spirit – of Australia's first *Defence Act* of 1903 was honoured. For this had specified that no man could be *compelled* to serve outside Australia. This provision reflected a long-standing suspicion of British imperial adventures, a suspicion widely shared among Australian progressives since the Boer War – a suspicion that was, for the moment, overwhelmed by the passions of war.

Indeed, up until this time Australia had been among the handful of progressive nations trumpeting even in its government nomenclature the novel proposition that the nation's military forces should be committed to 'defence', and defence only, shunning the idea of war beyond the shores of the nation. Formal titles told the story. From 1901 Australia had a 'Minister of Defence' rather than a Minister or Secretary of State for War (as Britain had), and a 'Department of Defence' rather than a War Office (as Britain had). Even the United States had a 'War Department'. (Britain, France, and the United States, for example, did not upgrade these titles until after the Second World War.) This proclaimed a reformist faith: other nations might contemplate wars in faraway places to extend their empires, but the new forward-looking Commonwealth of Australia did not. Or so it was imagined.

But in 1915, like all enlisting men, Ted Ryan would almost certainly be sent overseas. He would serve wherever he was sent, and he would serve under the British *Army Act 1881*. He was a 'volunteer' in signing up – but in a sense he was a volunteer no longer. Rather, he was a man shackled by an array of British military laws, practices and procedures for the duration of the conflict.

The precise legal situation of Ryan, and the more than 300,000 Australians who served overseas like him, deserves some close analysis. In passing Australia's *Defence Act 1903*, the Commonwealth Parliament – through a mixture of habitual deference to the imperial authorities in London and sheer legislative delinquency – had chosen simply to submit Australia's military personnel to the British *Army Act 1881* rather than to additional legislation reflecting Australia's own spirit. The only limitation specified at the time was that the British Act would apply in all its provisions, unless any of these were 'inconsistent' with Australia's own *Defence Act 1903*.[55] For Private Ryan, and for the many other Australians who were to face courts martial during the First World War, this would have profound consequences.

Young Harry's Ruse of War

Ted Ryan was in fact the last of the three brothers from the Ryan family of Broken Hill to enlist in the AIF in this way.

Perhaps the youngest brother Henry Martin Ryan, or 'Harry', had inspired his two older brothers to contemplate enlistment. He had joined up at Rosebery Park racecourse (now Eastlakes) in Sydney on 14 September 1914. The war had broken out only seven weeks before. Harry was aged just eighteen – too young to enlist.[56] The advertised minimum-age requirement for joining the AIF was nineteen years.[57]

What to do? Young Harry fibbed his way into the AIF. The dodge was simple: he had fronted up at the racecourse, the 'Light Horse Camp', and barked his eldest brother Ted's name, 'Edward James Ryan', as his own. He even gave Ted's exact age at that time, '23 years, 2 months'. Why? Harry was the only one of the three Ryan boys who was young enough to have been subject to Australia's pre-war scheme of 'compulsory military training' for boys aged 14 to 18. He had probably enrolled as a Senior Cadet under the first year of the scheme in 1911 when he was just 15. But if Harry gave his real name at the 'Light Horse Camp', this risked the authorities discovering his true age from the cadet rolls. So, by masquerading at his elder brother, Harry evaded the age requirement,

and the additional rule requiring youths aged 19 to 21 to obtain the permission of a parent or guardian before they could embark on what many imagined was to be the adventure of a lifetime – an expedition, overseas.[58]

So, Harry Ryan became 'Edward James Ryan, Service Number 672' in the files. He was allotted to the 13th Battalion. To keep things straight with the military, not surprisingly, Harry would maintain this false name in his official military records throughout the war, and presumably among his mates. The tale was a great family joke down the years. Indeed he would remain 'Edward James Ryan' officially to the end of his life, even though the family always called him Harry.[59]

Private Henry ('Harry') Martin Ryan, who falsely enlisted as 'Edward James Ryan', Service Number 672, probably Egypt, 1915 (courtesy of the late Beth Sutton).

Gone For a Soldier

The middle Ryan brother, Thomas Pearce Couch Ryan, or 'Tom', also unmarried and a labourer, was next to enlist. He joined the AIF in Perth on 13 January 1915.

Why did Tom decide to 'take the King's shilling' as the old phrase had it? No real evidence remains. But notably Tom joined up within days of news arriving in Perth of truly astonishing events in Broken Hill. On the morning of New Year's Day 1915, a long train left Broken Hill, containing 1,200 men, women and children, seated in 41 open-air mining trucks. They were looking forward to the annual picnic sports organised by the combined Manchester Unity Lodges. Just outside the city, the train suddenly came under rapid rifle fire from two men crouching behind a mound of earth. Nearby was an ice-cream cart flying the Ottoman flag. Two local men, one a young Afghan Afridi, an ice-cream vendor, and an older Indian man who had befriended him, had decided, desperately, to strike a tiny blow against the massed enemies of the Ottoman Empire – the people of Broken Hill. Three men and one woman were killed on or near the train, and seven people were wounded. Eventually, dozens of policemen, militia, and Rifle Club enthusiasts summoned to the scene pursued the two attackers to a rocky quartz outcrop called White Rocks just north of the town. In the gunfight that ensued, a bystander was killed, and then one of the attackers was killed outright and the other mortally wounded in a hail of fire. By nightfall a vengeful mob set fire to the empty 'German Club' building in Broken Hill. A crowd also threatened to destroy the local 'camel camp', blaming all Moslems for the tragedy, but the police blocked their path.[60]

The story of the attack on the picnic train was widely reported in the Perth press, so Tom and Ted could not have missed the fact that the outing was organised by the friendly societies dear to their uncle James Ramsay Mudie. They might even have imagined that there were members of his family on the train – although there is no family tradition saying so. Certainly, the two brothers would have recognised the scene of the firefight, near 'some white quartz rocks on a hill', as White Rocks, a childhood playground near their home at the corner of Brown and Zebina Streets.[61]

News of these dramatic and bloody events in Broken Hill may well have provoked Tom to step forward and volunteer to serve in the AIF.

On enlistment, Tom Ryan was aged just twenty-one. As his brother Ted was to do in September, he passed through the hands of Lieutenant Weaver at the Drill Hall in Francis Street, Perth. After his initial training at Blackboy Hill, a famous camp to the east of Perth, Tom left Fremantle aboard Her Majesty's Australian Troopship (HMAT) *Hororata* (A20) as one of the '11th Infantry Battalion – 5th Reinforcements', on 26 April 1915.

Unbeknown to Tom Ryan and all the men who tramped up the gangplank on that day, they were heading overseas in the immediate aftermath of a history-making day: on the previous day, 25 April, the men of the original 11th Battalion had rushed ashore at Anzac Cove on the Gallipoli peninsula – on the first as yet unchristened 'Anzac Day'.[62]

Tom Ryan and his comrades on HMAT *Hororata* were slated to reinforce this battalion upon arrival at Gallipoli.

It is very likely that Ted Ryan enrolled later that year in Perth with some hope of meeting up with his soldier-brother Tom overseas. Under the enlistment rules, brothers could request placement in the same units. Thus, Ted steered himself into the '14th Reinforcements of the 11th Battalion'. On paper at least, he was heading toward a reunion with Tom in that same Western Australian battalion serving on the Gallipoli peninsula.

Thus, in September 1915, when the real Ted Ryan enlisted in the AIF in Perth, Harry's masquerading as Ted a year earlier was undetected. As far as the military authorities were aware, there were simply two men called 'Edward James Ryan', from different states, and with the same age. But no one noticed anything amiss. In fact, before the war was over there would eventually be three men named 'Edward James Ryan' on the 'nominal roll' of the AIF.[63]

But the real Ted Ryan from Broken Hill would prove to be no ordinary soldier.

The three Ryan brothers, (L to R) Harry, Eddy (Ted), Tom, Broken Hill c. 1901-02 (courtesy of the late Beth Sutton).

Chapter 3

SOLIDARITY

BROKEN HILL, 1900 TO 1914

> That the Broken Hill workers condemn the efforts of the Australian section of the robber class to manufacture in this country a Dreadnought blood-drunkenness, with its accompaniment of insane racial hatred; and they further hasten to assure their comrades across the sea that they, in the splendid language of the international workingmen of an earlier day, hold that the workers of all countries are their friends, and the despots and exploiters of all countries are their enemies, recognising that all wars are made by and for the class that exploits the useful workers. That the workers of Broken Hill, in mass meeting assembled, send fraternal greetings to the workers of all other lands.[64]
>
> — Resolutions acclaimed by a mass meeting of workers on the Central Reserve, Broken Hill, 4 April 1909

Who knows what instincts, impulses, and spirits we may inherit from our parents and our childhood home? If a rebellious streak can be inherited, Edward Ryan senior had a full paint-tin to bequeath to his first-born child and namesake, Ted Ryan. But Ryan, the rebellious soldier-to-be, was also a child of Broken Hill and of the Mudie family. Very likely, something of Ted Ryan's combative spirit he inherited from the town where he grew to manhood – the mining town, famously tumultuous, and lauded in Labor circles as the crucible of Australian trade unionism – and from the Mudie family who fed and clothed him.

Growing Up with the Mudies

When 'Auntie Margaret' and 'Uncle Jim' Mudie, as the Ryan boys called them, gave a home to the three motherless children, Eddy (later 'Ted'), as noted above, was just eight years old, and his two younger brothers mere toddlers. From about 1900 to 1914, the Mudies and their many children were the key formative influences in the boys' lives.

A photo of the three lads taken early in the new century shows them in their Sunday-best clothes. Hair combed, collars in place, coats on. Their knickerbockers are a little short, some with torn edges – as hand-me-downs can be. But all three wear stockings, and polished boots. Harry and Eddy hold caps, while Tom holds a boater. Eddy is seated. Tom and Harry are standing, both draping a forearm over the back of Eddy's chair. Tom rests a hand on Eddy's shoulder. The boys look well – but their faces show no emotion.

Who were the boys' guardians? James Ramsay Mudie was a Scot by birth and he was proudly Scottish in outlook. Born in 1855 at Arbroath, a mill and fishing town on the North Sea coast of Scotland, he had arrived in Australia in 1880. There was always something of the Robbie Burns's spirit – that 'A man's a man for a' that' irreverence – about Mudie. He had worked as a sailor, a cook, and a miner. A formal photo from about 1896 shows him unsmiling, with his coat open, his tie askew, sporting a dark and straggly moustache, and tilting his head as he looks boldly back to the camera. In January 1900, about the time he became stepfather to the Ryan boys, Mudie was forty-five and employed by the Broken Hill Council as a caretaker of the Imperial Dam, just north of the town. It was part of Broken Hill's contentious water supply.[65] Here he was required to live on site, in a small house that he rented from the council.

James Ramsay Mudie and Margaret Nicholas Mudie, with their first two children, Beatrice and Ruby, c. 1896 (courtesy of Paul Mudie)

When the three Ryan boys arrived in the Mudie home, probably in 1900, James and Margaret already had four children of their own. A fifth arrived in 1901 (named Elizabeth Martin, after the Ryan boys' late mother) and a sixth in 1904. Taking in the three Ryan boys, therefore, was an act of great generosity on their part. Still more was required, as one birth followed rapidly upon another in the Mudie family. Another family photo, dating most likely from 1906, shows Eddy pictured with six of the Mudie children, four girls and two boys, all his juniors. Eddy's hand is on the shoulders of the youngest, Jim. The photo suggests he is their chief child-minder. By the time the Mudies' last child was born, in 1911 (and named Edward, presumably to honour Ted the child-minder), James and Margaret had nine children of their own, in addition to the three Ryan boys. Unless some were farmed out to relatives in Broken Hill and Moonta, there were twelve children and two adults in the Mudie house by 1911. That year, Eddy turned twenty and he seems to have taken 'Ted' as his preferred name. If still living in the Mudie household, he would have been the eldest of the twelve children.[66]

Eddy Ryan and the Mudie children, probably taken in Broken Hill, c. 1906.
Back row: Edward James 'Eddy' Ryan, Beatrice Mudie, Alma Mudie, Ruby Mudie.
Front row: Jim Mudie, Charlie Mudie, Elizabeth 'Betty' Mudie (courtesy of Paul Mudie)

James Ramsay Mudie evidently struggled for more than a decade out at the Imperial Dam – to provide a liveable home for this crush of children, to get a decent wage, and even to keep his job. Initially, the building into which the family was squeezed was very basic. Its deficiencies were evidently notorious, provoking arguments at the council. In September 1901, the council offered Mudie extra money to help with his rent until 'suitable accommodation' could be provided at the dam site.[67] Soon after it was proposed that a 'two-room cottage' be erected, with 'the caretaker to add to the building from the material of the existing one' – a scarcely generous offer, considering that in 1901 Mudie's household included Margaret, the five Mudie children, plus the three Ryan nephews.[68] Then, in 1902, Mudie only just survived a hostile report questioning his engineering competence. Fortunately, his supporters among the aldermen saved his job.[69] But the following year, with water running low at the dam, during one of Broken Hill's frequent 'water famines', council officers proposed putting Mudie on half-time. He stood up for himself, writing to the council. One supportive alderman told council that Mudie was 'a hero in his eyes for continuing in his position when he was so badly treated by the council. The house the council had provided for the caretaker to live in was a disgrace.'[70] The *Barrier Daily Truth*, the town newspaper owned by the trade unions, supported Mudie. The paper asserted that his critics on council had sought to have him 'hung, drawn and quartered'. It lambasted the hard-faced aldermen who 'talked and chaffed – and Mudie starved'.[71] In the end, he kept his full-time job. But it was demanding. In 1907 an alderman reported he was working 'about 60 hours a week'. His pay was very modest; it rose slowly from around £3 to just over £4 a week in 1911 (or roughly $470 a week in a rough real-wage equivalent in 2019), for seven days' work, with 4 shillings a week deducted for rent.[72] This was at a time when the 'basic wage' under the historic Australian 'Harvester Judgment' of 1907 was set according to the estimation that an unskilled labourer with a wife and just *three* children needed £2 and 2s per week to live a civilised existence (or roughly equivalent to $260 in 2019). Mudie was responsible for *ten* children in 1907. In light of all this, we may assume that in Mudie's crowded cottage out at the Imperial Dam, the Ryan boys undoubtedly experienced childhoods of some privation.

Margaret Mudie, like her sister Elizabeth, had learned her Christianity as a devout Primitive Methodist. The church was a social centre back in Moonta and in Broken Hill. She ensured that the Ryan boys joined her own children and learned their Bible stories at Sunday school. The family lore has it that the Jesus who held sway in this household was the lowly Nazarene carpenter, the friend of the poor, the preacher who prophesied that one day the last would be first and the first last, the rabble-rouser who drove the money-changers out of the temple.[73]

The home at the Imperial Dam was in an isolated setting just outside Broken Hill. It was an oasis of a kind, in a flat and arid landscape of bleached-orange sandy soil, with very few plants. There were vast horizons, tall skies of dazzling blue, and simmering summer heat. Stock was sometimes watered there. An occasional drowning and midnight suicide at the dam gave it a sad reputation. The Ryan and Mudie children were probably educated at the nearest state schools, first the little Round Hill School (in the recently established but struggling village of Taltingan, just outside Broken Hill), and later at the North Primary School in Broken Hill. Here the Ryan boys learned a beautiful handwriting style.

James Ramsay Mudie had no great public profile in Broken Hill. Evidently, like so many workers, he was a loyal trade unionist. He shared something of that collective spirit of 'self-help' characteristic of British and Australian organised labour in this period, which sat easily alongside his socialism. He had one particular passion: the cooperative movement. He was prominent in the local branch of the town's leading friendly society, the Manchester Unity Independent Order of Odd Fellows (IOOF).[74] At this time, the IOOF lodges, which were linked to the local trade unions, aimed to bring a degree of security, through social insurance and mutual aid, to all classes in the town.

What values did James and Margaret Mudie instil in their adopted nephews? Ted was the eldest of a tribe of children living in a very simple home, ruled by church-going but radical adopted parents. No doubt Ted was counselled to be responsible for all the children under his care. Scorning his own father's drunkenness, he learned to be frugal and sober. His daughter Beth recalls that he neither drank nor smoked. We know almost nothing of Ted Ryan's boyhood. But he may well be the young 'Edward Ryan' who was injured in a shooting accident while hunting near Broken Hill in May 1905, and then hunted on for two days before returning to town to face an operation to remove the bullet. If so, he was a boy of some resilience.[75]

And politics? There is no direct evidence of high-profile political activism on the part of James and Margaret Mudie in this early period. But decades later, the Mudie children would play very prominent roles in Labor and socialist politics in Broken Hill.[76] Just as the Mudies undoubtedly learned their Labor politics at home, the Ryans surely absorbed theirs at the Mudie hearth also. We may guess that the Ryan boys grew up in a home where the household gods were known by all to be both Christian and socialist.[77]

Broken Hill Turns to Parliament

Growing up in Broken Hill during the first decade of the new century, the three Ryan boys must also have absorbed something of the rough-and-tumble spirit of the pioneering town, dominated by the towering head-frames and whirring winding-gear that loomed over the mines along the famous long 'line of lode'. Outbursts of labour agitation – spirited and resilient – marked the city's history. The trade unions, especially those connected with the mining industry, were powerful and often quite radical in outlook.

In addition, trade unionism in Broken Hill could be strikingly internationalist in spirit. Broken Hill was not the only town to have a popular 'All Nations' hotel, but it was a very good fit here. The mining workforce, after all, was composed of many newcomers to the British colonies, people from nations often beyond the British Empire who were adventurous or desperate enough to work in the fearfully difficult conditions. For many, an international outlook became instinctive, and it guided action. In 1889, Broken Hill's unions had sent invaluable aid to the wharf labourers of London during the famous Dock Strike. For years to come, prominent British union leaders visiting Australia would trek all the way to Broken Hill to thank the locals for their generous display of international solidarity at the birth of the 'new unionism' in Britain – mass trade unions, for the unskilled as much as the skilled. They addressed big public meetings, urging the local labour movement forward to still greater activism. The fiery British trade union leader Ben Tillett, for example, visited Broken Hill in June 1898. The labour celebrity happily laid the foundation stone of the impressive Trades Hall building, on Blende Street, the central rallying point of labour agitation far into the future.[78]

Of course, labour circles in Broken Hill could sometimes show the same spirit of racism and chauvinism that often afflicted the wider Australian labour movement in its early days. 'White Australia' was a much-vaunted policy, eventually proclaimed in the national platform of the Federal Labor Party. Labor politicians often linked the issue of skin colour with cheap labour – 'coloured labour'. A plot to cheapen labour, they argued, drove Britain's rapacious imperialism. Sometimes 'White Australia' was used as a slogan for rallying unionists to the defence of higher wages and better conditions, and against the conspiracy of the 'boss class' to drive down the price of labour under the cover of Empire. In contrast, conservatives in Australia often talked up the need to import indentured coloured labour into the country, in order to develop the sparsely populated north, so the argument ran. In combating this, some trade unionists certainly descended into race-baiting.

But in Broken Hill, labour leaders could also be found denouncing racial prejudice against 'foreigners' in Broken Hill as a red herring, fomented by the 'boss press' to divide organised labour. Broken Hill's 'internationalists' discounted race and laced their speeches and journalism with appeals to the 'international solidarity of labour'.[79] The *Barrier Daily Truth* appealed to readers constantly to see that solidarity was 'the impregnable rock of Labor' and that 'before Australians are Empire glorifiers they should be national lovers'. Imperialism was denounced as 'necessarily tyrannical'.[80] The pages of the *Barrier Daily Truth* were closed to imperial bards like Kipling; they featured instead the radical Australian internationalist verse of Bernard O'Dowd, with his hymns to labour's ideal of 'Brotherhood' across the colour line. Swinburne's 'Song of Unity' was emblematic also, with its plea to stand firm against the kingdoms of injustice and oppression, because 'While three men hold together/ The kingdoms are less by three.'[81]

One issue above all others could arouse the labour movement in Broken Hill to united action: the disastrously dangerous working conditions in the mining industry. In the great pits and tunnels, death could come suddenly, from fatal accidents, falls and explosions, as men and machines ground away at the seams far below the surface – or it could come more insidiously, through foul air and dust, both below and above ground. The town was infamous for the danger of lead poisoning, or 'plumbism', produced by the smelting of lead. It afflicted mine-managers and workers, old and young. Toxic wastes fluttered down across the town. The disease known as 'miner's lung', complicated by pneumonia, also blighted many lives. Poor housing stock, overcrowded boarding houses, and inferior sanitation, worsened the periodic outbreaks of other infectious diseases.[82]

A series of savage industrial battles marked the history of the town from 1889 to the First World War. Strikes in 1889 and 1890 won the unions one big gain, minimum time-based wages, plus a cut in the working week from 48 to 46 hours. The employers fought back. In June 1892, the Mine Managers' Association attempted to break the unions by insisting on new pay-rates, to be based upon the ore produced. In response, the Amalgamated Miners' Association (AMA), the chief mineworkers' union, called a strike. The head frames fell silent. The striking workforce of 7,000 men stood together, for a remarkable eighteen weeks. Tempers sizzled. An effigy of Zebina Lane, chairman of the Mine Managers' Association, was burned in Argent Street – the Mudies' street at that time. The employers proved to be superior in organisation. The conservative state government, led by Sir George Dibbs, who had just returned from the UK sporting a new knighthood, decided to boost the police force in Broken Hill to protect the 1,500 labourers imported by the employers to help bust the unions. Slowly, the solidarity of the strikers collapsed, and they returned to work. It was a painful defeat. Then came the settling of scores. Eventually, six union leaders were imprisoned for 'unlawful conspiracy and inciting riots'. The victorious employers now refused to recognise the union, restored the 48-hour week, and imposed piecework rates. Union membership went into decline.[83]

But the union leaders had learned lessons. In Broken Hill, as across the nation, the industrial wing of the labour movement looked to parliamentary politics for redress. Organised labour in Australia in the 1890s, as in many places across the world, was mobilising in a new direction, aiming to capture political office, to wield power over legislation and the public purse, at local, state and national levels.[84]

'Social democracy' was a new power in many lands, from the Kaiser's Germany to Republican France, and even in Australia on the eve of its Federation. Ideologues in tune with this new movement stressed the need to 'civilise capitalism', if not overturn it. These 'social democrats' argued for state intervention, for the arbitration of industrial disputes, and for regulation to achieve minimum standards in employment. The message was simple: people should not have to sell their labour under circumstances that imperilled their health. They urged a virtual revolution in raising the public revenue, advocating a shift toward income-related taxation, in order to fund high quality public goods – schools, libraries, technical colleges, and hospitals – in order to extend opportunities to all for their self-development. Public need before private possessions, was the battle cry. Things deemed vital for a good society should be funded at the cost of the superfluous wealth of the very rich, not the essentials of the poor. In short, they wanted to strengthen social mobility, and dissolve entrenched privilege. Beyond the friendly societies, they urged state-sponsored social insurance, for mutual aid in facing the hazards of employment and life, with universal contributions and entitlements. Some urged that *international* minimum standards of life and labour should be the crusade of the future.[85]

Broken Hill's trade unions were often ground-breaking in this new quest for social justice through 'labour representation' in parliament. Just two years after the crushing of the strike of 1892, several of the defeated trade unions' leaders threw themselves into electioneering for seats in the New South Wales state Parliament in Sydney. In 1894, trade unionists Josiah Thomas and William Ferguson, the second a colleague of Edward Ryan senior, succeeded at the polls and set out to bring some new colour to the green parliamentary benches at Macquarie Street in Sydney. The federation of the new Commonwealth of Australia in 1901 brought the new national Parliament into Labor's sights across the nation. Again Broken Hill chose Labor: in the first national elections Josiah Thomas won the new federal seat of Barrier, and he transferred from Macquarie Street to the first Australian Parliament in Melbourne.[86]

At the beginning of the new century, Labor in Broken Hill had a tenacious grip on political power at every level. In 1900, the town became the first municipal district in Australia – possibly in the world – to have a Labor Mayor, Jabez Wright, and a Labor-controlled City Council.[87]

In the early years of the new century, visiting celebrities from the British Labour Party usually included Broken Hill in their Australian speaking tours. Most notably, Ramsay MacDonald MP, secretary of the Labour Party (and chairman of the Independent Labour Party, a radical group within the larger Labour Party), in the company of his wife Margaret, an accomplished speaker and feminist activist in her own right, visited Broken Hill for a few days in early December 1906, just a week before Australia voted in a federal election. Before arriving in the hot mining town, MacDonald had attracted the ire of the conservative press for speaking in Ballarat in support of a young James Scullin (the future Labor Prime Minister of Australia), who was challenging Prime Minister Alfred Deakin for his seat. MacDonald attacked Deakin as a man who always campaigned on the side of the Tories and against Labour when he visited 'the Old Country', a man with an 'imperialistic mind' who mixed with Britain's extreme imperialists – those who 'could haul down a clean Union Jack and put up a dirty one in its place'.[88] When the MacDonalds arrived in

Broken Hill, the Mayor hosted a public reception for them in the Town Hall, and both spoke on 'Socialism' at the Social Democratic Club, and later at the Trades Hall. Ramsay MacDonald stressed the need for unionists and socialists to combine in the Labor Party. 'Socialism was International', he declared, and praised Broken Hill Labor's progressive internationalism. He also refuted the mischievous claim that socialists were irreligious. 'Socialist ethics', he boldly suggested, 'were found in the Sermon on the Mount and the Four Gospels' – an assessment that would have appealed to the Christian socialists in the Mudie household. Eddy Ryan was fifteen when the MacDonalds visited Broken Hill; perhaps he was in the 'crowded and attentive audience' at one of his meetings.[89]

Keir Hardie MP, even more famous than MacDonald as a Labour idol, visited Broken Hill a year later. Hardie arrived spectacularly in the middle of a big dust storm. Then, flanked by the city's leading labour figures, he spoke from the stage of the Hippodrome theatre. The crowd was packed tight. As the press reported, for Broken Hill it was 'perhaps the largest number of citizens that has ever assembled in an enclosed building'. Hardie served up a British labour history lesson, hailing the radicals, trade unionists, and socialists of the 'Old Country' who had won crucial reforms in the last century, such as the boon of a more democratic suffrage and the first workmen's compensation laws. He predicted that the new British Labour Party, represented at last by some forty MPs following the election of January 1906, would soon help win more historic reforms. He predicted the overturning of 'the land monopoly', the establishment of old age pensions, and the winning of that most elusive emblem of domestic reform, Irish Home Rule. Cheers rang out. He repeated MacDonald's claim that labour took its ethics from the Sermon on the Mount. He told his audience of his passionate conviction that everywhere trades unionism was 'the foundation upon which every sort of Labour progress must be built'. But socialists and unionists must work together, he pleaded, so that the moderate Labour Party might slowly be converted to socialism. He ended on an internationalist note. To great applause, he told the throng that he looked forward to 'the time to come when they would be free, [and] when the quarrels between nation and nation would cease to be'.[90]

Perhaps a young Eddy Ryan listened to either or both of MacDonald and Hardie. Or perhaps he simply heard about these two visits to Broken Hill by the British Labour Party's founding heroes over the Mudie family's dinner table. If so, the chimes of childhood memory a decade later might have brought back such names as Ramsay MacDonald and Keir Hardie to Private Ted Ryan, while he convalesced in military hospitals in England in the summer and autumn of 1916.

Keir Hardie

The 'Gibraltar Of Unionism' Defies the 'Dreadnought' Mania

There was more industrial turmoil brewing in Broken Hill by late 1908. A new 'Combined Unions Committee', giving eleven unions a united voice, had achieved good wage increases in 1906 under a two-year agreement. In 1908, the union leaders began to agitate for a 44-hour week and higher time-based pay. Again, the mine managers and the unions faced off. The town's big mining companies sought to impose a 12.5% pay cut on mineworkers. The resulting strike lasted twenty weeks. Arbitration was attempted. There were violent confrontations, and the State Government again prosecuted leading unionists. The working-class community again closed ranks, shunning the hundreds of strike-breakers and armed police sent to the city.[91] Significantly, some pickets labelled themselves 'All Nations Pickets'.[92]

A feature of the strike was the leadership of another visiting British labour organiser, Tom Mann, a pillar of fire reminiscent of his friend and predecessor in Broken Hill, Ben Tillett. A gifted orator, Mann took on the role of chief rabble-rouser for the Combined Unions in late 1908, and was soon at the storm centre of the dispute.

Mann was special. He brought to Broken Hill, even more emphatically than MacDonald and Hardie, a strong focus upon 'internationalism'. This word, still relatively new at the time, reflected an ideal that was gathering support among many thinking people. At its heart lay the belief that the resolution of international problems – such as imperialist rivalry and war, the exploitation of domestic and colonial labour, or the barriers to commerce between nations – required stronger international law and institutions. In the two decades before the First World War, from chambers of commerce to trade unions, and from universities to political movements, there was an intensifying trend to 'internationalise' their meetings and perspectives. So, international trade fairs, exhibitions, and conferences of all kinds proliferated. New 'international federations' emerged, for trade unions, political parties, and various organisations promoting progressive causes, such as women's suffrage.[93]

Tom Mann was alive to this new mood. He frequently referred to labour as 'the great International movement.'[94] And Broken Hill audiences were receptive to this theme. Their crusading paper, the *Barrier Daily Truth*, was anything but insular. It frequently carried articles pointing to parallels between Australia, Britain, America, France and Germany, as the labour movement progressed under the stimulus of common ideals. The names of overseas labour and socialist personalities – such as Hardie and MacDonald in Britain, the French leader Jaurès, the German leader Bebel, and the American leaders Debs and Haywood – must have been familiar to readers.[95]

Mann's style may be swiftly depicted. For example, at the conclusion of a tub-thumping speech outside the Broken Hill Trades Hall in October 1908 he led the crowd in giving three cheers 'for the glorious cause of internationalism and the success of the men on the Barrier'.[96] Rhetorically, he sought to reconcile his own faith in internationalism with the locals' almost religious devotion to the slogan 'White Australia'. For instance, he told a vast crowd in January 1909 that he was 'a believer in true internationalism, and therefore refused to be chained down by the old animosities'. He expressed sympathy for the downtrodden across the colonial world. He was no Empire patriot. He was 'ashamed' of the lack of democracy in the British Empire for the coloured races but he conceded that the races 'were better apart'.[97]

The conservative New South Wales State Government, led by the Liberal-Reform premier Sir Charles Wade, soon targeted Tom Mann as the chief troublemaker in Broken Hill. He and other leading unionists were arrested in January 1909, and a local magistrate committed a group to face trial in April for unlawful assembly and riotous behaviour. Mann got bail. But under his controversial bail conditions, Mann agreed that he 'should not take part in the dispute within New South Wales but that such conditions should not apply outside the State'.[98] Protests erupted in Sydney against this effort to silence Mann. In Broken Hill, the Combined Unions Committee defiantly arranged for thousands of workers to travel by train just across the border to nearby Cockburn, in South Australia, to hear Mann speak, standing proudly just inside South Australian territory. Seeking convictions from a more compliant out-of-town jury, the government then moved the trial of Mann and four other union leaders to the country town of Albury. Mann was subsequently acquitted, but two other unionists were found guilty and jailed.[99]

These local events happened to coincide with a famous war scare in Britain that hypnotised public opinion there and soon had its echoes in Australia. British right-wing newspapers fomented the so-called 'Great Naval Scare' in early 1909, with sensational revelations accusing Germany of stealing a march on the Royal Navy by suddenly and secretly constructing more 'Dreadnoughts' – the famous all-big-gun ship of that time – while Britain's Liberal government dreamt of peace. This in turn touched off an outbreak of naval hysteria on the right in Australia. Ultra-nationalist conservatives raised a hue and cry, urging Australia's new Federal Labor government, led by Andrew Fisher, to fund an expensive battleship, a Dreadnought, as a 'gift' to the mother country, supposedly to save her in her naval race with Germany. These panic-merchants alleged that the reformist British Liberal government of Herbert Asquith and David Lloyd George was dithering in a socialistic fool's paradise of pension schemes while neglecting naval defence. In far away Australia, Fisher was accused of the same sin. His critics chorused: 'sea power' must come before 'socialism'. His supporters urged him to resist 'The Dreadnought Mania'.[100] This was the setting for the latest round of industrial trouble in Broken Hill in which Mann took the leading role.

Herbert Henry Asquith

The furore over Mann's bail conditions and 'the Dreadnought mania' sparked fiery internationalist and anti-war rhetoric from the leaders of Broken Hill labour. On Sunday 4 April 1909, at the height of public agitation over Mann's recent arrest, and the shifting of the trial of the trade unionists to Albury, a protest march, led by the Broken Hill City Band, drew a 'great crowd' to the Central Reserve in Broken Hill – memorably, while 'a violent dust storm' was gathering. The city's socialist and Labor organisations had planned the rally jointly. Harry Gray, one of the arrested unionists awaiting trial, proposed a spectacular motion. It denounced the 'insane racial hatred' behind the naval panic, and behind war itself, as an evil foisted on the people by 'despots and exploiters'. It poured scorn on 'war scares' as deliberate distractions trailed by 'the robber class' across the path of social progress. In his speech, Gray mocked the 'mad fever' behind Anglo-German rivalry. He declared he would be 'proud to be gaoled as an International Socialist'. Another speaker fulminated against the Dreadnought 'gift' campaign as 'one of the greatest exhibitions of slobber imaginable'. A third praised the cheering crowd for 'doing something to bring about the brotherhood of man' and for seeking 'to lift up the downtrodden workers in other lands'. The multitude carried Gray's motion without any dissent. The meeting ended with a stirring rendition of 'Song of Australia'. Here was a moment when Australian Labor's nationalism and internationalism were finely threaded together.[101]

The great strike of 1909 eventually ended with an equivocal victory for the unions, although splits between workers in Broken Hill, and in Port Pirie, left a bitter aftertaste. Arbitration vindicated the stand of the strikers against the pay-cuts, but it denied them the 44-hour week. The unions built a new peak body, the 'Barrier Labour Federation', with the mining unions providing the backbone.[102] Broken Hill basked in its reputation as 'the Gibraltar of Unionism'.

It is worth noting too, that the mooted Dreadnought-class battleship was never given to Britain. Rather, Deakin, and later Fisher, invested in building a naval force to be christened in 1913 as the 'Royal Australian Navy', while pledging behind the scenes to place these ships under the control of the British Admiralty upon the outbreak of any war.

Thus, the scene is set: here is the occasionally uproarious Broken Hill, home of the youthful Ryan brothers. No doubt their step-father, James Ramsay Mudie, guided them in their loyalties to the Labor cause. When things were at their hottest over the summer of 1908-1909, and Tom Mann was wowing the crowds in front of the Trades Hall, Eddy Ryan was coming up to his eighteenth birthday. Tom and Harry were in their mid-teens – impressionable ages. Living in the Mudie household, they could scarcely have resisted the siren song of labour solidarity, nor the message that 'despots and exploiters' were ready to rob the working people, in peace – and war.

Chapter 4

CHOOSING WAR

LONDON, MELBOURNE, BROKEN HILL, PERTH, 1914-1915

> Thus an Imperial Force about 75,000 strong [from the Dominions] is instantly under the orders of those who direct the movements of our armies. They will go without question and with eager alacrity, wherever they are sent. They will do what they are told to do. "Theirs is not to reason why."
>
> — 'Brothers in Arms', editorial, *The Times* [London], 13 August 1914

When the British Government declared war upon Germany, pulling the whole of the British Empire into the calamity, toward midnight on Tuesday 4 August 1914, the three young Ryan brothers were still living in Broken Hill. Ted was a very keen member of the popular Amalgamated Miners' Association Band, the leading trade union band in the city. On 14 July 1914, he attended the gaieties of the band's annual ball. He had been active in the band since 1910, and on the management committee since 1912.[103] But there is evidence that within a few short weeks or months after the outbreak of war, all three Ryan brothers had moved away from Broken Hill. The war, in different ways, would sweep them up and, in different ways, it would mark and maim them forever.

Harry was probably the first to go. In early September, he travelled to Lithgow, New South Wales, a mining and railway town west of Sydney. He stayed briefly in Lithgow's Mort's Estate with Mrs Mildred Seaton, a local Labor worker, who may have been a relation of the Mudie family with roots in Arbroath, Scotland.[104] Ted and Tom had also departed the Mudie household, but they travelled much further, all the way to Western Australia. Why? To find work, or just new horizons? It is impossible to be certain. But, like countless other Australians, their lives were upended by decisions made in faraway European capitals, and especially in London, by politicians, ambassadors, Foreign Office staff, generals, and admirals, quite unknown to them.

Hell-bent

Let us look briefly to these higher places, and ask how it was that the imperial government in London came to choose war in 1914. And what role did Australia's government play in this?

The essential story may be swiftly summarised. The crisis in Europe arose from a dispute in the Balkans between Serbia and Austria-Hungary. A local war between these two antagonists had broken out following Austria's brutal and foolish declaration of war on Tuesday 28 July. But an explosion of this local war into a European and world war was by no means inevitable, notwithstanding the networks of rival alliances and the willingness of diplomats to bluff and threaten. The European crisis had suddenly deepened over the weekend beginning Friday 31 July. Serbia's sponsor, Tsarist Russia, had decreed a general mobilisation against both Austria-Hungary and Germany and this was suddenly revealed in the British Parliament in London on the afternoon of that same Friday. Then on the evening of Saturday 1 August, Germany responded with a fateful declaration of war upon Russia.[105]

At that point, the British Government of Liberal Prime Minister Herbert Asquith, under pressure from the Conservative opposition and the Tory press, ceased to push for a diplomatic settlement and prepared the ground for Britain's rapid intervention. On the afternoon of Sunday 2 August, Asquith's Cabinet decided by a narrow margin to promise British naval support to France. Alliance fidelity, and fear of abandonment, trumped caution. In effect, this meant that Britain would enter virtually any European War in which France was engaged – whatever the cause. Britain's sudden choice to intervene, as a loyal ally of France and Russia, came before news had reached London of the ham-fisted German ultimatum to Belgium (on Monday 3 August) and before the German invasion of Belgium (on Tuesday 4 August). This was the occasion, but not the cause, of the British Empire's war, for the decision had been made on Sunday 2 August.

So controversial was the Asquith Cabinet's decision of Sunday that it prompted four of Asquith's nineteen Cabinet Ministers to submit their resignations over the next two days. Nowhere else in Europe did such a thing happen. The rebellious ministers were shocked that their Cabinet leaders, backed by threats to sink the government if defied, were absolutely determined to intervene in the looming war, essentially for reasons of solidarity with Russia and France – irrespective of the fate of Belgium.

Europe then slid over into the abyss. On Monday 3 August the German Government, mesmerised by the danger in the east from Russia, rushed forward to another declaration of war, this time upon Russia's ally in the west, France. The following morning, Tuesday 4 August, German troops began the invasion of Belgium. Berlin conceded publicly that the move was wrong, but beseeched Britain to understand that it was necessary, in order to save Germany from the perils inherent in a two-front war. The German move was diplomatically disastrous, costing Germany a great deal in world opinion. Most importantly, it gave London a new reason for entering the war – ostensibly, to defend Belgium, whose neutrality all were bound to respect by a treaty dating from 1839. So, deep in the evening of that same day, Tuesday 4 August, a small clique within the Asquith Cabinet, just five of the nineteen ministers who normally gathered at Downing Street, opted for an instant declaration of war against Germany. A hastily mustered and sparsely attended meeting of the King's Privy Council that same night formalised it. Many Radicals felt the government had stampeded the nation into war, but only a few criticised the decision publicly.[106]

It is seldom mentioned that, on that same day, the American President Woodrow Wilson cabled to the capital of every belligerent power an offer to use the United States as a mediating nation, to bring the Balkan dispute to the Permanent Court of Arbitration at The Hague. Over the next few weeks, cables in reply dribbled in from Britain and Europe – all conveying similar excuses. War – righteous, defensive war, against the wicked invader – was unstoppable, so they all pleaded. But, in fact, an alternative to the protracted disaster was always there to be chosen, from the first day, had there been the political will in the palaces, chancelleries, and parliaments of Europe.[107]

Meanwhile, Australia had leapt well ahead of the British decision. In the early evening of Monday 3 August, (that is, in the early morning of Monday 3 August, London time), a handful of ministers from the cabinet of Liberal Prime Minister Joseph Cook – in the middle of an election campaign and with the Parliament prorogued – sent an astonishing cable from Melbourne to London. It offered the 'imperial government' an expeditionary force of 20,000 men, to anywhere, for any objective, in any formation desired by London, and with Australia promising to meet the entire cost. Viewed from London, this was some forty hours before the British Cabinet finally decided upon a declaration of war at all.[108]

Did Australia go into the war with decent reluctance, with eyes open, and with a government determined to weigh the costs and objectives? And if Australian lives were to be placed in peril and lost, did the government ensure that those losses would be endured only for the sake of Australia's safety – and nothing else? Not a bit of it.

Of course, Australia could scarcely escape the war. Australia's belligerent status was decided upon by London, as a matter of law. The new federated Commonwealth was a self-governing 'white dominion' of the British Empire. But it had no powers in foreign policy, and certainly no constitutional power to choose neutrality. That said, Australia's decision makers were not captive: they had the power to decide when to offer military contributions, how much to offer, where to send troops and ships, and for what reason. In the decade before the war, Australia's freedom of action had been compromised; earlier governments had promised to hand over Australia's navy to British command upon the outbreak of war; and they had secretly prepared for – but not promised absolutely – to send an expeditionary force. So, by the outbreak of war, Australia's Government had raised expectations that narrowed its choices, but it was not so tightly tethered to London as to be in bondage. The Cabinet Ministers in Melbourne could decide upon a reckless immersion of the nation's lives and treasures in this world war, obedient to all of London's decisions. Or they could carefully husband those resources, and demand a say in the high diplomacy that would define the war aims for which Australians would surely die. They opted for recklessness.

Such recklessness prompted London to take Australia for granted – and the Empire's decision makers did exactly that.

Shadows of War – and Unemployment

How did this affect the Ryans and Mudies of Broken Hill? Very likely, soon after the outbreak of war, Harry had gone from Broken Hill to Lithgow. He was working there briefly for the government railways, either as a fitter or a baker – he gave different occupations in various enlistment and demobilisation papers. But, as we have seen, he turned up in Sydney in mid-September 1914, to enlist.

Ted and Tom were more adventurous. The railway to Western Australia was not completed until 1917, so the two brothers must have taken a ship from Port Adelaide to Fremantle at some point after August 1914.[109] In early 1915, they were sharing a house at 356 Barker Road, in Subiaco, a suburb of Perth. At that time, 'Subi' was a mostly working-class suburb. From this address Tom enlisted in the AIF in January 1915.

So it was that Harry enlisted in the AIF in Sydney, and joined a New South Wales battalion, the 13th Battalion, while Tom, and finally Ted, enlisted in Perth. Tom and Ted were eventually allocated to the predominantly Western Australian battalions, the 11th Battalion and the 51st Battalion respectively. A battalion, it is worth noting, was the key Australian unit to which the men felt their primary loyalty, identified by their common coloured shoulder flashes. A battalion was a formation of roughly a thousand men, generally commanded by a Lieutenant Colonel.

The River of Righteousness

Why, in the rush of youth, did the Ryans enlist?

Moral enthusiasms cannot be discounted. The Australian press, reflecting the British, was awash with the great moral issues said to be at the heart of Britain's war. The British leaders highlighted German guilt, and war crimes. The ear-worms planted early in the war – Germany's 'blank cheque' of support to Austria, Germany's 'violation of Belgian neutrality' (with its overtone of rape), the German chancellor's reported reference to the Belgian Treaty of 1839 as 'a scrap of paper', the 'Belgian atrocities', and Germany's problem of 'Prussian militarism' – would wriggle on for a century, and more. Supposedly, the Germans suffered from shameful moral infirmities. They were apparently uniquely blighted.

Britain bathed in a warming river of self-righteousness. Prime Minister Asquith told the House of Commons on 6 August 1914 that Britain was fighting for only two sacred, throat-catching reasons: first, 'to fulfil a solemn international obligation' toward neutral Belgium, and second, because Britain believed passionately that 'small nationalities are not to be crushed'.[110] In a speech at Dublin on 25 September 1914 Asquith added a grander goal designed to appeal to progressives: Britain sought, through war, 'the definite repudiation of militarism as the governing factor in the relation of states and of the future moulding of the European world'. Asquith promised that, after securing a victorious peace, Britain would build 'a real European partnership based on the recognition of common right, and established and enforced by a common will'.[111]

At the Guildhall in London on 9 November 1914 Asquith fashioned a famous summary of Britain's chivalrous goals, a statement that would be repeatedly quoted, not least by Asquith himself, as the only authoritative definition of Britain's war aims: 'We shall never sheathe the sword which we have not lightly drawn until Belgium recovers in full measure all and more than all that she has sacrificed, until France is adequately secured against the menace of aggression, until the rights of the smaller nationalities of Europe are placed upon an unassailable foundation, and until the military domination of Prussia is wholly and finally destroyed.'[112] According to Britain's leaders, the Empire was fighting for honour – simply for honour. Apparently, the idea of adding territorial conquests to the British Empire never crossed their minds.

In the opening weeks of the war, the bulk of the Australian press – including the trade union paper in Broken Hill, the *Barrier Daily Truth* – accepted these simplicities and went to war in full battle cry, trumpets blazing.[113] The cablegrams coming from Britain, censored at both the London and Australian ends, presented the war in stark terms, wrong and right. The received truths were unchallenged: Germany had started the war; Britain had intervened on the side of France (Russia was ignored) because it was the only possible response to a blackguard's bullying; Britain's objective was a grand moral ideal, to put right the world. The British cablegrams kept the Australian press focussed upon a narrow range of events, such as the German attack upon neutral Belgium, and the atrocities committed there by German troops (many of which did take place) – both providing a spectacular vindication of Britain's decision to enter the war. Controversies over Russian diplomacy during the crisis, and the Russian invasion of East Prussia, were avoided. According to the press it was all absolutely clear: the Empire was engaged in a giant act of international philanthropy, to cleanse the world of a monstrous wickedness. The Union Jack, it seemed, was woven from the very cloths of heaven.

The front-page headlines of the *Barrier Daily Truth* captured the spirit of righteous anger: 'WAR IN EUROPE. BELGIAN NEUTRALITY INVADED. MENACE TO ENGLAND'S

HONOR AND SHORES'. 'GREAT BRITAIN FORCED TO FIGHT. GERMAN TRICKERY AND INSOLENCE.' 'HEROIC STAND OF THE BELGIAN DEFENDERS.'[114] On 8 September, the *Barrier Daily Truth* even offered an editorial entitled 'The Glorious British Empire', fully embracing Britain's war as just, and praising Australia's offer of 20,000 men to be sent 'to fight in the British lines in Europe' – so all believed. The Dominions were displaying a 'marvellous unanimity'. 'All classes should be proud to belong to such a great Empire', preached the workers' paper.[115]

As in most of Australia, the bulk of organised Labor in Broken Hill accepted the justice of Britain's cause. The mother country was thought to be standing on a moral pinnacle and her statesmen were as archangels. It was a holy war, for Right. Therefore, when the Labor leader Andrew Fisher and his Federal Labor Party triumphed in the national elections of 5 September, the Broken Hill unions celebrated the victory as a patriotic boon. Labor, the party of social obligation, would lead the nation in a noble war, a collective effort, to save small nations in Europe from a cruel invader. Australian Labor rode with Britain, on a moral high horse.

Andrew Fisher (L) with Keir Hardie, 14 December 1907

But little cracks in the patriotic front in Broken Hill were discernible, even in the first weeks of the war, especially among the small more ideologically driven socialist groups to the left of Labor. This led to a spectacular incident of violence. In early September, on the eve of voting in the federal election, a crowd of outraged patriots decided to punish a group of anti-war demonstrators, who had allegedly jeered at a party of volunteers departing for Adelaide at Broken Hill's railway station. The flag-waving and song-singing enthusiasts for the war descended upon the city's 'Socialist Hall' and wrecked it.[116]

A month later a controversy erupted in the ranks of Ted Ryan's beloved AMA Band. The proud trade union musicians had a long-standing policy of not playing the 'National Anthem', that is 'God Save The King', at the end of their concerts. Some members wanted this policy honoured, and stoutly refused to play any 'patriotic music' to encourage recruiting. They insisted on sticking to the traditional workers' anthem, 'The Internationale', as the last piece in all concerts. Other band members threatened to withdraw from the AMA Band altogether unless it reversed the long-standing policy and embraced the 'National Anthem', as a patriotic gesture. Tempers were short on both sides. A special meeting of the AMA eventually struck a compromise: the AMA Band was instructed to finish concerts with *either* the 'National Anthem' *or* the 'Song of Australia'. Thus, 'The Internationale' vanished from the wartime concerts.[117]

'A State of Affairs in Broken Hill Unparalleled'

Much more serious worries soon engulfed the city – threats of mass unemployment.

Perhaps the Ryan brothers enlisted in the army in the generous spirit that clearly swept so many others into the AIF, in Broken Hill as elsewhere: to risk their lives valiantly in a quest to save others from harm in faraway places. But there is a strong chance that more material objectives were at play.

The collapse of employment in Broken Hill in August 1914, immediately upon the outbreak of war, almost certainly prompted all three Ryan brothers to leave the town. As war erupted in Europe, Broken Hill lost its most important customers – who happened to be German. Valuable contracts were cancelled. Sales of concentrates of zinc and lead to German firms ceased.[118] Thus, the bottom fell out of the employment market in Broken Hill – with a bang. In a sense, the crash in Broken Hill was emblematic of a much wider one, the crash of the grand international liberal project of the nineteenth century, inspired by men like Richard Cobden and John Bright. Most British liberals had firmly believed that commerce was the grand panacea that would sideline war as sure as rationality would displace irrationality. After all, who would wish to slaughter their customer? Instead, irrationality had triumphed in 1914.

The crisis at Broken Hill was immediate. On the second day of the war, the *Barrier Daily Truth* predicted that many mines would soon move to half-time operations.[119] The competing newspaper, the *Barrier Miner*, a privately-owned paper generally aligned with the employers, carried equally dark reports. It predicted that the mine owners 'would do their best to employ the men on half time' but might have to let up to half the workforce go, and government relief was vital to cushion the blow.[120] Half the workforce had been warned: ruin awaited them in Broken Hill. A week later the evening express train departing the city was stuffed full of 'single men who had been put out of work on account of the European crisis'.[121] The large North Mine closed for ten days on 13 August. 'The distress being felt here demands immediate action', editorialised the *Barrier Daily Truth*. With markets 'crippled', on 20 August the miners' unions and management met to discuss 'a state of affairs in Broken Hill unparalleled in any other part of the Empire'.[122] 'Distress Committees' and 'Relief Committees' began to operate in the city but with some spokesmen hinting that men could always consider the patriotic alternative to relief, enlistment. At the end of the month, the Silverton Tramway Company confirmed the exodus from the city: there had been a whacking 3,459 departures from Broken Hill and only 1,054 arrivals.[123] A nationwide search for jobs had begun for many workers.

Unemployment in Broken Hill soared. The overall statistics were stunning: almost 9,000 men had been employed in the Broken Hill mines in late 1913; after only three months of war in 1914 this total had dropped to 5,305.[124]

Mick Considine, soon to become Broken Hill's federal MP, would later insist that economic pressure had been a crucial factor in driving men from the city's mines to enlist in 1914. 'When the war started they would remember that a set was made against single men in Broken Hill and elsewhere.' Finger-pointing, in the midst of hard times, was a form of 'economic conscription', he complained.[125] This provoked bitter arguments that rattled on for years over whether or not men had been 'starved into enlistment' or were simply eager to volunteer for service.[126]

The economic collapse hit the city's Municipal Council quickly. In January 1915, the councillors heard from the Town Clerk that, as a result of the war, 'considerable difficulty' was expected in the council's finances in the coming year.[127] The very next month, the council, in a closed late-night session running over three hours, resolved to sack James Ramsay Mudie, after fifteen years of service as a caretaker. The exact reasons were hidden, suggesting it was not simply a matter of economy.[128] In any case, Mudie lost both his job and the house at the Imperial Dam. As a result, the large Mudie family was almost certainly cash-strapped, and probably in no position to assist the three Ryan boys after January 1915, even if they had opted to return to Broken Hill. Perhaps that added to the pressures to enlist.

Broken Hill's troubles were not unique. Much of Australia was reeling from the economic shocks of war. Unemployment figures across Australia in the third quarter of 1914 stunned the government. The Commonwealth Statistician reported that unemployment among trade unionists across the country had almost doubled, from 5.7 per cent in June to 10.7 per cent in October. There were big leaps in all states. Unemployment in the Ryans' home state of New South Wales climbed from 5.8 per cent to 9.3 per cent. Western Australia, where Ted and Tom were seeking work, showed a similar increase, from 6.3 per cent to 9.2 per cent. Joblessness in Victoria, Tasmania, Queensland and South Australia was well above 10 per cent.[129]

Therefore, perhaps the age-old recruiting sergeant, unemployment – or the threat of it – was directing Harry, Tom, and Ted, by a roundabout route, into the army. Certainly other Anzacs, when interviewed many years later, instantly suggested that hardship at home had hounded many a 'volunteer' into the ranks. For instance, why did Eric Abraham, and his four brothers enlist? 'Well you've got to remember that times were pretty tough in those days', Abraham replied to an interviewer. He recalled his eldest brother explaining his decision to enlist as a flight from the 'ghastly place' that was his failing farm, and saying 'anything is better than nothing'.[130] Why did Marcel Caux from Marrickville, whose Belgian parents were both dead, enlist? 'To get away from the terrible, tragic life I was leading ... It wasn't living really, it wasn't life. It was just existing', Caux reflected.[131]

The Ryan brothers' decisions to join up, therefore, perhaps reflected their need to fend for themselves, without the support of the proverbial 'little platoons' – parents. The brothers' parents were dead; the Mudie family was under pressure. A reminder of this came at enlistment. All three Ryan brothers faced a difficulty in nominating their next of kin. Harry gave only 'Mrs M. Seaton (Aunt)', from Lithgow, as his next of kin – possibly a relation, as noted above, but not his aunt. Tom gave his brother Ted's name and their last address together at Subiaco. When Ted enlisted, as we have seen, he gave the name of his uncle, James Ramsay Mudie of Broken Hill. Later, in letters to the Department of Defence, James Mudie would indeed describe the young soldier Edward James Ryan from Perth as 'my nephew and adopted son'.[132]

Exactly what motivated Ted in his decision to join up in September 1915, nine months after Tom, is guesswork. Perhaps the vivid reports in the Perth newspapers of the battles at Gallipoli affected him – especially as he believed that both his brothers were there.[133] Advertisements in the press during September 1915 pleaded that Western Australia needed to enlist 'an average of 25 men daily, merely to enable the troops she has already sent to the front to be maintained at their full and efficient strength'.[134] No doubt he felt a sense of solidarity with his two brothers. The prospect of seeing them again must also have been a powerful draw.

Or perhaps it was the lure of the six shillings a day (roughly equivalent to $32 in 2019), the advertised pay for a Private at that time. How secure was Ted Ryan in his employment in Subiaco in Perth in 1915? While living as a tenant at 356 Barker Road, Ted had found jobs as a 'storekeeper' and 'confectioner' with Mary Ann and John Burrows at a smallgoods store just around the corner at 135 Rokeby Road. Possibly Ted also worked at the connected shop next door, at number 133 Rokeby Road, the Ideal Tea Rooms, run fortuitously by Annie Kathleen Ryan – no relation, it appears. But Ted did endure some bad luck in Subiaco. Just a few days after Tom's enlistment in January 1915, fire damaged the house in which he lived in Barker Road.[135] He may have lost possessions; he may have been feeling the pinch. Probably he moved into a room with his employers, the Burrows family at 135 Rokeby Road, just across the road from

Subiaco's famous King's Hall, scene of recruitment meetings and public gatherings in aid of the wounded during 1915. That might have inspired him. At the Burrows' home, no doubt, Ryan also heard talk that their new son-in-law, William Bown, aged 22, only recently married to the Burrows' young daughter, Ethel, had decided to enlist. Bown joined up in August 1915, just a month before Ted, both giving 135 Rokeby Road as their home address.[136] Very likely, Ted felt under some moral pressure to follow Bown.

No doubt the thoughts of being reliably paid as a soldier, of being looked up to as a hero, and of travelling overseas, were all very alluring. Another West Australian, who enlisted at about this time, remembered exactly this intoxicating mixture of motives: 'Hero-worship and thoughts of the voyage and good times generally actuated by the fact that I would be receiving pay all this time weighed with me.'[137]

'A Gigantic Human Slaughterhouse'

When Ted Ryan followed his brothers' examples and enlisted in Perth in September 1915, his decision meant that all three Ryan brothers – three Broken-Hill-bred orphaned boys, now unskilled working-class young men, with no property – were all in the uniform of the AIF. Three small figures, on an enormous global stage.

Lifting our gaze to that enormous stage, we need to look not only to the battlefield but also to neutral Switzerland at this very moment. On 5 September 1915, only a fortnight before Ted Ryan enlisted, about thirty shadowy socialist dissenters gathered secretly in the small mountain village of Zimmerwald for a four-day conference to revive what had been the 'guiding star' of the socialist movement – a spirit of internationalism. As they travelled the short distance from Berne to Zimmerwald, the scarcely known Russian exile, Leon Trotsky, joked sourly how truly tragic it was that those socialist leaders loyal to internationalism could be squeezed into just four coaches for the journey. But they did not lack courage. They met in defiance of their warring governments, boldly meeting with 'enemies' abroad, risking prison, and planning for political action to bring forward an early peace. There, at a small guesthouse, the Villa Beau Séjour (which still stands), handfuls of socialist activists, from France, Germany, Austria, Russia, Italy, Switzerland, the Netherlands, the Balkans, Poland, Romania, and Scandinavia, debated the issues. No British socialists were present, for London had denied passports to two who had planned to come. The majority at Zimmerwald was still made up of men and women who were humanitarians to the marrow, and wary of the ultra-left's call for 'civil war' to end the war. Others, the soon-to-be-famous Vladimir Lenin and his few allies, were much more revolutionary in temper. But together they eventually hammered out a common manifesto on the basis of Trotsky's draft, decrying the God-fearing rulers who had transformed Europe into 'a gigantic human slaughterhouse'. The Zimmerwald Manifesto denied that this was a people's war. It demanded an end to the 'patriotic truce' upheld as 'sacred' on the domestic front by the so-called 'patriotic' pro-war politicians. It appealed to the working class 'to take up this fight for peace – for peace without annexations or war indemnities' – a slogan that would soon mobilise many minds. Truth-tellers everywhere were urged to challenge the fog-machines of propaganda and censorship that hid the politicians' real war aims. The people must restore peace. 'Never in the history of the world has there been a more urgent, a more noble, a more sublime task', pleaded the men and women of Zimmerwald.[138]

Leon Trotsky

Was this just a faint rumble of discontent from a forgettable and powerless underground? Certainly the Entente governments, by refusing passports to several moderate socialists, boosted the influence of the revolutionary left at Zimmerwald. The conference clearly lifted the spirits of those more adventurous souls, sickened by the war, willing to challenge the 'party truce', and press for a negotiated peace. Those dissidents were still the minority in the labour movements in 1915. But the raw emotions on display, and the deep revulsion against war voiced at Zimmerwald, would soon match the mood of millions of people across Europe.[139]

At first, in faraway Australia, only one small socialist newspaper had the contacts to ferret out reports on Zimmerwald in late 1915.[140] Just a year later, a well-organised public activism, surging up from the labour movement across Australia, would defeat the Hughes Government's referendum on conscription – a unique popular achievement in the history of this war. In that campaign, the people of Broken Hill would be among the first to mobilise, to rally for radical solutions, to denounce the continuing conflict, and to press for peace.

Amalgamated Miners' Association Band on a visit to Sydney, 1913

Chapter 5

'WIDER STILL AND WIDER'

CAIRO AND LONDON, MARCH 1915

Wider still and wider shall thy bounds be set,
God, who made thee mighty, make thee mightier yet.

— A.C. Benson, 'Land of Hope and Glory' (1902)

1915 was to be a huge year for the three Ryan brothers. After Ted's enlistment in September, all three sported the famous Norfolk-jacket, the dress tunic of the AIF. But let us digress a little and update the story of Ted's younger brothers, Harry and Tom, in early 1915.

When the Going Was Good

Trooper Harry Ryan (still known of course as 'Edward James Ryan', Service Number 672) of the 13th Battalion, the first of the brothers to volunteer, was already in Egypt. He and his comrades had departed Melbourne on board HMAT *Ulysses* (A38) on 22 December 1914, bound for Egypt. A week later, on 29 December, Harry had enjoyed his nineteenth birthday on board the troopship. HMAT *Ulysses* arrived at Alexandria on 31 January 1915.[141]

After disembarking, Harry Ryan's 13th Battalion established its camp on the aerodrome at Heliopolis in Cairo. During February and March 1915 the men were thrown into more military training. On 22 March, Major-General Sir Alexander Godley, the General Officer Commanding the 'New Zealand and Australian Division', which included the 13th Battalion, inspected the men in Cairo.[142]

If Harry was writing to his brothers, his letters must have set their minds racing. Their youngest brother had departed on a fabulous adventure, or so it seemed, an odyssey such as an orphaned boy from Broken Hill might never have hoped to enjoy – a sea voyage, on a grand ocean liner, to England, as the first volunteers believed, and to exotic and ancient places along the way. What an opportunity!

At that same time in March 1915, Tom Ryan, the second to volunteer, was still undergoing his basic training at a large camp at Blackboy Hill near Perth. He was in a group formally labelled as reinforcements for the 11th Battalion, which was already deployed in Egypt.

What stands out from the press coverage of the Blackboy Hill camp at this time is the number of concerts and edifying speeches provided for the men in camp, many from local religious figures, all stoking the fires of high moral enthusiasm. Tom Ryan, as a member of the Perth YMCA, may well have attended these. For example, on 16 March, a thousand soldiers listened to an illustrated talk in the large 'YMCA Military Tent', featuring the Anglican Dean of Perth, Henry Mercer, one of the most prominent among the Australian clerics ready to mix blood and holy water. The Dean spoke with fervour on the subject of 'Plucky Little Belgium', blessing that bright pearl of moral certainty in the minds of the men: that they were all engaged in a holy war for one noble goal, to liberate the people of Belgium.[143] (Years later, in Britain, Mercer would be found guilty of multiple frauds and he died disgraced in prison.) At the end of the month, twelve hundred soldiers watched a lantern-slide show, featuring photos of AIF soldiers already in Egypt. They listened to speeches and recitations, and sang popular patriotic songs, such as 'The Empire's Rally' and 'Kaiser Bill's Christmas Dinner'. But the big hit of the evening was the marching song 'Australia's Call to Arms', which provoked 'cheers and applause for some considerable time, and the soldiers joined in the chorus with gusto'.[144] That chorus ended with 'Three cheers for the British Union Jack!' The preceding verses included the lines:

And when in later years our history appears,
Let Australia's future sons be proud to say,
That their fathers, like our own, fought for rectitude alone,
To protect the weaker nations 'gainst the strong.[145]

'Fought for rectitude alone.' Here was the idealism of the men, and the Australian nation, writ large. The war was to be a just war, for the salvation of oppressed Belgians above all – not a war of expansion for the British Empire. Did those men in high office, those guardians of the young lives entrusted to the Empire's cause, in London and Melbourne, honour this spirit?

Another Spirit: 'Buccaneers'

During those months of training for Tom and Harry at the beginning of 1915, the men in high office determining the war aims of the British Empire did not stand still. Asquith's themes in his public speeches of 1914 – that Britain was fighting solely for Belgium, for small nationalities, and for 'public right' – scarcely matched the facts. A giddying escalatory spiral in war aims was under way.

In the first days of the war, as the British Cabinet launched schemes for the taking of all German colonies, Asquith – an incorrigible skirt-chaser – told his young lover, Venetia Stanley, how he had entertained his colleagues around the table, quipping that 'we looked more like a gang of Elizabethan buccaneers than a meek collection of black-coated Liberal Ministers'.[146]

As the war widened in late 1914 and early 1915, and as the list of captured German colonies in China, Africa, and the Pacific grew longer, another spirit possessed politicians in both Britain and Australia. Some boasted of the 'wider still and wider' bounds the British Empire had already achieved, and encouraged the public to demand still grander goals. Out of public view, detailed planning began for the aggrandisement of the British Empire. Saving Belgium and France from a cruel invader seemed to be only the first step. Germany would have to be punished. And there could be profit in punishment.

Increasingly, Britain's goal appeared to be not only the defeat but also the 'crushing' of Germany, both militarily and economically; the parcelling out among the victors of Germany's colonies; and the prosecution of a merciless blockade and land war until the Entente's armies achieved the occupation of Berlin itself. Such a military triumph would enable a dictated peace – supposedly the only path to safety.

Imperial orators got the headlines. Lord Curzon, an archetypal imperial figure on the right of British politics, told a public meeting in September 1914 that there could be no early peace: 'I should like to see the lances of the Bengal Lancers fluttering down the streets of Berlin, and like to see the dark-skinned Gurkha making himself at ease in the gardens of Potsdam.'[147] In December 1914, Austen Chamberlain (half-brother of Neville), a leading Tory, added his voice: 'Not till the German armies have been rolled back by the Russians on the east and by the other allies on the west, not until our forces meet in Germany, can victory be won or a lasting peace secured.'[148]

Liberal voices incited the same passions. In February 1915, Winston Churchill, First Lord of the Admiralty in Asquith's Liberal Government, paraded himself as a 'Mr Standfast'. 'The pressure on Germany will never be relaxed', he vowed in an interview in Paris, 'until she has surrendered unconditionally'.[149]

Loot for Russia, March 1915

Why then were Australians being sent to the Middle East – or the 'Near East' as most Englishmen called it – at all? For what exactly were so many young Australians, men like Harry and Tom Ryan, already risking their lives in that faraway place? Most Australians have been taught to be satisfied with the simplest of explanations: the campaign aim was to 'open up the Straits', and to 'knock Turkey out of the war', because the Ottoman Empire was allied to Germany. This is shallow stuff.

To understand the depth of the disaster, we must peek into the realms of high diplomacy – from which Australia was almost wholly excluded. In the first week of November 1914, the Ottoman Empire joined the ranks of the war-making governments. The unfortunate citizens of that empire were bumped into war, by a handful of hawkish ministers in Constantinople, and by steady German pressure. Moreover, the cause of Ottoman neutrality had been weakened when Russia, France and Britain, in badgering the Ottoman Government, had revealed their eagerness to grab what they could of the Ottoman Empire, if war erupted.[150] Thus, when Russia declared war upon the Ottomans on 2 November 1914, France and Britain followed loyally within days. In fact, British bombardments of the Turkish forts at the Dardanelles came two days before the formal declaration of war on 5 November.[151]

Soon Britain made conquests of Ottoman territory. An Indian Expeditionary Force seized Basra in the south of Iraq within three weeks of the war opening, in November 1914. British political officials travelling with the Indian force immediately assured local notables that the benefits of British rule over Basra would never be relinquished. Next, no less an imperial nabob than Lord Hardinge, Viceroy of India, visited Basra in February 1915 offering local officials 'the confident assurance' that Britain's 'more benign administration' was there to stay. Like-minded Empire builders in London pressed Hardinge's case for annexations in Iraq.[152]

Lord Hardinge

But London was guarded. Russian eyes – jealous eyes – were watching as Britain swallowed up Cyprus, Egypt, and signalled she might polish off Iraq as well. The mighty men of Whitehall were fully seized with the need to bribe Russia with something big to add to her own account to induce her to stay in the war, as a loyal ally. This now guided events.

The context is worth recalling: Tsarist Russia was at this time Europe's most oppressive autocracy. Concessions toward civil liberty, parliamentary government, and democracy, glimpsed at the time of the Revolution of 1905, had shrivelled under Tsar Nicholas II's reviving despotism following the defeat of the revolution, a despotism buttressed with French money. Anti-Jewish prejudice in Russia was so strong that even British Cabinet Ministers of Jewish ancestry could not visit Russia and Sir Edward Grey, Britain's Foreign Secretary, had repeatedly confessed his powerlessness to do anything about this, as recently as July 1914.[153]

From November 1914, suddenly a scramble for the whole of the Ottoman Empire captured the minds of the Entente's diplomats and war-planners. In Petrograd, the Tsarist elite saw the chance to win long-cherished territorial goals at the Straits; nothing less than the possession of Constantinople, the western coast of the Bosporus, the Sea of Marmora and its islands, southern Thrace, the coast of Asia Minor, and the Dardanelles. Sir Edward Grey encouraged Russia. In early November 1914, Count Benckendorff, the Russian Ambassador in London, known as 'old Benck' in diplomatic circles, reported to Petrograd assurances from Grey that 'the fate of the Straits and of Constantinople this time cannot be decided in any way except as conforms with our interest'.[154] On 13 November, Benckendorff assured his masters in Russia that King George V himself had generously promised him that 'as far as Constantinople is concerned, it is clear that this city must be yours'.[155]

Fear in London also hurried on the process. That is, fear of peace dawning. There was apprehension that Germany and Russia might soon agree to end their war, as both had suffered reverses in the fighting in 1914. British diplomats and Foreign Office grandees complained that President Wilson of the United States might soon offer mediation.[156] In January, reports from the British Embassy in Washington, where the Americans had sponsored private talks involving the British and German ambassadors, indicated German moderation. In Grey's words, the Germans had suggested 'that they would like peace and would agree to evacuate and compensate Belgium'.[157] This led some 'hawks' in London to see in the Gallipoli campaign a chance to head off an early peace. Britain, with the aid of colonial troops, should aim to win such a dazzling prize at the Straits that it could be used 'to bribe Russia to throw all her weight against Germany'.[158]

Count Alexander Benckendorff

For the British elite, the supreme goal was to keep Russia fighting, in the face of the military disasters Russia endured in East Prussia in late August 1914. Grey told the War Council on 3 March 1915, that Britain had to avoid 'anything in the nature of a breach with Russia, or any action which would incline Russia to make a separate peace'.[159] The very next day Sergei Sazonov, the Russian Foreign Minister, despatched to London an *aide-mémoire* demanding Russia's unconditional possession of Constantinople and the Straits. In return, Russia dangled in front of London and Paris the rich bait of a sweeping promise to support their future claims 'in other regions of the Ottoman Empire and elsewhere'; that is, a promise that when British and French eyes were kindling over a great carving up of the defeated Ottoman and German Empires, Russia would just sit and smile. Both Britain and France hesitated, and then quickly caved. At an audience with the Tsar and Sazonov at the Alexander Palace at Tsarskoye Selo near St Petersburg, Sir George Buchanan, the British ambassador, passed over a memorandum recording Britain's astonishing generosity: she was offering to Russia 'the richest prize of the entire war'. It was not possible to offer 'a greater proof of friendship', gushed the document.[160]

The handing over of the city of Constantinople and the Straits to Russian rule would indeed have been a stunning surrender of plunder on the part of the conquerors. Even the island of Imbros (Gökçeada) off the coast, one of the bases used by the British to attack Gallipoli, was to be gifted to Russia.

Thus, by the middle of March 1915, this so-called 'Straits and Persia Agreement' (See Appendix 6) was all stitched up. Cables were exchanged between Petrograd, Paris, and London. Ambassadors and Foreign Ministers signed solemnly, just as the men of Harry Ryan's 13th Battalion completed training in Egypt, and just as Tom Ryan and his fellow-soldiers at Blackboy Hill were singing of their passion to fight 'for rectitude alone'. This is how it happened – men clutching fountain pens bargained away ordinary men's lives. Just as Dylan Thomas would express it years later, 'The hand that signed the paper felled a city'.[161]

Sergei Sazonov

Under the terms of these diplomatic pledges, Russia was to gain a fabulous package of trophies. But Britain gained something to soften the blow. The old deal that had divided Persia, under the so-called Anglo-Russian Convention of 1907, was revisited.[162] Back then, Persia had been split into three 'spheres of influence': a northern zone for Russia, a southern zone for Britain, and a central 'Neutral Zone'. Now, under the new agreement, Russia accepted that the old neutral sphere, incorporating a long stretch of the coastline of the Persian Gulf, would be absorbed 'into an English sphere', while

Britain would allow Russia 'in return to be absolute mistress in her own sphere'. New lines on new maps were all agreed. Britain's share of supposedly neutral Persia had been inflated to half the country – more than 800,000 square kilometres, or an area more than twenty-five times the size of Belgium. Clearly the prospect of outright annexation hung over Persia, with British troops active in the south and Russian troops using northern Persia to attack the Ottomans. The Persian people, who had embarked on promising steps toward constitutional development in the early years of the twentieth century, were being sold down the river.

The phrase 'sphere of interest', of course, was code for a stretch of territory in which one avaricious foreign power would be dominant in all commercial opportunities. Oil was a bonus. Under the revised deal between Britain and Russia, the oil reserves in south-west Persia, first discovered in 1908 on a sixty-year 'concession' owned by the Australian mining entrepreneur William Knox D'Arcy, and then by a new company, Anglo-Persian Oil, were no longer in the 'neutral zone' but rather were firmly in British keeping.[163] And there were strategic advantages. Because Britain had pocketed the northern coastline of the Persian Gulf in her enlarged British sphere, London calculated that the boost to British power might help push Russian ambitions away from India and towards the Caucasus and Eastern Europe instead.

For all the diplomatic chatter, the Straits and Persia Agreement of March 1915 was meant to be strictly secret. Indeed, even seasoned British diplomats complained of a veritable 'war mania for secrecy' prevailing at the Foreign Office. For example, just prior to his despatch as the new British Minister to Persia in 1915, Sir Charles Marling was astounded to hear Grey tell him with a straight face that no agreement existed with Russia over the Straits and Persia. Marling thought this fantastic. Every other room in the grand Foreign Office building on Whitehall was alive with rumours, like rats in the rafters. The deal with Russia was, wrote Marling, 'a secret known to half the F. O.'; that is, that Russia stood to gain the great bulk of the plunder to be won through the Gallipoli campaign.[164]

There was the plan in a nutshell: a campaign to rob the Turkish people of their capital and its waterways, and gift them to Russia. Simple stuff – born of imperial and racial hubris. As many in London imagined, big imperial pounds could be pocketed at the price of some cheap colonial pennies, men from the Antipodes, who, under British command, would swiftly crush an enemy believed to be racially inferior. Of course, the British Parliament was told nothing of the diplomatic whys and wherefores behind the campaign. Also, Australians were told nothing. The big truth behind the campaign remained masked. But it can be stated plainly: Australians would soon die so that big prizes might be given to their mother country's ally – Russia.

While the British War Council in London discussed all this in early March 1915, Asquith remembered his joke from August 1914. 'We are a set of buccaneers sitting round a table', he told his ministers, again.[165] But it was no joke for those who would endure the campaign.

'The Spoils'

Meanwhile in London, Lewis Harcourt, Asquith's Colonial Secretary, who had been an opponent of Britain rushing headlong into war during the July crisis, somersaulted completely and began to plan for the big bold British Empire that victory would deliver. He appeared to imagine he had the world by the tail. On 25 March 1915, he circulated a document candidly entitled 'The Spoils' (See Appendix 7). He sketched on a grand scale, nothing less than a great re-shuffling of the territories possessed by Europeans in the colonial world where so many of the people of the planet had been divided into masters and servants. Harcourt began by assuming a complete success on the part of Britain and her allies and, thus, a capacity to 'dictate any terms'. A negotiated peace would not do.

What kind of peace with victory would Britain dictate? Harcourt recommended a great swag of British annexations or occupations in the Middle East, beginning with seizures in Mesopotamia, 'from the Persian Gulf to Baghdad'. Britain must also take, he urged, the Turkish port of Marmaris or the Greek island of Mytilene for strategic reasons; France could take Syria, while Britain (or the United States) could take Palestine. In Persia, as had just been foreshadowed, Britain must gain 'the neutral zone containing the oil fields and the province of Fars'; Britain must also obtain the transfer of the Persian capital south (for Teheran was in the Russian zone). Britain should also pocket the Turkish port city of Alexandretta (now Iskenderun) in order to command the Baghdad railway terminus.

Lewis Harcourt

Looking further afield, Harcourt swiftly redrew the map of Africa. If Italy entered the war, wrote Harcourt, Britain should swap British Somaliland for Italian Eritrea. All the captured German colonies in Africa should be held tight. The Union of South Africa must take and keep German South West Africa, unless Portugal should agree to swap it for valuable Portuguese colonies in the east (Mozambique); Britain must pocket German East Africa to complete 'the missing link' in the chain of possessions from the Cape to Cairo; Britain and France should divide equally both German Togoland and the Cameroons, or Britain might be more generous, but in return for being allowed to pocket all of the New Hebrides, and Djibouti (opposite Aden).

Next, he repackaged the Pacific. Britain and her Dominions should take the best of the German Pacific colonies, with Samoa going to New Zealand, and Australia keeping all other colonies south of the Equator. Japan should annex all Germany's colonies north of Equator, wrote Harcourt, notwithstanding the 'great trouble' this would cause with race-fixated Australia. Perhaps Britain might give France all of the New Hebrides, if Britain took all of the Cameroons, Togoland and Dahomey in Africa. To counter 'Australian prejudices' against French possession of all of the New Hebrides – an old Australian worry – Britain might look to 'sweetening the pill' by giving Australia not just the ex-German colonies but also the German island of Bougainville and the islands of the British Solomons.[166] In short, more trophies for Australia might help to shut her up.

Clearly, the river of righteousness was expected to produce a great deal of profitable flood-wrack for Britain. It was an astonishing programme of aggrandisement for an empire bragging to the world of its moral supremacy.

Chapter 6

GALLIPOLI

CAIRO, ANZAC COVE, LONDON, APRIL 1915

*[The] direct fruits of these operations will,
if the war is successful, be gathered entirely by Russia.*[167]

— Sir Edward Grey, British Foreign Secretary, to George Buchanan,
British Ambassador in Petrograd, 11 March 1915

As we have seen, by the time Ted Ryan joined the AIF in Perth in September 1915, his two brothers, Harry and Tom, were already serving under arms in the Middle East. Doubtless, Ted hoped to be reunited with them, somehow, in the tumult of war.

What were his two brothers doing?

Harry Ryan Gets Lucky

On 10 April 1915, the men of Harry Ryan's 13th Battalion marched away from their aerodrome camp at Heliopolis. They had no clear idea of what lay ahead other than combat. Over the next few days, the men were transported in several ships to the jumping-off point for the Gallipoli campaign, Mudros Bay on the Greek island of Lemnos, neutral Greek territory but occupied by British forces in early 1915. The 13th Battalion sailed from Lemnos on the morning of 25 April. They were not to be the very first to throw themselves ashore at Anzac Cove that day. Their ship arrived off the famous beach at 4.30 p.m. that afternoon, with the peninsula already the scene of intense fighting. The men waited for nightfall before they were tugged in small boats toward Anzac Cove. During that night, and into the early hours of the next day, the men 'disembarked under fire'. On 26 April they took up their positions at swiftly named places full of danger, at 'the head of Monash Valley', at Pope's Hill, and at Dead Man's Ridge.[168]

Was young Harry Ryan among them? It is not clear. An entry on his hand-written service record shows that Harry was hospitalised at 'Gallipoli' on 20 July 1915. But there was evidently some confusion. Almost four years later, on 20 May 1919, a record-keeping officer deleted the reference to Gallipoli, writing in explanation: 'I am informed this man was not on Gallipoli.' No source was given. Had Harry served there? Or did he serve only on a ship off Gallipoli? His brother, Ted, certainly believed he had been in the trenches and had been injured there, judging from his later letter to Ramsay MacDonald. But sadly, Harry's service record does not show all his movements during 1915 and the issue cannot be resolved.[169]

In any case, Harry Ryan was soon out of it. Perhaps someone picked out the fair-haired and fair-complexioned Harry as too young for battle. In any case, he got an 'ex-regimental' position in Cairo, outside the battalion. His records show that in July 1915, Harry was promoted to the rank of 'QMS', Quartermaster Sergeant, an NCO rank. Thus, he was busily engaged not in combat but as a mere cog in the supply chain for the war, arranging purchases and stores in Cairo.[170] He was lucky. But, in feeding the battle lines, Harry was still confronted by certain realities of this war. He would have witnessed the work of the 'Egyptian Labour Corps', some 50,000 Egyptian labourers, often poor men, compelled into difficult labour, for low pay, and sometimes very harshly treated by their British masters.[171]

New Blood

Tom, the middle Ryan brother, was soon up to his neck in combat. Tom's group of '5th Reinforcements' for the 11th Battalion was dropped at Anzac Cove in two batches, on 15 and 22 June 1915. Tom was in one or the other. The 11th battalion itself had landed at Gallipoli on the very first day of the campaign.

Tom Ryan and his companions joined a group of men at Gallipoli who had already endured several weeks of extraordinary hardship. By 5 May, casualties in the 11th Battalion were 36 killed, 200 wounded, and 197 missing. The men had also confronted the putrefying horrors of battle close up: for they had assisted in the recovery and burial of the dead from no man's land during the day-long armistice of 24 May.[172]

The 5th Reinforcements moved immediately into the trenches of their mates of the 11th Battalion at Boulder Dump Ridge. Within a week, all were engaged in another major combat. On 28 June, in an effort to distract the Turkish forces from moving reinforcements to the south, a neighbouring battalion made 'a demonstration' and the 11th Battalion was compelled to advance from its half-completed trenches. These movements drew 'heavy shrapnel fire' down on to the battalion. At the end of the day, the men had suffered more casualties, 21 killed and 42 wounded.[173]

By July, the 'War Diary' of Tom's 11th Battalion grew dark and pessimistic. The men's continuous hard work in trench construction, and 'mining and sapping', was 'proving a severe strain on them and they are more or less getting worn out. Many of them are suffering from nervous breakdown.' The arriving reinforcements now made up half the battalion, and the 5th Reinforcements especially – Tom's group – had 'not been sufficiently trained'. The battalion was crammed into a small area, where it suffered from 'continual shell fire'. More training was 'quite impossible' and the officers showed 'the strain of continuous duty', with sickness spreading. The commander of the battalion concluded: 'It is not in an efficient fighting state.'[174]

Then, early in the morning of 4 August, the 11th Battalion endured another 'fierce' surprise attack from the Ottoman forces, which captured parts of the battalion's trench line. Some six hours of bombing and bayoneting followed, as attackers and defenders surged back and forth, until the trench line was eventually recaptured. But the men still endured 'a heavy bombardment' and 'incessant rifle and M[achine] G[un] fire', and 'Bomb wounds'. A week later, the men went into reserve trenches for a short rest, and then back into the fray.[175] All of this Tom Ryan experienced.

On 21 August, Tom Ryan wound up at a Field Ambulance, and then a Casualty Clearing Station. Like so many others, he had succumbed to sickness. It was recorded as 'diarrhoea', but it was serious. The doctors soon despatched him to a hospital ship. He was hospitalised at Imbros, then at Mudros on Lemnos Island. His situation evidently caused great concern. At the end of the month, he was evacuated from Mudros to England with hundreds of others on the hospital ship *Esmeralda*. Tom's wounding and hospitalisation in London was reported in a 'Roll of Honour' in the Australian press in October 1915.[176] If Ted came across this item while he trained at Blackboy Hill, it must have dented his hopes of teaming up with Tom at Gallipoli, but no doubt added to his willingness to do his bit.

Loot for Italy: April 1915

A war-is-hell narrative does not come near to explaining this tragedy. We have to see well beyond the parapets to understand truly why men like Tom Ryan from places such as Broken Hill had ended up in those trenches in the first place. Here, once again, a brief excursion into high diplomacy completes the 'big picture'. From this different perspective, one may even cynically dub the Gallipoli campaign a success. For, among the various hopes floating the campaign had been the idea that it would bring neutral Italy into the war, on the side of the Entente – and it did.

Few histories of the campaign highlight this. But while preparations for the Gallipoli campaign were being made in March and April 1915, the British Foreign Office was duelling diplomatically with Britain's allies to strike a second big diplomatic deal to widen the war, the so-called 'Treaty of London' (See Appendix 8). Beginning in London in early 1915, Italian negotiators, the familiar trail of men in frock-coats and toppers led by the evocatively named Ambassador Guglielmo Imperiali, began to horse-trade, secretly, at the Foreign Office. The first British naval attacks on the Dardanelles in February naturally gave negotiations a kick along, for the Italian Government could scarcely hope to enjoy the spoils of war if it failed to enter it.

Those guiding the Italian negotiators from Rome were not by any means idealists. Baron Sidney Sonnino, who took the helm of Italy's Foreign Office in October 1914, was the key man. Cynical and unscrupulous, he was 'perhaps his nation's worst foreign minister'.[177] He was not above haggling with both sides over the price of Italy joining the war, or continuing to steer clear. He served the Italian Prime Minister, Antonio Salandra. Both men were authoritarians, contemptuous of Italian democracy. Both scented big booty on offer in this war; and both hoped to pick the top of the market in selling hundreds of thousands of Italian lives.

At first, the Russians made trouble: they did not want promises to Italy in the Balkans that might collide with their vision of a 'Greater Serbia'. The long stretch of coast along the Adriatic, the Dalmatian coast, was coveted by Serbia – Russia's protégé. Russia would take some persuading before agreeing to short-change Serbia.[178]

Widening the war was not easy. A majority of the Italian Parliament was opposed to war. Pope Benedict XV was opposed to war.[179] The Italian socialists and the peace movement were vehemently opposed, and had a significant following.[180] Moreover, Germany and Austria were bidding to keep Italy neutral. Concessions were proffered. But the Entente Powers sought to lure Italy's diplomats and politicians with such glittering spoils, such a bewitching array of territories and loans, that the Roman elite would agree to cajole, bribe, or overawe all the Italian opponents of war.

Pope Benedict XV

Timing was important. Asquith actually postponed the landings at Gallipoli for a fortnight because a setback there might 'result in choking off Italy'; that is, might give her an excuse to delay joining the war. Britain wanted the landings to be a last shoulder charge that would push Italy into signing up for war.[181] Synchronisation was needed, if greed was to supplant fear. It succeeded.

On 26 April 1915, the day after the landings at Gallipoli, the Australians were ashore, but still fighting hard for their slender foothold. Meanwhile, back in London, it all worked a treat. The diplomatic deal was closed. Grey and the ambassadors from Italy, France, and Russia affixed their signatures to the document. Just a little more than twenty-four hours after Australians and New Zealanders, amongst many others, began to die at Gallipoli, their blood helped seal the deal in London.

Why? With the British assuring the Italians that all had gone well at Gallipoli, they hastened to sign the so-called Treaty of London. Britain had called the top of the market. Italy's negotiators promised that Italy would enter the war against Austria-Hungary within one month.

In this way, the bill of sale for Italy's peace recorded a high price-tag. In return for entering the war, Italy was promised a bulging bag of annexations at the expense of Austria-Hungary, in the north of Italy, and along the Adriatic coast. The annexations would include the Trentino and the Southern Tyrol, up to the Brenner Pass; Trieste, and the provinces of Gorizia, and Gradisca, in the east; Istria up to the Quarnero, including the naval port of Pola; the Dalmatian coast as far south as Cape Planka, with neutralisation of the coast further south; the Bay of Valona (now Vlorë in Albania); and all the twelve islands of the Dodecanese (including Rhodes). The terms of the treaty contemplated the future transfer of hundreds of thousands of non-Italians to Italian rule. 'In the event of France and Great Britain increasing their colonial territories in Africa at the expense of Germany', Article 13 explained coyly, Italy would gain 'some equitable compensation' in Africa, too. New overlords, Italians, would push about the much pushed-about people of Africa if the demons in Berlin were licked.

Even bigger annexations were signalled, at the expense of the Ottomans. The Italians gained (under Article 9) a promise of 'a just share' in any eventual partition of the Ottoman Empire, in the region of Asia Minor surrounding Adalia (now Antalya, on the southern Turkish coast).

A cash splash was added. The Entente promised to Italy a fair chunk of any indemnity to be extracted from the losers in this war, and Britain offered immediately to facilitate a loan of £50 million. Gold for guns, and for glory – from London.

The lures were on the table. The plan again was simple: to batter down the front door of the Ottoman Empire, and so tempt the Italians to throw in their lot with the nations intent upon burglary there.

A determination to stomp upon any move to achieve an early peace guided one additional article in the Treaty of London, Article 15 – the anti-Vatican article. Under its terms, the diplomats agreed to block any peace efforts launched by Pope Benedict XV. They had not forgotten that this troublesome Pope had initially suggested the scandalous 'Christmas Truce' in the trenches of the Western Front at the end of 1914.[182] Thus, in the carefully drafted Article 15, the British, French, and Russians agreed to 'support such opposition as Italy may make to any proposal in the direction of introducing a representative of the Holy See [the Pope] in any peace negotiations or negotiations for the settlement of questions raised by the present war'.

Finally, characteristically now, under Article 16, all agreed that the whole treaty 'shall be held secret'.[183]

Secret, certainly for the men of Tom Ryan's group of reinforcements for the 11th Battalion at Gallipoli, who trudged up the gangplank of HMAT *Horarata* and departed Fremantle on the very day that the Treaty of London was signed, 26 April 1915. Thus, those Australians fighting at Gallipoli – including the men of Harry Ryan's 13th Battalion and Tom Ryan's 11th Battalion – became, in part, unknowing instruments in the goading of a mostly pacific people, the people of Italy, into a horrific war.

Blood for Oil

Behind the diplomacy lurked naked material interests, and 'strategic interests', which often served as a euphemism for the advancement of trade under an imperial banner. Strategic arguments in these terms certainly dominated in official British memoranda at this time, principally the long-standing obsession with the safety of British India. And that included trade.

In addition, new interests, especially oil, hovered in the background. With a view to securing oil supplies for the Royal Navy, only a month before the outbreak of the First World War, the British Government had invested £2 million to gain a majority shareholding in the Anglo-Persian Oil Company. This company hoped for victory at Gallipoli to guarantee British possession of the 'neutral zone' in Persia and with it, D'Arcy's oil. The Anglo-Persian Oil Company also owned the 'Turkish Petroleum Company', which had interests in other Ottoman territories confidently believed to be oil-bearing, mainly around Mosul in Mesopotamia. Victory over the Turks would secure these also. Another rival oil company, Royal Dutch Shell, part-Dutch and part-British, also had big interests at stake. Its oil fields in Romania and in the Baku in Russia had been suddenly shut off from world markets when the Ottomans closed the Straits in September 1914. The American company, Standard Oil, was eating up its market share of the war boom in oil. The opening of the Straits would help Royal Dutch Shell fight back. Such were the interests that men of property discussed, no doubt, in the comfort of London's Clubland as the campaign at Gallipoli unfolded.[184]

Meanwhile at the Foreign Office in Whitehall in mid-1915, the diplomat Maurice De Bunsen led a committee to clarify Britain's complicated war aims in the 'Near East'. De

Bunsen's men stressed strategic objectives to be secured in the aftermath of the Turks' defeat. The committee recommended the consolidation of British possessions in the Persian Gulf, but also the retention of Basra, in the south of Mesopotamia, which had been captured in 1914. De Bunsen highlighted the promising possibilities of winning control of oil around Mosul.[185]

Such were the material ambitions, essential to the campaign. Yet in many popular histories of Gallipoli, nothing shifts the focus from battle. In truth, the purposes underlying battle matter very much – surely, even more than battle itself. It was the men from the great embassies in Belgravia, Knightsbridge, and Mayfair, and those with whom they swapped banter at the Foreign Office, who determined the objectives of the war. It was the men in frock-coats who signed both the Straits and Persia Agreement in March 1915, and the Treaty of London in April 1915 – and in these were listed the war aims for which men perished.

But all this was veiled from the people. Instead, in their public addresses, British politicians held out to Australia and the other Dominions vague assurances of chest-swelling honours to come. For example, in May 1915, the British Conservative leader Andrew Bonar Law gave a public speech in this vein. He had just been appointed a Minister in a new national coalition government formed by Asquith to stave off political pressure from the Tories. Bonar Law told a big public meeting in London, designed to shower praise on the boundless patriotism of the Empire, that Britain's top-table politicians were thrilled by the loyal Dominions' support for the war. A grateful Bonar Law offered them a share in the glory – a chance to occupy Berlin! The brave Dominions, he promised, 'will not be the last to enter as conquerors the capital of an enemy'.[186]

This vision of slouch-hatted Australians swaggering down Berlin's *Unter den Linden*, the main boulevard in the German capital, was meant to flatter. But in truth it indicated yet another wild war aim for the British Empire, the conquest of Berlin itself – at an enormous cost in blood. And Australia's Government was being lured on, without complaint, into this ruinous project.

Worse still, Australia's Government, under Hughes's leadership from October 1915, seemed determined to sink deeper into the mire. Hughes revelled in the vulgarities of wartime politics. When the fact of failure at the Dardanelles became undeniable in December 1915, all those troops that had survived the bloody and under-resourced campaign were withdrawn to Egypt. But Hughes shunned any talk of failure. Instead he issued a personal 'Call to Arms', that is an official leaflet sent into every Australian home, pleading that another 50,000 volunteers must come forward to go overseas immediately, with 16,000 more required every month afterwards. He offered the remarkable retrospective prophecy that if Australia had only 'doubled' the numbers of men she had sent to Gallipoli, then 'the Australian armies would long ago have been camping in Constantinople, and the world war would have been practically over'.[187]

Andrew Bonar Law

Who would deploy these additional men? To what purpose? 'Ye Gods, did ever the nation have a bigger pair of blunderers at its head than Winston Churchill and Edward Grey', wrote Charles Bean in his private diary at Gallipoli. 'They blundered from opposite directions: Winston – from a brilliant instability; Grey from a stupid but honest density.'[188] Such truth-telling from Australia's chief war correspondent at Gallipoli was not for public consumption. Nor was Asquith's remark that those responsible for the British landings at Suvla in August, 'ought to be court-martialled and dismissed from the Army'.[189]

Catholics in the Ranks

Into the hands of such decision makers as Churchill, Grey, and General Sir Ian Hamilton, the Australian Government had committed the lives of the men of the First AIF. Needless to say, Australians – those at home, and those training in the sands in Egypt, all alike – still knew nothing about the diplomatic deals that had inspired the campaign and were carefully hidden behind all the moral fireworks ignited by London.

One more point is worth stressing. Between a fifth and a quarter of the men joining the AIF were Catholics, men of that persuasion having enlisted in rough proportion to their numbers in the Australian population.[190] Thus, there were plenty of Australian Catholics among the troops at Gallipoli. One of these was a nineteen year-old naval telegraphy officer from Glebe in Sydney, Norman Gilroy, who was on the transport ship SS *Bulla* just off the coast during the landings of 25 April 1915. He saw the 'innumerable' vessels 'carrying men and towing life boat and punts full of men ashore every minute'. He saw 'shell after shell' falling like dice among the troops as they landed, and some 'narrowly missing' the troopships standing off shore. One shell 'screeched overhead between the bridge and the mainmast' of Gilroy's ship.[191] Norman Gilroy – a future Catholic Cardinal and Archbishop of Sydney – was among those risking their lives. He would survive. Needless to say, no Australian at Gallipoli, Catholic or not, had the remotest idea that the men at the top in London, under Article 15 of the Treaty of London, had just agreed to sabotage any diplomatic initiative that Pope Benedict XV might launch to bring an early end to the shame of a war between Christians in Europe, and beyond. The veil drawn over such things was impenetrable.

Chapter 7

BAYONET STICKING

SUBIACO TO BLACKBOY HILL
SEPTEMBER 1915 TO FEBRUARY 1916

'In – out – on guard. Now with the short point into his bloody navel – in – twist – out with his guts on the point – in – out – on guard.'[192]

— Leonard Mann, AIF veteran, recalling his bayonet instructor's mantra during his training in 1917

Private Edward Ryan, in common with thousands of others enlisting in Perth, had instructions to return to the Drill Hall in Francis Street soon after his initial formal enlistment, and report ready for training. Married men were granted up to a month to put their affairs in order. Men with very little money generally reported quickly. In Ryan's case, he reported the very next day after enlisting, 22 September 1915.

All new recruits first listened to an address from the 'kindly and fatherly' Lieutenant Weaver. He spoke about 'discipline – rigorous military discipline, of course – efficiency, hygiene and leave'. Next, still in their civilian clothes, the men marched through the city toward Perth's central railway station, accompanied by a military band. One soldier recalled that the column of men, marching to the beat of a side drum, was 'cheered by the Crowds who turned out to give us a hearty send off'.[193]

Perhaps they felt the spirit conjured by Kipling in his story 'The Army of a Dream' a decade before: 'I rejoiced to the marrow of my bones thus to be borne along on billows of surging music among magnificent men, in sunlight, through a crowded town whose people, I could feel, regarded us with comradeship, affection – and more.'[194]

The newly-enlisted men were bound for Western Australia's largest training camp – Blackboy Hill.

Bayonet Land

Ted Ryan and his companions travelled first by train to a small station, Midland Junction, near Blackboy Hill. They then marched to the camp, which was set up on open ground beneath the Darling Ranges, about 20 kilometres east of Perth. Here Ted's brother, Tom, had trained in the early months of 1915.

The site was a maze of huts, tents and parade grounds. Up to 2,000 men could be housed here. It was a crush. The huts featured half-walls of galvanised iron, with canvas blinds that were rolled up in the daytime, and drawn down at night. Most men slept in these huts, with between 50 and 75 men squeezed into each one. Others slept in bell-tents, with six or seven men in each, sleeping with their feet toward the centre.[195]

Here Ryan was designated a 'Private', and attached to B Company in the 'No. 3 Depot Battalion' to begin training.

What was Blackboy Hill like? Sources for Ryan himself are so scarce that we must rely on the memoirs of other soldiers. For example, Walter Gillett, who passed through Blackboy Hill in early 1916, remembered bitterly his experiences there. He arrived 'hot, dirty, thirsty, my collar and cuffs reduced to a pulp, and dog tired'. He found the camp was in 'a pitiable state of systematic muddle'. Contradictory orders were barked at the men. Poor equipment was doled out. Dungarees and hats were tossed at them, indiscriminately, with no regard to size, leaving the soldiers to swap for something that fitted them. The military 'brains' excelled, as Gillett wrote, only in 'swank and humbug'. 'We wondered if we had joined the army or a circus.'[196]

The days passed in an endless round of 'physical jerks', games, 'squad drill', rifle practice, 'fatigue' duties, lectures, classes, and route marches. These drills were punctuated by notoriously invariable meals of stews, tea, bread and jam. There were nightly battles against 'bugs' infesting the huts. A vaccination day, and consequent short illnesses for many, was a reminder that overseas service was coming.[197]

The men trained from the first warning bugle at five a.m. to 'lights out' at 10 p.m. Visiting journalists from the Perth newspapers painted a picture of a hive of activity: artillery men were 'hard at it learning to manipulate their big guns', while in an abandoned quarry other men were 'learning the art of making the vicious little machine gun do its deadly work of spitting forth leaden death at the rate of 600 bullets per minute'. Elsewhere, the 'ordinary infantry' were busy 'learning bayonet fighting'.

'What do they do? Everything', wrote another admiring reporter. The energy of the innocent: 'Here a party rushes out of a trench, and with bayonets attacks fiercely stuffed bags hanging from a beam; there a company is busy learning to throw bombs from one trench into another – no easy business for a novice.' The flash and clash of bayonet skirmishing and bayonet sticking intrigued this particular reporter: 'In one corner men in leather jackets and huge masks are practising bayonet fighting.' The main lecturer in bayonet sticking, Sergeant Major Dunn, produced a little book on the subject. Devotee of the bayonet as he was, Dunn pleaded with the men not to be captivated by the romance of 'the spectacular and single combat form of fighting' but rather to remember to perfect their bayonet work for that moment when they all charged in 'a general assault'.[198]

Bayonet sticking captured many imaginations. It became part of the mass advertising for the war in Perth. For example, on 25 October 1915, a month after Ryan joined up, a 'GRAND MILITARY GYMKHANA' was held at the Royal Showgrounds in Claremont. Ironically, it was a day normally marking the 'Eight Hours Celebration', a labour holiday. War had displaced it. Now, top billing was given to 'BAYONET COMBATS – Open to N.C.O.'s and men, armed with the bayonet...' Next, for the entertainment of the crowds came the 'TEAMS BAYONET FIGHT – Each team to consist of one N.C.O. as leader and four privates; open to bona fide members of the A.I.F.'[199]

And after all this boosting of bayonets, did the soldiers actually use them in combat? Men from the 51st Battalion, in which Ryan served, were quite clear that the bayonet was rarely employed. Private William James Purvis was asked at interview if he ever used a bayonet. 'Never', he replied.[200] Lieutenant Baron Hay, an officer from the battalion, had the same reply: 'No. I never did. I haven't heard of anyone who did.'[201] Certainly, we know from many sources that other Australian soldiers did use the bayonet in battle. Corporal Archie Barwick from the 1st Battalion, for example, jotted down in his diary an incident in France in July 1916, when Australians advanced through a corpse-ridden, ruined French village, and 'were hunting the Huns like terriers do rats' and 'very few of them were taken prisoners, the bayonet was the weapon chiefly used'.[202]

But in training, it seems, the bayonet was rather overplayed, perhaps because it conjured up images of gallant knights from a pre-industrial age. In the imagined war, bayonets were to be indispensable; in the real war, flesh-shredding artillery would prove to be the big killer. As Private Ryan would soon discover.

Officer Class

Discipline at the Blackboy Hill camp was none too rigid. For instance, train travel caused a great rumpus. Passes for the railway trip to Perth were keenly sought. The soldiers believed that, having volunteered to serve, they should travel freely. There were violent scenes when the authorities sought to check that all departing soldiers had both passes and train tickets, pre-purchased, to stop widespread fare evasion. According to Gillett, on one occasion the men 'rushed' the railway officers, seized all tickets and scattered them like confetti among the milling crowd. The guard was called out, 'with fixed bayonets', but 'about 5,000 men' fled the camp and spent the day in Perth. 'We were all just thoroughly "fed up" with the foolery and humbug.'[203]

This may give a context to Ryan's first encounters with military discipline. In November, in Claremont, a seaside suburb of Perth with a showground used for military training, Ryan refused an order from 2nd Lieutenant Leonard Glover. He was one of the officers attached to Ryan's training battalion. Perhaps it did not help that Glover was a freshly-promoted junior officer. No doubt he sported a stiff-visored cap and a brand-new shiny Sam Browne belt: the emblems of the officer class. Glover was a relatively recent arrival from London, with a middle-class background and probably a strong British accent. He had gained his commission quickly, on the strength of recent service with the City of London Royal Fusiliers, a unit of the part-time British Territorial Force.[204] Possibly, Ted's jack-is-as-good-as-his-master convictions, drunk in with his mother's milk, and fortified by his father's fiery blarney, and then by the Mudie's Scottish radicalism, led him to bristle at shouted orders. On top of this was his trade union pride in being one of O'Dowd's 'rankers of the Bottom Dog Brigade'. All this in Ted's constitution must have collided with Lieutenant Glover's shining pride in his new status as an officer. The precise order that Ryan flouted is not recorded; he was simply charged with 'disobeying the lawful command of a superior officer'. For shame, he was fined five shillings.[205] The crime must have been minor, for only a month later Ryan was promoted to Corporal.

Nor did this first crime on Ryan's part interfere with his plans for overseas deployment. In November, he was initially listed among those to be sent to reinforce the 16th Battalion. But, presumably at his request, this was altered to '14th Reinforcements, 11th Battalion' – Tom's battalion – in December 1915.

Presumably, Ted preserved some hope of reuniting with Tom somewhere on the battlefront. However, he probably knew this was a long shot, especially if he had received a letter from Tom, or perhaps seen the press report that Tom was 'ill in hospital, London', indicating he had been wounded at Gallipoli and shipped out.[206]

'Trophies For the Nations that Captured Them'

Did Ted Ryan scan the pages of the newspapers for other things? Probably, as a thoughtful soldier might well do. Perhaps he noticed that there were already articles about 'war aims' and 'peace terms' being reported, from the British press. While Britain's secret diplomacy did not make it into the press, her propaganda did.

What was the war for? Charles Masterman, a former member of Prime Minister Asquith's Cabinet, had been given the task of producing propaganda for the war in 1914. Within weeks of the outbreak of war, he was the boss of a propaganda factory at Wellington House in London. It was Masterman himself who wrote a famous explanation of the war aims of Britain and her allies for a top-selling Liberal newspaper in November 1915. It went around the world.

Masterman sketched highly ambitious goals: Belgium must be restored to 'complete independence'; Germany must pay her an indemnity; France must have all of Alsace-Lorraine returned to her, and receive an indemnity; France must gain 'a natural and defensive boundary ... the Rhine', thus swallowing up much German territory in the west; 'German, Austrian, Russian Poland shall be united under the Tsar or a king appointed by him', thus swallowing up much German and Austrian territory in the East; 'Italy would receive the Trentino and the whole of Italy irredenta', at the expense of Austria-Hungary; Turkey must be 'torn to fragments'; Serbia must gain Bosnia-Herzegovina; 'the German fleet should be surrendered and either sunk or divided up among the Allies'; and German colonies must be 'trophies for the nations who conquered them'. Here was a grand programme of territorial grab.[207]

Many assumed this blueprint to be an authentic outline of the war aims that Britain must win in battle before peace could be contemplated. Masterman, after all, was close to the men in Asquith's circle. The article was widely reported in Australia.[208]

Britain's war aims – and therefore Australia's war aims – seemed to be growing with tropical speed.

But even more grand British war aims went unreported, for they were decided upon in more clandestine diplomatic bargains. From July 1915 to March 1916, British diplomats redoubled efforts to encourage an 'Arab revolt' against the Ottomans. Through the famous 'McMahon-Hussein Correspondence', Britain made certain promises to Arab leaders. Most importantly, in a formal exchange of letters between McMahon, the British High Commissioner in Egypt, and Hussein, the Sharif of Mecca, Britain induced the Arabs to rise in revolt. In return, Britain agreed to 'recognise and support the independence of the Arabs in all regions within the limits demanded by the Sharif of Mecca', making vaguely expressed exceptions for areas desired by Britain, such as Mesopotamia (Iraq), and areas desired by France, such as Syria. These agreements were secret.[209]

'Continental Despotism'

Parallel developments in British politics were ominous. In January 1916, the British Government crossed a red line in domestic policy: conscription. Compulsory military service for unmarried men was passed into law. Astonishing to many observers, it was Britain's still Liberal-led government that set aside the proud Liberal tradition of 'voluntarism'. For many decades, conscription had been seen as the despicable hallmark of 'Continental Despotism' – the policy of Napoleon, Bismarck, and the Tsar. Britain's Liberal ideals were sagging. The principle that a man should never be forced into military service abroad, a principle some argued was implicit in both the Magna Carta of 1215 and the Petition of Right of 1629, faded into history. Men could now be hunted into the war.[210]

Why? At bottom, it was a crude political deal. A general election in Britain would normally have been due after the expiry of the current parliament in January 1916 (the last election had been in December 1910 and British Parliaments had five-year terms). Behind the scenes, well-informed commentators saw the deal coming.[211] In the coalition Asquith had formed in May 1915, the Conservatives needed Asquith to persuade his Liberals to swallow conscription; the Liberals needed the Conservatives to prolong the life of the parliament. The Liberals in the Coalition were terrified that, unless the Tories in the Commons, and the Lords, voted for the extension of the term of the parliament from five years to six, they might face a 'Khaki Election' and 'the conscriptionists would sweep the country'.[212] To avoid this, Asquith ultimately gave in to Conservative demands for the conscription of unmarried men. As a result, the life of the parliament was extended, an election was postponed and Asquith clung to office. It set a cynical precedent. In fact, five times during the war, the incumbent parliamentarians would collude in this way to deny the British people a fresh election.[213]

With conscription bolstering the military ranks from January 1916, the British Government could look forward to a vast new supply of pressed men to throw into combat for its war aims – both known and unknown.

Sound and Fury

Soon after Ryan enlisted in September 1915, Australia's Labor Prime Minister, Andrew Fisher, retired, sick at heart. He accepted a position as High Commissioner in London. William Morris Hughes, a man with a much greater flair for populism, a kind of whistling kettle of perpetual outrage, replaced Fisher as Labor Prime Minister in late October 1915. Hughes's authoritarian impulses tempted him to use the emergency powers achieved by the Labor Government early in the war under the first *War Precautions Act 1914* much more vigorously and with very little scruple. The Act was frequently revised, and scores and then hundreds of *War Precautions Regulations* were decreed. They were used increasingly to crush dissent, buttress censorship, lock up 'aliens', and intimidate Hughes's political opponents. As ever, war was the solvent of principle. Arguably, the rule of persons displaced the rule of law in many cases.[214]

Once installed, Hughes announced he would soon be departing for London for top-level consultations. He departed from Sydney in January 1916, and travelled via the United States and Canada, arriving in Britain in March. In the heart of the Empire, he proved to be a political maverick. He was soon riding on the coat-tails of Lord Northcliffe, the flamboyantly aggressive pro-war and pro-conscription press mogul, owner of not only the prestigious *Times*, but also the fanatical *Daily Mail* and *Evening News* – 'red tops' in the spirit of the 'red tops' that we know today as coarse, sensationalist, right-wing, 'tabloid' mastheads. Hughes was welcomed into Northcliffe's circle and mesmerised by the stardust that his most raucous newspapers threw at his feet. Hughes, built like a shrivelled shrimp, was sold as a rough-diamond realist offering blunt truths and tough-guy solutions for every problem. With Keith Murdoch at his side, Hughes was soon band-wagon-riding with the leaders of a nationalist campaign designed to hound Asquith into accepting a second dose of conscription, this time for married men. Hughes's paint-by-numbers stump speeches on his 'Wake Up England' tour fed popular fury over German atrocities. Hughes was used to thinking in gargoyles; now in his speeches he conjured up terrible German faces, those of wicked German commercial agents who would stalk the globe again, he warned, undercutting Empire goods, underbidding British contractors, if Germany was not soundly defeated and economically isolated. Hughes manipulated the grief of the bereaved in demanding a more merciless war against the enemy, supposedly to redeem the deaths already endured. For the sake of the dead, he urged the rejection of all thought of a negotiated peace with Germany, 'the ravenous beast'.[215]

Lord Northcliffe

This time the military context was a crucial factor in the mix. The defeat of British forces by the Ottomans at Kut in Mesopotamia in April 1916, and the outbreak of a rebellion in Dublin, the historic Irish 'Easter Rising', created a sense of military crisis. In this context, Asquith capitulated to the Tories' demand for 'hard' conscription to turn the tide; therefore all men aged between 18 and 40, unmarried or married, and whatever their reservations about the war, would be forced to fight. And Hughes learned lessons.

In unexpected ways, Hughes added to tensions across the spectrum of British politics. Of course, a Labor Prime Minister visiting Britain – when Britain itself had never experienced a Labour Government – was a curious novelty. But Hughes amazed and appalled most of the leading figures of the British Labour Party, with his anti-German tirades, his enthusiastic support for a wider war, and his spruiking the 'capture of German trade' and a post-war 'trade war' as indispensable for victory. Hughes, in turn, shunned most British Labour leaders. Australian Labor newspapers reported the dissatisfaction felt at the top of the British Labour Party. They alleged that Hughes was swanning it up with the British ultra-patriots and imperial protectionists, such as Lord Milner and Leo Amery, and smearing all critics of conscription and the war as unpatriotic traitors. In Labor circles in Australia, it was feared that Hughes, fired-up and flattered by English Tories, would mount a campaign for conscription just as soon as he returned home, which was scheduled for mid-1916. His Labor critics prepared a wreath of rancour for him.[216]

Following all these events in the newspapers, as a thoughtful soldier from Broken Hill would, Ryan must have felt a rising sense of apprehension. He was in for a long war.

Chapter 8

SAILING

FREMANTLE TO SUEZ, FEBRUARY TO MARCH 1916

Interviewer: Did they all go willingly...?

Jesse Palmer: Well I think the trouble here must be faced. That there's so much unemployment. So many that had to – were scratching. And no dole that they have today. It was a case of having three meals a day, two changes of raiment, and five bob. They didn't get it all of course but it was something. Something for the family anyway. They went of course in their hundreds, because there were hundreds of unemployed.[217]

— Private Jesse Palmer, AIF veteran, interviewed 1995

On Saturday 12 February 1916, Ted Ryan and his companions took what would be, for some of them, a last Australian train journey, through the eucalyptus-dotted grasslands east of Perth. A steam train took them from Blackboy Hill toward Perth, and then straight on to the port of Fremantle.

Other soldiers who made that same journey have left accounts of the noisy send off they received. Private Ben Cohen, an engine driver from Perth, described it in detail in his diary. The first departing men 'with the band in the lead' marched out of the camp bound for the railway station, and received 'a great cheer' from the soldiers waiting in camp. Then, as the train wound its way toward Perth, the locomotive engine whistle was 'continually blowing to let the Citizens know we were coming'. Cohen recorded that 'at every station we passed we were given a great cheer'. When the train passed through the main railway junction in the city of Perth, 'all the Engines about were Crowing Cock a doodle do, which meant Hip, Hip, Hoolray [sic]'.[218] Finally, the train steamed on to the Fremantle dockside.

Warm-water Odyssey

Ted Ryan arrived at the wharf with just over two hundred other soldiers ready for embarkation for overseas service on that Saturday. Moored before them was the troopship HMAT *Miltiades*, designated as 'A28'. In peacetime, it was a small passenger liner normally working the Britain-Australia run. Appropriately enough for this military mission, the steamer was named after the fabled Greek general Miltiades, who had defeated the Persians at the battle of Marathon in 490 BC.

It was a very warm summer day, with the mercury rising past 32 degrees Celsius by noon.[219] Ryan lugged his gear up the gangplank with his brother-soldiers, and handed in his embarkation card. He was listed on the embarkation roll of the '11th Battalion, 14th Reinforcements' as an 'Acting Corporal'. The rank suggests his officers discerned in the young man from Broken Hill some potential for leadership among all these West Australians.[220]

No doubt, Ryan took his place, along with a swarm of other soldiers, leaning over the railings of the ship to wave to friends and family on the wharf. Ben Cohen, who went to Europe on the HMAT *Miltiades* on a later voyage, recalled some hi-jinx upon departure. 'The people ashore started throwing fruit up to us & and it was great fun catching the Oranges Etc. I caught 2 Oranges & 1 Peach and 1 plum.' The Blackboy Hill camp band played 'Auld Lang Syne' as HMAT *Miltiades* pulled away.[221]

Other soldiers who left from Fremantle about that time did not always remember the experience happily. Walter Gillett, who embarked a few months after Ryan, recalled the soldiers' resentment that friends and family were prevented from approaching the train at the wharf, and then were barred by 'a high picket fence (about ten feet high)' from getting too close to the boat to say goodbye. To add insult, the troops thronging the open decks of the ship were then surprised when their officers suddenly shouted orders for a roll call, below decks. When the roll call was complete, the men were disappointed to discover that the boat was already some distance from the wharf and they had missed their last chance to shout messages down to those waiting to farewell them. 'To think that the last action meted out to us in W.A. [Western Australia] should be so contemptible', recalled Gillett. As Fremantle disappeared in the wake of the ship, the troops 'wandered about aimlessly, silently, with thoughts all our own, and gloomy thoughts they were too'.[222]

Ryan's ship set sail in the Indian Ocean like almost all the troop transports, bound for Suez, via Colombo – again, a stunning adventure for a mining-town orphan and labourer to savour.

Travelling on board HMAT *Miltiades* with Ryan was another young man in his late twenties, Private David Harford, a labourer and miner like Ryan, from Albany. Harford's diary for the voyage offers glimpses of life on the troopship. The exotic sights that all were expecting came quickly: Harford carefully noted seeing a whale on the first day out, and later the appearance of dolphins, and the beguiling vision of an island that proved to be a mid-ocean mirage.

But two days out from Fremantle came a serious mishap for the men aboard HMAT *Miltiades*. She was a comparatively light vessel of only 7,814 tons. As Harford recorded, a 'very rough gale sprung up' with 'occasional big seas breaking on board'. On the morning of 15 February, great waves pummelled the ship, and broke over the deck, one 'completely wrecking [a] latrine in which were eight men'. The force of the wave and the collapsing latrine walls killed one man outright, broke the leg of a second, broke the arm of a third, and left others covered in bruises and scratches. A few days later, one of the severely injured men died. Death came early to HMAT *Miltiades*.[223]

This ship, as did all Australian troopships, soon revealed another stark reality. The army was a class-bound organisation. Gillett, for example, discovered that the soldiers had full use of the lower deck only. 'A guard was placed on the upper (or officers') deck, and no one was allowed there.'[224] The regime of training continued on board also. Men were exercised in 'running, jumping, physical jerks, or something of the like nature, to keep us "fit"'. Lectures on 'the latest man-destroying machinery were given by those who had taken a delight in studying such matters'.[225]

Imagineers of Peace

With Ted Ryan en route in February 1916, and his two brothers in Egypt, we might imagine that the war ensnaring all three Ryan brothers was now unstoppable. Not so. In fact, peace opportunities and peace activism on the world stage had coincided with key moments in all three Ryan brothers' journey-to-war stories.

Harry Ryan had spent the Christmas of 1914 on board HMAT *Ulysses* in the Indian Ocean. At the same time, as we have seen, along significant stretches of the Western Front, British and German soldiers briefly achieved their own spectacular and poignant 'Christmas Truce'.

As Tom Ryan was enlisting in the AIF in Perth in January 1915, American peace efforts had resumed. That month, American President Wilson's special emissary, Colonel Edward House, the enigmatic and softly spoken Texan, with a hat to match, began 'shuttle diplomacy' between London, Paris, and Berlin. He talked to all about the need for compromise, but was most sympathetic to the British. He quite understood, he wrote in his diary, that the British were eager 'to try out their new armies in the spring'.[226] House believed he had cultivated an especially warm relationship with Sir Edward Grey. 'His mind and mine run nearly parallel', he reported to President Wilson.[227] He was much more critical of others, finding most of the key men in the European capitals quite out of touch with their suffering people. House told President Wilson it was clear 'that the ruling class in France do not want peace, but that a large part of the people and the men in the trenches would welcome it'.[228] Soon House's efforts were hobbled by announcements from both sides of almost total economic blockades. Then, his compromise formula to end the conflict, a mutually agreed winding back of blockade warfare as a prelude to negotiations, was smashed by a tragedy – the German torpedoing of the liner *Lusitania* just off the Irish coast on 7 May 1915, with massive loss of life.[229]

This disaster occurred while Tom Ryan was on the high seas. He had departed Australia on 26 April 1915. Just two days later at The Hague in Holland, a grand conference opened, designed to inspire popular pressures for peace across the world –the famous 'International Congress of Women'. More than a thousand delegates came, from twelve countries, neutral and belligerent. Russia, France, and Serbia stopped their delegates from attending. London stopped all but a handful of British delegates from reaching The Hague. But Germany, Austria, and Hungary dared not prevent their delegations from attending. The famous American social worker and campaigner for women's suffrage, Jane Addams, was the inspirational organiser. It was a great success. The conference urged neutral mediation, open diplomacy, and international guarantees of a settlement, to end the war. At the end of the conference, emissaries carried the women's formula for peace to the various European capitals. This stimulated internationalist activism on the part of women's peace groups across Europe and America, and even in Australia.[230]

Jane Addams

American delegates depart from New York for the International Congress of Women at the Hague, April 1915

The US delegation at the International Congress of Women at The Hague, April 1915, showing Jane Addams, 2nd from the left in the front row.

The International Congress of Women in session in a large hall, the Dierentuin, in the Zoological Gardens at The Hague, April 1915

Well-credentialed internationalist academics and jurists were busy too. Earlier that same month, Dutch peace activists had founded the Central Organisation for a Durable Peace, also at The Hague. This 'think-tank', as we would call it today, attracted some of Europe's best and brightest jurists and scholars, who sought a formula for a compromise peace settlement and planned a new permanent international body to reinforce the peace in a post-war world.[231] 'Democratic control' of foreign policy was a common catch-cry. All of this pointed to the way forward.

There were parallels in many countries. In Britain, Radical MPs and dissenting socialists had founded the Union of Democratic Control (UDC) soon after the outbreak of war. It campaigned for the reform of 'secret diplomacy', opposed conscription, and urged a negotiated peace.[232] In Germany, the League for a New Fatherland (BNV) put forward a very similar programme. Albert Einstein was its most famous member.[233] In France, the 'League for the Rights of Man', and the 'Association for Peace Through Law', while cautiously supporting France's war of defence, advanced parallel ideas for a peace based on a new diplomacy, stronger international law and new multilateral institutions.[234]

More lobby groups soon emerged to promote the idea of a 'League of Nations' as the lynchpin of a new rules-based international order. The old order, based on mutual fear and a competitive arms race to deter war, had failed abysmally. In May 1915, liberal idealists founded a 'League of Nations Society' in Britain.[235] In neutral America, enthusiasts for arbitration founded a similar body, the 'League to Enforce Peace', in July 1915, to promote the concept of a peace underpinned by international guarantees.[236] To its left, a number of influential activist organisations emerged, such as the Woman's Peace Party and later the American Union Against Militarism, urging that President Wilson should both keep the United States out of war and step forward more boldly with an offer to mediate peace.[237]

Albert Einstein

More radically, by the time the battered nations of Europe reached the first anniversary of the outbreak of war in August 1915, full-throated criticism of the war was emerging from the left-wing factions of most of Europe's socialist and labour parties. Among socialists of the Independent Labour Party in Britain, among a dissenting minority in the French Socialist Party, and in the German, Austrian and Italian socialist parties, the demand for peace by negotiation and even a 'war on war' grew louder from a growing minority.[238]

In Germany especially, anti-war emotions seethed. In the Reichstag, the socialist deputies of the powerful German Social Democratic Party (SPD) held a quarter of the seats at the outbreak of war. In successive 'war credit' votes in the Reichstag from December 1914 onwards, the numbers of German socialists abstaining or opposing funds for the war grew each time, approaching one third of the SPD's Reichstag fraction. Courageous opponents of the war outside the parliament, men and women motivated by a humane idealism, also spoke up against any war of expansionism.[239]

In Britain also, dissent reached the parliament. While Ted Ryan was in training at Blackboy Hill in November 1915, a breakthrough moment came: dissenting parliamentarians of some eminence gave the first speeches at Westminster in favour of a diplomatic settlement of the war. Two mesmerised the House of Lords. Lord Loreburn, a former Liberal Lord Chancellor, and Lord Courtney, a passionate Quaker, implored national leaders to speak with greater honesty about war aims and to show a readiness to accept mediation. 'We are living now in a mist, and I think it is high time we stepped into the sunlight', declared Loreburn. Lord Courtney stressed that the military stalemate provided the chance for peace. 'The question is whether there is not an alternative to this unceasing strife. I believe there is', he told the House of Lords.²⁴⁰

Still more emphatic were the speeches that came from the green benches of the House of Commons over the following week. Three Liberal MPs, Charles Trevelyan, Arthur Ponsonby, and the Tasmanian-born Len Outhwaite, all pleaded for Britain to guard against war aims of aggrandisement and to search for peace by negotiation.²⁴¹ Even the pro-war Australian press reported on these speeches, but with hostility, wailing against the influence of these 'grumbling peers', 'cranks', 'injudicious politicians', and 'fault finders'.²⁴²

Then came a spectacular gesture in citizens' diplomacy from America. When Ted Ryan embarked on his voyage from Australia to Egypt in February 1916, for some weeks the newspapers had been carrying reports of another voyage – a spectacular trans-Atlantic peace initiative. A 'Peace Ship' had arrived in Europe.

Charles Trevelyan　　　　　　　　　　Arthur Ponsonby

Why a 'Peace Ship'? American peace activists had grown impatient with President Wilson's reluctance to host an international conference of neutral nations to end the war. President Wilson preferred his own 'lone wolf' diplomacy, relying on Colonel Edward House, whose never-failing flattery of Wilson had earned him the President's special trust. But a very rich and famous American had suddenly put the idea of a 'neutral conference' on the front page: Henry Ford. He decided to sponsor the liner *Oscar II* in December 1915, on a voyage carrying American peace delegates to Europe.

The aim was simple: to convoke a privately-sponsored 'neutral conference', inviting officially credentialed delegates to join their discussions, and thus prod the European neutrals – and perhaps Wilson – into joint action for peace. Thus, the body known as the 'Neutral Conference for Continuous Mediation' was established, first in the Grand Hotel in Stockholm in February 1916 – the same month that Ted Ryan embarked for war – and later at The Hague. The press pooh-poohed it as a stunt. But several northern neutral governments hailed the conference and sought representation. It did valuable work in promoting the outlines of a compromise peace. Deputations sent from the conference to the capitals of Europe then added to public pressures upon the warring governments to proclaim their war aims with clarity.[243]

Delegates of the unofficial Neutral Conference for Continuous Mediation, Stockholm, February 1916

While all this was happening, the three Ryan brothers had taken up arms. But developments on the 'peace front' in many places showed that the old pieties buttressing the war – victory, at any cost, in a holy war – were losing their power.

Exoticisms of Sea and Sand

HMAT *Miltiades*, with Ryan, Harford, and their two hundred brother-soldiers jostling for a view on deck, arrived at Colombo, in what is now Sri Lanka, on 22 February 1916, and dropped anchor outside the harbour. The ship berthed the next day. The men were allowed ashore on 24 February. For most it was their first glimpse of a non-white British possession. All was exotic, and mystifying. It was 'Columbia', as Harford misnamed Colombo in his diary. 'Plenty of Niggers', Harford recorded, revealing the common colour prejudice of the citizens of the white dominions of the Empire at this time. 'Nice place, but Beer not too good. Plenty of fruit. Bananas and pine apples etc. very hot climate.' A route march on a 'very hot day' tested the men before their return to the ship.[244]

The troopship slipped from its wharf at Colombo on 26 February, and charted its new course west, for Suez. Soon after, Harford marvelled at his first sight of British India; he could see tall mountains in the far distance as the ship skirted the coast. Tributes to the entrancing seascapes and wildlife of the oceans littered Harford's diary: '29th, 1pm, big shoal of porpoises sighted on Port Bow. 1st March, 3pm, Shoal of 8 whales passed just in front of vessel. Prow of ship just missed one big fellow. 2nd, Noon. Shoal of Dolphins.' Entering the Red Sea through the Bab al-Mandab Strait and heading north, the ship passed near the twelve volcanic islands, which the troops were told were the 'Twelve Apostles'.[245] No doubt Ted Ryan was similarly entranced.

The troopship arrived at the port of Suez at the head of the Red Sea on the morning of 8 March. Disembarkation was delayed for three days, so the men paced the decks, gazing at the shore. 'Coastline fringed by barren mountains', recorded Harford. Such barren mountains would have been a scarcely exotic sight for Ted Ryan from Broken Hill. At last, on the morning of 11 March 1916 the soldiers disembarked, and 'entrained' for Heliopolis, about ten kilometres northeast of the centre of Cairo. The train journey took until midnight that day.

Waking up the next morning in the maze of bell-tents and huts that was the Australians' camp at Heliopolis, the soldiers' Egyptian experience began with an early Church Parade. Free for the rest of the day, perhaps Ryan joined with Harford and others on a visit to the pyramids that first afternoon in Egypt. Harford threw a stone over one pyramid with a slingshot. He then climbed it, and carved his name at the top, as just about everyone did, and as French soldiers, all long dead, had done more than a century before.[246]

Rumbles from Broken Hill

Did letters from Broken Hill reach Ted Ryan here in Egypt? Very probably they did, for he was in Egypt for three months, and later, in England, he would write of receiving a great many. If so, he was almost certainly aware of the latest struggles in the life of the labour movement in his hometown. Moreover, incoming letters to the AIF were very rarely censored.[247]

What was the news from home? Health had become the focus of trade union activism in Broken Hill. The winning argument was simple: why should the producer be sacrificed to the product? On the eve of the First World War, the NSW Labor Government of Premier William Holman had acted in sympathy with the miners and appointed a Royal Commission to enquire into health issues arising from work in the mines. But, eclipsed by the urgencies of the war, the recommended reforms were delayed. So another major dispute erupted in Broken Hill during the second half of 1915. This time the unions' key objective was a 44-hour week for underground workers; that is, a demand that only a half-day should be worked on Saturdays. Less time worked underground, they argued, meant improved health prospects for miners.[248]

To achieve their half-day off, the underground workers resorted to Saturday afternoon strikes in January 1916 and were promptly sacked. Strike action widened. For weeks, the threat of violence hung over Broken Hill. The new federal Labor Prime Minister, Billy Hughes, lost patience with the strikers. Using tactics that would soon become wearily familiar, Hughes labelled those behind the dispute in Broken Hill as 'German sympathisers'.[249]

The dispute was eventually resolved, with a 44-hour week negotiated for the underground workers, in June 1916. But the political mood in Broken Hill was radicalising – and rapidly.

Waiting upon a New World

After arriving in Egypt in early March 1916, Ted Ryan began much more arduous training. Was it inevitable that he and his companions would fight in France over the coming months?

Let us pause once more and contextualise. Unbeknown to the three Ryan brothers, and millions in uniform and in mortal danger just like them, the chancelleries and embassies of the embattled nations of Europe at exactly this time were humming again with the possibilities of peace. In January and February 1916, Colonel House undertook a second mission to Germany, Britain, and France on behalf of President Wilson. House again encouraged all sides to moderate their war aims and prepare for an American-brokered compromise peace. He warned them of the 'terrible gamble they are taking in not invoking our intervention'[250]; and 'gamble' was the right word, for betting on victory was the ruthless gamble the ruling men on both sides preferred, in truth because they feared facing their exhausted people until they could hold something resembling a glittering trophy above their heads.

But there was an alternative. Just as Ted Ryan was getting to know Cairo in March 1916, Asquith's Cabinet at last contemplated a formal American offer of mediation, the fruit of House's mission. A final version was cabled from Washington, and written by President Wilson himself. It approved a deal only just struck by House and Sir Edward Grey (of which Paris had been informed). According to its terms, the United States was willing to summon a conference 'to put an end to the war', when Britain and France signalled 'the moment was opportune'; if Germany then refused a conference, or a reasonable settlement, the United States would '*probably*' enter the war. (The word 'probably' did not weaken the prospective offer; it merely preserved the legal reality that only Congress could declare war. But the enemies of negotiation seized on the word to discredit the deal.) This famous 'House-Grey Memorandum' was on the British Cabinet's table from March 1916.[251]

Colonel House (L) and Woodrow Wilson, 1912

Did the war-makers consider it carefully? Arthur Balfour, the former Conservative Prime Minister who had taken the post of First Lord of the Admiralty in Asquith's coalition, told his Cabinet colleagues, in his languid yet pitiless way, the plan was 'not worth five minutes thought'.[252] Later Lloyd George would fret at the prospect that peace might come before Britain had dealt the 'knock-out blow' to the German enemy; he advised that all peace talk should 'be very peremptorily stamped upon'.[253]

Thus, in their wisdom, Asquith's ministers looked upon the House-Grey Memorandum as a dead letter. It would never be activated.

If the ruling politicians in the tall, timber-lined rooms of power could not bring themselves even to contemplate peace, then other men and women – some idealistic, some fanatical – were ready to propound more revolutionary remedies to end the daily massacres at the front. A month after the Asquith Cabinet politely put aside House's offer, and just as the Australian forces in Egypt were honouring the first anniversary of the Gallipoli landings, another international conference of anti-war socialists convened in neutral Switzerland. This time almost fifty left-wing opponents of war reached the isolated Swiss mountain village of Kienthal, near Interlaken, with the winter snows still dusting the fabulous alpine landscape all around. For a week, from 24 April 1916, there in the dining room of the folkloric Hotel Bären (the 'Hotel Bear', which still stands), socialists from the most radical factions of a dozen European labour and socialist parties thrashed out the possibilities of making a 'war on war'.

Arthur Balfour

They built upon the passions of their Zimmerwald manifesto from 1915. The dining room of 'The Bear' rang with denunciations of imperialism and capitalism as the causes of war, and warnings that mild 'bourgeois' solutions, such as international arbitration, would not suffice to end war. Deliverance lay only in 'victorious socialism'. This time the socialist dissidents threatened the ruling classes with revolutionary class struggle to force a people's peace, with no seizures of territory and no economic slavery for anyone. It was agreed that all socialist and labour parties should defy the 'patriotic truce' and absolutely refuse to vote money for a continuation of the war. The more dogmatic and ruthless among the little company, men like Lenin and Gregory Zinoviev from the Russian delegations, wanted more – a commitment to a revolution to end the war. Within a year they would have their chance. The last morning of the conference was 1 May, the fabled May Day – 'the symbol of working class unity'. The little gathering of humanitarian socialists, dogmatic Marxists, dreamers and political exiles together watched the sunrise and honoured the moment.[254]

Far greater forces were at work though than could be encompassed by resolutions formulated at Kienthal. Among the increasingly hungry, cold, and bereaved working people of Europe – and even in the trenches – the mood was slowly swinging toward bitterness and radicalism. Outright hostility to the war could be heard among enlarging minorities across the European labour movement. Left-wing factions in all the major socialist and labour parties, in the nations at war and in the so-called 'northern neutrals', were questioning the fiction that the warring nations were honestly engaged in a defensive war, with no grand imperial claims. Even among Australian Labor activists, the demand for peace negotiations and the renunciation of 'imperialist war' was being voiced more and more confidently.

Mild liberal alternatives to the bloodshed were still on the table. In the spring of 1916, President Wilson sought to strengthen his vague standing offer of American mediation. On 27 May 1916, he addressed the well-heeled members of the American internationalist pressure group, the 'League to Enforce Peace' (LTEP), at the New Willard Hotel, in Washington. It was a historic speech. His audience included some wealthy philanthropists, as well as the key proponents of the 'new diplomacy' in America. Some more radical souls were in the audience, too, full of contempt for the old shibboleths of deterrence and the 'balance of power', and looking to President Wilson for a breakthrough to achieve peace in Europe. Wilson took a big risk. He committed the United States to enter a scheme for a League of Nations, based on a model of collective security. Thus, he offered the European war-makers a diplomatic revolution, with the backing of America: a peace based on new international 'guarantees of security' from a renewal of war, the object for which both sides claimed to be fighting.[255]

But the statesmen in Europe were again lukewarm in response. Huge battles were raging, around Verdun. More battles were being planned, for the summer, at the River Somme. The money was in, and the bets were down. Why call off the throw of the iron dice? Why not another round of fighting? The generals gambled on explosive power redeeming their losses. And General Haig, the British Commander of the British Expeditionary Force, was a high-roller in the casino of war. Battle, the politicians calculated also, might bring a healing victory and, incidentally, it might salvage their political fortunes. The dead soldiers, 'the fallen', it could be explained, forever and a day, had 'laid down their lives', had made 'the supreme sacrifice' – rather than had had their lives taken from them. So, President Wilson was rebuffed.

Ted Ryan would fight.

Chapter 9

SANDBOX

HELIOPOLIS TO HABIETA, MARCH TO MAY 1916

> Suez Canal. Awful place: nothing but Desert everywhere, nothing but sand and dust as far as an eye can see. Impossible to keep rifles and equipment clean, when wind blows all the desert seems to be in the air.[256]
>
> — Private David Harford, 51st Battalion, 2 April 1916

It must have seemed so utterly improbable to them. But in the northern spring of 1916, the three Ryan brothers, all labourers from Broken Hill, were briefly together in the ancient land of Egypt – this very ancient land of the bible stories that their Methodist mother had read to them. As the latest soldiers to invade Egypt scrambled over the great monuments, the mysterious relics of mankind's deep past lay all about them.

Imperial swap-shop: Egypt for Morocco – Morocco for Egypt

The more recent history of Egypt was just as mysterious to most of the uncomprehending young men of the AIF as the ancient history. Few would have been aware of the decades of rivalry between France and Britain for possession of Egypt and the Sudan. Few would have been aware of the significance of Alexandria, where so many of the Australians were arriving. During the Anglo-Egyptian war of 1882, British naval forces had shelled Alexandria. It was the moment that Britain launched the frantic race between the European powers to grab territory in Africa, known to history as the age of the 'New Imperialism'. Across the globe for a generation afterward, the Great Powers had jostled to extend their empires, dominating new lands and new peoples, and ensuring that the balance in the bargain between labour and capital in these lands of fresh opportunity could always be tilted toward the capital that lay in the hands of the foreign investor. Britain had occupied and governed Egypt from 1882, while preserving the fiction that Egypt was an autonomous province of the Ottoman Empire. French resentments over British high-handedness in Egypt bubbled away. War had almost erupted when French and British military expeditions came face-to-face at Fashoda, in Sudan, in 1898.[257]

To resolve these and other long-standing points of imperial rivalry, Britain had eventually done a deal with France in 1904. Under the secret terms attached to the so-called 'Entente Cordiale' (or 'friendly agreement') of April 1904, the fate of two valuable pieces of the Ottoman Empire had been decided. If 'by the force of circumstances', as the document put it delicately, Britain had to swallow up Egypt someday, French interests would be protected and France would not make trouble; and if 'by the force of circumstances' France had to swallow up Morocco someday, Britain would return the favour.[258] It was a typical imperial turf deal, a contract for prospective grab built on mutual if grudging respect for existing commercial interests, and the usual excuses for seeking new imperial territories beyond the reach of troublesome democracy, irksome trade unions, and the despised regulatory chill of Factory Acts. While scarcely mentioned by anyone, nonetheless it was this diplomatic deal from 1904 that partially explained why the men of the AIF were being deployed in Egypt a decade later.

And there were more recent complications. Soon after the declaration of war upon Ottoman Turkey in November 1914, Britain imposed martial law in Egypt and swiftly exercised her 'option', so to speak. First, the Ottoman territory of Cyprus was annexed outright. Second, on 18 December 1914, Britain declared that Egypt had become a 'British Protectorate', achieving annexation in all but name. As expected, Britain recognised a 'French Protectorate' over Morocco the very next day. Britain soon replaced the inconveniently pro-Ottoman Khedive (the local figurehead ruler of Egypt) with a pro-British Khedive, a client ruler. It was the crowning moment for all those British empire-builders who had aspired to take outright control of Egypt ever since the shelling of Alexandria in 1882.

Thus, the reality was complex: the men of the AIF were there in the Middle East for many reasons, but one of them was to make safe Britain's latest imperial acquisition – Egypt – from both the Ottoman Imperial Army and the local Egyptian nationalists. Of course, France also anticipated pocketing Morocco, sweeping away the concessions she had been forced to make to Germany during the dangerous international crises of 1905, 1908-09, and 1911. Such imperial rivalries were among the long-term causes of this catastrophic war and such were the deals the Anzacs were deployed to redeem and protect.

For the Ryan brothers, Egypt was simply the place an inscrutable fate had landed them, the utterly foreign yet strangely familiar desert landscape where they imagined they might meet up and muck in together. But very probably – it is impossible to be sure – they just missed out on seeing each other. At best, they may have shared a day of leave together. In March 1916, when Ted Ryan arrived in Egypt, the officers of the AIF were rearranging Australia's forces for fresh deployments, in France. When the reshuffling was all done, the three Ryan brothers would never fight together in the same unit.

Ted and Tom in the Land of the Pharaohs

It is very unlikely that Ted even saw his brother Tom in Egypt after his arrival on 11 March 1916. They were there together for about three weeks, but Ted had no leave, as he would later complain. At the time, the two brothers were in units more than a hundred kilometres apart.

On arrival in Suez, Ted's group of two hundred soldiers from HMAT *Miltiades* was still labelled as reinforcements for Tom's 11th Battalion. But things were not so simple in the AIF after Gallipoli. As is well known, in December 1915 the entire British 'Mediterranean Expeditionary Force', as it was more formally known, had been withdrawn from the Gallipoli peninsula. The surviving Australian troops, including Tom's 11th Battalion, were returned to Egypt at the end of the year.

But Private Tom Ryan was not amongst them. In fact, while Ted was on board HMAT *Miltiades* steaming toward Egypt in February 1916, Tom was coming to the end of a long period of convalescence in England. He had spent almost five months at Endell Street Military Hospital near Covent Garden in London. He was released in late February 1916, and despatched to Egypt. Tom arrived back in Egypt on 6 March 1916. He joined his old 11th Battalion at the military base at Serapeum, about 120 kilometres to the east of Cairo and near to the Suez Canal. Meanwhile, Ted's group of reinforcements arrived at Heliopolis near Cairo just five days later.

As chance would have it, the two Ryan brothers came close to being united in the same unit. But it was not to be. The officers who presided over the virtual doubling of the size of the AIF in Egypt at this time decided that Tom's 11th Battalion, just back from Gallipoli, was to be split, by the toss of a penny, on the parade ground, much to the 'consternation' of the veterans who were 'closer than brothers'.[259] Half would be transferred to the front lines in France very quickly as the backbone of a revitalised 11th Battalion, augmented by reinforcements, while the other half would remain behind in Egypt to help form the backbone of a new battalion, the 51st Battalion. Unluckily for the Ryan brothers, Tom was allocated to the first group and Ted would soon be allocated to the second.

So, at the end of March 1916, Tom left Egypt for France. He and his comrades filed aboard the British troopship HMT *Corsican*, and it steamed away from Alexandria, Egypt, on 30 March, bound for Marseille on the southern coast of France. As the 11th Battalion's war diary recorded, quite accurately, the men were joining the 'BEF', that is, the 'British Expeditionary Force'.[260]

Gallipoli had been a horrific experience for these men. A still greater trial of systematised mass killing on the Western Front in France during the summer of 1916 lay ahead.

When Harry Met Rose

Ted Ryan had a better chance of meeting his youngest brother, Harry – the brother who had borrowed his name to get into the ranks – in Egypt. They were both serving there, for about three months, from March to May 1916.

In January 1916, Harry's military career had moved in a new direction. He left military supplies and was attached to the 'Military Mounted Police' at Heliopolis. Harry's service record, showing his name as 'Edward James Ryan', gives few details. It seems possible that Harry was in Heliopolis when his brother arrived there on 11 March 1916. Ted's battalion was based there for three weeks. Intriguingly, someone offered Ted Ryan a post in the military police – according to a letter of Ted's to the Mudie family in Broken Hill published there in December 1916 – and it might well have been his brother Harry. However, as we shall see, Ted turned down the offer, and did not mention Harry.

Just one indication that Harry and Ted may have met survives. Among Ted Ryan's few surviving papers is a postcard of Harry, photographed in his uniform, and endorsed on the back 'To Ted, from his loving brother Harry'. The 'Carte Postale' was produced by a firm in Cairo, and is neither stamped nor dated. It shows Harry with the two stripes of a Corporal on his sleeve.[261] This matches Harry's own written account, a letter in his service file, explaining that he lost his post as Quartermaster Sergeant and reverted to the rank of 'Acting Corporal' when he entered the Australian Provost Corps, in February 1916. Perhaps Harry gave it to Ted in Egypt.

According to military records, in April 1916 Harry entered the 'Anzac Police'. His job was to enforce military law among AIF troops letting off steam in Cairo. There was evidently a lot to do. But, in any case, he was relatively safe compared with a soldier enduring life in the trenches. Two safe jobs had come his way, supply and the military police. He might well have thanked his lucky stars.

Harry's absorption in the Anzac Police and his release from the 11th Battalion may well have resulted from a fortuitous event in his personal life – his marriage in Cairo. At some point in early 1916, he formed a relationship with a dark-haired and 'dark-skinned' beauty called Rose, a woman with ethnic roots in Romania and Egypt. The couple soon married. Their baby daughter, Ruby Elizabeth, was born in Cairo in November 1916.[262]

Harry was fortunate indeed. And if Ted had taken a job alongside him in Cairo in the Anzac Police in 1916 he too might have been lucky. But, as we shall see, that was not to be.

Ted Ryan's Egypt

Meanwhile, upon arrival in Egypt in mid-March 1916, the group of reinforcements that had travelled on *Miltiades* from Fremantle had been formed into their Training Battalions. Ted Ryan's was designated the 3rd Training Battalion, and David Harford's the 7th. Immediately the men undertook days of parade drill, 'skirmishing drill', and route marches.[263] On one march, their officers pointed out Coptic Christian sites. Harford was impressed by a visit to 'Mary's Well' (at Al Humra, near Wadi al-Natrum, to the west of Cairo), known by tradition as a well created by Jesus for his family during their flight into Egypt. Harford was pleased also to see nearby an 'Avenue of Australian Eucalyptus trees on our way home'.[264] Such sights must have evoked memories of Bible stories, and of home, for many of the men.

Then, on 2 April, Harford's 7th Training Battalion was despatched by train from Heliopolis to Suez, to join the new 51st Battalion. On 20 April, Harford visited the 'old battlefield' near the town of Tel-el-Kebir, 'where Lord Wolseley and his men crushed the Arabs in 1882'. For men in training for a new war, these sights from the old campaign against the forces of the famous Egyptian nationalist, Ahmed Urabi, were poignant. The wrecks of empires gone and come, the human detritus of battles past, were strewn about for the contemplation of the men from Australia. 'Plenty of human bones lying about', wrote Harford in his diary, and 'the old trench lines are in a perfect state of preservation'.[265]

Happily we know something of Ted Ryan's experiences while training in Egypt from the one letter he wrote to the Mudie family in Australia that has survived. This letter, written from Perham Down in the autumn of 1916, happened to be given by his Uncle James for publication in the *Barrier Miner*. The paper made quite a splash with a series of soldiers' letters and it printed Ted's at the end of December 1916.[266]

Ted described being deeply impressed with Heliopolis. It was 'the first and best place we camped at in Egypt'. It was a 'tourist resort' on the edge of Cairo, built by various European companies, with 'wide streets, nice gardens, beautiful white buildings, and the architecture is the best'. At the top of his list was the luxurious Heliopolis Palace Hotel, with its fabulous 55-metre-high dome, built in 1911. It was used as an Australian hospital during the war. This splendid hotel and casino, and the Catholic Cathedral, Our Lady of Heliopolis, were 'two exceptionally fine buildings', wrote Ryan.

He travelled by electric tram on the short ride into the city of Cairo. But it repelled him. 'I think the less said about Cairo the better, as I think it is the most immoral place on this big piece of mud' – a reference, doubtless, to the widespread prostitution. But he did praise the fine hotels to be found in Cairo. These boasted 'nice lounges tables and an orchestra, and some of the hotels have moving pictures, and, of course you have your drinks in comfort'. There were 'dances every night', so that those seeking fun 'should never leave the hotel'.

But Ryan was most enchanted by 'The Barrage Gardens', a patch of glorious parkland laid out near the picturesque turreted Delta Barrage Bridge on the Nile, a favourite place for many soldiers. 'It has one of the prettiest gardens I ever saw', wrote Ryan. Other soldiers compared it to Sydney's Royal Botanic Garden.

Beyond Cairo, Ryan noted the harsh landscape and impoverished people. 'About the only thing one sees outside of the towns', he wrote, 'is an immense number of palm trees, donkeys, oxen, water wheels, and Egyptians with dirty robes and no boots.' To have no boots, as every working-class Australian boy knew, was a mark of poverty.

'Sweat, Sorrow, and Sore Eyes'

From Heliopolis, Ted Ryan's 3rd Training Battalion was shifted to the large camp at Tel-el-Kebir. Here Ted claimed to have been promoted to Sergeant, and to have been offered a position, full-time, on the instructional staff. Had he accepted this offer, he would most likely have been kept in Egypt, training other soldiers, 'but Billy Muggins declined with thanks'. He told his uncle that he had next been offered a position 'as a military policeman, known as an Anzac Police'. But he rebuffed it:

> I declined both these non-combatant jobs, as I thought a person who hadn't taken his chance in the firing line should not consider himself eligible to occupy a cold-footed job.[267]

Perhaps Harry was behind the second offer to Ted of a transfer to the Anzac Police. If so, Ted chose not to mention it. Perhaps an obvious complication scuttled the plan: if Ted had joined Harry, the authorities would have discovered that there were two men claiming to be 'Edward James Ryan', miraculously with the same birth date. Presumably Ted did not wish to reveal that Harry was masquerading under a false name – a fraudulent enlistment was not a good look for a man in the Anzac Police!

In any case, it is unlikely that Ted would have described the job as a 'cold-footed job' if he had known it came from Harry, and indeed that Harry had already jumped at such a job himself. Ted, as we know from his letter to Ramsay MacDonald, believed that his two brothers had both been knocked-about while serving at Gallipoli. Perhaps that fixed in his mind his own desire to fight. Ted stuck to his fighting unit. It was a fateful decision.

From Tel-el-Kebir, Ted Ryan was transferred to the AIF base at Serapeum just three weeks after Tom had departed from this same base bound for France. Serapeum was a bridgehead on the Suez Canal, clotted with tents in a desert landscape.

Here at Serapeum on 19 April, Ted Ryan and his fellow-soldiers from the 3rd Training Battalion were folded into the new 51st Battalion, their essential 'home' unit, comprising roughly a thousand men. Perhaps it was at this point that Ted discovered that his brother Tom was not among those already there – the 'old hands' from the 11th Battalion. He had departed for France at the end of March.

Maybe it was just as well that the three Ryan brothers were separated. In the same battalion there was always the chance of death for all three from just one shell. The English soldier-poet, 2nd Lieutenant Edmund Blunden, would later offer sobering reflections on this point. 'Brothers should not join the same battalions', he wrote, with one incident in his mind. 'When we were at the place where some of the wounded had been collected under the best shelter to be found, I was struck deep by the misery of a boy ... half-crying, half-exhorting over a stretcher when came the clear but weakened voice of his brother, wounded almost to death ... the effect was too surely a culmination of suffering.'[268]

The new 51st Battalion was only weeks old. It had been formally established at the beginning of March. It was 'purely a West Australian battalion', as the battalion war diary proudly recorded. But, of course, in line with frequent practice, the new commander was not Australian. Major Arthur M. Ross, born in India and educated at Rugby and Sandhurst, was a British officer formerly from the West Yorkshire Regiment who took command of the battalion as Lieutenant Colonel on 3 March 1916.[269] The Australians saw Ross as 'tall and sinewy, every inch a soldier' but haughty. On parades, he 'would jog his horse around through the ranks and say: "I think this man would like another guard tonight. Take his name sergeant!"'[270] He was old-school: he 'had great faith in cold steel'. The men recorded that, like the officers at Blackboy Hill, Ross lectured his troops directly. 'The infantryman's weapon is the bayonet', he told them.[271]

On joining the battalion, Ted Ryan faced instant demotion. As he explained in his letter home, it was the accepted practice that all those NCOs with temporary ranks in their training battalions would 'lose their stripes' as they entered the permanent battalions. 'I reverted to the ranks.' As plain old Private Ted Ryan, he joined A Company in the 51st Battalion.

The new battalion took its place in the expanded AIF. Those planning the structure of the force allocated the 51st Battalion to the 13th Infantry Brigade, along with three other battalions, the 49th, 50th, and 52nd Battalions. The commander of the brigade, William Glasgow, was a Queensland-born Australian. The 13th Infantry Brigade in turn was part of the 4th Division. Initially, the 4th Division was under the command of a British General, Sir Herbert Vaughan Cox and, unsurprisingly, in conformity with the prevailing sociology of the British Army, Cox was the product of elite schools, a Charterhouse man, a Sandhurst man, and an Indian Army officer.

More preparation for war followed for the men of the new 51st Battalion at Serapeum. They received their distinctive colour patches, a circle (indicating the 4th Division), horizontally divided, with a chocolate-brown half-moon sitting over light blue. The men were put through drills, route marches, 'exercises in Trench Warfare', 'Musketry',

'Night Operations' and 'Exercises in Attack'. One half-hour daily was spent on 'Bayonet Fighting and Instruction', and ten minutes on 'rapid reloading and firing'.

Serapeum, a large camp for the four battalions of the 13th Brigade, was notorious. Ryan wrote in his letter home of 'duststorms, flies, fleas, sweat, sorrow, and sore eyes'. Another soldier wrote that 'my recollections of this "Hell-on-earth" are anything but pleasant for apart from training that would break the heart of a lion, I think of thirst, sandstorms, full marching-order, outposts at night and flies and sand'.[272] Years later, a third soldier recoiled at his memories of being 'amongst the flies and eating sand'.[273] Water was in critically short supply, and the men were reduced to a ration of a bottle a day. The fine dust sickened some men, and one dust storm lasted for three days.[274]

Irritating encounters with class and privilege stayed in the minds of some soldiers. For instance, on 20 April, the Commander-in-Chief of the whole Egyptian Expeditionary Force, General Sir Archibald Murray, proudly escorting H.R.H. the Prince of Wales, inspected the men. The men were expected to put on a fine show. Wearing full packs and with fixed bayonets, they were ordered 'to dash 200 yards across soft sand', and then 'gaily leap' over four foot of barbed wire in order to storm a practice trench, 'while all the brass hats watched us on horseback'. Perhaps the British 'heads' imagined Australians 'could jump like Kangaroos', mused the men sourly. In a sullen protest, most soldiers soon gave up the charge, and 'walked the distance and leisurely occupied the trench'.[275]

An aquatic sports day in the Suez Canal broke the tedium. On 25 April the unit's war diary recorded that all enjoyed a holiday for the '1st anniversary of ANZAC DAY'. Inter-battalion games were arranged, and the 51st Battalion won the Divisional Aquatic Sports Relay Race, in the canal.[276] It was a last happy day for many.

The training continued into May 1916. A weekly route march required the men to march through sand. Musketry training on the firing range involved '5 rounds snap shooting and 5 rounds "thinning men"'. The men received their new Lee Enfield rifles, the Converted Mark III. There was extra practice for 'indifferent shots'. 'Lewis gun-firing and live bomb practices carried out from fire-trenches', noted the war diary.[277] That the men were being prepared to use the latest manufactured weapons for mass killing was clear – and each Sunday, as the war diary recorded, the men attended 'Divine Service as usual'.

In mid-May, the men of the 51st Battalion took their turn in the trenches of the 'Front Line Defences', fortifying the Suez Canal against any attack. 120 rounds of ammunition were issued to each soldier. Then at the end of the month, the men moved a few miles further east, to the trenches at Gebel Habieta. 'This is the place where we had to lie in the trenches waiting for the Turks', Ryan recalled later in his letter home. 'But we were unfortunate, as "Jacko" never put in an appearance.'[278]

Unfortunate? Apparently Private Ted Ryan, who had spurned the offers of a 'cold-footed job', was still eager for action.

Partitioning the Plunder

And for what? To what purposes were Ryan and his companions marching through sand in Egypt in early 1916? Did Australia's Cabinet ministers in Melbourne keep watch over the purposes to which Australian lives were being risked in this war? Did those commanding Britain's war, deploying the men destined to fill the war cemeteries, curb their appetites for plunder? Did they honour the spirit of 1914, namely, that men of generosity were stepping forward to wage a war of defence, with limited objectives – the liberation of conquered territories? Not a bit.

Again we must briefly explore events in the Cabinet rooms and grand state apartments of the governments at war. At exactly this time, a new series of secret agreements was concluded, principally between British and French diplomats. These inflated the objectives of the war much further. In essence, the trustees of the blood and treasure of the Empire in London agreed upon the partition of the whole of the Ottoman Empire.

The key British negotiator, Lieutenant Colonel Sir Mark Sykes, a Catholic Conservative MP, and his French counterpart, François Georges-Picot, a suave man with close links to the French Colonial Party, met frequently in London from late 1915 to draw up a grand bargain. Sykes reported to the War Committee on 16 December 1915, and got his riding instructions. The minutes are revealing. He warned the politicians that, if Britain were defeated in its wrestle with Ottoman Turkey, peril awaited. The fearful 'French financiers' (mentioned eleven times), 'a very evil force', would then do deals with the Ottomans to get their way. Competitive plans for 'railways' (mentioned five times) was a vital interest. Moreover, he feared Russia. Negotiating a peace before a military triumph, he cautioned, 'means ending the war with grave danger – *post*-war – to India, Egypt, and to the Entente, if Russia is unsatisfied with regard to an open port'. The solution? A 'great offensive' in the Middle East, and agreement beforehand with France to snaffle up the lot. And how to divide the spoils? Here Sykes famously pointed to a map and suggested, 'I should like to draw a line from the "e" in Acre to the last "k" in Kerkuk [*sic*]', that is, a line running almost a thousand kilometres, from the coast (of what is now northern Israel) to northern Mesopotamia (Iraq). France would take everything north of the line; Britain, under various guises, would take everything south of the line.[279]

Sykes and Picot reached a preliminary agreement in January 1916, which both Paris and London endorsed the next month. At Petrograd in March, Sykes and Picot got Russian approval. Grey then sent to Paul Cambon, the French ambassador in London, a letter confirming the famous terms on 16 May 1916. The 'Sykes-Picot Agreement' was in place.[280]

What 'Sykes-Picot Agreement'? We should remember that Australian lives – and many others – were lost in order to achieve it. So, we owe it to the dead that something is known of the plans within this famous agreement.

Sykes and Picot had wielded their red and blue coloured pencils over a vast map of the Ottoman Empire in the Middle East. Their deal illustrates the madness that may come upon men from staring at maps too long. In essence, the Entente planned to snatch everything. The map showed that Britain would directly rule a vast 'red' area, chiefly central and southern Mesopotamia, including Basra in the south and Baghdad in the north; France would directly rule a vast 'blue' area, chiefly all the Syrian and Lebanese coast, then a chunk of territory stretching north into the Ottoman Empire, from west of the port of Mersina (now Mersin in south-east Turkey), running as far north as Sivas (now in central Turkey) and then east toward Kurdistan.

Then came fudge. A large independent 'Arab State' or confederation was contemplated for the interior of Syria and Jordan (including Damascus) and stretching toward Mesopotamia, although Mosul was earmarked for France. But this 'Arab State' was to be divided into areas 'A' and 'B', where France and Britain respectively would exercise indirect control and thus gain economic dominance. An international regime was contemplated for a 'brown' area, chiefly the 'Holy Land' in Palestine, but a little separate pocket of 'red' to the north, on the Syrian coast, gave the two ports of Haifa and Acre to Britain.[281]

Through exchanges of notes with Russia in April and September 1916, Britain and France also agreed to big Russian gains at the expense of the Ottoman Empire in the north-east of Turkey and in the Caucasus, including the towns of Erzurum, Van, Bitlis, and Trebizond (now Trabzon) on the Black Sea.

Here was bounty beyond counting. The scramble for the Ottoman Empire was on.

Commercial ambitions pulsed in the text of the agreements. Articles were sprinkled with special provisions about who would build what railways and who would enjoy 'the priority of right of enterprise and loans' – all to advantage men with hungry eyes directing big firms in the great capitals of the Entente.

None of this was done in the sunlight. It was a dance of naked ambition in a members-only club. All were sworn to secrecy. Initially, even the Italians, who had been lured into the war in May 1915, were *not* told of this new agreement struck by their partners. But they would learn of it some months later anyway.[282]

Nor was the dividing of the spoils limited to the Ottoman Empire. During February 1916, while Ted Ryan was en route to Egypt, other bargains were being struck in London over former German colonies in Africa. On 23 February 1916, a well-prepared British official, Lancelot Oliphant, met Georges-Picot, who once again negotiated for France. Together they pored over maps of the German Cameroons. Self-effacingly, Oliphant asked Picot to kindly 'show us exactly what part of the *Kamerun* the French would like'. He complied, indicating 'in a casual way with a blue pencil' a generous helping for France but less than Oliphant had feared. Oliphant quickly agreed that Britain could graciously give away to France some 143,000 square miles of the former German colony, but keep 34,000 square miles for Britain, 'bigger that is than Scotland', as he boasted later.[283]

For such war aims were Australians risking everything. But no Australians – not the men in the Cabinet room on Treasury Gardens in Melbourne, not the anxious parents awaiting mail from their sons in the AIF, and certainly not the soldiers themselves eating sand in Egypt – learned anything at all of these war aims.

Private Edward James Ryan, full-length portrait, probably Egypt, 1916 – cropped, but originally endorsed 'best wishes, Ted' (courtesy of the late Beth Sutton).

The Happy Warrior – in a Norfolk Jacket

At some point during his sojourn in Egypt, like so many of his fellow-soldiers, Ted Ryan paid for a couple of studio portraits of himself in his military uniform to be taken, and he sent them home to the Mudie family in Broken Hill. One photo shows him seated, in front of a roughly painted canvas backdrop. He has written upon the photo the words,

'Best wishes, Ted'. Another, a close-up, shows him looking grim-faced, unsmiling, serious, and still very youthful in appearance. He has written 'Your loving nephew Ted' upon it. This one certainly was destined for his Uncle James and Aunt Margaret.

In the full-length portrait, he is staring impassively at the camera. He is wearing shorts, and the regulation tan boots and puttees. His campaign cap is at his feet. In both portraits, he wears that distinctive khaki military tunic of the AIF, with its rising-sun badge and scroll on the buttoned-up collar, proclaiming the 'Australian Commonwealth Military Forces', although he was now also a member of the 'Australian Imperial Force' (for which there was never any badge issued). This strange all-purpose jacket was formally known as the AIF's 'jacket service dress'.

Why strange? Our contemporary eyes are so used to seeing this standard AIF tunic that we probably fail to recognise what an incongruous garment it was for the soldiers. For it was modelled on the loose, pleated, single-breasted and belted shooting-jacket – the 'Norfolk jacket' – made famous by the corpulent Prince of Wales, later King Edward VII. He and his rich friends had made this jacket fashionable during their extravagant shooting parties that saw them blazing away at the birdlife on the Sandringham estate in Norfolk. Australian soldiers now donned the tunic, 'with its Norfolk-jacket cut', as if they were about to go on a jolly shooting expedition to pot grouse.[284]

The Egyptian photographer has given Ryan a long polished cane to hold in his right hand for the photo. He clutches its neck. Such a cane is definitely not part of the normal kit of a Private in the AIF. Perhaps the photographer feels that the cane lends a more authentic military air. Ryan clenches his other fist, and stares down the lens of the camera.

Here he is, Private Ryan, the happy warrior, ready for war.

Chapter 10

TO THE SHAMBLES

MARSEILLE, PARIS, FLEURBAIX, JUNE 1916

> *Interviewer:* And are you surprised that young people want to know about the war? That young people want to learn about it?
>
> *Private Thomas Talty:* Yeah. Yeah, well, you wouldn't be surprised … But I didn't know much about the First War either. 'Cos I was all around down the bloody trench. And I never got shot but by my bloody mates did.[285]
>
> — Private Thomas Talty, AIF veteran, interviewed 1998

On 1 June 1916, the 51st Battalion at Serapeum received stunning orders: the next destination was to be France. As part of the new 4th Division of the AIF, the battalion was to be thrown into battle on the Western Front.

The men spent three days quickly 'refitting and equipping'. Then, on 4 June, the men were marched 'in very hot, dusty weather' to meet two trains at the rail siding at Serapeum West. Then, all soldiers being issued with a waterproof sheet and a single blanket to ward off the chill of the evening, in their khaki drill they endured an overnight train journey to Alexandria on the Mediterranean coast. They arrived at the Gabbary Quay in Alexandria the next morning.

By 8 a.m. on 5 June the soldiers of the 51st Battalion were all aboard the British troopship HMT *Ivernia*, and soon after the ship set out on its five-day Mediterranean voyage, bound for Marseille on the south coast of France. Morale was 'middling': on the first night a combination of poor food and seasickness led almost all of the 3,000 aboard to dash for 'an urgent call'. The men were instructed to wear life-jackets for the whole voyage, as the officers feared a submarine attack. Four machine-guns periodically let loose into the blue ocean, which must have heightened tension, as part of the anti-submarine strategy. 'Good voyage', the war diary recorded.[286]

Ivernia arrived outside the port of Marseille early in the morning of 11 June. The great shining statue of the Virgin Mary on top of the city's tall Catholic basilica, Notre-Dame de la Garde, looked out over the grand harbour, an ageless icon of the city, and, according to the Catholic ideal, it offered the miraculous Mother's protection to all seafarers and, some must have hoped, to arriving soldiers. *Ivernia* entered the harbour at 5 p.m. Once the boat was docked, the men spent the night assisting in disembarking stores, guns and ammunition. Colonel Ross, the battalion commander, warned all that 'anyone caught breaking ship would be shot'. Just before half-past-ten on the morning of the next day, 12 June, the men clambered aboard one long train, 'a rake of cattle trucks', with twenty men per truck.[287] They began their journey north, toward the seat of the war – toward battle.

The Beauty of the Earth

It was a memorable train journey, over two-and-a-half days, from the far south of France to the far north.

The train travelled first through the countryside of Provence. There were two fixed stops per day for 'Halte-Repas' – meal breaks. The landscape was full of the scents of summer. It must have seemed that all the planet's chocolate-box prettiness was being poignantly trailed before the Australian troops, in the natural beauty of a French spring – the fields exploding into gold, and the orchards into flower – as they peered out through the train windows. 'I think the south of France is beautiful', Ryan wrote home very simply.[288]

Other Australian soldiers sent to the front by train from Marseille were also entranced. 'Beautiful view of the Rhone running alongside sometimes for miles. All the fruit trees in bloom. Women working the farms. Such beautiful country I have never seen before', wrote one.[289] Lieutenant George King of the 4th Battalion also wrote in his diary of this 'wonderful train journey' of three days and three nights. 'The charm of the South of France, in its very green gown of early spring, to our eyes, long tired with sand and desert, held us spell-bound.' King concluded 'Here surely is a land worth fighting for.'[290] For a young soldier such as Ted Ryan, used to the sights of the mostly gardenless homes and grassless pavements of the streets of Broken Hill, and the barren desert landscape surrounding the town, the journey through France in this lush season must have been captivating.

But it was hard going in the cattle trucks: there was barely room for twenty men to lie and sleep on the bare boards, ten men on each side. Incidents on the way excited class feeling and resentment. The troop train waited on sidings while 'Continental flyers' steamed past. At one station the men 'had a peep into a first-class compartment' with its 'satin covered seats like a dinky little parlour'. At Abbeville the train halted and the men tumbled out to stretch. A Red Cap with his pistol on his hip instantly confronted the men. 'Get back into that train, you chaps. How dare you get out without orders!' he barked.[291]

The train took the men of the 51st Battalion, now comprising just under a thousand men plus thirty-three officers, all the way to the small town of Caëstre, in the Nord Department, very near the border with Belgium. The men 'detrained' late in the evening of 14 June 'in a gentle drizzle of rain'. Guides explained the 'faint rumbling' the men could hear in the distance: 'Them's the guns, me boy.' Some might have heard the pounding of guns as a sound 'like distant surf'. The men then marched until dawn. At last they arrived exhausted at their first farm billets near the village of Meterin.[292]

It was 'a sleepy little village' with 'one crooked cobble-stone street'. The rural beauty of such places behind the lines caught many an Australian soldier's eye. 'Sides of roads are covered with poppies, cornflowers & many other species', wrote one.[293] But almost immediately the 51st Battalion resumed its training, with the usual 'Route marching and musketry'. Preparations intensified. Lewis Guns and gas helmets were issued. After a week, the men were marched about 20 kilometres to a position near the village of Sailly-sur-la-Lys, near Pétillon. Training in 'anti-gas measures' was included. A 'Scout Platoon' and a 'Grenade Platoon' were formed.

The front was now so close that officers reconnoitred the trenches into which the men were soon to be deployed, on rotation, relieving other Australian battalions in that sector of the line, near Fleurbaix.[294]

Late June 1916 was an ill-fated moment to arrive in the lines. Vast munitions had been amassed on the British side for the planned epic battle of the summer: it was the eve of the huge British offensive, just to the south, on the River Somme, a great crushing blow that was planned for 1 July 1916 – the 'season of liquidation'.[295]

'Trade warriors': Paris, June 1916

On their train journey up the Rhone Valley, the men of the 51st Battalion had seen 'old bent dames' at work in the fields. The Australians sympathised with them: 'These women of France would stand up, tears running down their cheeks, thinking perhaps of their own dear menfolk battling up north to keep out the invader', wrote one of Ryan's companions.[296] But were the Australians in France fighting only for its liberation? While the locomotive steamed north pulling the men of the 51st Battalion to the battlefront in June 1916, men of property and political power on the Entente side were gathering in conference in Paris. Bowler hats cloaked, they would meet in conference to draw up still more war aims – economic war aims. Clearly this vast war was not being fought simply to shift border-stones and national colours over the maps of Europe and the colonial world. Struggles over trade and resources were bound up in this conflict also.

Some background is vital. By this stage of the war, the Royal Navy's economic blockade of Germany was causing deep distress in many countries. Even the northern neutrals were affected, as the British intercepted the great bulk of trans-Atlantic trade, and 'rationed' even neutral states. Shortages of all kinds tormented the people. Food scarcity and high prices were very serious in Germany and Austria-Hungary. The draining of manpower from agriculture for the war effort worsened the impact of the 'hunger blockade'. After two years of war, premature deaths from malnutrition in Germany and Austria-Hungary, especially among the very young and the elderly, were already in the hundreds of thousands.[297] Lord Northcliffe told his top journalists candidly that Britain and Germany were engaged in a 'starving match'.[298] Indeed, Europe was on that slope toward total war, with no distinction made between combatants and civilians.

In Britain, the success of the blockade against Germany gave economic nationalism a big boost. Faith in the old dogmas of free trade had been fading since the turn of the century. The British promoters of the 'new protectionism' argued that after the war German commerce and investment should be banned, and not only from newly acquired territories but also from the British Empire as a whole – perhaps from all the victors' empires. Thus, German commercial, industrial, and financial enterprise could be suffocated, excluded from vast swathes of the globe.

In Britain, advocates of 'Tariff Reform' or 'Imperial Preference' (as protectionism was called), looked forward to the throttling of German competition. Extremists from the British Empire Union and the Anti-German Union demanded 'No German labour. No German goods. No German Influence. Britain for the British.' The British Empire, they argued, should become an economic fortress.[299] Pressures from this lobby rose steadily. In January 1916, Walter Runciman, Asquith's Trade Minister and a former Radical, promised the Commons that in future 'the resources of the British Empire shall be held, controlled, manipulated and used by Britishers for Britishers, first and foremost'. Goaded by protectionists, he went further, promising a 'new economic campaign' against Germany after the war, and arguing that 'it will be necessary for us, in making peace, to see to it that she does not raise her head', a wild threat of economic strangulation that was soon repeated far and wide in Germany.[300]

Asquith was so intimidated by the ceaseless demands for an economic 'war after the war' against Germany that he made a surprise appointment to the 'Inter-Allied Economic Conference' planned for Paris in June 1916. Perhaps he thought this might stifle the grievance gusher that was the Northcliffe press. The surprise choice was the clamorous Billy Hughes, the visiting Australian Prime Minister and darling of the ultra-patriotic German-baiting newspapers. During the early months of 1916, Hughes's roaring about German commerce as a 'monstrous cancer which is eating out the vitals of civilisation' and his shouts for more 'economic war' against Germany, saw him praised to the skies in the Northcliffe press. Asquith soon caved.

Caustic in his judgement was Raymond Asquith, the Prime Minister's son, an officer on the Western Front – where he would die later that year. He wrote to his wife Katherine that such mad decisions as the appointment of Hughes inspired him 'to devote my post-war energies to a crusade against the foulness and vulgarity of the modern world'. On Hughes, he was withering: 'To suggest ... that this man Hughes should represent the British Empire at an economic conference is almost as sensible as suggesting that Charlie Chaplin should do so.'[301]

The 'Inter-Allied Economic Conference' opened in Paris on 14 June 1916, just after the conclusion of the Sykes-Picot Agreement. Paris became vacation-land for all those looking to the war to deliver a big instalment of 'crony protectionism', as critics label it now. Not all business interests were agreed; not all their interests were aligned. Older firms, hoping for government assistance, looked for protection to exclude German competitors in imperial markets. Younger firms, hoping for international opportunities, were not convinced. The *Economist* was aghast. It was an old debate. Should economies be organised for producers or consumers? Should trade follow the flag, or be free to follow price and quality? Should governments help firms wrapped in the national flag to buy cheap and sell dear, while denying foreigners that chance?

The Paris Economic Conference would decide. Étienne Clémentel, the French Minister of Trade and Industry (1915-18), a convinced economic nationalist, presided. Here was a big stage upon which Hughes could strut. In his speech he called for a tighter blockade and for sweeping bans on *post-war* German commerce. The other members of the British delegation, Bonar Law, Lord Crewe, and George Foster, eventually accommodated Hughes's slogans and agreed to strengthen British proposals.[302]

The fruit of the conference, the 'Paris Resolutions', were necessarily written in imprecise terms. But in tone they owed much to Hughes. It was clear that the Entente nations were contemplating a kind of imperial self-sufficiency, a post-war trade bloc that would prohibit all trade with Germany for an indefinite period, supposedly so that the victors might look first to their own economic recovery. The 'economic warriors' in Britain were over the moon, and Hughes was revered as a hero.

These 'Paris Resolutions' were quickly released to the world's press. Britain, France, Russia, Italy, and Japan had publicly agreed to hobble the enemy countries' industry, commerce, and finance, and to convert the victorious empires into more self-sufficient imperial trade blocs, after the war. For British economic nationalists their vaunted ideal of 'tariff reform' – the 'new protection' – seemed close. After victory, so they promised, Britain would dominate in the export of industrial goods to her Empire, and the great bulk of British imports of natural products would come from her Empire. Trade would follow the flag – at last.

The German Right seized on the threat of a post-war boycott of all German commerce and trade. The Pan-Germans insisted that Germany's war was now very clearly a war of defence. Germany must fight on, they proclaimed, against a 'starvation peace'.[303] More fuel had been thrown on the fire.

Sacred Secrets

Thus, by the summer of 1916, when the Australian battalions were arriving at the front in France, the three key secret deals binding the Entente Powers, the deals that would prolong the war, were all in place: the Straits and Persia Agreement (March 1915), the Treaty of London (April 1915), and the Sykes-Picot Agreement (May 1916). On top of these had come the 'Paris Resolutions', uniquely in a public document, committing all to an economic 'war after the war'.

The secret diplomatic pledges, of course, remained hidden even from the representatives of the people in the British Parliament. A dozen times during 1915 and 1916, Radical and Labour MPs asked the Prime Minister and Sir Edward Grey if they could clarify Britain's war aims and peace terms.[304] Every time, the ministers dodged and weaved, and pleaded that secrecy must be respected, for the sake of alliance solidarity. Eventually, impatient MPs asked directly if it was true that Britain was fighting for Russian possession of Constantinople and the Straits, and for Italian dominance of the Adriatic. For example, on 24 May 1916, Ramsay MacDonald invited Grey to 'contradict the rumours' surrounding such secret treaties.[305] The sainted Sir Edward Grey fobbed him off. He replied that it was 'the duty of diplomacy' to focus completely on efforts 'to maintain the solidarity of the Allies'. Secrets were sacred – sunlight was scorned.[306]

Sir Edward Grey

Chapter 11

CARNAGE

FLEURBAIX TO ÉTAPLES, JUNE TO AUGUST 1916

Interviewer: How did you feel before you went into your first action?

Albert Linton: How did I feel? I felt rotten. Wouldn't you? Ha, ha, ha. The man that said he wasn't frightened, well, he's a liar. I've never seen anybody that when the shells are going over their head and bursting all around them, and they said they're not frightened. They're all huddled together …

— Private Albert Linton, AIF veteran, interviewed 1983[307]

The 51st Battalion was deployed in late June 1916 in a sector of the line near Fleurbaix that had already witnessed years of epic violence, destruction, and mass killing. It was a hell-scape. The battle of Neuve-Chapelle had been fought near here in March 1915, and several other battles since. Thousands of British, Indian and German soldiers had been killed on this stretch of ground, many so badly mangled that they were unidentifiable and churned into the mud and soil. Now many more stood poised, ready for the great British offensive on the Somme, counting down to 1 July. It would be a catastrophic campaign, with the dead carpeting the landscape.[308]

Here at the front most men had been killed – and many more would soon be killed – by artillery. The scale and brutality of what was happening in this mechanised fury had appalled H.M. Tomlinson, the British war correspondent, when he first witnessed it way back in late 1914:

> The mind of a witness in France is not stirred; it is stunned. One is speechless before the spectacle of men, not fighting in the way two angry men would fight, but coolly blasting great masses of their opponents to pieces at long range, and out of sight of each other, till a region with its wrecked towns and homesteads is littered with human bowels and fragments.[309]

Before the Deluge

It was much worse two years later. Hundreds of thousands of men lay entrenched, haunted no doubt by premonitions of being entombed. Sometimes they could catch a fleeting view of their enemies and sometimes, when they charged or raided, they were in each other's terrified faces with clubs and trench-knives. Enormities multiplied, night and day. Archie Barwick recorded in his diary an Australian raiding party that swooped on the enemy on the night of 27 June 1916. The men found 'that the German trenches were full of dead and dying men, and they killed all the survivors they found'.[310]

What was it like for soldiers of the 51st Battalion arriving for the first time in late June in the front line, exposed to the 'monstrous anger of the guns' – the sounds, the sights, the smells? For Private James Barber of the 51st, 'the infernal noise' of machine-guns was the worst. 'Does a man ever forget the first time he hears that noise?' It was like 'a thousand typewriters hammering away in the darkness'. The German machine guns had a 'peculiar chuckling sound', he wrote. 'It gave one an eerie creepy feeling, made the heart skip a beat.'[311]

Another Australian, Frank Weatherhead, remembered arriving at night, seeing 'strange lights' in the east, and hearing 'the full heavy rumble of the guns and foreboding full of menace'. There were 'moments of sickening dread as we waited under fire for the first time. Those moments were horrible.' He was face-to-face with 'a foul, filthy diabolical war ... I seemed part of the evil slime that surrounded us [and its] foetid atmosphere filled my lungs.'[312]

Some British soldiers have also left vivid pen-portraits. One recalled finding the fire-front both alluring and repellent, as he marched for the first time 'through darkness and ruined villages towards the flaring fair ground of the front'.[313] The eloquent soldier-novelist R.H. Mottram remembered hearing the shriek of shells for the first time as 'an unforgettable sound, as though the heavens, made of cheap calico, were being torn to lengths by some demonic draper'. Somewhere there were machine-guns jabbering away like 'some insane woodpecker'. Then came the 'low boom of "heavies", the sharper note of the field-guns, the whip-lash crack of rifles'.[314]

Nineteen-year-old Arthur Wheen, an Australian soldier who served in a sector of the front close to that of the 51st Battalion, went into the line in the summer of 1916 just a few weeks after Ryan. 'All the time', wrote Wheen, 'there was a crack, whiz, click clack rat-a-tat-tat tut tut tut tut tut tut tut of rifles and machine guns; whiz, bang, sigh of shrapnel; scream and burst of high explosive, and a howl as great chunks of iron and dirt flew.' He recorded his ultimate horror, of going down 'to the waist in sticky mud and cold water' so that 'I thought the mud was going to swallow me'.[315] And behind it all he remembered that the 'machine guns rattled like ten thousand demented devils'.[316]

And what sights might Ryan and his companions have seen? At night, the pyrotechnics of war were visible for miles behind. 'What a collection of fireworks!'

wrote James Barber. 'All colours of the rainbow, soaring into the blackness of the night.'[317] Flares entranced the soldiers. 'It was very pretty last night, you should have seen the bright flares', wrote Archie Barwick in late June 1916.[318] Some were hypnotised by the slowly falling and fading 'star-shell flicker from the line'.[319] For another soldier, the front was 'like looking into a stove full of glowing embers'.[320]

In a daylight march up to the line, the men surveyed vistas of violent death. Many were struck by the pathetic remnants of wrecked trees that lined the roads, 'rigid and silent as if sudden death had caught them and held them there'. Some surviving trees stood in the fields 'like giant corpses standing in tangled coils of barbed wire'.[321] Another remembered them as 'gaunt skeletons, crowned fan-shaped with splinters'.[322] And another recalled how 'torn camouflage fluttered from splintered trees' as the passing troops gazed up at their 'shiny shattered arms'.[323]

On arrival in the support trenches, and then the front line, the men confronted a landscape inundated with infamies. Across no man's land lay the human debris of battle, turning the landscape into a veritable charnel house. In summer 'the swathes of little brown bundles, with bones showing through, lay in nettles and grass'.[324] And everywhere, flies and rats. In the trenches, one soldier recalled that 'a legion of the fattest and longest rats he had ever seen were popping in and out of the crevices between the sandbags'.[325]

And smells? On the battleground there was always 'a whiff of the smell of butchers' shops in hot weather'.[326] One war correspondent remembered it as the 'familiar smell of the Somme, the smell of smouldering wood and offal ... The offal was all human'.[327] 'The wind came in puffs laden with an odour as of dead rats in an attic', wrote the volunteer American ambulance driver John Dos Passos.[328]

Lives in the Balance

Those Australians going into the trenches in June 1916 could scarcely have imagined the poignant conjunction of events that was taking place far beyond the battlefront. As they prepared to risk all, far away there was a telling confrontation between those determined to talk peace in the great chancelleries of Europe, and those determined to silence them.

While Ryan's 51st Battalion had been undertaking its sea voyage from Alexandria to Marseille, and then its long train journey north, arriving in the Fleurbaix sector of the front in late June 1916, one brave British woman had been undertaking her own peace mission – to Berlin. She was Emily Hobhouse, the famous British suffragist who had campaigned loudly against the Boer War, and had gained world renown for exposing Britain's tactic of herding women and children into 'concentration camps' where disease had killed almost 28,000 people.[329] From the beginning of the First World War, Hobhouse had been a trenchant critic. In early June 1916 she slipped from neutral

Switzerland into Germany, and then travelled north to German-occupied Belgium, in order to undertake her own investigations of social conditions. Then, on 17 June, she crossed over from Belgium back into Germany, planning to enquire into conditions for British citizens interned near Berlin. She completed her research.

Emily Hobhouse

She had a grander plan, too. Determined to cut through the diplomatic stalemate, Hobhouse used her contacts in the women's movement in Berlin to request a meeting with the German Foreign Minister, Gottlieb von Jagow, whom she had met years before. He took up the opportunity, inviting her to the German Foreign Office on the Wilhelmstrasse in the early evening of 19 June. Hobhouse found Jagow 'simple and natural and wholly unofficial in manner'. On a sofa by a window overlooking a darkening garden, the two spent an hour discussing the war and the possibilities for peace. 'I felt lifted into some sphere aloof from our blood-stained World', wrote Hobhouse. Jagow stressed that the balance of advantage in the war was, if anything, in favour of Britain. Germany had won great victories but had endured great defeats, such as at the Battle of the Marne; Britain, on the other hand, had achieved no great victories, but had endured *no* significant defeats. The tragedy was, as Jagow remarked, that if bloody-minded men were so determined the war 'could go on for years'. Nonetheless, the

German Chancellor was willing to discuss peace, as Jagow put it, '*not* from weakness but humanity'.³³⁰

Gottlieb von Jagow

In follow-up letters over the next week, Hobhouse made progress. She urged upon Jagow the crying need for a meeting between a German and an English statesman, on the sands of the Dutch coast, she suggested, 'say – at Scheveningen', to begin negotiations to end the war. If only face-to-face contact could begin, she pleaded. Jagow in reply depicted the leading British politicians as proudly unbending in recent speeches: Grey had petulantly told Parliament that Bethmann Hollweg had peddled 'a first-class lie' about Britain's diplomacy during the July crisis in 1914. Therefore, Jagow suggested, it was first 'for England to move in the matter'. Hobhouse asked Jagow to strengthen her hand when she reported on her mission, by giving her an assurance that if Britain did make an approach to Germany 'you [Jagow] would not reject it'. Jagow made the pledge. In a last letter to Hobhouse, he promised he would indeed 'not reject a proposal for informal conversations', but he asked her to keep silent regarding the fact that 'I [had] agreed in advance'.³³¹

German Chancellor, Theobald von Bethmann Hollweg

Hobhouse journeyed back to Britain via Switzerland and France. Soon after arriving at Southampton, on 28 June, she sent a cable to Sir Edward Grey at the Foreign Office. Full of confidence, she requested a meeting. Having received no reply, she wrote again from London the next day, 29 June, offering to give Grey an outline of her encouraging interview and correspondence with Jagow. Grey had his secretary send Hobhouse a note refusing to see her, but inviting her to put pen to paper.[332] As it happened, on those very days, 28 and 29 June, just as Hobhouse reached out to Grey, only to be rebuffed, Private Ted Ryan and his comrades were being primed-up to enter the front-line trenches in France for the first time. Hearts pounding.

Shell Burst

It was now the very eve of the Battle of the Somme. The 51st Battalion was to defend a half-mile of sand-bagged trenches and dug-outs in the 'Pétillon sector' of the front line, between the villages of Fleurbaix and Fromelles. The tour was scheduled to last 18 days, with the companies rotating. The soldiers of Ted Ryan's A Company, the last of the 51st Battalion to be deployed, slipped into their trenches on the night of 28-29 June. During the night, as the officers recorded, there was continuous rain and a lengthy bombardment. The shell-pocked mud trembled; the men huddled. They were all within the sweep of the scythe of death. Was Ryan confident or frightened? Perhaps it was as the British soldier Richard Aldington remembered it, when he looked back on the fate of a friend: 'Like a good many recruits, when first in the line he was inclined to be foolhardy rather than timorous.'[333] Who knows?

In any case, Ryan was indeed wounded during that first night in the front-line trenches. A German artillery shell did the damage. He was listed as 'wounded in action', suffering 'shell burns and abrasions'. Therefore, he must have been very near an explosion. The battalion war diary recorded that over the last five days of June, when the men manned the trenches, 'several bouts of heavy shelling were experienced'. The battalion's casualties were significant: five men were killed outright, another died quickly of wounds, and seventeen men and one officer were wounded from the shelling.[334] Ryan was one of the seventeen.

Private Ted Ryan had survived. But the terrible numbing brutality of a shell bursting very near must not be passed over quickly. Soldiers who endured such a shattering event have left scores of accounts. Private James Barber of the 51st Battalion recalled the impact of a 5.9 mm shell bursting on the back wall of a trench a few nights after Ryan's wounding. 'Outside the fire-step fifteen good Australians lay still, all that was left of them.'[335] Corporal Arthur Thomas of the 6th Battalion, fighting near Pozières on 24 July, wrote in his diary of a 'whirr – crash, a cruel scorching feeling on the head and face and a sickening concussion, for a shell had burst right handy'.[336] Archie Barwick of the 1st Battalion was nearby on that same day. 'All day long the ground rocked and swayed', he wrote in his diary. 'Men were driven stark staring mad and more than one of them rushed out of the trench, over towards the Germans.' Barwick recorded seeing men 'sobbing and crying like children'. One shell accounted for fifteen men, another for forty. Shells buried men 'by the dozen', some dead, some alive, and the living 'were frantically dug out again' by their mates. Some were 'pulled out in pieces, torn to ribbons'.[337]

Such events were branded into a soldier's consciousness. Even in the year 2000, the elderly Anzac veteran, Eric Abraham, told an interviewer in vivid detail how 'all of a sudden hell broke loose, behind me. My knees buckled up and I fell to the ground.' He was stunned. His body caved in. Abraham's officer told him immediately that there was no need for shame: 'If any bloke tells you he wasn't frightened of the shellfire the first time, he's a bloody liar and he's not here.'[338]

'Shell Burns and Abrasions – Face'

In the aftermath of his wounding, Ryan was evacuated. He took his place among the thousands transported from the front over the next few days and weeks, all 'clogging the wheels of the fighting machine', as the Somme battle raged.[339] He was admitted to the 3rd Australian Field Ambulance. There the doctors recorded his injuries more precisely: 'shell burns and abrasions – face.'[340]

The burns to Ryan's face tell us vital things about this incident. Ryan must have been very near to a bursting shell. It would have hit him with the force of a car crash at speed. Possibly he saw men ripped apart; possibly he saw men buried. Two men in the trenches with him died that night.[341]

Current medical research on the impact of bomb blasts on the human body highlights the array of injuries from the 'supersonic over-pressurisation shock wave' produced by high explosives. These include tissue tearing, damage to the hollow organs (the middle ear, bowel, lungs), damage to the ears causing tinnitus and vertigo, and damage to the central nervous system, such as 'concussion syndrome', 'intracranial, subdural and extradural haemorrhages', and, of course, post-traumatic stress disorder.[342] Thus, we must acknowledge that soldiers exposed to a blast very close to them could experience a very real concussion upon the brain, which can create a haunting sensitivity to similar sounds of battle in the future.

Added to this are the sights that Ryan very likely saw in the trenches during the rain of shells. This can be glimpsed in the memoirs of other soldiers.

In the spring of 1917, Lieutenant Eric Dark, a doctor working with the Australians' 9th Field Ambulance, witnessed one such incident right outside his advanced dressing station. As he watched a group of soldiers marching past there was 'a direct hit on a soldier, cutting off both his legs just above the knee; he fell onto the stumps of his thighs and, incredibly, took two or three stumbling steps before collapsing'.[343]

Frederick Manning, a Sydney-born soldier who served in the British Army, also saw a man 'blown into fragments by a high-explosive shell', and another 'torn into bloody tatters as if by some invisible beast'. It was 'infinitely more horrible to see a man eviscerated and shattered than to see him shot'. These incidents, he wrote, could reduce men to 'apathy and stupor', to 'bitter resignation', and to fitful sleep punctuated by 'convulsive agonies', and 'little whimperings which quickened into sobs, passed into long shuddering moans, or culminated in angry half-articulate obscenities'. As Manning wrote, any man who had endured 'the perilous instant' and had been 'half-stunned' might at any time fall back 'among the grotesque terrors and nightmare creatures of his own mind'.[344]

Lieutenant Blunden described the dazzling impact of shelling, the 'bright terrible phosphorous', the 'white hot fragments', and 'the fierce darts of the shrapnel'.[345] He also saw the effect of a direct hit upon a trench: 'The gobbets of blackening flesh, the earth wall sotted with blood, with flesh, the eye under the duckboard, the pulpy bone.' He remembered soldiers reduced to 'a kind of catalepsy' by the incident, and one sergeant muttering afterwards: 'It's a lie; we're a lie.'[346]

These are not just samples of evidence from gifted literary men. Scores of similar descriptions from ordinary Australian soldiers' diaries, letters, interviews, and from official Army documents and medical records, describe 'mentally maimed diggers' reduced to a pitiful state by shell shock following prolonged bombardments and near misses.[347]

Men Without Faces

From the field ambulance, Ryan was then shifted on 4 July to a British hospital on the coast, the '13th Stationary Hospital', in Boulogne. This was a hospital that had been hastily established in the early days of the war in the summer of 1914 in large industrial sheds near the wharves.[348] It had fifty ophthalmic beds, and specialised in treating facial and eye injuries. 'Shell wound face' was entered on Ryan's record. But he was lucky. His sight was safe. He was there for two days and then transferred to the nearby 1st Convalescent Hospital – 'wounded, mild'. On 7 July he was moved to the huge military base at Étaples, or 'Eatapples' as the troops called it. He would be treated there for a further fortnight.[349]

Ryan had endured only hours of battle. Then he had been among the wounded in ambulances, hospitals, and convalescent wards for about three weeks. The entire episode was not some brief encounter with war. In its aftermath, he was in the bowels of the beast. He undoubtedly witnessed gruesome sights among the seemingly endless stream of human wrecks on stained stretchers flowing through these medical facilities after the Battle of the Somme opened on 1 July. At Boulogne, being treated for a facial wound, Ryan doubtless saw in every other glance around his ward the worst of head injuries. Men without faces were there. Men breathing their last were there. Ryan must have heard eternity whispering down the wards. What he had seen with his own eyes, at Boulogne and Étaples, he believed in his soul.

We should not imagine that for a soldier to be taken to hospital was some kind of deliverance, there to be lulled by soft hands, plump pillows, and smooth sheets, with the war but a distant memory. Edgar Morrow, a West Australian soldier injured just after Pozières, witnessed things as a casualty behind the lines every bit as horrific as things he had witnessed in the front lines. He recalled his ambulance driver, after delivering him to hospital, cleaning out his ambulance as he looked on. There were 'armfuls of blood-soaked blankets' and 'stained stretchers', wrote Morrow. 'Blood was everywhere in the ambulance, and vomit on the floor.'[350]

Another Australian soldier, Fred Kelly, a machine gunner at the Battle of Fromelles in July 1916, testifies to the trauma of the aftermath. 'It was horrific', he recalled, 'when the wounded came back'. Kelly saw one 'very big man' wounded: 'this big fellah had no nose'. But no stretcher was at hand, so he had to walk out to get to medical assistance. Eighty years after the battle, Kelly declared that, of all the sights he had seen at Fromelles, watching that man walking away 'with just a hole in his face' was 'the thing that upset me the most'.[351]

The scenes to be witnessed in casualty clearing stations, hospital trains, and hospital wards could add up to a concentrated dose of horror – worse than the trenches. Frank Weatherhead remembered waiting on a stretcher at a dressing station 'all day', in 'tents full of haggard weary nervous and battered humanity' with 'groaning and cursing on all sides'. The scenes of battle 'kept burning my brain like sin'. Feeling 'sad and weary', he experienced no sense of relief that he was out of it. Then, on the hospital train, Weatherhead tried to summon sympathy for a man with a 'mangled hand', but he was soon overwhelmed by the fact that in that train 'we were a thousand and everyone has something wrong with him and everyone was in pain'.[352]

Hugh Walpole, the novelist who served with a Red Cross unit on the eastern front, was similarly devastated. In make-shift hospitals in Galicia, he remembered that 'the air was weighed down with the smell of blood and human flesh', with 'sighs and groans' as 'a perpetual undercurrent'. Walpole 'faltered' as he faced 'again and again bodies torn almost in half, faces mangled for life, hands battered into pulp, legs hanging almost by a thread'. It seemed that 'all the pain and torture would rise in a flood and overwhelm one'. 'The wounds were horrible', wrote Walpole. 'No man seemed to come into the room with an unmangled body. The smell rose higher and higher, the bloody rags lay about the kitchen floor, torn arms, smashed legs, heads with gaping wounds, the pitiful crying and praying, the shrill voices of the delirious.'[353]

Tending to the freshly wounded near the front, for months and years, even long-serving Australian ambulance staff could succumb to rebellious thoughts. In October 1917, young Private Frank Molony from the well-heeled eastern suburbs of Sydney, serving with the 1st Field Ambulance, was immersed in the stream of wounded men coming back from the 3rd Battle of Ypres (or Passchendaele), tending to them with the pathetically inadequate gauze for gashed bellies, splints for shattered limbs, and morphine for the maimed and dying. Off duty, he tried to take comfort, as he often did, in the pages of the *Anzac Bulletin*. From July 1916, this newspaper was assembled at Australia House in London by a team of publicists and distributed free, three times a week, to the men of the AIF in their camps in the UK and in the trenches.[354] Molony looked for words sculpted to inspire, the characteristically 'emphatic' and 'picturesque' words of Charles Bean, General Birdwood, or Sir Douglas Haig, the British commander of the British Expeditionary Force. Lost in the *Anzac Bulletin*, Molony tried to persuade himself that the bloodshed was a dire necessity. But this time it did not work. 'In the terrible elation that follows, I hate myself, hate and feel curses almost rise', he wrote. Then he recorded 'terrible nightmares' after reading reports of 'a successful, Christ "successful"! – a successful, God the word shivers horror, bombing of enemy hutments and billets.' He had been closing the eyes of dead men for too long.[355]

General Sir Douglas Haig

John Dos Passos experienced a similar epiphany as he tended the wounded in Italy. Talk of the righteous war turned his stomach. 'God it made you want to vomit to hear it', he wrote in January 1918.[356] In the summer of 1918 he volunteered to nurse wounded Americans at a base hospital near Paris. 'The night I particularly remember', he wrote, 'it was my job to carry off buckets full of amputated arms and hands and legs from an operating room'. He lost any simple faith in the justice of the war. 'Who could hold on to dogmatic opinions in the face of these pathetic remnants of shattered humanity?'[357]

Ryan's three weeks drifting among the human wreckage swept back from the battlefields of the Somme cannot be dismissed as a minor episode in his war. A few days hospitalised at Boulogne, and then a fortnight gazing at the men on stretchers, trolleys, and beds, probably pushed him to think hard about the battle, and 'the infinitesimal gains at the cost of enormous loss' as the soldiers knew so bitterly.[358] A smouldering doubt about the morality of this war began to kindle and flare.

'Crushed Hand and Nervous Breakdown'

Ryan returned to his 51st Battalion on 23 July with 130 other wounded men and fresh reinforcements. He had been away for 24 days. By this time the battalion was back in training behind the lines near the village of Halloy.[359] But here the men witnessed the hospital trains coming through, bearing 'shredded humanity' from the hellish fighting up ahead at Pozières. Investigating what lay ahead, their Battalion Commander, Lieutenant Colonel Ross, 'went up the line and he reported seeing more dead men than he had ever seen before in thirty years of soldiering'.[360]

Then came an emotional encounter. On 28 July, the men of the 51st Battalion lined the roads as their 'sister battalion' from Western Australia, the 11th, came back from Pozières. The men were 'covered with a thick growth of beard and with German helmets on their heads' but Ted's brother, Tom, was not among them. Ted may have searched the dirty faces in vain. There is every chance that he did not know that Tom had suffered shrapnel and gunshot wounds in France in May, and had been evacuated to England in June. In any case, the men of the two battalions, one fresh from the fighting, and one preparing to face battle imminently, spent their free time together that night. They were billeted in adjoining villages. There was much drinking and, no doubt, much mutual grieving over the faces and voices that the battle had taken from their thinned ranks.[361]

In early August, it was again the turn of the 51st Battalion, and the unit was moved near to the ruins of Albert, with its leaning Virgin, just behind the lines near Pozières – back to 'the roaring upheaval of earth'.[362] A return to the trenches was imminent. But during a battalion exercise on 7 August, Ted Ryan was injured for a second time – 'crushed L[eft] hand' was noted. The cause was not given. He was admitted to a Casualty Clearing Station.

The injury must have been disabling. For, after assessment, Ryan was transported from the front and hospitalised again at Étaples on the French coast on 16 August. This time the service files recorded two injuries: 'Crushed hand and nervous breakdown.' Clearly Ryan was still in the grip of shell shock. The situation was more serious than in the case of his first injury. He was transported to Calais, and then by the hospital ship *Newhaven* to England, with the words 'S. s[hock]' on his file.

In Ryan's service files are reminders of the torment these kinds of casualties could cause for relatives back in Australia. In early July, the Mudie household in Broken Hill received a telegram that Ryan had been wounded in France. James Mudie wrote to the Base Records Department in Melbourne on 20 July seeking more information about his nephew Ted, 'his address, what hospital he is in etc. as we have not heard from him since he left Australia'. On 27 July, the *Barrier Miner* did report that a 'Corporal E.J. Ryan, Broken Hill' was among the wounded.[363] But then an 'E.J. Ryan' was reported killed in the 197th Casualty List published on 22 August.[364] So, Mudie wrote to Melbourne again on 30 August asking if an 'E J. Ryan reported dead in the South Australian and Broken Hill press refers to no. 4635 Corporal E J. Ryan Wounded 51st Australian Infantry as the latter is my nephew and adopted son'. A week later Base Records replied with the comforting news: those newspaper reports of the death of an 'E.J. Ryan' had 'apparently referred to a soldier of the same name'. But the Mudie's Ted Ryan from Broken Hill was in hospital, 'wounded (mild)'.[365] Eight weeks of wondering were over. He was alive!

Margaret Mudie and James Ramsay Mudie, Broken Hill, c. 1916 (courtesy of Don Mudie).

Chapter 12

SHELL SHOCK

4th LONDON GENERAL HOSPITAL, CAMBERWELL, AUGUST 1916

> Got a direct hit … His hands were shaking violently, his eyes looked glazed, his face was a ghastly colour, and altogether he was a wreck … He was a pitiful sight, completely broken, right now. With every shell blast he ducked and eventually tucked himself in the corner cringing …[366]
>
> — Private Eric Abraham, AIF veteran, recalling a shell-shocked officer, Polygon Wood, 1917

Once admitted to the '4th London General Hospital', on Denmark Hill, in Camberwell, South London, on 26 August, Ryan's malady was recorded once again as 'S[hell] shock'. This hospital specialised in 'neurological cases', men from the trenches suffering from traumatic stress, such as Ryan. In fact, the words 'S. Shock', 'shell shock', and 'nervous breakdown' appear five times altogether in the handwritten entries within Ryan's service file.[367]

Bombardment

There can be no doubting Ryan's deep mental scars as a result of his shell shock. The two words can scarcely suffice to convey the horrific trauma. Those soldiers who experienced a barrage of shells have left descriptions of it as hellish and terrifying. Both the high explosive shells, and the shells that sent human-shredding shrapnel in all directions, could crush out faith in life itself. One shell might throw up a ton of earth, burying a group of soldiers alive; another might rend them to pieces, leaving 'abattoir refuse' littering the battlefield.[368] 'An artillery bombardment in full swing is hell itself let loose', Arthur Wheen wrote home. 'It's enough to scare the life out of a copper nail.'[369]

The diary of David Harford, the soldier who had sailed to Egypt with Ryan's group and was shipped to France a little after Ryan, tells us more. Harford was in the trenches very near to Ryan's in the autumn of 1916, and he preserved a memorable depiction of his fear, and numbing fatalism, under the ceaseless rain of artillery shells:

> October 14 [1916] ... terrific bombardment by enemy batteries. As bombardment increases in intensity we retire into our dugouts, not that they afford much protection we lie on the floor of our dugouts ... and listen to the awful bombardment, which is rapidly merging into a continuous roar. The ground trembles beneath me, and the air is charged with the acrid reek of high explosive fumes [.] In all this overcharged horror there comes as by a merciful dispensation of nature a certain insensibility to all fears, quite simple thoughts pass through our mind, so it is to end here: Here in his dark mildewed hole in the earth. ... I look around me at my damp rat-hole ... half way up in the corner a cluster of poison mushrooms or toadstools peer down at me. The centre one a little taller than the rest, seems to nod at me as it sways and trembles to the concussions of the terrible bombardments. One simply notes these things, fear of death having left one; and one prays only that [at] least it may prove one well placed shell, a crash of thunder and a lightning flash, to hurl us through the dark gates into eternity ... it is like nothing so much as a world ending in earthquake. The whole earth trembles until one is almost hurled upward ... Whether ANY of us will be alive when the bombardment ceases [.] Suddenly there is a concussion that seems to shake the breath out of my body, a big shell has burst very near ... One is astonished still to be living.[370]

Archie Barwick recorded in his diary a bombardment in July 1916, near the place that Ryan was injured, that lasted from dawn until 3 p.m. in the afternoon. He counted 75 shells landing on a patch of earth not larger than four acres in five minutes.

> [The shells] would frighten the bravest man on earth I'll bet [,] these enormous great shells they sound just like an express train rushing through the air, & when they explode it is more like a ton of dynamite exploding. [Y]ou can see them real plain sailing through the air on their frightful mission & everyone holds their breath & grip[s] themselves for the frightful concussion that arises from the explosion of these monsters. [T]hey threw earth & stone, & men too, or rather what is left of them, to a height of easily 300 feet. [W]ords fail to make anyone understand the terrible power possessed by these engines of destruction.[371]

Other Anzac soldiers have left moving accounts of the results. Marcel Caux recalled that 'you'd be shaking' and this would last 'for hours'. He was 'continually shell shocked'. The episodes 'had a deep effect on me', Caux explained.[372] Sergeant Jack Lockett recalled his first sight of a shell-shocked man, sheltering in a ditch, shaking uncontrollably. It 'frightened the life out of me.' After more than eighty years, recalling 'that shaking', he confessed 'it's pretty hard to talk now'.[373] Of his first experience under shell fire, Eric Abraham remembered : 'I was terrified and ashamed of myself ... My whole system was shut as never before ... The shock numbed my brain.'[374] Private Arthur Ebdon, a veteran of Fromelles, looked in despair at the remnants of his own platoon after two shells landed only thirty yards away. The men had been rendered speechless. 'There was my platoon ... No one spoke. They were all shell-shocked ... They were all shattered', Ebdon recalled.[375]

An Australian nurse, Sister Hope Weatherhead, treated shell-shocked men in hospitals in France from the summer of 1916. She remembered 'very pitiful cases', men struck 'dumb', and while others suffered 'paralysis of the limbs', some being 'so tremulous that they could not hold a cup of fluid in their hands'. The shell-shocked men could 'go quite mental' at the sound of anti-aircraft gunfire nearby.[376]

And the impact lasted. AIF veteran Private Jack Flannery remembered a man still suffering after his return to Melbourne in September 1919, keeping other soldiers awake with his nightmares in a hotel room they shared for the first three weeks. 'You couldn't sleep at night, see. Shell shocked. He'd get full, he'd get full, he was shell-shocked. By God. He'd get snakes, there'd be snakes: pink snakes and white snakes and German. Oh, God, he was in a bad way.'[377] Sergeant Jack Lockett recalled his 'nervous breakdown' after his return to Australia. 'I done the wrong thing, you see. I was living on my own.' He explained his restless fears, his disabling depression, his rising anxiety in any crowd, climaxing in his inability to go into the city of Melbourne without a friend to accompany him.[378] Ted Smout admitted to his own 'complete breakdown' from delayed shell shock. Smout knew from homeless men after the war that the terror could possess returned soldiers for many years afterward. 'A lot of them went for the grog you know.'[379] These examples could be multiplied, many times over.

The testimonies of Australian soldiers from more recent conflicts – Vietnam, Rwanda, Timor Leste, Iraq and Afghanistan – confirm all this: a horrific experience, from which a soldier survives, may nonetheless scar his mind and body indelibly.[380]

Blighty

In the summer of 1916, Ryan's shell shock and other injuries had been judged so severe that they necessitated his evacuation to England. But sadly, his one surviving undated letter to his Uncle James is curiously silent on his actual wounds. It does not describe the incidents, or the extent of his suffering. And there is no mention of shell shock.

Why? This letter was published in December 1916 in Broken Hill's *Barrier Miner*, a pro-conscription newspaper. Why there? Perhaps Mudie tried both papers. Perhaps he did not yet share or know of his nephew's views on conscription. In any case, publication came after the appointment of a military censor to enforce the censorship regulations at the rival *Barrier Daily Truth* paper, and as a result very few soldiers' letters appeared there.[381] The *Barrier Miner*, by contrast, carried dozens of soldiers' letters, and most certainly the paper's editor dutifully censored these, as the law required. This explains why Ryan's letter says almost nothing about his wounds, and is quite mild in spirit compared with his letter to MacDonald, which must have been written about the same time.[382]

Still, in the published letter Ryan did not pose as a warrior keen for action. He was quite open about being glad to have been evacuated from the battlefront. As is well known, many men were pleased to have got a 'gift wound' or a 'pearl blighty'. Ryan shared this feeling. He explained in his letter that he had been 'lucky enough to stop a "blighty". "Blighties", he continued, 'are the only things that are valued on the Somme. Anything that doesn't necessitate one's removal out of the firing line is considered worthless'. In the same way, another AIF soldier injured in 1917 remembered telling others 'exultantly' that his wound would get him to 'Blighty', that is, to England: 'I could see the envy in their eyes, and felt a spasm of sympathy for them in their misery.'[383]

In a perverse sense, Ryan had a lucky break. For whatever his personal suffering and injuries, he was to miss the worst of the fighting that consumed so many of the soldiers of the 51st Battalion around Mouquet Farm in mid-August and early September 1916. On 3 September, 176 men from the 51st Battalion were killed. Lieutenant Colonel Ross reported that total casualties over four days of fighting around the ruins of the farm were over 650. The battalion's officers were smashed. Of the thirteen officers who went forward, eight were killed outright, and 'only one has returned – and he wounded'. Ross reported, improbably, that the surviving soldiers were 'entirely cheerful'.[384]

Ryan had missed this disaster. But he had not escaped the sights of mangled men. In his letter home he wrote of the enormous losses he had witnessed and heard about, first at the casualty clearing station and later at the various hospitals. 'I don't know how the girls of Australia will get on for boys if this war lasts much longer, considering the number that are getting killed', he wrote grimly in his published letter home – a line that somehow escaped the attention of the censor.

He did try to convey to the family in Broken Hill something of the catastrophe unfolding in France. He recommended to his Uncle James that all Australians should watch the film 'the Battle of the Somme', a 'real good' film that he had just seen at the cinema. It depicted a bombardment of only 'a few minutes', he wrote, 'but it enables one to get an idea of what it is like to watch a bombardment on a five-mile front, or one that lasts days'. Ted added some statistics to hammer home the point, figures he may have gathered from survivors from the 51st Battalion, for they roughly match the figures in the battalion war diary. 'You can get some idea of what sort of a cutting up our battalion got when the whole of our twelve platoon officers were either killed or wounded, with the former in the majority.'[385]

Conscience – in Shock

Private Edward Ryan had survived a shell blast at close range. But, as we shall see, in the two years that followed, he would only just survive the military justice system. A long catalogue of offences would be recorded against him – eventually four charges of AWL ('Absent Without Leave', or 'AWOL' as the troops pronounced it), plus two charges of desertion.

Before we leap to judgement against him, it should be remembered that Ted Ryan would exhibit this defiance only after suffering two wounds in the summer of 1916, and after doctors had diagnosed shell shock on multiple occasions.

Such doctors were exceptional in 1916. The term 'shell shock' was probably coined in early 1915. After the Battle of the Somme in mid-1916, a veritable epidemic of it emerged. But it was under-reported, because the British authorities moved to restrict the use of the term from early 1917. In June, Haig's headquarters issued orders banning absolutely any diagnosis of 'shell shock' at the front, insisting on the tag 'Not Yet Diagnosed Nervous (NYDN)' for such cases.[386] The Australian records show that doctors persistently resorted to a score of such fudge words, ranging from 'neuralgia' to 'hysteria' to 'weak-mindedness' and 'premature senility', in order to avoid diagnosing the condition as the result of battle. Some suggested that a soldier's 'weak constitution' was the cause, rather than traumatic brain injury. In fact, the latest statistical studies of the AIF records show that shell shock led to the hospitalisation of some 41,800 Australian soldiers, one in seven of the troops that Australia sent abroad.[387] However, some doctors, with little knowledge of the deep psychological and physical distress involved, chose to play recruiting sergeant. As a result, 'damaged men were declared healthy, then sent back to the front, where they broke down again'.[388] This appears to have been Ryan's fate.

What was a shell-shocked soldier to do, a soldier who was both injured *and* had lost faith in the righteousness of the war? What kind of resistance could a soldier show, who had come to suspect the purity of British – and Australian – war aims, and to doubt that British political leaders were ready to explore ending the war on reasonable terms? Although Ryan was originally a volunteer, like all his fellow Australian soldiers, he scarcely remained a volunteer, in the real sense of that word, once under the thumb of military law. He had sworn loyalty to the King and promised to serve 'until the end of the War', plus four months – 'SO HELP ME, GOD'. He was a mere vassal to his King and his commissioned officers. What could a soldier do once he had decided that his own nation was deploying its army in pursuit of expansionist war aims?

Chapter 13

BROKEN DOLLS

BYFLEET, EDINBURGH, LONDON, SEPTEMBER 1916

> *A maiden met a man the other day,*
> *She looked at him and here's what she did say:*
> *'Why aren't you in khaki, or in navy blue,*
> *Fighting for your country like other fellahs do?'*
> *He looked at her with teardrops in his eyes,*
> *'Madam,' he said, 'you do not realise,*
> *That I once had my chance,*
> *Had my right leg shot off in France,*
> *I'm one of England's Broken Dolls!'*[389]
>
> — Popular song, 'England's Broken Dolls', 1916

At the 4th London General Hospital in Camberwell in late August 1916 the doctors again diagnosed 'shell shock' as Ryan's illness. According to Ryan's own account, he was then sent from the London hospital into the countryside. He spent at least a fortnight convalescing in a delightful setting, West Byfleet, an upper-middle-class village in Surrey, near Woking, to the west of London.[390] He was probably hospitalised first at the 'Blytheswood Auxiliary Hospital', a former private home, where a portrait of Lord Kitchener gazed down on the men in the dining room. He may also have had access to a nearby facility, 'Bleakdown Red Cross Hospital', newly set up in the clubhouse belonging to the Bleakdown Golf Club. Both were small military hospitals, with under forty beds, a matron, a physiotherapist, and a handful of volunteers and nurses. Both hospitals banned all liquor. But Ryan's late summer convalescence in Byfleet must have provided him with some consoling distractions, and memories to cling to over the next two very difficult years.

Ryan wrote home to Broken Hill that, in the 'sedate' town of Byfleet, 'I had the time of my life'. Gardens and the golf links surrounded the hospital. There was a croquet lawn in a courtyard, and a tennis court. 'We had a piano, phonograph, and library, and all sorts of inside games.' The recovering wounded soldiers could choose to 'do a bit of punting', very likely on the picturesque Basingstoke Canal that wound through the countryside nearby. 'I learnt to play lawn tennis at one of the nurse's homes', he reported.[391] So a friendship between Ryan and a nurse may have blossomed, but we have no detail. Other Australians at Byfleet were similarly entranced by this 'truly beautiful place'. One wrote home describing its 'grand walks', the 'avenues of fine oaks, elms, beeches, chestnuts', the 'real fairy dells', the berries of all kinds, and the canal with its 'pretty little one-arch bridge' on which the soldiers would gather to watch the canal traffic and the 'staid old horse' plodding the tow-path.[392]

Bucharest Bounces into War

But even as Ryan and thousands of other survivors from the Somme battles were convalescing, far away on the eastern front another escalation of the war was being prepared. Again, secret diplomacy preceded the explosion. After long negotiations, chiefly with Russia, but with Britain and France urging an agreement, the Romanian Government signed secret political and military deals, the 'Bucharest Conventions', on 17 August 1916. Romania agreed to enter the war on the side of Russia, Britain, and France. Romania was promised large annexations at the expense of Austria-Hungary: the bulk of Transylvania, about half the territory of Hungary (with a mixed population, Romanians in the minority), the Bukovina (majority Ukrainian), and the Banat of Temesvar (primarily Serbian). Britain supplied a loan of £40 million for Romania to purchase munitions. Just as the Germans had lured and bounced and bribed Bulgaria into joining the war on their side in September 1915, now the Entente did the same with Romania.[393]

More war aims were listed, and a new ally was gained for the British Empire, and for Australia, although scarcely one Australian soldier in a thousand could have pronounced the negotiators' names or the names of the Hungarian provinces they coveted, had these been divulged. Ten days later the killing began on the Romanian front. The war would prove to be calamitous for the Romanian people.

Tourist in Uniform

Before his final discharge from hospital, Ryan was granted two weeks' leave, the maximum normally granted. He travelled north to Scotland. The Mudie family's forebears hailed from Scotland, and his uncle, James Ramsay Mudie, had been born there. But sadly a letter from James giving the address of his sister (in Arbroath), so that Ted might catch up with his Scottish relatives, reached him too late. So, in the end he passed no time with a welcoming family as might have provided some real balm for a wounded soldier. Instead, he was a mere tourist.

Ted spent seven days in Edinburgh, and enjoyed watching a game of soccer there, but could not decide if it was superior to his favourite sport, Australian Rules Football.

He had a plan, he wrote, to move on to the Clyde shipbuilding works in Glasgow – one of the chief centres of industrial unrest, as it happened. But, as he explained, incessant rain had ruined his plan. Nonetheless, he was pleased with Scotland and the Scots, happily writing that 'the people treat the Australians well'.

Returning south, he spent eight days in London. Like countless AIF soldiers before and after him, Ryan sauntered about the historic buildings and surveyed the wonders of the great English capital, perhaps aided by a YMCA map-guide often issued to soldiers on leave. His letter home mentioned his visits to St Paul's Cathedral, Westminster Abbey, the Houses of Parliament, Buckingham Palace, the National Art Gallery, the Zoo, and the Tower of London.

But he sounded less than an enthusiastic tourist. The historic Tower of London was a disappointment. How could some plain stone room be thought interesting, he asked, just because 'some poor unfortunate was beheaded in it?' The trinkets of monarchy were also on display there, and they caught his eye. The expense of the collection of bejewelled crowns was notable, especially a great diamond in King George's crown. 'No doubt it is very pretty, but I would much rather have the money myself', he wrote bluntly.

He was happier distracting himself. He squeezed in more than eight theatre visits across his eight days in London! He sought solace in the soft seats and low lights of a string of famous ornate theatres. He proudly listed them: the Adelphi, Coliseum, Princes, London Pavilion, Prince of Wales, Palace, and the Garrick. He added that he had also visited two music halls. He saw a series of comedies and musicals, including 'The Girl from Ciro's', a French farce, and 'Broadway Jones', which featured a 'charming' girl who turns a man 'from the gay life of New York to the cares of running a chewing-gum factory in the wilds of Connecticut'. Here was fabulous escapism![394]

There were also some spectacular engineering feats to see in London. A true wonder was London's underground railway system, and especially the tube stations with their 'revolving staircases', that is, their escalators. Perhaps Broken Hill might boast of some similar advances by the time he could return there, he mused satirically in his letter home. 'I don't suppose I will know Broken Hill when I get back', he wrote wistfully, 'with its new water supply, and I suppose a new railway station. But I suppose I will be able to identify it by the number of duststorms.'

More serious things to be encountered in England struck home. Raised in Broken Hill, and thoughtful as he was, Ryan was alive to the scorching realities of life for the ordinary people of Britain. He was observing a class-bound society at war. He analysed it in his letter home, like a social investigator. Clearly the old country was riddled with injustice. He was appalled at the high cost of essentials. He rattled off a list of prices for bread, meat, eggs, and fruit – 'a terrible price'. He then listed the small salaries he had seen advertised in the newspapers, with married men on butchers' and bakers' delivery carts, for example, earning only 25 shillings a week, and a shipping clerk with some seventeen years' experience earning only £95 per year. He wondered 'how some people over here in England manage to get a living with wages so low and food so high'.[395]

The Spirit of Scotland

The two-week furlough had been bliss. He wrote of his longing to get back to the north again, just as soon as he could. 'I will try and get another trip to Scotland.' Perhaps at Christmas, he explained. 'I am living in hopes', he wrote home from Perham Down.

In fact, Ryan had travelled in Scotland at a time of intensifying political tension. Early in 1916, the government had reacted with despotic rigour to industrial unrest on the Clyde, arresting prominent critics of conscription and war, such as John Maclean, and exiling the leadership of the Clyde Workers' Committee from Glasgow.[396] Scotland was where the anti-war Independent Labour Party (ILP) – a radical faction of the Labour Party – was at its strongest. By the autumn of 1916, the ILP's campaigning for peace by negotiation was hotting up. The ILP newspapers, the Manchester-based *Labour Leader* and the Glasgow-based *Forward*, were cheering for the dissidents in the Labour Party and the Liberal Party who were noisily advocating for a peace of compromise to end the catastrophe consuming so much life in Europe.

It is not known whether Ted Ryan attended any political events in Scotland at all. (Under the *King's Regulations*, soldiers were forbidden to do so.)[397] He did not report any or, if he chose to include any accounts of these, such items might have been censored out, either at Perham Down (if he had given *this* letter to the officers) or at the *Barrier Miner*. We simply do not know.

But he may well have come across newspaper reports during his travels in Scotland during that autumn. For example, the Scottish Independent Labour Party Conference, which passed motions in favour of 'the settlement of the war by negotiation', was held in Edinburgh on 23 September. The last week of September was also the first anniversary of Keir Hardie's death – dubbed 'Keir Hardie Day' by Labour stalwarts. The much-loved working-class hero and founder of the Labour Party, and a lifelong critic of imperialism, militarism, and war, Hardie had opposed Britain's declaration of war in 1914. The Scottish Labour papers were filled with tributes. There were rallies in his memory in a dozen Scottish towns. Ramsay MacDonald, the most prominent of Labour's anti-war MPs, spoke at a series of events, addressing 6,000 people at Ayr on 30 September. At the main demonstration, on Sunday 1 October, St Andrew's Halls in Glasgow was thronged with 5,000 people, with many standing, to hear MacDonald honour the anti-war hero – the same hall in which Lloyd George had been shouted down by angry workers on Christmas Day 1915.[398]

According to Ryan's account of his leave, he overstayed by a single day. He had been granted fourteen days, 'and one I took made a total of 15', he boasted to his Uncle

James.³⁹⁹ It was a minor truancy, a small act of rebellion that appears to have gone unpunished. After his official discharge from hospital, at the expiration of his furlough, Ryan was ordered to appear at Perham Down. He was 'marched in' there probably on 2 October, and entered the 'No. 1 Command Depot'.⁴⁰⁰

If he had a heavy heart, Ryan was simply reflecting the mood of many AIF men. For example, Edgar Morrow, in a very similar situation to Ryan, wrote home from Perham Down at the end of his hospitalisation and convalescence in 1916 with blunt words: 'We only want to get home. I am tired of war.' Perham Down, he wrote, was just a place of 'captivity'.⁴⁰¹ Sergeant George Horan wrote to his father from Perham Down in early 1917: 'Most of our fellows think that England should be given to Germany with an apology for the state its in.'⁴⁰²

The Secretary of State for War Goes Rogue

Undoubtedly, during Ryan's last days of leave, or even as he travelled by train down to Perham Down, there were newspapers to devour from the W.H. Smith railway station news-stands. Ryan could not have missed the newspapers' reports on a political sensation: Lloyd George's famous 'knock-out blow' interview. This he had given to the leading American journalist, Roy Howard, in his War Minister's office in Whitehall on 28 September. Lord Northcliffe had helpfully arranged the interview.

What did the War Minister say? He bluntly warned the United States and all other neutrals not to offer mediation to end the war for there could be 'no outside interference at this stage'. Pressed by Howard, who asked if President Wilson should 'butt in' to bring peace, Lloyd George was emphatic. Britain would not 'tolerate' any 'humanitarians' with proposals for peace before the German menace was licked. 'Peace now or at any time before the final and complete elimination of this menace is unthinkable.' Comparing the war to a prize-fight, he argued that: 'The fight must be to a finish – to a knock-out.'⁴⁰³

The low tone of the interview was unmistakeable. Sporting analogies were littered throughout. 'The British soldier is a good sportsman', Lloyd George declared. He fought 'in a sporting spirit' and wanted 'a sporting chance'. He was 'a game dog'. 'He played the game. He didn't squeal.' British soldiers 'fought and died like sportsmen without even a grumble'. They did not whimper, especially 'now that the fortunes of the game have turned a bit'. There were 'no quitters' among the Allies, even when they were 'beaten all about the ring'. This allusion to a boxing match was only the first of many from Lloyd George.

On the other hand, Lloyd George did not hide the horror. He had just been to the front and had seen 'the door of hell'. He had seen 'myriads marching into the furnace'. But enduring it was glorious, he argued. The British dead had died for a reason: Britain indeed had 'invested thousands of its best lives to purchase future immunity for civilisation'. So, Britain must show 'resolve' and ignore 'the squealing done by Germans or done for Germans by probably well-meaning but misguided sympathizers and humanitarians'. Spain, the Vatican, and the United States – in fact, all the neutrals – must accept that they should not 'butt-in'. How long then might the war last? 'Time is the least vital factor', remarked Lloyd George, noting that twenty years had been required to defeat Napoleon in the early nineteenth century. Perhaps less than twenty years would be needed this time, he mused, but a long war it would be. So, no mediation could be considered – only more and more war, 'to a knock-out'.[404]

Needless to say, Lord Northcliffe's newspapers boomed this message loudest. 'NEVER AGAIN! BATTLE-CRY OF THE ALLIES. NO TIME FOR PEACE TALK. MR. LL. GEORGE'S WARNING TO NEUTRALS', shouted the headlines of *The Times*. The *Daily Mail* turned up the volume. 'HANDS OFF THE WAR! MR LLOYD GEORGE WARNS OFF NEUTRALS. WE WILL FIGHT TO A "KNOCK-OUT". AN INTERVIEW FOR AMERICANS. PEACE MONGERING FOR GERMANY IS UNFRIENDLY TO US.'[405] 'The British Armies in the field will be strengthened by them [Mr Lloyd George's words] in the knowledge that their valour and sacrifice are not going to be thrown away by the weakness of politicians at home', the editorial argued gallantly.[406]

A Game? A Dog? A Sportsman? Lives 'invested' at the front? The ring? A knock-out? One might easily imagine Ryan's reaction to this bombast. It was *the* political sensation in Britain, just as Ryan arrived at Perham Down. It deeply affected him.

Perham Down: 'How I hated the war!'

What was the great camp at Perham Down like? As one AIF soldier recalled, the troop train bound for Perham Down passed 'through some of the most beautiful country I had ever seen'. This lifted spirits. But the lads were not about to land in chocolate-box English countryside. Their trains mostly came through the rural splendours of Sussex, Surrey, and Hampshire, but then stopped at a small village nearest to their camp, Ludgershall, just inside Wiltshire, on the eastern edge of the giant Salisbury Plain Military Lands. The men then marched the short distance downhill to Perham Down. The camp was set in wasteland, much battered and bruised by military firepower. On arrival, some soldiers were pleased to discover that at least there were timber and galvanised-iron huts rather than mere tents for their new homes. It 'felt like a case of rising from rags to riches', one soldier remembered.[407] The huts were off the ground, and 'quite water proof'.[408]

But as winter approached, many soldiers soon decided they loathed the place. The intense cold and the 'hard boards' for beds robbed many of sleep – and good health. The camp was set in 'the most dreary part of dreary Salisbury Plains', one soldier complained.[409] Another told his parents that 'a bleaker or more desolate place would be hard to find'.[410] 'A limitless grey sky, muddy ground, the steamy huts with mud-covered floors, a rowdy crowd round a central stove, chill wetness everywhere. How I hated the war!'[411] Ludgershall offered little by way of distraction: two small pubs, a hotel, a decaying 15th century market cross in the High Street showing a 'Descent from the Cross', and nearby the mere foundations of a ruined 11th century royal castle. The British Army dominated all the surrounding villages, notably Tidworth and Bulford. There were some small hills near the camp, but neither the famed Stonehenge nor Salisbury was close enough to be visible. This was no tourist destination for Australians longing for a rural English idyll. (Today, the camp site is partly within the British Army's modern 'Swinton Barracks' and all that remains as reminders of the Australian presence is a Perth Road and a Fremantle Road.)

Here at Perham Down the soldiers endured weeks of tedious drills and instruction at the hands of a special 'Training Battalion'. There was the usual 'musketry' and 'bayonet fighting', with 'bayonet bags got up to represent the enemy'. There was plenty of 'hopping over', that is, practice in 'scaling trenches and hopping into the same'. And loads of 'doubling', that is, double-marching.[412] Drills could begin at 6 a.m. The drill instructor 'roars until his face is red'. The 'dreadful monotony' was 'soul-destroying'.[413] As one Corporal wrote home to his parents: 'These training camps are made very hard, so the men are glad enough to get away to the front.'[414]

Glad or sad, the men were headed for France and Belgium eventually. For whatever the hardships or comforts that the 'No. 1 Command Depot' offered, its purpose was clear: the wounded men were here to endure 'gradual hardening' and so to be made fit for still more war.[415]

No doubt a great disappointment for Ted Ryan upon arrival at Perham Down was confirmation that another chance to meet up with his wounded brother Tom had been lost. Perhaps Ted was unaware? Perhaps he knew? But the fact was that Tom Ryan, wounded and convalescing, had indeed been there in the little city of timber huts at Perham Down just a little more than a month before Ted's arrival. Tom had been invalided from France in May, with injuries to his left arm and leg, and shipped to England in June. After hospital, he had been sent to Perham Down on 27 July and then drafted back to his 11th Battalion in France on 21 August. So, Tom was gone from Perham Down only a few weeks previously.[416]

But for Ted Ryan there was at least one friend at the 'No. 1 Command Depot' at Perham Down, Private William Bown of the 9th Field Ambulance. He was the son-in-law of the same Burrows family that had employed Ted, at 135 Rokeby Road in Subiaco. As we have seen, Bill Bown and Ted had enlisted from this same address, Bill in August 1915 and Ted only a month later. Bown, wounded at the front in France in August 1916, was at the 'No. 1 Command Depot' from September to November. No doubt he had a store of searing experiences to relate to Ted Ryan.[417]

Broken Hill Echoes

There was also a big bundle of letters from Broken Hill waiting for Ted at Perham Down – he marvelled at the number. They must have been a revelation to him. These undoubtedly put him in touch with the changing mood of the people of Broken Hill.

At home, things were changing fast. The 44-hour-week dispute had ended in victory for the underground workers of Broken Hill in April 1916. The men got their Saturday half-day, and there were new minimum wage rates, and penalty rates for overtime.[418]

In the course of the dispute, two trade union leaders in particular had emerged as orators of talent, men who could stir a crowd, Percy 'Jack' Brookfield and Michael 'Mick' Considine. Both men were socialist idealists, and fervently internationalist in outlook. Both protested over the government's heavy-handed suppression of all critics of the war. Brookfield in particular denounced the war as a shameful slaughter; he claimed that it was fuelled by, and prolonged by, sordid commercial rivalries and imperialist ambitions. Through the leadership of Brookfield and Considine, the labour movement in Broken Hill was soon fiercely and overwhelmingly opposed to the ultra-patriots' suggested solution for flagging enlistments – conscription.

Michael Considine

Percy Brookfield,
portrait by C. H. Conlon, State Library of Victoria

In the middle of 1916, Brookfield had helped create a new mass organisation, 'Labor's Voluntary Army for Home Defence' (or sometimes 'Labor's Volunteer Army' – or just the 'LVA'), to resist conscription. Its name underlined the labour tradition: ready to defend the homeland, with volunteers, when war was incontrovertibly defensive, but suspicious of imperial adventures. A rally to launch this organisation attracted about five thousand people to the Central Reserve in Broken Hill at the end of July 1916. Tempers flared. Only a week after the founding of the LVA, violence broke out in the streets between opposing factions. The police arrested Brookfield. This prompted still larger crowds to rally in support of Brookfield and the LVA.[419]

Then, in late August 1916, Labor Prime Minister Hughes piloted through both his Cabinet and his Caucus, with some difficulty, a proposal for a referendum on conscription. The people would decide the issue. As the Parliament debated the necessary legislation, there was every indication that Labor was fracturing under the strain, with Hughes and his supporters sinking deeper into a nationalist populism.[420] The date for the referendum in Australia was fixed for Saturday 28 October 1916, but the soldiers overseas were to be given the chance to vote a fortnight earlier.

The truth about Hughes should be stressed. He had a long record of holding forth on the 'race peril' facing Australia – from Asian invasion. His absolute devotion to the cause of the British Empire sprang from the racial nightmares he had cultivated. His motives were clear: if Australia showed unfaltering loyalty to Britain, no matter what the cost in blood, treasure, and principles, then one day the British fleet, flying the White Ensign, would come to save White Australia.[421] Thus, his imperial subservience was fundamental, whatever froth he uttered about putting Australia first. On becoming Prime Minister in October 1915, Hughes had told Parliament: 'I do not pretend to understand the situation in the Dardanelles, but I know what the duty of this government is; and that is – to mind its own business, to provide that quota of men which the Imperial Government think necessary.'[422] In this spirit of absolute and unquestioning loyalty to the British Empire, men would be despatched from Australia by force – to anywhere, and for any cause – if Hughes could win the referendum.

In the face of Hughes's announcement that he would seek a mandate in a popular vote, the leaders of the LVA in Broken Hill redoubled their efforts to sink Hughes and his scheme. A rally and procession against conscription, beginning outside the Trades Hall, on the very eve of the referendum, attracted some seven thousand people. Clearly, public opinion in the Silver City was moving decisively against the war.[423]

Far away, after several weeks of renewed training at Perham Down in October 1916, Ted Ryan decided upon a bold step of his own to resist this war.

The postcard entitled 'Australians Parading for the Trenches', sold as *Daily Mail* War Picture, No. 40. This was the photograph featured in the *Daily Mail* and criticised by Private Edward Ryan. The caption on the reverse side read: 'These are the men who shortly after midnight of Sunday, July 23, 1916, took Pozières by a splendidly dashing advance through shrapnel, shell, and machine-gun fire.'

The original photograph on which the *Daily Mail* War Picture, No. 40, was based. In fact, the men photographed had not yet faced action in France and had only just received their steel helmets. The original caption at the Australian War Memorial reads: 'Outdoors group portrait of a battalion of the 6th Brigade that was newly arrived in Flanders from Egypt. The men are balancing their newly issued steel helmets on the ends of their rifles.'

Chapter 14

RAGE

PERHAM DOWN TO WESTMINSTER, OCTOBER 1916

Surely is anything that we are going to gain, worth such a human sacrifice as L[loyd] George is prepared to make?[424]

— Private Edward James Ryan, 18 October 1916

In his published letter from Perham Down to the Mudie family in Broken Hill in the autumn of 1916, Ted Ryan wrote of being thrilled to receive from home 'about 40 letters altogether'. And he wrote many replies. 'I have to write such a lot of letters that I think I will have to introduce carbon paper.'[425]

So, Ryan was 'in the loop' with regard to news from home. Undoubtedly he read of the shenanigans in Australian politics in general and of the political knife-fights breaking out at the beginning of the third year of war across Australia – and most certainly in Broken Hill. From family, and from fellow-unionists of the AMA, Ted undoubtedly learned of the doings of Brookfield, Considine, and the LVA, and the unprecedented activism against conscription and even against the war itself in his hometown. It would be astonishing if Ryan, after receiving his forty letters from Australia, was unaware of the deep fracture lines opening up in the ranks of Labor, as men and women of principle debated the rights and wrongs of the war.

If he received clippings from the *Barrier Daily Truth* for the first half of 1916 – or personal letters reflecting that paper's intensifying rage against the war – these could only have fortified his own seething hostility. By this time, Broken Hill Labor's daily newspaper was filled with articles denouncing conscription and the coercion of labour in Britain, scorning the idea that Australia should follow the mother country down the path of forced enlistment, and condemning the 'vampires' who were profiteering while advocating conscription and protectionism. The paper offered a most sympathetic coverage of peace activism from across the world.[426] In contrast, the paper tore strips off Prime Minister Billy Hughes, 'BILLY THE SHOWMAN', for developing a swollen head while in England and allowing himself to be steered by Tories and newspaper barons.[427] A selection of headlines serves to convey the paper's furious spirit: 'THE EMPIRE AND THE VAMPIRE', 'THE BLEEDER AND THE BLED', 'THE PERIL OF CONSCRIPTION', 'THE

IRON HAND: REVOLT OF THE BRITISH WORKERS', 'THE GIBRALTAR OF UNIONISM', 'CONSCRIPTION – TO BE OR NOT TO BE?', 'THE THREATENED HORROR OF CONSCRIPTION' and 'WANTED: A FIERY CROSS'.[428]

Ryan's own letter of defiance, therefore, mostly reflected his own personal experience, but undoubtedly there were also echoes of Broken Hill in it.

After a fortnight at Perham Down camp, on 18 October 1916, Private Edward Ryan sat down to compose his letter denouncing the sacrificial fantasy of war as advocated by the 'knock-out blowers' in both Britain and Australia. As we have seen, somehow evading the army censor, he sent the letter to James Ramsay MacDonald MP at the House of Commons in London. In so doing Ryan burst through that paralysing sense of 'powerlessness' that seemed to grip many soldiers in the ranks.[429] As Richard Aldington put it: 'It seemed insane to think that you had any individual importance.'[430] But Ryan set aside this kind of fatalism – and wrote.

Scottish Beacon

Ramsay MacDonald was Scottish in his accent and in his defiance. He was a handsome man, fifty years old in October 1916, with a shock of wiry, greying hair, and a straggly, wintry moustache. The war for him was a supreme tragedy. For years he had warned against the pernicious self-defeating arms race, and the danger of Britain being drawn in to a war on account of her virtual alliances with both France and Russia. The bloodshed haunted him. He was tortured by the monstrous bereavements brought down upon so many families by this war. Indeed, he did not have to imagine his empathy; he was well acquainted with heartfelt grief, having lost both his young wife Margaret, and a child, David, during the last years of peace. He was a passionate speaker, a man of conviction and charisma – and notoriety.

Since the death of the legendary cloth-capped labour leader, Keir Hardie, in September 1915, MacDonald was probably the most well-known opponent of the Great War in Britain. In a speech as Labour Party leader in the Commons on the afternoon of Monday 3 August 1914, MacDonald had pleaded for Britain to remain neutral and focus upon a diplomatic settlement. To no avail. Britain formally declared war deep in the evening of Tuesday 4 August. As we have noted, the next day, MacDonald urged his Labour MPs to enter a protest by abstaining on the Vote of Credit to fund the war. But the majority, overwhelmed by the passions of war, rebelled against him. Appalled, MacDonald resigned as chairman of Labour's parliamentary party. He devoted himself instead to the dissident minority of Labour MPs who, like him, were generally members of both the Labour Party and the radical Independent Labour Party founded by Keir Hardie, which was affiliated to the larger Labour Party.

Since August 1914, MacDonald had maintained his dissent. In the labour press, he criticised Sir Edward Grey's inconsistent and dishonest handling of the diplomatic

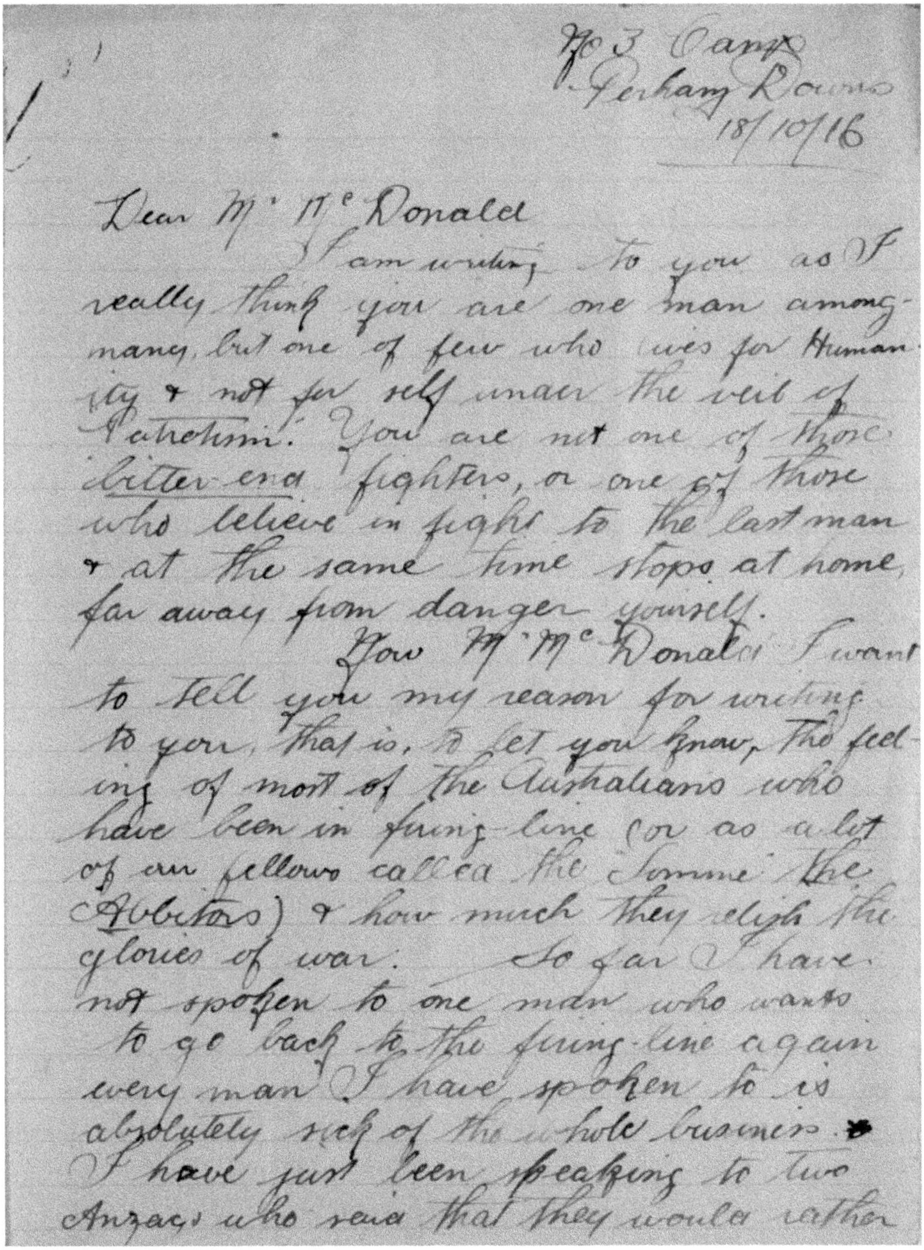

> No 3 Camp
> Perham Downs
> 18/10/16
>
> Dear Mr McDonald
> I am writing to you as I really think you are one man among many, but one of few who lives for Humanity & not for self under the veil of Patriotism. You are not one of those bitter end fighters, or one of those who believe in fights to the last man & at the same time stops at home, far away from danger yourself.
> You Mr McDonald I want to tell you my reason for writing to you, that is, to let you know, the feeling of most of the Australians who have been in firing line (or as a lot of our fellows called the Somme the Arbitors) & how much they enjoy the glories of war. So far I have not spoken to one man who wants to go back to the firing line again every man I have spoken to is absolutely sick of the whole business. I have just been speaking to two Anzacs who said that they would rather

The first page of Ted Ryan's letter to Ramsay MacDonald, 18 October 1916 (reproduced with the permission of the MacDonald family). See full transcript in Appendix 1.

crisis of July-August 1914, and he opposed the rapid escalation of the Entente's war aims. He took a leading part in September 1914 in the founding of the pressure group the Union of Democratic Control (UDC), which denounced the 'secret diplomacy' with Russia and France that had landed Britain in the disaster. As a result, from the very first weeks of the war, MacDonald had been dropped into a hate-spittoon by the ultra-patriotic press, accused of being on the side of the enemy, and no better than 'a paid agent' working for Germany.[431] The lowest of the pro-war papers, Horatio Bottomley's *John Bull*, even made a spectacular splash by breathlessly revealing what it considered to be a scandal – MacDonald's illegitimate birth. Intimidated by such gutter tactics on the part of his tormentors, MacDonald kept a low profile, in parliament at least, for many months. But the initially small cell of dissenters he had helped to create and build, the UDC, attracted much intellectual talent and raw energy, and grew steadily in stature as the paramount anti-war activist group in Britain.[432]

During 1916, MacDonald found his voice again in the House of Commons. He pleaded in a 'peace debate' in May 1916 for British war aims to be 'clearer and clearer'. It was vital in war, he argued, 'to make it perfectly clear to your enemy what your purposes are'. Extravagant war talk made it possible for Germany to 'misuse and misrepresent' Britain's purposes. War was not just a military problem; it was a political problem. So, Britain's leaders must disavow any intention of humiliating Germany or of tearing down her economic future. Wild talk of crushing and smashing 'Prussian militarism' was prolonging the war and consolidating Germany. Even if Britain succeeded in planting her General Staff Headquarters at Potsdam, he warned, militarism would not be expunged. Only the Germans could reform their own system. He rebuffed the complaint that he was 'a peace-at-any-price man'; those who saw infinite war as the only way to obtain peace were the truly reckless 'peace-at-any-price' fire-eaters. 'I am in favour of a peace which will express a new attitude of the international mind. Without that you can have no peace', he reasoned. And how to end the war? 'We want the neutrals to come in and help us to settle this War.'[433] Here was much far-sighted wisdom, rationally expressed, and courageously.

By the autumn of 1916, MacDonald was taking his message to public platforms across Britain. He was a leading figure in the public campaigns of both the ILP and the UDC, attracting large and enthusiastic audiences with his message of peace by negotiation. The men and women of the UDC were frequently encouraged by the enthusiastic support they received at these public meetings, especially in the industrial north of England and in Scotland.

MacDonald had also inserted himself into the conscription campaign in Australia. A number of personal letters from MacDonald to leading Australian Labor figures, attacking Hughes for his 'self-glorification', were widely published in the Labor and Catholic press in Australia from August 1916.[434] Hughes responded by abusing MacDonald in his public speeches as a man with a mind 'hopelessly narrow'.[435] The

Barrier Daily Truth published MacDonald's letter to an unnamed Australian Labor figure in August 1916. MacDonald wrote of his 'anger' and 'humiliation' at the antics of Hughes. 'He is the idol of everything that makes for Labor's enslavement', wrote MacDonald. Hughes's bombastic agitation for conscription during his tour of Britain in early 1916, MacDonald wrote, had 'DONE MORE THAN ANYTHING ELSE TO RIVET THE CHAINS OF REACTION, OF MILITARISM, AND OF PREJUDICES UPON THE MASSES OF THIS COUNTRY'. The words appeared in capitals in the *Barrier Daily Truth*.[436]

For a politically-minded soldier such as Ryan there were ample opportunities at Perham Down to catch up on political news such as this from Australia. One soldier wrote of 'a reading room' and 'a rather good library and an abundance of Australian papers and periodicals' at the camp – although how dated or wide the selection of newspapers may have been we cannot know.[437] But there is a strong chance that Ryan learned about MacDonald's controversial letters to Labor personalities in the Australian press, because many papers covered it. Or perhaps his correspondents from Broken Hill filled him in. Perhaps MacDonald's interventions in Australian politics gave Ted the idea of writing to MacDonald himself.

But it was a lucky thing that Ryan's letter reached MacDonald at all. Supposedly, letters addressed to MPs at the House of Commons were free from the censors' interference. But in June 1916, ultra-patriotic vigilantes at Westminster had sought to prevent soldiers from raising their grievances with MPs, pointing to 'Instruction No. 897' from the Army Council, which specified that soldiers with grievances must use army channels only.[438] Many such letters were intercepted. For example, in July an MP complained to Prime Minister Asquith that all letters to MPs from the ill-fated British Army in Mesopotamia had been 'severely censored' and some letters had been 'almost entirely wiped out'.[439] Outraged MPs complained in the House of Commons in 1916, and again in 1917, that soldiers writing to MPs had been punished.[440] Such was the parlous state of free speech in Britain after years of war, under the heavy hand of the censor and the brute fist of the emergency regulations of the *Defence of the Realm Act*. But, as we know, Ryan's letter got through to Westminster.

Hunting 'THE SHIRKER' into the War

The timing was also significant. When Private Ryan penned his letter to MacDonald on 18 October 1916, all soldiers at Perham Down had been assailed with propaganda 'circulars', as will be remembered, from Prime Minister Hughes, and from the British General Birdwood, the commander of Australian forces. Both implored them to vote 'Yes' in the first Australian 'Conscription Referendum'. The soldiers of the AIF abroad, given an early vote, were due to mark their ballots on the very next day. The Australian people would vote on 28 October.

Why was Hughes resorting to a plebiscite? The extremely divisive poll had been ordered by Hughes in order to help him overcome resistance to conscription in his own Federal Labor Party. A big 'YES' vote might sway resisters, he hoped. Hughes had led Labor for just a year. As mentioned, during his visit to Britain in the first half of 1916, the ultra-nationalist press had lionised him. He was a plain-speaking war-hawk, the kind of labour man whose Jingo language could keep working people and 'tuppeny Tories' loyal to the war. The experience had gone to his head. Hughes now hoped to push Australia down the British path of general conscription for overseas service.

The circulars that were prominently displayed and handed out to the troops at Perham Down, both Birdwood's 'Personal Message' and Hughes's 'Manifesto', were stunning pieces of propaganda. Birdwood claimed that the 'freedom' of Australia and the Empire was 'in danger of being turned into slavery by GERMANY'. The AIF's existing battalions, brigades, and divisions would be broken up, he warned, if more men were not pressed into the army. The lives of Australians would have been 'USELESSLY SACRIFICED if we relax our efforts in any way, until we have the Germans right down on their knees'. It was vital to catch 'THE SHIRKER' in the net of conscription. Birdwood finished with a plea to remember that the war was fought 'for the safety of our wives and children'.[441]

Hughes's two-page printed 'Manifesto' sought to press every button. He praised the troops who had 'added fresh lustre to the glorious name of Anzac'. But 'voluntaryism' had failed, he asserted. Australia was 'the freest democracy the world has ever known', he bragged, but she had to double the number of troops sent abroad in order to achieve 'decisive victory'. Why? The usual reasons: the Germans had 'deliberately provoked war' and deserved punishment; an early peace would be 'a hollow mockery'; and Germany had to be 'beaten to her knees' because she 'will never consent to the peace that the Allies want and are determined to have'. So, in bloody combat the Australian 'race' had to 'prove itself worthy'. The Australian troops should vote 'Yes', Hughes pleaded, to keep faith with France and Belgium, to avenge the 'foul outrages' of German troops, and to honour 'the debt [Australians] owe to Britain' whose 'mighty Navy' protected Australia. A 'Yes' vote from the troops would be 'a mighty shout across the leagues of ocean' to Australians at home. If they voted 'No', he asserted, 'they encourage the enemy'.[442]

The two circulars enraged Ryan. He was deeply incensed in particular at the accusation made in Hughes's circular that a 'No' vote would 'encourage the enemy'. Ryan saw straight through, in the words of a disillusioned war correspondent, 'the bottomless falsity' of this 'cheaper kind of current war psychology'.[443]

To understand Ryan's letter, some understanding of the push and pull of British politics at this precise moment is also important. As we have seen, by means of Lloyd George's 'knock-out blow' interview in late September, the energetic Secretary of State for War in British Prime Minister Asquith's coalition Cabinet had become the poster-boy of the ultra-patriotic press. All 'bitter enders' and 'knock-out blowers', as those urging still more intense warfare were known, were rallying behind Lloyd George. Lord Northcliffe, press baron *extraordinaire* and the most powerful reactionary nationalist voice in British politics, gave Lloyd George invaluable support.

Asquith, sensing a campaign orchestrated by the ultra-patriotic press to displace him as Prime Minister, sought to match Lloyd George's belligerence. In the House of Commons on 11 October, Asquith vowed to oppose any 'patched-up peace', arguing that Britain must keep faith with her dead – including his own recently killed son, Raymond – and fight on.[444]

Negotiations appeared to have been ruled out.

Rage – Against the War Machine

This was the immediate context in which one ordinary soldier, Private Ted Ryan, wrote to Ramsay MacDonald MP. Using up five full pages, he wrote in his elegant, twirling, formal script. He begged pardon for the obvious gaps in his education, and apologised for any 'mistakes in my spelling and grammer [*sic*]', which were certainly there – but none hid his passion.

Why MacDonald? Lloyd George's recent 'knock-out blow' interview and Asquith's parliamentary histrionics had dominated the press for a fortnight just before Ryan arrived at Perham Down. But, as we have seen, MacDonald was probably the politician with the highest profile among British advocates of peace in the pages of the newspapers that Ryan might have seen, including Australian papers – as a notorious advocate of peace. Certainly, in his speeches at Westminster from May 1916, MacDonald had urged Britain to moderate her war aims, to specify her peace terms, and to welcome neutral mediation. 'End this thing as quickly as you possibly can', the neutrals were saying to Britain. There was the way out. MacDonald begged Sir Edward Grey to miss 'no single opportunity which the men in the field give him to produce and widen out the basis of his coming peace'.[445] Then, in early September, MacDonald had been in the news again: tiny-minded pseudo-patriots had expelled him from his local club, the Moray Golf Club, near his family holiday home in Lossiemouth, in the far north of Scotland, because of 'his public utterances regarding the war'.[446] Most right-wing pro-war newspapers gleefully reported on MacDonald's victimisation.

Perhaps it is not a surprise that Ted Ryan chose a Labour politician called James Ramsay MacDonald to receive his letter. Very likely his name caught Ryan's eye because of his notoriety in the Hun-hating press, but also because he shared his first two names with Ryan's trade unionist uncle in Broken Hill, a proud fellow Scot, James Ramsay Mudie. Perhaps it was the Scottish link that prompted Ryan's letter? Did Mudie suggest it? Did Ted also remember the name MacDonald from his visit to Broken Hill in 1906? We cannot tell.

In his letter, Private Ryan began by lavishing praise on MacDonald as 'one of the few who lives for Humanity and not for self under the veil of Patriotism'. Clearly Ryan recognised the bare-knuckle politics emerging in Britain that autumn. 'You are not one of those <u>bitter-end</u> fighters', he wrote, 'or one of those who believe in fight to the last man & at the same time stops at home, far away from danger yourself'.

Ryan offered a voice fresh from the Somme. He quickly made plain his purpose:

> Now Mr McDonald [sic] I want to tell you my reason for writing to you, that is, to let you know the feeling of most of the Australians who have been in [the] firing-line (or, as a lot of our fellows called 'The Somme', The Abbitors [Abattoirs]) & how much they relish the glories of war. So far I have not spoken to one man who wants to go back to the firing-line again. [E]very man I have spoken to is absolutely sick of the whole business. I have just been speaking to two Anzacs who said they would rather be shot than face another bombardment like we received at Poziers [Pozières]. I have saw [sic] pictures of how the Anzacs come from the Somme out of the firing line bright & cheery, hirraying [hooraying] etc.
>
> Now I am going to tell you what they do feel like.

What were these 'pictures' that Ryan mentioned? Very probably, Ryan had come across a set of 'Official War Postcards' being widely sold at this time by Lord Northcliffe's *Daily Mail* – the newspaper that boasted it was 'The Soldiers' Paper'. Postcard Number 40 in the series of *Daily Mail War Pictures* was entitled 'Australians Parading for the Trenches'. This photo appeared in the *Daily Mail* and earned praise as the best of the series. It featured a large group of Australian soldiers, smiling at the camera, holding aloft their steel helmets balanced on their rifle barrels. The *Daily Mail* described this particular photo as 'one of the happiest' of the postcards. It rhapsodised over the 'atmosphere of gay good humour' and the 'laughing faces, wonderfully clear in detail'. 'The scene is full of life and gaiety', puffed the paper. Promoting the photo, the *Daily Mail* asserted: 'These are the men who shortly after midnight of Sunday, July 23, 1916, took Pozières by a splendidly dashing advance through shrapnel, shell, and machine-gun fire.' The implication was strong that the photograph showed the actual Aussie heroes of Pozières exultant, and eager to get back in the trenches for more combat, just *after* the battle.[447]

In fact, the photograph was misleading in several ways. The men caught by the camera 'full of life and gaiety' had not yet faced action. They were almost certainly men of the 6th Brigade, part of the 2nd Division, who had just received their British-made steel helmets – *before* any combat. Most units received their helmets soon after arriving in France. Moreover, the 6th Brigade was not involved in the capture of Pozières on 23 July at all. This bloody task had fallen to the men of the 1st Division. According to the war diary of the 6th Brigade, on 23 July the men were actually attending church parades.

They entered the wreck of Pozières four days later, relieving their comrades, and were 'shelled heavily all day'.[448] Thus, the captioning of the photograph by the *Daily Mail* and the accompanying article 'Heroes of Pozières' were simple examples of journalists recognising their 'duty of lying' in war.[449]

Ryan was not to know all these details. But he knew enough to give the lie to this type of war-whoop. Ryan had first-hand testimony to offer from the battle zone, and from his experiences in the field ambulances, casualty clearing stations, and hospitals behind the lines:

> I saw the second division of the Australians come out from the Somme. They had been in [the] firing line about a fortnight, & of course they had practically no sleep & I suppose less than 15 per cent of each battalion answered the final roll call.
>
> I went up to one of the Sergeants to ask him how he felt, & the reply I got was –for God's sake, cobber, don't talk to me to [sic] now, if you want to ask me any questions call round in about another 48 hours & I will do my best to answer you & it will give me time to realise that I actually came out of it alive. To every man its frightfulness was beyond their imagination.

At this point in his letter, Ryan sought to encourage MacDonald. He was well aware that the advocates of 'Peace This Autumn' and the advocates of 'the knock-out blow' were squaring off in British political debate.[450] Ryan let fly at Lloyd George and Asquith, both of whom preached against any 'premature peace' until Britain had achieved 'the crushing of Prussian militarism'.

> Of course, Mr McDonald I think you can imagine what the horrors of war are like but surely will us[e] your best to pull to their senses such men as Mr Asquith and Mr Lloyd George who are going to sacrifice hundreds of lives, rather I should have said thousands, make thousands of orphans, make thousands of cripples, make thousands face this hell.
>
> I often wonder if Lloyd George thinks when he is turning into his nice spring bed at night, that if the man in [the] trench who is exposed to all weathers, perhaps had no sleep for over [a] week & has his nerves strained to the uttermost, thinking that the next shell will most likely be the death of him, perhaps the sight of his chum who has had his brains blown out is a picture of horror in his brain, & the smell of his dead comrades is next to unbearable, agrees with him (L. George) that we don't want Peace, but we are out to crush Germany? No, that man doesn't say "hands of[f] Neutrals" & of course it is impossible for him to sing.

Sing? This last little barb was aimed at the Welsh-born War Minister's well-known habit of gathering friends for after-dinner around-the-piano hymn singing. Ryan had possibly seen reports in the press such as the story that had appeared in the *Daily Mail* in August of Lloyd George's appearance at the Welsh Eisteddfod in Aberystwyth. The War Minister, 'a high priest, not of politics but of psaltery' on that day, sang in a five-thousand-strong choir. Then he gave a speech, beating the nationalist drum, to the crowd gathered in a great tent set up in front of the Welsh National Library: 'Too long have the Welsh sung German and English tunes in their chapels. The old Welsh tunes suit the Welsh temperament', declared Lloyd George.[451]

Returning to Ryan's letter, he was clearly aware that war aims, and peace terms, were hot-button issues that autumn in Britain. Evidently, he also wanted to refute the common ultra-patriotic smear that those who wanted peace terms spelled out, and mediation tried, were 'pro-German' or even 'German peace agents'. Hughes had raised a storm of indignation in Australia with his repeated accusations that opponents of conscription were all 'the agents of Germany'.[452] The nefarious 'German peace agents' were Hughes's favourite political chew-toy. Because all three Ryan brothers were in the uniform of the AIF, Ted angrily asserted his conviction that he had the patriotic credentials to speak about the real attitudes of Australian soldiers.

He wrote on, in searing prose:

Now Mr McDonald why shouldn't we know what terms of Peace we are fighting for, why shouldn't we discuss what terms we are supposed to accept?

Has England still got her old ideal that of Conquer & not the supposed new ideal one of Peace?

Surely is anything that we are going to gain, worth such a human sacrifice as L. George is prepared to make [?]

Tomorrow is voting day for the Australian Forces and we have had Patriotic circulars handed to us from Gen. Birdwood & Premier Hughes asking us to vote Yes.

The majority of the soldiers who are in England have not yet been out to face the "music", & I think it is a good job for the "Yeses" that they haven't.

I suppose Mr L. George classes me in with that Group known as the German Peace Agents.

Our family consists of three boys & the three of us are on Active Service. One Brother is in the 13th battalion & was wounded once, (in Gallopoli [Gallipoli]). The other Brother was in the first reinforcements of the 11th Battalion & has been wounded twice. I have been slightly wounded twice. My Mother and Father are both dead, so I don't think our family has done much for Germany. But I am dreading the day when I will have to go into that hell again.

Now Mr McDonald, I hope you will do everything possible in your power to bring about a Peace & save this slaughter of Human Lives. Thanking you for what you have done, & thanking you in anticipation for what you are going to do.[453]

He signed off, 'Yours Peacefully, 4635, Pte. E.J. Ryan'. And he offered a defiant gesture in his postscript. He sought no shelter in anonymity. He turned over the last page of the letter, and in large letters he wrote down his full personal details, and his postal addresses, both at Perham Down and on active service in the field. He added: 'If at any time you <u>may</u> want to use my name or address you may do so. EJR'.

Australia's Siegfried Sassoon?

What happened? First, MacDonald did *not* use this letter in parliament. Had he done so, Private Ryan might have been as famous as 2nd Lieutenant Siegfried Sassoon, the well-connected British officer. Sassoon's angry statement 'that the war is being deliberately prolonged by those who have the power to end it' was read out by another British soldier-MP (the only one at Westminster who was *not* an officer), Corporal Bert Lees Smith, a Radical, to the House of Commons on 30 July 1917.[454]

MacDonald certainly did plead, again and again, for negotiations. He often raised the fate of the soldiers in the field when he put his case. The government should explore all diplomatic alternatives to the ruinous war, MacDonald argued, as a duty owed to the soldiers enduring the sufferings of war.[455] But he did not quote directly from Ryan's letter.

Nonetheless, Ryan's letter was certainly among those from a number of soldiers, which encouraged MacDonald. In December 1916 he preserved this in his diary: 'My information from both men and officers is that the war emotions of the home stayers are not those of the army, and that the army longs for peace and is grateful to those who are speaking peace.' The common soldier, he wrote, 'is revolutionary, I hear, because he sees how much political conservatism has been scrapped by the war'.[456] Undoubtedly, MacDonald was aware that defiant ordinary soldiers, even those thought to be suffering from shell shock, might be treated with great harshness, compared with officers.[457] Probably he thought it unnecessary to risk Private Ryan. He kept his name out of it.

In any case, this one combative Australian soldier would soon have trouble enough.

An Echo in the Cabinet

Was Ryan an isolated voice? Just a month after Ryan wrote his letter, Lord Lansdowne, a former Tory Foreign Secretary, architect of the Entente Cordiale, and leader in the House of Lords, submitted a memorandum (See Appendix 9) to Asquith's Cabinet. The Prime Minister had requested his ministers to undertake a fresh consideration of Britain's 'peace terms'. 'What does the prolongation of the war mean?' Lansdowne asked. 'Can we afford to go on paying the same sort of price for the same sort of gain?' It was the duty of decision makers to consider 'what our plight, and the plight of the civilized world will be after another year, or, as we are sometimes told, two or three more years of a struggle as exhausting as that in which we are engaged'. Britain's casualties were already over a million; the financial burden was 'almost incalculable'. 'We are slowly but surely killing off the best of the male population of these islands', Lansdowne lamented. 'Generations will have to come and go before the country recovers from the loss.'

Lord Lansdowne

Should the war be prolonged? Or should Britain be ready with peace terms? Lansdowne argued that Britain's leaders had a duty 'not to discourage any movement, no matter where originating, in favour of an interchange of views as to the possibility of a settlement'. A peace offer, perhaps even an armistice, was bound to come during the approaching winter. Britain must be ready. There were hopeful signs in Germany of moderation. 'From all sides come accounts of the impatience of the civil population and their passionate yearning for peace.' Lansdowne challenged Lloyd George directly: 'Let our naval, military, and economic advisers tell us frankly whether they are satisfied that the knock-out blow can and will be delivered.' If Britain chose still more war, with no credible prospect of a great military triumph, then 'the war with its nameless horrors will have been needlessly prolonged, and the responsibility of those who needlessly prolong such a war is not less than that of those who needlessly provoked it'.[458]

The Vote

Because it was the controversy over the Australian conscription referendum that had provoked Ryan to write, before moving on from his letter we can look ahead to the outcome of that battle.

How did the soldiers, and the people, ultimately vote? In mid-October 1916, a majority of the Australian soldiers abroad actually voted 'Yes', just as Hughes had hoped – but only by a small margin of 55.1% to 44.9%. AIF soldiers, just as Ryan claimed, recognised that a great many in their ranks were vehemently against conscription. Lance Corporal Jack Tarrant, a Queensland-born storeman and a Labor voter before joining up in August 1914, was one. Writing to his niece from France in November 1916, Tarrant told her how 'pleased' he was that 'the Non Conscripts had a victory'. 'We all voted here in the field and I think the Majority were against Conscription. I know I was and voted accordingly.'[459] A month later Tarrant told his sister that he was 'heart and soul' against conscription, and that the soldiers in France had been 'unanimously against the proposal'.[460] Soldiers remembered that when Australian troops in England were ordered into local theatres to hear Hughes speak on conscription, there was some unrest. As Sergeant Lockett recalled, 'the soldiers were all up agin it'.[461] Sergeant Horan agreed, that 'a large percentage' opposed conscription, because they did not want 'unwilling help'. The British had 'pampered Hughes and pulled his leg', wrote Horan.[462] Another soldier recalled being sick of the 'propaganda they put out. Cutting kiddies hands and all this off', and sick of the 'wholesale murder' that was war. He voted 'No'.[463] Certainly, the soldiers' final voting figures gave nothing approaching the roar for conscription that Hughes wanted. When the people went to the polls at the end of the month, and the soldiers' votes were added, the nation rejected conscription – just. The 'No' vote scored 51.6% and the 'Yes' vote scored 48.4%.[464] Incidentally, Ryan's hometown, Broken Hill, from which over 3,000 men had volunteered for the forces by 1916, voted 'No' to conscription with a solid majority of 8,922 votes to 3,858 votes.[465]

As a trade unionist from Broken Hill, Ryan must have taken heart: he was not isolated in his doubts about this war, not isolated in refusing to give a blank cheque to those who would expend his life and so many others in aggrandising empire. He was part of something big.

Chapter 15

A WINTER PEACE

PERHAM DOWN, DECEMBER 1916

> I say let those people who are in favour of forcing the war on at any price pay the penalty and not impose it on others as they are doing today. It is the old men in the House of Commons who cry out, 'We will fight to the last man'. WE! *They will not fight.* (Expressions of scorn). But I think they might do other work. When the question of the Conscientious Objector was before the House, they were saying, why should not the Objectors be sent to cut barbed wire in between the trenches? (Shame) But why should not these old men, who are in favour of fight to a finish, why should they not be utilised to cut barbed wire in front of the trenches? I would call upon those who are in favour of a fight to a finish in their own persons to pay the penalty which is exacted. (Hear, hear.)[466]

— Detective's notes, from the speech of Len Outhwaite, Tasmanian-born British Liberal MP, to a public meeting in favour of peace, Caxton Hall, London, 7 December 1916

After writing to MacDonald, Ryan was to spend another nine months at Perham Down camp, attached to the 'Hardening and Drafting Depot'. The sole purpose of the camp was to prepare men for their return to the front. The fact that Ryan was kept there for nine months, even though subject to periodic medical inspections, which were tilted toward finding soldiers fit and ready, testifies to the seriousness of Ryan's trauma and readily discernible shell shock. Perhaps this explains his selection in mid-October for transfer to a course in running a Quartermaster's Store, at Wareham, in Dorset, which would have led to a job in military supply rather than front-line service. But for some reason, not recorded in his records, this transfer did not take place.

In any case, Private Ryan did not simply sit out his time at Perham. During the winter of 1917-1918, he helped himself to two periods of AWOL, or 'French leave', as the soldiers called it. Evidently, there was something of the insurgent spirit in him, along with the wounds to mind and body.

What *precisely* inspired Ryan to these acts of indiscipline we shall never know. But we may speculate that, as a thinking soldier, he kept an eye on the press. He might have seen in early December reports in the *Daily Mail* – which we know he read – of a minor diplomatic sensation. Rumours had abounded for many months of a deal that Britain and France had made with Russia in March 1915, the Straits and Persia Agreement. The government repeatedly ducked questions about it in the House of Commons.[467] Then, on 2 December 1916, in an effort to revive flagging support for the war, Prime Minister Alexander Trepov revealed in the Russian Duma (the parliament) that Britain and France had indeed promised Constantinople and the Straits to Russia as spoils of war – the first official confirmation.[468] The 'secret' Straits and Persia Agreement of March 1915 was out.

Did Australians find out, either those at home or those serving abroad? The news was reported in very brief notes, one or two sentences, in the major Australian newspapers, some of which were apparently available at Perham Down.[469] Editorial comment was rare, with little beyond the expression of hope that Trepov's revelation might stimulate the pro-war forces in Russia.[470] When the reality of the news slowly hit home in Labor circles in Australia, there was anger. Australian lives – Russian war aims! Labor MPs scolded the Hughes Government in the Parliament. 'Now we discover that we are in the war for the purpose of giving Constantinople to Russia', railed William Finlayson, the Labor MP for Brisbane.[471] Needless to say, nothing about Trepov's speech appeared in the pages of the troops' newspaper, the *Anzac Bulletin*. Those fighting the war, apparently, had no need of such information about the purposes for which they 'sacrificing' their lives.

'French Leave'

Ryan was first found to be absent from Perham Down on 15 December 1916. We might well imagine him, mixing with soldiers on the little railway station at Ludgershall, slouch-hat set at a 'damn-your-eyes' angle, avoiding the 'jacks' as they inspected papers and permits in the trains and stations, crossing the streets to avoid them once in town. Where he spent his next five days of freedom is not recorded. Like so many others, his destination was probably London. He stayed away for five days, returning voluntarily to the camp on 19 December. On presenting himself to the camp's officers upon his return, he was immediately arrested. The charge: AWOL.

Australian troops showed some tolerance of the widespread resort to AWOL in their ranks, especially if the absconders scampered away from camps in England. In the autumn of 1916, Edgar Morrow wrote home from Perham Down boasting of how the men would cover up for each other. 'We "wag" it from the parade ground simply by deputing someone to answer when our names are called. I've done it often for others.' Then the men would 'stroll about out of sight of the camp until our pockets are full of nuts and our bellies full of berries. Then we lie in the soft grass in the sun and read, or talk about what we are going to do after the war.'[472]

The AIF veteran Eric Abraham remembered that the soldiers absconding were scarcely criminals in the eyes of other soldiers. AWOL was unremarkable. 'Oh, the only crime they committed my friend', Abraham told his interviewer, 'was being caught. Who cares about AWOL?'[473] It appears that Australian soldiers often played their 'volunteer' card as a shield to repel discipline on the matter of unauthorised leave. Another Australian recalled that, because 'we were all volunteers', the soldiers of the AIF 'could actually argue the point a little bit with our officers'.[474]

If Ryan argued the point on this occasion, he failed. Lieutenant Harry E. Shaw handed Ryan a summary punishment, probably after a dressing-down in the guardroom. Ryan's punishment was 'confinement to camp' at Perham Down for seven days, over the Christmas period, plus the forfeit of five days' pay. Commanding officers were actually permitted to hand out summary punishments to a maximum of 28 days – so Ryan's first punishment in England was relatively mild.[475] At the end of December, he was also transferred to the '13th Infantry Draft', at No. 4. Camp at Perham. This indicated that he was a step closer to being drafted back to the front.

Perham Down during winter was an especially harsh place to endure. One young Australian soldier, Jabez Waterhouse, was transferred from Perham Down to another camp nearby at Wareham in January 1917. He rejoiced in his good fortune. He wrote to his parents, 'I was very thankful to get away from the camp at Perham Downs; it was a Camp right in the middle of the Downs which for weeks on end were covered with snow & frost. This isn't all; the wind sailing across the Downs is like a sharp knife cutting right into the bone.' He explained that he had only been there for four days, but 'I thought I would die of cold'. It was 'simply cruel'.[476] An Australian cook at another camp at Durrington, a few miles away, wrote home in February 1917 that 'Australians are dying here I believe on an average of five per day with the cold'.[477]

Was Ryan extraordinary in chucking the war and simply bolting from Perham Down for a few weeks? Not at all. It is seldom realised just how many Australian soldiers rubbed up hard against military discipline – and walked away. Many disappeared from the ranks for a time, that is, they abandoned their training. They deserted, often only temporarily, but at an incredible rate from their camps across Britain. They were notorious for it.[478]

A 'Peace Note' – From Berlin

The five days of Ryan's truancy from the military camp at Perham Down, and his subsequent confinement, came during an astonishing but now forgotten moment in the history of the war – forgotten, that is, by historians fixated on battle. While Ryan was enjoying his first AWOL away from the snow-bound camp in mid-December

1916, suddenly the possibility of peace loomed out of the winter mists and flurries. A 'German Peace Note', and a week later an 'American Peace Note', appeared as public documents in newspapers across the world.

Again, let us depart from Ted Ryan's personal story to place it in a context of momentous significance. Why momentous? Imagine the Great War ending in the third winter of bloodshed, over the Christmas period of 1916. If peace had been restored, there would have been no American entry into the war. Very probably there would have been just the one post-war revolution in Russia, perhaps the milder revolution limiting or deposing the Tsar, as in March 1917; but no second, Bolshevik revolution, and therefore no descent into the monstrous parody of socialism that was Stalinist communism. Perhaps there would have been no post-war fascism in Italy, much less post-war debt, and maybe no Great Depression? If a liberal or social democratic Germany had evolved after a peace in 1916, which many commentators confidently expected, perhaps there would have been no Nazism in Germany. The lost opportunities are staggering (See Appendix 5 for a list, 1914-1918).

What happened to snuff out the possibility of peace?

On 12 December 1916, the German Government issued its Peace Note, igniting a flame of hope in many minds. The moderate conservative chancellor, Bethmann Hollweg, told the world that Germany and her allies (Austria-Hungary, Ottoman Turkey and Bulgaria) recognised the 'catastrophe' of a prolonged war that threatened to ruin Europe. So determined was the government to show that its Peace Note was a historic response to the people's genuine desire for peace and democratisation, it announced at the same time that the inscription '*Dem Deutschen Volke*', 'To the German People', would be placed in bold bronze letters on the pediment above the entrance to the people's parliament, the Reichstag building, to immortalise the moment. Yet the tone of the Peace Note was boastful. With an eye to the home front, Ludendorff had insisted on it.[479] Thus, Germany declared that her trench-lines were 'unshakeable'. But the Note also stressed that Germany and her partners were fighting only 'for the defence of their existence and freedom of their national development'. The essential fact stood out: to end 'the horrors of the war', Germany proposed 'to enter even now into peace negotiations'.[480] On the face of it, the conference could begin anywhere, with no preconditions. Bethmann Hollweg certainly aspired to success: he expected moderation to prevail at the negotiating table, and predicted that Germany could never resume fighting once talks began.[481]

The German Government, of course, was looking for a way out. With the German people beginning to starve, with the great bulk of the German colonial empire lost, and with all seaborne trade gone, moderates in Berlin genuinely hoped to negotiate peace and save something from the wreckage. Politically, the calculation was that, with a victory over Romania so recently achieved, a negotiated end to the war might save lives and at the same time save essentials of the old order in Germany from an inevitable post-war radical surge. On the other hand, recalcitrant right-wing German nationalists still hopeful for victory prayed that the Peace Note would fail.[482] They wanted to clear the way for another gamble – the resumption of unrestricted submarine warfare in the Atlantic, aimed at stopping the booming trade in war material between America and Britain.

German politics was polarised; people were hungry; and the political signs inside Germany were very mixed. Bethmann Hollweg had moved in a more moderate direction, both domestically and in foreign policy, holding out hopes for a 'new orientation' as he put it enigmatically. Most significantly, on 9 November 1916, in a major speech to the Reichstag, he had accepted the principle of compulsory arbitration of international disputes and the American plan for a League of Nations, to revolutionise diplomacy into the future.[483] Once the Peace Note was issued in December, he and his supporters had six weeks to achieve their compromise peace. Moderates in the diplomatic service had 'great hopes', but they also knew that they worked 'with a watch, so to speak, in their hands'.[484] If they failed, Hindenburg and Ludendorff could crusade for a renewal of war, on land and sea, without scruple.

The scene in the Reichstag on 12 December 1916 as Chancellor Bethmann Hollweg announces the sending of the German Peace Note

France showed the way – in swift rejection. One day after the release of the German Note, French Premier Briand in the French Parliament condemned the 'dupery' of

Berlin. He conceded that he had not yet seen the official text of Bethmann Hollweg's speech. Nonetheless, he brusquely denounced the peace offer as 'vague and obscure'. It was 'merely a ruse' to divide the Entente and 'deceive neutrals'.[485]

Next, only three days after the Note was issued, the authoritarian Tsarist Government – which had only just revealed the essentials of the Straits and Persia Agreement to the world – rebuffed the German initiative. The freshly-minted Russian Foreign Minister, Nikolai Pokrovksy, serving the new Prime Minister Trepov, did what he had to do to please his Tsar. He used his first speech in the Duma to lash out at the German Note. The Duma majority, basking in the recent news that Britain and France had indeed promised Constantinople to Russia, obediently passed a resolution recommending 'a categorical refusal' of the 'hypocritical' German peace offer.[486] The British, French, and Italian ambassadors in Petrograd were thrilled that Pokrovsky, whom they admitted was a man with 'no idea of foreign problems and diplomacy', had been so 'firm and frank' in rejecting peace.[487]

From Italy, the wily Baron Sonnino chimed in immediately. He warned the Italian Parliament that the Entente should not risk any parley, for this would raise in the common people's minds a 'false mirage of vain negotiations'.[488]

Sidney Sonnino

Thus were the standard lines peddled: the perils of a 'premature peace'; the Germans' devious 'peace trap'; the dishonour of making peace before 'victory crowns the just'; and the supposed inevitability of failure in negotiation. In truth, the Entente nationalists were playing into the hands of the Pan-German nationalists.

And Britain? Britain's new Lloyd George Government had been barely a week in office when Berlin released the Note. A virtual coup against the Liberal-led coalition of Asquith had been engineered in the first week of December. Asquith's coalition had been replaced by an improvised coalition led by David Lloyd George on 7 December. The Tories dominated. Not a single prominent Liberal joined the new coalition ministry. The Northcliffe press, and the Foreign Office grandees, hailed the self-proclaimed 'knock-out blow' government.[489] For example, Lord Bertie, Britain's ambassador to Paris, exulted that it had been installed, in the nick of time: 'what a mercy' that the 'pacifist' Sir Edward Grey had been tipped out of office before he and his kind had the chance to grasp at peace by negotiation.[490]

After taking over, Lloyd George had been sidelined by a bad cold. He would not speak in the House of Commons in response to the German initiative until 19 December. Meanwhile, the 'knock-out blow' mastheads scorned and scoffed at the German approach and lavished praise on Paris, Petrograd, and Rome for so promptly ruling out any negotiations.

In fact, a prompt rejection of the German Peace Note was exactly what the German right-wing nationalist extremists around Ludendorff and Hindenburg were hoping for. As the diplomatic historian Zeman has written: 'No one in London, Paris, Rome or Petrograd took Bethmann's offer for what it was: an action genuinely designed to put an end to the war, made in the teeth of fierce opposition at home.'[491]

'The Best News Since Bethlehem'

But on 18 December 1916, just a day before Lloyd George spoke, there was a fresh complication: the newly re-elected American President Woodrow Wilson at last acted decisively for peace. He issued his own Peace Note. Wilson had been encouraged to do so by the British Radicals of the Union of Democratic Control. They had been in contact with his special adviser, Colonel House, for many months.[492] The American Note made world headlines over the next few days. Wilson called upon all sides to specify their peace terms. Clearly, the United States stood ready at last to exert pressure to mediate the conflict. It was the best chance for peace in two and a half years.[493]

Lloyd George addressed the House of Commons as Prime Minister for the first time on 19 December. He began moderately. 'Any man or set of men who wantonly or without sufficient cause prolong a terrible conflict like this would have on his soul a crime that oceans could not cleanse.' But he refused to contemplate entering into any negotiations. Histrionically, he claimed that would be to 'put our heads into a noose with the rope end in the hands of Germany'. He then slipped back into a moderate tone. He proclaimed that the Entente was fighting on for a new formula: 'Restitution, reparation, guarantee against repetition – so that there shall be no mistake, and it is important that there should be no mistake in a matter of life and death to millions. Let me repeat again – complete restitution, full reparation, effectual guarantee.' He kept the Belgian bunting flying in the shop-front-window of Britain's war. He made no clean breast of Britain's wider territorial and economic war aims.[494]

Lloyd George was loyal to those who had lifted him into the saddle – the 'knock-out blowers.' And what kind of men now dominated in Lloyd George's new War Cabinet? It was a very right-wing clique, led by life-long imperialists, men like the ducal Lords Curzon and Milner, and the Tory leader Bonar Law. Australian lives were now, in truth, entrusted to men like Curzon, who had advised as early as the summer of 1915 that mass-butchery until victory was irresistible: 'If then two million (or whatever figure) more of Germans have to be killed at least a corresponding number of allied soldiers will have to be sacrificed to effect that object.'[495]

Lord Milner

Disappointed Radicals, former friends, and admirers, pleaded with Lloyd George, 'the People's David' of old, to think again. For instance, Henry Massingham, editor of the influential *Nation*, told Lloyd George the American offer was 'the best news since Bethlehem'.[496] He beseeched him to seek fame as the man 'who gave us peace and our children back again'.[497] But Lloyd George was immoveable.

Fatalists argued then – and some still do – that, in any case, there was no chance for peace. It is true that both sides had escalated their war aims far beyond their originally proclaimed intentions of defending territory. Assembling lists of booty that might bedazzle their bereaved peoples was a task that bewitched politicians and diplomats on both sides. Right-wing lobbies insisted on dictating the terms of any peace, once the enemy was rendered helpless. And not just in Germany. Clearly, the Entente Powers also had expansionist ambitions, and plans for a post-war boycott of all German commercial enterprise. The Ottoman Empire had already been partitioned, on paper.

'Bitter-enders' on every side had mobilised to suffocate the movement for peace. Using emergency powers, they succeeded: critics were silenced, meetings banned, mobs incited to intimidate anti-war gatherings, and moderates smeared as traitors.

The British pro-war press in particular indulged in a fabulously inconsistent campaign in December 1916 to sink any chance of peace. Supposedly, Germany was so weak she was bound to lose, so Britain must hold on; but Germany was so strong that negotiations could not be risked. Incited by Lloyd George's use of the word 'squealing' in his 'knock-out blow' interview, the newspapers argued that the Germans were so weak that they were indeed 'squealing for peace' in their Peace Note; yet sometimes in the same commentary, the Germans were depicted as so strongly placed at that particular moment that they would never negotiate in good faith.[498] The reality – that Germany was a house divided by bitter debates over the war – could not be admitted.

Was peace possible? The Americans certainly believed so. Colonel House negotiated with Bernstorff, the German Ambassador, across the winter of 1916-1917. House reported to Wilson on 15 January 1917 that the Germans' terms 'are very moderate and they did not intend to take any part of Belgium'. He noted Germany's public acceptance of the principle of arbitration and the plan for a League of Nations, and the agreement that Wilson's programme should be centre-stage at a coming peace conference. This gave 'a real basis for negotiations and for peace'. The next day he told Wilson that the United States could probably 'bring about peace much more quickly than I thought possible'. 'The Germans', wrote House, 'consent to almost everything that liberal opinion in democratic countries have demanded.'[499]

Hawkish historians pretend to *know* what would have happened if negotiations had commenced. They argue, pointing to German obstinacy, that failure was certain. We know no such thing. The only thing we know is that face-to-face negotiations in the public view were evaded.

The tragedy here is beyond forgiveness. Moderate Germans – socialists, liberals, and the more progressive Catholics – needed sound indications of moderation from the Entente side. They needed clarity and reassurance on the war aims of the Entente, from the Entente's leaders. They needed firm ground to stand upon, if they were to resist the German ultra-patriots. Such unambiguously moderate responses from the Entente never came.

So, obdurate men far from the battle zones, on both sides, strangled peace – again.

Australia and the Chance for Peace

And what of Australia?

The Hughes Government clung to the mulish clichés that fortified war: the 'danger of a premature peace', and the essential need to fight on 'to the bitter end' to obtain 'a just and lasting peace'. When news arrived of the German Peace Note, the Federal Parliament was sitting in Melbourne. Alfred Hampson, a Labor MP, asked Prime Minister Hughes if Australia might 'use its influence to bring about an honourable peace'. Nationalist MPs shouted at Hampson. Hughes mocked him, depicting him as a spokesman for Germany. Hampson's question, scowled Hughes, 'ought rightly be directed to Dr Bethmann Hollweg'.[500] Next day, James Mathews, another Labor MP, lashed out at the hecklers. 'The man who howls at a suggestion of peace is to my mind little better than a human beast. If he is so fond of war, he ought to be at the front.'[501]

What were the troops told? Again, the *Anzac Bulletin* is revealing. Its pages were generally filled with fortune-favours-the-brave stories, lists of soldiers decorated for their valour, and some humour, amidst stories from Australia. With peace being debated openly in the London papers, in December 1916 the *Anzac Bulletin* covered only those politicians in Australia heaping scorn on the German peace offer. Hughes's most gaudy lines in parliament were reproduced: Germany should be shunned, for she had outraged 'all laws human and divine', leaving the world 'bathed in blood and groaning in the agonies of war'. Peace would be 'a hollow mockery' without first forcing Germany to accept evacuations, indemnities, punishments, and 'effective guarantees'. The editor concluded that in Australia '*no* representative opinion favours the acceptance of the Peace proposals'.[502] The *Anzac Bulletin* then ignored the American Peace Note altogether while recommending in its Christmas edition the maxim, 'To the last drop and the last shilling' as a 'splendid phrase'.[503]

The truth is that Australia was never even consulted about the Entente's replies to the German and American Peace Notes. Instead, after the American note came in, Lloyd George sent a soothing telegram to Hughes, who read it in parliament. The war was being fought, Lloyd George asserted, 'for humanity and civilization'. He expressed confidence that Australia would fight alongside Britain 'however long the path to final victory'. He promised 'no faltering in our determination that the sacrifices which we, and you, have made, and have still to make, shall not be made in vain'.[504]

Such bilge sufficed. It was – and is – a common plea, but in reality a fraudulent appeal to a murderous loyalty to the dead. Wars must go on, supposedly, for the sake of the dead.

Was Australia's wartime government cautiously husbanding the lives of Australian soldiers abroad, ensuring they were fighting only for the nation's security, and not for the vanity of politicians? In the words of the historian Neville Meaney, while Hughes had been in Britain for four months during the first half of 1916, the British simply 'did not discuss their peace aims with him'. On the biggest issues, Lloyd George simply 'took the Dominions' assent for granted'.[505] Australia was scarcely regarded at all which is just how the ever-willing ally is always regarded. Indeed, in February 1917, when the German and American peace offers had been batted away by London, William Higgs, a Labor MP, asked Hughes in the parliament if a copy of the German peace proposals, and a copy of the 'Entente Reply to President Wilson', had been sent to Australia from London's Colonial Office – the official line of communication. If so, he asked if these could be 'printed for public information'? Astoundingly, Hughes replied with a simple 'No', to both questions. What could anyone conclude from this? Peace had been rejected by London; the Australian Government had not even been favoured with copies of the official documents; and so the Australian Government could not print them. Why had peace been suffocated? What terms were Australians to go on fighting for? The Hughes Government had not asked for any light to be shed on these matters – and did not get any.[506]

Needless to say, there were dissident voices in Australia. Labour newspapers began to point to rumours of the low diplomatic bargain by which Britain had drawn Italy into the war, a deal that made a mockery of the hand-on-heart professions of noble motives. 'If the whole truth of the sordid intrigues and aims in connection with this war were known, the people of the various nations would not sacrifice another life in such a conflict', speculated the *Australian Worker*. When all such truths came out, many would cry out to know why hordes of ordinary men should have died for 'commercial and imperial ambitions'.[507] And, not surprisingly, the *Barrier Daily Truth* was among those vehemently campaigning throughout December 1916 for the German and American peace offers to be grasped.[508] The paper kept up the barrage into January 1917, notwithstanding the presence of a military censor in the office. The *Barrier Daily Truth* was among those papers revealing that the Hughes Government, red-faced at the size of the 'No' vote among the troops, had hushed up the figures.[509] If Ryan eventually received copies of the *Barrier Daily Truth* – or again, letters from Broken Hill conveying its spirit – it must have stirred his seething passions on the matter of peace.

For all the Australian troops, the kicking of peace to the curb in 1916 meant that the hardships of 1917 and 1918 on the Western Front would be heaped upon the horrors already endured. And we should not doubt that the Australians at the front hoped for peace – even the most steadfast of them. A handful of samples must suffice. The troops' letters home – in spite of the censors – could include passages beseeching peace. 'It is time Europe saw the futility of this business', wrote Corporal Arthur Thomas in September 1916, while recording his still 'undoubted Faith' in the justice of the cause. In November, he wrote confidently that 'next year will see the end of this too horrible slaughter'. In December, he warned a brother not to volunteer but rather to 'KEEP WELL OUT OF THIS, we are not all going to be chopping blocks'. On New Year's Day he denounced the past 'year of hideous smashing waste & cruel foolery', and noted that on conscription 'most of the men here voted NO, their plight being awful'. At the end of January he wrote: 'I want nothing but to get away from this awful carnage & waste of splendid lives, such waste is terrific & God grant it will cease quickly.'[510]

Archie Barwick, similarly resolute in his belief that the Australians were right to fight, wrote on 1 July 1916: 'I firmly believe the end of the year will see the finish of this gigantic war, everything to me seems to point to it & I only hope I am right, for I am full up of it.'[511] When the peace proposals were first known in the trenches in mid-December 1916, he noted grimly that 'everyone seems to think that they won't be accepted by the Allies'. Only a week later, Barwick was still pessimistic, but opinions among his soldier mates had swung around completely: '[T]here is a pretty strong opinion that peace will come within a month or two but I am hanged if I can see how.'[512]

Bound to Fail – or Bound to Succeed?

Both the German and American peace notes of December 1916 were front-page news in the world's press. Soldiers and citizens in many nations could read them. Both notes clearly offered the prospect of the war ending by round-table negotiation – in Washington, perhaps, or Portsmouth, Maine, as the Russo-Japanese War had ended. The Entente Powers could scarcely ignore these notes. They would have to be debated in the Entente's parliaments. A public response was essential.

Any such negotiations were bound to fail anyway, screeched the 'knock-out blow' press. But advisers to the British Government in December 1916 gave exactly the opposite advice: negotiations were very dangerous because they were bound to succeed. All foresaw the reality: no negotiator could dare rise from the negotiating table without striking a bargain, so powerful would be the demand for peace arising from the suffering people of Europe. 'On no account must there be an armistice', David Davies, a personal adviser to Lloyd George, told the new Prime Minister. 'The army would be worse than useless afterwards – its morale would be impaired and it is problematical whether it would recommence the struggle.'[513] Foreign Office advisers agreed: even a short-term truce would tip Europe into peace, because 'once talks had started they could never be broken off'.[514] Eric Drummond, secretary to Arthur Balfour, the new Foreign Secretary, told Lloyd George that there must be 'no question of an armistice or a cessation of hostilities'. Let the Russians, French, and Italians turn down negotiations, he advised, and then Britain should rally behind them. 'Once negotiations have begun', Drummond explained, 'it will be difficult, in view of the war weariness in most countries, to break them off without trying to come to some sort of agreement.'[515]

The truth is quite clear: while the men in the cabinet rooms and chancelleries fumbled for excuses, Europe was teetering on the edge, between peace and war. All who sat in the grand, high-ceilinged rooms of power knew the unspoken secret: to begin negotiations meant that peace would break out – irresistibly – and the old order would be overwhelmed by the forces of change. Public opinion would demand that negotiators be locked metaphorically in a room, until they had hammered out a compromise peace. The war was like a spinning top, nearing exhaustion; if negotiations began, it would wobble, and tumble, into peace.

'Far Better Than What Actually Happened'

The peace that was lost over the Christmas of 1916 haunted many. 'Why couldn't it have ended rationally, as it might have ended, in 1916, instead of all that trumpet-blowing against a negotiated peace, and the ferocious talk of secure civilians about marching to Berlin?' So asked the young Vera Brittain in her diary on the day of the armistice in November 1918, when the victory was powerless to ward off the profound pain of the loss of her lover, Roland, in the war.[516] Even at the top there were regrets over this pathetically lost chance for peace. 'If a Wilson Peace in 1916 had brought real disillusionment with militarism, it would have been far better than what actually happened.'[517] This was the verdict of Sir Edward Grey in his memoirs.

Chapter 16

ESCAPADE

PERHAM DOWN TO ARBROATH, JANUARY-APRIL 1917

> 30 March: Russia is making good her opportunity to kick out her Monarchs and pro Germans, the Socialists have grasped the psychological moment & I believe it will go right through Europe [;] if it will be better for Britain remains to be seen, I fancy it will be worse, as she may have to disgorge territory.[518]
>
> — Corporal Arthur G. Thomas, letters to his parents from France, 30 March 1917

For Ted Ryan, who had shown his contempt for Lloyd George and the 'knock-out blowers' in his letter to Ramsay MacDonald in the autumn, the snuffing out of peace in December 1916 must have been sickening to read about. While he was playing truant from Perham Down in December 1916, the right-wing newspapers in particular were preaching for 'more vigorous prosecution of the war'. Presumably Ryan read in the press of the prompt French, Italian, and Russian rejections of both the German and American peace overtures. Lloyd George's rejection he may have read about when confined to barracks upon his return.

Very likely, Ryan was also receiving more letters from Broken Hill. If so, these must have emboldened him. At exactly this time, Broken Hill was in the forefront of a radical shift in Labor opinion across Australia. The defeat of the first conscription plebiscite in October 1916 had been a landmark moment. The heroes of the struggle against conscription in Broken Hill scooped up the political benefit and came to dominate local politics. Standing on radical anti-war platforms, 'Brookie' Brookfield would win the local Broken Hill seat of Sturt for Labor in a state by-election in February 1917, and then increased his majority in the general election for the New South Wales Parliament held on 24 March 1917; 'Mick' Considine would win the federal seat of Barrier for Labor in the federal election held on 5 May 1917. These two firebrands would soon become national figures – alternately canonized and demonised in a deeply divided Australia – as they widened the vision of the Broken Hill workers and led them in their resistance to conscription and war.[519]

'Special Marriage Leave'

It seems Ted Ryan's loathing of Perham Down got the better of him. Only a month after his confinement to camp over the Christmas of 1916, he committed a much more serious offence. He was found to be AWOL again – for almost five weeks.

Five weeks! The circumstances were telling. Ryan failed to return to Perham Down after a ten-day furlough, granted for 'special marriage leave' on 11 January. Such leave was not exceptional. A great many AIF soldiers did in fact get married while in the United Kingdom, and there was much colourful reporting on the 'Anzac Marriage Rush', and how alluring these fit men from the south seemed to be to British women.[520] But Ted Ryan's marriage plans apparently fell through. And then he was late, very late, in returning from leave. He was due back by 10 a.m. on 21 January but he did not show. Thus, back at Perham Down, a 'Court of Inquiry' was held into his case on 16 February, as per the military regulations. It officially recorded that Ryan was 'absent, without leave, from his duty' and that he was 'deficient' in absconding with all his clothes and equipment.[521]

Where was he? Ted Ryan had given his destination to the leave clerk as Arbroath, in Forfarshire, on the North Sea coast of Scotland, just north of Dundee. As we have noted, Ryan's Uncle James Mudie's relations still lived in this town. Presumably, this time Ryan had the address of the Mudie relatives. He had told his uncle in his letter home (as published in the *Barrier Miner* in December 1916) of his desire to return to Scotland after sampling the place on his first leave, as soon as he could.[522] So, it is reasonable to assume that he travelled north as planned, by rail, through the maze of mill towns and munitions works.

Assuming he made it all the way to Scotland this second time, we might well imagine that he picked up some rebellious sentiments there. Anti-war convictions were certainly strengthening in Scotland. If Ryan craved newspapers of the outlook of the *Barrier Daily Truth*, he would have found the Independent Labour Party's newspapers *Forward* and *Labour Leader* to his taste, and these circulated widely in Scotland. They documented the shift in opinion against the war, especially in the working-class towns and the local labour and trades councils of Scotland.[523] For example, in February 1917, it was the British Labour Party's 'Scottish Advisory Council' that broke with the still pro-war party majority and for the first time urged the wisdom of 'peace negotiations being opened without delay'.[524]

In the towns of Forfarshire, including Arbroath, by 1916 the social fissures were opening. In October 1916, just a month after Ryan's visit, the local trades and labour councils in Montrose, not far from Arbroath, began a series of big protests against high food prices caused by the war.[525] That same month, Sir Francis Webster, a leading Scottish Liberal and the most prominent industrialist in Arbroath, sensationally questioned the long war and the huge debts Britain was running up. Webster, who had lost one son at the front in 1914, attacked the government's slogan of waging war until 'Prussian militarism was crushed'. Addressing the Arbroath Chamber of Commerce, he declared that *he* for one 'was not out to crush Prussian militarism, but all militarism'. Exaggerated war aims were foolish, he argued, because they only roused 'a proud nation' like Germany to 'fight to the end'. Webster pleaded that Britain's ministers should 'be done with this talk'. If the enemy offered peace, 'let us hear and consider his proposals'.[526] Clearly, 'knock-out blow' opinion was fading and a much more critical spirit was taking hold in Arbroath and across Scotland.

Did Ryan spend his leave here in Arbroath? With no direct evidence, we are left to speculate. Ryan's sojourn in Scotland in January and February 1917 might well have strengthened his convictions about the war. On the other hand, perhaps it was not politics at all that detained him in Scotland. Perhaps his grasping at 34 days of extra leave was simply prompted by a painful but unremarkable complication in his personal life because when he did eventually turn up at Perham Down after his 'marriage leave' he was unmistakably unmarried. There was no certificate to display. Of course, it is also possible that the intended marriage was a ruse from the start.

Lily-White Goals – and Dark Designs

Because Ryan was free for more than six weeks during January and February 1917 – arranging to get married, or not – he had a chance to catch up on the world news beyond that covered by the newspapers at Perham Down. Let us explore some of the events well beyond the trenches reflected in the pages of the British press, and some events that were hidden.

As the President's offer of mediation in December 1916 had been released to all the great news agencies of the world, Britain and her partners decided they must concoct a public declaration politely rejecting it. This reply to Wilson would have to explain to the suffering people, really for the first time, what war aims the Entente Powers, from Liberal Britain to Tsarist Russia, were supposedly pursuing in common.

On 10 January 1917, Britain and her partners released the official 'Entente Reply to President Wilson' to the world. It smelled of roses – the usual vague generalities wrapped in perjuries. Apparently, the Entente Powers were innocent of all expansionist designs: they were 'not fighting for selfish interests'. Lloyd George's new slogan got a run: the Entente was searching innocently for 'reparation, restitution', and 'guarantees' against aggression. Blood was being spilled only to liberate Belgium, France, and Serbia, from their invaders, and to get just 'indemnities' for these nations' sufferings. Shiny ideological goals stood out, such as 'the reorganisation of Europe' along lines of nationality, the liberation of the oppressed nationalities inside Austria-Hungary, while achieving the 'expulsion' of the Ottoman Turks from Europe. To please Wilson, there was a vague expression of support for 'a league of nations'. According to this document, the Entente's soldiers, conscripts and volunteers alike, were dying for only the most generous, the most philanthropic and noble of purposes – to save mankind.

But certain war aims, enshrined in official Entente diplomatic exchanges over the preceding two and half years, were altogether missing in this new lily-white declaration, as if they had never been. For example, the protectionist schemes for an economic war after the war, as outlined in the well-publicised 'Paris Resolutions' of 1916, were simply not mentioned. Similarly, the fate of the captured German colonies was passed over without a word. The still darker secret treaties binding the coalition of Entente Powers together – the results of all the horse-trading between the likes of Grey, Sazonov, Delcassé, and Sonnino – were kept secret.[527]

Almost immediately after the official 'Entente Reply' was published, more secret cables and memoranda were being exchanged between the opulent ambassadorial mansions and the foreign office buildings in the Entente capitals. These carried details of still more deals. For instance, only two days after the 'Entente Reply' appeared, Aristide Briand, the French Premier, sent a private letter to Paul Cambon, his ambassador in London, at the embassy, Albert Gate House in Knightsbridge. It listed the bare minimum of France's actual war aims, as just agreed by the Briand Cabinet. The Franco-German border was the focus. France must have: the annexation of the German Saarland; the restoration of the Alsace-Lorraine frontier of 1790, without any plebiscite to gauge the wishes of the people; the end of German sovereignty in the Rhineland, with France achieving the 'neutrality' and 'provisional occupation' of the German province, through the territory's separation from Germany or even its partition by France – shorthand for annexation. A progressive frill was added: the letter expressed support for President Wilson's project of a 'League of Nations'.[528]

Over the winter of 1916-17, secret British documents were also drawn up in a similar spirit of grab. Sir Louis du Pan Mallet, a Foreign Office mandarin, chaired a 'Territorial Changes Committee', which had met from August 1916. It studied the alphabet soup of promises, treaties, agreements and understandings. Its report was submitted in early 1917. There were no surprises in its recommendations: Britain and her Dominions should retain all captured German colonies; Britain should negotiate territorial exchanges with France (because she might still be smarting over the British seizure of Egypt and Cyprus); in India, Britain should take the French outpost of Chandernagore but enlarge French Pondicherry; in the Pacific, Britain should gain France's eastern Pacific Islands while France should gain the New Hebrides; and in Africa, Britain should abandon claims in the Cameroons and in Darfur, in return for the cession from France of the islands of St Pierre and Miquelon, and fishing rights, off Newfoundland.[529]

Clearly, the slicing and dicing of the colonial world by the Entente's diplomats – while simultaneously planning to exclude Germany from it – was still an essential element of this protracted war.

Aristide Briand

All this, of course, was secret. But in the middle of Ted Ryan's 'marriage leave', came a public political sensation, which could not be kept out of the British press. Along with the rest of the world, Ryan undoubtedly had the chance to read news of an astonishing new departure from President Wilson – a public effort to back up his 'Peace Note'. On 22 January 1917, Wilson delivered to the Senate in Washington perhaps his most famous wartime speech, his so-called 'Peace Without Victory' speech. He argued passionately that a military victory for either side would be disastrous. Peace enforced by the victor upon the vanquished would rest 'as upon quicksand'. It would invite a war of revenge. If all genuinely wanted 'a lasting peace', then they should move to negotiate a settlement. 'Only a peace between equals can last', he declared. Therefore, 'it must be a peace without victory'. It was an eloquent plea to all the combatants to accept American mediation.[530] This was exactly the prospect that had inspired Ryan's letter to Ramsay MacDonald of October 1916.

Sadly, the great hopes raised by this speech were soon shattered. None of the powers responded formally. The pro-war British press ridiculed 'peace without victory' as the recipe of a weakling. Then, on 31 January, the German Government announced the resumption of unrestricted submarine warfare beginning the next day, thus threatening the British Navy's mastery of the Atlantic – and the war trade that rested upon it. The United States promptly broke off diplomatic relations with Germany, but did not declare war immediately. Two crowded months of tormenting political tension followed in the United States, with the forces urging peace pitted against those advocating war. Wilson agonised over his choice – then plumped for war, in late March.[531]

The Powers that Be

The American decision still hung in the balance when Ted Ryan returned to Perham Down voluntarily on 23 February 1917. He was still in uniform. He must have dodged the military police inspecting leave documents on the trains and at stations. Late in the evening of 23 February, Ryan was encountered by a Corporal F. South in a drying room – a favourite place, no doubt, to keep warm – at No. 2 Camp. There is no suggestion that he was hiding there, or sought to escape arrest. He was taken to the orderly room of No. 4 Camp and there placed 'under close arrest'. Ryan was accused of being an 'absentee' and 'admitted that he was'.[532]

This time Ryan was exposed to the risk of a much more serious punishment than a short period of confinement to barracks. The authorities had issued guidelines showing scales of punishment for short periods of AWOL up to seven days, generally the imposition of Field Punishment No. 2, with accompanying fines. But absences of over seven days had to be dealt with by a District Court Martial.[533] This body could impose much stiffer sentences. So, papers applying for a District Court Martial to deal with Ryan went up to the legal advisers at the headquarters for the Australian depots, Bhurtpore Barracks, at Tidworth, only a few kilometres away. Here at Tidworth the Australian officers handling courts martial worked and messed in barrack buildings with imperial names such as 'Candahar', 'Delhi' and 'Jellalabad' emblazoned on their entrances – all very evocative of the jewel-in-the-crown spirit that was taken for granted in military minds there. The papers initially sought to try Ryan for two crimes, both his 34 days of AWOL and his returning to Perham Down unmarried, after having sought marriage leave. Meanwhile, Ryan was held at Perham Down, in the Detention Compound for over six weeks.

New Worlds for Old

Incarcerated for all of March and early April, and deprived of access to newspapers under the rules of detention, Ryan would have had to rely on corridor gossip if indeed he learned anything at all about the truly epoch-making events taking place during that time.

The despotic Tsarist regime in Russia fell spectacularly on 15 March 1917. In the face of vast demonstrations in Petrograd, and the desertion of the city's troops to the side of the crowds, Tsar Nicholas II abdicated. The autocratic regime melted away, and Russia became a republic overnight![534] Over the next week, with varying degrees of insincerity, the war-makers in Paris and London and Rome issued formal statements welcoming Russia's spectacular turn toward democracy – through grimaces, with tears welling for the fallen Tsar, and with assurances that the war would go on.[535]

Tsar Nicholas II of Russia

In Russia, the cheers for the fall of the Romanovs were very real. In the heady first days of the March Revolution, the Tauride Palace in Petrograd, the home of the Duma, the Russian Parliament, was filled with the exultant soldiers and sailors whose mutinies and street demonstrations had helped to overthrow the three-hundred-year-old Romanov regime. They prompted the formation of a 'Soviet', or council, to sit at one end of the Tauride Palace, keeping watch over the Cabinet of the 'Provisional Government', drawn from the old Duma politicians, which met initially at the other end. Together, the men and women of the new Russia promised an end to despotism. There were sensational advances. Special proclamations ended the death penalty in the Russian Army, and freed political prisoners across Russia, progressive measures that the British Government explained it could not possibly emulate in its own army or in Ireland.[536] Everywhere, ordinary people were inspired and spoke of their hopes for the new Russia, with its generous civil liberties and a free press, remarkable for a nation still at war. A great new democracy was being born in Europe, a historic turn of inestimable value, if it could be sustained. The future was full of enormous possibilities – and also perils.

Unknown to almost all observers, the fall of the Tsarist government had thrown into doubt one last secret territorial deal that the regime had only just struck, with Paris. Gaston Doumergue, a veteran French politician and Minister of Colonies, had travelled to Petrograd to conclude a secret bargain with the Tsar and his advisers. The so-called 'Left Bank of the Rhine Agreement' (or 'Doumergue Agreement') was nutted out just days before the March Revolution.

The spirit of snatching and hoarding, fired by the diplomats' courage under no fire, produced this grand bargain. Its authors imagined the parcelling up of millions of people in Eastern and Western Europe into new domains after Germany's defeat. Russia agreed to support France's claim to the restoration of Alsace-Lorraine, and the seizure of the Saarland, and also the formation of separate 'neutral' states in the Rhineland, to be detached from Germany and aligned with France. In return, France granted Russia 'complete liberty' to fix her own boundaries with Germany and Austria. In short, France winked at Russian expansion in the east, while Russia winked at French expansion in the west. The diplomatic negotiations – conducted in Petrograd and scarcely controlled by the 'chaos' that reigned at the Foreign Ministry in Paris – were concluded on 8 March 1917.[537]

This latest diplomatic deal, of course, was all documented – in darkness.

But we should not imagine that only the benighted Russians and French did such things. Britain had been negotiating a number of diplomatic deals over the fate of captured German colonies. The most important of these, the secret Anglo-Japanese 'Balfour-Motono' agreement, giving to Japan the bulk of her Asian and Pacific conquests at Germany's expense, was concluded on 16 February 1917 – to head off the possibility of peace negotiations between Tokyo and Berlin.[538]

No secrets attended the next momentous event: the very public entry of the United States of America into the war in early April 1917, two months after breaking off diplomatic relations with Germany. Making his case for war to the Congress on 2 April, President Wilson set out the most idealistic reasons for America's intervention. 'The world must be made safe for democracy', he memorably proclaimed. 'Its peace must be planted upon the tested foundations of political liberty.' Indeed, Wilson denied all avaricious thoughts of territorial or economic seizures on the part of America.

> We have no selfish ends to serve. We desire no conquest, no dominion. We seek no indemnities for ourselves, no material compensation for the sacrifices we shall freely make. We are but one of the champions of the rights of mankind. We shall be satisfied when those rights have been made as secure as the faith and the freedom of nations can make them.[539]

The American declaration of war upon Germany came on 6 April 1917, in the wake of long debates and votes in both the House and Senate – with significant opposition. Constitutionally, only Congress could decide upon war. Thus, the United States did that very rare thing among the powers: it took a parliamentary vote for war ahead of the declaration – which came on Good Friday.

A little later, Wilson pointedly insisted that America would fight not as the 'ally' of Britain and her partners, but rather as an 'Associated Power'. The label advertised a crucial difference: as a progressive internationalist, Wilson did not share the imperialist and protectionist outlooks of those who directed the destinies of the Entente. And, in part, Wilson reasoned that by entering the war, America could liberalise the Entente's war. American blood, shed purely in the cause of democracy, would strengthen America's hands in fashioning the peace that must eventually come.

High-minded ideological goals were paramount, in American public debate and in official propaganda, as the nation was launched into the war. But domestic events belied this. Wilson's administration proved to be extremely illiberal on the home front. It very swiftly imposed conscription, under the banner of 'Selective Service'. The government then secured the passage of the draconian *Espionage Act* and *Sedition Act* and exploited these to repress all critics of the choice for war.[540]

All this cast doubt on Wilson's professed liberal motives for entering the war. Had he surrendered to the 'puppet-masters' of the 'war trust', the business and banking lobbies pressing for intervention? Doubters were aware that, with American loans to the Entente Powers flowing like a river of gold, and a vast trade in American munitions soaring in value, Wilson had allowed America's neutrality to become increasingly lop-sided. America's war boom saw the value of exports to Britain and Europe leap from $1.4 billion to $4.3 billion between 1914 and 1917.[541] The stock-tickers in New York noisily spat out the story of rising profitability. The case could be made that America was entering the war under the pressure of the mega-fauna that stomped through the jungle of vested interest – the gigantic 'warhogs', the financial and industrial interests, those who owned the kill-chains and profited so mightily from the war trade. America would fight, not so much to make the world safe for democracy, but rather to make the Atlantic safe for the arms trade.[542]

All this, no doubt, would have fascinated a politically aware soldier like Ryan. He had believed from the autumn of 1916 that the war should be ended by negotiation, and that the United States was the best hope for that cause. Now that hope was gone.

Accusers and Accused

Three days after America's entry into the war, on the morning of 9 April 1917, Ryan faced his District Court Martial in a hut at Perham Down.[543] A District Court Martial was one of four possible types of courts martial, each with increasing powers to punish and with generally diminishing rights for the accused, ranging from the rarely used Regimental Court Martial to the streamlined Field General Court Martial. Ryan's District Court Martial had the power to imprison him for a stretch not exceeding two years – and hard labour could be added.

As this was the first of four courts martial that Ryan would eventually face, it is worth stressing some essentials about the process. Courts martial were part of the structure of British army discipline; procedures adopted there were scarcely comparable with those in civilian courts. 'Military justice' was theatre – but serious theatre. The deterrence of indiscipline was the overall objective. 'The object of military law is to maintain discipline among the troops', announced the Manual of Military Law. This eclipsed any desire to uncover the complex truths behind any crime or any duty to pursue individual justice dispassionately.[544] Moreover, most of the officers sitting in judgment upon rankers were more or less clueless on the thicket of legal provisions governing the military courts. As even the British guide to courts martial (reprinted for Australian officers) put it, 'a large proportion of officers have little or no knowledge of Military Law'.[545]

The supposedly imperishable principles of British justice, proud liberal achievements for the protection of all, quickly withered under courts martial procedures. There was no 'presumption of innocence', no standard of proof 'beyond reasonable doubt', and no 'right to silence'. Nor did a court-martialled soldier receive one of the most elementary rights of Britons, as set out in the historic Magna Carta of 1215, namely the right to trial by one's 'peers'. The soldier was both investigated by and judged by his officers. Thus, a court martial existed on a different legal planet to that familiar in a civilian court of law.[546]

Hovering over every court martial were the British Army's rules and procedures, as outlined in the *Army Act 1881* (UK) under which Australians served – a daunting compendium of offences and punishments, showing, for example, a total of 111 offences that attracted trial by courts martial, including 29 offences for which the penalty was death.[547] Here the rigid distinctions between officers and men were meticulously maintained. As if from different worlds, officers and men faced different scales of punishments, and different procedures in courts of inquiry and courts martial. In practice, British knowledge and British precedents prevailed, and British officers often dominated in the command structures of the Australian camps and units.

How did it all work? Officers from Australian units who were drafted into a court martial, knowing little or no law, could consult various British guidebooks, most authoritatively the 948-page *The Manual of Military Law* published for the British War Office in July 1914, which incorporated the *Rules of Procedure* governing courts martial, and the *King's Regulations and Orders for the Army* (1912), with its 1,946 paragraphs. Helpfully, a dozen popular British cribs on military law also appeared, designed to plug the gaps in the officers' legal knowledge, such as Major R.L.C. Brooker's *Precis of Military Law and King's Regulations for Young Officers*, and later Lt-Col. S.T. Bannings's

Military Law Made Easy.[548] To assist the process of a court martial, the officers also received a printed pro forma document produced by the War Office, outlining the steps that they were required to follow. Spaces were left blank in the form to be filled in during the proceedings.

A swift survey of the officers fronting up at Ryan's District Court Martial on 9 April 1917 also reminds us of the military sociology on display – and the whiff of 'class justice'. Those 'duly sworn' to judge Ryan's case were led by the President of the court, Major Arthur England Johnson Croly, of the 11th Battalion. Croly was a graduate of Trinity College Dublin, the nephew of a London-based army colonel, a veteran of Gallipoli, and now second-in-command of the camp at Perham Down. Ryan faced also Captain Donald Duncan Buchanan, a former student of a famous private school, Newington College in Sydney, a grazier, aged in his early forties; and Captain George Bond, a 33-year-old clerk from Hobart, educated at Queen's College and Buckland's School, who had won a Military Cross at Pozières. Prosecuting Ryan was Captain Robert Humphrey Browning, MC. He did have legal training; Browning was a 31-year-old solicitor from Bathurst, and the son of a lawyer with chambers in Sydney's prestigious Phillip Street.[549]

These details serve to underline the fact that in a military trial such as this, the gap between the accused and his officer-judges was much more than the few paces that separated two tables in a hut. Those whose capped and pipped careers had been borne aloft by the privileges that class can bestow – and sometimes buttressed by meritorious performances in battle – faced the accused: in Ryan's case, a former orphan, a worker from the Broken Hill mines, and now a shell-shocked man of the lowest rank. A distinctly upper-class 'judge and jury' sat in judgement upon a man whose working life had made him familiar with the grimy faces and darkness of 'the pit'. The accusers and the accused were worlds apart.

The court martial papers show that the space reserved for 'counsel for the accused' was simply ruled through. Private Ted Ryan had no defence counsel, no 'prisoner's friend'. Under the 'Rules of Procedure' for courts martial outlined in the *Manual of Military Law*, all accused soldiers had the right to request a defending counsel or 'prisoner's friend', and to prepare their defence in advance with that 'friend'. Perhaps Ryan waived his right. Some historians suggest that the accused often declined a 'prisoner's friend', because in practice this duty was allocated to another officer (for only an officer could address the court), and it was realised how little he might do to defend the accused.[550]

But Ryan made it easy for the officers. He did not raise an objection to any of them, when formally asked if he did so. Then, charged with 34 days of AWOL, he promptly pleaded 'Guilty'. He did not cross-examine any of the witnesses appearing against him. The officers, of course, did not need to retire. The verdict was 'Guilty'.

The rules specified that at this point the court should consider a statement 'in mitigation of punishment'. Ryan told the court that he had already served in the army for 'a year and a half' and that he had been wounded in France near Pozières. Guilelessly, he made light of his decision to extend his leave. 'I was given a fortnight's furlough, but was having a good time so I overstayed my pass.' He noted he had 'only been up once before', meaning presumably up to London and the north, and that he 'meant to return but put it off from day to day'. 'I am willing to go back to the firing line', he added and, weighing the truth of this, we might recall that he had indeed rejected two opportunities for 'cold-footed jobs' in Egypt in 1916. Finally, he requested leniency. 'I had no leave until after I was wounded, and I have been waiting trial in military custody for 45 days on the present charge', he reminded the officers.

Significantly, Ryan did not advance any political objections to the war, nothing along the lines of his letter to MacDonald, written only six months before. In any case, such opinions were positively dangerous if offered 'in mitigation of punishment', and could only have weakened his chances of obtaining leniency.

Time already served gave him stronger grounds. He chose to highlight the long delay in summoning a court martial to try him. He was right: papers filed with the court martial show that applications from Perham Down seeking a District Court Martial for him had in fact gone up twice to the legal officers at nearby Tidworth, and had been 'returned twice for amendment'. Two difficulties had emerged. First, a witness who had offered to give evidence against Ryan regarding his allegedly fraudulent claim for marriage leave had been hospitalised and could not appear. Then, much to their embarrassment, the legal officers had discovered that Ryan's returning to camp unmarried was, in any case, not actually an offence under the *Army Act 1881*.[551] It had taken Major John J.A. Walker, the Officer Commanding the Drafting Depot at Perham Down, 32 days to get the proper formulation of his charge against Ryan on the 'Charge Sheet' ready for the court martial. Ryan was quite properly aggrieved.

Thus, having listened to Ryan's explanations, Major Croly, the President of the court martial, closed the court for the officers to deliberate on the sentence. Ryan was returned to prison, like all soldiers found guilty, knowing the verdict but not the sentence. The officers then decided upon a sentence: 42 days of detention. But Croly also wrote a 'Recommendation to Mercy' to accompany the papers. As in all courts martial, the verdict and sentence were provisional, until confirmed by a commanding officer. Indeed, under the rules, the officers had been all 'duly sworn' at the outset to do their duty and to keep the verdict and sentence secret as they awaited confirmation. So no one outside the court martial, least of all the accused cooling his heels in detention, would know the sentence in the immediate aftermath of a trial. Within a week, the papers lay on the desk of the British officer Brigadier-General Ewen Sinclair-Maclagan, at Tidworth (an officer whose mistakes early in the landings at Gallipoli are still regarded as fateful for the campaign).[552] He confirmed the verdict of guilty, but strained the quality of mercy in confirming the sentence: he agreed to remit just 20 days of the sentence.[553] Thus, Ryan remained in prison for another three weeks after his court martial, to be released on 30 April. And he lost pay. According to the Australian regulations, convicted soldiers generally lost their pay for the period of their absconding, and also their pay from the day a charge was laid against them to the day their punishment expired. Thus, Ryan lost altogether 100 days' pay, a total of £25 (roughly equivalent to $2,400 in 2019).

The whole experience must have been galling, and perhaps Ryan nursed a burning sense of resentment. Normally, soldiers went to a District Court Martial swiftly after their arrest and the whole procedure was wrapped up in ten days. Ryan had confessed his guilt, but on account of the incompetence of the officers in command of the courts martial procedures, after his 34 days of AWOL he had then served 45 days in custody awaiting trial, plus another 22 days of detention as his punishment, and consequently he had lost a lot of money.

Ryan's sentence was promulgated and read to a parade at Perham Down on 14 April, while Ryan was still in the detention barracks with two weeks left to serve. Probably he was not present at the parade. But these promulgations could be dramatic affairs. One diarist at Perham Down recorded an instance in October 1916 when a corporal, found guilty of desertion and punished with a demotion, was exhibited to other soldiers at a general parade and was 'stripped of his chevrons'. 'Charge and evidence read out by Camp Commandant in voice meant to be impressive but which [was] a thin squawk.'[554]

The truth is plain. Examples were being made of some to intimidate others. But delaying any return to the ghastly farce in France was not something shameful to many soldiers. Some soldiers at Perham Down who had seen action would openly boast in letters home that they felt 'pride in avoiding France for so long'.[555]

Revolution – and Revulsion of War

In one sense, Ryan's own small revolt against the war, revealed in his letter to MacDonald and in his two episodes of AWOL, was but a tiny local ricochet from a mounting barrage of criticism that was changing world opinion at the beginning of 1917 – and this represented a formidable challenge to the war-makers in London, Paris, Petrograd, Rome, and Melbourne. When Ryan was marched to his court martial at Perham Down in early April 1917, Britain and her partners were confronting simultaneously two momentous events: the Russian Revolution and the United States' intervention in the war. Both, in different ways, spelled trouble for the war-makers. And both would meet entrenched reaction.

The Russian Revolution clearly sprang from widespread popular revulsion against the war, and from a real loathing of those in power who were suspected of prolonging the war for imperialist goals. By no means was this movement confined to Russia. In April 1917, there was a wave of strikes in Germany against the hardships of rationing, and the strikers' leaders also accused the government of driving the nation to ruin for expansionist fantasies.[556] America's intervention in the war as an 'Associated Power' – a partner at a moral distance from the Entente – was not an unmixed blessing for the Entente. Huge economic weight was thrown into the struggle. But it also gave Wilson opportunities to make speeches upon true Liberal internationalist ideals, obliquely critical of Britain, France and Italy. This represented another serious challenge to Lloyd George who in his first months in office was hoping to invigorate enthusiasm for the war as a frankly imperial struggle. Thus, he had swiftly summoned an 'Imperial War Cabinet', including Dominion Prime Ministers, to meet in the spring of 1917.

The much more serious nature of the threat posed by the Russian Revolution was clear just two weeks into the upheaval. The Petrograd Soviet, elected from soldiers' regiments and workshops in the city, acting as a watchdog over the new Provisional Government, addressed an 'Appeal' to the world on 27 March. The Soviet claimed to speak on behalf of 'all the peoples who are being destroyed and ruined in the monstrous war'. It railed against all annexationists, everywhere; it urged democratisation, everywhere. It was time for 'concerted, decisive action in favour of peace'. How? 'We announce that the time has come to start a decisive struggle against the grasping ambitions of the governments of all countries; the time has come for the people to take into their own hands the decision of the question of war and peace.'[557]

On 10 April the Provisional Government of Russia, under pressure from the Soviet, followed this up with a declaration of new national war aims. It appeared to wash Russia's hands of all imperialism. It promised 'that free Russia does not aim at the domination of other nations, at depriving them of their national patrimony, or at occupying by force foreign territory, but that its object is to establish a durable peace on a basis of the rights of nations to decide their own destiny'.[558] British Labour and radical newspapers covered these stunning Russian events extensively and sympathetically. So too, far away, did Broken Hill's *Barrier Daily Truth*, although we do not know if any clippings ever reached Ryan.[559]

The crucial point is this: there were Private Ryans on every front ready to listen to this message, and they were not necessarily revolutionists. For the mood of revulsion against war that rippled through all the warring nations in 1917 drew upon age-old wisdom and millions of bereavements. For instance, in Britain it was but an echo of a song popular in the 1850s, and quoted constantly by peace advocates ever since:

Let the men who make the quarrels
Be the only men to fight.[560]

Chapter 17

RESISTANCE

PERHAM DOWN, MAY-JUNE 1917

Each was what every private soldier is, a man in arms against a world, a man fighting desperately for himself, and conscious that, in the last resort, he stood alone; for such self-reliance lies at the very heart of comradeship.[561]

— Frederic Manning, *The Middle Parts of Fortune* (1929)

Only a month after his first court martial, Ryan picked a much bigger fight: he resisted direct orders that he return to France. Found fit at last by the Medical Officers at Perham Down, he was warned that he must join a 'Draft Parade' on the evening of 8 May 1917 'in full marching order to proceed on draft overseas' or be found guilty of desertion. Ryan defied the warning. He did not show. However, bright and early the next morning, he voluntarily surrendered himself once again and was immediately arrested. He had not left the camp. This was just eight days after his release from detention at the end of April, as we have seen, at the end of his punishment for going AWOL beyond his 'marriage leave' in January and February.

'Desertion'

The commander of the Hardening and Drafting Depot, Major Cecil Tribe Knight, swiftly requested a court martial for Ryan. (Ironically, Knight would himself face investigations that same month over inefficiencies in his management of equipment for soldiers drafted from Perham Down, and before the year was out he would be returned to Australia as 'not fitted to command.')[562] Thus, after only a fortnight in the Detention Compound this time awaiting trial, Ryan faced his second District Court Martial at Perham Down on the afternoon of 22 May 1917.

Again, Captain Robert Browning prosecuted Ryan. Again, Browning alone had legal knowledge among the officers assembled to judge Ryan. Presiding over the scene was the President of the court, Major Michael Fitzgerald, a near fifty-year-old military officer and railway stores clerk from Goulburn, Irish-born but absolutely loyal (for he had been selected as an escort for King George V at the opening of Parliament in London two months before). Assisting him were Captain John Vincent Houlihan, a draftsman from St Kilda in his mid-twenties (who would soon be killed at Polygon Wood); and Lieutenant Fredrick William Lane, a twenty-eight-year-old Tasmanian civil servant, already suffering from deafness due to 'exposure'. Lane had once attended a Quaker-aligned school in Hobart, but had obviously forsaken his Quakerism, and would be killed in action in March 1918.[563] Again, there was no counsel appointed to appear for Ryan, no 'prisoner's friend'.

For the first time, Ryan faced the serious charge of desertion. This was formally described on the 'Charge Sheet': 'When on active service, deserting His Majesty's Forces' which was sloppy, for it should have said 'Service'. The typed sheet alleged that Ryan had absented himself from the drafting parade on the night of 8 May 'thereby avoiding proceeding overseas'. The implication was obvious: Ryan was assumed to have acted from cowardice. There was the nub of the matter. Lest there was any doubt, a presiding officer also recorded against the charge 'Section 12 (1) A. A.' This captured the essence of what was happening: Ryan was being court-martialled for desertion under section 12(1) of the *Army Act 1881* (UK), for which the maximum penalty was death.

It was, on the face of it, a clear case. Ryan had been warned, as were all soldiers being drafted overseas, that failing to appear would be punished as 'desertion'. This was indeed the longstanding pattern in the AIF – a warning that any soldier who went missing from a draft directed to ship out to France would face the charge not of AWOL but of desertion.[564]

Nonetheless, Ryan pleaded 'Not guilty'.

The court martial unfolded. Evidence was presented against Ryan. In practice, what really mattered to the officers in these cases was that the accused had been *warned* that he would face a desertion charge if he were a no-show. Company Sergeant Major James Bradford of the Hardening and Drafting Depot confirmed the fact. Two or three days before drafting, Ryan's name had been advertised on a 'Nominal Roll' on the company noticeboard as one of more than a hundred men of the 4th Division who were being sent back to France on 8 May. On the afternoon of that day, Bradford had witnessed the Drafting Officer warn these parading men, including Ryan, that they must return to the parade ground at 8.45 p.m. ready for their drafting overseas. Ryan was not present when the roll was called at 9 p.m. He was still absent when the draft marched out of Perham Down at 9.30 p.m., Bradford reported. An orderly, Acting/Sergeant Roy Alexander Scott of the Hardening and Drafting Depot staff, confirmed that Ryan had been among those warned.

But Ryan had not sought to escape the camp. His 'desertion' had been very short. The very next morning, at 6.30 a.m., Bradford noted, Ryan had 'reported to me' in uniform – just nine and a half hours after the parade roll call. He arrested him and placed him in the guardroom. But Bradford's evidence also showed that Ryan had immediately offered a reason for staying away – and a powerful one, from a soldier's perspective. 'I asked the accused', Bradford continued, 'why he hadn't gone with the draft and he replied that he wasn't going without his pay book as he hadn't had a pay for 3 months.' Pay was *the* issue, for Ryan.

Ryan declined to challenge any of the evidence against him.

Composing his defence, Ryan once again wisely left out of account the politics of the war. He chose to fight his case on purely practical grounds. Duly sworn, he argued that he was protesting over a matter of grim importance to every soldier – his pay. An officer recorded his evidence:

> About the end of February, 1917, I handed in my old Pay Book in to the Co[mpan]y office in order to get the new Pay Book. I inquired several times but could get no satisfaction as to the reason of my new Pay Book not coming to hand. Then again I inquired and ascertained that H[ead] Q[uarters] Tidworth had traced where my Pay Book was. For over two months I had not drawn any pay & wanted to get some before I went away.
>
> I consider I should not have been selected for draft until I had my new Pay Book. Both the O.C. & Sgt. Scott knew I did not have a Pay Book.[565]

Almost certainly later in this process, an officer further up the chain underscored in heavy blue pencil the second-last sentence, showing that Ryan had by his own admission decided to disobey his officers, asserting boldly that they were wrong to send him abroad without his Pay Book. Perhaps this officer put four heavy dark pencil strokes also against his claim that his immediate superiors knew of his missing Pay Book. This was to draw the attention of those tasked with confirming the sentence later.

Put simply, Ryan had protested that he was cold stony broke. Without a pay book, he would not be able to draw money in France from any Field Cashier. He would be fighting in France, for nothing – an intolerable injustice, in his view.

Significantly, the court martial papers record that the prosecutor 'declines to cross-examine the witness'. Ryan's evidence was simply taken down and read back to him, and was uncorrected. Perhaps there was a recognition here that Ryan's story of a lost pay book was hardly likely to be invented, as it could so easily be checked. If a soldier lost his pay book, he was required to lodge a Statement of Loss through his officers, and if a new book had been issued there would have been a record. And of course, Ryan had been recently locked up for weeks over the course of March and April and not able to pursue the matter of his pay book.

Other soldiers' experiences matched Ryan's. The procedure is clear: it was not uncommon for AIF troops to be ordered to surrender their pay books to their officers on the eve of their departure from Britain for overseas. 'Pay books were collected to prevent desertion', wrote one soldier diarist.[566] At Perham Down, pay books were collected and then returned to soldiers only after they had paraded for overseas draft and were loaded on to transports for France. Therefore, if Ryan had no pay book to begin with, this should have been clear to his officers.

And indeed, sometimes pay books *did* go missing, and replacing them took months. For example, one soldier, Jabez Waterhouse, reported that the 'Orderly Room' at Perham Down had lost his pay book in February 1917. Like Ryan, he had inquired repeatedly but 'got no satisfaction'. He was told to apply for a new one. In a letter home he complained that it 'may be anything up to three months before I am issued with a new one, I believe. All this time of course, I am unable to draw any pay.'[567] Another soldier, Arthur Giles, told his father in June 1918 that his pay book had been stolen, and he complained that it 'usually takes two or three months to get another'.[568]

Nevertheless, the officers sitting in judgement upon Ryan's case disregarded completely his defence based upon his pay book. It was immaterial, in their eyes. After taking all the evidence, the officers deliberated briefly on their verdict without Ryan present. When he was returned to the court the verdict was read to him. The court found him guilty of desertion, as charged. In accordance with the rules, Ryan was then returned to detention while the officers considered the sentence in closed court. Significantly, in all such courts martial the officers were sworn to keep secret the sentence, so Ryan would have been absolutely in the dark as to his punishment once he was returned to the cells.

This time, the officers opted for a punishment that was comparatively light considering Ryan had been found guilty of desertion.[569] The court recommended a sentence of another 30 days' detention. Perhaps the justice of Ryan's complaint over his pay book was silently conceded.[570] Once again, the verdict and sentence went 'upstairs' to Tidworth. This time, Major General Whiteside McCay, in command of the AIF depots in the UK, confirmed the verdict and sentence. Once again, a parade at Perham Down on 29 May heard the official 'promulgation' of the verdict and sentence. Ryan, of course, was still in the camp's Detention Compound, not to be released until 20 June, with plenty of time to calculate his loss of pay. The calculation this time was based on his 13 days of imprisonment awaiting trial, and his 30 days of detention: 43 days' lost pay, over £12 (roughly equivalent to $1200 in 2019). Not as disastrous as last time. But for a 'desertion' of just a few hours – in order to protest over his pay – he had ended up significantly out of pocket. No doubt this further inflamed his resentment over his treatment earlier in the year.

Was the missing pay book just an excuse to escape service? Perhaps for Ted Ryan it was emblematic of his oppression. As a class-conscious trade unionist, he must have found the loss of his pay an intense and provocative humiliation. He had inquired repeatedly for a new pay book, only to be dismissed by the camp's pay clerks and orderlies, then by his non-commissioned officers, and finally by his officers. Was it only a small thing? Or was it the kind of 'Prussianism' from the Australian officers that could jolt their soldiers into lashing out?[571] Sometimes seemingly petty humiliations could spark a wild response. As a Broken Hill miner, Ryan had been raised to see 'wagery' as the enemy, a marker of the oppression of his whole dusty class of mineworkers. As a Labor man, he knew his Henry Lawson, and the chip-on-shoulder spirit of his bold 'Second Class Wait Here'. Could Ryan stoically stomach being dismissed by those with military authority over him, and meekly return to France, to fight for his life, while waiting perhaps for months for access to any pay? No, instead he had chosen to rebel.

The Hammer of 'Desertion'

Was Ryan treated justly? Was he even correctly charged? A good case can be constructed that the charge of desertion was excessive, and should never have been formulated to cover a case of 'short desertion' such as his. It can even be argued that Ryan should have been acquitted, because the charge was so weak. In fact, a case can be mounted that he was the victim of ongoing abuse of the court martial system. After all, the distinction between short periods of AWOL and genuine desertion of the 'Service', with no intention of returning, a distinction which had long been maintained in British military law in the years leading up to the passage of the *Army Act 1881*, had been deliberately blurred since that date. Those officers who wrote their explanatory 'Notes' in the *Manual of Military Law* and the *King's Regulations*, and penned the popular cribs on military law, in the years between 1881 and the Great War, wanted the freedom to use the 'hammer' of a desertion charge to crush a spate of AWOL cases. And so they had blurred a crucial distinction in order to make examples of some men.

By the time Australian officers were making use of the 'hammer' of the desertion charges, the chapters and verses of the great bibles of military law could be cited. But in truth there were contradictory verses. For example, the *Manual of Military Law* (1914) spelled out that, for a charge of desertion to stick, the crucial 'criterion' was always the soldier's '*intention*'. Desertion fitted the bill only if the soldier clearly showed in his actions 'the intention of not returning' – the old understanding of desertion of the 'Service'. But then other 'Notes' on desertion opened up the field. They gave the example of a man who simply concealed himself in his barracks on the eve of despatch abroad, thus revealing his intention 'to escape some particular important service', thus 'shirking' his duty. This could be construed as covering Ryan's crime. Contradicting this, other examples conceded that a charge of AWOL should be preferred in cases of a 'short absence, unaccompanied by disguise, concealment, or other suspicious circumstances'.[572] Ryan fitted this description also, for he had not indicated an intention to desert the service altogether. Quite to the contrary, as the proceedings of the trial had shown, Ryan had been absent for just over nine hours, and then had surrendered, voluntarily, and in uniform, the morning after the draft parade that he refused to join. He had insisted he would serve, with a pay book. Arguably, the charge of 'desertion' against him was weak and ought never to have been levelled against him. A charge of disobeying an order filled the bill.

Bolting

Perhaps nursing a sense of injustice arising from his punishment over the missing pay book, Ryan again bolted from the camp at Perham Down only a week after leaving the Detention Compound. It was an odd and short-lived dash for a taste of freedom. Only four days later, on the evening of 1 July, he was apprehended, in uniform, by the military police at Kempton Park, outside London. Significantly, this was no pleasure garden but rather a military camp, about one hundred kilometres north-east of Perham Down. It was a former racecourse, not far from Hampton Court, that had been taken over by the British Army at the end of 1915. Perhaps Ryan was carousing with mates there. Or perhaps he was looking for his brother, Tom. In any case, he had not sought to clear out beyond the reach of the military. Nevertheless, he got the full treatment. For the first time, he was arrested and returned to Perham Down by the military police rather than simply turning up and surrendering at the camp as he had done previously.

The charge this time, his fourth in Britain, was the lesser one, AWOL. And there was no court martial. Instead, a week after his arrest, a simple punishment was imposed by his commanding officer: a sentence of 14 days of 'Field Punishment No. 2'. The days of imprisonment and punishment translated into a total forfeit of 26 days' pay, or £6 and 5 shillings (roughly equivalent to $560 in 2019).[573] 'Field Punishment No. 2' at Perham Down meant being imprisoned, and shackled intermittently, for a period not exceeding two hours a day, while undertaking hard labour as ordered but not tied to a fixed object, for this extra humiliation was specified for those sentenced to 'Field Punishment No. 1'.[574]

Ryan's record was now decidedly blotchy; it showed a pattern of repeated defiance. From December 1916 to June 1917, he had been found to be absent three times, and had once been found guilty of desertion. These offences all took place, it should be stressed, while Ryan was in camp in England, not in France.

What was happening? Perhaps Ryan was simply rebelling against the idea that soldiers were, in the words of one veteran, 'just beasts, herded and disposed of, counted and controlled, for such was the fate of the average infantryman'.[575]

Or perhaps his political opposition to the prolongation of the war, stated boldly in his letter to MacDonald in October 1916, was becoming more entrenched by the middle of 1917. Why? Certainly, in the reading rooms at Perham Down, Ryan had opportunities to follow the debates in the British press over the war. And clearly, he despised Lloyd George. He had every incentive, therefore, to read of the controversies that had erupted in Liberal circles following Lloyd George's spectacular unhorsing of Asquith as Prime Minister in December 1916. Was the Welshman's new 'coalition' government, so very heavily loaded with Tories, the creation of the ultra-patriotic press? Ryan had every reason to fear that Prime Minister Lloyd George, heading his own self-styled 'knock-out blow' coalition government, and immediately summoning an 'Imperial War Cabinet' rededicated to war, would toss aside every opportunity for peace by negotiation.

During his time at Perham Down, Ryan also received more mail from home. This would have carried news of intensifying quarrels throughout Australia, and especially in Broken Hill, over the war – a war alternatively denounced by 'anti-conscriptionists' as the work of the devil, or sanctified by 'pro-conscriptionists' as a struggle by avenging angels against German fiends from the depths of hell.

Whatever the mixture of motives behind Ryan's defiance, it is important to stress that he was by no means exceptional in his resistance to military discipline at Perham Down. No. 1 Command Depot's war diary shows that in May 1917 there were more than 2,500 men at Perham Down. Discipline was reported as 'very good' but in fact there were 517 incidents of indiscipline altogether, including the charging of 391 men for being 'Absent without leave', and 31 of these cases – including Ryan's – had been remanded for District Courts Martial. To house the throng of 'bolters' enduring punishment, the authorities established a new Detention Compound, surrounded by barbed wire, at the end of the month.

Soldiers going missing inside the camp, or legging it away, were daily events at Perham Down. To try to stem this tide of disaffection, many entertainments were ladled out. A band performed almost every night. The camp officers arranged spaces for boxing and billiards tournaments, and they expanded the reading and writing rooms, all in order to keep the men from breaking camp. Games, such as 'catch the greasy pig', featuring a larded-up piglet pursued by tumbling crowds of men, were introduced. 'The Perham Stars', a colourful entertainment troupe, also played for the men. Yet night raids by the camp police commonly found soldiers who had hidden themselves out of reach, in the practice trenches, in dugouts, and in haystacks and woods, on the small hills near the camp, as one report put it politely, 'with a view to an unfettered enjoyment of the English summer'.[576] Over time, the many sentences imposed on soldiers for going AWOL 'severely taxed the depot's detention accommodation'.[577]

The manner of Ryan's AWOL offences was pretty typical too. The reports of the Provost Staff, that is, the camp police, noted that most of these offences took place when soldiers, having been granted leave, chose to stay away. That is, they were soldiers who, like Ryan in January 1917, had decided to reward themselves with more leave than their passes indicated. So, they simply gave themselves an extended vacation from the tedium of training at Perham Down. The camp war diary was mellow on the subject: '[S]oldiers, having been through hospital and proceeding on furlough, feel inclined to make the best of the respite from right military discipline, and to take a short holiday over and above what has been officially sanctioned.'[578]

It is noteworthy also that the Australians were not unique in absconding. During 1917, every weekly issue of the *Police Gazette* in Britain listed long columns of names under the heading 'DESERTERS AND ABSENTEES FROM HIS MAJESTY'S SERVICE' – men reported as missing from all branches of the military in Britain. In addition, the paper listed hundreds of 'ABSENTEES UNDER THE MILITARY SERVICE ACT', Britain's conscription legislation. There were thousands of men listed. For example, the *Police Gazette* of 6 March 1917 listed a total of 1,653 absentees and deserters of all kinds on the run in Britain.[579]

But in mid-1917, Australian officers redoubled their efforts to repress AWOL in the AIF at their various depots in Britain. The tide of miscreants put great pressure on the legal teams at Bhurtpore Barracks, at Tidworth, as they sought 'to cope with the offence of AWL [AWOL].' An official report assembled a formidable mountain of statistics. There were 24,597 offences reported in 'Field Offence reports' for the six months from May to October 1917. Across the same period, there were 1,472 cases set down for trial by District Court Martial, 38 for trial by General Court Martial, and 1,325 Courts of Inquiry. The great bulk of these were for cases of desertion and AWOL.[580]

Action was required. In August, Major General James Whiteside McCay, the top man at the Bhurtpore barracks, issued special orders. He toughened up sentences, fines and forfeitures of pay. He produced a circular, decrying AWOLs, which he ordered to be exhibited in every hut. He argued that a man who went absent during training was delaying his return to the front, to do 'the fighting he promised to do'. The man who avoided an overseas draft was 'a pretty bad shirker who lays himself open to be called a worse name'. And yet, as McCay conceded, 'there is much A.W.L. in the A.I.F., though going absent is behaving like a rotter, and playing a dirty trick on the man at the front'. He pleaded with the men: 'I refuse to believe that we have as many rotters as the absentee figures would imply.'[581]

By the time this imploring circular was pinned up in the huts of Perham Down, Ryan was gone – to France. But neither he nor many others appear to have been persuaded by such appeals. The high rate of AWOL and desertion in the AIF, both in Britain and in France, would dip and peak, and then climb again as the Anzacs fought on into 1918.

FREEDOM

YPRES TO LE HAVRE, JULY-AUGUST 1917

> I enlisted to fight for a Peace without conquerors or conquered, as a Peace under those conditions does nothing to justify another war, either as a war of revenge by the <u>Conquered</u>, or a war of Glory and Patriotic land-grabbing by <u>Conquerors</u>.[582]
>
> — Private Edward James Ryan to his court martial, 12 September 1917

In mid-July 1917, only a few weeks after his latest AWOL and punishment, Ted Ryan was sent back to the shambles in France. If his service summary (See Appendix 3) is accurately dated, he was drafted out from Perham Down on 12 July 1917 apparently while still under sentence of periodic 'Field Punishment Number 2'. He was shipped via Southampton to the Australian base for the 4th Division at Le Havre, where he stayed for a fortnight. He was then loaded with others into a train for the front. He re-joined his old 51st Battalion near the front line at the end of the month.[583] The battalion was now under the command of an Australian-born officer for the first time, a Queenslander, Lieutenant Colonel John Ridley, appointed in February 1917 after the breakdown of Colonel Arthur Ross. Ridley was regarded as capable, but 'not an inspired leader'.[584]

Edmund Blunden remembered what happened when he returned to the British trenches from leave. 'One of the first things that I was asked in C Company dugout was, "Got any peace talk?"' Blunden recalled it as a rhetorical question, because he and his men felt only 'the endlessness of the war'. But his comrades did pose the question.[585]

If Ryan was asked, what might he have reported? We can only guess what public events he had followed in the newspapers while still at Perham Down up until his arrival back in the trenches in the high summer of 1917, and thereafter. But he was not about to abandon his settled convictions against the waste of this war.

1917: 'Peace With No Annexations and No Indemnities'

Was Ryan right? Was there a real chance for peace talks during 1917? Were the war-makers resisting this because they were still planning for aggrandisement? Let us take stock of the bigger picture – the war behind the war – once more.

Was the possibility of peace a mirage? That was certainly not what highly-placed people judged to be the case in 1917. Many on the Right of British politics – the advocates of ever more gambles with ever more men upon the battlefield in order to improve the nation's bargaining power at the diplomatic table – were terrified of peace breaking out. They predicted it, and they feared it. Viscount Esher, a veteran of Britain's Committee of Imperial Defence, and a confidante of generals, admirals, politicians, and of King George V himself, believed in the middle of 1917 that peace was just around the corner. Esher warned Lord Derby, the Secretary of State for War, in May 1917, just two months after the first Russian Revolution: 'We shall all go down before the new forces that are coming into the war. Thrones, aristocrats, plutocrats and all. Peace – a thoroughly dangerous peace – is clearly in sight.' To Lloyd George, Esher expressed it with threatening simplicity: 'We are on the high road to a peace such as no one ever dreamed of, arranged over the heads of statesmen, parliaments and armies.'[586]

In short, the pressure from below to end the war was steadily mounting, in many places. The governing piety of endless sacrifice in order to justify endless sacrifice came under challenge across war-wrecked Europe. There was a real possibility that peace might arrive irresistibly, propelled by the people's pain and their deepening disenchantment with strutting monarchs, and phrase-weaving politicians, diplomats and generals.

For a man like Ryan, there were indeed widely-reported political events that would have fascinated him, and high diplomatic events, hidden from view, that would have angered him because they vindicated so much of what he was saying.

For example, screened from the public, in the spring of 1917 various committees of the British War Cabinet were busily planning for the expansion of the Empire after victory. Committees led by the imperially-minded bluebloods, Louis du Pan Mallet, Lord Curzon, and Lord Milner, recommended a bewildering array of colonial swaps, seizures of territory, and punitive indemnities against the losers in this war.[587] Curzon's report amounted, in the words of one historian, to 'an annexationist's dream'.[588]

So ambitious were schemes for the parcelling up of Ottoman territory that one member of Lord Curzon's committee, the Tory Minister Austen Chamberlain, momentarily blanched. On 23 April 1917, he cautioned his colleagues that if the neutral powers learned of Britain's plans they might gain the impression 'that we were meditating the carving up of the world to suit our own interests'.[589]

Meanwhile, in the public realm, a king-tide of dissent was surging. In June 1917, urged by the Petrograd Soviet, Mikhail Tereshchenko, the Foreign Minister in the new Russian socialist-liberal coalition government, directly invited Russia's western allies to meet in order to revise their war aims downwards, and to prepare for peace negotiations. There was nothing secret about this approach. The Soviet's slogan, 'Peace with No Annexations and No Indemnities', first heard at Zimmerwald, was catching the public's imagination. The Entente leaders were embarrassed. They muttered inane generalities from the witchery of victory, politely sidestepped the real issues, and then brusquely dismissed the Russian invitation.[590]

Shielded from public scrutiny were more moments when opportunities for peace might have been seized. At The Hague in late June 1917, for instance, the neutral Dutch chaired meetings between British and German delegates on exchanging prisoners of war. Had there been the political will, these talks might have easily been broadened into peace negotiations. A British delegation, led by Lord Newton, met for a week with a German delegation, led by General Friedrich. The conference, observing all civilised conventions, worked from 25 June to 2 July. It was successful given its limited brief. But 'knock-out blowers' at the British Foreign Office, and among the politicians, had twisted arms to prevent the Lloyd George Government from authorising any wider discussion of peace diplomacy.[591]

At this time, there were signs inside Germany that the revolutionary ideas emanating from Russia, and the progressive ideas being advanced by America, were percolating irresistibly into the politics of the German Centre and Left. An 'Independent Social Democratic Party' was formed in April 1917, strengthening the anti-war forces on the German Left. In mid-July there was a breakthrough. A left-liberal majority in the German Reichstag pressed for the passage of a 'Peace Resolution', disavowing conquest and economic aggrandisement in the name of the German people. Moderate and humane deputies, from the Progressive People's Party, the Catholic Centre Party, and the Social Democratic Party, were cooperating together at last to force Chancellor Bethmann Hollweg's Government to come clean on Germany's war aims and negotiate 'a peace of understanding'.[592]

By July 1917, even Matthias Erzberger, the Catholic Centre Party leader pushing hard for the 'Peace Resolution' (in spite of his having flirted recklessly with 'annexationism' earlier in the war), began to mock the ultra-patriots as whack-jobs: 'One cannot pay any attention to the Pan-Germans, let them go berserk. It is cheaper to build sanatoria for them than to continue the war for another year.'[593] German politics were rapidly radicalising. At the height of the rumpus in Berlin, caught between those seeking democratisation and peace on the Left and those insisting on peace through a military conquest on the Right, Bethmann Hollweg resigned. The resolution was passed. Bethmann Hollweg's surprise right-wing replacement, Michaelis, then lasted only three months in office.[594]

Matthias Erzberger

While the 'Peace Resolution' furore erupted inside Germany, the more advanced parties in the Berlin Reichstag formed an 'Interparty Committee'. This group gained the right to meet even when the Reichstag was suspended, ramping up pressure on the government over the issues of democratisation, rationing, and peace.[595] Clearly the power of the dissenting forces inside Germany was slowly increasing.

But away from the prying eyes of the people, the German conservative and military elites persisted in planning for their peace of conquest. Why? As the industrialist Alfred Hugenberg had put it back in November 1914, the German Government would 'be well advised, in order to avoid internal difficulties, to distract the attention of the people and to give fantasies concerning the extension of German territory room to play'.[596] It was still the plan: only a fantastical victory could put a stopper on the rising social unrest inside emaciated Germany. So, three times during the spring and summer of 1917 the top German and later the Austrian negotiators met at Bad Kreuznach, in the Rhineland, bargaining – ever more unrealistically – over the plunder they still hoped to extract after imposing peace in east and west.[597]

In France also there were ominous signs. Earlier in that hot summer, the exhausted French army began to crack up. In May and June 1917, there were widespread mutinies. These led to more than three thousand courts martial and the conviction of more than twenty-three thousand French soldiers.[598] French politics too was radicalising. A former premier, Joseph Caillaux, the man who had negotiated away the threat of war with Germany provoked by imperial rivalry over Morocco in 1911, was emerging as the plausible spokesman for all those in France pressing for a negotiated peace.[599]

At the same time, the socialists of Europe were buoyant at the prospect of peace arising from the Petrograd Soviet's own project – a people's peace, with 'no annexations and no indemnities'. Dutch and Scandinavian socialists worked hand in glove with the Russians to convoke a great conference. European socialists were invited to Stockholm to frame the essentials of a moderate peace that could be supported by all progressive and democratic parties. The German and Austrian Governments did not dare forbid their socialists' attendance. Even radical opponents of the war were permitted to travel. Various socialist delegations arrived in Stockholm, and gathered in the headquarters of the Swedish Social Democratic Party, the *Folkets Hus* ('People's House') on the Norra Bantorget square in central Stockholm, ready to negotiate during that summer of soaring expectations of peace. They deliberated on the elements of a compromise peace. The putative 'Stockholm Conference' gave hope to all those on the Left who believed that a rising demand for democratisation and peace might force compromise.

But by mid-August, the Entente Powers and the United States had decided to stonewall: one by one they refused passports to their socialists to travel to Sweden. This paralysed the conference.[600] Who can say that a compromise program, let us imagine perhaps the Stockholm 'Sixteen Points', as might have emerged from Stockholm in 1917, would not have fired the idealistic imaginations of half the globe just as Wilson's 'Fourteen Points' were to do in 1918?

Again it is worth noting that many of these events gained sympathetic coverage in the *Barrier Daily Truth* during 1917 in spite of the local censor's scissors, and the intermittent prosecution of the editor.[601] In any case, it is unlikely that Ryan received direct inspiration from his hometown newspaper, unless his correspondents conveyed bits and pieces. More likely, he was putting together his indictment of the war based on what he had seen in France, and what he had managed to read in the newspapers in Britain, before being shipped back to France in July 1917.

Ryan could scarcely have trusted the *Anzac Bulletin*. Its 'Cable News from Australia' page regularly gave a megaphone to one politician above all others – Hughes. In various speeches leading up to his Nationalists' success at the federal election of May 1917, Hughes tub-thumped for war to the 'last man and last shilling', arguing that 'in no other way is it possible for Australia to be saved'. He claimed that Labor, his political home for decades past, was now 'in the hands of extremists', 'red-raggers', and 'disloyalists', men such as Percy Brookfield, recently elected in Broken Hill, whom Hughes named as typical of those who had 'no God, no Country, and no Flag' – an accusation Hughes deployed repeatedly. He argued for the essential and 'decisive victory'. 'We are against premature peace. We are for that lasting peace which can come only when the military despotism of Prussia is utterly destroyed.' Typically, the *Anzac Bulletin* featured Hughes's attack upon President Wilson's ideal of a 'Peace without Victory' as 'an appeal to the most craven, ignoble instincts'. The very few reports upon the Russian Revolution of March stressed that it was just a revolution against 'the peace intrigues of Germany'. Hughes assured readers that in Russia 'it is the head of the pro-German party that has fallen into the basket'. The Tsar's abdication, Hughes explained, meant that 'Russia is going to fight to a finish' with her 'irresistible' army. The *Anzac Bulletin* also covered repeatedly Hughes's promotion of his cherished 'trade war' against Germany, his attacks upon Ramsay MacDonald for seeking to travel to Stockholm, and his typical abuse of all those associated with the Stockholm Conference project as 'peace cranks' and 'secret agents of Germany masquerading as pacifists'.[602] War – only war – could save civilisation; such was the unvarying diet fed to the troops. Ryan, and no doubt other like-minded soldiers, would have found the *Anzac Bulletin* next to useless as a news source.

To the Shambles – Again

The timing of Ted Ryan's return to the trenches was potentially disastrous. It was the eve of General Haig's appallingly costly Third Battle of Ypres (or Passchendaele), which opened on 31 July 1917 – the worst of 'the sodden atrocities of 1917'.[603] At that time, the men of the 51st Battalion were stationed just behind the lines near Kemmel, in Belgium, preparing to take their turn in the line. The Ypres landscape lay before them – as the soldier poets described it, that 'ever yawning tomb', that muddy landscape 'where blood's the only coloured thing'.[604] The unit undertook intensive training in early August – a week of mornings devoted to 'Bayonet Fighting', 'Skirmishing', 'Gas drill', 'Musketry exercises, Rapid Loading', combined with route marching on alternate days. Every afternoon for an hour-and-a-half the men were put through their paces in 'Scouting, Bombing, Lewis Gun, Signalling, Rapid Wiring, First Aid, Guards and Sentries, Saluting and Compliments'.[605] It was a taxing schedule, no doubt, especially for any shell-shocked man.

On the morning of Sunday 12 August, some 450 to 500 men from the battalion paraded and then joined work gangs undertaking 'fatigue work', according to the unit's war diary. This meant ordinary labouring, on such tasks as 'salvage, cable laying, carrying, wiring and constructing support trenches'.[606] The men were to work during that day 'in the Forward Area', but not directly in the front-line trenches.

But on that morning, Ryan was found to be absent. After just a fortnight back with his unit, he had walked away.

To The Sea

Why? Perhaps he was driven to desperate measures by irresistible provocations. Maybe it was simply the sound of artillery, or even the smell of it, that tipped Ryan, as it tipped so many former shell-shock victims, over the edge.

There are countless documents testifying to the twin torments of artillery: the maddening sound, and the high explosive shells that produced upheavals of earth, burying soldiers alive.[607] Arthur Wheen, for example, wrote home of artillery that was 'the music of a pandemonium both day and night'. 'They scream and howl, rush, race and sail screech whistle, whirr and whiz awfully ... and boom bang and tear, without intermission.'[608] 'Shell fire', wrote Private Frank Weatherhead, 'has all the torments of Hell crammed right into your brain till your head seems to burst and you are no longer responsible for your actions'.[609] Edmund Blunden wrote of 'the mental torture' of a steady bombardment. At every blast 'our scalps seemed to be lifted and jarred with acute pain'. The smell of high explosive, coming off the 'dingy green masses of smoke' – lyddite – was an unforgettable presence in hot shell holes after a blast. [610] That stalking pungent scent could break a former shell-shocked soldier's self-control.

Many such soldiers also suffered from tinnitus (a perpetual ringing in the ears) as a result of a shell bursting very near. Exposure again to the sounds and smells of artillery, even while in training, or working near the forward area, might excite the condition. Perhaps tinnitus recurred in Ryan, and catapulted him toward making his dash for liberty.

Or perhaps it was the countless sights of atrocity that soldiers encountered. 'Dead men lay everywhere, in every attitude', Wheen wrote of the scenes confronting him in No Man's Land. 'Limbs and scraps of men were strewn among the shell holes.'[611] One British veteran remembered an artillery shell landing among men and producing a nightmare vision, reminiscent of 'a coster's barrow spilt among the traffic and splashes of fruit on the pavement'.[612] More graphically, another recalled the 'grotesquely mangled' bodies, and 'the putrefying mass of charred human flesh', all amidst 'the stinking ooze' – realities of war.[613]

Or perhaps it was a visceral revolt against militarism itself. Dos Passos, the troubled American ambulance driver, who got into strife for denouncing the war in his table-talk and letters home from the front, wrote a novel about a deserter that was published after the war. It paralleled his personal experiences. In the case of Dos Passos, his insurgency sprang from an irresistible desire to 'shake off the mud of common slavery', to be free of 'the miserable dullness of industrialised slaughter', and to escape 'the hideous farce of making men into machines'. He felt 'like a toad hopping across a road in front of a steamroller'. He longed to throw off 'the humiliating agony of this servitude'. He felt only contempt for those orators back home who sought to justify the war with their 'glittering, soap bubbles to dazzle men for a moment', their 'vast edifice of sham', and their 'gigantic phrases that floated like gaudy kites high above mankind'. The 'soggy despair throbbed in him like an infected wound' – until he escaped. Then he felt 'like a man who has come out of a dark cellar'.[614] Flight, clearly, could be a euphoric, cleansing sprint toward freedom.

Whatever the trigger, Ryan's latest rebellion was very serious. If he survived his wandering behind the lines, he would stand accused for the second time of the serious crime: 'When on Active Service Deserting His Majesty's Service'. In fact, he had absented himself while his unit was just behind the front. He had walked away – not from the firing line, but from a fatigue duty behind the line. However, according to the strict letter of military law, he had deserted the field of battle.

Ryan walked a long, long way – to the sea. Undoubtedly he had to dodge officers, and military policemen. He could have melded in with other Australian troops, but with difficulty, for his colour patch of the 51st Battalion would have marked him as a man in the wrong place. He had to find shelter, and food, and directions – so it is likely someone sympathetic to his plight assisted him. He was eventually apprehended by the military police on his thirteenth day of freedom, 25 August 1917. He was arrested in the small hours of darkness, at 3.35 a.m., at the darkened railway station near the wharves of Le Havre, on the French coast. Here was the Australian base where he had been just a month before. Somehow, Ryan had threaded his way to the Atlantic coast, more than 300 kilometres to the west.

How did he do it? We shall never know. Perhaps like-minded soldiers shielded him, helped him, or looked the other way? Almost certainly, considering the distance, he hitched a ride. By some mixture of means, he journeyed back to the west, along the choked capillaries feeding the open wound of the war. There were unforgettable images along the way: Mottram remembered 'that eternal procession of men, men, mules, limbers, men, guns, ambulances, men, lorries going on and on like some gigantic frieze'.[615] What Ryan did, what sights he saw, how he escaped detection, what food if anything he managed to eat, will all remain undiscovered. But his intention was clear enough: presumably he was attempting to reach the sea, and then England.

Siren Calls: Stockholm and the Vatican

Who can estimate what was in his mind while Ted Ryan was on the run? His private terrors must have absorbed him.

But once again to understand the full scale of the catastrophe in Europe in 1917 – made worse by the squashing of opportunities to end it – we should again change our vantage point, back up, and look to the wider public realm. For political events were being played out that reflected exactly the convictions Ryan had outlined in his letter to Ramsay MacDonald nine months previously: the need for wild war aims to be resisted and for a compromise peace settlement to be attempted.

Two events in August 1917 draw the eye.

First, at the moment Ryan escaped from the front line on 12 August, a major political furore had just erupted in Britain. Arthur Henderson, the mild-mannered Labour Party man with two sons at the front, the blunt-speaking trade unionist who had so far been loyal to Lloyd George and had been appointed to his War Cabinet in December 1916 to symbolise working-class patriotism, suddenly broke ranks. In early August he had come to the conviction that he must support the projected international socialist conference at Stockholm, and press for British representatives to go. He had been sent to Russia in the summer of 1917 to rally pro-war opinion; but he had seen that the war was more and more discredited there because the Entente Powers refused to wash their hands of imperialist goals. He foresaw that Russia's young democracy might go down the gurgle hole of history if the war was prolonged. So, upon his return, Henderson guided his party to an astonishing decision: to send delegates to the proposed conference at the Social Democratic headquarters in Stockholm. British delegates should be there, he insisted, to sit down with neutral, German, and Austrian socialists. Moderates should talk to moderates. The nuts and bolts of a negotiated peace should be worked out. On 10 August, an enraged Lloyd George promptly sacked Henderson. In the aftermath of this sensation, the British Labour Party shifted to the Left, with key leaders joining socialists and radicals in urging the revision of war aims and a negotiated end to the war. The alliance between Labour and Lloyd George's 'knock-out blow' coalition was over.[616]

Second, while Ryan made his improbable journey toward Le Havre in August 1917, there was a major diplomatic development that slowly percolated into the world's press: Pope Benedict XV issued a new peace proposal, and the Vatican publicly released this on 10 August. It was studded with Wilsonian rhetoric, pointing the way toward a new international order. The Papal Note urged the acceptance by all of the principle of international arbitration, so that at last 'the moral force of right should be substituted for the material force of arms'. The Pope pleaded for the winding back of war aims by all in order to achieve a negotiated settlement. It would be based upon 'the true freedom and community of the seas', the 'reciprocal condonation' of all war costs and damages, and the 'reciprocal restitution' of all seized territories, including Belgium and the captured German colonies. There were to be no annexations, for anyone. Into the future, a new international organisation would guarantee the peace deal, enforcing 'sanctions' against any state refusing arbitration of international questions. All would agree to the 'simultaneous and reciprocal reduction of armaments'. Territorial disputes, urged the Papal Note, should be resolved in a 'spirit of equity and justice' through round-table negotiations.[617]

This was undoubtedly a spectacular diplomatic initiative, for Catholics everywhere to admire and be stirred to action – if they could read the full text. But strict censorship in Australia allowed only summaries to appear in the newspapers. The pro-war press savaged it anyway, as a German-inspired trick. Catholics had to wait for more than a month for the full text to appear.[618] Meanwhile, the leaders of the Entente governments, led by London, prepared to squash the Papal initiative as they had agreed they would do in the secret Treaty of London of April 1915.

Then, President Wilson stepped in ahead of his partners, whom he did not consult, to answer the Pope. He struck an uncompromising tone, typical of the new 'line' that he had adopted since taking the United States into the war in April 1917. Within months, Wilson, the former idealist advocate of a negotiated peace without victory, had transformed himself into an angry advocate of the doctrine of peace *through* victory.

Fugitive expectations that Wilson might still favour a negotiated end to the war swiftly faded. He refused to support Russian diplomatic efforts to achieve a compromise peace during 1917. He failed to challenge his new Western partners on their imperialist aims, clearly believing that he could not liberalise these until Americans had fought, and until Britain and France were 'financially in our hands'.[619] He came to believe passionately that only if the United States entered the war with total commitment could he prevail in the democratic peacemaking and nation-building that he envisioned would follow after victory – a peace without conquest. So war 'to make the world safe for democracy' was retailed everywhere by American propagandists as if it were the eleventh commandment. As the French journalist and politician André Tardieu would write: 'When Americans fall in love with an idea, even if their enthusiasm does not last, it is always intense.'[620]

Wilson was steadily more vehement in his attacks on Berlin. For example, in his Flag Day Address of 14 June 1917, he had depicted the German Government and its 'military masters' as despotic, implacable and unworthy of trust – and thus it was impossible for him to recognise them as a partner in negotiations. Sounding very much like Hughes, Wilson denounced the 'sinister intrigue' for an early peace being pursued in the West by the 'agents and dupes' of Berlin.[621] (A few months later, Wilson would publicly denounce American pacifists for their 'stupidity.'[622]) If Ted Ryan had become aware of this big shift in Wilson's invective – the Wilson whom he had so admired for his peace initiative in December 1916 – it could only have added to his disgust at the lengthening war, and possibly fuelled his determination to abandon it.

In any case, on 27 August 1917 Wilson was the first of the Western leaders to reject forcefully the Pope's Note, after less than three weeks' deliberation in Washington. In a unilateral and brusque reply to the Vatican, he ruled out a compromise peace with the 'ambitious and intriguing government' in Berlin.[623] He could not 'take the word of the present rulers of Germany as a guarantee of anything that is to endure', he declared. This suggested that America was demanding regime change. Wilson appeared to call upon 'the German people' to stage a revolution against the 'irresponsible' militarists in Berlin, who had 'secretly planned to dominate the world'. He was not entirely one-eyed: he also took a swipe at all plans on all sides for 'selfish and exclusive economic leagues' after the war which displeased London and Paris. But, much relieved by Wilson's tough rhetoric denouncing Germany's leaders, Britain and France chose to ignore the Pope's offer and to shelter behind Wilson's reply, while ignoring his little dig at their plans for economic war after the war. The British Foreign Office warned the government that it was best to avoid all discussion of a united reply to the Pope, for clarifying war aims was 'very undesirable just now' considering that revolutionary Russia favoured the winding back of imperial ambitions. So Lloyd George's Cabinet eventually decided in late August to issue no formal British reply to the Pope at all, and to urge Britain's allies to fall in behind the hollow pretence that Wilson's idealistic war aims exactly matched their own.[624]

The Germans did reply formally to the Vatican in mid-September. It was a relatively progressive document, embracing the ideals of future disarmament, 'obligatory arbitration', and new supra-national organisations.[625] But the German elite spoiled the moment. By a mixture of deception, cajolery, and practical arguments, the moderate committee representing the pro-peace Reichstag majority was persuaded not to push for a specific public disavowal of any German intention to retain Belgian territory in the official reply to the Pope ahead of any talks. The pan-Germans wanted no such surrendering of this valuable bargaining chip in advance, although a back down in negotiation was widely expected. Thus, while hundreds of thousands of hapless soldiers on both sides faced battle in the hellish landscapes around Ypres and Passchendaele through the autumn of 1917, the stonehearted men from the Cabinets, chancelleries, and foreign offices stumbled about evasively and allowed another peace opportunity to founder.[626]

Would Ryan have known any of this? Probably not. While on the run from 12 August, and indeed after his arrest on 25 August, Ryan had as much chance as any other soldier in the battle-zone of following the latest diplomatic news – practically none. Generally no reading matter was given to prisoners. And again, if by chance Ryan caught sight of the ubiquitous *Anzac Bulletin*, he would have been no wiser. It blotted out all inconvenient news. Judging from its pages from August-September 1917, neither the Henderson affair nor the Papal Peace Note ever happened. But probably Ryan needed no special knowledge of the tall hypocrisies of the summer and autumn of 1917 to strengthen the anti-war convictions that he had first expressed at Perham Down a year before.

Perhaps Ryan was just like Dos Passos, who in August 1917 was working with his team of ambulance men near Verdun. 'The war is utter damn nonsense – a vast cancer fed by lies', Dos Passos wrote in his diary, just two days before Ryan was arrested. 'Of all the things in this world a government is the thing least worth fighting for. None of the poor devils whose mangled dirty bodies I take to the hospital in my ambulance really give a damn about any of the aims of this ridiculous affair.'[627]

Once arrested in the darkness at Le Havre on 25 August, Ryan was immediately imprisoned. Then, over the next few days, under close arrest, he was allocated to a group of soldiers being sent east, for the front, and returned to his 51st Battalion – for punishment.

The Château de Bomy, scene of Private Ryan's first Field General Court Martial, 12 September 1917, at which he was sentenced to death.

Chapter 19

DEFIANCE – AND DEATH SENTENCE

CHATEAU DE BOMY, SEPTEMBER 1917

Tears came and sobs ... and I couldn't help them ... dressing a shattered body, out in the night, by the cold hard thin light of the moon. Hatred surges up, and [all] the while you're cutting blood and mud soaked tunics – feeling life blood thick on the stretcher, & winding white gauze over slowly welling blood and a muddied wound. Stretchers in the ankle mud – and their mates around the chaps they've carried over.... 'Andy hasn't been dressed' – 'Over here digger.' Oh God, if I die I'm Australian.
And then poor bodies lie under blankets ... two chaps came over to me and said, 'He died mate! What will we do – he only came out of the line tonight, can we take him away in the morning?' And I wrote the dead boy's name on a ticket, and pinned it on the blanket.[628]

— Private Frank H. Molony, 1st Australian Field Ambulance, 27 October 1917

On 11 September 1917, Brigadier-General William Glasgow, commander of the Australian 13th Infantry Brigade, comprising four infantry battalions, which included Ryan's 51st Battalion, ordered a Field General Court Martial to try Private Ryan. At that time, all the battalions of the 13th Brigade were in training once again, well behind the lines, near the village of Matringhem, about 73 kilometres to the south-west of Ypres. But because Ryan was to be charged with desertion, and was thus formally on trial for his life, the court martial was almost certainly held higher up, at the staff headquarters of the 4th Infantry Division – although the place of the court martial is not recorded on the surviving stripped-down account of the proceedings. At that time, the staff had taken possession of the beautiful eighteenth-century pile, the Château de Bomy, some five kilometres north-east of Matringhem. On the balance of probabilities, this is where the court martial was convened.

Rough Justice

The *Field* General Court Martial was the most intimidating of the four types of courts martial available. At these courts martial, the procedures were slimmed down in the interests of swift 'justice', if the meaning of the word may be stretched. Thus, various protections for the accused that had a hit-and-miss existence anyway in the District Courts Martial and in the General Courts Martial were often entirely absent in the rules governing the Field General Courts Martial. Yet the latter had the power to sentence a soldier to death. Clearly, the dilutions in the rules of procedure pointed the way toward 'rough justice': only three officers were needed to sit at the court martial, and only minimum rank was required; the pre-trial rights of the accused were severely curtailed; his rights to representation and advice during the court martial were withdrawn; there was no minimum twenty-four-hours' notice of the start of the trial; and the documents to be recorded were minimal.[629] Not surprisingly, the conviction rates at the Field General Courts Martial were significantly higher than in other types of courts martial.[630]

The military authorities were supposed to have recourse to this inevitably harsh brand of courts martial when military exigencies made it 'not practicable' to summon the General or District Court Martial. However, class prejudice was clearly at work in the streaming of rankers toward Field General Courts Martial, and of officers toward General Courts Martial. The British statistics (which covered the colonial forces) provided clear evidence of systematic injustice. Practicability was supposed to dictate the choice for a Field General Court Martial when abroad. Supposedly, military exigencies rendered it impossible to try ordinary soldiers serving abroad, with the minimum safeguards of the General Court Martial in place, but almost invariably it was possible to try officers by this means. Thus, the overwhelming bulk of those who endured Field General Court Martial abroad were soldiers, while almost all officers were funnelled to a General Court Martial – with a minimum of five brother-officers to judge them.[631] Of course, it was in quest of better discipline in the ranks that the ordinary soldiers endured the rougher end of military justice.

Thus, on the first page of Private Ryan's court martial record, 'Army Form A. 3', the 'Form for Assembly and Proceedings of Field General Court Martial on Active Service', a pre-printed statement appeared: 'And whereas I am of opinion that it is not practicable that such offences should be tried by an ordinary General Court Martial.' Nothing was required to substantiate the claim, and nothing was written down. The idea conjured out of thin air, of course, was that some kind of military emergency – shrapnel screeching, fire and flame – dictated this resort to something near to the fabled 'drum-head' court martial. In fact, Ryan's court martial, like so many others, was being convened at some distance from the front, in a Brigade Headquarters.

The Higher Powers at the Château de Bomy

At this point in the war, the AIF's courts-martial teams had set aside separate days of the week to hold courts martial for the different Australian divisions. Wednesdays had been established as a 'courts-martial day' for soldiers from the 4th Division. Thus, it was at the grand Château de Bomy that Ryan faced his Field General Court Martial on Wednesday 12 September 1917.

The setting of the trial no doubt had its own power to intimidate. The perfectly symmetrical Château de Bomy still stands. It had been built in white stone for an eighteenth-century French noble family, just before the decade of revolutionary events in France had smashed the fortunes of such families. This relic of the late feudal age was three-storeys high, counting the rooms in the ceiling space. It featured two narrow wings extending forward from the main building, with superb tall windows overlooking a private park and lawn for games. Prisoners arriving under guard might have paused to admire the grandeur of the building, park and gardens, before crunching their way over the gravel drive, then entering a hall and an anteroom to await their turn for justice. The sight of high-ranking military officers, with red tabs, Sam Browne belts, and swagger sticks, clanking across the parquetry inside, could only have added to the sense of powerlessness endured by the accused. And the timber-panelled rooms, with their tapestries, gilt, mirrors, and ornate fireplaces, impressed everyone, not just the men under guard. One Australian courts-martial officer, Athol Lewis, wrote of the 'magnificent grounds' surrounding such châteaux, and of one especially grand room used for the trials, which 'had some magnificent furniture in it – & good old paintings'.[632] Class hierarchies were woven into the whole system. Lewis had noticed this upon joining the other courts-martial officers at the request of General John Monash. First, Lewis had visited the general's headquarters, had been informed of his promotion, and then immediately invited to dine in the officers' mess for the first time. Lewis was struck by the numbers of fellows he met in the mess whom he immediately remembered as chums from his private school and law studies at Melbourne University. Old pals and old times were rediscovered.[633]

The wording of the charge against Ryan at the Château de Bomy was significant: 'When on active service deserting his Majesty's Service'. The *Army Act 1881* (UK) specified under section 12 that soldiers could face a death sentence if they deserted 'when on active service'. This was defined as being the case when soldiers were 'engaged in operations against the enemy', or were 'in a country or place wholly or partly occupied by the enemy', or were 'in military occupation of any foreign country'. Such deserters were indeed 'liable to suffer death'.[634] As noted previously, the AIF men in France served under the British *Army Act 1881*. A note on the court-martial papers again preserved the fact: Ryan was to be tried under 'A.A. Sect. 12 (1a)' – the *Army Act 1881*. Thus, on the face of it, he was on trial for his life.

A Coy 51st Battalion
France

Sir,

The following statement is my conscientious reasons for my past conduct being such as it is.

Previous to enlisting as a soldier in the Australian Army that Germany intended to crush her European enemies & by so doing had adopted the policy of "might is right" which is opposed to the ideals of Humanity & Civilisation. About eleven months ago, England to my mind adopted the same policy towards Germany. England's policy at that time consisted of no peace-conference until Germany was crushed so as to teach them a lesson of virtue. When the war had reached this stage, it was no longer a war of resistance.

Statements like the following: "Hands off Peace-makers, hands off America!" "We must crush Germany now, once & for all", proves that England's policy was one of aggression. Our Premier Mr Lloyd George gambled with Human lives to obtain those ends. The Premiers statements goes to prove that it was only a gamble. Instead of telling America to keep her hands off, he is telling us that America is the balance of power.

I enlisted to fight for a Peace without conquerors or conquered, as a race under those conditions as nothing to justify

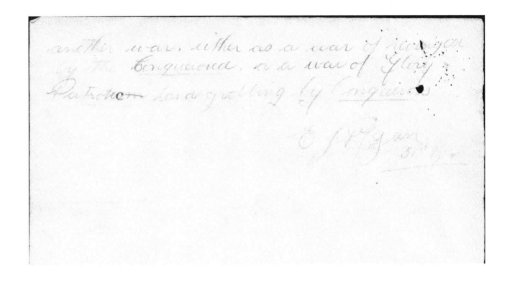

The first page of Ted Ryan's statement to his court martial, 12 September 1917.
See full transcript in Appendix 2.

But the court martial records show that the men in the stiff-visored caps were not quite so distant from the accused this time.[635] For one thing, they were comparatively young. By the autumn of 1917, officers running courts martial 'in the field' in France were certainly younger than those whom Ryan had faced at the camp at Perham Down. Of course, they were still 'officer class', and still wielded ultimate power from behind their emblems of separate status, their pipped epaulettes, shining buttons, glistening boots and Sam Brownes. Of course, there was no jury to impress. Ryan's chief prosecutor was Major Charles Fortescue, DSO, MC, a rapidly promoted 24-year-old officer, a graduate from the expensive Toowoomba Grammar School, a jeweller in civilian life who had joined up within days of the outbreak of war, and had served at Gallipoli. But assisting him were two more humble-born men. Lieutenant Philip Herman Weston was a 26-year-old 'dairy hand', English-born, who had joined up early, in Adelaide in September 1914. Completing the line-up was Lieutenant William James Hall, a 27-year-old teacher from Hughenden, Queensland, who had been in the forces for just a little over a year. As usual, none of these men had legal training.

The surviving records bear testimony to cut-down justice. There was no Courts Martial Officer or Judge Advocate present. There was no 'Charge Sheet', and no 'Summary of Evidence', as might have been useful in pre-trial defence preparations. Indeed, there is no record of Ryan being given an officer to act as his legal counsel, that is, to act as 'friend of the accused'. He had no counsel.

Private Ryan Tells His Truth

Again, Ryan did not make it easy for his accusers: he pleaded 'Not guilty'. If he was to go down, he would go down swinging. So, the evidence against him had to be assembled.

It was formidable. The first witness, Corporal Charles Town, explained that he had been acting as Ryan's Sergeant when he warned him on the evening of 11 August that he must parade the next morning at 7.15 a.m. ready for a 'fatigue' – labouring. Town saw Ryan that morning at 7.10 a.m. But five minutes later he was gone. He instituted a search, in vain. A second witness, Lance Corporal B.C. March, a British military policeman, described seeing Ryan at the end of his adventure: in the Gare des Voyageurs, the railway station, at Le Havre, at about 3.35 a.m. on 25 August. He had immediately arrested him. Showing their determination to put Ryan under the harrow, the President of the court had ordered March to travel a great distance to appear at the court martial. To complete the prosecution, an officer then produced Ryan's 'conduct sheet', his 'B122' form, providing 'Evidence as to Character.' Of course, this showed his record of various AWOLs, and his two courts martial – all damning stuff so far as the officers were concerned.

Ryan's chance to defend himself then came. For the first time in his encounters with the military justice system, he did not keep hidden his political objections to the war. It was the centrepiece of his defence.

Ryan declined to speak. But he produced a gritty written statement. Undated, and hand-written in his fine script, this was explosive. It outlined his continuing political objections to the prolonged war, and to the rapidly escalating war aims of the British – so far as he knew them. The proceedings of the trial show that the document was 'read over' by the officers, which probably means that it was read in silence rather than aloud.

In two pages, Ryan explained his purpose: he wanted to give an explanation of his 'consciencous [sic] reasons', as he described them, for his 'past conduct'. He had enlisted, he wrote, from generous and moral motives, to resist aggression. Germany, he explained, had planned 'to crush her European enemies and by so doing had adopted the policy of "might is right" which is opposed to the ideals of Humanity and Civilisation'. But he had come to realise, he argued, that Britain was little better. He harked back directly to the themes of his letter to Ramsay MacDonald of October 1916, in which he had complained bitterly about Lloyd George's 'knock-out blow' interview and his reckless spurning of American offers to mediate peace:

> About eleven months ago, England to my mind adopted the same policy[636] towards Germany. England's policy at that time consis[ted] of no peace-conferences until Germany was crushed so as to teach them a lesson of virtue. When the war had reached this stage, it was no longer a war of resistance.

Statements like the following – hands off Peace-makers – hands off America: We must crush Germany now, once and for all, proves that England's policy was one of aggression. Our Premier Mr Lloyd George gambled with Human lives to obtain those ends. The Premier's statements goes [sic] to prove that it was only a gamble, instead of telling America now to keep her hands off, he is telling us that America is the balance of power.

I enlisted to fight for a Peace without conquerors or conquered, as a Peace under those conditions as [does?] nothing to justify another war, either as a war of revenge by the Conquered, or a war of Glory and Patriotic land-grabbing by Conquerors.[637]

Here was a passionate, politically inspired, and consistent protest against the war. The phrase 'Peace without conquerors' directly recalled Wilson's 'Peace without Victory' speech. But notably, Ryan did not mention more recent developments, such as the socialists' Stockholm conference and the Pope's peace offer. Possibly he was unaware of them. Lloyd George was still in his sights. Here was a private soldier scolding the British Prime Minister – on paper! It was the war-makers' determination to repel mediation that had sickened Ryan back in the autumn and winter of 1916, and he dwelt upon it still. He must have been aware of the two stupendous international events of the spring of 1917: the Russian Revolution, and the hopes for peace it ignited, on the one hand, and the American decision to enter the war, and the dwindling of hope for an early peace on account of it, on the other. But Ryan did not mention Russia – a wise move. Rather, his statement signalled his bitterness over the irony that Lloyd George, who had rebuffed America as a neutral mediator to end the war in late 1916, was now preaching the indispensability of America as the decisive force buttressing Western power in 1917. Clearly, Ryan had at least some knowledge of the complex international debates provoked by American intervention in this protracted war, now entering its fourth year.

And clearly this soldier from Broken Hill was not merely interested in saving one special Private Ryan. He wanted the war ended, and all the lowly 'Private Ryans' saved.

Echoes of Broken Hill – and Beyond

What lay behind Ryan's convictions? His judgements of world events, such as they were presented in the British press? Or was Ryan motivated at all by the political news from Australia? We know that he had expressed fierce disapproval of Hughes at the time of the conscription referendum in October 1916. What Australian news might have shaped his opinions since then?

It cannot be established with certainty that mail from his friends and family in Broken Hill was reaching him at the front. He had written proudly of his big bundle of mail waiting for him at Perham Down in October 1916. But in France since July 1917?

We simply do not know. But even if nothing had followed Ryan to France, something of the spirit of Broken Hill seems to have possessed him. At the very least, he might have learned from his earlier mail that the war machine he was serving in France was more and more controversial back home in Australia. The Labor movement in Broken Hill, as ever, had been in the vanguard of a push against the conscription and war. Letters Ryan received up until his departure from Perham Down in mid-July 1917 may well have fired his rebellion.

In fact, a spirit of defiance in the face of war, such as Ryan demonstrated in August and September 1917, had driven many to political agitation in Australia at exactly this time.

The defeat of the first conscription referendum in October 1916 had set the scene. Hughes's decision to walk away from the Federal Labor Party following his defeat was a political bombshell. Then, Hughes had negotiated behind the scenes with the Opposition for a coalition that could preserve his prime ministership. Hughes, the inveterate Labor bruiser, eventually chose to team up with conservative men who had been his political enemies for half a lifetime. This provoked volcanic political passions. Instantly, the majority faction of the Federal Labor Party turned on Hughes as a despicable 'rat'. Labor was full of contempt for his 'Australian National War Government' as it grandly and controversially christened itself. In Hughes's Cabinet of twelve men sat five formerly Labor Ministers – also despised as 'rats'. Labor, bitterly divided, went down before Hughes and his new Nationalist allies in the federal election of 5 May 1917. Bizarrely, the result indicated that a majority of the Australian people rejected conscription, and yet a majority still endorsed a pro-war government. This did nothing to cool tempers. To say the least, throughout 1917 Australians remained deeply divided on the seemingly endless war.

A spectacular proof of this division came at the beginning of August 1917 in Sydney. A great strike began among railway and tramway workers at the Eveleigh Railway Workshops and the Randwick Tramsheds. It spread rapidly. Eventually, more than 77,000 workers joined the mass strike.[638]

The stoppage unleashed the poisonous politics of loyalty and disloyalty. The strikers were smeared as 'disloyalists', betraying the AIF and siding with Germany. The government invited 'loyalists' to help break the strike of these 'traitors'. Feelings ran high. But in spite of the huffing and puffing against the strikers' treachery from politicians, preachers and editors, supporters of the strike flocked to the frequent demonstrations in Sydney, with mass meetings of unprecedented size. Eventually, up to 100,000 people filled the Sydney Domain to voice their backing for the strikers. At the head of one column of marchers, returned AIF men displayed a large banner, which read 'WE WHO FOUGHT IN THE TRENCHES ARE FIGHTING FOR AUSTRALIAN DEMOCRACY AT HOME'.[639]

On the face of things, the mass strike that began in Sydney was simply about a despised new 'card' system of measuring productivity at work – 'Taylorism', as it was called. But controversies over conscription, high prices, and the justice of the war itself bubbled to the surface during the dispute. Strikers denounced the Hughes Government for the relentless victimisation of all critics of the war. The government in turn sought to shut the mouths of pacifists of all brands, Labor MPs, women peace activists, troublesome Catholic priests, mild-mannered Quakers, and the firebrands of the 'Wobblies' (as the members of the 'Industrial Workers of the World' group, or IWW, were known). All were smeared as 'German sympathisers'.

The nets of emergency power in the hands of the government, the scores of regulations issued under the *War Precautions Act 1914*, reinforced by the *Unlawful Associations Act 1916*, caught many men and women of the labour movement, from the handfuls of genuine 'revolutionaries' to the many more ordinary trade unionists and even Labor parliamentarians who happened to speak critically of the British Empire and its war. In Catholic circles most especially there was criticism of harsh British policies in Ireland, which had been under martial law since the Easter Rising of 1916. The Hughes Government, fortified by its power to rule virtually by decree and buttressed by the fanatically pro-war press, had great power to intimidate all such critics – scurvy knaves in its eyes. But, as the crowds demonstrating in Sydney in August 1917 showed only too clearly, many tens of thousands of people were willing to stand up against the catcalls of 'traitor', 'disloyalist' and 'pro-German'.[640]

Events inside Australia echoed events in Europe. The radical spirit in Australian Labor circles had been inspired in part by the first Russian Revolution of March 1917, the mass action that had created the republic. Agitation for peace and democratisation stoked unrest in many nations in the aftermath of the collapse of Tsarism. As we have seen, demands for a negotiated end to the war grew louder in strike-bound and famished Germany in April 1917, where a new breakaway anti-war socialist party, the Independent Socialist Party of Germany (USPD) had been formed. The dream that the war might be ended in Stockholm captivated many on the European left. In Britain, a powerful gathering of labour leaders and trade unionists at Leeds in June, the so-called 'Leeds Convention', welcomed the March Russian Revolution, urged the revision of the Entente's imperialist war aims, and demanded a negotiated peace. The Papal Peace Note of August 1917 both reflected and encouraged this new mood. Wherever people's lives and fortunes were being ruined by war, voices were rising in protest.[641]

One soldier standing in a gilded room in the Château de Bomy on that autumn day in 1917 to receive his sentence was in no way a mere grumbler in the ranks. What Ryan put down on paper at his court martial was a denunciation of the war-makers' vainglory such as could be heard at many labour gatherings across Australia, and the world. Ryan's accusations – that the war was a war of conquest and that those directing it had slammed the door on good prospects for peace – were the same accusations thrown at the men of the governing classes, in city squares and in parliaments across Europe and America, and in far away Broken Hill.[642]

Why did the war-makers insist on war until the enemy was crushed? Why did they shun 'peace traps' as they always called them? Why did the 'bitter-enders' – the 'never-endians' as critics dubbed them – insist upon gambling so extravagantly with human lives, until the enemy was on his knees? Why did they demand a dictated peace? After all, Wilson himself had argued before entering the war that only a 'peace without victory' could last. Of course, Wilson had changed his mind by the summer of 1917, joining Paris and London in denying socialists their passports to Stockholm. Could it be true that the war was really a crusade for high ideals, for democracy and civilisation, as Wilson now insisted? Or were all out for glory, land-grabbing, economic gain, and their own political salvation through victory?

In Ryan's statement at the Château de Bomy, one could catch the spirit of 1917 – a seething spirit of defiance.

Death Sentence

Of course, Private Ryan's political objections to the war could never have saved him at his court martial. The officers judging his case had no choice. Their duty was to preserve military discipline, whether they sympathised or not with Ryan's political objections. The officers had to be worried that soldiers choosing to walk away, for whatever reason, left more work for others to do, and thinner lines facing the enemy. Ryan, they knew, had made his choice and would have to face his punishment.

Some officers may even have shared Ryan's cynicism about the purposes of the long war. One British soldier famously recalled an officer addressing his men while flourishing contemptuously a pamphlet entitled *Allied War Aims*. 'I've got some bumff here I'm supposed to read to you', he said. 'But you've heard all this balls before.'[643] Perhaps, more than a few AIF soldiers shared Ryan's convictions. Certainly, men under fire can be forgiving toward those soldiers who break ranks.

None of that mattered in this court martial. Ryan was stuck fast in the net of military law.

Therefore, on 12 September 1917, Major Charles Fortescue, Lieutenant Weston, and Lieutenant Hall predictably found Ryan guilty of the crime of desertion. Following the procedures laid down, a detail of soldiers would then have taken Ryan away from the court room to detention. At this point, he knew his verdict, but not his sentence.

The three officers judging Ryan would have moved immediately to the next stage of the court martial, the sentencing. All three had to agree if 'Death' was the decision. But 'Death' it was. The slim record of the court martial was signed by Fortescue, as President, and sent up the line of command for confirmation. Probably later, one officer underlined the word 'Death' in blue pencil on the court-martial record for the attention of the senior ranking officers. Thus, Ryan became one of only 121 Australian troops actually sentenced to death by Australian courts martial during the Great War.[644]

Those officers in authority above the court considered the matter of confirmation over the next fortnight. The British commander of the AIF's 4th Division, Major General Ewen Sinclair-Maclagan, signed up on 19 September, but he reserved the matter: he directed that Ryan be held in detention, that is, near at hand, and not despatched to a permanent prison until General Birdwood, Commander of the First Anzac Corps, had looked at the documents. He sent these on to Birdwood for final confirmation of the verdict and death sentence. Would Ryan be executed? Birdwood entered his decision and signed on 24 September: 'I commute the sentence to 5 yrs P.S. [Penal Servitude] and confirm the finding and sentence as now commuted.'[645] Ryan's new battalion commander, Lieutenant Colonel Ridley, signed on 5 October, and finally the verdict and sentence were 'promulgated' by being read to the 51st Battalion on that day. Probably, Ryan found out only on that day.

Why was Ryan not shot? Answering that question requires a little exploration of the context. During 1916 and again in 1917, General Birdwood (the British general in command of Australian forces from December 1914) had repeatedly pressed the Australian Government to get tough and agree to the use of the death penalty to deter desertion. He argued that executions were vital in order to restore discipline among the Australians. 'I cannot help feeling that the power of inflicting this, and possibly the carrying out of it in one or two cases, would at once put a stop to desertion, which is, as you see, becoming prevalent', Birdwood wrote to Defence Minister George Pearce in May 1917.[646]

High-ranking Australian officers agreed. For instance, at various times, those in the command structure directly above Ryan's 51st Battalion, namely Brigadier William Glasgow of the 13th Brigade, and Major General Sir William Holmes, commander of the 4th Division (from January 1917 until his death at the front in July), had backed up Birdwood in his plea for executions.[647] Major General Sir Charles Rosenthal, of the 4th Australian Divisional Artillery, was another who recommended capital punishment. On 4 July 1917 he preserved one such decision in his diary: 'This morning I attended to various papers including several Court Martials. I found it absolutely necessary to recommend the death sentence in the case of 4 men guilty of desertion.' Later that same afternoon Rosenthal distracted himself from such distasteful duties, recording proudly that he had 'attended at the Bailleul Town Square to meet His Majesty King George'.[648] Rosenthal never wavered in his conviction. Toward the end of the war, he even went public in his support for the death penalty.[649]

Officers on the courts-martial circuit also pressed for executions. Lieutenant Edwin Brissenden, a King's Counsel, wrote back to his friend Mr Justice Ferguson at the Supreme Court House in King Street, Sydney, in September 1917, the very month Ryan was tried: 'I don't expect you hear much of these things in Australia but there is desertion, and it is regrettable that the foolish sentiment of the old ladies in Melbourne won't let us shoot a few.' By 'the old ladies' he meant, of course, the Ministers of the Australian Government. Brissenden argued that 'rank, calculating, dishonourable Cowardice' had to be crushed. He cited the cases of three young men who had left the front line in the hours before combat. In previous battles, he conceded, they had been 'buried' or 'stunned, by shells' and lived 'under constant rain, and under shell fire that never let up'. Such men, wrote Brissenden, were typical of those who had reached the point where they had simply told themselves 'I've had as much as I can stand – I want a rest'. In Brissenden's opinion, these young soldiers who had 'drifted out' of the line had been rightly sentenced to death, but then their sentences had been commuted. The 'British rule of thumb method' would have been far better, the ghoulish Brissenden reasoned because a man who was 'always a bad soldier and shirker' should be shot.[650]

Brissenden was not exceptional. The permanent President of all Field General Courts Martial in the 4th Division, Major Arthur Hyman, a lawyer from Sydney, recalled returning to Divisional Headquarters after his round of courts martial to be confronted with staff officers asking: 'How many men have you hanged today?'[651]

None were hung. None were shot. To allow the death penalty following a court martial, the Hughes Government would have had to amend the controversial section 98 of Australia's own *Defence Act 1903*. Section 98 was quite precise: 'No member of the Defence Force shall be sentenced to death by any court-martial except for mutiny, *desertion to the enemy*, or traitorously delivering up to the enemy any garrison, fortress, post, guard, or ship, vessel, or boat, or traitorous correspondence with the enemy; and no sentence of death passed by any court-martial shall be carried into effect until confirmed by the Governor-General.'[652] Thus, there were only *four* grounds for a death sentence at a court martial. Most notably, mere desertion could not of itself attract a death sentence – only desertion to the enemy side, an exceedingly rare thing.[653] In practice, therefore, the Australian Parliament in 1903, borrowing from earlier colonial legislation, had happily carved out real protections for Australian troops from the 29 offences under which they might otherwise have been sentenced to death under the British *Army Act 1881*.

Yet, as in the case of Ted Ryan's Field General Court Martial, Australian officers passed death sentences, in undeviating loyalty to the *Army Act 1881* knowing that these sentences were, after all, contingent. In effect, they waited upon the General Officer Commanding to commute them, at the moment of 'confirmation' of the sentence, trusting that he would recognise that he was bound to do so under Australia's *Defence Act 1903*.[654]

What was really happening here? Australian officers were clearly embarrassed by the rising tide of AWOL, desertion, and consequent courts martial. Perhaps some officers cherished the hope that the accumulation of death sentences might add to the weight of the case for change, and so hurry on the day of reckoning for deserters.

Thus, the number of death sentences handed down by Australian courts martial kept increasing during 1916 and 1917, before falling away in 1918.[655]

Why did the Hughes Government not move to expose the men of the AIF to the wider threat of capital punishment under the British *Army Act 1881*?[656] Hughes himself clearly had no compunctions. In April 1915, arguing for the death penalty under Australia's War Precautions Bill, he had told the Parliament: 'Death is no new thing, and the death penalty is not new. If a man deserves death, why should he not get his deserts?'[657] But in the lead-up to the first conscription referendum in October 1916, the Hughes Government was clearly loath to do anything to raise suspicion on the issue. This would have been politically uncomfortable for two reasons. First, talk of capital punishment was in the air, because the radical Queensland Labor government of Premier T.J. Ryan (an anti-conscriptionist) had introduced a bill to abolish all capital punishment in that state in August 1916, provoking much publicity before it was defeated.[658] Second, there had been some bad press. The British military authorities' shipping of 30 conscientious objectors to the front in May and June 1916, in order to court martial and then execute them, had only just been averted by last-minute pleas to the British Government from Radical MPs. This and similar stories on the mistreatment of conscientious objectors were splashed about in the pages of the anti-conscriptionist press in Australia.[659] In this context, the Hughes Government wisely offered no hint that it contemplated any amendment to the *Defence Act 1903* that might lead to death sentences for conscripts. Neither Hughes nor Pearce objected to firing squads at the front from positions of principle. Both conceded the military case for shooting deserters. But political expediency dictated their choice. They saw the vehemence of opposition to both conscription and executions. In November 1916 Pearce explained to Fisher, the former Labor Prime Minister installed as High Commissioner in London, that he feared 'bloodshed' in Australia if the government had moved to impose conscription by legislation.[660]

During 1917, the Hughes Government came under fresh pressure from both Australian and British military authorities, and from Lloyd George's Government. Perhaps there was renewed hope among the British and the Australian top brass that the Hughes Government, fortified by its federal election victory in May 1917, might be encouraged to change the law. They offered a blizzard of statistics to show that the swell of bolters in the AIF was directly attributable to the Australian ban on executions at the front.[661] Behind the scenes, the Australian Government sought the opinion of Robert Garran, the Solicitor-General, and in June 1917 he confirmed the essential fact: under Australian law, the British *Army Act 1881* did apply to the men of the AIF, but 'save so far as it is inconsistent with the Defence Act'. A month later the Cabinet decided not to seek 'at this juncture' any amendment to the *Defence Act 1903* 'in reference to Sentence of Death as punishment for desertion'.[662]

In August 1917, the British military leaders were panting again for Australian executions. Significantly, this was at exactly the moment General Lavr Kornilov, the Tsarist-minded Russian Commander who would soon attempt a counter-revolutionary coup, was crusading for the restoration of the death penalty on the Russian front – and winning much applause from British generals.[663] Sir Douglas Haig was in the vanguard of the renewed effort to twist Australian arms. From his château at Montreuil in France, the church-going Haig, working through the Colonial Office in London, pressed the case upon Melbourne. Haig asserted that the levels of AWOL and desertion in the AIF's divisions were 'four times greater' than in other British divisions. Freedom from the death penalty was to blame for it was a 'privileged position' exploited by Australian troops. 'Unless [the] Commonwealth Government agree to place their troops under [the] Army Act without any restrictions as regards [the] death penalty', Haig warned, '[the] fighting efficiency of these divisions will deteriorate to an extent which may gravely affect [the] success of our arms.' Shooting condemned men, Haig offered mildly, would be used 'very sparingly' and only where 'an example' was 'urgently required'. But Hughes's Cabinet again opted to sit tight, deciding only that Hughes would 'place the position of the Government on his question before the Government of the United Kingdom'.[664] In September, Pearce gave an explanation to Birdwood, arguing that news of firing parties despatching Australians at the front would have a 'disastrous effect on recruiting'.[665]

Was there something of an orchestrated campaign, with the cooperation of Australian officers, to get Melbourne to change its mind? The evidence is suggestive rather than conclusive. Leading officers were clamorous for executions at the front. The British generals agitating along with Haig included Birdwood, Rawlinson, Godley, Gough and Plumer. The Australian generals included John Monash, J.G. Legge, H.B. Walker, E.A. Wisdom, and Rosenthal. Monash told his wife in July 1917 that the government's refusal to amend the law to allow executions was 'having a very bad effect on discipline'. Monash explained that he was strongly urging Pearce 'that in some clear case of cowardly desertion, the law should take its course. One single execution', he argued, 'will stop the rot which is setting in'.[666] The Australian officers did direct that sentences handed down by courts martial – including death sentences – must be solemnly read at battalion parades, clearly in an effort to intimidate the troops. Some claimed that the great bulk of the Australian officer corps favoured executions. Lieutenant Colonel W.A. Ralston believed he spoke for 'the majority of officers' in the AIF in lamenting the ban on firing squads despatching deserters. He wrote home from France complaining that desertion was a plague 'in every battalion'. His explanation was blunt. 'In the British or any other army these men get shot.' Who was to blame? He levelled his accusation: '[O]ur Australian government will not give us the power, so to the standing disgrace of Australia these men go free, do no work, draw more pay than any other soldier in the world and take the time of good men in guarding them, when they would otherwise be working. This matter is felt very keenly by the majority of officers in the A.I.F.'[667]

Perhaps it was a case of the officers and the men in the ranks gradually finding each other out. The officers wanted to use the threat of death to discipline the men; the men in turn came to see that there was an element of theatre at play. In the end, no one was shot. Archie Barwick, for example, had cottoned on to the folklore by October 1917. He listened to harsh prison sentences being read out to his parading battalion. Then he noted in his diary that Australian courts martial were punishing clear cases of desertion by convicting bolters of the lesser crime of AWOL, in contrast to the death sentences inflicted upon British rankers. Barwick reasoned that 'we are under the Imperial Government in practically everything but as regards punishments the Australian authorities refused to allow the death penalty to be inflicted on Australians without first getting the consent of our Government'. Personally, Barwick felt that 'a little shooting would do no harm'. In fact it might be become essential, he jotted down, especially if conscription brought more and more 'rotters' into the ranks of the AIF.[668]

It did not happen. During 1918, death *sentences* became rare. Political developments help to explain the slide in numbers. In December 1917, conscription was rejected at a second referendum in Australia. During the bitter campaign, some anti-conscription speakers pointed to the danger of executions at the front in the wake of conscription. The death penalty, they warned, faced conscripted men in every other army.[669] The 'No' vote resolved matters. There would be killing galore on the Western Front during 1918 but the men of the AIF would not be ordered to kill each other.

Only in September 1918 did the Australian Government come clean on the 'push' for executions that it had resisted. Acting Prime Minister William Watt (Hughes was again in Britain) conceded in Parliament in Melbourne that Haig, Birdwood, and other commanders had indeed made 'strong representations' during 1917, urging an amendment to the *Defence Act 1903* so that convicted Australian deserters could be shot. But the Cabinet had decided against it. And there was no going back. Watt confirmed the plain facts as they stood: for a soldier of the AIF to be 'liable to the death penalty, he must actually desert *to the enemy*'.[670]

Thus, neither Ted Ryan, nor any one of the 121 Australian soldiers handed a death sentence during the war, was ultimately executed in contrast to the British experience. British courts martial did deliver death sentences, and in a small minority of cases, firing squads of soldiers were assembled to take the lives of their fellow soldiers. Some 343 British soldiers were executed in this way during the Great War, selectively, as a deterrent ('to encourage the others' as Napoleon once put it).[671] These killings were advertised. The 'General Routine Orders' issued by British Headquarters, and seen by Australian officers, frequently headlined these death sentences and executions, in a transparent effort to intimidate all rebels in the ranks.[672]

It is tempting to argue that the death sentences handed to Ryan and more than a hundred others by Australian courts martial were, in the strict sense, illegal. Certainly, it was open to the Australians directing the courts martial processes in the AIF to read section 98 of Australia's *Defence Act 1903* as an instruction to each and every court martial. The wording was quite plain: 'No member of the Defence Force shall be sentenced to death by any court-martial' except, as we have seen, in four very limited circumstances. Was it an instruction to avoid even a *sentence* of death, leave alone actual executions? They chose not to read it this way. Instead, they relied on the British *Army Act 1881* that declared all death sentences emerging from courts martial to be 'not valid', *until* the General Officer Commanding confirmed the final sentence which meant, in practice, commutation of death sentences. Australian officers sat in judgement at the courts martial of Australian soldiers. This was official policy.[673] But at every court martial, it seems, loyalty to British practice was allowed to eclipse respect for Australian law.

Was Ryan's court martial by any measure just? Was he in any position to mount his defence? And were the officers at his courts martial qualified to administer justice? Standards fell far below those recommended by the British authorities. Lieutenant General George Fowke, the British Adjutant General, issued instructions to all units in early 1918 reminding officers at courts martial that a soldier on trial for his life needed 'the utmost assistance of every kind in his defence'. Convening officers should appoint a 'friend of the accused', and wherever possible they should select an officer 'who is a barrister or solicitor', or at the very least someone 'who by reason of ability and discretion will be able to present the case of the accused adequately to the Court'. Fowke pleaded that officers should do nothing 'to derogate from the right of the accused' to select his own counsel. Defending counsel had to be given 'sufficient time' to prepare their defence and to consult with the accused.[674] There is no indication in Ryan's courts martial papers that he received any such assistance.

A contemporary Australian soldier's judgement upon such courts martial was damning. In late 1918, Edwin Corboy, a twenty-two-year-old wounded ex-soldier, a veteran of the fighting around Ypres, was elected Labor member for Swan upon his return from the war. In November, Corboy would tell the federal Parliament of the grave deficiencies of the courts martial system. He explained that he had seen 'really savage sentences' imposed on soldiers, for trivial offences 'that a civil magistrate would have laughed at'. The injustices stung him. When it came to death sentences, he argued, it must be remembered:

> ... that accused persons in the Army are not able to secure proper representation at their trial. Ninety-nine men out of 100 are not conversant with one-fifth of the provisions of the *Army Act*, and do not know how to defend themselves. That is not just to the accused whose life is trembling in the balance. He should have the right

to be represented by a man who is trained in legal matters, and who is able to put up a decent fight for the accused's life.[675]

Corboy had witnessed British practices. He told the story of a conscripted nineteen-year-old British soldier who 'lost all control of himself' after 'three hours of the heaviest drum fire imaginable' – and ran. Accused of desertion, he was swiftly executed in the public square of Ypres. Australia's 'soldier citizens' should never be on trial for their lives before a court martial, declared Corboy – Australia should shake free of the 'grip of militarism'.[676]

We should note at this point that the Americans in the First World War also decided they would never shoot a single deserter; that in 1930 the British reconsidered their decisions and scrubbed the death penalty for desertion from their military law; and that during the Second World War, no British or Commonwealth soldier was shot for desertion.[677] These facts leave the Australian and British officers' strenuous 'push' for the execution of AIF deserters during the First World War exposed as the wrong-headed, mess-jacket bravado that it was.

Stifling the Peace

The records will show it forever: Ted Ryan was found guilty of desertion and sentenced to death. But questions must haunt us. Was Ryan correct in the accusations he made at his court martial? Was it true that the British and Entente governments had allowed their war aims to be enlarged again and again? Had they recklessly thwarted opportunities for peace, even after three years of bloodshed?

Let us turn again briefly to the men in power and their high diplomacy. At the very time Ryan was under sentence of death in mid-September 1917, following his court martial, the British Cabinet was considering yet another peace offer from Berlin. This had arrived through Spanish channels from the German Foreign Minister, Richard von Kühlmann. The Germans' opening gambit was quite moderate. As conveyed to the British, peace could be made on this basis: 'Cession of Alsace-Lorraine by Germany; Restoration of Serbia; Territorial Concessions to Italy; Colonial Concessions to Great Britain; Restoration of Belgium'. Secret hand-written minutes of the British War Cabinet for 24 September show that some ministers wanted this offer buried instantly. One warned that if Russia found out that such moderate terms were on the table, she might 'get out of the war'. Lloyd George even argued against informing the Americans: 'At present, we wanted the U.S.A. to fight and there was no need to discuss questions of peace with them.' The supposedly uncompromising Germans appeared ready to compromise. The British leaders were embarrassed. These remarks offer chilling insights into the minds of great men for whom great wars are fought.[678]

Richard von Kühlmann

Three days later, the War Cabinet discussed the matter again. Lloyd George had just been across the Channel to Boulogne to talk to the new French Premier, Paul Painlevé. Lloyd George reported: the German offer 'is serious', he said, but the French were divided over how to respond. Ex-premier Briand wanted to talk to the Germans, to explore ending the war; but ex-premier Ribot, the Foreign Minister, and President Poincaré wanted to smother the idea. Briand had been forbidden to pursue projected back-channel talks with a German envoy in Lausanne. 'What M. Painlevé seemed to fear', said Lloyd George, 'was not that the German offer was <u>not bona fide</u>, but that it was <u>bona fide</u>'! Painlevé had explained to Lloyd George that if it was known that German terms were so mild, then he 'doubted whether France would continue fighting'. Lloyd George agreed. He expressed to the War Cabinet his own 'doubts as to whether in the event of such an offer this country would continue the war'. Lloyd George also shared disquieting news from the front. He reported that 'an officer at the front had told him that the men, who for the first two years had never discussed such matters, were beginning to talk among themselves of what we were fighting for. They would fight for Belgium, but not for conquest ...'[679] Men just like Ted Ryan.

DEFIANCE – AND DEATH SENTENCE | 217

Alexander Ribot

The next day, the War Cabinet listened patiently as General Sir William Robertson complained that the French wanted the British to take on more of the front, but were keeping back in their depots their own French boys who were to turn 20 years of age in 1918 until the following spring. Compared with the French, Robertson observed, Britain was admirably profligate. 'He remarked that we were sending to the front all our men who were over 19.'[680] No one challenged this. Lloyd George's Ministers, with steady eyes it seemed, were willing to fight to the last twenty-year old, ploughing under the rising generation, if need be and, in their view, needs must.

But whatever the youth of Britain's soldiers being pressed into the lines, her statesmen were in no hurry to respond to the latest German peace offer. With Lloyd George's approval, Balfour waited over a fortnight, from 18 September until 6 October, before informing the ambassadors of France, America, Japan, Italy and Russia in London of the German approach. Britain, he said, awaited a formal offer. But Kühlmann, personally a moderate who did not believe in a military resolution of the war, was caught in the pincers of German domestic politics. He feared that to announce publicly, in advance of negotiations, that Germany would give up Belgium, would be to squander his main bargaining chip and embolden Paris and London to insist on all of Alsace-

Lorraine as well. In fear of his pan-German critics, Kühlmann then hobbled his own peace initiative by denying in the Reichstag on 9 October that he had ever intended to include Alsace-Lorraine in any deal – implying that in his judgement concessions in Belgium were more important to Britain. Two days later Lloyd George responded, killing off all hopes. In a public speech, he suddenly backed France unequivocally in her demand for the return of all of Alsace-Lorraine, without plebiscite.[681] To complete the disaster, the ultra-nationalist reactionaries in Paris then drove Painlevé from office as a wobbler. The hardliners in Berlin would later strike against Kühlmann for admitting his conviction that the war could not be ended by military means. Thus, on both sides irrationality had triumphed again, and the German offer languished. Of course, the public was never told that a German peace offer had been left dangling.

While all these discussions in the British War Cabinet took place, the Third Battle of Ypres was pressed forward, climaxing in the Battle of Passchendaele in November. Australia's casualties were 38,000, including some 12,000 killed and missing.[682]

Once more, the politicians and diplomats, the guardians of the lives of the soldiers, had dragged their feet, and peace was scuppered. Peace may have been tantalizingly close. We shall never know.

Chapter 20

CONFINEMENT

CAESTRE, SEPTEMBER TO DECEMBER 1917

> Still lists in 'Base Orders' come out of men who have been court-martialled and shot for 'desertion' and 'showing cowardice in front of the enemy'. What is cowardice? And who are the officers in charge to judge [?]. He who is without sin amongst us, tell him cast the first stone, and judge not, lest ye be judged [;] how could any of these officers answer then?
>
> — Private Frank H. Molony, 1st Australian Field Ambulance, 13 September 1916 [683]

Following his court martial, Private Edward James Ryan was imprisoned initially for almost three months within the '1st Anzac Corps Reinforcement Camp', set up on the Caëstre-Fletre road, behind the lines.[684] Ryan might have recognised the town of Caëstre. The men of the 51st Battalion had arrived there before, on the very eve of their first action in France, in June 1916. They were dog-tired then, after their long train journey from Marseille. Long, long ago, it must have seemed, as Ryan awaited his fate.

The Condemned Man

Ryan must have believed execution was unlikely, but not impossible. Then, according to the British pattern, there might have been a blindfold at dawn, a firing party at five paces with men drawn from Ryan's own unit, wavering rifles aimed at the condemned man, manacled and tied to a chair or a post, a paper disk over his heart, a chaplain as the last man to walk away, an officer with a loaded pistol to finish the job and an early morning death parade of the whole battalion to witness the execution.[685]

The fact that Australians had not been executed following death sentences came to be well-known.[686] On the other hand, the death sentences for desertion were publicised and read to Australian troops on parade by their commanding officers.[687] The British 'General Routine Orders', listing the names of executed British soldiers, were also read to parades.[688] Rumours circulated that Australian executions *had* happened. For instance, Major Aubrey Wiltshire, who would sit on many courts martial, recorded in his diary his own firm belief that at least two men had been executed at Gallipoli.[689] Soldiers must have apprehended that it was possible for the policy of no executions to be reversed by the pro-conscription government in Melbourne, or perhaps evaded by an officer intent on some wild action to curb indiscipline. It was always possible that official policy might buckle under the weight of the officers and their legal advisers, who clearly favoured it. The chance of it was there. Could a condemned man have banished this from his mind?

When would Ryan have known his sentence? As we have seen, following his court martial and death sentence on 12 September 1917, a fortnight elapsed before General Birdwood recorded his commutation of Ryan's death sentence – unwillingly, as we know. No firing squad. The verdict, sentence, and merciful commutation were then 'promulgated' when the details were read to the parading 51st Battalion on 5 October. This was three weeks after Ryan's court martial. Probably only then did Ryan learn, while imprisoned at the reinforcement camp at Caëstre, that he had been sentenced to death, but that he would not be shot, and instead faced five years in prison. The accompanying financial penalty he could easily have calculated himself: he would lose all the pay from the moment of his absconding to the end of his sentence. The pay clerks entered the details on his 'Statement of Service': 'Total Forfeiture: 5 years and 31 days'. The stoppage was confirmed for pay book 125985/4.[690]

It was a grim outlook. But a kind of fortune had favoured Ryan, and all those Australians similarly sentenced to death. Political circumstances back home had saved them – not the politicians, not the military commanders, and not the officers drafted into courts martial to judge them. Their lives had been spared for reasons of political expediency. Thus, a British military prison awaited Ryan. A long period behind bars was likely. The official documents specified there would be no reconsideration of his term of imprisonment until 9 November 1918, more than a year away.[691]

An Exceptional Anzac?

How rare was Ryan's crime? Was his desertion an instance of an exceptional lack of discipline? Those who hope that every Australian war story is a see-how-great-we-are story might assume that Ryan was just one of a tiny number of recalcitrant men – mere bad apples, at the bottom of the barrel – among all those plucky Anzacs.

Not so. Any temptation to place Ryan on the very margins can scarcely survive a hard look at the statistics. During the first half of 1917, the five Australian Divisions in France reported a total of 171 AIF soldiers deserting the field, an average of almost 35 men per division. The remaining 57 Divisions of the BEF reported only 506 desertions in total, an average of less than nine men per division – less than a third of the Australian average.[692] And the Australian numbers steadily increased. Courts martial for desertion among AIF soldiers serving overseas climbed from 288 in 1916, to 1,283 in 1917, and then to 1,807 in 1918. Comparisons were embarrassing. The AIF figures for deserters facing courts martial overseas were, as one historian concludes, 'four times higher than in any other division in the British Army'.[693]

Clearly, the much-vaunted Anzac spirit could include a determination to get the hell out of the battle zone.

Private Ryan – and the Lord

But a sceptic might ask a deeper question. Was Ryan's rebellion pointless? Was peace already in the lost-cause basket? Were his pleas for a diplomatic settlement by the autumn of 1917 ultimately naïve and futile – the views of a forgettable rump of opinion? This is far from accurate. The European people's revulsion of war had already produced epoch-making revolutionary events in Russia, and there was a rising tide of anti-war opinion in most of the warring nations, including Britain.

While Ryan was kept in military detention from the late autumn of 1917-18, a number of spectacular political developments in Britain showed that the opinions of men like Ryan were gaining traction in many places – high and low.

For example, in late November 1917 – just after Lenin's seizure of power in Russia – Lord Lansdowne, no longer in Cabinet but still one of the most prominent Tories in England, wrote a spectacular letter (See Appendiz 10) to the London *Daily Telegraph*, a conservative paper, urging a compromise peace. It echoed an earlier secret Cabinet memorandum of his from November 1916. After another year of stupendous waste at the fronts, he had decided to go public. 'We are not going to lose this war', Lansdowne reassured his readers, 'but its prolongation will spell ruin for the civilised world, and an infinite addition to the load of human suffering which already weighs upon it'. He was impatient with those ultra-patriots who asserted that Germany's guilt in starting the war was all that mattered. He responded that the war's 'wanton prolongation would be a crime, differing only in degree from the criminals who provoked it'. What was the war for? Security was the most important objective to be obtained from the war, he wrote. But victory would be useless if the nations were utterly exhausted. The war must be ended, therefore, wrote Lansdowne, 'in time to avert a world catastrophe'. The people of Europe held the key to the restoration of peace, Lansdowne added provocatively, for the people were aware that the war 'has already lasted too long'. Mass revolt might end the war, he hinted. He implored the rulers to contemplate peace talks, before all Europe was shattered.

To prepare the way for peace, Lansdowne wanted war aims revised downward. And he wanted the war aims of the Entente and the United States harmonised, at last, in reality. He denounced the 'deplorable' plans for a 'boycott' of Germany commerce after the war ended – plans dear to Billy Hughes.[694] He wanted the Western Powers together to appeal over the heads of the German militarists and Pan-Germans, to the people of Germany, who honestly desired only to defend their homeland. In fact, inside Germany, Lansdowne's intervention did encourage influential liberals and moderates, especially in the German foreign ministry. They hoped for some moderation in Britain's position that might lead to negotiations before the horrors of another spring offensive in 1918 were unleashed.[695]

But in Britain, Lansdowne, the noble lord from the great estate at Bowood, was met with orchestrated hysteria in the 'fight to the finish' press: he was a 'white-flagger', a 'mischief-maker', a 'boche-lover', a decrepit old aristocratic 'pacifist' flirting with 'treason' – the usual choice pickings from the slurry of slurs. His argument for compromise was drowned out in a great hue and cry against his 'defeatism', fanned by the war-at-any-price newspapers. Lansdowne was gibbeted, as it were, on every editorial hill controlled by such press barons as Lords Northcliffe and Beaverbrook, for the crime of questioning the war. Frightened as ever by these right-wing crusading mastheads, the Lloyd George Government abandoned Lansdowne. He was left to rot before the public gaze, with key government spokesmen hiding the truth that he had in fact consulted a number of key men, including Balfour, Lloyd George's Foreign Secretary no less, before sending his letter to the *Daily Telegraph*.

Predictably, the *Anzac Bulletin* carried Hughes's damning and inane assessment of the furore to the men of the AIF: Lansdowne was allegedly the tool of 'a clique of doctrinaire pacifists and pro-German agents'.[696]

Nonetheless, Lansdowne's plea that a diplomatic settlement should be attempted, after more than three years of battlefield stalemate, crowned by the recent horrors of Passchendaele, attracted noisy support. Leading British Labour politicians, dissenting Liberal MPs, Radical economists, and many of the leading lights in the progressive international movement crusading for the League of Nations project, rallied to Lansdowne's defence. A public campaign was launched. Lansdowne's chief organiser was Francis Hirst, a respected former editor of *The Economist*. Big-minded people, such as the historian Gilbert Murray, the radical economists Henry Brailsford and John Hobson, the internationalist thinkers Goldie Dickinson and Bertrand Russell, and the feminists and suffragists Helena Swanwick and Sylvia Pankhurst, were among those courageous spirits who came out to defy the 'never-endians'. So too, the two Liberal peers who had first pleaded for negotiations back in November 1915, Earl Loreburn and Lord Courtney, now rushed to declare their warm support for Lansdowne. War aims must be credibly moderate, and then peace was entirely possible, they argued. But Lansdowne's own Tory party rained a torrent of curses upon him.[697]

In stunning contrast, many soldiers backed Lansdowne. Sir John Simon, a leading British Liberal, visiting troops at the front, found strong support: the men doing the fighting in France, he discovered, were 'not nearly such fire-eaters as some of those who speak in their name'.[698] Many others observed this. 'Every soldier I know, my husband, and also my brother (who is fighting at Amiens), now think Lord Lansdowne right', as one woman wrote to Hirst.[699]

Was the peace-by-negotiation movement in Britain at this time the preserve of a mere handful of men and women from a tiny pacifist playpen in the corner? Not at all. The results of by-elections in Britain in early 1918 showed that nearly half the electors in constituencies in the north of England could cast votes for a peace-by-negotiation candidate, in spite of overwhelmingly pro-war newspapers and the harassment of peace candidates by the government. At a by election at Keighley in April 1918, the peace-by-negotiation candidate for the Independent Labour Party got 32.5 per cent of the vote. Next, in May 1918, a by-election was held at Wansbeck, a mining constituency just north of Newcastle. The 'win-the-war' Coalition candidate, Robert Mason, a shipowner, faced Eb Edwards, the openly peace-by-negotiation candidate from the Northumberland Miners Association. Spooked, the government did its best to hamper Edwards; his election agent was suddenly arrested and locked up during the campaign as a conscientious objector. Mason got home with 5,814 votes; but remarkably Edwards garnered 5,267 votes – a very respectable 47.5 per cent. When the results were shouted from an upper window of the Morpeth Town Hall to a large crowd in the market square, Edwards' supporters erupted in cheers, elated that their peace candidate had almost carried the day. Labour journalists covering the event were in no doubt that 'peace by negotiation was *the* issue in the election', and impressed that Edwards' performance was 'so astonishingly good'.[700] The wind was changing.

And the Australian troops in France? Again the loyal Archie Barwick, promoted to sergeant during 1917, gives us a glimpse into Australian opinion in the trenches. In late 1916 he had predicted that 'surely by the time next December comes round it will be all over & we will be back in sunny Australia'.[701] Now, a year later, he lamented his fate in his diary: '[A]ll the boys are feeling the same way ... everything military is getting hateful to us all, people in Australia or England don't long for this war to finish any more than we do I'll bet, & as the days go past we hate it more & more.'[702] Corporal Arthur Thomas had told his family back in August 1917 that: 'I don't want to ever go back to the lines.' In January 1918 he wrote that 'peace is more evident than ever & the great day is looming bright & glorious.' A week later he wrote again that 'the pace for peace has set in properly & no doubt the people will bring it about quicker than any other method.'[703]

But the pro-war British newspapers continued to vilify Lansdowne, as he periodically renewed his call for negotiations during the first months of 1918, and the editors shouted for war 'to the bitter end'. Edmund Blunden witnessed this public flogging meted out to Lansdowne while on leave in England, and was disgusted: such a spirit, masquerading as love of country, was despicable callousness on the part of the stay-at-homes, as he put it, 'the crystallisation of dull civilian hatred on the basis of "the last drop of blood"' – other people's blood, of course.[704]

Chapter 21

DARKNESS

DUNKIRK AND CALAIS, DECEMBER 1917 TO AUGUST 1918

And anybody that's been ninety days in a pommie military prison knows all about it too![705]

– Gunner Harry Sennett, AIF veteran, interviewed 1990

After three months in the Australian prison compound, on 6 December 1917 Ryan began his journey, hand-cuffed and under guard, to a British-run prison camp. He entered No. 10 Military Prison just outside Dunkirk on 10 December 1917 to continue serving his sentence of five years – a prisoner, so to speak, of the war-machine. On the face of it, he might have expected his stretch to last until September 1922. But quite soon, there was an indication that some leniency might be in the offing. Just before the Christmas of 1917, his sentence was formally reduced: down from five years to two years of imprisonment but 'hard labour' was added.

No. 10 Military Prison was a prison camp, for about 400 men, built on low-lying and swampy land, exposed to the sea, fog and wind of the Channel. Fenced in behind the wire, the prisoners were crowded in to bell-tents at night, sleeping 'sixteen to eighteen men each'. A New Zealand conscientious objector who was imprisoned there remembered that the warders and guards aimed to 'cow down' new prisoners, 'and so for the first hour we were rushed about, yelled at, bullied, and had all manner of threats and warnings hurled at us'. The men were deprived of their woollen underwear upon arrival, increasing their suffering from the cold. The warders, mainly civilians from British prisons, systematically humiliated and insulted the prisoners. Food was poor; hard labour was constant; letters were forbidden. Any resistance was punished with pointless drills, Field Punishment Number 1, and periods of solitary confinement.[706]

At some point early in 1918, Ryan was transferred with other Australian soldiers the short distance from the prison at Dunkirk to another British prison camp, the No. 7 Military Prison at Vendroux, Les Attaques, inland from Calais. Here he was placed under the governorship of one Major J.J. Hardinge – a rather brutish prison governor soon to be infamous. Hardinge's prison camp, if anything, was worse than No. 10.

Deepening Night

How exactly the officers and guards treated Ryan as an individual prisoner at these two prisons we can never know for certain. There is no record of him committing any additional crime while imprisoned, so probably he was spared special torments. But the evidence points to a prison regime for all that was harsh, even deliberately vindictive and cruel.

The procedures and punishments at No. 7 Military Prison, Les Attaques, were notorious. Some captives have left eye-watering records. Robert Price, a British conscientious objector – a Christian pacifist of total commitment – was imprisoned at Les Attaques a few months before Ryan, in June 1917. According to Price, prisoners like him could be confined in cells for up to fourteen days at a time. They could be handcuffed for twenty-four hours a day, manacled with arms behind their backs during the day, and by their hands, pinioned in front, during the night. He witnessed soldiers being savagely beaten by officers with the buckle-ends of their belts, as they struggled with their mocking and spiteful tormentors.[707]

Those Australian soldiers sent for punishment to various other British prisons in France have left records that tell of similar mistreatments. Henry Sennett was imprisoned for ninety days in a 'pommie prison' for shooting a mule, after the beast kicked him in his face. He spent his days on his knees, being ordered repeatedly to occupy himself 'wiping and cleaning the toilets, scrubbing the floors, any dirty job that was about'. 'You had to scrub the same floor two or three times', he recalled. When he and a colleague rebelled, they climbed on to the roof of the prison; they then dared the guards to retrieve them. The roof-top resisters relished the moment, for 'as they come up we kicked them or hit them'. 'By Jeez we paid the penalty after', said Sennett. 'We got hit with everything but the kitchen sink.' After his release, Sennett and his companions took their revenge. They happened to meet some of their former prison guards enjoying a night out on the town at Beaulieu and, as he recalled, 'we had the pleasure of belting them'.[708]

Australian soldiers mistranslated 'Les Attaques' as 'The Attic'. We may gain some more detail on conditions here if we look forward just a few months from Ryan's term of imprisonment. In early March 1919, the Prison Governor, Major Hardinge, faced a serious riot at 'The Attic'. Almost one hundred prisoners, the great bulk of them Australian, revolted against their mistreatment. They complained of a regime of cruelty, unnecessary manacles, poor food, and bitter cold. They were overwhelmed, charged with mutiny, and found guilty by a Field General Court Martial.[709]

In May 1919, the scandal of 'Les Attaques' became public. A British Labour newspaper, the *Daily Herald*, printed the complaints of the soldiers against Hardinge and his regime: prison guards and officers were accused of viciously assaulting prisoners, placing them in irons and handcuffs, and providing too few blankets during cold weather. Ultra-patriots in the British Parliament actually raised the Hardinge issue, as an instance of the Labour press being so unpatriotic as to blacken the name of a fine officer by repeating false allegations against him. The relevant Minister, Henry Forster – later Lord Forster, Governor-General of Australia – came to Hardinge's rescue, grandly denied all the prisoners' complaints, and rounded on the *Daily Herald* for printing such 'libellous statements'.[710]

However, official enquiries into the conditions at 'The Attic' following the riot in March 1919 revealed a credible catalogue of abuses with many witnesses. The prisoners complained of food that was 'never varying', 'often rotten', 'improperly cooked', 'dirty', and 'unwholesome'. They suffered from neglect of their illnesses, such as 'scabies' and venereal disease. In winter, they sickened in 'unbearable, freezing' iron and cement cells, where 'icicles hung from the ceilings'. The jailers made frequent use of 'figure eights', that is, handcuffs, placed on men for 'petty affairs', such as 'missing buttons'. There were screaming matches as men were 'ill-treated with whips in their cells', and scenes of bedlam as prisoners fought back, with the teeth of some being 'knocked out'. Conscious of their 'status' as volunteer-soldiers, the Australians complained that they were prevented from talking to Australian officers. Their letters were limited to only one censored letter per month. The captives accused guards of confiscating tinned food found in parcels from Australia, because they 'were only allowed soap and toothpaste'. They reported that 'no reading material was ever allowed'. Sanitation was wretched, with a score of men sharing only 'one dish of water' for washing, while foul toilet tins were kept in cells in all weathers. Finally, the men charged their jailers with stealing their Australian clothes and personal possessions: 'rings, money and watches not being returned on leaving prison'.[711] It was a remarkably consistent record of austere policies and vicious incidents.

Ryan endured confinement in this British prison for the first eight months of 1918.

'Bolshie-leaks'

Let us zoom out once more and survey what was happening beyond the prison bars. Again, from late 1917 until his release the following summer, Ryan missed momentous events that would have intrigued him and revelations that again vindicated the essential criticisms he had made of the war. Let us juxtapose some of these landmark events on the grand high-diplomatic stage of the war along with the tally marks, as it were, recording Ryan's imprisonment.

When Ryan entered the British-run No. 10 prison camp near the coast at Dunkirk in December 1917, he had already endured four months of imprisonment since his arrest for desertion in August. Winter had descended across the battlefronts and upon the prisons. But during that same time, for a brief period on the international stage, peace looked possible, even likely.

On the Eastern Front, various ceasefires had been in place for some weeks. Then, at the shell-smashed town of Brest-Litovsk in Russian Poland, on 15 December 1917, an official armistice was signed between the Central Powers and the new Bolshevik-led Russian Government.[712] Half the catastrophic European war appeared to be fizzling out. The Russians urged the Western Powers to send representatives to join them in ongoing peace talks at Brest-Litovsk, so that the war could be ended at last in a general peace. With an eye to Wilson and maximum publicity, the Germans even accepted the astonishing Russian proposal that these peace talks should be conducted openly – in the face of the world's press. More private feelers, and much 'megaphone' diplomacy, involving almost all the belligerents, accompanied these big developments on the Eastern Front. But the Western Powers steadfastly refused to come to any peace conference initiated by the new socialist regime in Russia – the 'Russian terrorists' as some dubbed them. The possibility that socialists might mediate peace – and scoop up the political benefit – was seen as a grave danger.[713]

The context is vital to understand the power of the moment. In mid-November 1917, Lenin's new coalition government, prompted by Leon Trotsky, his Commissioner for Foreign Affairs, had begun to publish the so-called 'Secret Treaties' from the archives of the Russian foreign ministry, in order to spotlight the Western Powers' imperialism and to ignite popular demands for a general peace. These were the treaties made between the Tsarist government and Britain, France, Italy and Japan, during the conflict. Among others, the complete texts of the Straits and Persia Agreement of March 1915, and of the Treaty of London of April 1915 – the two diplomatic agreements that underpinned the Australians' campaign at Gallipoli – were revealed to the world for the first time.

There was pressure not to publish. The pro-war *New York Times* grudgingly published only short extracts on 25 November 1917.[714] The radical New York *Evening Post* had to wait until late January before publishing complete texts.[715] But in Britain, the influential Liberal *Manchester Guardian* did not wait, publishing damning summaries of the diplomatic revelations on 26 November 1917.[716] Then, of huge significance, the same paper published on 12 December 1917 the complete texts of the Straits and Persia Agreement of March 1915, and of the Franco-Russian Left Bank of the Rhine or Doumergue Agreement of March 1917, in which both powers had agreed to support each other in gobbling up territory in western and eastern Germany.[717] The ferociously hungry Entente cat was well and truly out of the bag.

As the New Year dawned in January 1918, Ryan was shifted to the notorious prison 'The Attic' near Calais. It was his fifth month of imprisonment. Now very likely he shared his cell or bell-tent with various other 'deserters' and 'absentees', and with political dissidents, as we have seen, including pacifist and political conscientious objectors from Britain and New Zealand. Such men – had they access to newspapers – would have been intrigued to read of the astonishing events of that winter, in politics, and in diplomacy, all indicating an intensifying struggle between those determined to end this war by military might alone, and those urging round-table negotiations. But almost certainly they languished without any knowledge of the great earthquakes in world politics that were shaking certainties everywhere.

London witnessed one breakthrough. Sensing great danger in the air following the Russian diplomatic revelations of November and December 1917, Lloyd George decided that he must at least go through the motions of outlining more cautious war aims for Britain. He would re-badge himself as a moderate. He deliberately chose to deliver an impassioned address to a select trade union gathering at the Caxton Hall in London on 5 January 1918, in an effort to revive among the working class a faith in this war as a righteous war. He conceded: 'When men by the millions are being called upon to suffer and die, and vast populations are being subjected to suffering and privations of war on a scale unprecedented in the history of the world, they are entitled to know for what cause or causes they are making the sacrifice.' And so? Lloyd George insisted that Britain was now fighting only for 'self-determination', and the liberation of people cruelly subjected to foreign rule – in Belgium, in Poland and in Austria-Hungary. Apparently, Britain was not fighting to extend her empire at all. The captured German colonies were not necessarily to be retained, Lloyd George suggested; rather, they were simply held in trust, until the peace conference could decide their fate. Posing boldly as a magnanimous peacemaker, he even promised that Britain, when victorious, would not 'attempt to shift the cost of warlike operations from one belligerent to another' – a promise he would later seek to evade during the period of peacemaking at the end of the war.[718]

He pipped Wilson. Just a few days later, on 8 January, Wilson delivered his famous 'Fourteen Points Address' to a joint session of Congress. It marked more credible moderation in war aims on Wilson's part, in an effort to rally public support in America and in the Entente nations for a march toward victory, in this 'the culminating and final war for human liberty'. But he spoke only for the United States. There was no coordination with his partners in Europe. Open diplomacy, open markets, freedom of the seas, disarmament, democracy for all – these were the watchwords that spangled his Fourteen Points. He played with fire: he promised a peace based on 'self-determination' for all, a phrase that suggested there might even be tentative steps toward global de-colonisation. There must be 'an absolutely impartial adjustment' of all colonial claims at the war's end, he declared, which suggested Germany might not lose all her colonial empire. He disavowed all ideas of indemnity and closed imperial economic systems, committing the United States to stand for free trade and against protectionism. This appeared to pit America against the Entente's protectionist 'Paris Resolutions' of 1916. All nations, Wilson predicted, would move to disarmament under the peace terms. And, crowning the edifice of a just and lasting peace, he promised a

League of Nations, so that stronger international law and institutions would put an end to war, forever.[719] Here was an epoch-making challenge to war-makers, on both sides.

However, hopes for peace raised by Wilson were within weeks severely dented by a bellicose declaration. The Supreme War Council, a military body dominated by France and Britain, met in early February at the luxury Trianon Palace Hotel, at Versailles. The leaders here decided to end all talk of negotiation with Germany. Lloyd George's slipperiness was on display. No doubt, just as all those present were thinking sceptically of his recent moderate speech at the Caxton Hall, Lloyd George brazenly told the Supreme War Council that indeed, in his view, 'no body was bound by a speech'.[720] So on 4 February the Council (in reality, the British and French leaders) released a communiqué summarising their decisions, the so-called 'Versailles Declaration': this announced that the Entente's top men had all agreed that 'the only immediate task before them lay in the prosecution with the utmost vigour ... of the military effort of the Allies'.[721] Thus, the 'knock-out blowers' had concocted another blanket 'No' to peace negotiations.

Once again, the extremists on one side had come to the rescue of the extremists on the other. Once again, the British, French and Italian men of war who wanted a 'fight to the finish' had proclaimed that negotiations were impossible, that talk of peace was a profanation, and that the elusive victory was indispensable. They invited a spring offensive.

As the spring thaw arrived in March 1918, the war was to be renewed in an orgy of violence on the Western Front. Hindenburg and Ludendorff, representing all those in the German ruling elite who hoped that something approaching victory might stave off the drift to democracy and even revolution inside Germany, had planned a great new offensive – a last offensive. It was born of the desperate hope that Germany might yet win big military gains in France before millions of Americans arrived to strengthen the lines. Dubbed 'Operation Michael', the offensive opened on the Western Front on 21 March. Conscripted, under-fed, and under-resourced young German men and boys were thrown into the fight against their counterparts on the other side of the wire. For a brief period, the British and French lines crumpled.

Peace Talk: 'Very Reasonable and Worthy of Consideration'

Was the negotiated peace that so many dissidents had been urging unmasked as utterly illusory by this almighty clash of firepower in France?

If we step back once again, we may see a dozen forks in the road that might have been taken before the bloodshed was resumed in March 1918. The roads not taken were well marked, and repeatedly if tentatively explored, before the warring nations' leaders recalled the explorers and returned to the road of war. The reality is that, during 1917, and even into the spring of 1918, peace chatter was incessant – but mostly out of public hearing. That very fact meant that the chatter could be cut short, without the risk of a mass uprising at the back of the negotiators. But it would be foolish to assume that, because no road toward a negotiated peace was ultimately taken, there had been no forks in the road.

Just a few peace initiatives might be mentioned.

Perhaps the most significant was the so-called 'Sixtus affair'. After the death of Franz Josef, the old Austro-Hungarian Emperor, in November 1916, the new youthful and intensely Catholic royal couple, Emperor Karl I and Empress Zita, believed it was their destiny to restore peace. Karl sought to use his brother-in-law, Prince Sixtus of Bourbon-Parma, a member of the former French Royal Family at that time serving in the Belgian army, as an intermediary in secret negotiations with France. In a private letter of March 1917 carried by Sixtus to the French, Karl gave much ground: he accepted that peace would require the restoration of both Serbia and Belgium, and the return of Alsace-Lorraine to France. Lloyd George and Ribot were keen to pursue this feeler, but the Italians feared that their war aims against Austria (territorial gains promised under the secret Treaty of London of 1915) might be sacrificed in any peace deal. Thus, at the conference of St Jean de Maurienne in April 1917, the Italians vehemently opposed even a separate peace with Austria. The British and French feared wrecking the alliance with Italy. The negotiations went cold. For months, the Austrian leaders vacillated, at one point appearing willing to push the Germans into general peace talks, while at another appearing determined to preserve alliance solidarity, as hope for salvation by battle waxed and waned. Later, in March 1918, Clemenceau, who called all peace talk treachery, decided to blow up the whole affair. Acting unilaterally and recklessly, he suddenly released the private letters of the Emperor Karl, discrediting him as disloyal in German and Austrian eyes, and thus derailing any hope of Austria undertaking diplomatic talks behind the scenes to prepare the way for peace.[722]

Linked to this saga, for some months during 1917 a series of confidential talks took place, initially in Fribourg in Germany, between Nikolaus Revertera, an Austro-Hungarian diplomat, and Abel Armand, a French officer. These gave glimpses of hope that Germany would ultimately offer concessions on both Belgium and Alsace-Lorraine.[723] In September 1917, Briand, the former French Prime Minister, and Oscar van der Lancken, the Governor of German-occupied Belgium, were on the verge of talks in Lausanne-Ouchy, Switzerland, to explore possible concessions on both sides. Then the ageing Alexander Ribot, French Foreign Minister, suddenly banned Briand from making the approach. He stayed home. Had the talks gone ahead, the two grand hotels on Lake Geneva, chosen for the two delegations, the Hôtel du Château and the Hôtel Beau-Rivage, might have been famous forever as the cradles of peace.[724] Well-connected aristocrats tried to push the cause along, too. From March 1917, Lady Walburga Paget, whose son Sir Ralph Paget was an English diplomat, dispatched a series of letters to Maria Christina, Queen of Spain, urging Spanish diplomats in Madrid and Brussels to press forward British-Austrian peace talks. She soon fell foul of crusty old conservatives in the Foreign Office, such as Lord Hardinge, who sternly warned both Pagets, mother and son, to butt out. Hardinge never saw a peace feeler he liked.⁷²⁵

Emperor Karl of Austria

In the summer of 1917 contacts proliferated. Peace talks in The Hague between Sir Walter Townley, the British ambassador, and Count Ludwig Széchényi, an Austrian diplomat who had served in London before the war, seemed close. A middleman, Ferdinand Leipnik, was confident of compromise. But by October 1917, Balfour had concluded that the Austrians were indeed 'obviously anxious for peace' – but not for the separate peace that London wanted, a peace that would leave Germany weakened and exposed. He told Townley that, therefore, 'the best course seems to do nothing and to let events develop'.⁷²⁶

This was typical. In late 1917, Britain's men of power authorised a number of secret approaches to isolate Germany by luring both Austria-Hungary and Ottoman Turkey toward separate peace deals – while always suppressing talk of a general peace. In dealing with both Vienna and Constantinople, the British still shifted uneasily between plotting for partition and bargaining for peace. Partition meant inciting rebellion inside both the Austrian and Turkish empires, by promising liberation for their subject peoples. Bargaining for an early peace came always with the caveat: no broadening of the talks. Austria must be lured toward the betrayal of Germany, not a big peace table.

Testing the waters for such a bargain, General Jan Smuts, a member of Lloyd George's War Cabinet, travelled secretly to Geneva in December 1917 to meet the former Austro-Hungarian ambassador to London, Count Mensdorff – just at the moment Ryan was entering the prison in Calais. Nothing resulted. Smuts reported that a frustrated Mensdorff asked, 'Why were we going on fighting?' Lloyd George wanted a victory. 'If another year of this destruction had to pass', warned Mensdorff, 'the position of Europe and civilization, already so pitiable, would indeed be beyond repair'.[727] Philip Kerr, Lloyd George's private secretary, followed in Smuts's wake with a mission to Berne in March 1918. Here he met another Austrian envoy. Both efforts failed because Britain insisted that Austria-Hungary, if she wanted a soft peace, must abandon alliance solidarity and strike out for a separate peace. Austria wavered, but ultimately hoped to mediate a general peace. The British refused to budge. Foreign Office mandarins were appalled that general peace talks might lead to unconscionable compromises, such as the return of some German colonies.[728]

The Lloyd George Government also explored some astonishing back channels. Five times between June 1917 and October 1918, the British entrusted vast sums to none other than the notorious arms manufacturer Basil Zaharoff. His role? He was to meet with Ottoman officials in an attempt to bribe them into withdrawing from the war. Zaharoff, 'Zedzed' as he styled himself, was ever hopeful. He solicited 'chocolate' for his services – a Knight Grand Cross of the British Empire. But he achieved no decisive diplomatic breakthrough, and won no 'chocolate'.[729]

What of the men of God in Christian Europe? To their credit, several progressive church leaders in Europe sought to jump-start Christian pressure for peace. Swedish Archbishop, Nathan Söderblom, took a leading role. From July 1917, the British Council for Promoting an International Christian Meeting pressed for British acceptance of Söderblom's proposals for a conclave of Christian church leaders to discuss a diplomatic settlement. But most British Anglican bishops held aloof. Most Scandinavian and several church leaders from neutral nations went ahead anyway, meeting in Uppsala in December 1917. Encouraged, Söderblom called for a second Christian conference to promote peace in February 1918. Balfour, the British Foreign Secretary, warned Anglican Bishops that, whatever they decided, he would issue no passports for any such conference.[730]

Again, German-British talks on exchanging of prisoners of war might have provided another open moment. Meetings were resumed at The Hague in June 1918. Lloyd George briefly flirted with the idea of widening these parleys, but the War Cabinet was reluctant.[731] This time, the more conservative Sir George Cave led the British delegation, with Lord Newton reduced to a supporting role. Still, Newton was optimistic. 'We had not been there long', he recalled, 'when it came to my knowledge that the Germans were acutely, almost passionately, anxious to enter upon peace negotiations'. He was told that the Germans 'were willing to evacuate Belgium and to pay an indemnity, and that there was no intention of retaining territory in Alsace and Lorraine'.[732] But Cave had been directed to stall, saying that he had 'no instructions' to talk peace. Balfour, the Foreign Office elites, and the Tory press, had all pulled strings to keep the talks at The Hague strictly limited to one subject – prisoners of war.[733] Nonetheless, on Newton's return to London, Lloyd George gave him fifteen minutes to put the case for taking up the German feelers that had reached him. As usual Lloyd George was tentative, musing that the 'only question was whether [the] moment [is] opportune'. He 'would think it all over carefully'. And nothing happened.[734]

Through all of this, the British press often insisted that there was no realistic alternative to the grinding war because the wicked Germans would never leave Belgium unless battered out by brute force. The myth of German inflexibility on Belgium served the 'fight-to-the-finish' brigade well. But the evidence contradicts this. British diplomatic sources are littered with indications that the civilian inner circles in Germany considered Belgium only as Berlin's biggest bargaining chip. Clearly, many in Berlin thought it foolish to announce Germany's unconditional abandonment of Belgium before peace negotiations began, just as London refused to say that a single captured German colony might be returned.[735] For Berlin, fudging on the issue of Belgium pacified the Pan-Germans on the home front. So instead, Berlin's diplomats gave out many loud hints, and many British analysts believed them to be true, that Germany intended to give up Belgium. Assurances of this were given to the Americans in 1916-1917 and to the British in the Kühlmann peace initiative of September 1917.[736] General Haig himself admitted it. Clutching his newly-presented Field Marshal's baton on 2 January 1918, Haig told King George V that his troops did not want to fight so that France might regain Alsace, or Italy seize Trieste: '[T]hey realise that Britain entered the war to free Belgium and to save France. Germany is now ready, we have been told, to give all we want in these respects.'[737]

Thus, tragically, the great issues at stake in 1918 were all to be resolved by force and by force alone. Both sides were to blame for this. Pressures for peace and democratisation were simmering, in revolutionary Russia, in Germany, in France, and especially in Italy ever since major military setbacks there in October 1917, but were suppressed. Everywhere the war was kept going, but only with great difficulty. Over the winter of 1917-1918, some of Lloyd George's colleagues privately confessed their regrets about choosing ongoing war. For instance, David Davies, a key member of Lloyd George's secretariat, wrote to a friend in January 1918 lamenting 'our folly in not convening a conference six or nine months ago'.[738] Similarly, in March 1918, General Jan Smuts, a popular member of Lloyd George's War Cabinet, conceded that the 'psychological moment for negotiating with Germany, if we wished to negotiate, was last July and August'.⁷³⁹ Instead, the British elites had banked on the Third Battle of Ypres, or Passchendaele, to deliver a victory. Nothing like it had materialised.

Were men like Ted Ryan, therefore, unrealistic to imagine compromise? Was a negotiated peace only the dream of 'soft-conscienced men'? What of the men of iron? In fact, Australia's own Lieutenant General Monash saw that the prospect of peace by negotiation was very real. When the Germans made their 'Christmas Peace Offer' during the peace talks at Brest-Litovsk in late 1917, Athol Lewis, a young member of a family friendly with Monash, visited him at his divisional headquarters in a château in Steenwerck, near Armentières. As noted previously, Lewis was about to be appointed a courts-martial officer. He chatted to Monash alone in his room. After polite enquiries over the health of his mother and father, Monash showed him photographs of the German lines at Ypres before and after a devastating bombardment. Then Monash surprised him. Lewis preserved the moment in his diary: '[Monash] ... thought the peace offer in yesterday's *Times* said to have been made by the Germans to the USA for the Allies here very reasonable and worthy of consideration.'⁷⁴⁰

Epitaph

Who were the realists? Who were the idealists? Those surveying daily the human cost of the machines cutting a swath through those stumbling into action saw through the claims of the supposed 'realists' with their never-failing faith in more war. For example, Private Frank Molony, as he tended the wounded at his field ambulance stations in October 1917, reflected bitterly on the insane 'militarism' he witnessed daily, and its devilish work. He provided a suitable epitaph for so many.

> All day long the youth of the world, with minds strung to breaking point march to the line; their eyes seeing skeleton ruins, gaping holes, and sudden showers of high flung earth and bricks – on happily just the man in front of him ...
>
> All day long the Artillery are drawing to their guns long lines of mule teams laden with sudden compacted deaths, and all day long the unladen mules go back ... save those the shell struck.
>
> And all along the road the old men sweep and clear – fill in and stamp hard the new torn hole – move aside the dead horse team, and the splintered limber or wagon.
>
> The youth of the world winds up and down the road, to and fro through the low valleys, climb carefully the low ridge, and die suddenly or slowly, or comes back elated or dulled.
>
> The roads are full of the beauty of the world, and the terrible horror of war.⁷⁴¹

Chapter 22

SENTENCE SUSPENDED

CALAIS TO AMIENS, AUGUST 1918

Interviewer: What were some of the songs they sang in the estaminets?
Alfred Hayden: Oh that's the only one. 'We want to go home'.
Everyone joined in that …

Interviewer: Did you feel that?
Alfred Hayden: Oh yeah.[742]

— Private Alfred George Hayden, AIF veteran, interviewed 1985

In mid-August 1918, almost a year after his arrest for desertion, Ryan learned that the authorities had suspended his prison sentence.

Why? In essence, Ryan was released from prison under the British *Army (Suspension of Sentences) Act 1915*. The Act has been compared to the pre-war 'Cat and Mouse Act' that was used to torment suffragettes, who could be locked up under harsh conditions, force fed, then released, and then locked up again. The provisions of the *Army (Suspension of Sentences) Act 1915* gave similar powers to the military authorities; they could supplement the numbers at the frontline periodically by taking men from military prisons. At the will of the military elite, the soldiers could be told their sentences were suspended, and they were returning to the front. They would then soldier on, under the usual military laws, plus the threat of being bundled back to prison to resume their original terms of imprisonment if they reoffended in any way.

After the war, a US Senate inquiry into military justice heard evidence from Lieutenant Colonel Rigby, the Judge Advocate of the American Army, about the British system. Rigby reported that British commanders were determined that jailed soldiers should not feel they were 'getting out of danger'. Thus, through the use of suspended sentences, 'between 30,000 and 40,000 men were restored to the colours during the war'. British officers had boasted of even higher figures, suggesting they had 'restored from their detention barracks during the war 54,000 men, roughly'. 'Undoubtedly many of them died in battle', Rigby told the Senators. 'They found their system working very successfully. They are really very proud of it.'[743]

Thus, just one of the many soldiers released in this way, Ted Ryan was escorted from 'The Attic' prison camp near Calais on 18 August 1918, and returned to the 51st Battalion at the front two days later.

What was the real state of the war – and the diplomatic possibilities of ending it – to which he was returning? Ryan could hardly have known. While he had endured his total of eleven months in detention, which included the bleak winter months of 1917-18, he was almost certainly cut off from all war news – from both the battlefront and the homefront. For Ryan, darkness had prevailed.

Fighting On – In the Dark

And not only Ryan. Over those same months, the Australian people had their best chance to put under sunlight the precise purposes for which Australian soldiers were risking life and limb – but they would be permitted barely a chink of light. In the aftermath of the second Russian Revolution of November 1917, as noted previously, there was a spectacular unveiling of diplomatic secrets in just a few newspapers in Britain and America. So, before resuming Ryan's story at the front in August 1918, we must again raise the narrative beyond the horizon line of the trenches and see how these international events affected Australia.

As winter descended in late 1917, knowledge of the 'secret treaties' released by the Bolsheviks in the wake of their seizure of power was spreading in Britain and America. The *Manchester Guardian*'s revelations in December 1917 of the diplomatic exchanges known as the 'Constantinople and Persia Agreement' of March 1915 should have attracted some attention in Australia, for they exposed the true objectives of the Gallipoli campaign, the winning of sweeping gains at the Dardanelles, for Russia. The *Manchester Guardian* followed this first unmasking of diplomatic secrets on 18 January 1918 by printing the full text of the secret Treaty of London.[744] Similarly, informed Australians might have gobbled this one up. The document, signed on 26 April 1915, showed that the Gallipoli campaign had helped hurry Italy into the war, by holding out a share in the booty to be wrenched away from the Ottoman Empire. Again, Australians had died at Gallipoli for these secret objectives. Especially irksome to Australian Catholics would have been the revelation that the Entente partners had agreed under Article 15 to stand united against any peace initiative of Pope Benedict XV.

Any reader of these documents might instantly have seen that Britain and her partners were pursuing much territorial plunder. The war, embarked upon with so much fanfare by the British Empire as a great moral crusade to save France and Belgium, had clearly been transformed into a war of international brigandage: to dismember the Ottoman Empire, to expand Russian territories in eastern Europe, at the Straits and in the Caucasus, to give France a great slice of German territory in the Rhineland, and to strip Germany of all her colonies. Behind it all, and openly stated, was not just a plan to shift flags on maps, but a plan to sweep away German commercial and financial competition, especially in the Middle East and Africa.

Here was a turning point. But would Australians be permitted to learn anything of these carefully curtained truths? Not if the Hughes Nationalist Coalition Government could prevent it. It was the choice of that government to leave Australians fighting on – in the dark. The government was not about to clarify the war aims beyond the daily gruel of the essential need for a holy victory over the German monsters in order to redeem the souls of the Australian dead.

Why? First, context is vital. In December 1917, when the 'secret treaties' were first appearing in some foreign newspapers, the Hughes Government had its eyes firmly fixed on the coming second referendum on conscription, due just before Christmas. Revelations of the purposes behind the three years of combat so far might imperil the victory of conscription at the polls! So, the Hughes Government wheeled out its heaviest censorship machinery. By maintaining the existing strict control over the cables bringing news to Australia, by the censorship of the press, and by resorting to outright prohibitions, the government proceeded to limit any knowledge in Australia of these diplomatic deals. A news blackout descended – as an act of state policy.[745]

On 12 December 1917, George Pearce, as Minister of Defence, beefed this up, announcing a big bundle of 'Prohibited Publications', under Regulation 28AB, one of more than one hundred special regulations that the Government proclaimed under the *War Precautions Act 1914-1916*. The official *Commonwealth of Australia Gazette* listed more than 220 books, pamphlets, newspapers and journals that were suppressed, overnight. Anyone found in possession of them risked very heavy fines and imprisonment. The net was flung wide. Radical, internationalist, and pacifist publications of all kinds were banned. On the 'banned list' were not just Australian, British and American titles, but also dozens of publications from Russia, Italy, Ireland, India, and from various neutral states in Europe. The prestigious overseas dailies that had actually first published the secret treaties, the *Manchester Guardian* and *New York Times*, were probably regarded as too powerful to ban outright. Control of the cable news served to screen the Australian public from revelations in them. But smaller fry, such as the leading British Labour newspapers the *Labour Leader* and *Forward* (where the 'secret treaties' were indeed soon be reprinted) were prohibited. A bizarre vindictiveness was at work. For example, the American press magnate, William Randolph Hearst, had for some years opposed American intervention in the war.[746] So, everything from his stable was barred, including the scarcely subversive *Good Housekeeping*, *The Motor*, *Motor Boating*, and *Harper's Bazaar*.[747]

Thus, the government's boot pressed down harder on the windpipe of criticism of the war. It tried other methods also to stifle dissent and to manipulate the electorate in a second referendum on conscription. The voting day was announced suddenly for 20 December 1917, with only a minimum amount of time – two days – until the electoral rolls were closed for fresh enrolments. In addition, for the first time, this national referendum was to be held on a working Thursday, rather than on a Saturday, making it a little more difficult for working-class voters to get to the voting places.[748]

A new cascade of pro-conscription propaganda fell upon Australia's soldiers in France and Britain, pleading for them to register a 'Yes' vote, as an act of loyalty to their dead cobbers, and as inspiration for those at home. Yet some soldiers in their letters home persistently denounced conscription. For example, Lance Corporal Jack Tarrant, a champion of a 'No' vote in the ranks in 1916, had told his various correspondents throughout 1917 that he was still a 'No' man, because, looking about in France and Britain, he saw that 'conscription leaves poverty and depression behind'.[749] Tarrant added that he had 'no faith' in Hughes's Government. He lamented that 'it is simply murder to see the fine young Australians who are paying the penalty never to return to their native land'.[750] When conscription was again rejected at the polls, he wrote from France that he was still 'a great Anti Conscriptionist and of course was very pleased to see the people of Australia turn it down'.[751] The result stunned Hughes and his supporters. They were once again especially embarrassed by the soldiers' vote, because an even slimmer majority had voted in favour of conscription than in October 1916.[752]

Over the months that followed, Hughes's Government redoubled its efforts to suffocate dissent in liberty-loving Australia. It banned more anti-war publications. The astonishingly reactionary mind-set of the government was often on display. For example, in February 1918, Pearce banned a famous book – Karl Liebknecht's pre-war study *Militarism and Anti-Militarism*, a fierce denunciation of militarism in Europe, written by a leading socialist now languishing in prison in Germany. But he was German, so Australia suppressed his anti-militarist masterpiece incongruously, in the fourth year of a war supposedly waged to suppress 'Prussian militarism'.[753] Similarly, on Anzac Day 1918, the government criminalised anything produced by the 'Union of Democratic Control' (or UDC), Britain's leading left-Liberal internationalist pressure group in which Ramsay MacDonald was still prominent. Thus, the UDC's most popular pamphlet, Seymour Cock's *The Secret Treaties*, first published in England in April 1918, was suppressed.[754] The Australian big city newspapers carried long lists headed 'PROHIBITED: PAPERS YOU MUST NOT READ'.[755]

These same main city newspapers buried reports of the 'secret treaties' as they joined in a great roar of complaint over Russia's 'betrayal' of the cause of Britain and her allies. The Labor-aligned newspapers managed to give publicity to summaries – but rarely complete texts – of the diplomatic secrets unveiled by Trotsky. One was the *Barrier Daily Truth*. It predicted that the Hughes Government would 'do its damnedest to prevent the vulgar herds from browsing among the details of those records of chicane and treachery'.[756]

And so it did. The extraordinary energy of Hughes's 'Australian National War Government' in tightening censorship extended to Parliament itself. During January 1918, Federal Labor MPs began to debate war aims. They advocated the Wilsonian war aims that had been endorsed by the British Labour Party, and attacked the 'Welsh Kaiserism and Prussianism' of Hughes.[757] But they were hamstrung in revealing whatever details of the 'secret treaties' they might have known by threats of prosecution. Intimidation reached even into the debating chambers. In February 1918, Pearce directed the military police to impound packets of printed speeches, taken directly from *Hansard*, by James Catts, a Labor MP from Sydney. They were seized from a Labor party room inside the federal Parliament in Melbourne. Labor protested loudly – but in vain.[758] Hughes's MPs permitted the Parliament to doctor its own records of debate. In late September 1918, Pearce secured a resolution of the Senate allowing 'the omission' from *Hansard* of anything that might offend an ally of Britain or threaten the successful prosecution of the war.[759] The House of Representatives authorised the doctoring of its *Hansard* in a similar way on 2 October 1918.[760]

Nonetheless, Australia's Parliament did debate war aims during 1918. In early April, Hughes put a resolution vowing that Australia would 'fight on to secure a victorious peace and the freedom of the world'. Labor proposed an amendment urging instead an 'honourable peace', and declaring that the House was 'not opposed to peace by negotiation'. Labor MPs denounced Hughes and his 'tyrannous censorship' for suppressing all informed discussion of war aims. William Higgs, a Queensland Labor MP, complained that even Wilson's famous 'Fourteen Points' speech had 'not been reported in full in any daily newspaper in Australia'. 'I say that the people of Australia are being kept in the dark about what is happening in the world.' Labor MPs criticised the government for backing imperialist plans for territorial conquest and the crushing of German commerce. When the Labor amendment was lost on party lines, the ebullient Nationalist MPs sang 'God Save the King'.[761]

But inside the Labor Party, peace activists were steadily shifting opinion. During the early months of 1918, four of the state Labor parties adopted resolutions urging 'that immediate negotiations be initiated for an International Conference' to determine 'equitable terms of peace'. In May 1918, the Sydney Trades and Labour Council denounced suggestions that Labor assist in recruiting and instead called upon workers everywhere to press their governments 'to secure immediately an armistice on all fronts and initiate negotiations for peace'. Then the powerful NSW Labor conference in early June came out strongly against the war and recruiting. The path-changing moment came on 25 June, when the Inter-State Conference of the Labor Party in Perth agreed to urge the Allies to come clean, that is, to issue a new 'clear authoritative statement' of war aims in accord with the 'publicly declared objects' for which Australia had entered the war in 1914 – 'liberty, democracy, and the independence of small nations'. Labor defiantly opposed any more recruiting for overseas service until the Allies announced their 'readiness to enter into peace negotiations under the basis of no annexations, no penal indemnities'. But fear of the censor forced the party to cut out much of the debate in the official *Report* of its own conference.[762]

Indeed, the censor's hot breath was felt upon all those in the party determined to expose the 'secret diplomacy' prolonging the war. Federal Labor MPs could criticise, but only in general terms, the revelations in the 'secret treaties'. On Anzac Day 1918, James Catts offered 'a short list' of what had been revealed in London and New York over recent months. Nationalist MPs taunted Catts for speaking in 'parables'. Catts shot back, 'I am not allowed to deal with the mass of evidence in my possession'.[763] Not until June 1918 did a Labor MP, Mick Considine from Broken Hill, read into *Hansard* the texts of the Straits and Persia Agreement of March 1915 as given in the *Manchester Guardian* while responding to a shout from a Nationalist MP that 'there are no such secret treaties'.[764] The censorship suppressed reporting of the speech in the newspapers. Very late in the war, other Labor MPs did boldly denounce the 'secret treaties' while warning that their denunciations might disappear from *Hansard*.[765]

As a result of such censorship and intimidation, most Australians remained in the soupiest fog about the purposes of the war. Apart from avid readers of the Labor press, most Australians never had a chance to learn that the Gallipoli campaign had been aimed at seizing big trophies for Russia, to keep her in the war, or that the Anzacs' landing at Gallipoli on 25 April 1915 had been cynically used as a lever to tip Italy into the war. Most never learned that France and Russia had agreed upon mutual aggrandisement on Germany's western and eastern frontiers, a deal that underwrote the long war on the Western Front that cost so many Australian lives. Most remained ignorant of the string of colonial deals London had struck with France and Japan. The tangible purposes of the war, the territorial seizures and special economic privileges sought in order to further enrich already rich men, all remained hidden.

Instead, the British people – and the Australian people – were offered a shamelessly laundered version of Britain's war aims. Britain's well-funded National War Aims Committee plundered progressive statements from the British Labour Party in late 1917 and from Lloyd George in early 1918 to show that Britain was fighting not for imperial gain but for a new democratic future for all of mankind. One especially disingenuous propaganda pamphlet asserted that Britain was:

> … seeking no selfish or predatory aims of any kind, pursuing, with one mind, one unchanging purpose: to obtain justice for others, that we may thereby secure for ourselves a lasting peace. We desire neither to destroy Germany nor to diminish her boundaries; we seek neither to exalt ourselves nor to enlarge our empire. We fight for the common salvation of all from the perpetual menace of militarism and the curse of recurrent wars. We aim at nothing which we cannot openly state before all men.[766]

Such was the fantasy offered to the ordinary people. Did it work? Not if recruiting is any guide. Only a comparative trickle of men enlisted in Australia during 1918. The government responded with desperate efforts to frighten the people with propaganda images of an unspeakably evil Germanic monster poised to gain victory unless more men came forward to volunteer. The campaign flopped. A planned AIF 6th Division was abandoned. Clearly doubts about the purity of the British Empire's cause were percolating far beyond the Labor benches.[767]

But probably nothing about these controversies in Australia reached Ryan or his fellow prisoners at 'The Attic' during the early months of 1918. Similarly, precious little of it reached the soldiers of the AIF in the lines in France or in the camps in England. The *Anzac Bulletin* left the men clueless about the purposes for which they were being pressed to fight on – and on. This trench newspaper continued to act as a noisy relay station for ultra-patriotic opinion in Australia. It gloried in the indispensable victory that was always just around the corner, mocked talk of 'secret treaties', abused 'pacifists' whose ideals allegedly 'cloaked treachery to the nation', scolded all the 'weak-framed people' who advocated diplomatic compromise, and warned of the grave peril of 'a negotiated peace' to the Empire, because 'if the war becomes even a drawn game – we are lost'.[768]

Scarcely a drip of news appeared in the *Anzac Bulletin* about the tumultuous events in Russia, other than Hughes's assertion that the Bolshevik Revolution in November was the work of 'the insidious propaganda of pacifists and German agents'.[769] Nothing appeared about the revelations of 'secret diplomacy' over the winter of 1917-18, and nothing about President Wilson's progressive speeches during 1918, challenging the old conceptions of great-power politics and protectionism. Not even Wilson's world-famous 'Fourteen Points' of January 1918 got a mention (until Hughes set out to rubbish them in late 1918).[770]

In a sense, all soldiers were like the survivors of mustard gas attacks, depicted in the iconic painting 'Gassed' by John Singer Sargent: the men stumbling on, blindfolded in gauze, with their hands on each other's shoulders or tugging on each other's packstraps. As the British advocate for a negotiated peace, Israel Zangwill, put it: 'This is the true "fog of war" – that we no longer see each other, that we hack blindly in the dark at the monstrous images we have made of each other.'[771]

Brest-Litovsk and the Last German Offensive, March 1918

In the face of the massive German offensive into France beginning on 21 March 1918, it is easy to blot out all this dishonesty and fudge, and point fixedly instead to the reality of German aggression. The Germans, after all, imposed an annexationist peace treaty upon Bolshevik Russia in early March 1918, the Brest-Litovsk Treaty. Under its terms, beneath the cover of extending a dubious 'independence', the Germans took a great swag of the former Russian imperial borderlands (mostly non-Russian in population), including Finland, the Baltic provinces of Estonia, Livonia, Courland, and Lithuania, (later Estonia, Latvia, and Lithuania), and Russian Poland and the Ukraine, under varying degrees of autonomy and German tutelage. (Under a supplementary treaty in August, Russia also had to pay an indemnity of six billion gold marks to Germany.[772])

There was much huffing and puffing in London against the cruelty of the Brest-Litovsk Treaty. In Hughes's words, dished up to Australia's troops, it was 'living proof of the perfidy of the real purpose of Germany'. He lamented that '[Russia's] head was now poised on the bloody pike of the Germans'.[773] Of course, as their own 'secret treaties' had revealed, France and Russia had contemplated big bites of their own into territories in western and eastern Europe respectively, and all the Entente nations were still planning to gobble up great hunks of the Ottoman Empire in the Middle East, and beyond, with Britain playing the role of apex predator. Further afield, events soon revealed the double-standards at work: just a fortnight after the German Reichstag ratified the Brest-Litovsk Treaty (against the abstentions and protests of the German socialists), Japanese forces began to arrive in Vladivostok, with British and American support. The numbers of Japanese troops climbed steadily toward 70,000. The catastrophic Western intervention in Russia, aiming at a Tsarist restoration, was launched.[774]

The hypocritical chorus of pots calling kettles black resounded through the press for months. Brest-Litovsk became a rhetorical token; but it was scarcely convincing go-to evidence of singular German evil. Certainly, there were men of power in Berlin who had no intention of genuinely independent nations emerging from the former Tsarist empire in eastern Europe under German tutelage; similarly, there were men of power in London, Paris, and Rome who had no intention of genuinely independent nations emerging in the future across the Middle East, in the Rhineland, or on the eastern shores of the Adriatic, under the victors' tutelage. In reality, none of the Western decision makers actually wished to see the Russian borderlands returned to Bolshevik Russia – not in 1918, and not in the future.[775] Moreover, the six billion gold marks extorted from Russia in 1918 was soon to be dwarfed by the enormous sum for 'reparations' imposed upon Germany in the aftermath of the Versailles Treaty: a total of 152 billion gold marks.[776]

It is true that, in this chaos of grab and vengeance, there was no 'moral equivalence' between Germany and her enemies but neither was there a moral gulf. Some historians are inclined to pass over the family resemblance in war aims asserting that, in the face of the German offensive of March 1918, the Western forces were at least fighting a just defensive war for democracy.[777] This would be to lose sight of the vast colonial spoils that were still fundamental to the conflict – in Africa, Asia, the Pacific, and especially in the Middle East.

Those at the centre of power in London did not lose sight of them. For example, Maurice Hankey, the secretary to the British War Cabinet, could be charmingly candid. In August 1918, he pressed the case that Britain should not surrender the oil fields of Mosul, in Mesopotamia, to France, or to anyone. Hankey advised Balfour, Lloyd George's Foreign Secretary, that oil would be absolutely vital for 'the next war'. In fact, Persian and Mesopotamian oil were 'the only big potential supply that we can get under British control'. Therefore, as Hankey put it, 'the control over these oil supplies becomes a first class British War Aim'.[778]

Last Gasp

At exactly this moment, mid-August 1918, Private Edward Ryan was freed – to fight for all those war aims, known and unknown.

His original five-year sentence, revised down to two years with hard labour in December 1917, was now suspended – not quashed. Thus, the threat of being returned to prison if he offended again hung over him. There was another crucial matter: his pay. After his death sentence was commuted to five years of imprisonment, his total forfeiture of pay had been calculated at five years and thirty-one days. Was this forfeiture also revised down to two years in December 1917? In short, was he back on the payroll immediately upon suspension of his sentence or would he have to wait? This was unclear upon his release in August 1918. If the stop order on his pay was not suspended, he would be waiting for his next pay until at least December 1919. As we shall see, this issue would soon drive Ryan to a last act of indiscipline.

Why was he released? A simple fact: more men were required for the five Australian Divisions at the front. For this reason, Ryan was taken from the British prison at Les Attaques near Calais and returned to the Australian authorities. He was not free, of course. He was sent back to his old unit at the front.

Private Ryan re-joined the 51st Battalion near the village of Rosières-en-Santerre on 20 August, a few kilometres to the east of Villers-Bretonneux. The battalion was now under its third commander, Lieutenant Colonel Robert Christie, a Queenslander, appointed in October 1917. The battalion had just moved into reserve trenches, relieving an American unit, near Harbonnieres. Here the men spent the next four days, doing salvage work in 'very warm' weather. There was some relief. They had a chance to bath in communal baths on leaving the trenches, and were then bussed to billets at Rivery, just to the north-east of Amiens.[779] Two weeks of training followed in the Amiens area, including tactical exercises, range finding, and firing practices in the moat surrounding the ancient citadel of Amiens – the familiar thunder of shellfire and gunfire, and the familiar scents of lyddite and cordite – all painful no doubt for any shell-shock case.

Ryan was back, as one British veteran described it, in that 'riot of ghastliness and horror, of inhumanity and negation'.[780] The Australian Colonel, Aubrey Wiltshire, was just as evocative in February 1918, writing in his diary of the 'whine of shell and whiz of bullet' and 'the aftermath of stinking corpses and living pain'. Wiltshire lamented that 'War is becoming scientific murder as soft flesh and blood have no chance against hard steel.'[781]

How could a man freshly released from prison, with Ryan's record of shell shock and his convictions about the waste of this criminal war, fit into his old battalion, after almost a year? He may well have encountered a spirit of killing abroad in the battalion that revolted him. For some soldiers, a vow to take revenge for the deaths of their friends spurred them onward. Some months before, on Anzac Day, 25 April 1918, Captain Billy Harburn of the 51st Battalion had told his men: 'Kill every German you see, we don't want any prisoners, and God bless you.' 'No Prisoners' was Harburn's direct order on that day.[782] Awarded a Military Cross in June 1918, Harburn was still with the 51st Battalion when Ryan rejoined the unit in August 1918. Other soldiers of the 51st Battalion certainly remembered their officers' boastful stories, that may or may not have been true: one officer sought to impress them by describing his shooting of six Germans after their capture in Noreuil, waving his pistol as he explained airily, '[w]e can't take prisoners (bang)', 'we gotta mop this village up (bang)', and 'the only good Fritz (bang) is a dead Fritz (bang)'.[783]

Certainly such stories were not exceptional. Private Alf Hayden remembered an officer in his 1st Battalion saying: 'I'm gonna kill every German I see.' Hayden also recalled another soldier, 'Bob Christie' – not the commander of the 51st Battalion – bragging of killing at least ten wounded Germans. Hayden related a clash between Christie and an English officer who scolded Christie for being 'cruel' in killing these 'all unarmed men'. 'I get six bob a day to kill 'em, and I'm gonna kill 'em, until they kill me', Christie had replied.[784]

The Australian soldier, Arthur Wheen, who would in his post-war life enthusiastically translate Remarque's *All Quiet on the Western Front*, knew that all sides were capable of atrocity. A decade after the war ended, he would write disdainfully of those Hun-haters who still thought only of 'German grossness'. 'I should not mind compiling some of my experiences of British ditto for their edification. They won't admit that the bestiality was wherever the war was', wrote Wheen. He could tell of British cruelties that 'would make their tears forever flow'.[785]

Of course, not every soldier thought like Christie, or like Wheen. As the Australian, British, and American forces advanced across France in the late summer and autumn of 1918, enjoying greater and greater superiority in firepower and supplies, some soldiers found the mood of exultation impossible to resist – a let-the-machine-guns-do-the-talking spirit of retribution. After all, the British and French enjoyed overwhelming superiority in mobile armour: the Germans had at the most only 40 tanks (half of them captured machines), while the British and French had some 4,000 by late 1918.[786] The Americans were arriving in vast numbers. Victory beckoned! It was, wrote Australian Corporal Downing, an advance that 'no adventurous soul could wish to miss'.[787]

Others found that spirit impossible to share. The one-sidedness of the struggle troubled some. Increasingly, the AIF faced disaffected, ill-equipped, under-fed, conscripted, German youths.[788] They were tossed into these battles not to win the domination of Europe, but rather to improve Germany's bargaining position. In the words of one historian, the Germans fought to stem the Western powers' advance simply so that they 'could negotiate peace on terms that were not devastatingly one-sided'.[789] German soldiers captured by Australians during 1918 were offered a meal and instantly 'woofed their food like starved mongrels'. 'They ain't soldiers', said an American looking on.[790] The veteran Eric Abraham remembered being shocked by the physical condition of the German prisoners that were taken in the last months of the war. Increasingly, they were young and half-starved. 'Shocking damn thing', he recalled. 'Originally they were well-built, well-fed, good-looking soldiers. That was in 1916. I used to see them going back. 1918 they were pasty-faced blokes, ill-kempt, didn't look like soldiers even, although they had their uniforms on. Totally different. They were out on their own, down to bedrock, the German nation was, down to bedrock.'[791]

The Château de Bovelles, scene of Private Ryan's second Field General Court Martial, 15 October 1918.

Chapter 23

ON STRIKE

RIVERY TO BOVELLES, SEPTEMBER-OCTOBER 1918

Interviewer: Australian soldiers, your cobbers, how were they regarding the war, during their time in France?

Ern Morton: It wasn't discussed much but I know that the majority, yes I could say the majority, were opposed to the war.[792]

— Private Ernest Morton, AIF veteran, interviewed 1985

On 5 September 1918, after a fortnight's training at Rivery, the 51st Battalion received its 'warning order' from its immediate superiors in the chain of command, the staff of the AIF's 13th Infantry Brigade: the battalion was to move by bus, in stages, east to the forward area near Péronne, on the Somme, beginning the next morning, 6 September.

But Ryan was not with them. At a roll call that morning, an hour before the buses departed, Ryan was found to be absent. The buses left Rivery without him. He had drifted away. And he would be gone for eleven days.

The Retiring Enemy – and the Walking Man

What incident propelled him again toward flight? Was it the order to move forward? Was Ryan consciously avoiding combat?

Probably. Some readers will say that he walked away from his fellow-soldiers to whom he owed loyalty. Others will say that he walked away from the demonic war in which he did not believe. Some will weigh his abandonment of 'mates' as the ultimate wrong. Others will weigh his abandonment of the war as a choice for release from moral compromise, a choice that was fundamentally right. Those of us who have never had to weigh the rights and wrongs of this question in our own lives should be loath to judge.

Another consideration is relevant. From Ryan's point of view, he was refusing to join in the pursuit of an enemy that was retiring anyway. He might well have regarded that pursuit as futile. The officers of Ryan's 51st Battalion in early September 1918 certainly told the men, to buck them up, that the tide of battle had turned very much in their favour. They did not expect that any hard fighting lay immediately ahead. The battalion's intelligence officers spelt out the fact: 'The enemy is retiring on the Australian Corps front closely pressed by our advanced guard', their report read.[793] The battalion's objective was 'to penetrate as far as possible into the enemy's ground *without becoming involved in any serious action*'.[794] As events turned out, the battalion spent a few more days in the support area behind the lines after Ryan's disappearance on 6 September. On one day, the men bathed in the River Somme. They entered the front-line positions on 10 September, and advanced the next day. 'Opposition was slight and our casualties light', recorded the battalion's war diary. 'Enemy very quiet.' 'Enemy offered little resistance.' On 21 September, the men were relieved. They fell back to 'poor' and 'dirty' billets behind the lines in the village of Guignemicourt. During those last days of desultory fighting, the battalion lost a total of seven killed and 54 wounded. Fighting there was. But, putting this in perspective, the total of evacuations due to sickness in the battalion during this same period was 44.[795]

Another soldier, Stan Nixon of the 16th Battalion, remembered those last days of fighting. The German troops 'seemed to have lost all interest in everything'. Nixon was sickened by what he saw, 'day after day. It is just this murder.' He resolved 'to fire at their legs'. Why? 'They got a woman and kids at home, just the same.'[796]

So, yes, Ryan missed the last of it. Where did he go, and what was he doing?

Drifting, it would seem – and possibly confused. Again, he must have been dodging officers and the military police for the eleven days he was missing, perhaps hiding his battalion's shoulder patches, and surviving by mixing in with other troops. Then a British soldier, Sergeant Fred Illger of the 8th Sherwood Foresters, when directed by an officer, arrested Ryan as 'a straggler' on a road behind the lines near Corbie on 16 September. Ryan had in fact been wandering just a few kilometres away from his battalion. Having moved east, Ryan was actually nearer to the front than he had been when he disappeared from the battalion. The British unit handed him over to the officers of the 51st Battalion when they arrived at Guignemicourt. Probably Ryan was held in the 4th Division's own 'Divisional Field Punishment Compound' when it was established on 1 October at Picquigny, on the banks of the River Somme, just a few kilometres to the north of Bovelles.[797]

Flight

How did other Australian soldiers regard their comrades who took flight from their battalions? How did they regard those men who sought escape from the war through a self-inflicted wound? Or even through suicide? Some were moved to sympathy.

At his advanced dressing station, Private Frank Molony was one of the more generous in judging fellow soldiers at their end of their endurance. On 30 August 1917, he treated a British soldier 'with a bullet through his face'. Molony privately decided it was a self-inflicted wound from the soldier's own rifle, fired twice. But Molony was prepared to mark the wound down officially as 'accidental'. He sympathised: 'There's no incentive in his mind, and no hope. He's the result of the Army's discipline, and he was the type they shoot for "cowardice". They shoot for cowardice, and award for heroism, and everyone has come to know the vague invisible dividing line.'[798]

Sergeant Eric Evans, of the 13th Battalion, recorded in his diary in June 1918 an attempted suicide. 'A chap cut his throat yesterday in the wood at the bottom of the camp.' He had been 'very depressed and threatened to do it'. He was found 'lying naked, covered in blood' and was saved. Evans did not condemn him. Rather, he wrote, 'there is a certain amount of guilt in the mess that we didn't take heed of his warnings'.[799]

And 'deserters'? In the great confusion at the Western Front during the last months of fighting, it was not uncommon to encounter 'stragglers'. One Australian soldier, Private Gissing, recorded in his diary in March 1918 his reluctance to arrest several British deserters whom he encountered, deciding instead to warn them to report back to their units as soon as possible.[800] By contrast, in August 1918, a Private Clifford Geddes had no time for Australian deserters, complaining in his diary of his disgust at 'having to tramp after these brutes that clear out'.[801]

Reluctance to judge was more typical among the troops. Toward the end of the war, Australian soldiers would express quite openly to their own families how near they had come to breaking down. For example, writing from a British hospital a few days before the armistice, Private Frank Weatherhead told his father that his wound had 'seared his brain', so that he now 'trembled like a leaf' even at the sound of a train whistle. His nerves were 'severely unstrung'. 'Modern action is the most nerve racking and tragic that anyone is called on to face and it is bound to break the stoutest heart if he is forced to stick it.' 'Many a time', he admitted, 'I have been tempted to run or to sacrifice anything to get out of it'. A wound was to him a blessed relief, because 'shell fire is worse than death'.[802] Just after the war, a soldier's history of the AIF 24th Battalion conceded that some men 'funked it on the way to the trenches', but the author had no harsh words for them, because 'the agonies men were called upon to endure were never meant for flesh and blood'.[803]

Even Australian officers sitting on courts martial privately expressed sympathy for bolters. For example, Major Aubrey Wiltshire had mixed feelings, even as he regularly handed out sentences of 10 years' penal servitude to soldiers for desertion. Wiltshire recorded as early as the autumn of 1916 that it was 'very noticeable that more men are deserting than formerly – generally good men too'. He confided to his diary his understanding of the typical deserter's story. Such a man had usually experienced combat, but then 'seen his mates blown out each time and at last his nerve fails and he disappears until after the battalion comes out. A heavy penalty is then his. Pathetic!'[804]

Field General Court Martial

After a month of imprisonment, Ryan faced his fourth court martial, another Field General Court Martial, on 15 October 1918.

By this time the whole world, even soldiers in the line, were conscious that the end of the war was near. Bulgaria and Turkey had sued for peace at the end of September. Germany had applied for an armistice on 5 October. It was revealed to the world's press. President Wilson and the new reformist German Government, a liberal-Catholic-socialist coalition led by Prince Max of Baden, were soon exchanging cables that were republished in the press, in an amazing display of the kind of 'open diplomacy' that Wilson, the progressive internationalist, had promised in his 'Fourteen Points' in place of the old 'secret diplomacy'. There was talk that an armistice, ending it all, was imminent.

In October 1918, all the battalions of the Australian 13th Infantry Brigade were engaged in some perfunctory training around Bovelles, behind the lines, about ten kilometres west of Amiens. The officers had set up their Brigade Headquarters in the beautiful Château de Bovelles, another grand eighteenth-century pile. 'This Château is glorious – very pretty garden and grounds', wrote a young Major James Churchill-Smith. 'From my window I can get a clear view of Amiens and Villers-Bretonneux.'[805] The officers enjoyed tennis on the château's court during the day, and bridge in the evenings. Meanwhile, the soldiers were billeted in the surrounding village's houses. They still had much to endure: the officers noted that the men's billets were 'very dirty', and 'a good deal of influenza' was appearing.

This, of course, was but a local episode of the influenza pandemic that would soon kill many millions of people across the world, including in greatest numbers the malnourished poor, the elderly and the young, in war-ravaged Europe and in the Middle East, over the winter of 1918-1919. The influenza virus hitched a ride on those troops and workers shunted about in this global clash of empires. Likely sources included American servicemen transported to Europe after contracting the infection from poultry farms in Kansas, sick soldiers mixing at the British army base at Étaples, and sick Chinese labourers shipped to the western front by the British. About 135,000 of these unfortunate indentured Chinese labourers had been transported from the captured German port of Qingdao to Europe via the United States during the winter of 1917-1918. By whatever means it came to Europe, the pandemic was yet another poisoned gift delivered to the world through the disasters of imperialism and war.[806]

But for the Australian soldiers in October 1918, the hot war seemed to be winding down at last. Those units resting were likely to stay resting. Amusements were needed. The officers at staff headquarters of the 4th Division began planning a boxing tournament for the entertainment of the troops.[807] The officers of the 13th Infantry Brigade looked to their men's comforts. Brigade and battalion committees organised a series of sporting events, including an athletics carnival for all the battalions. The brigade war diary noted that a concert hall was erected at the village of Guignemicourt, for the divisional concert party 'The Smart Set', and for lectures and debates, all in order 'to keep the men amused during the long winter evenings'.[808] Weirdly – or aptly, at the climax of a great imperial struggle in which racial consciousness was never far below the surface – AIF troops were often invited to debate the White Australia policy.[809]

Meanwhile, at 13th Brigade Headquarters, at the Château de Bovelles, plans were also made for the next round of courts martial. Three soldiers were listed for trial on 15 October 1918, all from the brigade's battalions. Two men, including Ryan, were to face charges of AWOL, and one other man a charge of desertion.

The day of Ryan's trial was a dull day, with heavy showers in the morning. There was also an important visitor from London who arrived at Bovelles that same day: Prime Minister Hughes. He likely visited the headquarters of the 13th Infantry Brigade at the château during the day. He was touring the front, still playing up to the British press as an ultra-patriotic attack dog, being photographed giving rousing speeches to the Australian troops. The men of the 50th Battalion, and the 51st Battalion, Ryan's battalion, were ordered to parade at an aerodrome near Bovelles at 11 a.m. to listen to Hughes.[810] Of course, Ryan was not on parade. But the bleak serendipity was remarkable: Hughes, whose inflammatory pro-conscription circular distributed to troops at Perham Down had so angered Ryan in 1916, was hosted at Bovelles on the very day of Ryan's trial.

The officers of the court martial were assembled at the château when they returned from the parade for Hughes. At 12.30 p.m., Major James Churchill-Smith took his place as President of the Field General Court Martial – a court constituted under the same diluted 'drum-head' procedures as Ryan had faced in September 1917. Churchill-Smith was a well-connected young man from a very prosperous Adelaide family; the Savoy Hotel in London was his favoured canteen when on leave. He was the holder of a Military Cross for gallantry, and a staff officer at 4th Division Headquarters. The day of the court martial happened to be his cake-and-candles day: 'My birthday – getting old. (24 yrs)', he recorded in his diary.[811] The other members of the court martial were also young. There was Captain Arnold Meredith Moulden, a 23-year-old barrister from Adelaide, and the travelling specialist in courts martial for the 4th Division. There were also two officers who had been rankers: Lieutenant James Anthony Menzies, a 26-year-old carpenter from Queensland, recently promoted from the ranks; and Second Lieutenant James Richard Bridger, a 22-year-old cotton trimmer from Maclean, New South Wales, also promoted from the ranks, just two months before. Bridger was drawn from Ryan's own 51st Battalion, which was unusual for military justice was meant to be blind.[812] Lieutenant Raymond F. Lade of the 50th Battalion, a 29-year-old Tasmanian solicitor, prosecuted. Two months later, Lade himself would be admitted to hospital in London, under the 'NYD' ('Not Yet Determined') label – meaning shell shock.[813] So here at Bovelles, ironically, one shell-shocked victim was prosecuting another.

The usual form lay on the table for the officers to complete during the court martial, 'Army Form A. 3'. The same slimmed-down procedures made for a quick trial: no 'Charge Sheet', no 'Summary of Evidence', and only minimal documentation for the officers to complete. Significantly, once again, the surviving papers show no sign of a 'prisoner's friend' being present to defend Ryan. But fortunately for Ryan, this time it was the lesser crime, AWOL, not desertion, that was listed as his offence. Because he had not appeared with the battalion at Rivery when buses were taking men back to the 'forward area' on 6 September, he might well have been charged with desertion, again. The circumstances of his walking away from his battalion were not so very different from August 1917, when his escape from a fatigue duty had resulted in a charge of desertion, a guilty verdict, and a death sentence. What was different this time? The war was clearly sputtering to its end and the Australian battalions were all resting. Churchill-Smith had been jubilant in his diary on 4 October over news of the Turks' 'giving in', and he had jotted down his prediction that Austria would soon follow, and 'then Goodbye to Germany'. Just two days before Ryan's trial, Churchill-Smith had recorded in his diary again, 'Good news in paper of Peace talk and advances'.[814]

But Ryan was not going meekly back into prison. He again pleaded 'Not Guilty'. As in September 1917, he would fight the charge.

Two pages of pencilled scrawl preserve the proceedings of the trial. Evidence was presented from witnesses. Private Harry Bowra from the 51st Battalion confirmed that Ryan had been absent from that roll call at Rivery on 6 September. Perhaps Bowra, a very young soldier from Kalgoorlie, felt under some pressure to show loyalty to the officers; only months before he had suffered 14 days' Field Punishment No. 2 for 'allowing prisoners to escape'.[815] Then, the British soldier who had arrested Ryan as a straggler, Sergeant Fred Illger, gave his testimony. He explained that he had doubts about Ryan after seeing him on the Corbie road, 'owing to his actions'. He did not elaborate. Then, 'acting under instructions, I arrested him' – the words perhaps hinting at some reluctance on his part. Possibly Ryan had struck him as a man in a confused state. 'I don't think he was trying to dodge me', added Sergeant Illger.

Ryan's case, of course, was hopeless. But he defended himself. This time he chose not to argue over the politics of the war. Under oath, he offered a simple explanation for his walking away, which echoed his complaints of May 1917. He protested against the injustice that he was soldiering on, after his release from prison, without pay. How? He told the court that his sentence of five years' imprisonment, with its accompanying forfeiture of pay, had been reduced to two years in late 1917. That sentence had then been suspended in August 1918, enabling his release from prison and return to the front. But, he protested, his pay had not been restored – or he believed it had not. 'A large debit was put in my pay book for a sentence of which part had been suspended', he alleged. This suggests he was in possession of his pay book and was disputing an entry under 'Forfeitures'. 'I thought it was unfair that I should forfeit pay for time I had not done. So I went AWOL', he told the officers bluntly. Someone underlined this confession in blue pencil strokes in the court record. He had admitted his crime. But from Ryan's point of view, he was on strike.

The weight of the complaint was clear. If Ryan was soldiering without pay, while under a suspended sentence, he was being treated as a convict at the front line. He was on strong ground. The official Paymaster's handbook specified that, from the date of a soldier's arrest, his pay book would carry the entry 'Pay Ceases'. But the handbook also specified that the forfeiture of pay of an imprisoned soldier should be lifted the day after the suspension of his sentence.[816] Ryan's service record certainly preserves the initial stop-order: 'Total Forfeiture. 5 years & 31 days.' This hand-written entry reflected the fact that his original death sentence had been commuted to five years of imprisonment. But no further entries revised this, neither when his sentence was further commuted to two years in December 1917, nor when he was released in August 1918. Nothing was recorded about the forfeiture being lifted. It was meant to be automatic. But if Ryan's pay book had been swiftly restored to him upon his departure from prison, he probably saw the original 'Pay Ceases' entry, unamended – and reacted angrily. He would scarcely have invented this argument, as his paybook was presumably readily available for checking. But courts martial did not exist to test the motives behind AWOL – just to punish it.

Perhaps he was the victim of vindictive neglect, or of an innocent bureaucratic delay. After all, the AIF Paymaster and his pay corps were based in London. Delays in resolving disputes over pay, and as we have seen in the issuing of new pay books, inevitably arose. Ryan may well have acted impulsively, before the lumbering bureaucracy restored his pay. Significantly, he walked away from his unit only 19 days after being released from prison, so there is a chance that he simply acted too hastily. In any case, his patience had snapped.[817]

As it turned out, none of the officers at Ted Ryan's court martial disputed, sought to disprove, or even investigated his claim. The matter of pay was irrelevant. That bore upon Ryan's motive, which was also irrelevant. Ryan was probably removed from the court for a brief time to allow the officers to discuss the case, and then returned to it to hear the officers' verdict: 'Guilty'. Next, as procedure demanded, the court moved to consider any mitigating factors, which usually revolved around 'evidence of character'. The prosecutor submitted a certified copy of Ryan's 'B122' form, his much-blemished record of offences and punishments. In response, Ryan called no 'evidence of character' and declined to offer any further statement. There was no point. Nothing there would help him.

Sentencing followed. The sentence this time was relatively mild: Ryan faced fifty days of 'Field Punishment Number 2'. Lieutenant Colonel John Whitham, the brigade commander, confirmed it. Lieutenant Colonel Robert Christie, Ryan's battalion commander, signed up also, promulgating the verdict and the sentence at a parade of the 51st Battalion on 19 October, just four days after the court martial. Another prison stretch awaited Ryan.[818] Later, Ryan's pay card recorded the financial penalty accompanying his sentence: 'Total Forfeiture 80 days.'[819] This amounted to £24 (roughly equivalent to almost $2000 in 2019). This was a slightly softer penalty in terms of loss of pay than he might have expected.

Note the mildness of the punishment overall. For whatever reason – either sympathy with a shell-shocked soldier, or in a forgiving spirit inspired by rumours of an armistice any day that might release them all from the maw of the war – the officers of this court martial were notably more charitable toward Ryan than those who, just a year before, had handed him a death sentence for desertion.

Chapter 24

FIELD PUNISHMENT

FLIXECOURT, OCTOBER TO NOVEMBER 1918

> Passed the Detention Camp where defaulters are imprisoned. Saw the posts to which men are chained daily for No. 1. Field Punishment. This is true, and a disgrace to any Nation professing to fight for liberty.[820]
>
> — Private W.J. Allsop, Diary, 1 March 1916

This time Ryan was incarcerated for his 50 days of field punishment not in a British military prison but in the 'Australian Corps Field Punishment Compound'. On 19 October 1918, he entered the compound. At that time, this moveable prison had just been shifted from the La Chapelette near Péronne to the small town of Flixecourt, on the River Somme, to the north-west of Amiens.[821]

Soldier of Misfortune

The regime in the various AIF Field Punishment Compounds was austere, but was clearly less extreme than in the British prisons that Ryan had endured at Dunkirk and Calais. A recently-promoted Captain Reuben P. Penna was in command of the 'Australian Corps Field Punishment Compound'. Under the Australian rules, prisoners such as Ryan who had been sentenced to Field Punishment Number 2 could be kept in irons, handcuffs, or fetters, for two hours, between 2 p.m. and 4 p.m., 'for not more than three out of four consecutive days', and up to a maximum of 21 days – but not tied to a fixed object. (Those soldiers unlucky enough to be sentenced to Field Punishment No. 1 were tethered to posts in view of their fellow prisoners for two hours a day – hog-tied to the war machine.) For all prisoners there was a round of parades, drill, and labouring. Rations were reduced: 'Tea, biscuit and bully beef only.' There was no reading matter, 'except for sacred literature and drill books', and no tobacco or alcohol. Prisoners slept on the floor of a guardroom overnight. Talking with guards or anyone outside the compound was forbidden. Total silence was imposed after 'lock-up time'.[822]

Ryan was still undergoing this punishment when the armistice was signed on 11 November 1918. He was kept imprisoned until the end of December 1918.

Fighting On – To Exhaustion

Was Ryan just one bad Anzac among a handful of disaffected troops in 1918? The final statistics tell a very different tale. The AIF as a whole was exhausted.[823]

But before we review the statistics, the diary of Corporal Arthur Thomas from the 6th Battalion may serve to give voice to the men still fighting in the spring and into the summer of 1918. 10 April: 'Yesterday's march was a terror ... Forty eight of us in a cattle truck, very uncomfortable ... Reached our destination after thirteen hours.' 13 April: 'We are being rushed everywhere and sleep as we stand, it is awful.' 18 April: 'Becoming monotonous, too long on this job ... We have been under shell fire since Xmas.' 22 April: 'It is absolutely treacherous moving about.' 23 April: 'Yesterday was a day of horrors, the barn we were in was intensely shelled ... We are having heavy casualties because going and coming is very hazardous.' 27 April: 'This is my seventh day in the trenches and am feeling jaded and tired and sick to the heart of the whole damnable foolish episode.' 28 April: 'I have been in trenches since Jan[uary], four months.' 30 April: 'We were relieved last night and I never in my life felt so weary.' 1 May: 'An English officer committed suicide this morning ... We are being shelled and these farm houses are death traps. We lost all but four [men] in five platoon through a shell bursting in on the men ... The men are all suffering from shell shock.' 3 May: 'Salvos of big [shells] were crashing about our ears and hellish excitement everywhere, more men were caught. Christ how long is such absurdity to last?' 19 May: 'We are breaking down, flesh and blood can't stand two years of this without bad results ... Our chaps put a trench mortar into Jerry's post and the cries and groans made me shiver. It makes a man hate war to the full.' 4 June: 'Fritz seems furious and he pounded hell out of us and we came right through his barrage, on a death trap road ... It is very nerve racking to be constantly under shell fire and horrors and dirt and filth, I am sick and tired of the blasted show, it is cruel.' 5 June: 'Last night, another night of horrors.'[824] An artillery shell killed Corporal Thomas three days later.

Thomas's jottings in denunciation of the war were by no means rare. The Censorship Department advising Field Marshal Haig at British General Headquarters in July 1918 circulated extracts from many intercepted letters, showing deep dissatisfaction, letters that troops had tried to post home – including Australians. One soldier from the 1st Division wrote in June that the British were 'sticking the dirt into the Aussies a treat'. Prison, or mutiny, began to look like good options to this soldier. 'It's a barstard [sic] in the line and it's a barstard out. A man would be better in the clinc [prison] doing a couple of years. Nothing would please me more than to see our blokes jib.' Another wrote in July: 'they are treating us like dogs, all the boys are fed up with it as they won't give us any rest, I think they want to kill all the Australians'.[825]

Bleeding Out – Breaking Out

Troops as exhausted as this were bound to break, even as their new Australian-born commander, Lieutenant General John Monash pushed them, in his own words, 'relentlessly' in the summer of 1918. He believed in the maxim: 'Feed your troops on victory.'[826]

But clearly victory was not sufficiently heady a spirit to hold them all together. In the most well-known incident, more than a hundred men from the Australian 1st Battalion, including NCOs, mutinied just behind the lines near the village of Hargicourt on 20 and 21 September 1918. They refused all orders as a protest against the sudden cancellation of a rest period that had been promised. In mid-October, various courts martial sat to judge the cases of 118 men charged with both mutiny and desertion. All but eleven were found guilty of desertion, and imprisoned.[827]

The mutiny stood at the peak of a formidable pile of similar cases. The Australian figures show the monthly total of Field General Courts Martial, trying cases of both AWOL and desertion, had increased from 544 cases a month in May 1918 to 716 cases a month in October 1918 – from a force of about 90,000.[828]

Similarly, the numbers of Australian soldiers serving prison terms in France and Britain during the last year of the war remained high. Taking a snapshot from July 1918, the figures show that at that time, military prisons held a total of 782 Australian soldiers, or almost eight AIF soldiers per thousand. This compared with British figures of less than one per thousand, while other colonial troops were imprisoned at a rate of less than two per thousand.[829]

Leading British officers often fumed about the Australians' lack of discipline. 'The Anzacs are very brave men, but they are simply a mob in uniform', wrote one officer in 1917.[830] Field Marshal Haig circulated figures in March 1918 showing that nine Australian soldiers per thousand were in prison, compared with only one British soldier per thousand. Still eager for executions, Haig hotly protested again that this was 'greatly due to the fact that the Australian government refuses to allow capital punishment to be awarded to any Australian'.[831] Lieutenant General Sir George H. Fowke, Adjutant General to the British Armies in France, supported Haig. Fowke complained that the percentage of AIF soldiers in France enduring prison during the six months ending in August 1918 had climbed to a rate '17 times greater than the whole of the British Expeditionary Force'.[832] As discussed earlier, in the minds of these red-tabbed staff officers, the prospect of Australians shooting Australians was just the sort of nightmare required to buck up these renegades of the AIF.

Official weekly AIF figures from the summer of 1918 provide a snapshot of the problem. Each and every week, from 1 June to 3 August 1918, the total of AIF men listed as 'absent' was in the hundreds: 364, 343, 343, 339, 277, 404, 441, 441, 459, and 439.[833] In September 1918, the totals were 711, 722, 687, and 646.[834] In October 1918, they were 665, 603, 613, and 578. When Ryan was court-martialled and sent to prison in October 1918, he was one of 106 men of the 4th Division so punished.[835] The next month, the month of the armistice, there were still 150 cases. The officers actually took comfort from such figures. 'The General Discipline of the troops throughout the month was very good', beamed the Assistant Provost Marshal of the Australian Corps in his official diary.[836]

The courts-martial officers, such as Lieutenant Athol Lewis, who were closer to the action, were more realistic. The work was burdensome. Lewis recorded that he had sat on 16 courts martial on a single day in May 1918, and 13 on another day in November 1918.[837]

During the spring and summer of 1918, Lewis learned that the numbers of Australian deserters on the loose behind the lines had become notorious. They were reported to have formed gangs of marauders, raiding farms and supply lines to get food. At that time, Lewis wrote of two incidents pointing to the presence of these brigands, quite close to General Monash's headquarters at St Gratien. On 28 April, two officer friends, a Captain Hyde and a Lieutenant Irwin, told Lewis that they had been enjoying a pre-dinner canter on their horses when they encountered an Australian deserter, who looked 'very comfortable', living in a makeshift shelter in the woods. Hyde arrested him, and told Irwin to ride on. Ironically, Hyde was soon thrown from his horse and was assisted back to Monash's headquarters by the prisoner! A few days later, Lewis and another officer were walking in the same beautiful wildflower-littered woods known as the 'Bois de Mai' when they saw a lone Australian soldier, 'an Infantry man out with a rifle & he dodged quickly out of our way'. Lewis learned it was not at all unusual. He confided to his diary the story circulating among the officers that 'the woods harbour quite a lot of our fellows who're living regular Kelly gang existences, every now & then raiding neighbouring farms'.[838]

Even after the armistice, the British authorities continued to supply Monash with embarrassing sets of comparative tables reflecting badly on discipline in the AIF in 1917 and 1918: the figures on courts martial convictions for desertion – three to four times the British rate – pointed to a deepening spirit of disillusionment among the Australians.[839]

This prompted officers at the headquarters of the Australian Corps to take a hard look at the evidence themselves in December 1918. Their official report asserted that serious crimes over the last six months of the war – assaults, looting, robberies with violence, thefts from homes, damage to property, drunkenness and rowdiness – were mainly the work of 'a large body of deserters and absentees who were hiding, evading capture in the woods in the Somme Valley about Corbie-Amiens-Picquigny'.

A 'round up' of the 'culprits' in this area in early November 1918 netted 75 men, long-term absentees. The report acknowledged that clearly the 'most serious' breaches in discipline in the AIF undoubtedly arose from the high rates of desertion and AWOL.[840]

The same picture emerges on a smaller scale, inside the AIF's 4th Division, which included Ryan's 51st Battalion. The 4th Division's Courts Martial Officer, Captain Arnold Moulden, as will be remembered, sat on Ryan's court martial in October 1918. Moulden's official diary for that month survives. It lists more than eighty courts martial in the AIF's 4th Division, including Ryan's case, for October 1918. It shows also that Moulden attended ten courts martial on one day during that month. Offences to be judged would range from AWOL – Ryan's crime – to drunkenness, using disorderly language, prejudicing good order, self-infliction of a wound, escaping once arrested, allowing other prisoners to escape, and finally desertion. The great majority of courts martial judged cases of AWOL and desertion, with 'escaping from confinement' also quite common.[841] It was only marginally better in November 1918, even after the armistice, with 45 courts martial. On one day, 20 November, Captain Moulden attended courts martial for 21 soldiers in turn, overwhelmingly cases of AWOL and desertion. Significantly, some men were on trial for allowing prisoners to escape, indicating some sympathy in the ranks for those accused of walking away from the war.[842]

When the war ended, the numbers of Australian soldiers in military prisons in France was 811, and the figure kept rising until a peak of 1,153 was reached in February 1919. The number in British prisons in England stood at 434 in May 1919.[843]

Trauma

Why so many? It is only in recent years that researchers have revealed the enormous numbers of traumatised men in the ranks of the AIF. Official figures reveal that just under 5,000 soldiers of the AIF during the First World War were actually discharged because of 'war related psychological trauma'.[844] But this almost certainly underestimates the dimensions of this crippling hardship.

At least one Australian commander, Major General Talbot Hobbs, Commander of the 5th Division, could see the inside of the problem. On 17 July 1918, Hobbs warned his officers of the 'great injustice' of sending all AIF men accused of desertion or AWOL to prison following court martial. There were recent cases, Hobbs argued, in which men found guilty of these crimes 'were discovered to be men suffering from nervous breakdown – men who were utter wrecks from a nerve point of view and totally unfit for front line work'. Such men were 'undoubtedly entitled to consideration', yet the courts martial had ignored their 'mental condition'. Hobbs stressed one case in which he thought it 'criminal' to have sent a man in such a nervous state back into the firing line in the first place.[845] Similarly, when about 60 'strikers' from the 59th Battalion refused to advance in September 1918, General 'Pompey' Elliott, commander of the 15th

Brigade, was advised that 'one and all' in that battalion were 'suffering from excessive fatigue, loss of sleep and nervous strain' and were at 'the limit of endurance'.[846]

Meanwhile, the punishments inflicted to deter AWOL and desertion in the AIF sparked controversy back home in Australia during 1918. In May, George Pearce, the Defence Minister, announced that the government would publish in newspapers the names of those guilty of 'desertion from the firing line'. The men would be publicly dishonoured, announced Pearce, 'as a deterrent'. Next, Pearce introduced a stop on all payments to dependents of Australian soldiers who were deemed to have deserted, after 80 days of absence without leave to punish the soldiers' kin. These measures provoked passionate debates in Parliament. Members complained about the unfairness of courts-martial procedures for the lower ranks, the harshness of punishments, the deprivation of food, the pitiful mental state of many of the deserters, and the unfairness of the government in seeking to shame men and publicly humiliate their families.[847] By October 1918, local Labor organisations were petitioning against all this because, as they argued, 'in most cases the men are suffering mentally from shell shock'.[848]

Clearly, there were many men like Private Ted Ryan. His injuries, his convictions regarding the war, and his repeated acts of defiance were not at all exceptional. He was just one angry, exhausted, and traumatised Anzac soldier, among many.

Who can tell exactly how many were just like him? Certainly, hatred for the war eclipsed all other emotions for many veterans in the long run. In June 1998, Lieutenant Harry Angel was the second-oldest surviving AIF veteran from the First World War. He was interviewed about his war experiences. He was asked: 'What is the one thing you most remember about the war?' He replied instantly, with gravel in his voice: 'Get out of it!'[849]

… Chapter 25

RETURN

FROM BELGIUM TO BROKEN HILL, 1919

The armistice took place while we was in Amiens. And what – what a joyful day it was. My word, to think the whole thing had ended. Yeah … Oh terrific, terrific. To think we – the sail boat – we got back in Australia after so many years there. No more fear![850]

— Private Bill Richardson, AIF veteran, interviewed October 1984

As peace descended over the devastated terrain of northern France and Belgium in November 1918, the Australian forces were among those that moved east, through the embers of war, into Belgium, as part of a mooted 'March to the Rhine'. But in mid-December, this decision was reversed. The Australians would be spared the sights of wild-eyed and hungry children gathered expectantly around their smoking cookers in the Rhineland – as British troops were soon to behold, so painfully.[851] Instead, the Australians were going home.[852] So, Australian battalions moved forward only as far as Belgium, generally by train, unhindered, without a shot being fired, leaving behind a landscape that millions of men had fought over for more than four years.

The miserable Australian Corps Field Punishment Compound was also on the move. It was originally intended that it would remain behind the lines in France. But documents suggest it was shifted more than 200 kilometres east into Belgium, and was functioning at Florennes, about thirty kilometres to the south-east of Charleroi, on Christmas Day 1918. Very likely Ryan spent Christmas in 'the cage' there.[853]

Meanwhile, the 51st Battalion had also moved further east, into Belgium. Over four days in mid-December, the men marched in stages from Sivry, just inside the Belgian border, to their destination, Bouvignes-sur-Meuse, near Namur. On 19 December, royalty paid a visit. David, the playboy Prince of Wales (the future King Edward VIII), with his page-boy prettiness and his decorative staff officer's uniform on display, called upon the 51st Battalion at Bouvignes for the day, 'passing through the billets and chatting to the men'.[854] On Christmas Day, the men arranged a grand dinner for themselves, and 'a dance until midnight in the large factory which was largely attended by the local ladies'. The Prince of Wales was back again on New Year's Eve to smile and award medals to

16 men of the battalion at the nearby village of Dinant (scene of a horrific massacre of civilians by vengeful German troops in the early weeks of the war in 1914).[855]

Ryan missed the royal visits. According to his service record, he was released from the Field Punishment Compound and returned to the 51st Battalion on 30 December 1918.[856]

Running on Empty

Ryan rejoined a battalion at rest and happily awaiting its return to Australia. In December, no doubt with ineffable relief, the men had handed in their steel helmets and box respirators to the Quartermaster. The fighting really was over. For the next two months, the men of the battalion passed their time in their winter quarters, organised into educational and recreational classes of all kinds. There were lectures, games, 'pillow fights', boxing tournaments, cross-country races, and dances. Then came liberation – for some. On 9 January 1919, 53 men classed as 'enlistments from 1915' departed, grasping at an early return to Australia as a reward for their long service. On 20 January, 73 more men followed, and on 29 January another 79 were let go. Of course, in light of his record, Ryan was not among them. Orders had specified that 'men who have misbehaved' must not get home earlier than 'men who have behaved themselves and done their duty'.[857] For those waiting it out with the battalion, the officers arranged more recreations. During February 'the most popular form of amusement in the evening was dancing, as dances were arranged for three nights each week and on the night of 16th a fancy dress was held and was largely attended by the troops and civilians in numerous fancy costumes'. However, the weather was bitter. There were up to twenty centimetres of snow in mid-February; it was still snowing in late March 1919.[858]

For three weeks in mid-March, Ryan was posted on a special task, outside the battalion. He was sent into Namur for 'Detached Duty' with the 'Namur Guard', guarding a large supply dump. It was uneventful. He came back to the battalion with 31 other men in early April. By this time the remnants of the battalion were moving back to the west, billeted at Le Roux, not far from Charleroi. The thinning ranks of the Australian battalions necessitated the combination of the 49th, 50th and 51st Battalions. A few days later, the men marched a few kilometres further to Aiseau, a mining town. Here a large concert hall was commandeered for more 'dances and concerts'. Courtesy of the manager of the local coalmine, the men had access to the hot water of the pithead baths – luxury!

Eventually, Ryan's turn came. On 13 April, he was 'marched out' with 11 officers and 111 men, in 'Quota No. 35', one of the very last 'quotas', bound for England. The men marched 13 kilometres to the railhead at Charleroi. A train then took them across France, and eventually to the wharves near the Australian base at Le Havre – the same wharves where Ryan had been arrested after making his solo journey of escape, from near the front line to the sea, in August 1917.[859]

On 22 April 1919, Ryan was among a mixed group of soldiers who boarded a troopship at Le Havre. They saw the last of France disappear behind them, landing the same day at Southampton. A few days before, a legal formality had been cleared up: the remaining unexpired part of Ryan's sentence of two years' imprisonment with hard labour, dating from his court martial in September 1917, was remitted. We may guess that his pay was also restored, his first payment for eighteen months.[860]

Ryan's group left Southampton by train immediately. Next day, 23 April, they arrived at the AIF's large Hurdcott Camp, actually a string of camps near the village of Compton Chamberlayne, to the west of Salisbury. It was another little town of rough huts, no doubt very reminiscent of Perham Down. But here at Hurdcott, in 1917, a large outline-map of Australia, enclosing the word 'Australia', had been cut into the chalk of the green hillside overlooking the camp, originally by men in detention. (It is now restored.)[861] It gazed down upon the men of Ryan's group for the next eight weeks as they waited their turn for a ship home.

Cooling their heels at Hurdcott, Ryan and his companions would miss the two parades staged by Australian troops through London, on 25 April, Anzac Day, when the Prince of Wales took the salute outside Australia House, and on 3 May, when the King's message was handed out to the troops, telling of his hopes that their victory would 'assure peace to their children and children's children'.[862]

Not all who saw it were uplifted. Henry Mond, a disillusioned British officer, son of an English Cabinet Minister, watched the Australian soldiers as they passed on 3 May. He was moved to a bitter poem lamenting this 'empty triumphal'. It was 'made of old to please/ The gaping crowds, the wealthy at their ease', he wrote. 'Hollow and hollow' was the tramp of the 'living souls caught living in machines'. He denounced the 'golden heap of perjuries' that had fed the war, and looked forward to an avenging angel, 'knife in hand', rushing forward to clear the world of the 'master perjurers', and then 'with the welter of their blood, the floors/ Shall rot and crash upon the throne of Mars'.[863]

'Fine Phrases ... Dark Thoughts'

Meanwhile, what had victory purchased? In his letter to Ramsay MacDonald in 1916, and at his court martial in 1917, Ryan had accused those directing the war in London of being possessed by a spirit of conquest. He had argued that imperialist war aims were driving on the war, and that a negotiated peace should have been tried. Was he right? How did the period of peacemaking in early 1919 turn out?

While the men of the 51st Battalion passed their time amid the snows of Belgium during the winter of 1918-1919, the armistice held, and the treatymaking began. Just over the border, inside Germany, the final episodes in this tragically prolonged war unfolded: a new German Government was brought to power by a revolution but was effectively isolated by the victorious powers, the political forces in the defeated nation became murderously polarised, civil war loomed, and the population continued to suffer. For the German people, the war did not end with the armistice.

The unhappy tale of the peacemaking may be swiftly told. The United States, Britain, France, and Italy had promised in their pre-armistice correspondence with Germany on 5 November 1918 that they would draw up peace terms strictly in accord with President Wilson's progressive program – for a peace without conquest.[864] But Germany had descended into confusion and powerlessness. Desperate to confirm the peace, revolutionary sailors had provoked nation-wide unrest in the first days of November 1918. This provoked a peaceful transfer of power from the last Chancellor of the *Kaiserreich*, Prince Max of Baden, to a six-man social-democratic Cabinet in Berlin on 9 November. That new government then accepted the advice of the military elite that even the toughest armistice terms must be signed, and so they were, on 11 November. Over the next month, Germany's military forces disintegrated in a largely spontaneous demobilisation, and the conquering western armies advanced, unopposed, into Belgium and the Rhineland, just as the armistice specified.[865]

The statesmen of the victorious powers were horrified by Germany's shift to the Left. The new socialist government in Germany was shunned. The victors refused to contemplate any measures that might have consolidated democracy inside Germany. The armistice terms were applied rigorously. Most harshly and controversially, the economic blockade of Germany remained in force. Emergency food assistance was grudgingly given in April 1919 – too late for tens of thousands. The continuing 'starvation blockade' saw the total of German civilians killed by malnutrition continue to mount beyond the three-quarters of a million dead estimated to have perished already by the time of the armistice.[866]

In Britain, the political forces that had gathered under the banner of the 'knock-out blow' during the war now proceeded to poison the peacemaking. A revealing incident underlining this took place in London a few days before Christmas 1918. Lloyd George had rushed to exploit the moment of victory by plunging the nation into a general election. His 'Make-the-Germans-Pay' election campaign had just ended in the triumph of his Tory-dominated Coalition. President Wilson was expected soon in England, on his way to the Paris Peace Conference. The Imperial War Cabinet met to plan for Paris, with Hughes and other Dominion Prime Ministers present. Those around the table discussed quite frankly how Wilson's progressive ideals could be opposed and Britain's empire enlarged on the back of the great victory over Germany. Edwin Montagu, one of the few Liberals present, was appalled at the ministers' evident determination to plan for 'a peace of the old style'. Sarcastically, he told them it would be 'very satisfactory if we could find some convincing argument for not annexing all the territories in the world.' Later, Montagu penned a furious letter to Balfour, the Foreign Secretary. He singled out Australia's Prime Minister Hughes as one of the worst hypocrites of 'the flag-waving type' men 'who want to go to any place because we can', while declaring: 'Good God, Sir, isn't it splendid to be a British subject.' The open hostility to Wilson's progressive ideals distressed Montagu, especially considering all the pious wartime speeches about the high moral values for which Britain was supposedly fighting. 'Is it not our only hope that President Wilson is just as much a humbug as we all are', he observed bitterly. He lamented the 'unhappy spectacle' he had just witnessed: the 'trusted of the Empire, the custodians of the future, the translators of victory, the instruments of lasting peace' were all conspiring together to sabotage Wilson, just in case 'he meant what he said'. 'And we are going into these negotiations with our mouths full of fine phrases and our brains seething with dark thoughts.'[867]

The bad faith that Montagu saw at work fatally compromised the whole process of peacemaking. There was the chance for something better – but it slipped past. For example, in an effort to gain credit with the victors, the new social-democratic German Government held early elections in January 1919 for an assembly to fashion a new democratic constitution in Weimar. A strong majority of socialists and liberals in coalition was elected in favour of democracy, peace, and the Wilsonian internationalist program. Germany stood at a turning point. If the peacemaking went well, the war would be forever discredited as a swindle, and those democratic reformers who had secured the armistice for Germany in November 1918 – with promises of Wilsonian protections – would be celebrated as heroes. If the peacemaking went badly, they would be condemned as traitors – the 'November criminals'.

Lloyd George, Vittorio Orlando, Georges Clemenceau, and Woodrow Wilson, Paris, 1919

Throughout the months of peacemaking, the victorious powers simply refused to negotiate peace with the new German Government in any meaningful way. After months of haggling among themselves, Clemenceau eventually presented 'the conditions of peace' to the German delegation on 7 May 1919 in an elaborate ceremony at the gleaming Trianon Palace Hotel, on the edge of the Great Park at Versailles. Clemenceau told the Germans there would be no opportunity for any face-to-face negotiations. That was the point of hanging on until military victory was achieved – peace could be imposed.

The Lost Peace

The treaty reflected a victory on the part of the old world over the new. Certainly Wilson gained agreement to set up the League of Nations, as the emblem of the 'new diplomacy', which he hoped would set right the flaws in the peace settlement. But this new League of Nations looked very much like a victors' club, with Germany and Russia excluded. Wilson, weakened by illness and political reversals at home in the mid-term elections, had given way on all of the most significant territorial, colonial, and economic points. Germany had to accept responsibility for all the damage inflicted upon the victors by the war, and to acknowledge an open-ended total of 'reparations' – clearly a fudge word to mask the demand for a phantom payment, all the victors' war costs, which right-wing campaigners hoped to impose upon Germany, and thus rebuff proposals for wealth taxes and capital levies in their own countries.

The high expectations raised by Wilson were smashed. German opinion was devastated. Great banners were unfurled at public demonstrations in Berlin, reading 'Only the 14 Points'. The victors threatened to resume invasion and to reimpose a total blockade upon Germany if her government resisted signature. With the Rhineland occupied, resistance was impossible. Germany sent two delegates – a prominent anti-war socialist and a Catholic liberal – to sign the peace treaty, under protest, on 28 June 1919.[868]

The impact of this traumatic period of peacemaking upon German politics was disastrous. The builders of Weimar were discredited; the Western victors gave mouth-to-mouth resuscitation to the German nationalist right; and democracy was indelibly associated in the German public mind with national humiliation.[869]

Two vignettes illustrate the destructive political impact of the treaty terms, and especially the damage done to the Weimar Republic's fledgling democracy, by the foolish exclusion of Germany from any genuine role in negotiations for the peace.

First, an American visiting Berlin in the aftermath of the armistice remembered a conversation with a right-wing German nationalist at an elite hotel. He asked the American what kind of peace terms might come from the period of peacemaking? '"Military terms", was the reply. "But what about Wilson?" "In spite of Wilson," said the American sadly. "Thank God," exclaimed the German, "for in that case we shall overcome the revolution and secure our national freedom so much sooner.'"[870]

Second, the German socialist, Toni Sender, a lifelong internationalist, remembered the moment when the final terms were revealed. 'It was in the early morning hours of June 17, 1919, as I was alone in my editorial office in Frankfurt that the text of the peace treaty as dictated by the Allies reached me. My hearts skipped beats as I read it. Is it possible – such a blow, such a humiliation to the young Republic? Had they forgotten all their promises – or had they fooled us?'[871]

The peace had been botched. The new internationalism was hobbled, western liberalism across the globe was very much discredited, and extremist politics emboldened. Those who had misspent the soldiers' blood in prolonging the war had now misspent the soldiers' victory in imposing the peace.

Just as Ryan had feared, there was no peace without conquest.

'Starvation ... That is How You Will Exact Any Terms From Germany'

Australia's role in this was to help to sabotage the 'Wilsonian Moment'. Prime Minister Hughes had returned to Britain in June 1918. For the next six months, he whirled his political bullroarer for war to the bitter end – and a profitable peace. As the end of the conflict approached, he campaigned for vengeance, and the crushing of the German economy after victory. He gladdened the hearts of reactionaries and chilled the hearts of liberals. In August 1918, the leading British Liberal newspaper the *Daily News* claimed he had no equal in the 'violation of the decencies of public life'.[872]

What did Hughes do as peace descended?[873] He was infuriated by Lloyd George's promises to Colonel House in Paris in early November 1918 that Britain was ready for armistice and would honour the Wilsonian program in her peacemaking. He publicly denounced Lloyd George and derided Wilson. He depicted the Fourteen Points – with their 'open covenants of peace', 'freedom of navigation upon the seas', invaded territories 'restored' rather than war costs extorted from the vanquished, and even an 'absolutely impartial adjustment' of contested colonies – as a betrayal of the great victory.

Hughes had no higher ideal for the peace conference than the restoration of the old international disorder, with the losers in the Great War reduced to penury and weakness. The future would be as the past: weak international institutions; the colonial world divided up and ruled from Europe; the big nations locked in a perpetual quest for military superiority, all jealously guarding their right to make war, all relying again on the old diplomacy and the 'balance of power'. In Hughes world, the only guarantee of peace was fear.

Hughes spoke up, as he imagined it, for Australia, but almost always in a bad cause. He pressed Lloyd George to seek an indemnity from Germany (in spite of Lloyd George's specific promise not to do so at Caxton Hall in January 1918, repeated in the so-called

'Lansing Note' of 5 November, just a week before the armistice). Crusading for a more punitive payment, Hughes led an Imperial War Cabinet sub-committee on 'Indemnity' urging that Germany pay a huge bill for the war. Constantly, Hughes colluded with Britain's press barons and the protectionist lobby to promote this agenda during the British general election suddenly called by Lloyd George for December 1918.

Arriving at the Paris Peace Conference in January 1919, Hughes continued to harass both Wilson and Lloyd George. On the conference's 'Reparation and Indemnities Commission' he again boomed the case for a punitive indemnity. He worked his press contacts to keep up an agitation for a post-war economic boycott of Germany. He loudly resisted Wilson's attempts to bring international oversight to all European colonisation, demanding unfettered control for Australia of her captured German colonies. Wilson's plan was eventually watered down to the so-called 'mandates' system – scarcely very different to annexation – under which the nations granted possession of the former German colonies were simply obliged to report on their administration to the League of Nations. Hughes also fiercely resisted any racial equality clause being built into the new diplomatic order that Wilson advocated. Thus, Hughes had a hand in a long-term disaster: the historic movements for self-determination emerging in the colonial world, disillusioned with the liberal democracies' hypocrisy on display at Versailles, turned increasingly to international communism for inspiration.

Hughes's vindictiveness toward Germany was especially heartless. As the people of Germany and Austria-Hungary faced the twin torments of the hunger blockade and the influenza pandemic during the winter of 1918-1919, Hughes was unmoved. He told the Imperial War Cabinet 'that 85% of the German people are as bad as the ex-Kaiser ever was, and are as deserving of death'.[874] In the eight months following the armistice of November 1918, it is estimated that an additional 245,000 Germans died as a result of the blockade.[875] Hughes opposed emergency food shipments being sent into Germany in the spring of 1919, remarking that 'starvation would do anything. That is how you will exact any terms from Germany.'[876]

In the aftermath of the catastrophe of this Great War, this was the blinkered vision – not to say the vicious temper – of Australia's wartime leader.

Hughes took his seat in the dazzling Hall of Mirrors at the Palace of Versailles when the treaty was signed on 28 June 1919. He had insisted upon Australia's separate representation and signature. Some Australian nationalists were impressed. But it was a gesture masking the reality of the record. On the most critical issues during the long war, Hughes had let London make the key decisions. He had been effusively loyal to the British imperial cause, in almost everything – for the sake of 'White Australia'.[877]

Georges Clemenceau, Woodrow Wilson, and David Lloyd George, leave the palace of Versailles after the signing of the treaty, 28 June 1919

After arriving home, in the golden glow of victory, Hughes gave a triumphal speech in the Parliament on the Versailles Treaty in September 1919. He stressed the wickedness of the 'blood-guilty' Germans, 'the peril in which we stood' in the face of the German threat to Australia, and, Hobbesian to the last, the continuing danger from Germany in 'this commercial war, this war of life and death for all the peoples of the earth'. He honoured the sacrifice of young Australians, their 'invincible valour', and 'the high ideals for which these boys died'. Of course, he maintained that 'complete and decisive victory' had redeemed the losses of 'our bravest and best'.

But, as ever, Hughes's own trumpet was nearest his lips. He blew it while explaining the one big disappointment out of the Peace Conference – the Germans were not being hounded for *all* the war costs of the victors, as they should have been, but rather only for 'reparations'. The British were to blame, he claimed, for they had not sufficiently resisted Wilson's foolish Fourteen Points. However, if *he* had had his way in Paris, *he* would have got all the victors all their war costs, and Australia would have had no war debt. Thus, Hughes insisted, the treaty was 'unjust' – to Australia.

Hughes dwelt upon the imperishable things that the men of the AIF had won for the nation. 'They died for the safety of Australia. Australia is safe. They died for liberty, and liberty is now assured to us and to all men.' But he had nothing to say about the tediously long lists of imperial articles in the Versailles Treaty – the great totem of the victory for which Australians had also assuredly died. For instance, Articles 141 to 154 expunged all of Germany's rights in Morocco and Egypt, in favour of French dominance in Morocco and British dominance in Egypt – just as had been foreshadowed secretly at the birth of the Entente Cordiale between Britain and France in 1904.[878] Those articles indicated as clear as day that the war was indeed the bloody climax of the age of the New Imperialism. Hughes talked instead of the supposedly indestructible things that he had brought safely home to Australia: he mentioned democracy, twice; and he hailed his preservation of 'White Australia', seven times.[879]

The 'Soupship *Chronic Disease*'

Just a week before the signing of the Versailles Treaty, Private Edward Ryan began his journey home. On 21 June 1919, he and his fellow-soldiers, drawn from several depleted battalions, travelled by train from Hurdcott to Devonport. In the afternoon, they filed on board the former North German Lloyd passenger liner *Königin Luise*. The ship had been recently surrendered to Britain under interim 'reparations' arrangements and was serving as an Orient Line troopship still under its old German name. It took a day to load. One digger diarist on board was Ben Cohen, who had enlisted from Perth and trained at Blackboy Hill like Ryan. He described the scene: from the crowded railings of the ship high-spirited soldiers looked down upon the wharf as some soldiers' wives and families joined the long queues of troops lined up to mount the gangway. So, 'as each Motor Car arrived with a Digger and his Bride, they received a cheer and good natured barrack which all enjoyed'.[880] The couples and families were accommodated aft. The troops jostled for hammocks on the stuffy lower decks. Soon they would prefer to sleep on the open decks, under the stars.

The troopship *Königin Luise* departed Devonport in the early evening of Sunday 22 June. 'Our decks and rigging were crowded with Diggers and cheers from the Wharf and Boats were returned by the Boys, whilst the Band on board played "Good Bye-e-e" and "Auld Lang Syne"', Cohen recorded. They were bound for Australia at last, via Durban. Each day now, they were one day nearer real peace. In fact, the troops departed at the height of press speculation over whether the treaty drawn up in Paris would be signed, or whether war would be resumed. News that peace – of a kind – had been signed reached the men after they had been at sea for a week.

As seasickness hit, the soldiers soon renamed the *Königin Luise* the 'Soupship *Chronic Disease*'. The spirit on board hovered somewhere between dance-on-the-tables and shoot-out-the-lights – except that it was a 'dry' ship. There was a piano on the hatch above the soldiers' deck and Cohen wrote that 'it is played all day'. Soon a Sports Committee and Concert Party were formed. The band on board was in constant demand, providing dances for the married couples, and backing sing-alongs and a Song Service for the troops. There were even competitions between the various messes to decorate tables with knives, forks and spoons in various displays.

Hilarity reigned. For the entertainment of the troops, mock trials were begun a few days into the voyage, a 'Diggers Court of Injustice'. A jury of 'twelve untrue and unjust men' sat in judgement, mainly upon officers and NCOs accused of comical crimes. There were 'roars of laughter' as Lords of Misrule victimised officers. But Privates were also tried, charged with running 'a gambling school'. A 'Private Ryan' was listed among the men of the 'other ranks' who was 'tried', in good humour – and if it was Private Edward James Ryan, it was undoubtedly the happiest of his wartime trials.[881]

There were a few incidents though. A crewman fell overboard during a lifebelt parade and was successfully rescued by a lifeboat, only to be arrested later for threatening to strike the captain. Cohen noted one throat-catching moment: as the ship crossed the line, and the stars wheeled above the ship in the night sky, the Southern Cross was visible low on the horizon for the first time.

The cage of discipline rattled. After docking in Durban on 14 July, the men were ordered to form up on the wharf in order to march into town – but the men simply melted away, walking into town just as they wished, catching trams, and spending the day in the hotels. There was some drunkenness over the next three days. There were difficulties in getting all the troops back on board for a departure on 16 July. The ship's horn blasted again and again in warning. Ironically, after only hours at sea, the ship had to return to Durban when a shortage of fresh water was discovered. Again, the 'hotels were opened and soon were filled and very busy'. Finally, the next day, to the strains of 'Home Sweet Home', the ship departed Durban for Fremantle. Ted Ryan had his twenty-eighth birthday on 29 July as the ship crossed the Indian Ocean. In the early evening of Saturday 2 August, as Cohen recorded, 'a cheer rang out' from soldiers gathered thickly at the railings as someone spotted the lighthouse on Rottnest Island. They would all be home by morning.

Tugs nudged the troopship *Königin Luise* toward the jam-packed Victoria Quay in Fremantle, near Perth, on a rainy morning, on Sunday 3 August 1919. The ship 'was one mass of khaki', wrote a journalist. 'Jubilant "Aussies" were perched everywhere, and as they scanned the faces below and recognised their excited friends and relations their faces lit up with smiles and they waved in return and cheered themselves hoarse.' Thousands were on the wharf to greet the men. A military band struck up. 'Everyone was in ecstasies.'[882]

Ted Ryan was among more than a thousand Australian soldiers who spilled off the ship that day – five years to the day, 3 August 1914, since the Australian Government had cabled to London its extraordinary offer of an expeditionary force of 20,000 men, to serve the British empire, anywhere, for any objective, under British command – before Britain had decided to declare war at all.[883]

The men moved down the gangway, handed in their disembarkation cards, and submitted to a medical and dental inspection. Private Edward Ryan responded to the medical men's questions as to whether he was suffering from wounds or illnesses while 'on service' with a simple 'No'. Asked to describe his own condition, he replied 'Good'. The doctors then formally recorded that they had found his heart, lungs, other organs and hearing all 'Clear'. Needless to say, there was no question, and no examination, to ascertain Ryan's psychological fitness – in spite of shell shock appearing in his service file. 'F.D.' was the final decision swiftly recorded: 'fit for discharge'. In addition, the assessment 'PENSION ASSISTANCE NIL' was added to his repatriation file. The date of discharge was set for one month in advance, 2 September 1919.[884]

A Welcome Committee of volunteers was present on the shoreline to provide refreshments as the men emerged from their medical examinations. Then, before leaving the wharf, each man had to pay three shillings for a railway and tram ticket for his period of leave in the city of Perth.

Ten days later, Ted Ryan received a final payout of £63, nineteen shillings and eleven pence (roughly equivalent to $5,074 in 2019). It is impossible to be certain from the surviving documents exactly how this sum was calculated, or if it disproves or vindicates Ryan's claim that his pay had been unfairly stopped for a period after the remission of his sentence in August 1918. By the time he arrived back in Fremantle in August 1919, his period of service in the AIF had been just under four years. He had served for a total of 1,412 days, at the standard pay of six shillings a day. His paycard shows that the clerk did record the large financial penalty that had been imposed upon Ryan – by the clerk's calculation, a total forfeiture of 582 days' pay during his time in uniform, or more than 41% of his pay.[885]

Later that month, Ted Ryan sailed on another troopship, the *City of Exeter*, from Fremantle to Adelaide, South Australia, and was listed in the press among soldiers 'not expected who returned'.[886] He was travelling home, to Broken Hill. His Uncle James Ramsay Mudie had told the local press that he was happily expecting his return.[887] Precisely when Ted arrived is not clear, probably in late August 1919. In any case, it was a homecoming to the Mudie family, with at least six children still at home, then at 673 Beryl Street. It was evidently a time of some hardship. For Ted's Uncle James was twice listed in June and December 1919 as receiving relief work provided by the Broken Hill City Council 'to deal with cases of urgent distress'.[888] Ted was home.

Chapter 26

AFTER THE DELUGE

FROM BROKEN HILL TO WAHROONGA, 1919 TO 1943

And the dead number many I know ... and one I remember before the others was a Sergeant North. One leg was compound fractured, the other amputated at the knee ... for a whole day he marvellously fought death ... He struggled for life strong against death ... but he died, and the pettiness and littleness of life about went on. Away across the world a home was to know agony and pain.
And the ultimate gain? Down the generations lying histories that tell of a wounding war; of brave men and nobleness.[889]

— Private Frank H. Molony, 1st Australian Field Ambulance, 29 September 1917

All three Private Ryans from Broken Hill survived the war. The three Ryan brothers' experiences were scarcely comparable, one a military policeman, one a decorated and much wounded man, and one a rebel court-martialled four times. This pattern is a reminder of the random destruction that can be visited upon people's lives when the devil of war is unleashed. All three brothers had experienced great disruption, and some hardship. But, in a sense, both Ted and Tom were sacrificed to the war, while the youthful Harry, delivered by chance into the ranks of the military police in Cairo, was shielded from the worst of it.

Harry Ryan's Cairo

The youngest brother, Harry, certainly was the most fortunate. As will be remembered, while masquerading as his brother 'Edward James Ryan', he served for most of the war as a military policeman in Egypt – a 'jack' as the soldiers called them. His marriage to Rose in Cairo, and the birth of Ruby in late 1916, probably saved him from service beyond Egypt.

In 1919, Harry elected to stay in Cairo with Rose and Ruby following his demobilisation. He worked for an Italian pharmaceutical firm, and then as a procurements officer for the British Army. He and Rose eventually had four children in Cairo, Ruby, Ernest, Elsie and Jack. (Their first-born child, Ruby, would later marry a British soldier, Les Francis, in Cairo, and their child, Bob Francis, would go on to be a famous radio personality in Adelaide from the 1960s to the 2000s). In the 1920s, Harry and Ted were long-distance letter writers. Harry sent photographs of his children, pointing out landmarks in the background from Cairo and Port Said that he knew Ted would remember from his war experiences in Egypt. He signed off his letters, 'Your loving brother Harry Ryan'.[890] The wars of the youngest and eldest Ryan brothers were poles apart – but there was no break in affection.

Harry visited Australia briefly in 1939, when the three brothers met, as it turned out, for the last time. He returned to Australia for good in 1947 and died in Adelaide in 1961.

Tom Ryan, Military Medal – and AWOL

Tom Ryan returned home to Australia in May 1918, bearing multiple wounds – shell wounds to the arm and leg, a gunshot wound to the chest, a shell wound to the left shoulder, and a complex fracture of the left arm. He had also been recommended for the Distinguished Conduct Medal (DCM) for bravery in March 1917, during an advance by the 11th Battalion at Le Barque, in late February. Tom Ryan went out 'again and again' to 'a very exposed place', during heavy shelling, to restore telephonic communications. 'He set a fine example of courage and determination throughout', read the recommendation.[891] But in the event the recommended decoration was downgraded and Ryan was given only the more common Military Medal. Tom Ryan was not quite the model medal-proud soldier: after leaving his troopship in Melbourne, he defied orders to report to a military hospital, prompting a court of enquiry and a finding of AWOL against him just before his formal discharge at the end of 1918.[892] Like Ted, there was a rebellious streak in Tom.

Tom stayed in Melbourne for a few years after the war, and there, in 1920, Tom married Ellen 'Nell' King.[893] Tom was soon a father to twin girls, Helen and Mary. The family moved to Sydney and Tom found work as an accountant. Tom joined the public service, working in Sydney for the federal Department of Health, and later in the accounts section of the Repatriation Department, which dealt with returned soldiers. Working in that position, no doubt, he encountered documents every day testifying to the long lingering hardships of the first and second world wars. He retired aged 60 in 1953.[894]

Tom died of a stroke in May 1964, soon after suffering a fall. He had stumbled as he rushed to avoid a speeding car on the street outside his home in suburban Wollstonecraft, Sydney. Proud of his military service, the family ensured his Military

Medal and his AIF number were recorded on the plaque marking his grave at the Macquarie Park cemetery in Sydney.

Ted Ryan's Balms of Peace

Perhaps not surprisingly, Ted was the least lucky.

After returning to Broken Hill, Ted Ryan worked as a labourer, a sawyer, and then as an engine driver at various BHP mines. He passed the engine drivers' examinations for electric engines in 1922, and became a fully-qualified engine driver in 1925. Work was uneventful, except for an accident at the British Mine sawmill in 1923, when he stepped back upon a sharpened saw and cut his leg, landing him briefly in hospital.[895] During this period, Ted lived for some time at the Returned Soldier's Hostel in Broken Hill, the former 'Resch's Palace Hotel', a grand property once owned by the German beer magnate, Emil Resch, interned during the war, then purchased by the Mine Managers' Association in 1919 and given to the Returned Soldiers' League for a nominal rental. Ted Ryan may be the 'J. Ryan' who took part in the Returned Soldiers' Debating Society in 1922, taking the progressive side in several debates.[896] He may be the 'E. Ryan' who was an office-bearer in the Workers' Educational Association from 1923 to 1925.[897] He may be the 'E. Ryan' who spoke to the 'Sturt Juvenile Rechabites (girls)' in April 1926 on 'the evils of strong drink' – speaking with a conviction traceable to his father's fate.[898] Thus, he sought no leadership roles, but neither did he seek obscurity.

Sometime in 1925, Ted Ryan met a young nurse, Mary Cameron McDonald (always known as Marie), in Broken Hill – her surname another piece of serendipity.[899] Marie had obtained her nurse's certificate in Sydney in 1920 and rose quickly to be a theatre sister at Sydney's Royal Prince Alfred Hospital by the mid-1920s.[900] There, as it happened, she treated many injured ex-soldiers, and knew of their sufferings, in mind and body. Seeking a change, she had opted for a 'bush' experience, nursing in the countryside, and she chose Broken Hill. She was working in the North Broken Hill Baby Health Centre in April 1925.[901] Ted and Marie fell in love. Marie came from a prosperous family. Her mother Sarah's family, the MacPhersons, had gained wealth in wheat farming as pioneers in the Narrandera district of New South Wales.[902] Her father, Murdoch McDonald, had been a prominent grazier in Victoria. After his death, Marie lived with her mother and sisters in a fine home in solidly middle-class Roseville on Sydney's North Shore. In choosing a working-class man from Broken Hill as her husband, Marie crossed a class line. But Marie had a radical instinct, and was dismissive of some of her family's pretensions. According to family sources, during the courtship, as ardent republicans, both Marie and Ted decided to drop the 'Royal' whenever they spoke of the 'Prince Alfred' hospital.

Marie returned to Sydney in June 1926 to prepare for the marriage. Ted was to follow in September. At that time, Ted was a motor driver and engine driver at the South

Blocks mine in Broken Hill. He was still boarding at the Returned Soldiers' Hostel. Evidently, he got on with his fellow boarders. Perhaps Ted had kept his own war record quiet, or perhaps the other residents were a charitable lot and took all ex-soldiers as they found them. In any case, he was not resented. On the eve of his departure to Sydney to be married, his ex-soldier mates gathered to farewell him and to make a presentation. The secretary of the local Returned Soldiers' League and manager of the hostel, the former Lieutenant James Ross Charlton (an ardent conscriptionist during the war) congratulated Ted on his forthcoming marriage and presented him, as was customary, with a 'gold-mounted fountain pen'.[903] Marie and Ted Ryan were married at the Presbyterian Scots Church in Sydney in late September 1926. Ted's brother Tom was his best man, and Marie's sister Christina her bridesmaid.[904]

The couple crossed the Tasman immediately to Auckland, New Zealand, where a friend made good on a promise of work for Ted, as an engine driver. The newly-married couple lived in Parnell. They had two children there. First came a daughter Elizabeth Margaret, or 'Beth' as she was known (named in honour of Ted's mother), a 'blue baby' who was lucky to survive. Then came a son, Ross Marlen.

Ted and Marie Ryan with their daughter and son returned to Sydney in July 1932. They settled in Wahroonga, a northern well-to-do suburb, distant from the city. Originally characterised by large mansions on spacious blocks, the suburb was opened up to cheaper housing developments in the 1930s. Ted and Marie settled at 10 Hampden Avenue, a much humbler street then than it is today. At the end of the street, there were Italian market gardens. The songs of Italy filtered into the Ryans' own garden, as Beth remembered, where Ted was a keen planter and weeder.

Beth and Ross walked through the bush to the small local state primary school at Turramurra North, a 'one-woman school' in those days. Later, Beth went to Hornsby Girls High School. Beth recalls Ted as a wonderful, loving father, 'very funny', and 'thrilled to have a family of his own'. He scarcely spoke of the war to his young family. Beth recalls only her mother reporting that Ted spoke eloquently on the misery of life in the trenches, where men laboured 'up to their knees in mud' and learned to rest and sleep by 'lying upright against the slope of the trench'.[905]

While living on Sydney's upper North Shore, Ted Ryan appears never to have lost his rebellious Broken Hill spirit. He was active in local Labor politics in the mid-1930s. He joined the new Lindfield branch of Australian Labor Party (ALP), which met in the local hall at St Alban's Anglican Church. He was active in the ALP's State Electorate Council for Gordon. In 1936, he was caught in the crossfire in factional warfare in the state Labor Party over Jack Lang's domination of the NSW branch of the party. Ryan aligned himself with 'the industrial movement', that is, the dissident trade unionists opposing Lang's so-called 'Inner Group' of supporters. But the Lindfield branch was pro-Lang. After special meetings and two close votes, in November 1936, Ryan was suspended from his local branch for six months for 'disruptive tactics' – an ironic charge, for the Lang forces were often accused of these![906] Apart from this, he sought no high profile in politics. He had one significant political friendship: with a young lawyer 'of leftist inclination', Ken Wilberforce Tribe (whom Ted called Ken 'Willinghorse' Tribe, on account of his enthusiastic activity on so many fronts). At his law office, Ken Tribe, the humble-born scholarship boy and chorister who had made good at the elite Sydney schools, St Andrew's Cathedral School and Shore School, spent time with Ted, the Broken-Hill-born miner and four-times court-martialled soldier. They sympathetically discussed labour politics, fascism, communism, history, and music, across the class divide. Tribe would later be a major patron of the Sydney musical scene, leading the Musica Viva group, which successfully promoted chamber music.[907]

Ted and his brother, Tom, remained close. As both lived on Sydney's North Shore, they saw a good deal of each other. Their very different wars – at least on paper – did not come between them. There was no break between the one soldier, who had won the Military Medal for his bravery, and the other soldier, who had faced a death sentence for his defiance of war. 'Uncle Tom' and 'Aunty Nell' loaned their car to Ted for family outings. On weekends Tom's twin girls, Mary and Helen, played with Ted's children, Beth and Ross, at many family get-togethers, often at the popular Bobbin Head picnic ground, close to Ted's home.

Marie was focused upon raising her two children and does not appear to have maintained her nursing registration. But she did campaign for progressive causes. Citing her nursing experiences, she publicly urged more sex education in schools in order to combat the scourge of venereal disease.[908]

In his spare time, Ted pursued an intense self-education. He read voraciously in the field of ancient history, borrowing many books from the Sydney City Library. He was especially absorbed by ancient Greek history, explaining to his children that in the history of the Greek Commonwealth and in its famous 'democratic' Agora lay the roots of modern democracy and civil liberty.

A Thief in the Night

Ted found employment as an electric-crane driver at a number of factories, and eventually worked at Australian Consolidated Industries (ACI), a large glass factory in the city of Sydney. This involved shift work. After one late shift on Monday 18 October 1943, he travelled by train home as usual to his nearest station, Wahroonga. Soon after midnight, Ted was bicycling from Wahroonga station to his home, in Hampden Avenue. In a nearby street, Braeside Street, a tree-lined road with many large historic mansions with their tennis courts and grand gardens, just a few minutes from his home, Ted collided with another cyclist travelling in the opposite direction. Ted was thrown to the ground, and badly injured. He died of head injuries the next day in Hornsby District Hospital. It was twenty-seven years and a day since he had written his letter of outrage to Ramsay MacDonald, greeting him as 'Yours peacefully' in his effort to do something to save all those Private Ryans he had witnessed being sacrificed on the Western Front.

There was a coronial inquiry at Hornsby. The District Coroner found that Ted's death was a regrettable accident. *Both* cyclists, he reported, had been 'riding without lights'.[909]

But a story often told in the family afterwards amended that verdict. A few weeks after Ted's death, his widow, Marie, received a letter from a couple who would not divulge their names. They had been canoodling in waste ground on Braeside Street very near to where the accident happened, and were amazed to find a lit bicycle lamp tossed through the air and landing near their struggle-rug. Embarrassed, they kept away from the scene of the accident. But in their anonymous letter, they expressed condolences, and assured Marie Ryan that Ted's bicycle had been lit. This accorded with the family's conviction that Ted always carefully maintained his lamp. Nor were wartime brownout regulations to blame. These had been eased during 1943 for Sydney's streetlighting and for all vehicles, and cyclists were required to ride with a lamp after sunset. He had been an unlucky, not a reckless cyclist.

Ted Ryan died aged just 52. He had lived humbly: upon his death his entire estate was valued at only £380 (roughly equivalent to $26,100 in 2019).[910] His grave, also in Macquarie Park cemetery, in the Methodist section, bore no military emblems. Indeed the grave is without any headstone, neither for Ted, nor for Marie, whose remains were interred there upon her death in 1974. Ted Ryan had survived a close shell blast, and much else, during the Great War, only to have his life violently taken from him in a simple bicycle accident, on a suburban street, years later. His only daughter Beth was aged 16 and his only son Ross aged 11. As Ted had grown up motherless in his teenage years, his children would grow up fatherless in theirs – two more, among millions, deprived of their father during those terrible years of the Second World War.

But these bare outlines of three lives changed by the war can scarcely convey the deeper impact. All three Ryan brothers had been wounded in body. We can only guess what visions and voices came for them at night. We can only guess at the inner sufferings of these three young men, and their families, the 'slow violence' that war can do for decades to come – 'the heart-break at the heart of things'. As George Eliot wrote long ago, there are 'robberies that leave man or woman forever beggared of peace and joy, yet kept secret by the sufferer – committed to no sound except that of low moans in the night, seen in no writing except that made on the face by the slow months of suppressed anguish and early morning tears'.[911]

Chapter 27

A VINDICATION

Interviewer: What are your thoughts today about war? About the First World War, about any war?

Thomas Talty: Oh, it was a shocking turn out. Should never have happened. That's what I think about it. And I wouldn't go again to another war. ... Terrible tragedy. ... Bugger them. If they want to start a war let them go themselves. None of the big fellahs went. It was all these privates, went over the top.[912]

— Private Thomas Talty, AIF veteran, interviewed 1998

Private Edward James Ryan was one of many who were assailed by doubts about the ultimate ends of this war. How shall we evaluate his defiance?

Should we judge him? We should be cautious. Frederic Manning, the Australian-born veteran of the Great War, put it this way: soldiers disliked civilians showing any 'readiness to judge others, who had at least submitted to the test'. It was a kind of breach of loyalty, explained Manning, for anyone who had never been so sorely tried, 'to set up as a judge'.[913] It is a warning to us.

But first, let us clear the decks.

Peace – Impossible or Irresistible?

Was there a chance for a negotiated peace during the First World War? Or was it a hopeless cause?

During the fighting, pro-war slogans were the 'white noise' of the war: 'seeing it through' until the 'knock-out blow', a 'fight to the finish', and war 'to the bitter end'. Supposedly, all German 'peace traps' had to be rejected, because the Germans had no intention of compromising. A negotiated peace was impossible.

In fact, there is no consensus among historians on this issue. Some popular writers grandly declare that there was no 'credible shortcut to peace'.[914] But this is conjecture masquerading as certainty. In fact, over many decades dissenting scholars have offered hopeful estimates of the chances of peace.[915] The prominent military historian Keith Jeffery reminds us that as each diplomatic initiative to end the war was squandered, the potential for peace had not 'evaporated', but rather 'was extinguished' by deliberate acts of state policy.[916] A recent study of the international peace movement during the war concludes that the 'truth is that if a handful of men in key positions, or just some of them, had decided to end the war by a negotiated settlement, if could have happened almost immediately'.[917]

But were the obstacles simply too great? In fact, much evidence suggests exactly the opposite. For example, when the German Foreign Minister Kühlmann made his peace offer in the autumn of 1917, critics in Paris and London argued not that talks were foredoomed to fail but rather, that they must be avoided precisely because any start in talks would signal the end of war. Arthur Balfour, the British Foreign Secretary, mused that 'it would be impossible to continue the war with vigour, or even to continue it at all, if the Powers once reached the stage of discussing terms round a table'.[918] In other words, the men who always publicly talked down the chances of peace insisted privately that peace must be smothered in its infancy – lest it smother the war itself.

German singularity?

Another rationalisation for the mass slaughter persists: German wickedness was a singular evil.[919] Was the *Kaiserreich* unique in its aggressive imperialism, unparalleled in its despotism, and incomparable in its militarism – with no credible moderate opposition with whom to make peace? This is to force the fright mask of 'Prussian militarism' down upon every political faction inside Germany. Perspective is needed. We should not fall into the trap of insisting, as ultra-patriots did during the war, 'that the German grey is jet-black and British grey snow-white'.[920] Moreover, a focus upon German evils may distract us from seeing the *systemic* evils at work in European imperialism, militarism, authoritarianism, and in the secret statecraft of elite diplomats. Through these systemic evils, the war was decades in the making, and the proximate causes scarcely compare with the systemic causes. The best comparative studies of the war reveal eccentric monarchs, reckless military advisers, duplicitous diplomats, and rapacious men of empire, in every warring nation – not just in Germany.[921]

Nor was Germany a solid monolith of unteachable 'Prussianists'. Rather, the *Kaiserreich* was a bitterly divided society, held together, ironically, by the persistence of the war.[922] The push for peace inside Germany had real heft. In the words of one specialist historian, 'it is difficult to avoid the conclusion that the Central Powers ... were far more willing to countenance something approaching a compromise peace than the Entente'.[923]

Many thought peace might come quickly. For example, James Gerard, the American Ambassador in Berlin, told Colonel House in February 1915 that 'if a reasonable peace is proposed now' Berlin would grab at it in 'a matter of days, even hours'.[924] Matthias Erzberger, the moderate Catholic Centre Party politician behind the Reichstag's 'Peace

Resolution' in July 1917, agreed. 'If I had an opportunity in the near future to have a talk with Lloyd George or Balfour or one of their authorised agents', he told a reporter, 'we could probably agree in a few hours upon a basis of peace and reconciliation, so that official peace negotiations could then follow immediately'.[925] Some German diplomats agreed. Baron von Romberg, German Ambassador in Switzerland during the war, was optimistic. 'I am rather firmly of the opinion', declared Romberg, 'that as soon as we should have taken our seat at the conference table, at least in the year 1916, we would never again have drawn the sword in defence of a single one of our demands regarding annexation'.[926]

The 'bitter-enders' on both sides fiercely maintained that the enemy was hostile to all compromise. It was a self-serving fiction. Historians see hostility toward an early peace as a callousness characteristic of the elites on both sides. 'It does not suffice simply to describe the resistance to such an outcome in Germany', writes Roger Chickering.[927] Holger Afflerbach, an expert on the diplomatic history of the war, laments that the Germans' efforts for peace 'were systematically ignored and ridiculed by Paris and London'. He scolds the British, who 'failed to use their room for manoeuvre'. By 1917, the 'hardliners on both sides were now keeping each other in power'. Afflerbach also questions the alibi often given out that Germany was uniquely aggressive. As he reminds us, the Entente's war aims were 'in some respects even more ambitious'.[928]

But, some say, surely the possibility of a German victory and her domination of Europe justifies the long war. The case is scarcely proven. As early as the autumn of 1914 many in Berlin's governing circles, from General Falkenhayn to Chancellor Bethmann Hollweg, recognised that the German army's failure to win swiftly in the West was disastrous, and a compromise peace the only way out.[929] Certainly from March 1917, with submarine warfare failing to turn the tide in the Atlantic, influential moderates in Berlin and Vienna knew that a peace on the basis of the *status quo ante bellum* was probably the best outcome that could be negotiated, even if the Central Powers' military forces could win more ground by some herculean effort.[930] The balance of advantage against the Central Powers was clear. In quick time, Germany had lost its entire seaborne trade, its overseas empire, and its access to world markets – and her people were starving. In the long run, American intervention after April 1917 was bound to crush her. German victories over devastated lands in Eastern Europe in 1917-1918 yielded her little. The so-called 'Bread Peace' of Brest-Litovsk imposed on Russia in 1918 failed to extort bread in any quantity. Germany's final offensive in the West did not bring her to the brink of victory. That last roll of the dice was a vain effort to improve her bargaining position. Even a more successful last German thrust in the spring of 1918 could not have given Germany and her allies the power to have dictated anything like a 'Victory-Peace' across the globe.[931]

In the final analysis then, can we possibly *know* for certain what were the chances of compromise? It was never clear how far or near peace might have been. But we should remember that history is one improbability after another. If we believe in our humanity and rationality, we have to believe that peace stood a chance.

War for Democracy?

Another dearly loved excuse for the prolongation of the war persists, the belief that the political masters in the West made war only for the most idealistic of reasons – for the sake of democracy. This is a naïve position. Notwithstanding Wilson's evident sincerity about this goal, most of the other Western leaders, not to mention the Tsar and his government, were never driven by a courageous desire to cleanse the world of despots and build democracy.

In Britain, the claim that both the wartime governments led by Asquith and Lloyd George were gallantly battling on for democracy's sake was always mostly a fraud. Lord Selborne, a dissatisfied Tory who had resigned from Asquith's Coalition Government in 1916, spoke for this collective mind: 'We cannot conceal from ourselves the fact that in a life and death struggle such as this [war], intelligently directed autocracy has an immense advantage over democracy.'[932] In a revealing moment, Robert Cecil, the aristocratic under-secretary at the Foreign Office, told the House of Commons in October 1916 that the government had 'the responsibility to govern the country' and 'cannot share that responsibility with the House of Commons or with anybody else – not during the War'.[933]

Everywhere, enthusiasm for the war and enthusiasm for democracy were at opposite ends of the political spectrum. Certainly this was the case in 'knock-out blow' Britain, and in Hughes's Australia. Everywhere reactionaries directing the seemingly 'forever war' hoped not for the flourishing of democracy after the war, but rather to shove victory down the throat of social progress.

The Russian Revolution intensified this thinking. Lord Curzon mocked the 'wild worship of so-called democracy' that the Russian revolution had conjured everywhere.[934] The British Commander himself, General Sir Douglas Haig, typified the reactionary instinct. Haig explained to General Sir William Robertson that a crucial reason to keep fighting in 1917 was because, in the aftermath of a great victory, '[t]he chief people to suffer would be the socialists who are trying to rule us all'.[935] Keith Murdoch, the journalist closest to Hughes, wrote the stark truth about this in a private letter to General 'Pompey' Elliott in May 1918: 'I admit that democracy must be cast aside by all patriotic men if the labouring classes become selfish and indolent under the authority it gives them.'[936]

Lord Curzon

The chancelleries, embassies, and military headquarters of Britain's allies were similarly cluttered with reactionaries. Many of those men invariably insisting on war 'to the bitter end' would not have crossed the road for democracy. They believed in it like they believed that the meek would inherit the earth – not at all.

Was Military Victory Certain?

We must face yet another powerful argument for the long war: that the leaders in the West decided to fight on unswervingly because they *knew* that military victory was just around the corner. This is wisdom after the event. Just as Private Ted Ryan argued, the 'knock-out blowers' were gamblers, not prophets. For example, discussions in Lloyd George's War Cabinet in October 1917, while the Australians were suffering terrible casualties during the Passchendaele disaster, reveal a Cabinet wracked with doubt. After surveying Haig's plans for taking the fight to Germany in 1918, the War Cabinet decided they 'did not provide a convincing argument that we could inflict a decisive military defeat on Germany on the Western Front next year'. Indeed, the Cabinet concluded at that time that there was 'no reasonable probability of a decisive victory'.[937] This was not a debate between those who knew that victory was coming in 1918 and 'defeatists' who had lost the faith. No one knew that victory was coming in 1918.[938]

The harsh truth is this: the Entente's decision makers favoured a *long* war, because they hoped that in a protracted struggle they were more likely to win, eventually – at enormous cost. As Robert Lansing advised President Wilson as early as August 1915, the Entente Powers were shunning mediation and choosing ever more war 'on the theory that Germany and Austria cannot stand the waste of men and resources resulting.'[939]

Understanding Private Ryan in Context

How then shall we *understand* Private Ryan?

Let us remind ourselves of Ryan's record. Altogether, he faced six serious charges, four of AWOL, plus two of desertion. On three of these six occasions, Ryan surrendered himself to his officers. On the three other occasions, he was arrested as a soldier on the run. His two disappearances from the 51st Battalion in France were, of course, the most problematic blotches on his record. On both of these occasions, he was missing for more than a week. By any measure this was desertion. But never did Ryan actually abandon the front line under fire.

Two facts stand out. First, *all* Ryan's escapades took place *after* his wounding. He was wounded twice at the front in the summer of 1916, and then diagnosed multiple times as a man suffering from shell shock. Second, all Ryan's 'crimes' were committed *after* he wrote down his statement condemning the war as a foul disaster, needlessly prolonged.

We who have never experienced the fist of war upon our faces should consider the testimony of those who have. They tell us that a man unluckily near to a shell burst feels 'a flash, as when a blast furnace door is swung open, and a roar that started white and went red'.[940] They tell us that those who have seen a trench 'all splashed with arms and legs' are changed forever.[941] They tell us that those who have cradled 'a man whose head was broken as a flower-pot may be broken' remember it forever.[942] It was the Queensland-born veteran of the AIF, Tom Talty, who told his interviewer succinctly: 'We were all nervous wrecks after that First World War.'[943]

Were men such as Talty and Ryan simply displaying the 'weakness' of the odd ordinary soldier? No, because the records show that officers could also succumb. The first commander of Ryan's 51st Battalion, Colonel Arthur Ross, was put on sick leave and then relieved of his command in February 1917, after his brother officers found him no longer fit to lead. As his adjutant put it, Ross 'did not recover from the shock of the Pozières losses'.[944] Similarly, Lieutenant Colonel Walter Cass 'relinquished' his command of the 54th Battalion in August 1916 following his hospitalisation for 'debility'. In fact, he had angrily denounced 'wholesale murder' at Fromelles.[945]

The bottom lines help us to see that Ryan was but one of a great throng of men who had had enough. The total number of courts martial convened in the AIF (both in Australia and overseas) was formidable. Historians have variously estimated the total to be somewhere between 20,000 and 30,000, with most giving a figure nearer 20,000. The most thorough statistical study of crime and punishment in the AIF by Edward Garstang finds that during the entire war, there were 'approximately 23,000 courts martial for 331,184 Australians in the AIF'. This was a much higher rate than in the New Zealand or Canadian forces, as Garstang stresses: 'One in fourteen Australians, one in fifty New Zealanders, and one in twenty-five Canadians faced a court martial.'[946]

If we look more precisely at the phenomenon of desertion, it emerges clearly that a significant number of men in the AIF – to play with a well-known phrase – wished by any means to *quit* the Western Front. The total number of courts martial *convictions for desertion* in the AIF (both in Australia and overseas) during the war has been estimated at 4,101.[947] But this clearly underestimates the total number of desertions. We must add in those soldiers who were charged with AWOL rather than desertion during 1918, even when their absences lasted longer than seven days (Ryan being one, in October 1918). And we must add in those deserters who were never apprehended. For example, when the war ended, more than 900 Australian soldiers, declared to be 'illegal absentees', were still at large in France and England. They were offered a return to Australia during the demobilisation period and most never faced a court martial.[948] The total number of deserters from the AIF, therefore, must have exceeded 5,000.

'It Is Absurd To Talk About Men Being Brave or Cowards'

Some readers may wish to judge Private Ted Ryan harshly. The case for the prosecution is simple. Ryan signed up. He promised to serve. He promised to fight and repel the King's enemies. He owed his mates unswerving loyalty. He was a deserter, a shirker – a man who shrank from the test of battle.

Again, veterans of the conflict generally refused to throw about such epithets. For example, Alex Ellis, veteran and author of the AIF's 5th Division's history, admitted that 'thousands of men sick almost to death, physically enervated, nervously bankrupt' had cracked and buckled under the strain of the war. Many chose 'to creep away for a week and sleep in some dingy cellar and then to return to the battalion headquarters and say, "I was knocked up. I have been away for a sleep and a rest."' Many soldiers were guilty of quitting the war in this way – indeed, guilty of desertion, wrote Ellis, 'if that constitutes desertion'.[949]

Richard Aldington, the famous British soldier-poet, vehemently denied that men under fire either had courage or had none:

Any man who spent six months in the line ... and then claimed that he had never felt fear, never received any shock to his nerves, never had his heart thumping and his throat dry with apprehension, was either superhuman, subnormal, or a liar ... There were very few – were there any? – who could resist week after week, month after month of the physical and mental strain. It is absurd to talk about men being brave or cowards.[950]

Similarly, Sergeant George Horan of the AIF told his father: 'I reckon there is no such thing as a "hero" – just men "acting naturally".'[951] The Australian Lieutenant George Baron Hay, an officer from Ryan's 51st Battalion, agreed. Hay was interviewed late in his life. He discounted 'courage' in war. Asked what gave him 'the courage to get over the top', he replied dismissively: 'It wasn't courage. You had to go. Everyone was doing it.'[952]

A stern judgement against Ryan ignores his motives and simply insists that he should have done his duty, and stuck by his mates.

Can it be so simple? The idea that duty trumps all has haunted men of principle across the decades. For example, Dietrich Bonhoeffer, the anti-Nazi German Christian theologian, reflected on this from his prison cell during the Second World War. Should bewildered soldiers stifle their doubts and take 'the path of duty'? As Bonhoeffer wrote: '[W]hen men are confined to the limits of duty, they never risk a daring deed on their own responsibility, which is the only way to score a bull's eye against evil and defeat it. The man of duty will in the end be forced to give the devil his due.'[953]

Those determined to find Ryan 'guilty' might contemplate a simple question. When a nation's political leaders callously prolong a war, and a shell-shocked soldier walks away from that war – which is the greater crime?

Learning from Private Ryan

The case for Ted Ryan places him in the 'big picture' and sees the profound moral conundrum he faced. We know, both from his letter to Ramsay MacDonald in October 1916, and from his statement to his court martial in September 1917, that Ryan held consistent, principled, political objections to the war.

Was he right? He accused the decision makers of fighting on, and suppressing peace, in order to redeem a brace of secret diplomatic deals – on every side. Surely Ryan was absolutely correct in his indictment.

To understand Ryan even more uncomfortably we might ask ourselves what would we have given up in Ryan's situation? Our finger, our hand, our arm – or indeed life itself – for the war aims of 1914-1918? For the Entente's territorial war aims in the Middle East, Africa, and the Pacific? For the squashing of German commercial enterprise across the globe? For Russia's plans to gain all of Poland and Galicia in the east, while France gained all of the Rhineland in the west? For Japan's ambitions in

China? After all, these were among the war aims to which Australia was signed up, by way of London.

Believing this carnival of killing was wrong, did Ryan's moral responsibility evaporate in the face of his oath to serve George V, the British King-Emperor? What is a man of principle and conscience to do?

The issue of conscience in the ranks is not being raised here out of time and place. It was raised in Australia *before* the war. When Australian parliamentarians debated the first *Defence Act* in 1903, the individual soldier's conscience came up. Arguing for the famous 'voluntary clause' ultimately included in the *Defence Act*, Henry Bournes Higgins, the prescient Radical, stressed how evil it was that 'any class' of men 'might be called upon in virtue of their oath, and on pain of imprisonment or death by shooting, to take part in quarrels in the making of which they have had no hand, and of which they may or may not approve'. War, after all, if not an essential duty for the defence of the nation, was 'the most horrible of crimes'. Men should not fight 'without regard to the justice of the case or to any considerations of right or wrong'. Higgins gave the example of Britain's Opium War as a bad cause. 'We do not want our men to be dragged into a war that may be against their conscience.' One astonished MP interjected, asking Higgins if soldiers 'usually consider the rights or wrongs of a war?' Higgins replied: 'If they do not they ought to do so. The absurdity of the position is that these men, because they are poor, are treated as being willing to sell their services to the country, as if they had no conscience of their own.'[954] Higgins won the argument: only volunteers could be despatched overseas to fight.

A decade later, Australian soldiers found themselves to be mere cogs in a gigantic war machine, churning through countless men. What moral responsibility did one of them have if he came to the conviction that he was being trained, armed, and goaded to take the lives of other men, for a cause in which he had no conscientious faith?

The rights and wrongs are not clear-cut. Philosophers have long debated them. As far back as the sixteenth century, the Italian philosopher Vitoria argued that: '[I]f the war seems patently unjust to the subject, he must not fight, even if he is ordered to do so by the prince.' Conscience was supreme. It was wrong for soldiers to kill others 'in bad faith', wrote Vitoria, because 'if their conscience tells subjects that the war is unjust, they must not go to war even if this conscience is wrong'.[955]

In every war, such appeals to conscience divide us. For some, obeying orders is the supreme duty, for it serves to protect the soldier's comrades. Others, aware of the atrocities almost always inseparable from war, argue that every soldier has an additional duty, a duty of diligence, that cannot be evaded, to find out the true causes and true objectives of the enterprise to which he or she is committing their body and soul. That duty eclipses all others.[956]

Lines of Duty – Conundrums of Resistance

In one sense, the line of least resistance for any soldier is to follow the tightly drawn line of military duty; to sink into the great mass of men, perhaps while evading any direct share in the bloodshed.

During the Great War, surely, many soldiers did this. They suppressed their doubts, immersed themselves fatalistically in the moment, and refused to think deeply about the changing rights and wrongs of the long war. For instance, Gordon Carter, a young Australian officer and veteran of Gallipoli, wrote to his parents about casualties on the Western Front in November 1916: 'Lives go faster than in Gallipoli and one gets a sort of fatalistic feeling and honestly it's not the least good thinking about anything except your job.'[957]

But some went further and, in the end, dodged the business of killing. Private Ernest Morton, for example, had enlisted in the AIF very early, in September 1914, served at Gallipoli, and then in various Machine Gun Companies in France. He was wounded and hospitalised more than once. He remembered encountering a 'mortally wounded' German officer, 'a young chap, be in his late teens', during the fighting on the Western Front in 1918. This German spoke perfect English. 'He prayed to me to kill him. Put him out of his misery.' Morton could not. 'From that time on', as Morton recalled, 'I turned against war' and 'never did anything in the war'. He refused to fire his machine gun. He took no more lives. 'I'm not going to have anything at all to do with this', he said to himself.[958]

Some others wished they had found the courage to chuck it – and walk away. Arthur Graeme West, a British ranker promoted to Second Lieutenant, confessed in his diary in September 1916 that he had come to sympathise with the reviled pacifists. It was the 'uselessness' of the war that repelled him. He reflected that 'had I been in full possession of my reasoning powers when the war began, I would never have joined the army'. He was 'caught in a net', he wrote. 'Now it all looks to me so absurd and brutal that I can only force myself to continue in a kind of dream-state.' He granted that for Britain and France to resist Germany was right, in the beginning. But 'why go on? Can no peace be concluded?' Exactly as Ryan would write in his letter to MacDonald the following month, West jotted down his bitter conviction that 'no peace can be worse than this bloody stupidity'. It was 'maddening' to see men 'accepting it all as necessary'. He wished he had 'stood apart' at the outset. 'To defy the whole system, to refuse to be an instrument of it – this *I* should have done.'[959] West was killed at Bapaume in April 1917.

Still, other soldiers slogged on, with rising passion, all the way to the armistice of November 1918. Clearly, most Australian soldiers stayed with the war, obeying orders. Archie Barwick, whose pride in being Australian and whose faith in the justice of the cause never faltered, was one of these. But even Barwick could mix a big dose of disillusionment into the nationalism preserved in his diary in late 1918. The insurgent thought gripped him, that wars beyond the Australian continent should never be contemplated again: '[N]ever no more for me, the only time I would fight again is in defence of my own country, I would never go out of "Aussie" again seeking stoush, I have had my fill of it, at the same time I am glad I came to this[,] I will never regret it as long as I live.'[960]

As the Australians captured more and more German prisoners in the last weeks of the war, some of the victorious Australian soldiers began to feel an overwhelming sense of kinship with the defeated. Interviewed some eighty years after the events, Charlie Mance, a Private in the 22nd Battalion, remembered seeing 'Germans everywhere' who had surrendered, awaiting escorts to prison compounds. Walking with the German prisoners, Mance recalled that 'one bloke showed me his wife's photos'. Mance's interviewer asked if this had prompted him to doubt the war? 'You must have questioned why this was all happening? Why all this fighting?' In responding, Mance remembered more of the scenes of the mass surrender of German soldiers, some injured, some near death, late in the war:

> Well, when you look at it, when we got down there, in France, and you see a lot of Germans, wounded, and blokes was reading the last rites on them, they're just the same as you. Young blokes! I could see a couple of our blokes laying there. No different![961]

Clearly enough, Ryan was far from being the only soldier, Australian or otherwise, to be struck by an irresistible sense of fellowship with *all* other soldiers tossed into the bonfire of war, an irresistible conviction that our common humanity must limit – and eventually triumph – over war itself.

Private Ryan – and Ourselves

Is it courageous to suppress all moral doubts – and fight? Is it right simply to go on soldiering, while secretly longing for escape, 'to keep right on to the end of the road' as the music-hall troubadour of the war, Harry Lauder, urged? Or is it more courageous to defy all the pressures of the moment, to weigh loyalty to mates against loyalty to conscience, and simply walk away?

What *should* Ted Ryan have done? Should he have been loyal, unto death, like so many others? Should he have faced the kill-or-be-killed conundrum? Should he have trusted the men directing the war, because they were men of integrity who knew, after all, how to achieve a lasting peace? Were they? Did they?

We should remember that these were class-ridden societies at war. The two men ultimately responsible for the prolongation of the war on the British side, Asquith and

Lloyd George, Britain's two wartime Prime Ministers, had no deep sympathy for the dim hordes of working-class men in uniform.[962] Lloyd George sought to repress his feelings for the wounded. Visiting France in February 1916, Lloyd George visited a man, the son of a friend, hospitalised with a gunshot wound to the head. Later he repeatedly told his lover, Frances Stevenson, 'I wish I had not seen him'.[963]

Ted Ryan defied this class-fuelled callousness and followed his conscience. Does he stand disgraced – as a deserter? Or does his war teach us some vital things? It reminds us that Australia's wars have been fought mostly by young unmarried men, with little property, from the working class. It reminds us that there were opponents of war even within the ranks of the fighting men. It reminds us that, once wars begin, the objects of war are seldom limited to the loudly advertised noble goals, for which so many men generously enlist. It reminds us that there are always alternatives to long wars, and that some soldiers huddling in trenches could glimpse them.

Looking beyond the trenches, as Ryan did, we see the tragedy of the war anew: in imperial escalation, in thwarted peace opportunities, and in the folly of an Australian government so committed to war that its troops and people were urged to fight on – in darkness.

Private Ryan's war shows us, to ourselves, more completely.

When contemporary Australians lavish praise upon 'the Anzac spirit', we would do well to remember it whole: the men's fierce democratic outlook, their fanatical egalitarianism, and their radical collective spirit. Ryan's story, like so many other Anzac stories, shows us that the men of the AIF often displayed a cheeky suspicion of king-and-country simplicities. In the midst of mounting horror, the men fought above all for each other, to win through to safety – certainly not to win through to victory for the sake of the war-makers' imperial aims. The fabled mateship of the troops, their solidarity, often morphed into a brotherhood of defiance. Their mateship included a strain of *radical* mutuality – an ideal scarcely recognised by some promoters of 'the Anzac spirit' today.

Supposedly victory would vindicate everything in this most ruinous of wars. But what is remarkable listening to the interviews of Australian soldiers of the First World War, many years after victory was theirs, is the frequency of denunciations of the war from the lips of the men themselves – the victors. Sergeant Jack Lockett was asked by his interviewer: 'What do you think the war achieved?' 'Bloody well nothing, bloody well nothing', he replied. 'War was fought, I couldn't see much out of it. Some of these bloody heads ought to be put in it.'[964] Lockett explained that he did wonder upon his return to Australia 'what the devil we were all over there for'. Why did the war go on? 'Only money', Lockett softly lamented. 'What was it all for? What was it all for? All them soldiers, sixty odd thousand killed', he mused. Asked if the war was not the war to end all wars, Lockett interrupted, 'Oh yes, it was all that! Wars to end all wars. But it made a damn lot o' wars. Still makin' 'em!'[965] Similarly, Private Thomas Talty, the only one of three brothers from the one Queensland family to have survived the war, faced similar questions in his interview. 'Were you disappointed? You went to the Great War. The Great War was called the War to End all Wars wasn't it?' 'Sure', he replied, 'that's what they told us it was, but it never ended them'.[966]

Is it true that victory consoles all, and reassures us that our men's lives were not lost in vain? The 'not in vain' card was played often during the Great War. For example, on the eve of the first conscription referendum in late October 1916, Lieutenant General Birdwood supplied Prime Minister Hughes with a made-to-order statement designed to shepherd the voters into the polling booths to vote 'Yes'. The troops demanded conscription, argued Birdwood. 'The Anzacs feel sure that Australia will see sacrifices already made are not in vain', Birdwood's statement began.[967] It appeared in all the Australian pro-conscription newspapers on the eve of polling day, among dozens of similar appeals juggling with the phrase 'not in vain'. Thus, were the corpses of soldiers who had already gone west rolled out rhetorically to be used as recruiting sergeants for still more men to feed the war machine. It was typical – and timeless. And yet no victory ever raised the dead. Private Ryan rebelled against it all. It is still painfully relevant.

We cling to our faith that wars of defence are right and necessary, as a last resort. Yet seldom are they incontrovertibly wars of defence, and seldom are they incontrovertibly a last resort. But once begun, wars must go on, we are told, so that dead soldiers shall not have died in vain. Is it not the truth that wars should end, so that more soldiers shall not die for vanity?

APPENDICES

APPENDIX

Private Edward J. Ryan's letter to Ramsay MacDonald

18 October 1916

No 3 Camp
Perham Downs
18/10/16

Dear Mr McDonald [sic]

I am writing to you as I really think you are one man among many, but one of the few who lives for Humanity and not for self under the veil of Patriotism. You are not one of those bitter-end fighters, or one of those who believe in fight to the last man & at the same time stops at home, far away from danger yourself.

Now Mr McDonald I want to tell you my reason for writing to you, that is, to let you know the feeling of most of the Australians who have been in [the] firing-line (or, as a lot of our fellows called 'The Somme', The Abbitors [Abattoirs]) & how much they relish the glories of war. So far I have not spoken to one man who wants to go back to the firing-line again. [E]very man I have spoken to is absolutely sick of the whole business. I have just been speaking to two Anzacs who said they would rather be shot than face another bombardment like we received at Poziers [Pozières]. I have saw [sic] pictures of how the Anzacs come from the Somme out of the firing line bright & cheery, hirraying [hooraying] etc.

Now I am going to tell you what they do feel like.

I saw the second division of the Australians come out from the Somme. They had been in [the] firing line about a fortnight, & of course they had practically no sleep & I suppose less than 15 per cent of each battalion answered the final roll call.

I went up to one of the Sergeants to ask him how he felt, & the reply I got was – for God's sake, cobber, don't talk to me to [sic] now, if you want to ask me any questions call round in about another 48 hours & I will do my best to answer you & it will give me time to realise that I actually came out of it alive. To every man its frightfulness was beyond their imagination.

I am a very poor hand at this corresponding business & no doubt my education could stand a lot of improvement, so I ask you to excuse mistakes in my spelling & grammer [sic].

Of course Mr McDonald I think you can imagine what the horrors of war are like but surely will us [use] your best to pull to their senses such men as Mr Asquith and Mr Lloy[d] George who are going to sacrifice hundreds of lives, rather I should have said thousands, make thousands of orphans, make thousands of cripples, make thousands face this hell.

I often wonder if Lloyd George thinks when he his [is] turning into his nice spring bed at night, that if the man in [the] trench who is exposed to all weathers, perhaps had no sleep for over [a] week & has his nerves strained to the ut[t]ermost, thinking that the next shell will most likely be the death of him, perhaps the sight of his chum who has had his brains blown out is a picture of horror in his brain, & the smell of his dead comrades is next to unbearable, agrees with (him L. George) that we don't want Peace, but we are out to crush Germany? No, that man doesn't say "hands of [sic] Neutrals" & of course it is impossible for him to sing.

Now Mr McDonald why shouldn't we know what terms of Peace we are fighting for, why shouldn't we discuss what terms we are supposed to accept?

Has England still got her old <u>ideal</u> that of <u>Conquer</u> & not the supposed new <u>ideal</u> one of <u>Peace</u>?

Surely is anything that we are going to gain, worth such a human sacrifice as L. George is prepared to make [?]

Tomorrow is voting day for the Australian Forces and we have had Patriotic circulars handed to us from Gen. Birdwood & Premier Hughes asking us to vote <u>Yes</u>.

The majority of the soldiers who are in England have not yet been out to face the "<u>music</u>", & I think it is a good job for the "Yes es" that they haven't.

I suppose Mr L. George classes me in with that Group known as the German Peace Agents.

Our family consists of three boys & the three of us are on Active Service. One Brother is in the 13th battalion & was wounded once, (in Gallopoli [Gallipoli]). The other Brother was in the first reinforcements of the 11th Battalion & has been wounded twice. I have been slightly wounded twice. My Mother & Father are both dead, so I don't think our family has done much for Germany. But I am dreading the day when I will have to go into that hell again.

Now Mr McDonald, I hope you will do everything possible in your power to bring about a <u>Peace</u> & save this slaughter of Human Lives. Thanking you for what you have done, & thanking you in anticipation for what you are going to do.

I remain, Yours Peacefully
4635. Pte. E.J. Ryan
51st Battalion Australian Forces

The following appears on the back of the final sheet of the letter:
(Present Address)
C/o   No 3 Camp
      Perham Downs
      Ludgershall
      Hants

(Active Service Address)
  A Coy, 51st Battalion
      13th Brigade
          4th Division
              A I Forces

P.S. If at any time you <u>may</u> want to use my name or address you may do so. EJR

Source:
  Ramsay MacDonald's Papers (The National Archives, Kew, UK)
  TNA: PRO/30/69/1160, f. 108

APPENDIX

Private Edward J. Ryan's Statement to his Court Martial

12 September 1917

A Coy 51st Battalion,
France

The following statement is my consciencous [sic] for my past conduct being such as it is.

Previous to enlisting as a soldier in the Australian Army [I believed] that Germany intended to crush her European enemies and by so doing had accepted the policy of might-is-right which is opposed to the ideals of Humanity and Civilisation.

About eleven months ago, England to my mind <u>adopted the same policy</u> [these words underlined in blue by his prosecutors] towards Germany. England's policy at that time consis[ted] of no <u>peace-conferences</u> until Germany was crushed so as to teach them a lesson of virtue. When the war had reached this stage, it was no longer a war of resistance.

Statements like the following – hands off Peace-makers – hands off America: We must crush Germany now, once and for all, proves that England's policy was one of aggression. Our Premier Mr Lloyd George gambled with Human lives to obtain those ends. The Premier's statements goes to prove that it was only a gamble, instead of telling America now to keep her hands off, he is telling us that America is the balance of power.

I enlisted to fight for a Peace without conquerors or conquered, as a Peace under those conditions as [does?] nothing to justify another war, either as a war of revenge by the <u>Conquered</u>, or a war of Glory and Patriotic land-grabbing by <u>Conquerors</u>.[968]

APPENDIX 3

Private Edward James RYAN, 4635, Service Summary

1915:
    21 Sept: enlists Perth, Western Australia, and trains at Blackboy Hill Training Camp.
    9 Nov: charged with disobeying a lawful command, and fined five shillings.

1916:
    12 Feb: departs Fremantle on troopship *Miltiades* bound for Egypt.
    10 Mar: disembarks, Suez, Egypt.
    Mar-Apr: trains in Egypt, at Heliopolis, Tel-el-Kabir, Serapeum, and Habieta.
    19 Apr: allocated to new 51st Battalion at Serapeum.
    5 June: 51st Battalion departs Alexandria on troopship *Ivernia* bound for Marseille.
    12 June: 51st Battalion disembarks Marseille, France, begins train journey to Caëstre.

FIRST WOUNDING
    28-9 June: wounded in action by shell burst in the trenches, Fleurbaix sector.
    29 June: admitted 3rd Australian Field Ambulance **'shell burns and abrasions, face'**.
    4 July: to 13th Stationary Hospital (Ophthalmic), Boulogne.
    5 July: to No. 1 Convalescent Hospital, Boulogne.
    7 July: transfers to 4th Division Base Depot, Étaples.
    23 July: rejoins 51st Battalion from base.

SECOND WOUNDING
    7 Aug: injured during 51st Battalion training exercises.
    8 Aug: admitted Casualty Clearing Station with **'crushed left hand'**.
    16 Aug: admitted hospital, Étaples, with **'crushed hand and nervous breakdown'**.
    26 Aug: embarks Calais for England on hospital ship *Newhaven*.
    26 Aug: admitted 4th London General Hospital, Camberwell, with **'S[hell] Shock'**.
    Sept: convalescence at Blytheswood and Bleakdown Hospitals, West Byfleet, Surrey.

LEAVE

Sept: granted period of leave, seven days in Edinburgh and eight days in London.

PERHAM DOWN, ENGLAND

2 Oct: enters Perham Down, No. 1 Command Depot, Hardening and Drafting Depot.

18 Oct: **writes to Ramsay MacDonald denouncing war and urging negotiations.**

19 Oct: AIF soldiers' vote in first Conscription Referendum.

15 to 19 Dec: takes off from camp without leave for five days, returns voluntarily.

19 Dec: CHARGE: AWOL (5 days), summary punishment (no court martial): 7 days confinement to camp, plus forfeits 5 days' pay.

1917:

FIRST COURT MARTIAL – THE EXTENDED 'MARRIAGE LEAVE' AWOL

> 11 Jan: granted ten days 'marriage leave' to Arbroath, Scotland.
>
> 21 Jan to 23 Feb: extends his leave by 40 days.
>
> 23 Feb: arrested Perham Down, No. 2 Camp, after returning voluntarily.
>
> 23 Feb-8 Apr: in prison awaiting trial for 45 days.
>
> **9 Apr: DISTRICT COURT MARTIAL, Perham Down: CHARGE 'AWOL' (40 days), pleads GUILTY. Finding GUILTY. SENTENCE: 42 days detention (plus forfeits 100 days' pay, £25).**

SECOND COURT MARTIAL – THE 9 HOUR PAYBOOK 'DESERTION'

> 8-9 May: refuses to parade for departure overseas to France without new paybook, then surrenders himself next morning at Perham Down.
>
> 9-22 May: in prison awaiting trial for 13 days.
>
> **22 May: DISTRICT COURT MARTIAL, Perham Down. CHARGE 'DESERTION' (9 hours). Pleads NOT GUILTY, arguing wrong to send him to France without his paybook. Finding GUILTY. SENTENCE: 30 days detention (plus forfeits 43 days' pay).**

27 June-1 July: takes off from camp without leave for 5 days, until apprehended by Military Police at Kempton Park near Richmond.

9 July: CHARGE: AWOL (5 DAYS), summary punishment (no court martial): 14 days Field Punishment No. 2, plus forfeits 26 days' pay.

12 July: proceeds to France, via Southampton, to return to 51st Battalion.

THIRD COURT MARTIAL – THE 14-DAY 'DESERTION' TO LE HAVRE

> 12 Aug: found missing from fatigue duty with 51st Battalion, near Kemmel, Belgium.
> 25 Aug: arrested at the wharves, Le Havre.
> 26 Aug-11 Sept: in detention awaiting trial for 17 days.
> 12 Sept: **FIELD GENERAL COURT MARTIAL, Chateau de Bomy. CHARGE 'DESERTION' (14 days). Pleads NOT GUILTY, arguing principled political objections to a war of conquest, unnecessarily prolonged. Finding GUILTY. SENTENCE: DEATH.**
> 24 Sept: sentence commuted, 5 years penal servitude (plus forfeits 5 years' and 31 days' pay).

10 Dec: admitted No. 10 British Military Prison, Dunkirk.
23 Dec: sentence of 5 years commuted to 2 years 'Imprisonment Hard Labour'.

1918:
18 Aug: sentence suspended, released from No 7 Military Prison, Vendroux, Les Attaques (Calais).
20 Aug: returns to 51st Battalion, reserve trenches, Rosières-en-Santerre, France.

FOURTH COURT MARTIAL – THE 11-DAY AWOL BEHIND THE LINES

> 6 Sept: found missing from 51st Battalion at Rivery before move to forward area.
> 6-16 Sept: wanders near the front before arrest as a straggler near Corbie.
> 15 Oct: **FIELD GENERAL COURT MARTIAL, Chateau de Bovelles. CHARGE: AWOL (11 days). Pleads NOT GUILTY, arguing debit in pay-book unfairly retained. Finding GUILTY. SENTENCE: 50 days of Field Punishment No. 2 (plus forfeits 80 days' pay).**

19 Oct: confined in Anzac Corps Field Punishment Compound, Flixecourt.
30 Dec: released and returned to 51st Battalion, Bouvignes-sur-Meuse, Belgium.

1919:
Jan-Apr: with 51st Battalion, Bouvignes-sur-Meuse, Belgium
Mar: guard duties, Namur.
22 Apr: shipped to England via Le Havre, enters Hurdcott camp.
21 June: embarks for return to Australia on troopship *Königin Luise*.
2 Aug: disembarks Fremantle, then by ship to Adelaide, and returns to Broken Hill.

APPENDIX

WAR AIMS AND SECRET TREATIES OF BRITAIN AND THE ENTENTE POWERS

1914-1918

The Pact of London, 4 September 1914 (PUBLIC)

Russia's 'Thirteen Points' outlining annexations, September 1914 (SECRET)

Britain declares annexation of Cyprus, protectorate over Egypt, Nov. 1914 (PUBLIC)

Britain promises not to return captured Basra (Iraq) to Ottoman rule, Nov. 1914 (PUBLIC)

Japan's Twenty-One Demands on China, January 1915 (SECRET)

British promises of annexations to Serbia, February-May 1915 (SECRET)

The Straits and Persia Agreement, 8 and 12 March 1915 (SECRET)

Lewis Harcourt Cabinet Document, 'The Spoils', 25 March 1915 (SECRET)

Théophile Delcassé's 'Terms of Peace' for France, 11 April 1915 (SECRET)

The Treaty of London, 26 April 1915 (SECRET)

Japan's ultimatum to China on remaining Thirteen Demands, May 1915 (PUBLIC)

De Bunsen Committee on 'Asiatic Turkey', 30 June 1915 (SECRET)

The 'McMahon-Hussein correspondence', July 1915-March 1916 (SECRET)

The Sykes-Picot agreements, January-May 1916. (SECRET)

Paris Economic Conference, 14-17 June 1916 ('Paris Resolutions') (PUBLIC)

The Bucharest Conventions, 17 August 1916 (SECRET)

The Paget-Tyrrell Foreign Office war aims memorandum, August 1916 (SECRET)

The Entente Reply to President Wilson, 10 January 1917 (PUBLIC)

The Briand-Cambon letter, on French war aims 12 January 1917 (SECRET)

British promise not to return captured German colonies, 31 January 1917 (PUBLIC)

Mallet 'Territorial Changes Committee' report, January to April 1917 (SECRET)

Colonial agreements re captured German colonies and other territories (SECRET)

- August 1914 – Anglo-French deal on partition of German Togoland
- February 1916 – Anglo-French deal on partition of the German Cameroons.
- 3 July 1916 – Russo-Japanese deal on partition of China, Manchuria, and Mongolia.
- February 1917 – Anglo-Japanese 'Balfour-Motono' deal re German & Chinese territories

Franco-Russian 'Left Bank of the Rhine' or Doumergue Agreement, 14 February-8 March 1917 (SECRET)

St-Jean-de-Maurienne Agreements, 19 April 1917 (SECRET)

Imperial War Conference, London, commits to 'imperial preference', April 1917 (PUBLIC)

Curzon Committee report on territorial war aims, 28 April 1917 (SECRET)

Milner Committee report on economic and non-territorial war aims, 1 May 1917 (SECRET)

French Chamber of Deputies resolution on war aims, 5 June 1917 (PUBLIC)

Italian declaration of a protectorate over Albania, June 1917 (PUBLIC)

London Conference widening territorial changes agreed at St-Jean-de-Maurienne Conference, 7-8 August 1917 (SECRET)

Lloyd George vows to return Alsace-Lorraine to France, 11 October 1917 (PUBLIC)

British Labour Party produces 'Memorandum of the War Aims', 28 December 1917 (PUBLIC)

Lloyd George's Caxton Hall Address, 5 January 1918 (PUBLIC)

National War Aims Committee produces 'The War Aims of the British People', February 1918 (PUBLIC)

Official declarations of support for new nations in Eastern Europe to be created from the Austro-Hungarian Empire, Summer 1918 (PUBLIC)

APPENDIX

LOST OPPORTUNITIES FOR A NEGOTIATED PEACE

1914-1918

President Woodrow Wilson's peace initiative, suggesting arbitration at the Hague Court (4 August 1914 – renewed 18 August 1914)

German diplomatic approaches to Russia through Denmark (winter 1914-15)

Ambassadorial mediation (German-British), Washington (September-December 1914)

Spontaneous Christmas truce on the Western Front (December 1914)

Robert La Follette's Peace Resolution in US Senate urging US-led neutral mediation to achieve a negotiated peace (8 February 1915)

The first Colonel House Mission to Britain and Europe (January-May 1915)

Dutch Anti-War Council's private attempts to mediate between Germany and Britain (April-October 1915)

International Congress of Women, The Hague (April-May 1915)

International Congress of Women delegations to the European capitals (May-July 1915)

Gildemeester-Bernstorff (Dutch-German) approaches to President Wilson in support of mediation (May-June 1915)

Dutch Government peace initiatives for an official Neutral Conference under US leadership (July-September 1915)

Ford 'Peace Ship' takes US peace activists to Europe to launch an unofficial Neutral Conference for Continuous Mediation (December 1915)

Neutral Conference for Continuous Mediation begins meetings, Stockholm (February 1916)

Törring-Waxweiler (Belgian-German) conversations (November 1915-February 1916)

The Second Colonel House Mission to Britain and Europe (January-February 1916)

House-Grey Memorandum on US mediation for a negotiated peace (February 1916)

Japanese-German peace negotiations, Stockholm (March-May 1916)

President Woodrow Wilson's speech to the US League to Enforce Peace (May 1916)

Emily Hobhouse's one-woman 'peace mission' to Berlin (June 1916)

Sweden, Norway, Denmark agree to propose a Neutral Conference on neutral rights (September 1916)

Asquith Cabinet discussions on peace terms – Lord Lansdowne's two Memoranda in support of negotiations (November 1916)

Bethmann Hollweg speech to the Reichstag accepting a League of Nations and compulsory arbitration of international disputes (9 November 1916)

German and American Peace Notes (12 and 18 December 1916)

Francis Hopwood attempted Anglo-Austrian negotiations, Copenhagen (February-March 1917)

Erzberger-Kolyshko (German-Russian) talks, Stockholm (March-April 1917)

Lady Paget's letters to Queen Maria Christina of Spain, urging support for a peace with Austria-Hungary (March-October 1917)

Prince Sixtus-Emperor Karl peace initiatives (December 1916-June 1917)

First German-British negotiations on the exchange of POWs, The Hague (June-July 1917)

The Stockholm Socialist Conference proposal (May-August 1917)

Russian proposal for an Inter-Allied Conference to revise war aims (May-June 1917)

Zaharoff-Kerim (British-Ottoman) talks (June, November 1917, and January, August, October 1918)

The Henry Morgenthau Mission to the Ottoman Empire (July 1917).

The Reichstag 'Peace Resolution' (July 1917)

Széchényi-Townley (Austrian-British) attempted talks, via the intermediary Ferdinand Leipnik, The Hague, Netherlands (July-Dec. 1917)

Papal Peace Note (10 August 1917) and German Reply (17 September 1917)

Armand-Revertera (French-Austrian) talks, Switzerland (7, 9, 22 August 1917)

Lancken-Briand (German-French) attempted talks, Lausanne-Ouchy, Switzerland (September 1917)

The Kühlmann peace initiative via Villalobar, The Hague and Spain (September-October 1917)

Lord Lansdowne's 'Peace Letter' to the *Daily Telegraph* (29 November 1917)

Smuts-Mensdorff (Anglo-Austrian) talks, Geneva, Switzerland (18-19 December 1917)

Brest-Litovsk talks (Russo-German) and German Christmas peace offer (December 1917-January 1918)

Lloyd George's 'Caxton Hall' speech, Wilson's 'Fourteen Points' and 'Four Principles' speeches, Central Powers' replies, and Herron-Lammasch (US-Austrian) negotiations (January-February 1918)

Kerr-Skrzynski (Anglo-Austrian) talks, Berne, Switzerland (March 1918)

Swedish Archbishop Söderblom's Christian peace conferences, Uppsala, Sweden (December 1917 and February 1918)

Second German-British negotiations on the exchange of POWs, The Hague (June-July 1918)

APPENDIX

The Straits and Persia Agreement

Sometimes known as 'The Constantinople Agreement', of March 1915 (CAB 37/126/33)

In this Britain and France promised to give Russia the spoils of the Gallipoli campaign, in return for Russian agreement to annexations elsewhere in the Ottoman Empire for France and Britain, and in Britain's case in return also for agreeing to give Britain the so-called neutral zone in Persia (between the British and Russian zones, as divided in 1907). This deal underpinned the Gallipoli campaign.

[This Document is the Property of His Britannic Majesty's Government.]
Printed for the use of the Cabinet. May 1915.

SECRET.

[35812]   No. 1.

Sir G. Buchanan to Sir Edward Grey.—(Received March 27.)

(No. 44. Secret.)
Sir,   Petrograd, March 13, 1915.

IN accordance with your instructions, and after consultation with my French colleague, I informed the Minister for Foreign Affairs yesterday morning that, subject to the war being prosecuted to a successful conclusion and to the desiderata of Great Britain and France in the Ottoman Empire and elsewhere being realised, His Majesty's Government would agree to the Russian *aide-mémoire* on the subject of Constantinople and the Straits, which his Excellency had handed to me on the 4th March, and of which I have the honour to transmit a copy herewith.

I at the same time gave his Excellency an *aide-mémoire* to the above effect, embodying your telegram No. 329 of the 10th March, though, in order not to compromise the cypher, I had been obliged to alter the sequence of the words.

I then read to him and left with him a memorandum, in which I have recorded the observations which you had, in your telegram No. 43, Private and Secret, of the 11th instant, instructed me to make on the subject of our assent to the Russian demands.

Copies of both these documents are enclosed.

After expressing in warm terms his satisfaction at receiving this communication, his Excellency said that he had no objections to raise to any of the desiderata of His Majesty's Government, with the sole exception of the conversion into an English sphere of the present neutral sphere in Persia. The question of railways made it very difficult for Russia to renounce all her existing rights in that sphere, and, if she did, she would have to ask us to allow her in return to be absolute mistress in her own sphere.

After some further conversation on the subject, I told his Excellency that I had been instructed to make personally to the Emperor the same communication which I had just made to him, and enquired when I could have the honour of an audience. M. Sazonof replied that this would not be at all easy to arrange, as His Majesty was leaving the next morning for the front, and would probably be engaged with audiences all the afternoon, as he himself was to have one late in the evening. I then suggested that, as the Emperor would probably wish to consult him before replying to the communication which I had been instructed to make, His Majesty might perhaps consent to receive us both together. This his Excellency kindly arranged, and I accordingly accompanied him to Tsarskoe.

I have, in my telegram No. 54, Private and Secret, of yesterday's date, reported that the Emperor, in the course of our audience, authorised me to inform you that he consented in principle to the neutral sphere being incorporated in the British sphere, but that M. Sazonof will probably insist on our giving in return some assurances as to Russia's liberty of action in her own sphere.

I have, &c.
GEORGE W. BUCHANAN.

Enclosure 1 in No. 1.

Aide-mémoire communicated by M. Sazonof, March 4, 1915.

LE cours des derniers événements amène Sa Majesté l'Empereur Nicolas à penser que la question de Constantinople et des Détroits doit être résolue définitivement, selon les aspirations séculaires de la Russie.

Toute solution serait insuffisante et précaire si la ville de Constantinople, la rive occidentale du Bosphore, de la mer de Marmara et des Dardanelles, ainsi que la Thrace méridionale jusqu'à la ligne Enos-Midia, n'étaient désormais incorporées à l'Empire de Russie.

[664]

2

De même, et par nécessité stratégique, la partie du littoral asiatique comprise entre le Bosphore, la rivière Sakharia et un point à fixer sur le golfe d'Ismid, les îles de la mer de Marmara, les îles d'Imbros et de Ténédos devront être incorporées à l'Empire.

Les intérêts spéciaux de la France et de la Grande-Bretagne dans la région ci-dessus désignée seront scrupuleusement respectés.

Le Gouvernement Impérial se plaît à espérer que les considérations ci-dessus seront accueillies avec sympathie par les deux Gouvernements alliés. Lesdits Gouvernements alliés sont assurés de rencontrer auprès du Gouvernement Impérial la même sympathie pour la réalisation des desseins qu'ils peuvent former en d'autres régions de l'Empire ottoman et ailleurs.

Pétrograde, le 19 février (4 mars), 1915.

Enclosure 2 in No. 1.

Aide-mémoire communicated to M. Sazonof, March 12, 1915.

SUBJECT to the war being carried on and brought to a successful conclusion, and to the desiderata of Great Britain and France in the Ottoman Empire and elsewhere being realised as indicated in the Russian communication herein referred to, His Majesty's Government will agree to the Russian Government's *aide-mémoire* relative to Constantinople and the Straits, the text of which was communicated to His Britannic Majesty's Ambassador by his Excellency M. Sazonof on the 19th February (4th March), 1915.

Petrograd, February 27 (March 12), 1915.

Enclosure 3 in No. 1.

Memorandum.

HIS Majesty's Ambassador has been instructed to make the following observations with reference to the *aide-mémoire* which this Embassy had the honour of addressing to the Imperial Government on the 27th February (12th March), 1915.

The claim made by the Imperial Government in their *aide-mémoire* of the 19th February (4th March), 1915, considerably exceeds the desiderata which were foreshadowed by M. Sazonof as probable a few weeks ago. Before His Majesty's Government have had time to take into consideration what their own desiderata elsewhere would be in the final terms of peace, Russia is asking for a definite promise that her wishes shall be satisfied with regard to what is in fact the richest prize of the entire war. Sir Edward Grey accordingly hopes that M. Sazonof will realise that it is not in the power of His Majesty's Government to give a greater proof of friendship than that which is afforded by the terms of the above-mentioned *aide-mémoire*. That document involves a complete reversal of the traditional policy of His Majesty's Government, and is in direct opposition to the opinions and sentiments at one time universally held in England and which have still by no means died out. Sir Edward Grey therefore trusts that the Imperial Government will recognise that the recent general assurances given to M. Sazonof have been most loyally and amply fulfilled. In presenting the *aide-mémoire* now, His Majesty's Government believe and hope that a lasting friendship between Russia and Great Britain will be assured as soon as the proposed settlement is realised.

From the British *aide-mémoire* it follows that the desiderata of His Majesty's Government, however important they may be to British interests in other parts of the world, will contain no condition which could impair Russia's control over the territories described in the Russian *aide-mémoire* of the 19th February (4th March), 1915.

In view of the fact that Constantinople will always remain a trade *entrepôt* for South-Eastern Europe and Asia Minor, His Majesty's Government will ask that Russia shall, when she comes into possession of it, arrange for a free port for goods in transit to and from non-Russian territory. His Majesty's Government will also ask that there shall be commercial freedom for merchant-ships passing through the Straits, as M. Sazonof has already promised.

Except in so far as the naval and military operations on which His Majesty's Government are now engaged in the Dardanelles may contribute to the common cause of the Allies, it is now clear that these operations, however successful, cannot be of any advantage to His Majesty's Government in the final terms of peace. Russia alone will, if the war is successful, gather the direct fruits of these operations. Russia should therefore, in the opinion of His Majesty's Government, not now put difficulties in the way of any Power which may, on reasonable terms, offer to co-operate with the Allies. The only Power likely to participate in the operations in the Straits is Greece. Admiral Carden has asked the Admiralty to send him more destroyers, but they have none to spare. The assistance of a Greek flotilla, if it could have been secured, would thus have been of inestimable value to His Majesty's Government.

To induce the neutral Balkan States to join the Allies was one of the main objects which His Majesty's Government had in view when they undertook the operations in the Dardanelles. His Majesty's Government hope that Russia will spare no pains to calm the apprehensions of Bulgaria and Roumania as to Russia's possession of the Straits and Constantinople being to their disadvantage. His Majesty's Government also hope that Russia will do everything in her power to render the co-operation of these two States an attractive prospect to them.

Sir E. Grey points out that it will obviously be necessary to take into consideration the whole question of the future interests of France and Great Britain in what is now Asiatic Turkey; and, in formulating the desiderata of His Majesty's Government with regard to the Ottoman Empire, he must consult the French as well as the Russian Government. As soon, however, as it becomes known that Russia is to have Constantinople at the conclusion of the war, Sir E. Grey will wish to state that, throughout the negotiations, His Majesty's Government have stipulated that the Mussulman Holy Places and Arabia shall under all circumstances remain under independent Mussulman dominion.

Sir E. Grey is as yet unable to make any definite proposal on any point of the British desiderata; but one of the points of the latter will be the revision of the Persian portion of the Anglo-Russian Agreement of 1907 so as to recognise the present neutral sphere as a British sphere.

Until the Allies are in a position to give to the Balkan States, and especially to Bulgaria and Roumania, some satisfactory assurance as to their prospects and general position with regard to the territories contiguous to their frontiers to the possession of which they are known to aspire; and until a more advanced stage of the agreement as to the French and British desiderata in the final peace terms is reached, Sir E. Grey points out that it is most desirable that the understanding now arrived at between the Russian, French, and British Governments should remain secret.

Petrograd, February 27 (March 12), 1915.

APPENDIX 7

LEWIS HARCOURT'S CABINET DOCUMENT, 'THE SPOILS'

25 March 1915

In this Harcourt, Colonial Secretary, outlined a package of possible British annexations across the globe, to counterbalance the annexations granted to Russia and France. (CAB 63/3 pp. 104-107 - the relevant four pages from CAB 63/3)

March 25 1915

[This Document is the Property of His Britannic Majesty's Government.]

Printed for the use of the Cabinet. March 1915. (1915) 13.

SECRET.

104

"THE SPOILS."

WE seem to be forced by the possible capture of Constantinople into a premature discussion of a division of the yet unacquired spoils of the whole war.

As I am specially concerned with German colonies, I am drawn into the consideration of the whole question.

The following observations are based on the presumption that the Allies are completely successful and able to dictate any terms they choose to Germany, Austria, and Turkey.

1. I assume that we shall retain some part of Mesopotamia, possibly as far as from the Persian Gulf to Bagdad, mainly on the ground stated by Lord Crewe that this fertile land would give an outlet for Indian emigration.

2. If Persia became involved in the war it would be desirable that part of the neutral zone containing the oil fields and the province of Fars should pass under British control.

3. It would also be an advantage, in view of Russian predominance in Northern Persia, if the capital and seat of Government could be transferred from Tehran to some more southern or eastern town.

4. It has been suggested that, if Russia is at Constantinople, we should occupy Alexandretta—

   (a.) to command the Bagdad Railway terminus,
   (b.) as a naval base to protect Egypt and our sea route to India from Russian attack.

5. (a) Seems to necessitate our control or occupation of all Mesopotamia and the Bagdad Railway, which would be a costly and onerous obligation, though with great expenditure on irrigation the valley of the Euphrates would probably be made very fertile and perhaps remunerative.

6. As to (b), Alexandretta does not seem by any means an ideal naval base for the protection of Egypt against Russian attack.

It is an open roadstead and the cost of a harbour would be considerable.

For purely naval purposes the fine harbour of Marmarice on the mainland due north of Rhodes, or the island of Mitylene, with its great land-locked inlets, would seem to be preferable. Mitylene commands the exit from the Dardanelles and the Gulf of Smyrna.

But I am very doubtful whether we should be wise to add to the number of our hostages to fortune in the Mediterranean.

[449]

APPENDIX

7. France claims Syria and the Taurus, but it is not certain that this is intended to include Alexandretta.

I think it would be unfortunate if France became the guardian of the Christian Holy Places in Palestine.

I should like to see them in British hands, (and perhaps governed from Egypt), or, if that is impossible, I have heard a suggestion that they might be under the protection of the United States.

8. If Italy comes into the war it might be possible, and would be advantageous to us, to exchange British Somaliland, which is contiguous to Italian Somaliland, for the Italian Erithrea, on the Red Sea, which adjoins the Soudan and Abyssinia. We might, if necessary, give them some accommodation at Solum on the frontier of Tripoli and Egypt for this object.

9. All the German possessions in the Pacific have now been taken from her.

Samoa is under the control of New Zealand, Japan is temporarily in occupation of all the islands north of the equator, and Australia all the islands south of the equator. It is out of the question to part with any of the territories now in the occupation of Australia and New Zealand.

Japan evidently intends to claim the possession at the end of the war of all the islands she is now occupying, with the possible exception of Yap.

I fear that this will cause great trouble with Australia, especially as regards the Marshall Islands, the trade of which has been, even under German rule, exclusively with Australia.

The United States is not likely to be pleased at Japanese extension eastward in the Pacific.

10. There remain the German colonies in Africa, all of which I assume we shall have captured by the end of the war.

11. If German South-West Africa is occupied by the Union Government, it must obviously be retained as part of the British Empire, unless the Union Government and Portugal were willing to exchange it for the Portuguese possessions on the east coast of Africa, including Delagoa Bay, Beira, and Mozambique. This exchange would effect a consolidation of Portuguese and British territory, and probably be to the advantage of each; but it is not likely to be acceptable to the Portuguese, who would be incapable of governing the German population.

12. German East Africa forms the missing link in the chain of British possessions from the Cape to Cairo.

It would make an admirable colony for Indian emigration of the class which wants to trade and not to cultivate, assuming that the latter will be provided for in Mesopotamia.

The German railway, now complete, from Ujiji on Lake Tanganyika to Dar-es-Salaam on the coast, will in future tap and carry a large part of the trade of the Belgian Congo, and will deprive our Uganda Railway of much of the traffic which it now obtains from Ruanda and the southern half of the Victoria Nyanza.

13. Togoland is in the joint occupation of French and British forces.

It could be—

> (a.) divided: approximately half going to the British Gold Coast and Ashantee, and the other half to French Dahomey; but, in any division, it

would be difficult to allot the only port, Lomé, and the single railway up to Kamina;
- (b.) given to the French;
- (c.) given to the British, in each case in consideration of some advantage elsewhere.

If it was retained by the British, a deal might be made with the French to obtain also the part of Dahomey which separates Togoland from Nigeria, so as to form all our possessions in the Gulf of Guinea into a solid and continuous territory.

14. The Cameroons are being invaded, and presumably captured, by a joint French and British force. France is employing, and will probably continue to employ, a larger land force than ours. But we provided the whole of the naval assistance which alone made possible the initial capture of the capital, Duala, and the railway.

It might be assumed that we should equitably be entitled to half the Cameroons, but at the most I do not think we should require or could usefully occupy more than one fourth of it.

The French will undoubtedly desire a large share of it, and especially that part which was taken from them by Germany at the time of Agadir.

We might ourselves retain very much less than one-fourth of the area, but what it is essential that we should have is the northern railway (about 80 miles) from Duala to Baré; Mount Cameroon on the coast, which will make a perfect sanatorium for the whole of West Africa; and the town and harbour of Duala, which in enemy hands could easily be made an impregnable and menacing naval base against our West and South African commerce.

15. We want from France two things—
- (a.) their share of the Condominium in the New Hebrides;
- (b.) their small settlement of Jibuti opposite Aden, which controls the mischievous arms traffic to Abyssinia and Central Africa.

To obtain these we can offer France—
- (c.) three-fourths of the Cameroons (instead of one-half), *plus* our half share of Togoland;
- (d.) or, if we wish to retain all Togoland and acquire Dahomey, we can offer France *all* the Cameroons except Mount Cameroon and Duala, and in such a wide settlement we could throw in the Gambia, which is an object of great desire by the French; but the cession of the Gambia would be very unpopular in this country, and arouse much public and Parliamentary criticism and agitation.

16. Alternatively we might surrender to France *our* share of the New Hebrides Condominium as compensation, with nearly the whole of the Cameroons, for our possession of Togoland and Dahomey.

This would be an impossible suggestion in ordinary times of peace, owing to Australian prejudices, but as Australia is now to acquire such a large amount of new Pacific territory she might at this moment be induced to agree to it.

In order to sweeten the pill, I should not object to giving Australia also the German island of Bougainville and our adjoining islands of the Solomon Group.

17. And, lastly, we might take this opportunity of restoring to China, with or without a consideration, the costly folly of Weihaiwei.

L. H.

March 25, 1915.

APPENDIX

The Secret Treaty of London

26 April 1915

This is the treaty under which Italy agreed to enter the war, within a month, and outlined the territorial gains that would flow to Italy when peace was made. The landings at Gallipoli helped secure the Italian signature and entry into the Great War in May 1915.

Published in 1920 as 'Agreement between France, Russia, Great Britain and Italy, signed in London April 26, 1915', Parliamentary Paper, cmd. 671

MISCELLANEOUS. No. 7 (1920).

261

AGREEMENT

BETWEEN

FRANCE, RUSSIA, GREAT BRITAIN AND ITALY,

SIGNED AT LONDON, APRIL 26, 1915.

Presented to Parliament by Command of His Majesty.

LONDON:
PRINTED AND PUBLISHED BY
HIS MAJESTY'S STATIONERY OFFICE.

To be purchased through any Bookseller or directly from
H.M. STATIONERY OFFICE at the following addresses:
IMPERIAL HOUSE, KINGSWAY, LONDON, W.C. 2, and
28, ABINGDON STREET, LONDON, S.W. 1;
37, PETER STREET, MANCHESTER;
1, ST. ANDREW'S CRESCENT, CARDIFF;
23, FORTH STREET, EDINBURGH;
or from E. PONSONBY, LTD., 116, GRAFTON STREET, DUBLIN.

1920.

[Cmd. 671.]   *Price 1d. Net*

Agreement between France, Russia, Great Britain and Italy.

Signed in London April 26, 1915.

D'ORDRE de son Gouvernement, le Marquis Impériali, Ambassadeur de Sa Majesté le Roi d'Italie, a l'honneur de communiquer au Très Honorable Sir Edward Grey, Principal Secrétaire d'État de Sa Majesté britannique pour les Affaires Étrangères, et à leurs Excellences M. Paul Cambon, Ambassadeur de la République française, et M. le Comte de Benckendorff, Ambassadeur de Sa Majesté l'Empereur de Toutes les Russies, le mémorandum suivant :

Mémorandum.

Article 1ᵉʳ.

Une convention militaire sera immédiatement conclue entre les états-majors généraux de la France, de la Grande-Bretagne, de l'Italie et de la Russie; cette convention fixera le minimum des forces militaires que la Russie devra employer contre l'Autriche-Hongrie afin d'empêcher cette Puissance de concentrer tous ses efforts contre l'Italie, dans le cas où la Russie déciderait de porter son principal effort contre l'Allemagne.

La convention militaire réglera la question des armistices, qui relève essentiellement du commandement en chef des armées.

Article 2.

De son côté, l'Italie s'engage à employer la totalité de ses ressources à poursuivre la guerre en commun avec la France, la Grande-Bretagne et la Russie contre tous leurs ennemis.

Article 3.

Les flottes de la France et de la Grande-Bretagne donneront leur concours actif et permanent à l'Italie jusqu'à la destruction de la flotte austro-hongroise ou jusqu'à la conclusion de la paix.

Une convention navale sera immédiatement conclue à cet effet entre la France, la Grande-Bretagne et l'Italie.

BY Order of his Government the Marquis Imperiali, Ambassador of His Majesty the King of Italy, has the honour to communicate to the Rt. Hon. Sir Edward Grey, His Britannic Majesty's Principal Secretary of State for Foreign Affairs, and to their Excellencies M. Paul Cambon, Ambassador of the French Republic, and to Count de Benckendorff, Ambassador of His Majesty the Emperor of All the Russias, the following memorandum :—

Memorandum.

Article 1.

A military convention shall be immediately concluded between the General Staffs of France, Great Britain, Italy and Russia. This convention shall settle the minimum number of military forces to be employed by Russia against Austria-Hungary in order to prevent that Power from concentrating all its strength against Italy, in the event of Russia deciding to direct her principal effort against Germany.

This military convention shall settle question of armistices, which necessarily comes within the scope of the Commanders-in-chief of the Armies.

Article 2.

On her part, Italy undertakes to use her entire resources for the purpose of waging war jointly with France, Great Britain and Russia against all their enemies.

Article 3.

The French and British fleets shall render active and permanent assistance to Italy until such time as the Austro-Hungarian fleet shall have been destroyed or until peace shall have been concluded.

A naval convention shall be immediately concluded to this effect between France, Great Britain and Italy.

Article 4.

Dans le traité de paix, l'Italie obtiendra le Trentin, le Tyrol cisalpin avec sa frontière géographique et naturelle (la frontière du Brenner), ainsi que Trieste, les comtés de Gorizia et de Gradisca, toute l'Istrie jusqu'au Quarnero et y compris Volosca et les îles istriennes de Cherso, Lussin, de même que les petites îles de Plavnik, Unie, Canidole, Palazzuoli, San Pietro di Nembi, Asinello, Gruica, et les îlots voisins.

Note.

La frontière nécessaire pour assurer l'exécution de l'article 4 sera tracée comme suit :

Du Piz Umbrail jusqu'au nord du Stelvio, elle suivra la crête des Alpes rhétiennes jusqu'aux sources de l'Adige et de l'Eisach, passant alors sur les monts Reschen et Brenner et sur les hauteurs de l'Oetz et du Ziller. La frontière ensuite se dirigera vers le sud, traversera le mont Toblach et rejoindra la frontière actuelle des Alpes carniques. Elle suivra cette frontière jusqu'au mont Tarvis, et après le mont Tarvis la ligne de partage des eaux des Alpes juliennes par le col Predil, le mont Mangart, le Tricorno (Terglou) et la ligne de partage des eaux des cols de Podberdo, de Podlaniscam et d'Idria. A partir de ce point, la frontière suivra la direction du sud-est vers le Schneeberg, laissant hors du territoire italien tout le bassin de la Save et de ses tributaires; du Schneeberg la frontière descendra vers la côte de manière à inclure Castua, Mattuglia et Volosca dans le territoire italien.

Article 5.

L'Italie recevra également la province de Dalmatie dans ses limites administratives actuelles en y comprenant au nord Lisarica et Tribania, et au sud jusqu'à une ligne partant sur la côte du cap Planka et suivant vers l'est les sommets des hauteurs formant la ligne de partage des eaux de manière à laisser dans le territoire italien toutes les vallées et cours d'eau descendant vers Sebenico, comme la Cicola, la Kerka, la Butisnica et leurs affluents. Elle recevra aussi toutes les îles situées au nord et à l'ouest de la Dalmatie depuis Premuda, Selve, Ulbo, Scherda, Maon, Pago et Patadura au nord, jusqu'à Meleda au sud en y comprenant Sant' Andrea, Busi, Lissa, Lesina, Tercola, Curzola, Cazza et Lagosta, ainsi que les rochers et îlots

Article 4.

Under the Treaty of Peace, Italy shall obtain the Trentino, Cisalpine Tyrol with its geographical and natural frontier (the Brenner frontier), as well as Trieste, the counties of Gorizia and Gradisca, all Istria as far as the Quarnero and including Volosca and the Istrian islands of Cherso and Lussin, as well as the small islands of Plavnik, Unie, Canidole, Palazzuoli, San Pietro di Nembi, Asinello, Gruica, and the neighbouring islets.

Note.

The frontier required to ensure execution of Article 4 hereof shall be traced as follows :—

From the Piz Umbrail as far as north of the Stelvio, it shall follow the crest of the Rhetian Alps up to the sources of the Adige and the Eisach, then following the Reschen and Brenner mountains and the Oetz and Ziller heights. The frontier shall then bend towards the south, cross Mt. Toblach and join the present frontier of the Carnic Alps. It shall follow this frontier line as far as Mt. Tarvis and from Mt. Tarvis the watershed of the Julian Alps by the Predil Pass, Mt. Mangart, the Tricorno (Terglu) and the watersheds of the Podberdo, Podlaniscam and Idria passes. From this point the frontier shall follow a south-easterly direction towards the Schneeberg, leaving the entire basin of the Save and its tributaries outside Italian territory. From the Schneeberg the frontier shall come down to the coast in such a way as to include Castua, Mattuglia and Volosca within Italian territory.

Article 5.

Italy shall also be given the province of Dalmatia within its present administrative boundaries, including to the north Lisarica and Tribania; to the south as far as a line starting from Cape Planka on the coast and following eastwards the crests of the heights forming the watershed, in such a way as to leave within Italian territory all the valleys and streams flowing towards Sebenico—such as the Cicola, Kerka, Butisnica and their tributaries. She shall also obtain all the islands situate to the north and west of Dalmatia, from Premuda, Selve, Ulbo, Scherda, Maon, Pago and Patadura to the north, up to Meleda to the south including Sant' Andrea, Busi, Lissa, Lesina, Tercola, Curzola, Cazza and Lagosta, as well as the neighbouring

environnants et Pelagosa, à l'exception seulement des îles Grande et Petite Zirona, Bua, Solta et Brazza.

Seront neutralisées :

(1.) Toute la côte depuis le cap Planka au nord jusqu'à la racine méridionale de la péninsule de Sabioncello au sud, de manière à comprendre toute cette péninsule; (2) la partie du littoral commençant au nord à un point situé à 10 kilom. au sud de la pointe de Ragusa Vecchia descendant au sud jusqu'à la rivière Voïussa, de manière à comprendre le golfe et les ports de Cattaro, Antivari, Dulcigno, Saint-Jean de Medua, Durazzo, sans préjudice des droits du Monténégro résultant des déclarations échangées entre les Puissances en avril et mai 1909. Ces droits ne s'appliquant qu'au territoire actuel monténégrin ne pourront être étendus aux territoires ou ports qui pourraient être attribués au Monténégro. En conséquence, aucune partie des côtes appartenant actuellement au Monténégro ne. pourra être neutralisée. Resteront en vigueur les restrictions concernant le port d'Antivari auxquelles le Monténégro a lui-même consenti en 1909; (3) et, enfin, toutes les îles qui ne sont pas attribuées à l'Italie

rocks and islets and Pelagosa, with the exception of Greater and Lesser Zirona, Bua, Solta and Brazza.

To be neutralized :—

(1) The entire coast from Cape Planka on the north to the southern base of the peninsula of Sabbioncello in the south, so as to include the whole of that peninsula; (2) the portion of the coast which begins in the north at a point situated 10 kilometres south of the headland of Ragusa Vecchia extending southward as far as the River Voïussa, in such a way as to include the gulf and ports of Cattaro, Antivari, Dulcigno, St. Jean de Medua and Durazzo, without prejudice to the rights of Montenegro consequent on the declarations exchanged between the Powers in April and May 1909. As these rights only apply to the present Montenegrin territory, they cannot be extended to any territory or ports which may be assigned to Montenegro. Consequently neutralisation shall not apply to any part of the coast now belonging to Montenegro. There shall be maintained all restrictions concerning the port of Antivari which were accepted by Montenegro in 1909; (3) finally, all the islands not given to Italy.

Note.

Les territoires de l'Adriatique énumérés ci-dessous seront attribués par les quatre Puissances alliées à la Croatie, à la Serbie et au Monténégro :

Dans le Haut-Adriatique, toute la côte depuis la baie de Volosca sur les confins de l'Istrie jusqu'à la frontière septentrionale de Dalmatie comprenant le littoral actuellement hongrois et toute la côte de Croatie, avec le port de Fiume et les petits ports de Novi et de Carlopago, ainsi que les îles de Veglia, Pervichio, Gregorio, Goli et Arbe. Et, dans le Bas-Adriatique (dans la région intéressant la Serbie et le Monténégro), toute la côte du cap Planka jusqu'à la rivière Drin, avec les ports importants de Spalato, Raguse, Cattaro, Antivari, Dulcigno et Saint-Jean de Medua et les îles de Zirona Grande, Zirona Piccola, Bua, Solta, Brazza, Jaclian et Calamotta. Le port de Durazzo resterait attribué à l'État indépendant musulman d'Albanie.

Note.

The following Adriatic territory shall be assigned by the four Allied Powers to Croatia, Serbia and Montenegro :—

In the Upper Adriatic, the whole coast from the bay of Volosca on the borders of Istria as far as the northern frontier of Dalmatia, including the coast which is at present Hungarian and all the coast of Croatia, with the port of Fiume and the small ports of Novi and Carlopago, as well as the islands of Veglia, Pervichio, Gregorio, Goli and Arbe. And, in the Lower Adriatic (in the region interesting Serbia and Montenegro) the whole coast from Cape Planka as far as the River Drin, with the important harbours of Spalato, Ragusa, Cattaro, Antivari, Dulcigno and St. Jean de Medua and the islands of Greater and Lesser Zirona, Bua, Solta, Brazza, Jaclian and Calamotta. The port of Durazzo to be assigned to the independent Moslem State of Albania.

ARTICLE 6.

L'Italie recevra l'entière souveraineté sur Vallona, l'île de Sasseno et un territoire suffisamment étendu pour assurer la défense de ces points (depuis Voïussa au

ARTICLE 6.

Italy shall receive full sovereignty over Valona, the island of Saseno and surrounding territory of sufficient extent to assure defence of these points (from

nord et à l'est, approximativement jusqu'à la frontière septentrionale du district de Chimaru au sud).

Article 7.

Si l'Italie obtient le Trentin et l'Istrie conformément aux termes de l'article 4, la Dalmatie et les îles de l'Adriatique dans les limites indiquées dans l'article 5 et la baie de Vallona (article 6), et si la partie centrale de l'Albanie est réservée pour la constitution d'un petit État autonome neutralisé, elle ne s'opposera pas à ce que les parties septentrionale et méridionale de l'Albanie soient, si tel est le désir de la France, de la Grande-Bretagne et de la Russie, partagées entre le Monténégro, la Serbie et la Grèce. La côte à partir de la frontière méridionale de la possession italienne de Vallona (voyez l'article 6) jusqu'au cap Stylos sera neutralisée.

L'Italie sera chargée de représenter l'État d'Albanie dans ses relations avec l'étranger.

L'Italie accepte, d'autre part, de laisser dans tous les cas à l'est de l'Albanie un territoire suffisant pour assurer l'existence d'une frontière commune à la Grèce et à la Serbie à l'ouest du lac d'Ochrida.

Article 8.

L'Italie recevra l'entière souveraineté sur les îles du Dodécanèse qu'elle occupe actuellement.

Article 9.

D'une manière générale, la France, la Grande-Bretagne et la Russie reconnaissent que l'Italie est intéressée au maintien de l'équilibre dans la Méditerranée et qu'elle devra, en cas de partage total ou partiel de la Turquie d'Asie, obtenir une part équitable dans la région méditerranéenne avoisinant la province d'Adalia où l'Italie a déjà acquis des droits et des intérêts qui ont fait l'objet d'une convention italo-britannique. La zone qui sera éventuellement attribuée à l'Italie sera délimitée, le moment venu, en tenant compte des intérêts existants de la France et de la Grande-Bretagne.

Les intérêts de l'Italie seront également pris en considération dans le cas où l'intégrité territoriale de l'Empire ottoman serait maintenue et où des modifications seraient faites aux zones d'intérêt des Puissances.

Si la France, la Grande-Bretagne et la Russie occupent des territoires de la Turquie d'Asie pendant la durée de la

the Voïussa to the north and east, approximately to the northern boundary of the district of Chimara on the south).

Article 7.

Should Italy obtain the Trentino and Istria in accordance with the provisions of Article 4, together with Dalmatia and the Adriatic islands within the limits specified in Article 5, and the Bay of Valona (Article 6), and if the central portion of Albania is reserved for the establishment of a small autonomous neutralised State, Italy shall not oppose the division of Northern and Southern Albania between Montenegro, Serbia and Greece, should France, Great Britain and Russia so desire. The coast from the southern boundary of the Italian territory of Valona (see Article 6) up to Cape Stylos shall be neutralised.

Italy shall be charged with the representation of the State of Albania in its relations with foreign Powers.

Italy agrees, moreover, to leave sufficient territory in any event to the east of Albania to ensure the existence of a frontier line between Greece and Serbia to the west of Lake Ochrida.

Article 8.

Italy shall receive entire sovereignty over the Dodecanese Islands which she is at present occupying.

Article 9.

Generally speaking, France, Great Britain and Russia recognise that Italy is interested in the maintenance of the balance of power in the Mediterranean and that, in the event of the total or partial partition of Turkey in Asia, she ought to obtain a just share of the Mediterranean region adjacent to the province of Adalia, where Italy has already acquired rights and interests which formed the subject of an Italo-British convention. The zone which shall eventually be allotted to Italy shall be delimited, at the proper time, due account being taken of the existing interests of France and Great Britain.

The interests of Italy shall also be taken into consideration in the event of the territorial integrity of the Turkish Empire being maintained and of alterations being made in the zones of interest of the Powers.

If France, Great Britain and Russia occupy any territories in Turkey in Asia

guerre, la région méditerranéenne avoisinant la province d'Adalia dans les limites indiquées ci-dessus sera réservée à l'Italie, qui aura le droit de l'occuper.

during the course of the war, the Mediterranean region bordering on the Province of Adalia within the limits indicated above shall be reserved to Italy, who shall be entitled to occupy it.

Article 10.

L'Italie sera substituée en Lybie aux droits et privilèges appartenant actuellement au Sultan en vertu du Traité de Lausanne.

Article 10.

All rights and privileges in Libya at present belonging to the Sultan by virtue of the Treaty of Lausanne are transferred to Italy.

Article 11.

L'Italie recevra une part correspondant à ses efforts et à ses sacrifices dans l'indemnité de guerre éventuelle.

Article 11.

Italy shall receive a share of any eventual war indemnity corresponding to her efforts and her sacrifices.

Article 12.

L'Italie déclare s'associer à la déclaration faite par la France, la Grande-Bretagne et la Russie à l'effet de laisser l'Arabie et les lieux saints musulmans en Arabie sous l'autorité d'un pouvoir musulman indépendant.

Article 12.

Italy declares that she associates herself in the declaration made by France, Great Britain and Russia to the effect that Arabia and the Moslem Holy Places in Arabia shall be left under the authority of an independent Moslem Power.

Article 13.

Dans le cas où la France et la Grande-Bretagne augmenteraient leurs domaines coloniaux d'Afrique aux dépens de l'Allemagne, ces deux Puissances reconnaissent en principe que l'Italie pourrait réclamer quelques compensations équitables, notamment dans le règlement en sa faveur des questions concernant les frontières des colonies italiennes de l'Érythrée, de la Somalie et de la Lybie et des colonies voisines de la France et de la Grande-Bretagne.

Article 13.

In the event of France and Great Britain increasing their colonial territories in Africa at the expense of Germany, those two Powers agree in principle that Italy may claim some equitable compensation, particularly as regards the settlement in her favour of the questions relative to the frontiers of the Italian colonies of Eritrea, Somaliland and Libya and the neighbouring colonies belonging to France and Great Britain.

Article 14.

La Grande-Bretagne s'engage à faciliter la conclusion immédiate, dans des conditions équitables, d'un emprunt d'au moins £50,000,000 à émettre sur le marché de Londres.

Article 14.

Great Britain undertakes to facilitate the immediate conclusion, under equitable conditions, of a loan of at least 50,000,000*l.* to be issued on the London market.

Article 15.

La France, la Grande-Bretagne et la Russie appuieront l'opposition que l'Italie formera à toute proposition tendant à introduire un représentant du Saint Siège dans toutes les négociations pour la paix et pour le règlement des questions soulevées par la présente guerre.

Article 15.

France, Great Britain and Russia shall support such opposition as Italy may make to any proposal in the direction of introducing a representative of the Holy See in any peace negotiations or negotiations for the settlement of questions raised by the present war.

Article 16.

Le présent arrangement sera tenu secret. L'adhésion de l'Italie à la

Article 16.

The present arrangement shall be held secret. The adherence of Italy to the

déclaration du 5 septembre, 1914, sera seule rendue publique aussitôt après la déclaration de guerre par ou contre l'Italie.

Après avoir pris acte du mémorandum ci-dessus, les représentants de la France, de la Grande-Bretagne et de la Russie, dûment autorisés à cet effet, ont conclu avec le représentant de l'Italie, également autorisé par son Gouvernement, l'accord suivant :

La France, la Grande-Bretagne et la Russie, donnent leur plein assentiment au mémorandum présenté par le Gouvernement italien.

Se référant aux articles 1er, 2 et 3 du mémorandum, qui prévoient la coopération militaire et navale des quatre Puissances, l'Italie déclare qu'elle entrera en campagne le plus tôt possible et dans un délai qui ne pourra excéder un mois à partir de la signature des présentes.

En foi de quoi les soussignés ont signé le présent accord et y ont apposé leurs cachets.

Fait à Londres, en quadruple original, le 26 avril, 1915.

(L.S.) E. GREY.
(L.S.) IMPERIALI.
(L.S.) BENCKENDORFF.
(L.S.) PAUL CAMBON.

Declaration of the 5th September, 1914, shall alone be made public, immediately upon declaration of war by or against Italy.

After having taken act of the foregoing memorandum, the representatives of France, Great Britain and Russia, duly authorised to that effect, have concluded the following agreement with the representative of Italy, also duly authorised by his Government :—

France, Great Britain and Russia give their full assent to the memorandum presented by the Italian Government.

With reference to Articles 1, 2 and 3 of the memorandum, which provide for military and naval co-operation between the four Powers, Italy declares that she will take the field at the earliest possible date and within a period not exceeding one month from the signature of these presents.

In faith whereof the undersigned have signed the present agreement and have affixed thereto their seals.

Done at London, in quadruplicate, the 26th day of April, 1915.

(L.S.) E. GREY.
(L.S.) IMPERIALI.
(L.S.) BENCKENDORFF.
(L.S.) PAUL CAMBON.

II.

Déclaration par laquelle la France, la Grande-Bretagne, l'Italie et la Russie s'engagent à ne pas conclure de paix séparée au cours de la présente Guerre européenne.

LE Gouvernement italien ayant décidé de participer à la présente guerre avec les Gouvernements français, britannique et russe et d'adhérer à la déclaration faite à Londres le 5 septembre, 1914, par les trois Gouvernements précités,

Les soussignés, dûment autorisés par leurs Gouvernements respectifs, font la déclaration suivante :

Les Gouvernements français, britannique, italien et russe s'engagent mutuellement à ne pas conclure de paix séparée au cours de la présente guerre.

Les quatre Gouvernements conviennent que, lorsqu'il y aura lieu de discuter les termes de la paix, aucune des Puissances alliées ne pourra poser des conditions de paix sans accord préalable avec chacun des autres Alliés.

II.

Declaration by which France, Great Britain, Italy and Russia undertake not to conclude a Separate Peace during the course of the Present European War.

The Italian Government, having decided to participate in the present war with the French, British and Russian Governments and to accede to the Declaration made at London, the 5th September, 1914, by the three above-named Governments,

The undersigned, being duly authorised by their respective Governments, make the following declaration :—

The French, British, Italian and Russian Governments mutually undertake not to conclude a separate peace during the course of the present war.

The four Governments agree that, whenever there may be occasion to discuss the terms of peace, none of the Allied Powers shall lay down any conditions of peace without previous agreement with each of the other Allies.

8

En foi de quoi les soussignés ont signé la présente déclaration et y ont apposé leur cachets. Fait à Londres, en quadruple original, le 26 avril, 1915. (L.S.) E. GREY. (L.S.) IMPERIALI. (L.S.) BENCKENDORFF. (L.S.) PAUL CAMBON.	In faith whereof the undersigned have signed the present Declaration and have affixed thereto their seals. Done at London, in quadruplicate, the 26th day of April, 1915. (L.S.) E. GREY. (L.S.) IMPERIALI. (L.S.) BENCKENDORFF. (L.S.) PAUL CAMBON.

III.

DÉCLARATION.

LA Déclaration du 26 avril, 1915, par laquelle la France, la Grande-Bretagne, l'Italie et la Russie s'engagent à ne pas conclure de paix séparée au cours de la présente guerre européenne, restera secrète.

Après la déclaration de guerre par ou contre l'Italie, les quatre Puissances signeront une nouvelle déclaration identique, qui sera rendue publique à ce moment.

En foi de quoi les soussignés ont signé la présente déclaration et y ont apposé leur cachets.

Fait à Londres, en quadruple original, le 26 avril, 1915.

 (L.S.) E. GREY.
 (L.S.) IMPERIALI.
 (L.S.) BENCKENDORFF.
 (L.S.) PAUL CAMBON.

III.

DECLARATION.

The Declaration of the 26th April, 1915, whereby France, Great Britain, Italy and Russia undertake not to conclude a separate peace during the present European war, shall remain secret.

After the declaration of war by or against Italy, the four Powers shall sign a new declaration in identical terms, which shall thereupon be made public.

In faith whereof the undersigned have executed the present Declaration and have affixed thereo their seals.

Done at London, in quadruplicate, the 26th day of April, 1915.

 (L.S.) E. GREY.
 (L.S.) IMPERIALI.
 (L.S.) BENCKENDORFF.
 (L.S.) PAUL CAMBON.

APPENDIX 9

Lord Lansdowne's Secret Memorandum to the Cabinet

13 November 1916

In this, Lansdowne cast doubt on the idea of achieving military victory, pointed to the enormous cost in life and treasure, and put the case for an attempt to be made at achieving a negotiated peace. (CAB 37 159/32)

[This Document is the Property of His Britannic Majesty's Government.]

Printed for the use of the Cabinet. November 1916.

CONFIDENTIAL.

MISCELLANEOUS 223 RECORDS

THE members of the War Committee were asked by the Prime Minister some weeks ago to express their views as to the terms upon which peace might be concluded. I do not know whether there has been a general response to this invitation, but the only reply which I have seen is one written last month by the First Lord of the Admiralty, in which he deals at some length with the problems which might have to be discussed at any Peace Conference. Mr. Balfour observes truly that these questions cannot be profitably examined except upon an agreed hypothesis as to the military position of the combatants at the end of the war, and he proceeds to assume, though merely for the sake of argument, that the Central Powers, either through defeat or exhaustion, have to accept the terms imposed upon them by the Allies.

I venture to suggest that the attention of the War Committee might with advantage be directed to a somewhat different problem, and that they should be invited to give us their opinion as to our present prospects of being able to "dictate" the kind of terms which we should all like to impose upon our enemies if we were in a position to do so.

We are agreed as to the goal, but we do not know how far we have really travelled towards it, or how much nearer to it we are likely to find ourselves even if the war be prolonged for, say, another year. What will that year have cost us? How much better will our position be at the end of it? Shall we even then be strong enough to "dictate" terms?

It seems to me almost impossible to overrate the importance of these considerations, because it is clear that our diplomacy must be governed by an accurate appreciation of them.

We have obtained within the last few days from the different Departments of the Government a good deal of information as to the situation, naval, military, and economic. It is far from reassuring.

From the President of the Board of Trade we received on the 26th October a most interesting and carefully compiled memorandum tending to show the daily growing shortage of tonnage and its consequences. Mr. Runciman comes to the conclusion that our shipbuilding is not keeping pace with our losses, and that, although the number of our vessels is down, the demands on our tonnage are not diminished. We must look forward to depending more and more on neutral ships, but we can be under no illusions as to the precarious nature of that resource. I do not think I exaggerate when I describe this most important document as profoundly disquieting. But in a later memorandum, dated the 9th November, the President paints the picture in still gloomier colours, and anticipates, on the advice of his experts, "a complete breakdown in shipping .... much sooner than June 1917."

The President of the Board of Agriculture has recently presented to the Cabinet his report on Food Prospects in 1917. That report goes to show that there is a world's deficit in breadstuffs, that the price of bread is likely to go higher, that there has been a general failure of the potato crop, that the supply of fish is expected to be 64 per cent. below the normal, that there is considerable difficulty in regard to the supply of feeding-stuffs, that the difficulties of cultivation steadily increase, that land is likely to go derelict, the yield to decline, and the number of livestock to diminish greatly.

Lord Crawford's later note, dated the 9th November, on Home Food Supplies, shows that these anticipations were not unduly pessimistic. The position has, he tells us, become much worse, and, owing to the inroads made upon the agricultural population by the demands of the army, it is in some parts of the country "no longer a question of maintaining a moderate standard of cultivation, but whether cultivation will cease."

Turning to our naval and military resources, we have a report from the First Lord of the Admiralty, dated the 14th October, from which we learn that, in spite of the tremendous efforts which we have made, the size of our Home Fleets is still insufficient, that we have nearly reached the limit of immediate production in the matter of capital ships, that we have not got nearly enough destroyers to meet our needs for escort and anti-submarine work, that we shall certainly not have enough for our Allies, and that the position in regard to light cruisers is not much better. From the same report we may infer that the submarine difficulty is becoming acute, and that, in spite of all our efforts, it seems impossible to provide an effectual rejoinder to it. The increasing size of the enemy submarines, the strength of their construction (which will apparently oblige us to rearm our merchantmen with a heavier gun), and their activity in all parts of the world, point to the same conclusion.

The papers which we have from time to time received from the General Staff and from the War Committee prove that in the matter of man-power we are nearing the end of our tether. The last report of the Man-Power Distribution Board seems, in particular, to sound a grave note of warning. The unexhausted supply of men is, they tell us, now very restricted, and the number available can only be added to by a still further depletion of industry. In the meanwhile Ireland still declines to add to the available supply the 150,000 men who would be obtainable from that country, and I am not aware that any serious attempt is to be made to secure them.

All these seem to me to be very serious factors in the calculation which it is our duty to make. It will be replied, and no doubt truly, that the Central Powers are feeling the pressure of the war not less acutely than we feel it, and I hope we shall also be told that our staying powers are greater than theirs; but, even if this be so, it is none the less our duty to consider, after a careful review of the facts, what our plight, and the plight of the civilised world will be after another year, or, as we are sometimes told, two or three more years of a struggle as exhausting as that in which we are engaged. No one for a moment believes that we are going to lose the war; but what is our chance of winning it in such a manner, and within such limits of time, as will enable us to beat our enemy to the ground and impose upon him the kind of terms which we so freely discuss?

I do not suppose for an instant that there is any weakening in the spirit of the people of this country, and I should hope, although I do not feel absolute confidence on the subject, that the same might be said of our Allies; but neither in their interests nor in ours can it be desirable that the war should be prolonged, unless it can be shown that we can bring it to an effectual conclusion within a reasonable space of time.

What does the prolongation of the war mean?

Our own casualties already amount to over 1,100,000. We have had 15,000 officers killed, not including those who are missing. There is no reason to suppose that, as the force at the front in the different theatres of war increases, the casualties will increase at a slower rate. We are slowly but surely killing off the best of the male population of these islands. The figures representing the casualties of our Allies are not before me. The total must be appalling.

The financial burden which we have already accumulated is almost incalculable. We are adding to it at the rate of over 5,000,000l. per day. Generations will have to come and go before the country recovers from the loss which it has sustained in human beings, and from the financial ruin and the destruction of the means of production which are taking place.

All this it is no doubt our duty to bear, but only if it can be shown that the sacrifice will have its reward. If it is to be made in vain, if the additional year, or two years, or three years, finds us still unable to dictate terms, the war with its nameless horrors will have been needlessly prolonged, and the responsibility of those who needlessly prolong such a war is not less than that of those who needlessly provoked it.

A thorough stock-taking, first by each Ally of his own resources, present and prospective, and next by the Allies, or at all events by the leading Allies, in confidential consultation, seems indispensable. Not until such a stock-taking has taken place will each Ally be able to decide which of his desiderata are indispensable, and whether he might not be prepared to accept less than 20s. in the £ in consideration of prompt payment. Not until it has taken place will the Allies as a body be able to determine the broad outline of their policy or the attitude which they ought to assume towards those who talk to them of peace.

I think Sir William Robertson must have had some such stock-taking in his mind when he wrote the remarkable paper which was circulated to the Cabinet on the 31st August. In that paper he expressed his belief that negotiations for peace in some form or other might arise any day, and he urged that "We need therefore to decide without loss of time what our policy is to be, then place it before the *Entente* Powers, and ascertain in return what are their aims, and so endeavour to arrive at a clear understanding before we meet our enemies in conference." The idea may, for all I know, have been acted upon already.

Many of us, however, must of late have asked ourselves how this war is ever to be brought to an end. If we are told that the deliberate conclusion of the Government is that it must be fought until Germany has been beaten to the ground and sues for peace on any terms which we are pleased to accord to her, my only observation would be that we ought to know something of the data upon which this conclusion has been reached. To many of us it seems as if the prospect of a "knock out" was, to say the least of it, remote. Our forces and those of France have shown a splendid gallantry on the western front, and have made substantial advances; but is it believed that these, any more than those made in 1915 with equally high hopes and accompanied by not less cruel losses, will really enable us to "break through"? Can we afford to go on paying the same sort of price for the same sort of gains?

Judging from the comments supplied by the General Staff I should doubt whether the Italian offensive, however successful, is likely to have a decisive effect.

At Salonica we are entangled in an extraordinarily difficult enterprise, forced upon us, against our better judgment, by our Allies, and valuable only because it occupies enemy troops who would otherwise be fighting the Russians and the Roumanians. On the Russian and Roumanian frontiers we shall be fortunate if we avoid a disaster, which at one moment seemed imminent. General Brusiloff's language is inspiring, but is it really justified by the facts? The history of the Russian operations has been very chequered, and we shall never, I am afraid, be free from the danger of miscarriages owing to defective strategy, to failure of supplies, to corruption in high places, or to incidents such as the disastrous explosion which has just lost us 10,000 tons of munitions at Archangel.

Again, are we quite sure that, regarded as political rather than military assets, our Allies are entirely to be depended upon? There have been occasions upon which political complications have threatened to affect the military situation in France. I quote the following sentences from a letter written a few days ago by a very shrewd Frenchman: "Rappelez-vous bien que la démocratie française n'est pas menée par son gouvernement; c'est elle qui le mène: un courant d'opinion publique en faveur de la cessation de la guerre pourrait être irrésistible. . . . . Au feu, le soldat français se battra toujours comme un héros: derrière, sa famille pourra bien dire: en voilà assez!" Italy is always troublesome and exacting. Sir Rennell Rodd, in a despatch dated the 4th November, asks us to take note of the fact that there are already in Italy "certain symptoms of war weariness and discouragement at the protraction of the struggle. . . . . Great Britain is represented as the only country anxious to prolong the struggle *à outrance* for her own ends. . . . . It would be wrong to pretend that there exists here the same grim determination to carry through as prevails in Franc

and in the British Empire." The domestic situation in Russia is far from reassuring. There have been alarming disorders both at Moscow and in Petrograd. Russia has had five Ministers of the Interior in twelve months, and the fifth is described as being by no means secure in his seat.

Our difficulties with the neutrals are, again, not likely to diminish. It is highly creditable to the Foreign Office that during the last two years we have escaped a breakdown of our blockade policy, which, in spite of continual obstruction and bad faith, has produced excellent results; but we have been within an ace of grave complications with Sweden and the United States. As time goes on the neutrals are likely to become more and more restive and intolerant of the belligerents, whose right to go on disturbing the peace of the civilised world they will refuse to admit.

I may be asked whether I have any practical suggestion to offer, and I admit the difficulty of replying. But is it not true that, unless the apprehensions which I have sketched can be shown, after such an investigation as I have suggested, to be groundless, we ought at any rate not to discourage any movement, no matter where originating, in favour of an interchange of views as to the possibility of a settlement? There are many indications that the germs of such a movement are already in existence. One cannot dismiss as unworthy of attention the well-substantiated reports which have come to us from time to time upon this subject from Belgian, Scandinavian, Japanese, and Russian sources, or such circumstantial stories as those told in Sir Esme Howard's despatch of the 24th August as to the meeting held at Prince Lichnowsky's house, and in Lord Eustace Percy's memorandum as to the intimations made by the Rector of the Berlin University. The debates in the Reichstag show that the pacificist groups are active and outspoken. From all sides come accounts of the impatience of the civil population and their passionate yearning for peace.

It seems to me quite inconceivable that during the winter we shall not be sounded by some one as to our readiness to discuss terms of peace or proposals for an armistice. Are we prepared with our reply? Lord Crawford has dealt with the question of an armistice. I am not sure that I agree with some of his suggestions, but I am sure that he is right in holding that an unconditional refusal would be inadmissible.

As to peace terms, I hope we shall adhere stedfastly to the main principle laid down by the Prime Minister in the speech which he summed up by a declaration that we could agree to no peace which did not afford adequate reparation for the past and adequate security for the future, but the outline was broadly sketched and might be filled up in many different ways. The same may be said of the not less admirable statement which he has just made at the Guildhall, and of the temperate speeches which the Secretary of State for Foreign Affairs has from time to time delivered.

But it is unfortunate that, in spite of these utterances, it should be possible to represent us and our Allies as committed to a policy partly vindictive and partly selfish, and so irreconcilably committed to that policy that we should regard as unfriendly any attempt, however sincere, to extricate us from the *impasse*.

6

The interview given by the Secretary of State for War in September last to an American correspondent has produced an impression which it will not be easy to efface. There may have been circumstances of which I am unaware, connected perhaps with the Presidential election, which made it necessary to announce that at the particular moment any intervention, however well meant, would be distasteful to us or inopportune. He said, indeed, that "the world must know that there can be no outside interference *at this stage*"—a very momentous limitation. For surely it cannot be our intention, no matter how long the war lasts, no matter what the strain on our resources, to maintain this attitude, or to declare, as M. Briand declared about the same time, that for us too "the word peace is a sacrilege." Let our naval, military, and economic advisers tell us frankly whether they are satisfied that the knock-out blow can and will be delivered. The Secretary of State's formula holds the field, and will do so until something else is put in its place. Whether it is to hold the field, and, if not, what that something else should be, ought surely to depend upon their answer, and that again upon the result of the careful stock-taking, domestic and international, which, I hope, is already taking place.

L.

The above note had been written before the discussion which took place at to-day's Cabinet, from which we learned that the War Committee had already decided to take important steps in the direction which I have ventured to indicate.

L.

November 13, 1916.

APPENDIX

Lord Lansdowne's letter to the *Daily Telegraph* [London]

29 November 1917 (from the Telegraph Historical Archive).

In this, Lansdowne repeated the arguments of the memorandum from a year before, and pointed to the need to wind back extravagant war aims, and embrace more progressive aims, in harmony with those of the United States, in order to attempt peace by negotiation.

CO-ORDINATION OF ALLIES' WAR AIMS.

LETTER FROM LORD LANSDOWNE.

To the Editor of "The Daily Telegraph."

Sir,—We are now in the fourth year of the most dreadful war the world has known; a war in which, as Sir W. Robertson has lately informed us, "the killed alone can be counted by the million, while the total number of men engaged amounts to nearly twenty-four millions." Ministers continue to tell us that they scan the horizon in vain for the prospect of a lasting peace. And without a lasting peace we all feel that the task we have set ourselves will remain unaccomplished.

But those who look forward with horror to the prolongation of the war, who believe that its wanton prolongation would be a crime, differing only in degree from that of the criminals who provoked it, may be excused if they too scan the horizon anxiously in the hope of discovering there indications that the outlook may after all not be so hopeless as is supposed.

The obstacles are indeed formidable enough. We are constantly reminded of one of them. It is pointed out with force that, while we have not hesitated to put forward a general description of our war aims, the enemy have, though repeatedly challenged, refused to formulate theirs, and have limited themselves to vague and apparently insincere professions of readiness to negotiate with us.

The force of the argument cannot be gainsaid, but it is directed mainly to show that we are still far from agreement as to the territorial questions which must come up for settlement in connection with the terms of peace. These are, however, by no means the only questions which will arise, and it is worth while to consider whether there are not others, also of first-rate importance, with regard to which the prospects of agreement are less remote.

Let me examine one or two of these. What are we fighting for? To beat the Germans? Certainly. But that is not an end in itself. We want to inflict signal defeat upon the Central Powers, not out of mere vindictiveness, but in the hope of saving the world from a recurrence of the calamity which has befallen this generation.

What, then, is it we want when the war is over? I know of no better formula than that more than once made use of, with universal approval, by Mr. Asquith in the speeches which he has from time to time delivered. He has repeatedly told his hearers that we are waging war in order to obtain reparation and security. Both are essential, but of the two security is perhaps the more indispensable. In the way of reparation much can no doubt be accomplished, but the utmost effort to make good all the ravages of this war must fall short of completeness, and will fail to undo the grievous wrong which has been done to humanity. It may, however, be possible to make some amends for the inevitable incompleteness of the reparation if the security afforded is, humanly speaking, complete. To end the war honourably would be a great achievement; to prevent the same curse falling upon our children would be a greater achievement still.

This is our avowed aim, and the magnitude of the issue cannot be exaggerated. For, just as this war has been more dreadful than any war in history, so we may be sure would the next war be even more dreadful than this. The prostitution of science for purposes of pure destruction is not likely to stop short. Most of us, however, believe that it should be possible to secure posterity against the repetition of such an outrage as that of 1914. If the Powers will, under a solemn pact, bind themselves to submit future disputes to arbitration; if they will undertake to outlaw, politically and economically, any one of their number which refuses to enter into such a pact, or to use their joint military and naval forces for the purpose of coercing a Power which breaks away from the rest, they will, indeed, have travelled far along the road which leads to security.

We are, at any rate, right to put security in the front line of our peace demands, and it is not unsatisfactory to note that in principle there seems to be complete unanimity upon this point.

In his speech at the banquet of the League to Enforce Peace, on May 28, 1916, President Wilson spoke strongly in favour of

A universal association of nations . . . to prevent any war from being begun either contrary to treaty covenants or without warning and full submission of the cause to the opinion of the world.

Later in the same year the German Chancellor, at the sitting of the Main Committee of the Reichstag, used the following language:

When, as after the termination of the war, the world will fully recognise its horrible devastation of blood and treasure, then through all mankind will go the cry for peaceful agreements and understandings which will prevent, so far as is humanly possible, the return of such an immense catastrophe. This cry will be so strong and so justified that it must lead to a result. Germany will honourably co-operate in investigating every attempt to find a practical solution and collaborate towards its possible realisation.

The Papal Note communicated to the Powers in August last places in the front rank:

The establishment of arbitration on lines to be concerted and with sanction to be settled against any State that refuses either to submit international disputes to arbitration or to accept its awards.

This suggestion was immediately welcomed by the Austrian Government, which declared that it was conscious of the importance for the promotion of peace of the method proposed by his Holiness, viz., "to submit international disputes to compulsory arbitration," and that it was prepared to enter into negotiations regarding this proposal. Similar language was used by Count Czernin, the Austro-Hungarian Foreign Minister, in his declaration on foreign policy made at Budapest in October, when he mentioned as one of the "fundamental bases" of peace that of "obligatory international arbitration."

In his despatch covering the Allied Note of Jan. 10, 1917, Mr. Balfour mentions as one of the three conditions essential to a durable peace the condition that

Behind international law and behind all treaty arrangements for preventing or limiting hostilities some form of international sanction might be devised which would give pause to the hardiest aggressor.

Such sanction would probably take the form of coercion applied in one of two modes. The "aggressor" would be disciplined either by the pressure of superior naval and military strength, or by the denial of commercial access and facilities.

The proceedings of the Paris Conference show that we should not shrink from such a denial, if we were compelled to use the weapon for purposes of self-defence. But while a commercial "boycott" would be justifiable as a war measure, and while the threat of a "boycott," in case Germany should show herself utterly unreasonable, would be a legitimate threat, no reasonable man would, surely, desire to destroy the trade of the Central Powers, if they will, so to speak, enter into recognisances to keep the peace, and do not force us into a conflict by a hostile combination. Commercial war is less ghastly in its immediate results than the war of armed forces, but it would certainly be deplorable if after three or four years of sanguinary conflict in the field, a conflict which has destroyed a great part of the wealth of the world, and permanently crippled its resources, the Powers were to embark upon commercial hostilities certain to retard the economic recovery of all the nations involved.

That we shall have to secure ourselves against the fiscal hostility of others, that we shall have to prevent the recurrence of the conditions under which, when war broke out, we found ourselves short of essential commodities, because we had allowed certain industries, and certain sources of supply, to pass entirely under the control of our enemies, no one will doubt, subject however to this reservation, that it will surely be for our interest that the stream of trade should, so far as our own fiscal interests permit, be allowed to flow strong and uninterrupted in its natural channels.

There remains the question of territorial claims. The most authoritative statement of these is to be found in the Allies' Note of Jan. 10, 1917. This statement must obviously be regarded as a broad outline of the desiderata of the Allies, but is anyone prepared to argue that the sketch is complete, or that it may not become necessary to re-examine it?

Mr. Asquith, speaking at Liverpool in October last, used the following language:

No one pretends that it would be right or opportune for either side to formulate an ultimatum, detailed, exhaustive, precise, with clauses and sub-clauses, which is to be accepted verbatim et literatim, chapter and verse, as the indispensable preliminary and condition of peace.

"There are many things," he added, "in a world-wide conflict such as this, which must of necessity be left over for discussion and negotiation, for accommodation and adjustment, at a later stage."

It is surely most important that this wise counsel should be kept in mind. Some of our original desiderata have probably become unattainable. Others would probably now be given a less prominent place than when they were first put forward. Others again, notably the reparation due to Belgium, remain, and must always remain in the front rank, but when it comes to the wholesale rearrangement of the map of South-Eastern Europe we may well ask for a suspension of judgment and for the elucidation which a frank exchange of views between the Allied Powers can alone afford.

For all these questions concern our Allies as well as ourselves, and if we are to have an Allied Council for the purpose of adapting our strategy in the field to the ever-shifting developments of the war, it is fair to assume that, in the matter of peace terms also, the Allies will make it their business to examine, and if necessary to revise, the territorial requirements.

Let me end by explaining why I attach so much importance to these considerations. We are not going to lose this war, but its prolongation will spell ruin for the civilised world, and an infinite addition to the load of human suffering which already weighs upon it. Security will be invaluable to a world which has the vitality to profit by it, but what will be the value of the blessings of peace to nations so exhausted that they can scarcely stretch out a hand with which to grasp them?

In my belief, if the war is to be brought to a close in time to avert a world-wide catastrophe, it will be brought to a close because on both sides the peoples of the countries involved realise that it has already lasted too long.

There can be no question that this feeling prevails extensively in Germany, Austria, and Turkey. We know beyond doubt that the economic pressure in those countries far exceeds any to which we are subject here. Ministers inform us in their speeches of "constant efforts" on the part of the Central Powers "to initiate peace talk." (Sir E. Geddes at the Mansion House, Nov. 9.)

If the peace talk is not more articulate, and has not been so precise as to enable his Majesty's Government to treat it seriously, the explanation is probably to be found in the fact, first, that German despotism does not tolerate independent expressions of opinion, and second, that the German Government has contrived, probably with success, to misrepresent the aims of the Allies, which are supposed to include the destruction of Germany, the imposition upon her of a form of government decided by her enemies, her destruction as a great commercial community, and her exclusion from the free use of the seas.

An immense stimulus would probably be given to the peace party in Germany if it were understood:

(1) That we do not desire the annihilation of Germany as a Great Power;

(2) That we do not seek to impose upon her people any form of government other than that of their own choice;

(3) That, except as a legitimate war measure, we have no desire to deny to Germany her place among the great commercial communities of the world;

(4) That we are prepared, when the war is over, to examine in concert with other Powers the group of international problems, some of them of recent origin, which are connected with the question of "the freedom of the seas";

(5) That we are prepared to enter into an international pact under which ample opportunities would be afforded for the settlement of international disputes by peaceful means.

I am under the impression that authority could be found for most of these propositions in Ministerial speeches. Since the above lines were written, (1), (2), and (3) have been dealt with by our own Foreign Minister at the public meeting held in honour of M. Venizelos at the Mansion House.

The question of "the freedom of the seas" was amongst those raised at the outset by our American Allies. The formula is an ambiguous one, capable of many inconsistent interpretations, and I doubt whether it will be seriously contended that there is no room for profitable discussion.

That an attempt should be made to bring about the kind of pact suggested in (5) is, I believe, common ground to all the belligerents, and probably to all the neutral Powers.

If it be once established that there are no insurmountable difficulties in the way of agreement upon these points, the political horizon might perhaps be scanned with better hope by those who pray, but can at this moment hardly venture to expect, that the New Year may bring us a lasting and honourable peace.—I am, Sir, your obedient servant,

LANSDOWNE.

Lansdowne House, Nov. 28.

ABBREVIATIONS

AIF	Australian Imperial Force
AMA	Amalgamated Miners' Association
ANZAC	Australian and New Zealand Army Corps
AWM	Australian War Memorial
AWL	Absence Without Leave
'AWOL'	The soldiers' slang for Absence Without Leave
BDM	Births, Deaths, and Marriages
BEF	British Expeditionary Force
CPD	Commonwealth Parliamentary Debates (Hansard), Australia
DORA	Defence of the Realm Act
DSO	Distinguished Service Order
FO	Foreign Office
HC Deb	House of Commons, Debates (Hansard), UK
HL Deb	House of Lords, Debates (Hansard), UK
HMAT	His Majesty's Australian Troopship
HMT	His Majesty's Troopship
HO	Home Office
ILP	Independent Labour Party
LVA	Labor's Volunteer Army
MC	Military Cross
MLMSS	Mitchell Library manuscripts
MP	Member of Parliament
NAA	National Archives of Australia
NLA	National Library of Australia
PRO	Public Record Office (now The National Archives)
SPD	Social Democratic Party of Germany
TNA	The National Archives (UK)
UDC	Union of Democratic Control
UK	United Kingdom
UNSW	University of New South Wales
USPD	Independent Social Democratic Party of Germany
YMCA	Young Men's Christian Association

NOTES

1 Charles Trevelyan, 'Nationalism Decadent', *The UDC*, Vol. 3, No. 2 (December 1917), 170.
2 E.J. Ryan to Ramsay MacDonald, 18 Oct. 1916, MacDonald Papers, TNA: PRO/30/69/1160 f. 108.
3 Much of the detail of Ryan's war experience is based on his service records. See Private Edward James Ryan, Service Number 4635, NAA: B2455. Other family details come from Beth Sutton, née Ryan, the daughter of Ted Ryan, whom I interviewed in 2016 and 2017 in Maryville, Newcastle, Australia.
4 Jabez Waterhouse to his father, 17 Jan. 1917, MLMSS 2792 (K 21692/Folder 17) (Mitchell, Library).
5 Wessex Archaeology, *Perham Down World War I Practice Trenches, Salisbury Plain, Hampshire: Archaeological Evaluation Report* (Ref: 113940, Salisbury, 2017).
6 On Perham Down, see T.S. Crawford, *Wiltshire and the Great War: Training the Empire's Soldiers* (Marlborough, Wiltshire, 2012), and Trevor Rowley, *The English Landscape in the Twentieth Century* (London, 2006), 335.
7 Sydney James Stutley, Diary, 6-7 Oct. 1916, MLMSS 3045/Item 2 (Mitchell Library).
8 No 1. Australian Command Depot, War Diary, Oct. 1916, AWM4, 33/16/1.
9 Edgar Morrow, *Iron in the Fire* (Carlisle, 2006), 27.
10 Thomas Alcock, war narrative, MLMSS 1609/Item 2 (Mitchell Library).
11 David Marquand, *Ramsay MacDonald* (London, 1977), Ch. 9.
12 'Personal Message from General Birdwood to Members of the A.I.F', and Hughes, 'Manifesto to Australian Soldiers', in 'Message re Referendum', Birdwood Papers, AWM 3DRL/3376 13/2 (Australian War Memorial). The words in capitals are in the original.
13 E.J. Ryan to Ramsay MacDonald, 18 Oct. 1916, MacDonald Papers, TNA: PRO/30/69/1160 f. 108. Underlining in original.
14 Kevin J. Fewster, 'Expression and Suppression: Aspects of Military Censorship in Australia during the Great War', unpublished PhD thesis (UNSW, 1980), 64. The officers had full barrows of censorship work to do anyway. In a typical month, the camp handled 60,000 letters and 11,000 parcels, and all outgoing mail was theoretically subject to censorship. No 1. Australian Command Depot, War Diary, July 1917, AWM4, 33/16/5.
15 Section 55 of the Australian *Defence Act 1903* brought all Australian military forces under the disciplinary provisions of the *Army Act 1881* (UK), 'save so far as it is inconsistent with this Act.'
16 *Army Act 1881* (UK), section 5, paragraph 5 (5). See also sections 42 and 46 of the *Army Act 1881* (UK).
17 For example, see Paragraph 453: 'An officer or soldier is forbidden to publish in any form whatever, or communicate, either directly or indirectly, to the press, any military information, or his views on any military subject, without special authority.' *King's Regulations and Orders for the Army* (1912), 105. See also Paragraph 439 on 'Redress of Grievance', and Paragraph 461 on 'Treason and Mutiny'.
18 Paragraph 40, in War Office, *Manual of Military Law* (London, 6th ed, 1914, reprinted 1917), 412.
19 *The London Gazette*, 11 Aug. 1914, Regulations 21 and 27. Amendment of Regulation 21, issued under the *Defence of the Realm Act 1914*, issued on 1 Sept. 1914: 'No person shall by word of mouth or in writing spread reports likely to cause disaffection or alarm among any of His Majesty's forces or among the civilian population.' TNA: HO 45/10690.
20 George B. King, Diary, 30 Sept. 1916, MLMSS 1801 (Mitchell Library).
21 James Mathews, *Commonwealth Parliamentary Debates*, 14 Dec. 1916, 9932, (henceforth *CPD*).
22 E.J. Ryan to Ramsay MacDonald, 18 Oct. 1916, MacDonald Papers, TNA: PRO/30/69/1160.

23 'Government Water Supply', *Barrier Miner*, 7 Mar. 1889, and Erik Eklund, *Mining Towns: Making a Living, Making a Life* (Sydney, 2012), 37.
24 R.J. Solomon, *The Richest Lode: Broken Hill 1883-1988* (Sydney, 2008), 214-17, and 'The Water Question' and 'Government Water Supply', *Barrier Miner*, 7 March 1889, 'Municipal Council', *Barrier Miner*, 28 Feb. 1890, and 6 June 1890.
25 'Municipal Council', *Barrier Miner*, 28 Feb. 1890.
26 'Municipal Council', *Barrier Miner*, 17, 31 Jan.1890, 'A Lively Scene', *Barrier Miner*, 6 Feb. 1890, 'Arrest of an Alderman', *Barrier Miner*, 13 Feb. 1890.
27 'Enginedrivers and Firemen', *Barrier Miner*, 16 Jan. 1890, 'Threatened Labor Difficulty', *Barrier Miner*, 2 Apr. 1890, 'Ferguson's Case', *Barrier Miner*, 3 Apr. 1890.
28 W.W. Phillips, 'Christianity and its Defence in New South Wales, circa 1880 to 1890', unpublished PhD thesis (ANU, Canberra, 1969), 4-5, 30-31. The Primitive Methodists, the Wesleyan Methodist Church, the Bible Christian Church, the United Methodist Free Church, and several smaller organisations, formed the Methodist Church of Australasia in January 1902.
29 'Moonta', *Wallaroo Times and Mining Journal*, 23 Nov. 1867.
30 'Police', *Yorke's Peninsula Advertiser*, 12 Sept. 1884.
31 Elizabeth Martin Couch was born on 10 October 1867 at Moonta Mines in South Australia. On 24 August 1886, she married Frederick Riter. Frederick died on 25 January 1888. See Death Certificate, NSW BDM 13703/1888.
32 Marriage Certificate for Edward James Ryan and Elizabeth Martin Riter, NSW BDM 2721/1890.
33 South Australian District Birth Certificate Transcript for Edward James Ryan, showing he was born at Moonta Mines, Daly District, South Australia, registered 20 Aug. 1891.
34 See Birth Certificates for Thomas, NSW BDM 8940/1893, and for Harry, NSW BDM 7670/1896.
35 'Municipal Elections: Burke Ward', advertisement from Edward Ryan, *Barrier Miner*, 5 Feb. 1891.
36 'A Strained Relationship', *Barrier Miner*, 25 June 1891.
37 'Small Debts Court: Kerin V. Ryan', *Barrier Miner*, 17 Aug. 1891.
38 'Warden's Court', *Barrier Miner*, 28 Aug. 1891.
39 'In Bankruptcy', *NSW Government Gazette*, 7 July 1893.
40 'The Open Cut Fatality', *Barrier Miner*, 15 Dec. 1897.
41 'Police Court', *Barrier Miner*, 9 Dec. 1896, 'The same "Old Drunk"', *Barrier Miner*, 29 Nov. 1898, 'Police Court', *Barrier Miner*, 4 Apr. 1899, 'Police Court', *Barrier Miner*, 23 Nov. 1899.
42 Death Notice placed by Edward Ryan, *Barrier Miner*, 7 Dec. 1899, and 'Magisterial Inquiry', *Barrier Miner*, 8 Dec. 1899.
43 Death Certificate for Elizabeth Martin Ryan, NSW BDM, 12572/1899. Death Notice placed by Edward Ryan, *Barrier Miner*, 7 Dec. 1899, and 'Magisterial Inquiry', *Barrier Miner*, 8 Dec. 1899. Death Certificate for Elizabeth Ryan, NSW BDM 12572/1899.
44 'Police Court', *Barrier Miner*, 18 Aug. 1904, 15 Aug. 1905, 27 Oct. 1905, 18 Dec. 1905, 24 Apr. 1906, 10 May 1907, 29 Nov. 1907, 'A Licensing Prosecution', *Barrier Miner*, 24 Jan. 1911.
45 'The Military Contingent for England', *Albany Advertiser*, 29 Apr. 1897, 'Our Soldiers: Appointment and Promotions', *The Daily News* [Perth] 29 Jan. 1915.
46 'Recruiting: to the Editor' from Clement Middleton, *The Daily News* [Perth], 10 Aug. 1915; 'O'Shea's Complaint', *The Daily News* [Perth], 'Recruiting in Perth', *The West Australian* [Perth], 16 Oct. 1915.
47 'Peeps at People', *Sunday Times* [Perth], 9 Jan. 1916.
48 'Western Australia: Recruiting Campaign', *The West Australian* [Perth], 1 July 1916, 'Recruiting', *The West Australian* [Perth], 5 Sept. 1916.
49 'Recruiting in Perth', *The West Australian* [Perth], 22 Sep. 1915
50 More than half of the AIF was 25 years of age or younger, and 81% were unmarried. Jane Beaumont (ed), *Australian Defence Sources and Statistics* (Melbourne, 2001), 116.
51 See Appendix, 'Social Statistics of the First AIF', in Graham Seal, *Inventing Anzac: The Digger and National Mythology* (St Lucia, 2004), 173.

52	'General Secretary's Report', *Australian Worker*, 10 Feb. 1916, *Sydney Morning Herald*, 17 Feb. 1916.
53	Walter Edward Gillett, memoir, 'A "Chat" from Khaki', 5, MLMSS 1585 (Mitchell Library).
54	Attestation Paper, in Private Edward James Ryan, Service Number 4635, NAA: B2455. Italics added.
55	In a telling indication of Australia's very slow passage to full independent nationhood, Australian military personnel continued to serve under the British *Army Act 1881* (UK) until 3 July 1985 when changes specified under new Australian legislation finally commenced.
56	Henry Martin Ryan Birth Certificate, NSW BDM 7670/1896.
57	'The Expeditionary Force', *Sydney Morning Herald*, 11 Aug 1914: 'Youths under 19 will not be accepted.' See also 'Rolling Up' and 'Volunteers', *Sydney Morning Herald*, 15 and 17 Aug. 1914.
58	Ten days before Harry enlisted, Senator Edward Millen, the Minister for Defence, announced that 'the ages for enrolment have been fixed at from 19 to 45 years. In the case of volunteers under 21 years of age, the consent of the parent or guardian will be necessary', *Sydney Morning Herald*, 4 Sept. 1914. The upper age limit of 45 years was an increase on the initially announced limit of 38 years (with 38 being the upper limit in the British Army). On 3 June 1915 Senator George Pearce, the Minister for Defence, announced that because 'recruiting has shown a marked falling off lately, the ages for enrolment were now fixed from 18 to 45.' *The Daily Telegraph*, 4 June 1915.
59	Private Edward James Ryan, Service Number 672, NAA: B2455, is in fact the service record of Edward's brother Harry Ryan. I owe this information to Beth Sutton, née Ryan, daughter of Ted Ryan. The Birth Certificate of Henry Martin Ryan, 7670/1896, NSW BDM, gives his date of birth as 29 December 1895. He died on 7 October 1961 and was buried as 'Edward James Ryan' in Adelaide.
60	R.H.B. Kearns, *Broken Hill 1915-1939* (Broken Hill, 1975), 4-6.
61	'Sensational Shooting Case', *The West Australian*, 2 Jan. 1915, 'Broken Hill Sensation', *The West Australian*, 4 Jan. 1915, 'Broken Hill Sensation', *The Western Mail*, 8 Jan. 1915.
62	Private Thomas Pearce Couch Ryan, Service Number 2055, NAA: B2455, and 11th Battalion Nominal Rolls, 1 to 8 Reinforcements, AWM8, 23/28/2. Ryan is mislabelled as 'Thomas Pearce *Conch* Ryan' in the NAA: B2455 series.
63	According to the Nominal Roll, at AWM133/46.
64	'Working-class Unity', *Barrier Daily Truth*, 5 Apr. 1909.
65	'Municipal Council', *Barrier Miner*, 12 Jan. 1900.
66	The children of James and Margaret Mudie, and their birth dates, were: Beatrice Mary (1892), Ruby Pearl (1894), Alma Couch (1896), Charles Adamson (1899), Elizabeth Martin (1901), James Ramsay (1904), Agnes Margaret Jane (1906), Thomas Henry (1908), Edward Glover (1911).
67	'Municipal Reports', *Barrier Miner*, 21 Sept. 1901.
68	'The Council', *Barrier Miner*, 18 Oct. 1901.
69	'The Imperial Dam', *Barrier Miner*, 18 Apr. 1902.
70	'The Council', *Barrier Miner*, 17 Apr. 1903 and 1 May 1903, 'The City Council Monthly Meeting', *Barrier Miner*, 30 Nov. 1910.
71	'Councillors in Confab', *Barrier Daily Truth*, 8 May 1903.
72	'City Council', *Barrier Miner*, 30 Jan. 1907, and 'The City Council', *Barrier Daily Truth*, 28 July 1911. The conversion to equivalent real wages in 2019, allowing for inflation, has been calculated via the MeasuringWorth web-based tool https://www.measuringworth.com/calculators/australiacompare/
73	Information from interviews with Beth Sutton and Don Mudie.
74	'Octogenarians Born in Scotland Die Same Day', *Barrier Miner*, 22 May 1935. Mudie was active in the Trades and Labourers' Union. In later years, he was President of the Old Age Pensioners' Association in Broken Hill and a member of the Workers' Industrial Union of Australia.
75	'A Shooting Mishap', *Barrier Miner*, 25 May 1905.
76	Multiple sources show that, from the 1920s to the 1960s, several of the male children of James and Margaret Mudie were actively involved in progressive, anti-fascist, and humanitarian causes, in the trade unions and politics of Broken Hill, especially in the

77 Amalgamated Engineering Union, the Australian Labor Party, and the Communist Party of Australia.
77 For information on the Mudie and Couch families, I am grateful for the research of Greg Bateman, Don Mudie, Doug Jones, Jenny Camilleri, and Chris Nilsen, and for interviews with Beth Sutton.
78 R.H.B. Kearns, *Broken Hill 1894-1914: The Uncertain Years* (Broken Hill, 1974), 13.
79 On the record of internationalism in the Broken Hill labour movement, and the ongoing opposition to racist politics, see Sarah Gregson, 'Foot Soldiers for Capital: The influence of RSL racism on interwar industrial relations in Kalgoorlie and Broken Hill', unpublished PhD thesis (UNSW, 2003), and Sarah Gregson, 'Defending Internationalism in Interwar Broken Hill', *Labour History*, 86 (May, 2004), 115-136.
80 For example, 'The Impregnable Rock of Labor', and 'They Say', *Barrier Daily Truth*, 26 May 1905.
81 For example, 'Democratise the World', *Barrier Daily Truth*, 12 July 1907. Swinburne's poem 'A Song in Time of Order' (1852) was popular in Australian labour circles.
82 R.J. Solomon, *The Richest Lode: Broken Hill 1883-1988* (Sydney, 2008), 207, 218-222, R.H.B. Kearns, *Broken Hill, 1883-1893* (Broken Hill, 1977), 59.
83 Bradon Ellem and John Shields, 'Making the "Gibraltar of Unionism": Union Organising and Peak Union Agency in Broken Hill, 1886-1930', *Labour History*, 83 (Nov. 2002), 65-88, Kearns, *Broken Hill, 1883-1893*, 46.
84 Paul Robert Adams, *The Best Hated Man in Australia: the Life and Death of Percy Brookfield, 1875-1921* (Glebe, 2010), 8-13.
85 For an introduction, see Bede Nairn, *Civilising Capitalism: the Labor Movement in New South Wales 1870-1900* (Canberra, 1973).
86 Adams, *Brookfield*, 13.
87 Michael Hogan, 'Municipal Labor in New South Wales', *Labour History*, 72 (May 1997), 123.
88 'A Labor Rally', *The Ballarat Star*, 27 Nov. 1906, 'Prime Minister Attacked', *Daily Telegraph* [Sydney] 28 Nov. 1906, 'The Federal Campaign', *The Advertiser* [Adelaide], 26 Nov. 1906, 'Mr Ramsay MacDonald', *The Argus* [Melbourne], 27 Nov. 1906. In the election of 12 December 1906, Deakin retained the seat of Ballarat, 12,331 votes to 6,305 for Scullin. MacDonald's tour of Australia began in Sydney in October 1906.
89 'Ramsay MacDonald in Broken Hill', and 'Ramsay MacDonald at the Trades Hall', *Barrier Daily Truth*, 7 Dec. 1906.
90 'Mr Keir Hardie's Visit', *Barrier Miner*, 9 Dec. 1907, and Keir Hardie, 'In South Australia', *Labour Leader*, 6 Mar. 1908.
91 Ellem and Shields, "Gibraltar of Unionism", 70-72.
92 Adams, *Brookfield*, illustration, between 191-193.
93 For an introduction, see F.S. Lyons, *Internationalism in Europe, 1815-1914* (Leyden, 1963).
94 See 'Port Pirie is Coming Into Line', 'Labor in Sweden', and 'Situation at Port Pirie', 'Disintegration', *Barrier Daily Truth*, 2, 14, 19, 28 Nov. 1908.
95 For example, 'Our Labor Observatory', 'International Bureau', *Barrier Daily Truth*, 26 July 1907, 'A Working-class Victory', *Barrier Daily Truth*, 2 Aug. 1907, 'Politics and Persons', *Barrier Daily Truth*, 30 Aug. 1907.
96 'Saturday Night's Meeting', *Barrier Miner*, 19 Oct. 1908.
97 'Saturday Night's Mass Meeting', *Barrier Miner*, 18 Jan. 1909.
98 'Mann's Bail Conditions', *Evening News* [Sydney], 28 Jan. 1909, 'The Broken Hill Lockout', *The Worker* [Wagga], 4 Feb. 1909.
99 Adams, *Brookfield*, 16-17.
100 For example, 'The Dreadnought Mania: Plutocratic, Jingoistic and Party Move', *Barrier Daily Truth*, 2 Apr. 1909.
101 'Working-class Unity', *Barrier Daily Truth*, 5 Apr. 1909 and 'The Trial at Albury', *Barrier Miner*, 5 Apr. 1909.
102 Adams, *Brookfield*, 15-18.
103 'A.M.A. elections', Barrier Miner, 28 June 1910, 'A.M.A', *Barrier Miner*, 11 Dec. 1912, 'A.M.A. Band Ball', *Barrier Miner*, 15 July 1914. A photograph of the A.M.A. Band from 1913 is among Ted Ryan's very few papers, in the possession of Beth Sutton.

104 'Mrs Seaton', obituary, *Lithgow Mercury*, 7 Dec. 1925.
105 For the most even-handed and authoritative exploration of the July-August 1914 crisis, see Christopher Clark, *Sleepwalkers: How Europe Went to War in 1914* (London, 2012).
106 For critical accounts of Britain's descent into war, see Keith Wilson, 'The British Cabinet's Decision for war, 2 August 1914', *British Journal of International Studies*, 1, 2 (1975), 148-159, Duncan Marlor, *Fatal Fortnight: Arthur Ponsonby and the Fight for British Neutrality in 1914* (London, 2014), and my own Douglas Newton, *The Darkest Days: The Truth behind Britain's Rush to War, 1914* (London, 2014).
107 Bryan to Penfield [US Ambassador in Austria-Hungary], 4 Aug. 1914, *FRUS, Supplement 1914*, 42.
108 The Governor-General [of Australia] to the Secretary of State [Harcourt] (received 6.20 p.m., 3 August 1914), in The Parliament of the Commonwealth of Australia, *European War: Correspondence Regarding the Naval and Military Assistance Afforded to His Majesty's Government by His Majesty's Oversea Dominions*, No. 10 (printed 11 Nov. 1914), in The Parliament of the Commonwealth of Australia, *Papers Presented to Parliament, Vol. V, Session 1914-17*, 1434. For a critical account of Australia's decision-making, see my own Douglas Newton, *Hell-bent: Australia's Leap Into the Great War* (Melbourne, 2014).
109 Passenger lists are incomplete for ships arriving in Fremantle from Port Adelaide in 1914. For example, the ship 'Dimboola' arriving with a passenger 'Ryan', *Daily News* [Perth], 24 Aug. 1914, or 'Indara' arriving with a passenger 'Ryan', 'and 53 in steerage', *Daily News* [Perth], 23 Sept. 1914.
110 HC Deb 06 August 1914 vol 65 c2079.
111 'Ireland in the Fighting Line', *Times*, 26 Sept. 1914.
112 'Ministers on the War', *Times*, 10 Nov. 1914.
113 The trade union and Labor newspaper of Broken Hill, the *Barrier Daily Truth*, was owned by the Barrier District Australasian Labor Federation from 1899.
114 *Barrier Daily Truth*, 5, 6, 7 Aug. 1914.
115 'The Glorious British Empire', *Barrier Daily Truth*, 8 Sept. 1914.
116 'Socialist Hall Wrecked', *Barrier Miner*, 5 Sept. 1914.
117 'The AMA Band and the National Anthem', *Barrier Miner*, 5 Oct. 1914, and 'Matters at the Barrier', *Daily Herald* [Adelaide], 12 Oct. 1914.
118 'The Proprietary', *Barrier Miner*, 4 Aug. 1914.
119 'Barrier Mines May Work Half Time', *Barrier Daily Truth*, 6 Aug. 1914.
120 'How the Commonwealth and State Government can provide ample work and wages for every man in Australia', *Barrier Miner*, 6 Aug. 1914.
121 'The Position Locally', *Barrier Daily Truth*, 13 Aug. 1914
122 'The Result of the Conference', *Barrier Daily Truth*, 21 Aug. 1914.
123 'The Effect Locally: The Exodus', *Barrier Daily Truth*, 27 Aug. 1914.
124 Kearns, *Broken Hill 1894-1914*, 67, Adams, *Brookfield*, 28, Solomon, *The Richest Lode*, 261.
125 'The Preliminary Ballot', *Barrier Daily Truth*, 14 Aug. 1916.
126 'Brookfield and Soldiers', *Barrier Daily Truth*, 16 Sept. 1917.
127 'Council Estimates for 1915', *Barrier Miner*, 30 Jan. 1915.
128 'A Late Sitting', *Barrier Miner*, 26 Feb. 1915; 'City Council Sits Late', *Barrier Daily Truth*, 26 Feb. 1915.
129 'Unemployment in Different States', *Western Mail*, 29 Jan. 1915, 'News of the Day', *The Age*, 6 Jan. 1915.
130 Eric Abraham, interviewed 25 January 2000, Australians at War Film Archive, Archive number: 2541. UNSW.
131 Marcel Caux, interviewed 13 June 2003, Australians at War Film Archive, Archive number: 502. UNSW.
132 J.R. Mudie to Base Records Officer AIEF, 30 Aug. 1916, Private Edward James Ryan, Service Number 4635, NAA: B2455.
133 For example, 'The Dardanelles Fighting', *The West Australian* [Perth], 21 June 1915, 'From the Firing Line', *The Sunday Times* [Perth], 29 Aug. 1915, 'Heroism: Deeds of Great Daring', *The West Australian* [Perth], 27 Sept. 1915.
134 'The Country's Need', *The West Australian* [Perth], 14 Sep. 1915.

135 'A Subiaco Call', *Daily News* [Perth], 18 Jan. 1915.
136 For these details, I am grateful to Claire Greer, who kindly shared with me her research on AIF enlistments from the suburb of Subiaco, Perth. Service record of William Stanley Bown, Service Number 6431, NAA: B2455.
137 Gillett, memoir, 'A Chat with Khaki', 4, MLMSS 1585 (Mitchell Library).
138 Angelica Balabanoff, *My Life as a Rebel* (New York, 1938), 135-138, 'The Zimmerwald Manifesto', in Marc Ferro, *The Great War, 1914-1918* (London, 1973), 184-188, Julius Braunthal, *History of the International: 1914-1943* (London, 1967), Ch. 2., David Kirby, *War, Peace and Revolution: International Socialism at the Crossroads 1914-1918* (New York, 1986), 78-80.
139 F.L. Carsten, *War Against War: British and German Radical Movements in the First World War* (London, 1982), 36-42.
140 'Peace Conference of Socialists', *The Socialist* [Melbourne], 26 Nov. 1915.
141 13th Battalion War Diary, Nov. 1914, Dec. 1914, and Jan. 1915, AWM4, 23/30/1, 2 and 3.
142 13th Battalion War Diary, Feb. 1915, AWM4, 23/30/4.
143 'News and Notes', *The West Australian*, 16 Mar. 1915, and 'Y.M.C.A. Military Tent', *The West Australian*, 17 Mar. 1915.
144 'Concert at Blackboy Hill', *The West Australian*, 29 Mar. 1915
145 'Australia's Call to Arms', words by Teeby, music by E.R.B. Jordan, Brisbane, 1914. Object 178540338, National Library of Australia (NLA).
146 Asquith to Stanley, 6 Aug. 1914, in Michael and Eleanor Brock (eds), *H.H. Asquith Letters to Venetia Stanley* (Oxford, 1985), 158.
147 'Gurkhas in the Gardens of Potsdam', *Times*, 11 Sept. 1914.
148 *Morning Post*, 16 Dec. 1914.
149 Churchill interview with *Le Matin*, reproduced in *Economist*, 6 Feb. 1915.
150 Kemal H. Karpat, 'The Entry of the Ottoman Empire into World War I', *Belleten*, LXVIII, 253 (2004), 24-36, and F.A.K. Yasamee, 'Ottoman Empire', in Keith Wilson (ed), *Decisions for War, 1914* (New York, 1995).
151 Chris Roberts, *The Landing at Anzac, 1915* (Sydney, 2015), 25.
152 V.H. Rothwell, 'Mesopotamia in British War Aims, 1914-1918', *The Historical Journal*, 13, 2 (June 1970), 273-294.
153 See the Foreign Office debate in the House of Commons, HC Deb 10 July 1914 vol 64 cc1383-463.
154 Benckendorff, quoted in W.A. Renzi, 'Great Britain, Russia and the Straits, 1914-1915', *Journal of Modern History*, 42, 1 (1970), 6.
155 Benckendorff quoted in C. Jay Smith, 'Great Britain and the Straits Agreement of 1914-1915 with Russia: the British Promise of November 1914', *American Historical Review*, 70, 4 (1965), 1031. See also A.L. MacFie, 'The Straits Question in the First World War, 1914-18', *Middle Eastern Studies*, 19, 1 (Jan. 1983), 50.
156 Lord Bertie to Grey, 27 Nov. 1914, Bertie Papers, FO 800/166, cited in M.G. Ekstein-Frankl, 'The Development of British War Aims: August 1914-March 1915', unpublished PhD thesis (University of London, 1969), 237.
157 Grey to Buchanan, Bertie, and Greene, 11 Jan. 1915, Grey Papers, FO 800/75, quoted in Ekstein-Frankl, 'Development of British War Aims', 242-3. On ambassadorial mediation, see Arthur Link, *Wilson: The Struggle for Neutrality, 1914-1915* (Princeton, 1960), Ch. VII.
158 Ekstein-Frankl, 'Development of British War Aims', 256.
159 War Council Minutes, 3 Mar. 1915, TNA: CAB 42/2/3.
160 The Straits and Persia Agreement is within Buchanan to Grey, 13 Mar. 1915 (containing Sazonov's 'Aide-mémoire', 4 Mar. 1915, and Grey's 'Aide-mémoire' and accompanying 'Memorandum', 12 Mar. 1915), CAB 37/126/33. See also Aaron S. Kliemann, 'British War Aims in the Middle East in 1915', *Journal of Contemporary History*, 3, 3 (July, 1968), 237-251, and William A. Renzi, 'Great Britain, Russia, and the Straits, 1914-1915', *Journal of Modern History*, 42, 1 (1970), 1-20.
161 Dylan Thomas, *The hand that signed the paper* (1935), in Dylan Thomas, *Miscellany* (London, 1963), 25.

162 'Convention signed on August 31, 1907, between Great Britain and Russia containing arrangements on the subject of Persia, Afghanistan, and Thibet', *British Parliamentary Papers*, cd. 3750.

163 Oliver Bast, 'British Imperialism and Persian Diplomacy in the shadow of World War I (1914-1921)', in The British Council, *Didgah: New Perspectives on UK-Iran Cultural Relations* (London, 2015), 87.

164 Keith Wilson (ed), *West Meets East: An English Diplomat in the Ottoman Empire and Persia, 1890-1918: the unfinished autobiography of Sir Charles Marling* (Istanbul, 2010), 92-5.

165 Harcourt Cabinet Memorandum, 10 Mar. 1915, Harcourt Cabinet Memoranda 1915, Harcourt Papers.

166 Lewis Harcourt, 'The Spoils', Cabinet Paper, 25 Mar. 1915, TNA: CAB 63/3/104-7.

167 Grey to Buchanan, 11 March 1915, quoted in C.J. Lowe, 'Britain and Italian Intervention, 1914-1915', *Historical Journal*, 12, 3 (1969), p. 544.

168 13th Battalion War Diary, April 1915, AWM4, 23/30/6.

169 Trooper Edward James Ryan (in fact, the service record of Henry Martin Ryan), Service Number 672, NAA: B2455.

170 Trooper Edward James Ryan, Service Number 672, NAA: B2455. See Ryan to Officer of Base Records, 26 Nov. 1924, giving his own record of the dates of his promotions, within this file.

171 David R. Woodward, *Hell in the Holy Land: World War I in the Middle East* (Lexington, 2006), 36.

172 11th Battalion War Diary, May 1915, AWM4, 23/28/2.

173 11th Battalion War Diary, June 1915, AWM4, 23/28/3.

174 11th Battalion War Diary, July 1915, AWM4, 23/28/4.

175 11th Battalion War Diary, Aug. 1915, AWM4, 23/28/5.

176 'Roll of Honour', *Western Mail* [Perth], 22 Oct. 1915.

177 Richard Bosworth, 'Italy's Wars of Illusion, 1911-1915', in Andreas Gestrich and Hartmut Pogge von Strandmann (eds), *Bid for World Power? New Research on the Outbreak of the First World War* (Oxford, 2017), 198.

178 Paul du Quenoy, 'With Allies Like These, Who Needs Enemies? Russia and the Problem of Italian Entry into World War', *Canadian Slavonic Papers*, 45, 3/4 (Sept-Dec. 2003), 409-440.

179 His encyclical, Ad Beatissimi Apolostolorum, promulgated on 1 Nov. 1914, denounced the war: 'The combatants are the greatest and wealthiest nations of the earth; what wonder, then, if, well provided with the most awful weapons modern military science has devised, they strive to destroy one another with refinements of horror.' See John F. Pollard, *The Unknown Pope: Bendedict XV (1914-1922) and the Pursuit of Peace* (London, 1999).

180 James A. Young, 'The Consulta and the Italian Peace Movement, 1914-18', in Solomon Wank (ed), *Doves and Diplomats: Foreign Offices and Peace Movements in Europe and America in the Twentieth Century* (Westport, 1978), 154-177.

181 Hankey Diary, 6-9 Apr. 1915, Maurice Hankey, *The Supreme Command, 1914-1918* (London, 1961), 300-301, and Grey to Bertie, 10 Apr. 1915, FO371/2244, cited by William A. Renzi, *In the Shadow of the Sword: Italy's Neutrality and Entrance into the Great War* (New York, 1987), 208.

182 Malcolm Brown and Shirley Seaton, *Christmas Truce: The Western Front, December 1914* (London, 1994) 37.

183 'Agreement between France, Russia, Great Britain and Italy, signed at London, April 26, 1915', *British Parliamentary Papers*, Miscellaneous No. 7, Vol. 50, Cmd. 671.

184 On the oil issue, see Ann Gower Matters, 'Imperialism in Iraq, 1914-1932: Asking For Trouble', unpublished PhD thesis (Flinders University, 2015), Martin William Gibson, 'British Strategy and Oil, 1914-1923', unpublished PhD thesis (University of Glasgow, 2012). The vast historiography includes Gregory P. Nowell, *Mercantile States and the World Oil Cartel, 1900-1939* (Ithaca, 1994), Marian Kent, *Oil and Empire: British Policy and Mesopotamian Oil, 1900-1920* (London, 1976), and Marian Kent, *Moguls and Mandarins: Oil, Imperialism and the Middle East in British Foreign Policy 1900-1940* (New York, 2013).

185 Aaron S. Kliemann, 'British War Aims in the Middle East in 1915', *Journal of Contemporary History*, 3, 3 (July, 1968), 237-251.
186 *Telegraph* [London], 20 May 1915.
187 Hughes, 'The Call to Arms', *Sydney Morning Herald*, 15 Dec. 1915
188 Charles Bean, Diary, 25 Sept. 1915, AWM: 3DRL606/17/1.
189 Asquith to Kitchener, 20 Aug. 1915, quoted in George H. Cassar, *Asquith as War Leader* (London, 1994), 119.
190 Seal, *Inventing Anzac*, 173.
191 Norman Gilroy, Diary 25 Apr. 1915, MLMSS 2247/Item 1 (Mitchell Library).
192 Leonard Mann, *Flesh in Armour* (2014), 107.
193 'Western Australia: Popularising Recruiting', *West Australian* [Perth] 13 June 1916, and Benjamin Alfred Cohen, Diary, undated, MLMSS 1844/1 (Mitchell Library).
194 Rudyard Kipling, 'The Army of a Dream', in *Traffics and Discoveries* (London, 1904), 282.
195 Benjamin Alfred Cohen, Diary, undated, MLMSS 1844/1 (Mitchell Library).
196 Gillett, memoir, 12-15, MLMSS 1585 (Mitchell Library).
197 Gillett, memoir, 20-24, 29, 31-2, MLMSS 1585 (Mitchell Library), and Benjamin Alfred Cohen, Diary, undated, MLMSS 1844/1 (Mitchell Library).
198 'Bayonet Fighting at Blackboy Hill Camp', and 'A Great Transformation', *Sunday Times* [Perth], 13 and 20 Sept 1914, 'Blackboy Camp: Daily Routine Described', *Westralian Worker*, 17 Dec. 1915, and review of W. Dunn, *The Use of the Bayonet*, 'News and Notes', *The West Australian*, 6 July 1916.
199 'Eight Hours Celebration', *The Swan Express* [Midland Junction] 15 Oct. 1915.
200 William James Purvis, interview, 1976, OH4103/6 (State Library of Western Australia).
201 George Baron Hay, interview, 11 Nov. 1976, OH4103/3 (State Library of Western Australia).
202 Archie Barwick, Diary, 23 July 1916, MLMSS 1493/Box 1/Item 4 (Mitchell Library).
203 Gillett, memoir, 24-26, MLMSS 1585 (Mitchell Library).
204 Leonard Charles Glover service records, NAA: B2455. Glover was later one of the many missing, presumed killed, with the 28th Battalion at Pozières in July 1916.
205 Private Edward James Ryan, Service Number 4635, NAA: B2455.
206 'Western Australia – The Roll of Honour: 91st and 92nd Casualty List', *The West Australian* [Perth], 15 Oct. 1915.
207 'The Only Possible Peace Terms', *Daily Chronicle* [London] 15 Nov. 1915.
208 For example, 'Peace Terms', *The Sun* [Sydney], 17 Nov. 1915, 'Terms of Peace', *Southern Times* [Bunbury] 2 Dec. 1915, 'Terms of Peace', *The Collie Miner*, 4 Dec. 1915.
209 McMahon to Grey, 18 Oct. 1915, and minutes on this, and Grey to McMahon, 20 Oct. 1915, in C.J. Lowe and M.L. Dockrill (eds), *The Mirage of Power. Vol. 3. The Documents. British Foreign Policy, 1902-22* (London, 1972), 527-31.
210 Douglas Newton, '"A Real Heritage of the English People": British Liberalism and "Continental Despotism"', in Robin Archer, Joy Damousi, Murray Goot, and Sean Scalmer (eds), *The Conscription Conflict and the Great War* (Clayton, 2016), 14-36.
211 'Sir John Simon's Speech', *Manchester Guardian*, 6 Jan. 1916, Letter to the editor by 'One of the 200', 'Conscription', *Nation*, 22 Jan. 1916.
212 Frances Stevenson diary, 31 Jan. 1916, in A.J.P. Taylor (ed), *Lloyd George: A Diary by Frances Stevenson* (London, 1971), 90.
213 The Parliament and Registration Bill, extending the life of the parliament, was debated in the Commons, HC Deb 20 December 1915 vol 77 cc59-87, and in the Lords, HL Deb 06 January 1916 vol 20 cc819-50. It passed the Lords on 25 January 1916, see HL Deb 25 January 1916 vol 20 c969. The life of the parliament was extended five times altogether during the war, January and August 1916, April and November 1917, and July 1918.
214 For a recent survey, see Catherine Bond, *Law in War: Freedom and Restriction in Australia during the Great War* (Sydney, 2020).
215 Fitzhardinge, *Little Digger*, 69-94, Jill Kitson, *Patriots Three* (Sydney, 2005), Parts II and II.
216 'European Socialists and the War', *Australian Worker*, 20 Jan. 1916, 'Mr Hughes Attacked', *Australian Worker*, 30 Mar. 1916, 'Mr Hughes', *Australian Worker*, 13 Apr. 1916.

217	Transcript of interview with Jesse Palmer (Service Number 63958), Australian Army Medical Corps AIF, 1916-1919, interviewed by Peter Rubinstein for 'Voices from the Great War', 28 November 1995, Sound item S03437 (AWM).
218	Cohen, Diary, 29 Jan. 1917, MLMSS 1844/1.
219	'Warm Weather', *The Daily News* [Perth].
220	Embarkation Roll, 14th Reinforcements for the 11th Battalion, AWM8, 23/28/4.
221	Cohen, Diary, 29 Jan. 1917, MLMSS 1844/1 (Mitchell Library).
222	Gillett, memoir, 36-38, MLMSS 1585 (Mitchell Library).
223	Private David Harford, Diary, 13,15 Feb. 1916, AWM: 1DRL/0335 (Australian War Memorial).
224	Gillett, memoir, 39, MLMSS 1585 (Mitchell Library).
225	Gillett, memoir, 40, MLMSS 1585 (Mitchell Library).
226	House Diary, 11 Feb. 1915.
227	House to Wilson, 14 Mar. 1915, Seymour (ed), *Intimate Papers I.*, 401.
228	House to Wilson, 14 Mar. 1915, Charles Seymour (ed), *The Intimate Papers of Colonel House. Vol. I. Behind the Political Curtain* (London, 1926), 401.
229	Charles E. Neu, *Colonel House: A Biography of Woodrow Wilson's Silent Partner* (Oxford 2015), Chs 13-14.
230	David S. Patterson, *The Search for Negotiated Peace: Women's Activism and Citizen Diplomacy in World War I* (New York, 2008).
231	Madeleine Z. Doty, *The Central Organisation for a Durable Peace, (1915-1919)*, Published PhD thesis (University of Geneva, 1945). G. Lowes Dickinson and J. Allen Baker attended for Britain, and Walther Schücking, Ludwig Quidde, Otto Lehmann-Russbüldt, and Kurt von Tepper Laski for Germany.
232	Marvin Swartz, *The Union of Democratic Control in British Politics during the First World War* (Oxford, 1971).
233	Karl Holl, *Pazifismus in Deutschland* (Frankfurt, 1988), Part III.
234	Norman Ingram, 'The Enduring Legacy of 1914: Historical Dissent, the *Ligues des droits de l'homme*, and the Origins of 'Pacifisme nouveau style', in *Synergies Royaume-Uni et Irlande*, 4 (2011), 85-94.
235	Henry R. Winkler, *The League of Nations Movement in Great Britain, 1914-1919* (New Brunswick, 1952), 50.
236	Warren F. Kuehl, *Seeking World Order: The United States and World Organization to 1920* (Nashville, 1969), 184-191.
237	For recent surveys, see Michael Kazin, *War Against War: The American Fight for Peace, 1914-1918* (New York, 2017) and Amy Aronson, *Crystal Eastman: A Revolutionary Life* (New York, 2020).
238	Austin van der Slice, *International Labor, Diplomacy, and Peace 1914-1919* (Philadelphia, 1941), Ch. 3, Braunthal, *History of the International, Vol. 2*, Ch. 2, Kirby, *War, Peace and Revolution*, Ch. 4.
239	Carl Schorske, *German Social Democracy 1905-1917: the Development of the Great Schism* (New York, 1955), Ch. XI, David Welch, *Germany, Propaganda and Total War, 1914-1918: the Sins of Omission* (London, 2000), 172-3, A.J. Ryder, *The German Revolution of 1918: A Study of German Socialism in War and Revolt* (Cambridge, 1967), 57-8, J. Shand, 'Doves Among Eagles: German Pacifists and their Government during World War I', *Journal of Contemporary History*, X (1975), 95-108, Alexander Watson, *Ring of Steel: Germany and Austria-Hungary at War, 1914-1918* (London, 2014).
240	HL Deb 08 November 1915 vol 20 cc181-230.
241	Ponsonby, HC Deb 11 Nov. 1915 vol 75 cc1450-1459; Trevelyan, HC Deb 15 Nov. 1915 vol 75 cc.1557-1563; Outhwaite, HC Deb 15 Nov. 1915 vol. 75 cc1598-1604.
242	For example, 'Peace by Negotiation', *West Australian* [Perth], 17 Nov. 1915, 'Fault-Finders', *Daily Post* [Hobart], 11 Nov. 1915, 'Grumbling Peers', *Maitland Weekly Mercury*, 13 Nov. 1915, and 'Injudicious Politicians', *Sydney Morning Herald*, 20 Nov. 1915.
243	Barbara S. Kraft, *The Peace Ship: Henry Ford's Pacifist Adventure in the First World War* (New York, 1978), Ch. 11.
244	Harford, Diary, 22-26 Feb. 1916. AWM: 1DRL/0335.
245	Harford, Diary, 27 Feb. to 4 Mar. 1916. AWM: 1DRL/0335.

246 Harford, Diary, 8-12 Mar. 1916, AWM: 1DRL/0335.
247 Eric Dark, war narrative, 32, MLMSS 5049/Item 5 (Mitchell Library), and Fewster, 'Expression and Suppression', 69.
248 Kearns, *Broken Hill 1915-1939*, 11.
249 Adams, *Brookfield*, 36-8, Fitzhardinge, *Little Digger*, 63.
250 House Diary, 14 Feb. 1916.
251 Arthur S. Link, *Wilson: Confusions and Crises, 1915-1916* (Princeton, 1964), Ch. IV, Joyce Williams, *Colonel House and Sir Edward Grey: A Study in Anglo-American Diplomacy* (Lanham, 1984), Ch. IV, 'Memorandum of Sir Edward Grey', 22 Feb. 1916 and House to Grey, 8 Mar. 1916, in Seymour (ed), *Intimate Papers II*, 200-02.
252 Secret addendum to the proceedings of the War Committee, 21 March 1916, TNA: CAB 42/22/16, and see Hankey's minutes on the War Committee meeting of 21 March 1916, TNA: CAB 42/11, cited in John Milton Cooper, 'Note: The British Response to the House-Grey Memorandum: New Evidence and New Questions', *Journal of American History*, 59, 4 (1973), 961.
253 Lloyd George, quoted in Sir William Robertson, *Soldiers and Statesmen, 1914-1918* (London, 1926), Vol. I, 280.
254 Braunthal, *History of the International*, Vol. 2, 49-52, Kirby, *War, Peace and Revolution*, 82-83, Carsten, *War Against War*, 86, Balabanoff, *My Life as a Rebel*, 138-141.
255 Thomas J. Knock, *To End All Wars: Woodrow Wilson and the Quest for a New World Order* (Princeton, 1992), 75-81.
256 Harford, Diary, 2 April 1916, AWM: 1DRL/0335.
257 For a popular account, see T. Pakenham, *The Scramble for Africa: The White Man's Conquest of the Dark Continent, 1876-1912* (New York, 1992), and for the classic anti-imperialist account see Wilfred S. Blunt, *The Secret History of the English Occupation of Egypt* (Dublin, 2007, originally published 1907).
258 'Declaration between the United Kingdom and France Respecting Egypt and Morocco, together with the Secret Articles Signed at the Same Time', 8 Apr. 1904, (printed Nov. 1911) *British Parliamentary Papers*, Cd. 5969.
259 Captain C. Longmore, *Carry On!* (Perth, 1939), 13. 'Barb', 'The 51st Over There', *Western Mail* (Perth), 23 Apr. 1936. Two brothers, Private Alan Howard Barber and Private James Norman Barber, who served in the 51st Battalion, compiled this history, with the assistance of other veterans. It appeared in the *Western Mail* in weekly instalments in 1936-37.
260 Private Thomas Pearce Couch Ryan, Service Number 2055, NAA: B2455, and 11th Battalion War Diary, March 1916, AWM4, 23/28/12.
261 Harry Ryan to Ted Ryan, undated postcard, in possession of Beth Sutton.
262 Rose Ryan died 16 May 1990, aged 92, and is buried in the Jewish section of Centennial Park Cemetery, Pasadena, Mitchum City, South Australia. Ruby's birth date of November 1916 can be estimated from Harry Ryan's demobilisation documents, Form 534, dated 9 February 1919, filed with his enlistment papers, NAA: B2455. This gives her age as 2 years and 4 months. Ruby Elizabeth Francis (née Ryan) died 2 July 1996 and is buried in Centennial Park Cemetery, Adelaide.
263 Harford, Diary, 13, 14, and 15 Mar. 1916, AWM: 1DRL/0335, and the service records of David Bernard Harford, Service Number 2844, NAA: B2455.
264 Harford, Diary, 14 Mar. 1916, AWM: 1DRL/0335.
265 Harford, Diary, 13 Apr. 1916, AWM: 1DRL/0335.
266 'Private E.J. Ryan', *Barrier Miner*, 31 Dec. 1916, is an undated letter from Ted Ryan to his uncle and guardian, James Ramsay Mudie, at Broken Hill. It is the only letter from Ted Ryan that survives.
267 'Private E.J. Ryan', *Barrier Miner*, 31 Dec. 1916.
268 Edmund Blunden, *Undertones of War* (Harmondsworth, 1938), 45.
269 51st Battalion War Diary, March 1916, AWM4, 23/68/1.
270 Barber, 'The 51st Over There', *Western Mail*, 23 Apr. 1936.
271 Barber, 'The 51st Over There', *Western Mail*, 14 May 1936.
272 George B. King, Diary, 1 Mar. 1916, MLMSS 1801 (Mitchell Library).

273	Albert Charles Linton, interviewed by Alistair Thomson, 12 June 1983, Sound item S01318 (AWM).
274	Barber, 'The 51st Over There', *Western Mail*, 23 Apr. 1936.
275	Barber, 'The 51st Over There', *Western Mail*, 23 Apr. 1936.
276	51st Battalion War Diary, April 1916, AWM4, 23/68/2.
277	51st Battalion War Diary, May 1916, AWM4, 23/68/3.
278	'Private E.J. Ryan', *Barrier Miner*, 31 Dec. 1916.
279	War Committee. 'Meeting held at 10, Downing Street on Thursday, December 16, 1915', 'Evidence of Lieutenant-Colonel Sir Mark Sykes, Bart., M. P., on the Arab Question'; TNA: CAB 24/1/51.
280	Robert H. Lieshout, *Britain and the Arab Middle East: World War I and its Aftermath* (London, 2016), Christopher M. Andrew, and A.S. Kanya Forstner, *France Overseas: The Great War and the Climax of French Imperial Expansion* (London, 1981), 74-5, Ch. 4, Marian Kent, 'Great Britain and the End of the Ottoman Empire 1900-1923' in Marian Kent (ed), *The Great Powers and the End of the Ottoman Empire* (London, 2005), 165-198, and Grey to Cambon, 16 May 1916, in E.L. Woodward and R. Butler (eds), *Documents on British Foreign Policy 1919-1939*, First Series, Vol. 4 (London, 1952), 244-7.
281	The original 'Map of Eastern Turkey in Asia, Syria, and Western Persia', signed by Sykes and Picot, 8 May 1916, is in TNA: MPK1-426, originally from FO 371/2777.
282	Paul C. Helmreich, 'Italy and the Repudiation and the Anglo-French Repudiation of the 1917 St-Jean-de-Maurienne Agreement', *Journal of Modern History*, 48, 2 [On Demand Supplement] (June 1976), 104, and Edward Peter Fitzgerald, 'France's Middle Eastern Ambitions, the Sykes-Picot Negotiations, and the Oil Fields of Mosul, 1915-1918', *Journal of Modern History*, 66, 4 (Dec. 1994), 697-725.
283	Peter J. Yearwood, 'In a Casual Way with a Blue Pencil: British Policy and the Partition of Kamerun', 19, V.H. Rothwell, *British War Aims and Peace Diplomacy, 1914-1918* (Oxford, 1971), 11-12, Gaddis Smith, 'The British Government and the Disposition of the German Colonies in Africa', in Prosser Gifford and Wm. Roger Louis (eds), *Britain and Germany in Africa: Imperial Rivalry and Colonial Rule* (New Haven, 1967), 275-299.
284	For example, see Corporal Norman Campbell, AIF, 'The Coat That Fits Every Body', *The Northern Herald* [Cairns], 9 Feb. 1917.
285	Private Thomas Lawrence Talty, interviewed by Peter Rubinstein, 26 June 1998, Sound item S03426 (AWM).
286	51st Battalion War Diary, June 1916, AWM4, 23/68/4. Barber, 'The 51st Over There', *Western Mail*, 30 Apr. 1936.
287	Barber, 'The 51st Over There', *Western Mail*, 30 Apr. 1936.
288	Private E.J. Ryan', *Barrier Miner*, 31 Dec. 1916.
289	Geoffrey Bell Hughes, Diary, 25 Mar. 1916, MLMSS 3923 (Mitchell Library).
290	George B. King, Diary, 1 Apr. 1916, MLMSS 1801 (Mitchell Library).
291	Barber, 'The 51st Over There', *Western Mail*, 30 Apr. 1936.
292	Barber, 'The 51st Over There', *Western Mail*, 30 Apr. 1936, and John Dos Passos, *Mr Wilson's War: From the Assassination of McKinley to the Defeat of the League of Nations* (New York, 2013), 260.
293	Geoffrey Bell Hughes, Diary, 18 July 1916, MLMSS 3923 (Mitchell Library).
294	51st Battalion War Diary, June 1916, AWM4, 23/68/4.
295	C.E. Montague, *Disenchantment* (London, 1934), 164.
296	Barber, 'The 51st Over There', *Western Mail*, 30 Apr. 1936.
297	Table II, in N.P. Howard, 'The Social and Political Consequences of the Allied Food Blockade of Germany, 1918-19', *German History*, 11, 2 (June 1993), 166, and see C. Paul Vincent, *The Politics of Hunger* (Athens, Ohio, 1985).
298	'Message from the Chief', 6 Feb. 1917, quoted in J. Lee Thompson, *Politicians, the Press, and Propaganda: Lord Northcliffe and the Great War, 1914-1919* (Kent, Ohio, 1999), 124.
299	On 'anti-German economics' see Marc Trachtenberg, '"A new Economic Order": Etienne Clémentel and French Economic Diplomacy during the First World War', *French Historical Studies*, 10, 2 (1977), pp. 315-341, Forrest Capie, 'Pressure for Tariff Protection in Britain, 1917-31', *Journal of European Economic History*, 9, 2 (1980), esp. pp. 432-3, Robert

300. HC Deb 10 Jan. 1916 vol 77 cc1299-394, and HC Deb 23 Feb 1916 vol 80 cc713-78.
301. Raymond to Katherine Asquith, 7 April 1916, in John Jollife (ed), *Raymond Asquith: Life and Letters* (London, 1987), 255.
302. Peter Spartalis, *Diplomatic Battles of Billy Hughes* (Sydney, 1983), 28-34, and L.F. Fitzhardinge, *The Little Digger, 1914-1952: William Morris Hughes, A Political Biography*, Vol. II (Sydney, 1979), 121-137.
303. Welch, *Germany, Propaganda and Total War*, 199.
304. For examples of ministers refusing to nominate terms of peace or war aims in response to questions, see: Fred Jowett's question to Grey, HC Deb 11 February 1915 vol 69 c699; David Mason's questions to Asquith, HC Deb 12 July 1915 vol 73 c652, and HC Deb 12 July 1915 vol 73 cc652-3; and Sir William Byles's question to Asquith, HC Deb 21 July 1915 vol 73 c1492.
305. HC Deb 24 May 1916 vol 82 cc2192.
306. HC Deb 24 May 1916 vol 82 cc2202.
307. Private Albert Charles Linton, interviewed by Alistair Thomson, Sound item S01318 (AWM).
308. British forces would lose 432,000 casualties, including about 150,000 killed outright and another 100,000 seriously wounded and maimed. Robin Prior and Trevor Wilson, *The Somme* (Sydney, 2006), 301.
309. H.M. Tomlinson, 'A War Note for Democrats', *English Review*, Dec. 1914, 75.
310. Archie Barwick Diary, 27 June 1916, MLMSS 1493/Box 1/Item 3.
311. Barber, 'The 51st Over There', *Western Mail*, 30 Apr. 1936.
312. Francis Weatherhead to his mother, 20 Nov. 1918, in Muriel E. Clampett (ed), *My Dear Mother* (Melbourne, n.d.), 229.
313. Montague, *Disenchantment*, 136.
314. R.H. Mottram, *The Spanish Farm Trilogy, 1914-1918* (London, 1927), 9, 13, 275.
315. Arthur Wheen to his sister Agnes, 28 July 1916, in Tanya Crothers (ed), *We Talked of Other Things: the Life and Letters of Arthur Wheen, 1897-1917* (Longueville, 2011), 46.
316. Wheen to his sister Lily, 16 Sept. 1916, *We Talked of Other Things*, 55.
317. Barber, 'The 51st Over There', *Western Mail*, 14 May 1936.
318. Archie Barwick Diary, 30 June 1916, MLMSS 1493/Box 1/Item 3.
319. Mottram, *Spanish Farm*, 13.
320. John Dos Passos, *Three Soldiers* (London, 1997), 150.
321. Morrow, *Iron in the Fire*, 60.
322. Mottram, *Spanish Farm*, 275.
323. Dos Passos, *Three Soldiers*, 144, 148.
324. Montague, *Disenchantment*, 161.
325. Richard Aldington, *Death of a Hero* (London, 1929), 324.
326. C.E. Montague, *Action* (London, 1928), 45.
327. H.M. Tomlinson, *All Our Yesterdays* (London, 1930), 390-1.
328. John Dos Passos, *One Man's Initiation: 1917* (London, 1920), 97.
329. Jennifer Hobhouse Balme, *To Love One's Enemies* (Cobble Hill, 1994), 474.
330. Hobhouse to Jagow, 18 June 1916, Jagow to Hobhouse, 19 June 1916, in Jennifer Hobhouse Balme, *Agent of Peace: Emily Hobhouse and Her Courageous Attempt to End the First World War* (Stroud, 2015), 99, 100, and Jennifer Hobhouse Balme, *To Love One's Enemies* (Cobble Hill, 1994), 552.
331. Hobhouse to Jagow, 20 June 1916, Jagow to Hobhouse, 20 June 1916, Hobhouse to Jagow, 21 June 1916, and Jagow to Hobhouse, 21 June 1916, in Balme, *Agent of Peace*, 100-103. On Grey's insult toward Bethmann Hollweg, see HC Deb 24 May 1916 vol 82 c2201.
332. Emily Hobhouse Journal, 28 June 1916, in Balme, *Agent of Peace*, 115.
333. Aldington, *Death of a Hero*, 326.
334. 51st Battalion War Diary, June 1916, AWM4, 23/68/4.
335. Barber, '51st Over There', 7 May 1936.
336. Arthur G. Thomas, Diary, 24 July 1916, AWM 3DRL/2206.

337	Archie Barwick, Diary, 24 July 1916, MLMSS 1493/Box 1/Item 4.
338	Eric Abraham, interviewed 25 Jan. 2000, Australians at War Film Archive, Archive number 2541.
339	Mottram, *Spanish Farm*, 267.
340	Private Edward James Ryan, Service Number 4635, NAA: B2455.
341	On the night of 28-29 June, two men from the 51st Battalion were killed, Matthew Newton (SERN 2745), labourer, aged 42, James Jeffery Cross (SERN 3804), labourer, aged 24. Arthur George Every (SERN 3823), telegraph messenger, aged 18, was wounded on 27 June and died of wounds on 29 June.
342	S.H. Goh, 'Bomb blast mass casualty incidents: initial triage and management of injuries', *Singapore Medical Journal*, 50, 1 (2009), 101-106.
343	Eric Dark (future husband of the Australian novelist Eleanor Dark), war narrative, MLMSS 5049/Item 5 (Mitchell Library).
344	Frederic Manning, *The Middle Parts of Fortune* (London, 2014, first published 1929), 4, 8, 14-15.
345	Edmund Blunden, *Undertones of War* (Harmondsworth, 1938), 68, 133, 195.
346	Blunden, *Undertones of War*, 67.
347	For example, Richard Lindstrom, 'The Australian Experience of Psychological Casualties in War, 1915-1939', unpublished Ph. D thesis, Victoria University of Technology, 1997, Ch. 1, 'Shell shock: the Australian infantryman's perspective', and Michael B. Tyquin, *Madness and the Military: Australia's Experience of the Great War* (Loftus, 2006), Ch. 3, 'Through a Glass Darkly'.
348	Stephen Wynn and Tanya Wynn, *Women in the Great War* (Barnsley, 2017), 101.
349	Private Edward James Ryan, Service Number 4635, NAA: B2455.
350	Morrow, *Iron in the Fire*, 10.
351	Frederick 'Fred' John Kelly (Service Number 2599), 1st Battalion at Gallipoli, transferred to the 53rd Battalion, 14th Machine Gun Company, and then 5th Machine Gun Battalion, interviewed by Peter Rubinstein, 8 January 1997, Sound Item, S03419 (AWM).
352	Francis Weatherhead to his father, 5 Nov. 1918, Clampett, *My Dear Mother*, 226.
353	Hugh Walpole, *The Dark Forest* (London, 1929), 116, 191-2.
354	The *Anzac Bulletin* was edited by Henry Casimir Smart, a Boer War veteran, journalist, and friend of Charles Bean.
355	Frank H. Molony, Diary, 27 Oct. 1917, MLMSS 2883/Item 4 (Mitchell Library).
356	Dos Passos, Diary, 1 Jan. 1918, in Townsend Ludington (ed), *The Fourteenth Chronicle: Letters and Diaries of John Dos Passos* (Boston, 1973), 115-6.
357	John Dos Passos, *The Best Times: An Informal Memoir* (New York, 1966), 69-70.
358	Mottram, *Spanish Farm*, 92.
359	51st Battalion War Diary, July 1916, AWM4, 23/68/5.
360	Barber, '51st Over There', *Western Mail*, 7 May 1936, Neville Browning, *Fix Bayonets: The History of the 51st Battalion AIF* (Bayswater, WA, 2000), 26.
361	Browning, *Fix Bayonets*, 26.
362	Mottram, *Spanish Farm*, 176.
363	'Australians in Action: 187th Casualty List', *Barrier Miner*, 27 July 1916.
364	'The Australians: 197th Casualty List', *The Register* [Adelaide] 22 Aug. 1916, and 'Australians in Action: 197th Casualty List', *Barrier Miner*, 22 Aug. 1916, giving 'E.J. Ryan' as among the dead from Western Australia.
365	J.R. Mudie to Base Records Officer, 20 July and 30 Aug. 1916, Base Records Officer to J.R. Mudie, 7 Sept. 1916, in Private Edward James Ryan, Service Number 4635, NAA: B2455. See 'Australian Casualties: List no. 197', *Barrier Daily Truth*, 23 Aug. 1916.
366	Eric Kingsley Abraham, recorded memoir, 21 June 1990, Sound item S04443, Part 3 (AWM).
367	See 'Casualty Form – Active Service' (B. 103 Form), Private Edward James Ryan, Service Number 4635, NAA: B2455.
368	C.E. Montague, *Rough Justice* (London, 1926), 278.
369	Wheen to Lily, 16 Sept. 1916, *We Talked of Other Things*, 55.
370	Harford, Diary, 14 Oct. 1916, AWM: 1DRL/0335.
371	Barwick, Diary, 24 July 1916, MLMSS 1493/Box 1/Item 4.

372 Marcel Caux, interviewed 13 June 2003, Australians at War Film Archive, Archive number: 502. UNSW.
373 Jack Lockett, interviewed 11 Jan. 2000, Australians at War Film Archive, Archive number: 2539. UNSW.
374 Eric Kingsley Abraham, recorded memoir, 21 June 1990, Sound item S04443, Part 2 (AWM).
375 Arthur Cyril Ebdon, interviewed 29 Feb. 1992, Sound item S02097, Part 1 (AWM).
376 'Overseas War Record of Sister Hope Weatherhead (1915-1919)', in Clampett, *My Dear Mother*, 152.
377 Jack Flannery, interviewed by Alistair Thomson, 1 May 1983, Sound item S01312 (AWM).
378 Jack Lockett, interviewed by Peter Rubinstein, 22 Jan. 1997, Sound item, S03435.
379 Ted Smout, interviewed 8 Apr. 2002, Australians at War Film Archive, Archive number: 1145. UNSW.
380 The Vietnam veteran, Greg Lockhart, remembers a rocket attack against a South Vietnamese unit he was advising in October 1972 that killed four Vietnamese and injured twenty. Lockhart likens the short barrage of eight rockets to 'the deafening sounds beneath a railway bridge when a speeding train roars overhead.' In another incident in November 1972, Lockhart survived a mine that exploded under his jeep. 'Suddenly there was an explosion, a pile of black smoke, and through shock waves I was riding flames of white light.' He recalls a 'splitting of consciousness' and 'a sense of dissociation.' He saw himself, from above, 'floundering through clinging fumes.' In Lockhart's experience, a near miss of this kind could become the hinge around which a soldier's earlier and later lives would turn. Greg Lockhart, interview, 28 February 2018, and see Greg Lockhart, 'Preface and Acknowledgements' to *The Minefield: An Australian Tragedy in Vietnam* (Crows Nest, 2007), xiv. On the impact of the War in Iraq on an officer, see John Cantwell, *One Australian's War on Terror* (Melbourne, 2013).
381 The censor was Lt.-Col Dyke, Adams, *Brookfield*, 66. For a sample of an anti-conscription letter in the *Barrier Daily Truth*, see 'What a Soldier Says', 17 Jan. 1916. As early as March 1915, the editor of the *Barrier Daily Truth* complained that the censor was instructing the paper that 'we are not to publish matter with a view to checking the stream of recruits.' This was 'an assumption of power which it is not with the censor to wield.' See editorial, 'Militarism and What It Means', *Barrier Daily Truth*, 2 Mar. 1915.
382 See Deputy Chief Censor (Australia), *Rules for the Censorship of the Press* (1917), Section 15, paragraph (ix): 'Gruesome details of wounds or mutilations which would disturb the public or cause pain to relatives of the wounded or killed are not to be published.'
383 Morrow, *Iron in the Fire*, 21.
384 51st Battalion War Diary, Sept. 1916, AWM4 23/68/7. 'Addenda to Report: The Morale of the Men'. See also the reports of soldiers of the battalion captured on 51st Battalion, AWM30 B11.3, and 'Western Australian War Memorials 51st Australian Infantry Battalion', from RSL Highgate Sub-Branch.
385 'Private E.J. Ryan', *Barrier Miner*, 31 Dec. 1916.
386 Stefanie Caroline Linden and Edgar Jones, 'Shell shock Revisited: An Examination of the Case Records of the National Hospital in London', *Medical History*, 58, 4 (Oct. 2014), 519-545. See 'General Routine Order' (GRO) 2384, issued 13 June 1917, quoted in Mark Osborne Humphries, *A Weary Road: Shell Shock in the Canadian Expeditionary Force, 1914-1918* (Toronto, 2018), 231. From September 1917, officers and soldiers claiming mental disability from shellfire had to document their nearness to an exploding shell on Army Form W3436. See Anthony Richards (ed), *Report of the War Office Committee of Enquiry into "Shell Shock"* (Cmd. 1734), (reprinted London, 2014), IX, and Fiona Reid, *Broken Men: Shell Shock, Treatment and Recovery in Britain 1914-30* (London, 2010), 166.
387 See David Noonan, 'War Losses (Australia)', in the online *International Encyclopedia of the First World War* (2016), at 1914-1918-online.net, and David Noonan, *Those We Forget: Recounting Australia's Casualties of the First World War* (Melbourne, 2014), 70-82, 128.
388 Jay Winter, *Remembering War: The Great War between Memory and History in the Twentieth Century* (Yale, 2006), 54, Jay Winter, 'Shell Shock and the lives of the Lost Generation', in Ashley Ekins and Elizabeth Stewart (eds), *War Wounds: Medicine and the*

	Trauma of Conflict (Auckland, 2010), 28-40, Edgar Jones and Simon Wessely, *Shell Shock to PTSD: Military Psychiatry from 1900 to the Gulf War* (Hove, 2005), 17.
389	Australian lyrics of a parody of the Al Jolson hit 'Baby Doll' (Nov. 1916). Lyrics of the British version vary slightly, and were probably written by W.M. Harris, a British soldier. See George Simmers' research blog: https://greatwarfiction.wordpress.com/2013/05/23/one-of-englands-broken-dolls/
390	'Byfleet Bleakdown Hospital', *Surrey Advertiser*, 23 Sept. 1916, 'Presentation to Miss M.K. Duff', *Surrey Advertiser*, 7 Oct. 1916, 'Wounded Soldiers' Christmas', *Surrey Advertiser*, 30 Dec. 1916.
391	'Private E.J. Ryan', *Barrier Miner*, 31 Dec. 1916.
392	Corporal T.A. Saxon, 'Letters from Our Boys', *Violet Town Sentinel*, 2 Oct. 1917.
393	V.N. Vinogradov, 'Romania in the First World War: The Years of Neutrality, 1914-1916', *International History Review*, 14, 3 (Aug. 1992), 452-461. 'Memorandum for Romanian Minister', 19 July 1916, *British Documents on Foreign Affairs: Reports and Papers from the Foreign Office Confidential Print, Part II, Series H, The First World War*, Vol. 2 (Washington, 1989), 334. On Bulgaria, see David Stevenson, *The First World War and International Politics* (Oxford, 1988), 59-61.
394	The plays included 'The Girl from Ciro's', a comedy-farce (The Garrick), 'Broadway Jones' (Prince's Theatre), 'Mr Manhattan', a musical (Prince of Wales), 'High Jinks', a musical comedy (Adelphi), 'Pick-a-dilly', musical (London Pavilion), and 'Bric-a-Brac', musical (Palace). See also, 'Broadway Jones Revived', *Times*, 7 Sept. 1916, describing an audience of 2,000 wounded soldiers who came as guests of the management.
395	'Private E.J. Ryan', *Barrier Miner*, 31 Dec. 1916.
396	Robert Keith Middlemas, *The Clydesiders* (London, 1965), 71, B.J. Ripley and J. McHugh, *John Maclean* (Manchester, 1989), Ch. 4, and for a recent survey see Maggie Craig, *When the Clyde Ran Red: A Social History of Red Clydeside* (Edinburgh, 2018), Ch. 15.
397	*King's Regulations* (1912), paragraph 451.
398	See 'The ILP Vindicated: Scotland's Faith', *Labour Leader*, 28 Sept. 1916, and 'The Keir Hardie Demonstrations', 'Scotland and Keir Hardie', *Labour Leader*, 5 Oct. 1916, and 'Keir Hardie's Memorial', *Forward*, 7 Oct. 1916, and Craig, *When the Clyde Ran Red*, Ch. 14.
399	'Private E.J. Ryan', *Barrier Miner*, 31 Dec. 1916.
400	The date is unclear. Ryan's 'Casualty Form – Active Service' (B. 103 Form), lists the date of his marching in to Perham Down as 27 Sept., but his discharge from the 4th London General Hospital as 2 Oct. A typed record of service lists the date of his arrival at Perham Down as 2 Oct. Private Edward James Ryan, Service Number 4635, NAA: B2455.
401	Morrow, undated letter [1916], *Iron in the Fire*, 26-27.
402	George Horan to his father, George Horan Papers, MLMSS 1468/Item 2 (Mitchell Library).
403	'Never Again!', *The Times*, 29 Sept. 1916.
404	'Never Again!', *The Times*, 29 Sept. 1916.
405	'Hands Off The War!', *Daily Mail*, 29 Sept. 1916.
406	'Hands Off!', *Daily Mail*, 29 Sept. 1916.
407	Eric Kingsley Abraham, recorded memoir, 21 June 1990, Sound item S04443, Part 1 (AWM).
408	Jabez Waterhouse to his father, 17 Jan. 1917, MLMSS 2792 (K 21692/Folder 17) (Mitchell, Library).
409	George B. King, Diary, 30 Sept. 1916, MLMSS 1801 (Mitchell Library).
410	Jabez Waterhouse to his father, 17 Jan. 1917, MLMSS 2792 (K 21692/Folder 17) (Mitchell, Library).
411	Morrow, *Iron in the Fire*, 44.
412	Thomas Alcock, war narrative, MLMSS 1609/Item 2 (Mitchell Library).
413	Morrow, *Iron in the Fire*, 46, 53.
414	Arthur G. Thomas, letter to his family from Lark Hill, 30 Aug. 1917, AWM 3DRL/2206.
415	Charles Bean, *Official History of Australia in the War of 1914-1918, Vol. III, The Australian Imperial Force in France, 1916* (12th edition, 1941), 170.
416	Private Thomas Pearce Couch Ryan, Service Number 2055, NAA: B2455.
417	William Stanley Bown, Service Number 6431, NAA: B2455.
418	Adams, *Brookfield*, 44.

419   Adams, *Brookfield*, 58-63.
420   Robin Archer, 'Labour and Liberty: The Origins of the Conscription Referendum', in Archer, et al. (eds), *Conscription Conflict*, 40.
421   Greg Lockhart, "We're so Alone': Two Versions of the Void in Australian Military History', *Australian Historical Studies*, 120 (Oct. 2002), 389-97, and Greg Lockhart, 'Race Fear, Dangerous Denial: Japan and the great deception in Australian history', *Griffith Review*, 32 (2011), and Peter Cochrane, *Best We Forget: The War for White Australia 1914-18* (Melbourne, 2018).
422   *CPD*, 29 Oct. 1915, 7022. I am grateful to Dimity Torbett for this reference.
423   Adams, *Brookfield*, 73.
424   E.J. Ryan to Ramsay MacDonald, 18 Oct. 1916, MacDonald Papers, TNA: PRO/30/69/1160. Punctuation added.
425   'Private E.J. Ryan', *Barrier Miner*, 31 Dec. 1916.
426   Samples from the *Barrier Daily Truth*: 'Peace Alliance', 4 Jan. 1916, 'The Ford Peace Delegates', 14 Jan. 1916, 'Leibknecht's Greetings', 24 Jan. 1916, 'The Women's Peace Party', 5 Apr. 1916, 'Let There Be Peace', 1 Aug. 1916.
427   Samples from the *Barrier Daily Truth*: 'Billy the Showman', 3 Apr. 1916, 'Mr Hughes's Superlatives', 23 June 1916, 'Philip Snowden on Hughes', 27 June 1916.
428   Samples from the *Barrier Daily Truth*: 3, 4, 6, 10, 14, Jan. 1916, 30 Mar. 1916, 3 Apr. 1916, 10 & 23 & 29 June 1916, and 'The Preliminary Ballot', 14 Aug. 1916.
429   'I was sick from powerlessness', wrote the Australian artist and soldier, James Stuart MacDonald. He described his reaction in these terms when he witnessed Australian officers commandeer a lawn tennis court behind the lines in June 1918, by putting up a sign 'FOR OFFICERS ONLY', and loudly telling ordinary soldiers to keep away. J.S. MacDonald to his wife, 14 June 1918, James Stuart MacDonald letters, MLMSS 2874 (Mitchell Library).
430   Aldington, *Death of a Hero*, 294.
431   'Helping the Enemy', editorial, *The Times*, 1 Oct. 1914.
432   David Marquand, *Ramsay MacDonald* (London, 1977), Chs 9-10.
433   HC Deb 24 May 1916 vol 82 cc2189-2198.
434   For example, 'Feeling of Humiliation', *Daily Standard* [Brisbane], 9 Aug. 1916, 'Ramsay MacDonald and W.M. Hughes', *Daily Standard* [Brisbane], 12 Sept. 1916 (letter dated 20 Apr. 1916), *The Socialist* [Melbourne], 18 Aug. 1916, *The Catholic Press*, 12 Oct. 1916. Philip Snowden sent a similar letter; 'Message to Australians', *Bendigo Independent*, 24 Oct. 1916.
435   'Hocusser Hughes', *Truth* [Perth], 12 Aug. 1916.
436   'Australia's Re-Action: British Laborites Humiliated', *Barrier Daily Truth*, 16 Aug. 1916. See also J.R. MacDonald, 'Open Letter to a Conscientious Objector', *Barrier Daily Truth*, 3 Oct. 1916, but Ryan could not have seen this before he wrote his own letter to MacDonald.
437   Morrow, *Iron in the Fire*, 48.
438   See Major Newman's question to Mr Tennant, HC Deb 27 June 1916 vol 83 cc708-9, and Mr Nield's question to Mr Forster, HC Deb 09 November 1916 vol 87 cc425-6W.
439   HC Deb 18 July 1916 vol 84 c. 858.
440   'Soldiers' letters to M. P.'s', *Common Sense*, 10 Nov. 1917, records complaints from six MPs.
441   'Personal Message from General Birdwood to Members of the A.I.F', in 'Message re Referendum', Birdwood Papers, AWM 3DRL/3376 13/2 (Australian War Memorial). The words capitalised are in the original.
442   Hughes, 'Manifesto to Australian Soldiers', in 'Message re Referendum', Birdwood Papers, AWM 3DRL/3376 13/2.
443   Montague, *Disenchantment*, 53.
444   'No Patched-Up Peace', *The Times*, 12 Oct. 1916.
445   For example, see Macdonald's speech, HC Deb 24 May 1916 vol 82 cc2188-2197.
446   'Mr Ramsay MacDonald and his Golf Club', *Manchester Guardian*, 31 Aug. 1914, 'Mr Ramsay MacDonald and the Moray Golf Club', *Aberdeen Journal*, 2 Sept. 1914.
447   'Heroes of Pozières', *Daily Mail*, 31 Aug. 1916. The postcard is available at Museums Victoria, at Items MM 90948 and ST 39405. See also 'The Daily Mail: War Postcards', *Daily Mail*, 7 Sept. 1916.

448	The original photograph can be seen at AWM EZ0003. The AWM caption explains that the men were 'newly arrived in Flanders' and had 'newly issued steel helmets' and one man from the 26th Battalion is identified. The 26th Battalion arrived in France on 21 March 1916 and into the trenches on 12 April. See 26th Battalion, War Diary, Mar. & Apr. 1916, AWM4, 23/43/8-9, and 6th Brigade, War Diary, July 1916, AWM4, 23/6/11.
449	Montague, *Disenchantment*, Ch. VIII.
450	For example, Charles Buxton, 'Peace This Autumn', *The UDC*, Sept. 1916.
451	'Mr Lloyd George as Singer: Welsh Instead of German Hymn Tunes', *Daily Mail*, 19 Aug. 1916.
452	For example, Henry Boote, 'A Challenge to Mr Hughes', *Australian Worker*, 21 Sept. 1916.
453	E.J. Ryan to Ramsay MacDonald, 18 Oct. 1916, MacDonald Papers, TNA: PRO/30/69/1160 f. 108. Underlining in original.
454	HC Deb 30 July 1917 vol 96 cc1797-8.
455	HC Deb 12 February 1917 vol 90 cc339-50, HC Deb 20 February 1917 vol 90 cc1244-9, HC Deb 26 July 1917 vol 96 cc1480-1496, and Ramsay Macdonald, 'The Big Push', *The UDC*, Oct. 1916.
456	Ramsay MacDonald, Diary, 21 and 24 Dec. 1916, MacDonald Papers, TNA: PRO/30/69/1753.
457	See MacDonald Diary, 27 Feb. 1918, MacDonald Papers, PRO 30/69/1953 and Gerard J. De Groot, *Blighty: British Society in the Era of the Great War* (London, 1996), 166, Taylor Downing, *Breakdown: The Crisis of Shell Shock on the Somme, 1916* (London, 2016), 89-91.
458	Lord Lansdowne, untitled Cabinet Memorandum, 13 Nov. 1916, TNA: CAB 37/159/32.
459	Jack Tarrant to Una, 11 Nov. 1916, courtesy of Graeme and Trish Sawyer, also available in John George Tarrant Correspondence, 1914-1918, State Library of Queensland, SLQ Box 16045.
460	Jack Tarrant to Cissy, 8 Dec. 1916, Tarrant Correspondence.
461	Sergeant Jack Lockett, interviewed by Peter Rubinstein, 22 Jan. 1997, Sound item, S03435.
462	George Horan to his father, 23 Feb. 1917, George Horan Papers, MLMSS 1468/Item 2 (Mitchell Library).
463	Stanley William Nixon, interview, 1976, OH4103/6 (State Library of Western Australia).
464	Murray Goot, 'The Results of the 1916 and 1917 Conscription Referendums Re-examined', in Archer, et al. (eds), *Conscription Conflict*, 131-2, 111.
465	Paul Adams, 'Labor's Volunteer Army: The Fight Against the 1916 Conscription Referendum in Broken Hill', *Australian Folklore*, 22 (2007), 121, 133.
466	Outhwaite, cited in CID intelligence report on an anti-war meeting held at the Caxton Hall, London, 7 Dec. 1916, TNA: HO144/1459/316786/2. I am grateful to Duncan Marlor for this reference.
467	For example, see Snowden's question, HC Deb 16 November 1916 vol 87 c979979.
468	'Russia and the Dardanelles', *Daily Mail*, 4 Dec. 1916, and 'Victory at All Costs: Russian Premier's Statement', *Times*, 4 Dec. 1916.
469	For example, 'What Russia Will Get', *Sydney Morning Herald*, 5 Dec. 1916, 'Constantinople's Future', *Argus*, 5 Dec. 1916, 'Russia and Constantinople', *Age*, 5. Dec. 1916.
470	'Misconceptions in Russia', *Sydney Morning Herald*, 5 Dec. 1916.
471	*CPD*, 28 Feb. 1917, 10721.
472	Edgar Morrow, undated letter [Oct. 1916] quoted in Morrow, *Iron in the Fire*, 51.
473	Eric Abraham, interviewed 25 Jan. 2000, Australians at War Film Archive, Archive number 2541.
474	Albert Charles Linton, interviewed by Alistair Thomson, 12 June 1983, Sound item S01318 (AWM).
475	Jim Waddell, 'From Federation to Armistice: The Earliest Army Legal Officers', in Bruce Oswald and Jim Waddell, *Justice in Arms: Military Lawyers in the Australian Army's First Hundred Years* (Newport, 2014), 11. Lieutenant Harry E. Shaw would have a very bumpy experience himself in the army in the years that followed; he was found guilty at courts martial for various crimes in 1916 and 1917, including being drunk and striking two superior officers. He was finally declared 'unfit for general service' in February 1918. See Harry Edmund Shaw, Lieutenant, NAA: B2455.
476	Jabez Waterhouse to his father, 23 Jan. and 4 Feb. 1917, MLMSS 2792 (K 21692/Folder 17) (Mitchell Library).

477 Jeremiah Tarrant, to Cis, 15 Feb. 1917, Tarrant Correspondence.
478 Roger Beckett, 'The Australian Soldier in Britain, 1914-1918', in Carl Bridge, Robert Crawford, and David Dunstan (eds), *Australians in Britain: The Twentieth Century Experience* (Melbourne, 2009), Ch. 6, especially Table 6.2.
479 Konrad H. Jarausch, *The Enigmatic Chancellor: Bethmann Hollweg and the Hubris of Imperial Germany* (New Haven, 1973), 253.
480 'Proposals for Peace Negotiation Made by Germany, 12 Dec. 1916', and 'Note of the German Government to the Vatican Regarding the Peace Proposals', 12 Dec. 1916, in Scott (ed), *Official Statements of War Aims and Peace Proposals*, 2-5.
481 Wolfgang Steglich, *Bündnisscherung oder Verständigungsfrieden. Untersuchungen zu dem Friedensangebot der Mittelmächte von 12. Dezember 1916* (Göttingen, 1958), 183.
482 Hans Gatzke, *Germany's Drive to the West: A Study of Germany's Western War Aims during the First World War* (Baltimore, 1966), 161-9. For example, see Zimmermann's confession, in Gerhard Ritter, *The Sword and Scepter: The Problem of Militarism in Germany, Vol. III, The Tragedy of Statesmanship – Bethmann Hollweg as War Chancellor (1914-1917)* (Coral Gables, 1972), 290.
483 W.H. van der Linden, *The International Peace Movement during the First World War* (Almere, 2006), 409, and Jarausch, *Enigmatic Chancellor*, 250.
484 Evidence of Baron von Romberg, in *Official German Documents relating to the World War, Vol. 1: The Reports of the First and Second Sub-committees of the Committee appointed by the National Constituent Assembly to inquire into responsibility for the war, together with the stenographic minutes of the Second Subcommittee and Supplements thereto* (New York, 1923), 181, 184.
485 'Speech of Premier Briand on the Peace Proposals in the French Chamber of Deputies, 13 Dec. 1916', in Scott (ed), *Official Statements of War Aims and Peace Proposals*, 7-8.
486 'Speech of Nicholas Pokrovsky, Russian Minister of Foreign Affairs, in the Duma, 15 Dec. 1916', and 'Resolution of the Russian Duma Against Acceptance of the German Peace Proposals, 15 Dec. 1916', in Scott (ed), *Official Statements of War Aims and Peace Proposals*, 9-11.
487 Maurice Paleologue, *An Ambassador's Memoirs* (London, 1923), 718-9.
488 'Speech of Baron Sonnino, Italian Minister for Foreign Affairs, in the Chamber of Deputies, 18 Dec. 1916', in Scott (ed), *Official Statements of War Aims and Peace Proposals*, 12.
489 J. McEwen, 'The Struggle for Mastery in Britain: Lloyd George versus Asquith, December 1916', *Journal of British Studies*, XVIII (1978), 131-156
490 For example, Lord Bertie to Hardinge, 16 and 20 Dec. 1916, Hardinge Papers 28 (Cambridge University Library).
491 Zeman, *Diplomatic History*, 118.
492 Lawrence W. Martin, *Peace Without Victory: Woodrow Wilson and the British Liberals* (New Haven, 1958).
493 'An Appeal for a Statement of War Aims', 18 Dec. 1916, in Arthur Link (ed), *The Papers of Woodrow Wilson*, Vol. 40 (Princeton, 1982), 273-6.
494 HC Deb 19 December 1916 vol 88 c1334.
495 Curzon, 'Registration and military service', 21 June 1915, quoted by David French, 'The Meaning of Attrition, 1914-1916', *English Historical Review*, 103, 407 (Apr. 1988), 398.
496 H.W. Massingham to Lloyd George, 22 Dec. 1916, Massingham Papers, MC 41/87 (Norfolk Record Office).
497 H.W. Massingham to Lloyd George, 25 Dec. 1916, Massingham Papers, MC 41/87.
498 For example, 'Our Unbeaten Army', *Aberdeen Journal*, 5 Oct. 1916, and see Richard Holt, in the House of Commons, HC Deb 11 October 1916 vol 86 c131.
499 House to Wilson 15 and 16 Jan. 1917, in Link (ed), *The Papers of Woodrow Wilson*, Vol. 40, 478 and 493.
500 *CPD*, 13 Dec. 1916, 9714.
501 *CPD*, 14 Dec. 1916, 9928.
502 'Australian Opinion on Peace Proposals', *Anzac Bulletin*, 20 Dec. 1916. Italics added.
503 'Famous War Phrases', *Anzac Bulletin*, 27 Dec. 1916.
504 *CPD*, 20 Dec. 1916, 10283.
505 Neville Meaney, *Australia and World Crisis, 1914-1923* (Sydney, 2009), 44, 59, and 247-8.

506 *CPD*, 8 Feb. 1917, 10324.
507 'Motives!', *Australian Worker*, 4 Jan. 1917.
508 For example, 'Peace on Earth', 14, 15 Dec. 1916, and 'The Peace Proposals', 22, 23, 24, 25, 29 Dec. 1916, and 'Peace in the Air', *Barrier Daily Truth*, 30 Dec. 1916.
509 'The Soldiers' Vote', *Barrier Daily Truth*, 28, 30 Dec. 1916.
510 Arthur G. Thomas to his family, 21 Sept., 6 and 26 Nov., 1916, 1 and 29 Jan. 1917. AWM 3DRL/2206. The words capitalised are in the original.
511 Barwick, Diary, 1 July 1916, MLMSS 1493/Box 1/Item 3.
512 Barwick, Diary, 11 and 18 Dec. 1916, MLMSS 1493/Box 1/Item 7.
513 David Davies, handwritten memo 'The German Peace Proposals', Dec. 1916, David Davies Papers, C. 4/1 (National Library of Wales).
514 Rothwell, summarising Guy Locock to Hankey, 16 Dec. 1916, Lloyd George Papers, F/60/2/2, cited by V.H. Rothwell, *British War Aims and Peace Diplomacy 1914-1918* (Oxford, 1971), 61.
515 E. Drummond to Lloyd George, 15 Dec. 1916, enclosing E. Drummond, 'German Peace Proposals', 14 Dec. 1916, FO 800/197/97-8 and 101-2.
516 Vera Brittain, *Testament of Youth* (London, 1933), 461.
517 Grey of Fallodon, *Twenty Five Years* (London, 1928), Vol. II, 132.
518 Arthur G. Thomas to his family, 30 Mar. 1917, AWM 3DRL/2206.
519 Adams, *Brookfield*, 88, 104, and Chs 2-7.
520 For example, 'Beauty and the Anzacs', *Pall Mall Gazette* [London], 25 Aug. 1916, 'Anzac Marriage Rush', *Daily Mail* [London] 13 Oct. 1916. It is estimated that 20,000 wives fiancées and children of Australian troops and munitions workers were returned to Australia during 1919. See Ekins, 'Australians at the end of the Great War', 177.
521 'Record of the Declaration of a Court of Inquiry', 16 Feb. 1917, in RYAN Edward J. (Private): Service Number – 4635 : Unit – 51st Battalion, Australian Imperial Force : Date of Court Martial – 9 April 1917, NAA: A471, 19556.
522 'Private E.J. Ryan', *Barrier Miner*, 31 Dec. 1916.
523 For example, William Stewart, 'Travels in Scotland', *Forward* [Glasgow], and 'It Grows', *Forward* [Glasgow] 9 Mar. 1918.
524 'Scottish Notes', *Daily Herald*, 3 Feb. 1917.
525 'Food Prices Protest Meeting', *Montrose, Arbroath and Brechin Review*, 20 Oct. 1916.
526 'Socialist War Points', *Forward* [Glasgow], 18 Nov. 1916, and 'Remarkable Speech on War Debt', *Forward* [Glasgow], 11 Nov. 1916.
527 'Entente Reply to President Wilson, January 10, 1917', in Scott, *Official Statements of War Aims and Peace Proposals*, 35-38.
528 David Stevenson, *French War Aims Against Germany, 1914-1919* (Oxford, 1982), 48-51.
529 William Roger Louis, *Great Britain and Germany's Lost Colonies, 1914-1919* (Oxford, 1967), 70- 3, Erik Goldstein, *Winning the Peace: British Diplomatic Strategy, Peace Planning, and the Paris Peace Conference 1916-1920* (Oxford, 1991), 14.
530 'An Address to the Senate', 22 Jan. 1917, in Arthur Link, ed. *The Papers of Woodrow Wilson*, Vol. 40, 1916-1917 (Princeton, 1982), 533-539.
531 The best account is Kazin, *War Against War*, Ch. 4.
532 RYAN Edward J. (Private): Service Number – 4635 : Unit – 51st Battalion, Australian Imperial Force : Date of Court Martial – 9 April 1917, NAA: A471, 19556.
533 An undated letter from early 1916 from the Deputy Adjutant and Quartermaster General I Anzac Corps, quoted in Graham Wilson, *Accommodating the King's Hard Bargain: Military Detention in the Australian Army 1914-1947* (Newport, 2016), 147.
534 The most complete history is E.N. Burdzhalov, *Russia's Second Revolution: The February 1917 Uprising in Petrograd* (Bloomington, 1987).
535 For example, Lloyd George expressed the conviction that the new Russian government had been formed with the express purpose of carrying on the war 'with increased vigour'. *HC Deb 19 March 1917 vol 91 cc1536-8*. Moving a formal motion of congratulation to the Duma, Bonar Law also spoke of his 'feeling of compassion for the late Czar.' *HC Deb 22 March 1917 vol 91 cc2085-94*.
536 On the death penalty: *HC Deb 04 April 1917 vol 92 c1278*. On Ireland: *HC Deb 22 March 1917 vol 91 cc2024-5*.

537 Stevenson, *French War Aims*, 52-6.
538 Ian Nish, *Alliance in Decline: A Study of Anglo-Japanese Relations 1908-1923* (Oxford, 1972), Ch. XI.
539 'An Address to a Joint Session of Congress', 2 Apr. 1917, Arthur Link (ed), *Papers of Woodrow Wilson* (Princeton, 1983), Vol. 41, 525.
540 The best survey is H.C. Peterson and Gilbert C. Fite, *Opponents of War, 1917-1918* (Madison, 1957).
541 Michael S. Neiberg, *The Path to War: How the First World War Created Modern America* (Oxford 2016), 99.
542 For example, see the speeches by Senators George Norris and Robert La Follette in the US Senate on 4 Apr. 1917, *Congressional Record*, 65 Cong., 1 Sess., 212-214 and 223-236, the contemporary pamphlet, Scott Nearing, *The Great Madness* (1917) and John Milton Cooper, 'The Command of Gold Reversed: American Loans to Britain, 1915-1917', *Pacific Historical Review*, 45, 2 (May 1976), 209-230, Stuart D. Brandes, *Warhogs: A History of War Profits in America* (Lexington, 1997), and Hugh Rockoff, 'Until It's Over, Over There: the U.S. Economy in World War I', in Stephen Broadberry and Mark Harrison, *The Economics of World War I* (Cambridge, 2005), 310-343.
543 RYAN Edward J. (Private): Service Number – 4635: Unit – 51st Battalion, Australian Imperial Force: Date of Court Martial – 9 April 1917. NAA: A471, 19556.
544 *Manual of Military Law*, (Ch. II, para. 2), 6. The *Manual of Military Law* suggested that, in order to crush a spate of offending, sometimes 'an example may be necessary' and officers had to consider 'the effect to be produced on the military body to which the offender belongs, rather than in reference to the act of the individual himself', (Ch. V, para. 85), 50. Similarly, *King's Regulations* contemplated the possibility that the 'state of discipline' might create a situation that 'renders a serious example expedient', *King's Regulations*, (para. 552), 125.
545 The Adjutant General's Branch, *Circular Memorandum on Courts Martial, for the Use of Convening and Staff Officers, and of Officers Giving Instructions on this Subject* (London, 1916), 5. A version of this pamphlet with the same title was printed in Melbourne by the Government Printer, no date.
546 In 1998, the High Court of Australia stressed the gulf between courts martial and civilian courts that had always existed: 'A court martial is not a court of law. Although it is obliged to dispense justice it has been held that it does not exercise the judicial power of the Commonwealth. It is a body constituted, ordinarily, by lay people. The participation of a member with legal training would be wholly accidental.' See *Hembury v Chief of the General Staff* (1998) 193 CLR 641; [1998] HCA 47 per Kirby J at para [72].
547 The offences and punishments are conveniently summarised in Wilson, *King's Hard Bargain*, Table 1, 54-60.
548 Among at least a dozen publications, see S.T. Banning, *Military Law Made Easy: with appendices of the examination papers, fully answered with references to the official books* (London, 1908) and Major R.L.C. Brooker, *Precis of Military Law and King's Regulations for Young Officers* (1917), noted by Diane Kaye De Bellis, 'Stories of Australian Deserters in World War 1', unpublished PhD thesis (University of South Australia, 2014), 89. The Adjutant General's Branch of the Staff, at British General Headquarters, produced various pamphlets, such as *Circular Memorandum on Courts Martial, for the Use of Convening and Staff Officers, and of Officers Giving Instructions on this Subject* (1916) and a later version in June 1917 written by Major Francis Seward Laskey, *Circular Memorandum on Courts-martial for Use on Active Service* (London, 1917). See also Wilson, *King's Hard Bargain*, 64-65.
549 Records for these officers are also available in the personnel files at NAA: B2455.
550 See Rule 87: 'An accused person may have a person to assist him during the trial, whether a legal adviser or any other person. A person so assisting him may advise him on all points and suggest the questions to be put to witnesses.' See also Rule 13 on procedures for the preparation of defence. War Office, *Manual of Military Law* (1914), 578 and 622. De Bellis, 'Australian Deserters', 94.

551	Lieut-Col J. Knox (Tidworth) to Judge Advocate General, London, 1 May 1917, in Court martial papers, Ryan, E.J. (Private), 9 Apr. 1917, NAA: A471, 19556.
552	Chris Roberts, *The Landing at Anzac 1915* (Sydney, 2015), 86.
553	Court martial papers, Ryan, E.J. (Private), 9 Apr. 1917, NAA: A471, 19556.
554	Sydney James Stutley, Diary, 7 Oct. 1916, MLMSS 3045/Item 2 (Mitchell Library).
555	Morrow, *Iron in the Fire*, 41.
556	Carsten, *War Against War*, 124-128, and Watson, *Ring of Steel*, 479.
557	From *Izvestiia*, Number 15, 28 Mar. 1917, reproduced in Alfred Golder (ed), *Documents of Russian History, 1914-1917* (New York, 1927), 325-6.
558	Scott, *Official Statements of War Aims and Peace Proposals*, 95-96.
559	See for example, 'Politics in Russia', *Barrier Daily Truth*, 30 Mar. 1917, and the many articles entitled 'Russia's Upheaval' and 'Russia's Rebirth' that appeared in its pages during July 1917.
560	Henry Richard MP, at a Liberal meeting at Merthyr, 10 Nov. 1885, in *South Wales Echo*, 11 Nov. 1885 and quoted in HC Deb 19 March 1886 vol 303 c1396. The words come originally from Charles Jeffreys and Charles William Glover, 'Jeannette's Song', c. 1848, from W.H. Eburne, *The Conscript's Vow* (Edinburgh, 1852); see John Gittings, *The Glorious Art of Peace: From the Iliad to Iraq* (Oxford, 2012), 123.
561	Manning, *Middle Parts of Fortune*, 202.
562	Cecil Tribe Knight, Major, NAA: B2455.
563	Service records for these officers are available at NAA: B2455.
564	Richard Blundell, Diary, 3 Sept. 1915, MLMSS 750 / Item 1 (Mitchell Library).
565	Court martial papers, Ryan, E.J. (Private), 22 May 1917, NAA: A471, 7299. Underlinings in the original.
566	Richard Blundell, Diary, 3 Sept. 1915, MLMSS 750/Item 1 (Mitchell Library).
567	Jabez Waterhouse to his father, 4 Feb. 1917, MLMSS 2792 (K 21692/Folder 17) (Mitchell Library).
568	Arthur Giles to J.C. Giles, 19 June 1918, MLMSS 1841 (Mitchell Library).
569	Under the *Army Act 1881* (UK), the District Court Martial had the power to sentence Ryan to a term of up to two years' imprisonment.
570	Court martial papers, Ryan, E.J. (Private), 22 May 1917, NAA: A471, 7299.
571	For example, James Stuart MacDonald to his wife, 14 Aug. 1918, MacDonald letters, MLMSS 2874 (Mitchell Library): 'Disappointment has turned this job into a hateful one ... The fraudulency of it all! The opportunity this militarism presents for putting pressure on one! The war won't be of any use unless it discredits it. I notice the growth of Prussianism in the army all along – a state of affairs foreign to the very principle of Australia.'
572	*Manual of Military Law* (1914), 18-20, Paragraphs 13 to 20 provide guidelines on 'Desertion, Fraudulent Enlistment, and absence without leave.' Paragraph 13: 'The criterion between desertion and absence without leave is *intention*.' Italics in original. The *Manual* offered examples in every direction. Paragraph 16: 'A man who absents himself in a deliberate or clandestine manner, with the view of shirking some important service, though he may intend to return when the evasion of service is accomplished, is liable to be convicted of desertion just as if an intention never to return had been proved against him. Thus if a man on the eve of the embarkation of his regiment for foreign service, or when called out to aid the civil power, conceals himself in barracks, the court will be quite justified in presuming an intention to escape the important service on which he was ordered and in convicting him of desertion.' Paragraph 19: 'The fact that a soldier surrenders is not proof by itself that he intended to return, even though he is in uniform at the time of surrender.' However, Paragraph 20 specified: 'In any case of doubt as to whether one or the other offence has been committed, the court should find the prisoner guilty of the less offence.'
573	Included with record of offences, Court martial papers, Ryan, E.J. (Private), 12 Sept. 1917, NAA: A471, 10237.
574	See 'Rules for Field Punishment' (under section 44 of the *Army Act 1881*), in *Manual of Military Law* (1914), 721.

575   Mottram, *Spanish Farm*, 627.
576   'No 1 Australian Command Depot', War Diary, May 1917, AWM4, 33/16/2.
577   See 'Records of No. 1 Command Depot relating to District Courts Martial, 1914-18 War', NAA: AWM221.
578   'No 1 Australian Command Depot', War Diary, May 1917, AWM4, 33/16/2.
579   *Police Gazette*, 6 Mar. 1917.
580   Appendix B, in 'Work of the Deputy Assistant Judge Advocate General's Department, 30 Apr. to 29 Oct., 1917', in 'A Staff, Headquarters AIF Depots in UK, Apr-Oct. 1917', War Diary, AWM4, 1/67/1.
581   Circular Memo. No 123, 9 Aug. 1917, in 'A Staff, Headquarters AIF Depots in UK, Apr-Oct. 1917', War Diary, Apr-Oct. 1917, AWM4, 1/67/1.
582   Item A, court martial papers, Ryan, E.J. (Private), 12 Sept. 1917, NAA: A471, 10237. Underling in original. Slightly amended to correct the grammar.
583   51st Battalion, Field Returns, 4 Aug. 1917, lists Ryan arriving on 29 July 1917, AWM25 861/9 Part 323.
584   Lieutenant-Colonel Thomas S. Louch, quoted in William Francis Westerman, 'Soldiers and Gentlemen: Australian Battalion Commanders in the Great War 1914-1918', unpublished PhD thesis (UNSW Canberra, 2014), 274-275, 307.
585   Blunden, *Undertones of War*, 25.
586   Esher to Derby, 31 May 1917 and Esher to Lloyd George, 31 May 1917, quoted in Keith Wilson, *A Study in the History and Politics of "The Morning Post"* (New York, 1990), 146.
587   Louis, *Lost Colonies*, 70- 3, D. Stevenson, *The First World War and International Politics* (Oxford, 1988), 112.
588   G. Smith, 'The British Government and the Disposition of the German Colonies in Africa', in P. Gifford and W. Louis (eds), *Britain and Germany in Africa* (New Haven, 1967), 288.
589   Chamberlain on 23 April 1917, quoted in Erik Goldstein, *Winning the Peace: British Diplomatic Strategy, Peace Planning, and the Paris Peace Conference, 1916-1920* (Oxford, 1991), and see Stevenson, *First World War and International Politics*, 112.
590   Rex Wade, *The Russian Search for Peace: February-October 1917* (Stanford, 1969), Ch. V.
591   Lord Newton, *Retrospection* (London, 1941), 236-40, John Yarnall, *Barbed Wire Disease: British and German Prisoners of War, 1914-1918* (Stroud, 2011), 162.
592   Wilhelm Ribhegge, *Frieden für Europa: Die Politik der deutschen Reichstagsmehrheit 1917/18* (Essen, 1988), 171-199.
593   Erzberger, quoted in K. Epstein, *Matthias Erzberger and the Dilemma of German Democracy* (New York, 1971), 190.
594   Jarausch, *Enigmatic Chancellor*, 373-378.
595   Erich Mathias and Rudolf Morsey, *Der Interfraktionelle Ausschuss 1917/18*, 2 vols. (Düsseldorf, 1959).
596   Hugenberg, quoted in Gordon A. Craig, *Germany 1866-1945* (Oxford, 1986), 364.
597   See the record of discussions at Kreuznach, in Gerald Feldman (ed), *German Imperialism, 1914-1918: The Development of a Historical Debate* (New York, 1972), 32-34, and Ottokar Czernin, *Out of the World War* (London, 1919), 157-159.
598   Neil Hollander, *Elusive Dove: The Search for Peace During World War I* (Jefferson, 2014), 165-9, John Williams, *Mutiny 1917* (London, 1962).
599   Rudolf Binion, *Defeated Leaders: The Political Fate of Caillaux, Jouvenel, and Tardieu* (New York, 1960), Ch. 6.
600   L.P. Morris, 'The Russians, the Allies and the War', *Slavonic and East European Review*, 50 (January 1972), 29-48, Wade, *Russian Search for Peace*, Chs IV and V, Michael Kettle, *The Allies and the Russian Collapse: March 1917-March 1918* (London, 1981), David Kirby, *War, Peace and Revolution: International Socialism at the Crossroads 1914-1918* (New York, 1986).
601   For example, 'Freedom's Greatest Fight', 5 July 1917, 'Russia's Rebirth', 10 July 1917, 'Germany's Peace Formula', and 'Germany's Internal Throes', 18 July 1917, 'Stockholm Peace Conference', 16 Aug. 1917, *Barrier Daily Truth*. On the prosecution of the editor, W.D. Barnett, see 'Militarist Set against the BDT', *Barrier Daily Truth*, 14 July 1917.
602   For example, see in the *Anzac Bulletin*, 'Peace without Victory' and 'Mr Hughes on the Trade War', 7 Feb. 1917, 'Mr Hughes on the Revolution in Russia', 21 Mar. 1917, 'Manifesto of

the Prime Minister of Australia: To Australian Soldiers on Active Service', 4 Apr. 1917, 'The Aims and Objects of the Ministerial Party' and 'Mr Hughes and Mr Ramsay MacDonald', 11 Apr. 1917, 'Mr Hughes on Pacifists', 20 June 1917, 'A Cunning Trap', 15 Aug. 1917.

603 Mottram, *Spanish Farm*, 379.
604 R.H. Mottram, *Ten Years Ago* (London, 1928), 76, and Arthur Graeme West's poem 'God! How I hate you, you young cheerful men', in Nigel Jones (ed), *Diary of a Dead Officer: Being the Posthumous Papers of Arthur Graeme West* (London, 2007), 148.
605 'Syllabus of Training for the week ending 1 Aug. 1917', in 51st Battalion War Diary, August 1917, AWM4, 23/68/18.
606 51st Battalion War Diary, August 1917, AWM4, 23/68/18.
607 Lindstrom, 'Psychological Casualties', 54, Downing, *Breakdown*, 216.
608 Wheen to his father, 22 Nov. 1916, *We Talked of Other Things*, 63.
609 Francis Weatherhead to his father, 5 Nov. 1918, Clampett, *My Dear Mother*, 224.
610 Blunden, *Undertones of War*, 82, 89, 205, 219.
611 Wheen to his father, 16 Dec. 1916, *We Talked of Other Things*, 67.
612 Guy Chapman, *A Passionate Prodigality* (Southampton, 1985, first published London, 1933), 59.
613 Mottram, *Spanish Farm*, 204, 353.
614 Dos Passos, *Three Soldiers*, 166, 176, 214, 224, 278, 288, 295, 349. The novel is autobiographical.
615 Mottram, *Spanish Farm*, 620.
616 Mary Agnes Hamilton, *Arthur Henderson: A Biography* (London, 1938), Ch. VII, J.M. Winter, 'Arthur Henderson, the Russian Revolution and the Reconstruction of the Labour Party', *Historical Journal*, 15, 4 (1972), 753-73.
617 'The Peace Proposals made by His Holiness the Pope to the Belligerent Powers on August 1, 1917', House of Commons Parliamentary Papers, Cmd. 261 (1919).
618 'The Pope's Peace Note to the Nations', *Freeman's Journal* [Sydney] 23 Aug. 1917, and 'Full Text of the Pope's Peace Note to Warring Powers', *The Catholic Press* [Sydney], 27 Sept. 1917.
619 Wilson to House, 21 July 1917, *Wilson Papers*, vol. 43, 236. 'England and France *have not the same views with regard to peace that we have by any means. When the war is over we can force them to our way of thinking, because by that time they will, among other things, be financially in our hands; but we cannot force them now.*' Italics in original.
620 André Tardieu, *France and America: Some Experiences in Cooperation* (New York, 1927), 234, quoted in Seymour (ed), *Intimate Papers*, Vol. III, 304.
621 'A Flag Day Address', 14 June 1917, *Wilson Papers*, vol. 42, 498-504.
622 'An Address in Buffalo to the American Federation of Labour', 12 Nov. 1917, *Wilson Papers*, vol. 45, 14.
623 'President Wilson's Reply to the Pope's Peace Note, August 27, 1917', in G. Lowes Dickinson (ed), *Documents and Statements relating to Peace Proposals and War Aims* (London, 1919), 550-52.
624 On the British reaction to the Pope's Note, see Wolfgang Steglich, 'Die Haltung der britischen Regierung zur päpstlichen Friedensaktion von 1917', in Wolfgang Steglich (ed), *Die Verhandlungen des 2. Unterausschusses des Parlamentarischen Untersuchungsausschusses über die päpstliche Friedensaktion von 1917* (Wiesbaden, 1974), 365-409, especially 396-7, and Minutes of the War Cabinet, 27 Aug. 1917, TNA: CAB 23 3/72.
625 'The German Chancellor's Reply to the Pope's Peace Note, September 19, 1917', in Dickinson, *Documents and Statements*, 53-55.
626 On the history of the Papal Peace Note, see Robert Althann, 'Papal Mediation during the First World War', *Studies* [Ireland], 61, 243 (1972), 219-240, Gatzke, *Germany's Drive to the West*, Ch. IV, Welch, *Germany, Propaganda and Total War*, Ch. 6. On the German position, see the introduction to Wolfgang Steglich (ed), *Der Friedensappell Papst Benedikts XV vom 1 August 1917 und die Mittelmächte* (Wiesbaden, 1970), 1-17.
627 Dos Passos, Diary, 23 Aug. 1917, in Ludington (ed), *Fourteenth Chronicle*, 92.
628 Frank H. Molony, Diary, 8 Oct. 1917, MLMSS 2883/Item 4 (Mitchell Library).

629 See the rules covering a Field General Court Martial, in *Manual of Military Law*, (para. 105-123), 631-636.
630 War Office, *Statistics of the Military Effort of the British Empire During the Great War 1914-1920* (London, 1922), 644.
631 *Statistics of the Military Effort*, Part XII, Discipline, 641-673.
632 Athol Lewis, Diary, 10 May 1918, Athol Hugh Lewis Papers, AWM: PR00897, Item 22.
633 Athol Lewis, Diary, 3 May 1918, Athol Hugh Lewis Papers, AWM: PR00897, Item 22.
634 *Manual of Military Law* (1914), containing the *Army Act 1881*, showing Section 12 (1), regarding desertion, and Section 189 providing a definition of 'on active service', 390 and 553.
635 Court martial papers, Ryan, E.J. (Private), 12 Sept. 1917, NAA: A471, 10237. Incidentally, these papers are half the length of those of Ryan's District Court Martial at Perham Down, showing that the procedures of a Field General Court Martial were of a summary nature by comparison.
636 These words were underlined in blue by Ryan's prosecutors.
637 Item A, court martial papers, Ryan, E.J. (Private), 12 Sept. 1917, NAA: A471, 10237. Underlining in original.
638 See Laila Ellmoos, 'Historical Overview', and Lucy Taksa, 'The Great Strike and Its Impact', in Laila Ellmoos and Nina Miall (eds), *1917: The Great Strike* (Sydney, 2017), 14-24.
639 Ellmoos and Miall (eds), *1917, The Great Strike*, 39.
640 For surveys of the rising opposition to war in Australia see Robert Bollard, *In the Shadow of Gallipoli: The Hidden History of Australia in World War I* (Sydney, 2013) and Verity Burgmann, *Revolutionary Industrial Unionism: the Industrial Workers of the World in Australia* (Cambridge, 1995).
641 For surveys, see Carsten, *War Against War*, Kirby, *War, Peace and Revolution* and David Stevenson, *1917: War, Peace, and Revolution* (Oxford, 2017).
642 For samples from the *Barrier Daily Truth*, see 'Let There Be Peace: the Voice from the Vatican', 17 Aug. 1917, 'Pope's Peace Proposals', 21 Aug. 1917, 'The Great Strike', 22 Aug. 1917, 'Stockholm Peace Conference', 23 Aug. 1917, 'Why Men Strike', 27 and 29 Aug. 1917, 'Mightier than the Sword', 31 Aug. 1917.
643 Henry Williamson, *The Patriot's Progress* (Stroud, 1999, first published London, 1930), 91.
644 Wilson, *King's Hard Bargain*, 66. Edward John Garstang, 'Crime and Punishment on the Western Front: the Australian Imperial Force and British Army Discipline', unpublished PhD Thesis, Murdoch University, 2009, 28, establishes that of these 121 death sentences, 117 were handed down in France.
645 Court martial papers, Ryan, E.J. (Private), 12 Sept. 1917, NAA: A471, 10237.
646 Birdwood to Pearce, 22 May 1917, Birdwood Papers, Series 7, Letters to Pearce, 3 DRL/3376 (AWM).
647 Garstang, 'Crime and Punishment', 24.
648 Sir Charles Rosenthal, Diary, 4 July 1917, MLMSS 2739/vol.1 (Mitchell Library).
649 Rosenthal told American journalists in London: 'The Australian Army was the only force which, unfortunately, had not the death penalty, and, therefore had an unenviable record of desertions.' 'Australia's Army', *Barrier Miner*, 6 Nov. 1918.
650 E. Brissenden to Mr Justice Ferguson, 11 Sept. 1917, Sir David Gilbert Ferguson Correspondence, MLMSS 2858/Box 1/Folder 5 (Mitchell Library).
651 Quoted from a letter of A.W. Hyman to C.E.W. Bean, 3 Jan. 1939, in Oswald and Waddell (eds), *Justice in Arms*, 30.
652 *Defence Act 1903* (Cth), italics added.
653 Aaron Pegram, *Surviving the Great War: Australian Prisoners of War on the Western Front, 1916-1918* (Cambridge, 2020), 20, 83. Pegram establishes that, of the 3,400 Australians charged with desertion, none was found guilty of desertion to the enemy, and only two probable cases were identified but not prosecuted.
654 Under the British *Army Act 1881*, the 'sentence' of death at any court martial, British or Australian, was deemed 'not to be valid' until the 'confirming authority', the GOC, promulgated it.
655 De Bellis, 'Australian Deserters', 76.

656 The pioneering work on this topic is Richard Glenister, 'Desertion Without Execution: Decisions that saved Australian Imperial Force deserters from the firing squad in World War I', unpublished Honours thesis (La Trobe University, 1984).
657 Hughes on the War Precautions Bill No. 2, *CPD*, 23 Apr. 1915, 2625.
658 R.N. Barber, 'The Labor Party and the Abolition of Capital Punishment in Queensland, 1899-1922', *Queensland Heritage*, 1, 9 (Nov. 1968). For example, see 'Abolishing Capital Punishment'.
659 Will Ellsworth-Jones, *We Will Not Fight: The Untold Story of World War One's Conscientious Objectors* (London, 2008), Chs 10 to 13. On death sentences for conscripted men, see 'A Boon for the Brute', *Australian Worker* (Sydney), 6 July 1916.
660 Pearce to Fisher, 21 Nov. 1916, quoted in Glenister, 'Desertion without Execution', 53.
661 For example, 'Decypher of Cablegram from the Secretary of State for the Colonies', 3 Feb. 1917, and the representations from Lieut-General A.J. Godley (6 July 1917), General Hubert Gough (2 March 1917), Field Marshal Douglas Haig (24 Jan. 1917), H.C. Holman (7 Feb. 1917), G.H. Fowke (23 Feb. 1917), Lieut-General William Birdwood (11 Dec. 1916), General Henry Rawlinson (7 Jan. 1917), and Lieut-General William Birdwood to Secretary Department of Defence, Melbourne, 18 July 1917, in 'Application of Death Penalty in the AIF', NAA: MP367/1, 403/8/354.
662 Robert Garran, 'Opinion' on 'Application of Imperial Army Act to Australian Imperial Force', 7 June 1917, and Cabinet Minute, 25 July 1917, in the name of Minister for Defence (Senator George Pearce), in NAA: A6006, 1917/7/25, both reproduced in De Bellis, Appendix B to 'Australian Deserters'.
663 Michael Kettle, *The Allies and the Russian Collapse: March 1917-March 1918* (London, 1981), 76.
664 'Decipher of cablegram received from Secretary of State for the Colonies dated London, 23rd August 1917, 12.55pm', in 'Application of Death Penalty in the AIF', NAA: MP367/1, 403/8/35.
665 Pearce to Birdwood, 20 Sept. 1917, in Glenister, 'Desertion Without Execution', 53.
666 Monash to his wife, 19 July 1917, in War Letters of General Monash, Vol. 2, Monash Papers, 3DRL/2316 (AWM), and Glenister, 'Desertion Without Execution', 28 and Appendix B.
667 A.W. Ralston to Healey, 24 Nov. 1917, in Ralston Family Correspondence, 1891-1935. MLMSS 1713/Item 1 (Mitchell Library).
668 Barwick, Diary, 24 Oct. 1917, MLMSS 1493/Box 2/Item 11.
669 See anonymous letters to Pearce dated 16 Dec. 1917, citing a returned soldier warning an anti-conscription public meeting about the death penalty at the front, in the file 'Application of Death Penalty in the AIF', NAA: MP367/1, 403/8/35.
670 Acting Prime Minister William Watt, *CPD*, 26 Sept. 1918, 6429. Italics added.
671 Garstang, 'Crime and Punishment', 15, 28.
672 See William Finlayson, *CPD*, 26 June 1918, 6440.
673 For example, this was reaffirmed in Lieutenant General G.H. Fowke, 'Courts Martial on Members of the Australian Imperial Force', 23 Sept. 1918, AWM27, 363/28.
674 'Circular Memorandum: Courts-Martial – Defence of Accused in cases which may involve and award of the death penalty', 11 Mar. 1918, AWM27, 363/28.
675 Edwin Corboy, *CPD*, 22 Nov. 1918, 8253.
676 Edwin Corboy, *CPD*, 22 Nov. 1918, 8254.
677 Glenister, 'Desertion Without Execution', 57, 59.
678 Minutes of the War Cabinet, 24 Sept. 1917, TNA: CAB 23/16/2.
679 Minutes of the War Cabinet, 27 Sept. 1917, TNA: CAB 23/16/2. Underlining in original.
680 Minutes of the War Cabinet, 28 Sept. 1917, TNA: CAB 23/4/15.
681 On the Kühlmann affair, see the introduction to Wolfgang Steglich (ed), *Der Friedensappell Papst Benedikts XV vom 1 August 1917 und die Mittelmächte* (Wiesbaden, 1970), 1-17, Wolfgang Steglich (ed), *Die Friedensversuche der kriegführenden Mächte im Sommer und Herbst 1917* (Stuttgart, 1984), LIX-XCIII, David Woodward, 'David Lloyd George, a Negotiated Peace with Germany, and the Kühlmann Peace Kite of September 1917', *Canadian Journal of History*, 6, 1 (1971), 75-93, and David Stevenson, *1917: War, Peace, and Revolution* (Oxford, 2017), 261-267.
682 Jane Beaumont, *Broken Nation: Australians in the Great War* (Crows Nest, 2013), 362.

683   Frank H. Molony, Diary, 13 Sept. 1916, MLMSS 2883/Item 1 (Mitchell Library).
684   Australian Corps Reinforcement Camp, War Diary, Aug. 1916-Nov. 1917, AWM4, 33/2/1.
685   David Johnson, *Executed at Dawn: British Firing Squads on the Western Front 1914-1918* (Stroud, 2015), 35-7. Gerard Oram, '"What alternative punishment is there?" Military Executions During World War I.' Unpublished thesis (Open University, 2000), 174-5.
686   'The Death Penalty and AIF', *Anzac Bulletin*, 15 Aug. 1917.
687   Edward Luders, Diary, 21 Oct. 1916, MLMSS 3045/Item 2 (Mitchell Library).
688   Oram, 'Military Executions During World War I', 14.
689   A.R.L. Wiltshire, Diary, 27 Jan. 1916, MLMSS 3058/Box 1/Item 4 (Mitchell Library).
690   'Statement of Service', Private Edward James Ryan, Service Number 4635, NAA: B2455.
691   Court martial papers, Ryan, E.J. (Private), 12 Sept. 1917, NAA: A471, 10237.
692   Garstang, 'Crime and Punishment', 24.
693   Garstang, 'Crime and Punishment', 28. The statistics are from Glenister, 'Desertion Without Execution', Figure 1, 24-5. Adding in courts martial for desertion from camps in Australia pushes the totals even higher: 657 in 1916, 1,400 in 1917, and 1,887 in 1918.
694   Lansdowne, 'The Co-ordination of Allied War Aims', *Daily Telegraph* [London], 29 Nov. 1917.
695   Gerhard Ritter, *The Sword and the Scepter: the Problem of Militarism in Germany*, Vol. IV (Coral Gables, 1973), Ch. 5, and Eberhard Demm, 'Une Initiative de Paix Avortée: Lord Lansdowne et le Prince Max de Bade', *Guerres Mondiales et Conflits Contemporains*, 40, 159 (1990), 5-19.
696   'Mr Hughes on Lord Lansdowne', *Anzac Bulletin*, 7 Dec. 1917.
697   Douglas Newton, 'The Lansdowne "Peace Letter" of 1917 and the Prospect of Peace by Negotiation with Germany', *Australian Journal of Politics and History*, 48, 1 (2002), pp. 16-39.
698   John Simon to Herbert Samuel, 28 Dec.1917, Samuel Papers, A/155/V/6 (Parliamentary Archives).
699   G.S. Payne to Francis Hirst, 7 Apr. 1918, Hirst Papers (Bodleian Library, Oxford).
700   'The Wansbeck Election: Near Win for Labour and Peace', *Labour Leader*, 6 June 1918. At by-elections where peace-by-negotiation candidates stood, the results were 15% at Ayrshire North (11 October 1916), 23% at Rossendale (13 February 1917), 7% at Stockton-On-Tees (20 March 1917), 6.5% at Aberdeen South, 32.5% at Keighley (26 April 1918), and 47.5% at Wansbeck (28 May 1918). I thank Duncan Marlor for research on these by-elections.
701   Barwick, Diary, 1 Dec. 1916, MLMSS 1493/Box 1/Item 7.
702   Barwick, Diary, 27 Dec. 1917, MLMSS 1493/Box 2/Item 11.
703   Arthur G. Thomas to his family, 30 Aug. 1917, 29 Jan., 4 Feb. 1918, AWM 3DRL/2206.
704   Blunden, *Undertones of War*, 206.
705   Harry Percival Sennett, interviewed 13 Sept. 1990, Sound item S01686 (AWM).
706   Garth C. Ballantyne, in H.E. Holland, M.P., *Armageddon or Calvary: the conscientious objectors of New Zealand and the process of their conversion* (Brooklyn, 1919), 95-104.
707   Price listed his place of punishment as 'No. 5 Military Prison, Les Attaques'. See Robert Price, in Peter Brock (ed), *'These Strange Criminals': An Anthology of Prison Memoirs by Conscientious Objectors* (Toronto, 2004), 85-6.
708   Gunner Henry Percival Sennett (20199), interviewed 13 Sept. 1990, Sound item S01686 (AWM).
709   Garstang, 'Crime and Punishment', Ch. 6, HC Deb 06 June 1919 vol 116 c2427W.
710   HC Deb 26 May 1919 vol 116 cc822-3 and HC Deb 12 May 1919 vol 115 cc1336-7.
711   Garstang, 'Crime and Punishment', Ch. 6, based on documents in AWM10, 4304/7/60.
712   Ribhegge, *Frieden für Europa*, 201-249.
713   Ritter, *Sword and the Scepter*, Vol. IV, Ch. 2, Watson, *Ring of Steel*, Ch. 12, J. Wheeler Bennett, *Brest-Litovsk: The Forgotten Peace, March 1918* (New York, 1938).
714   'Trotzky Bares Russia's Compacts', *New York Times*, 25 Nov. 1917.
715   Michael Wreszin, *Oswald Garrison Villard, Pacifist at War* (Bloomington, 1965), 84. The New York *Evening Post* published texts of the secret treaties on 25, 26, 28 Jan. and 2 Mar. 1918.
716   'Russia and Secret Treaties: Terms Published', *Manchester Guardian*, 26 Nov. 1917.
717   'The Russian "Secret Documents": Full Text', *Manchester Guardian*, 12 Dec. 1917.
718   David Lloyd George, *British War Aims: Statement by the Right Honourable David Lloyd George, January Fifth, Nineteen Hundred and Eighteen* (New York, 1918).

719	Woodrow Wilson, 'An Address to a Joint Session of Congress', in Link (ed) *Papers of Woodrow Wilson*, Vol. 45 (Princeton, 1984), 534-9.
720	Supreme War Council, Minutes, 'Procés-Verbal', 2 Feb. 1918, in TNA: CAB 25/120, 306.
721	'Supreme War Council', *The Times*, 4 Feb. 1918, and David F. Trask, *The United States in the Supreme War Council: American War Aims and Inter-allied Strategy, 1917-1918* (Middletown, 1961), 48.
722	See Tamara Griesser-Pe ar, *Die Mission Sixtus: Österreichs Friedenversuch im Ersten Weltkrieg* (Wien, 1988), Elisabeth Kovács, *Untergang oder Rettung der Donaumonarchie? Band 1: Die Österreichische Frage: Kaiser und König Karl I. (IV.) und Die Neuordnung Mitteleuropas* (1916-1922) (Wien, 2004), and Elisabeth Kovács, *Untergang oder Rettung der Donaumonarchie? Politische Dokumente aus internationalen Archiven* (Wien, 2004), and James and Joanna Bogle, *A Heart for Europe* (Leominster, 1990).
723	Steglich (ed), *Die Friedensversuche*, XIV-XXXVIII, and 1-93.
724	Olivier Lahaie, *La guerre secrete en Suisse (1914-1918): Espionage, propaganda et influence en pays neuter pendant la Grande Guerre. Tome 2: 1916-1917* (Paris, 2017) 367-372.
725	Steglich (ed), *Die Friedensversuche*, XXXVIII-XLVII.
726	Balfour to Townley, 8 Oct. 1917, in Steglich (ed), *Die Friedensversuche*, 219, and XCIII-CVIII.
727	Smuts, 'Conversations with Count Mensdorff', 20 Dec. 1917, in Steglich (ed), *Die Friedensversuche*, 314, and CVIII-CXXVIII.
728	Wilfred Fest, *Peace or Partition: the Habsburg Monarchy and British Policy, 1914-1918* (London, 1978), 160-176 and 204-07. For example, see Horace Rumbold to Balfour, 3 Dec. 1917, bearing Lancelot Oliphant's minute: 'This does not look promising: a peace conference on the basis of return of territory, e.g. African colonies!' Steglich (ed), *Die Friedensversuche*, 289-290.
729	Keith Hamilton, 'Chocolate for Zedzed: Basil Zaharoff and the secret diplomacy of the Great War', in Keith Hamilton (ed), *Foreign and Commonwealth Office Historians: Records of the Permanent Under-Secretary's Department* (London, 2005), 27-41.
730	Clive Barrett, *Subversive Peacemakers: War Resistance 1914-1918: An Anglican Perspective* (Cambridge, 2014), 162, 164, Bengt Sundkler, *Nathan Söderblom: His Life and Work* (London, 1968), 188-209.
731	Minutes of the War Cabinet, 6 June 1918, TNA: CAB 23/6.
732	Newton, *Retrospection*, 261, and Lord Newton, Diary, 26 June 1918, Newton Papers (Laughton).
733	Earl of Derby, Diary, 9 June 1918, in David Dutton (ed), *Paris 1918: The War Diary of the 17th Earl of Derby* (Liverpool, 2001), 41, and Reading to Lansing, 7 June 1918, *Papers Relating to the Foreign Relations of the United States, Supplement 1, The World War, Vol. 1* (Washington, 1933), 251.
734	Lord Newton, Diary, 1918, Newton Papers.
735	For discussion of the evidence on Germany's intentions toward Belgium, pointing to Bethmann Hollweg's willingness to offer concessions in mid-1917 (commitments given to the Papal Nuncio Pacelli), and Chancellor Michaelis's greater caution after the fall of Bethmann Hollweg, see Steglich, 'Einleitung', in his *Der Friedensappel Papst*, 4-6. Typical is Rumbold to Balfour, 3 Dec. 1917, transmitting the views of Count Károlyi, the Hungarian statesman, that 'Germany has no intention of retaining Belgium. There has been no official public statement to this effect because Germany wishes to obtain concessions in return for the surrender of Belgium.' Steglich (ed), *Die Friedensversuche*, 287.
736	For example, Joseph Clark Grew to Robert Lansing, 21 Dec. 1916, House to Wilson, 15 Jan. 1917, *Wilson Papers*, vol. 40, especially 434 and 477. On British diplomatic opinion, see Rennell Rodd to Lord Hardinge, 20 Oct. 1916, Hardinge Papers, and Rennel Rodd to Arthur Balfour, 30 Jan. 1917, Lloyd George Papers, quoted in Youssef Taouk, 'The Roman Catholic Church in Britain during the First World War: A Study in Political Leadership' unpublished Ph. D (Western Sydney University, 2003), 246.
737	Haig Diary, 2 Jan. 1918, in Robert Blake (ed), *The Private Papers of Douglas Haig, 1914-1919* (London, 1952), 277.
738	David Davies to T.O. Gavransky, Davies Papers, C 3/25, National Library of Wales.

739   Smuts quoted in C.P. Scott Political Diary, 20 March 1918, Scott Papers, Box 134, John Rylands Library.
740   Athol Lewis, Diary, 26 Dec. 1917, Athol Hugh Lewis Papers, AWM: PR00897, Item 19. The reference is to the article 'The Kaiser's Peace "Terms": New Propaganda Move', *Times*, 24 Dec. 1917.
741   Frank H. Molony, Diary, 8 Oct. 1917, MLMSS 2883/Item 4 (Mitchell Library).
742   Private Alfred George Hayden, interviewed by Richard White, 10 February 1985, Sound item S04348 (AWM). See also Morrow, *Iron in the Fire*, 76.
743   See the evidence of Lieut. Col. W.C. Rigby, 25 Sept. 1919, reporting an interview with General Sir B.E.W. Childs, 10 July 1919, in *Establishment of Military Justice: Hearings before a Subcommittee of the Committee on Military Affairs, United States Senate, Sixty-Sixth Congress* (Washington, 1919), 457, and 642-645.
744   'The Allies' Treaty with Italy', *Manchester Guardian*, 18 Jan. 1918.
745   See Deputy Chief Censor (Australia), *Rules for the Censorship of the Press* (1917), Section 11, banning 'Statements likely to cause disaffection or alarm, or to prejudice his Majesty's Forces or Foreign Relations', 7.
746   W.A. Sandberg, *Citizen Hearst* (New York, 1961), Ch. 9.
747   *Commonwealth of Australia Gazette*, No. 215, 12 Dec. 1917.
748   Goot, 'The Results of the 1916 and 1917 Conscription Referendums Re-examined', in Archer, et al. (eds), *Conscription Conflict*, 114.
749   Tarrant to Una, 24 May 1917, Tarrant to Kit, 28 June 1917, Tarrant Correspondence.
750   Tarrant to Una, 24 Oct. 1917, Tarrant Correspondence.
751   Tarrant to Una, 15 Feb. 1918, Tarrant Correspondence.
752   Goot, 'Conscription Referendums', in Archer, et al. (eds), *Conscription Conflict*, 131-2, 111. The soldiers' vote was much closer in December 1917: 'Yes' by a margin of 52.5% to 47.5%.
753   *Commonwealth of Australia Gazette*, No. 23, 21 Feb. 1918.
754   *Commonwealth of Australia Gazette*, No. 58, 25 Apr. 1918.
755   *Daily Herald* [Adelaide], 12 Jan. 1918.
756   For example, 'Trotsky's Revelations', *Barrier Daily Truth*, 1 Mar. 1918, and see 'Trostky's Revelations', *Daily Standard* [Brisbane], 18 Mar. 1918, 'More Secret Treaties', *Daily Standard* [Brisbane], 23 Apr. 1918, 'Aims of Conquest', *Worker* [Brisbane], 16 May 1918, 'Secret Treaties and Trotsky', *Westralian Worker*, 14 June 1918, 'Secret Treaties', *Australian Worker* [Sydney], 4 July 1918.
757   *CPD*, 15 Jan. 1918, 2955-2973, and 18 Jan. 1918.
758   *CPD*, 5 Apr. 1918, 3646-3679.
759   *CPD*, 26 Sept. 1918, 6385.
760   *CPD*, 2 Oct. 1918, 6560-72.
761   *CPD*, 4 Apr. 1918, 3595-3646. The quotation from Higgs is at 3601.
762   Murray Perks, 'A New Source on the Seventh A.L.P. Federal Conference, 1918, *Labour History*, 32 (May, 1977), 75-79, and 'Australian Demand for Negotiation', *Labour Leader*, 22 Aug. 1918. On Vere Gordon Childe's activism in Labor circles to secure these resolutions in favour of a negotiated peace, see Terry Irving, *The Fatal Lure of Politics: The Life and Thought of Vere Gordon Childe* (Clayton, 2020), 86-88.
763   *CPD*, 25 Apr. 1918, 4187-8.
764   *CPD*, 12 June 1918, 5803-04.
765   For example, James Mathews, *CPD*, 2 Oct. 1918, 6571.
766   C. McCurdy (ed), *War Aims of the British People* (London, 1918).
767   Emily Robertson, 'A much misunderstood monster: The German ogre and Australia's final and forgotten recruiting campaign of the Great War', *History Australia*, 13, 3 (2016), 351-367. In 1918, the government aimed for enlistments at the rate of 7,000 a month; it achieved a rate of 2,500 a month.
768   For example, among many snippets in the *Anzac Bulletin*, see 'Mr Hughes on Mr Lloyd George's Speech', 11 Jan. 1918, 'Meaning of a German Peace', 24 May 1918, 'Labour and the War', 28 June 1918, 'Australian Pacifists', 16 Aug. 1918, 'War Aims Propaganda', 30 Aug. 1918, 'Australia and the Pacific', 27 Sept. 1918.
769   'Australia and the Empire', *Anzac Bulletin*, 23 June 1918.

770 'Germany's Pacific Possessions', *Anzac Bulletin*, 29 Nov. 1918, 'Australia at the Conference', *Anzac Bulletin*, 14 Feb. 1919.
771 Zangwill, *The War for the World*, 196.
772 John Wheeler Bennett, *Brest-Litovsk: The Forgotten Peace, March 1918* (New York, 1971), Appendix V, and 345.
773 'The Meaning of the German Advance', *Anzac Bulletin*, 3 May 1918.
774 John Bradley, *Civil War in Russia, 1917-1920* (London, 1975), 66, Evan Mawdsley, *The Russian Civil War* (Boston, 1987), 100.
775 Under the armistice terms of November 1918, and again in the Versailles Treaty of June 1919, the victors would specify that German troops in the east were *not* to withdraw until they deemed it 'desirable'; they did not demand a complete withdrawal until late August 1919. See Clause 12 of the Armistice Terms and Article 433 of the Versailles Treaty. See Scott, *Official Statements of War Aims and Peace Proposals* (Washington, 1921), 477-483 and *The Treaty of Versailles and After: Annotations of the Text of the Treaty* (Washington, 1947), 743.
776 Germany demanded six billion gold marks in money, securities and goods from Russia as 'reparations' under a supplementary treaty to Brest-Litovsk in August 1918. The victors over Germany in 1919 eventually demanded a total of 152 billion gold marks in 'reparations' (20 billion under article 235 of the Versailles Treaty, plus 132 billion through the Reparations Commission in 1921), more than 25 times the figure that the Germans had imposed upon Russia. See Geoffrey Barraclough, *Factors in German History* (Oxford, 1946), 143, David Kent, *The Spoils of War: The Politics, Economics, and Diplomacy of Reparations 1918-1932* (Oxford, 1989), 11, Leonard Gomes, *German Reparations 1919-1932: A Historical Survey* (London, 2010), 7.
777 For example, Bruce Gaunson, *Fighting the Kaiserreich: Australia's Epic within the Great War* (Melbourne, 2018).
778 Hankey to Balfour, 1 Aug. 1918, in 'Petroleum situation in the British Empire and the Mesopotamia and Persian oilfields', CAB 21/119, quoted in Helmut Mejcher, 'Oil and British Policy towards Mesopotamia, 1914-1918', *Middle Eastern Studies*, 8, 3 (1972), 386.
779 51st Battalion War Diary, August 1918, AWM4, 23/68/30.
780 From the Preface of Herbert Read, *Naked Warriors* (London, 1919), quoted in Bertram Lloyd, *The Paths of Glory: A Collection of Poems written during the war, 1914-1919* (London, 1919), 6.
781 A.R.L. Wiltshire, Diary, 11 Feb. 1918, MLMSS 3058/Box 1/Item 17 (Mitchell Library).
782 Roy William Harburn, Service Number 961, B2455. Quoted in C.E.W. Bean, *Official History of Australia in the War of 1914-1918, Vol. V: The Australian Imperial Force in France during the Main German Offensive, 1918* (8th Edition, 1941), 580 and 591.
783 Barber, '51st Over There', *Western Mail*, 28 Jan. 1937.
784 Private Alfred George Hayden, 1st Infantry Battalion, interviewed by Richard White, 10 Feb. 1985, Sound item S04348 (AWM). Hayden identifies the soldier who defied warnings against killing the wounded as 'Bob Christie', probably J.R.C. Christie of the 1st Battalion.
785 Wheen to Miss Lewers, 18 Apr. 1929, *We Talked of Other Things*, 55.
786 Jim Beach, 'British Intelligence and German Tanks 1916-1918', *War in History*, 14, 4 (Nov. 2007), 454-475.
787 Corporal Jimmy Downing, quoted in Ross McMullin, *Pompey Elliott* (Melbourne, 2008), 463.
788 Ryan Edward Zroka, '"If only this war would end": German Soldiers in the Last Year of the First World War', unpublished PhD thesis, University of California, San Diego, 2013.
789 McMullin, *Elliott*, 470.
790 James Stuart MacDonald to his wife, 4 July 1918, MacDonald letters, MLMSS 2874 (Mitchell Library).
791 Eric Abraham, interviewed 25 January 2000, Australians at War Film Archive, Archive number: 2541. UNSW.
792 Ernest Morton, interviewed by Alistair Thomson, 21 June 1985, Sound item S01322 (AWM).
793 51st Battalion War Diary, Appendix 11A, '51st Battalion Order No. 85a', dated 7 Sept. 1918, AWM4, 23/68/31.

794 51st Battalion War Diary, Appendix XX, 'Report on Operations carried out by the 51st Battalion during the period 10th [to] 24th September 1918' dated 28 Sept. 1918, AWM4, 23/68/31. Italics added.
795 51st Battalion War Diary, 5, 6, 11, 14, Sept. 1918, and 'Intelligence Summaries' included as Appendix XV, AWM4, 23/68/31.
796 Stanley William Nixon, interview, 1976, OH4103/6 (State Library of Western Australia).
797 'Administrative Instruction No. 92', 1 Oct. 1918, 4th Division, HQ Administrative Staff, War Diary, Oct. 1918, AWM4, 1/49/31, Part 1.
798 Frank H. Molony, Diary, 30 Aug. 1917, MLMSS 2883/Item 3 (Mitchell Library).
799 Eric Evans, Diary, 6 June 1918, in Patrick Wilson, *So Far From Home* (East Roseville, 2002), 179.
800 H.E. Gissing, Diary, 30 Mar. 1918, MLMSS 1845/Item 6 (Mitchell Library).
801 Clifford M. Geddes, Diary, 22 Aug. 1918, MLMSS 2763/Item 2 (Mitchell Library).
802 Francis Weatherhead to his father, 5 Nov. 1918, in Clampett, *My Dear Mother*, 223-4.
803 W.J. Harvey, *The Red and White Diamond* (Melbourne, 1920), 34, quoted in Glenister, 'Desertion Without Execution', 60.
804 A.R.L. Wiltshire, Diary, 26 Nov. 1916, MLMSS 3058/Box 1/Item 8 (Mitchell Library).
805 James Churchill-Smith, Diary, 25 Sept. 1918, PRG 1159/1/3 (State Library of South Australia).
806 Laura Spinney, *Pale Rider: the Spanish Flu of 1918 and How It Changed the World* (London, 2017).
807 4th Australian Division, Administrative Staff HQ, War Diary, Oct. 1918, AWM4, 1/49/31 Part 1.
808 51st Battalion War Diary, Oct. 1918, AWM4, 23/68/32, 13th Infantry Brigade War Diary, Oct. 1918, AWM4 23/13/33.
809 Robert Saunderson Hamilton, Diary, 12 Dec. 1918, MLMSS 2769/Item 2 (Mitchell Library). During the war, and after the armistice, AIF troops often debated this set topic. For example, see Thomas Alexander White, Diary 18 May 1917, 3 June 1917, MLMSS 965/vol. 3 (Mitchell Library), Archie Barwick, Diary, 20 Dec. 1918, MLMSS 1493/Box 3/Item 16 (Mitchell Library).
810 51st Battalion War Diary, Oct. 1918, AWM4/23/68/32, 13th Infantry Brigade War Diary, Oct. 1918, AWM4 23/13/33.
811 James Churchill-Smith, Diary, 15 Oct. 1918, PRG 1159/1/3.
812 Wilson, *King's Hard Bargain*, 64.
813 Lieutenant Raymond Freear Lade, Service Number 2725, NAA: B2455.
814 James Churchill-Smith, Diary, 4 and 13 Oct. 1918, PRG 1159/1/3.
815 Private Harry Bowra, Service Number 7692, NAA: B2455.
816 See Chief Paymaster, A.I.F., *Instructions to Pay Representatives of the Australian Imperial Force* (London, 1918), 99. This recorded that: 'If a soldier is released from prison on a partly served sentence, (i.e., it is suspended) the forfeiture incurred will be for the period from the date of the award to, and including, the date of suspension or remission.'
817 Unfortunately, discrepancies in the financial penalties recorded on Ryan's service papers, that is, inconsistencies between his 'Statement of Service' forms, his 'Casualty Form – B103', and the conduct sheets 'B122' in his courts martial records, render it impossible to determine whether Ryan's pay was unfairly docked in this period. His pay card does not resolve the matter. See RYAN, Edward James, SERN: 4635][WWI paycard], NAA: K1143.
818 Court martial papers, Ryan, E.J. (Private), 15 Oct. 1917, NAA: A471, 17295.
819 RYAN, Edward James, SERN: 4635 [WWI paycard], NAA: K1143. Under the regulations, pay was normally stopped from the day a soldier disappeared to the day his sentence expired, which in Ryan's case would have been 114 days.
820 W.J. Allsop, Diary, 1 Mar. 1916, MLMSS160/Item 1 (Mitchell Library).
821 Australian Corps, HQ, Administrative Staff, War Diary, Oct. 1918, showing Table A, 'Moves', 8 Oct. 1918, AWM4, 1/37/7, Part 2.
822 Wilson, *King's Hard Bargain*, 172-3.
823 See Ashley Ekins, 'Fighting to Exhaustion: morale, discipline and combat effectiveness in the Armies of 1918', in Ashley Ekins (ed), *1918: Year of Victory. The end of the Great War and the shaping of history* (Auckland, 2010), 111-129, and Ashley Ekins, 'Australians at the End of the Great War', in Hugh Cecil and Peter H. Liddle (eds), *At the Eleventh Hour: Reflections, Hopes and Anxieties at the Closing of the Great War, 1918* (Barnsley, 1998), 157-180.

824 Arthur G. Thomas, Diary, 1916-1918, extracts from typescript, AWM 3DRL/2206.
825 Extracts from 'Censorship Dept. Report to the C-in-C., July 1918', reproduced in John Terraine, *Impacts of War 1914 and 1918* (London, 1970), 172-3.
826 Lieutenant General Sir John Monash, *The Australian Victories in France in 1918* (London, Ch. XVII).
827 Greg Raffin, *Mutiny on the Western Front: 1918* (Newport, 2018), 106-126.
828 Ekins, 'Fighting to Exhaustion', 127, and Wilson, *King's Hard Bargain*, 178.
829 Garstang, 'Crime and Punishment', 39.
830 Brigadier-General Sir Robert Ludlow's diary, October 1917, quoted in Peter Scott, 'Law and Orders: Discipline and Morale in the British Armies in France', in Peter Liddle (ed), *Passchendaele in Perspective: The Third Battle of Ypres* (Croydon, 2013), 363.
831 Haig, Diary, 3 Mar. 1918, in Gary Sheffield and John Bourne (eds), *Douglas Haig: War Diaries and Letters, 1914-1918* (London, 2005), 386.
832 Lieutenant General G.H. Fowke, Adjutant General, to Judge Advocate General, War Office, 12 Aug. 1918, quoted in Ekins, 'Fighting to Exhaustion', 112.
833 Garstang, 'Crime and Punishment', Table 2.2, 40.
834 Australian Corps Assistant Provost Marshal, War Diary, Sept. 1918, AWM4, 3/2/11.
835 Australian Corps Assistant Provost Marshal, War Diary, Oct. 1918, AWM4, 3/2/12.
836 Australian Corps Assistant Provost Marshal, War Diary, Nov. 1918, AWM4, 3/2/13.
837 Athol Lewis, Diary, 31 May and 14 Nov. 1918, Athol Hugh Lewis Papers AWM: PR00897, Items 23 and 25.
838 Lewis, Diary, 28 April and 3 May 1918, AWM: PR00897, Item 22. See also Captain N.A. Nicholson, quoted in Bill Gammage, *The Broken Years: Australian Soldiers in the Great War* (Ringwood, 1975), 218.
839 According to the British figures, for the first six months of 1917, convictions at courts martial for desertion for the five Australian divisions averaged 34.2 men per division, compared with a British figure for their 57 divisions of only 8.87 men. Throughout 1918, each month the average number of convictions at all courts martial for the Australian divisions was three to four times the figure for the British divisions. Report from Keith Officer, supplying figures from the British Adjutant General, 17 Nov. 1918, in Monash, Personal Files, Book 21, 3 Oct.-24 Nov. 1918, Monash Papers, AWM 3DRL/2316 (Australian War Memorial).
840 'Discipline of the Australian Corps, July-November, 1918', in Australian Corps, HQ, Administrative Staff, War Diary, Dec. 1918, AWM4, 1/37/9.
841 'War Diary of Fourth Australian Divisional Court Martial Officer for October 1918', in Administrative Staff Headquarters, 4th Division, War Diary, Oct. 1918, AWM4, 1/49/31 Part 2.
842 'Court Martial Officers' Diary', in Administrative Staff Headquarters, 4th Division, War Diary, Nov. 1918, AWM4, 1/49/32 Part 2.
843 Ekins, 'Fighting to Exhaustion', 113.
844 Richard Lindstrom, 'Psychological Casualties', 1. See also Tyquin, *Madness and the Military*.
845 Hobbs, 5th Division CM no. 61, 17 July 1918, in AWM25 807/1, quoted by Wilson, *King's Hard Bargain*, 179-80.
846 Medical report, quoted in Ross McMullin, *Pompey Elliott* (Melbourne, 2008), 486.
847 *CPD*, 26 June 1918, 6425-6440 and *CPD*, 26 Sept. 1918, 6409.
848 'Deserters from AIF', *Western Argus*, 1 Oct. 1918, and *The Week* [Brisbane], 11 Oct. 1918.
849 Lieutenant Harold Lionel Angel, 'Harry', interviewed by Peter Rubinstein 24 June 1998, Sound item S03448 (AWM).
850 Bill Richardson, interviewed by Roger Davis, 11 Oct. 1984, Sound item S04838 (AWM).
851 Douglas Newton, *British Policy and the Weimar Republic, 1918-1919* (Oxford, 1997) 242-243.
852 'First Amendment to Instruction No. 11 "March to the Rhine"' 8 Dec. 1918, in Australian Corps, HQ, Administrative Staff, War Diary, Dec. 1918, AWM4, 1/37/9.
853 Australian Corps, HQ, Administrative Staff, War Diary, Dec. 1918, 'Australian Corps "Q" Summary', 25 Dec. 1918, shows the 'Australian Corps Field Punishment Compound' at Florennes AWM4, 1/37/9. (An undated 'Location List' in this file also places the compound at Poulainville in France.) See also Routine Order No. 209, 28 Dec. 1918, in AWM4, 13/7/33.
854 51st Battalion War Diary, Dec. 1918, AWM4, 23/68/34.

855 51st Battalion War Diary, Dec. 1918, AWM4, 23/68/34. On the massacres at Dinant, and in surrounding villages, in August 1914, see John N. Horne and Alan Kramer, *German Atrocities 1914: A History of Denial* (New Haven, 2001), 44-52.
856 We must presume Ryan was returned after leaving prison in December 1918. However, the 51st Battalion War Diary does not list the arrival of a soldier, un-named, from prison, until February 1919.
857 For example, 'First Amendment to Instruction No. 11, "March to the Rhine"', 8 Dec. 1918, Australian Corps, HQ, Administrative Staff, War Diary, Dec. 1918, AWM4, 1/37/9
858 51st Battalion War Diary, Jan. 1919, AWM4, 23/68/35, 51st Battalion War Diary, Feb. 1919, AWM4, 23/68/36, 51st Battalion War Diary, March 1919, AWM4, 23/68/37.
859 51st Battalion War Diary, April. 1919, AWM4, 23/68/38.
860 Private Edward James Ryan, Service Number 4635, NAA: B2455.
861 See on line the work of Sharon Soutar, for the organisation 'Historic England', and Helen Roberts, for the 'Map of Australia Trust', at map-of-australia.com
862 'Anzac Day in London', *Argus*, 28 Apr. 1919, and 'On the March', *Sun* [Sydney], 7 May 1919.
863 Henry Mond, 'A Dirge on the Triumphal March of the Australian Forces through London, May 1919', from *Poems of Dawn and the Night* (London, 1919), 22.
864 See 'Wilson's Fourth Note', incorporating the promise of the 'Allied Governments', 5 Nov. 1918, in *Preliminary History of the Armistice* (New York, 1924), 143-4.
865 Among dozens of accounts, one of the best is still A.J. Ryder, *The German Revolution of 1918: A Study of German Socialism in War and Revolt* (Cambridge, 1967).
866 Vincent, *Politics of Hunger*, 141, 170, and N.P. Howard, 'The Social and Political Consequences of the Allied Food Blockade of Germany, 1918-19', *German History*, 11, 2 (June 1993).
867 Minutes of the Imperial War Cabinet, 18 and 20 Dec. 1918, CAB 23/42; Montagu to Balfour, 20 Dec. 1918, Balfour Papers, 49748. On British hostility toward the German Revolution of 1918-1919, see my own study, Douglas Newton, *British Policy and the Weimar Republic, 1918-1919* (Oxford, 1997).
868 Among scores of histories of the peacemaking, see in particular Arno J. Mayer, *The Politics and Diplomacy of Peacemaking* (London, 1967), Klaus Schwabe, *Woodrow Wilson, Revolutionary Germany, and Peacemaking, 1918-1919* (Chapel Hill, 1985), and Margaret Macmillan, *Peacemakers: The Paris Conference of 1919 and Its Attempt to End War* (London, 2001).
869 See Richard Bessel, *Germany After the First World War* (Oxford, 1993).
870 John W. Wheeler-Bennett, *Hindenburg: The Wooden Titan* (New York, 1967), 288.
871 Toni Sender, *The Autobiography of a German Rebel* (London, 1940), 133-4.
872 Editorial, *Daily News*, 1 Aug. 1918.
873 The narrative that follows on Hughes's role in the peacemaking is based on my study, Newton, *British Policy and the Weimar Republic*, especially 71-9, 207-11, 292-4, 350, 355, 393, 395-7.
874 Minutes of the Imperial War Cabinet, 20 Nov. 1918 TNA: CAB 23/43.
875 Howard, 'Allied Food Blockade', 162, 166.
876 Frederick Eggleston Diary, 9 Mar. 1919, Eggleston Papers, MS 423/6/58 (National Library of Australia).
877 Studies of Hughes's performance during the war and at Versailles include Spartalis, *The Diplomatic Battles of Billy Hughes*, Fitzhardinge, *Little Digger*, W.J. Hudson, *Billy Hughes in Paris: The Birth of Australian Diplomacy* (Melbourne, 1978) and Peter Cochrane, *Best We Forget: The War For White Australia* (Melbourne, 2018).
878 See *The Treaty of Versailles and After: Annotations of the Text of the Treaty*, 292-298.
879 *CPD*, 10 Sept. 1919, 12163-79.
880 Details of the voyage that follow are from Benjamin Alfred Cohen, Diary, 1 Mar.-23 June 1919, and 28 June-12 Aug. 1919, MLMSS 1844/7-8 (Mitchell Library).
881 *Diggers Defence Act: Souvenir of Diggers Supreme Court assembled to carry into effect the sections, provisions and conditions contained in the above mentioned Act / Australian Imperial Forces on board the troop and family ship 'Konigin Luise', at sea* (Printed in

	Durban, 1919). There were two Private Ryans on board, 4635 Private E.J. Ryan, and 4322 Private T.F. Ryan. See 'Coming Home', *The West Australian*, 23 July 1919.
882	'Konigin Luise Arrives', *The West Australian*, 4 Aug. 1919.
883	Munro Ferguson to Colonial Office, 3 Aug. 1914, quoted in Newton, *Hell-bent*,13.
884	RYAN, Edward James – Service Number – 4635, Repatriation Files, NAA: PP2/8, R18661.
885	RYAN, Edward James [SERN:4635] [WWI paycard], NAA: K1143.
886	'The City of Exeter Troops', *The Register* [Adelaide], 23 Aug. 1919. Two doctors signed off on Edward Ryan's fitness, one a very young recently qualified doctor, Dr. Eric Francis Erby.
887	'Personal', *Barrier Miner*, 28 July 1919.
888	'Relief Work', *Barrier Miner*, 28 June 1919 and *Barrier Daily Truth*, 6 Dec. 1919.
889	Frank H. Molony, Diary, 29 Sept. 1917, MLMSS 2883/Item 4 (Mitchell Library).
890	For example, Harry to Ted Ryan, 5 Aug. 1929, in Beth Sutton's possession.
891	'Recommendation File', AWM28, 2/305, and 'Presentation of Honours and Rewards, 1st Division, March 1917', AWM28, 2/523.
892	Private Thomas Pearce Couch Ryan, Service Number 2055, NAA: B2455.
893	Marriage Certificate, VIC BDM, 1949/1920.
894	*Commonwealth of Australia Gazette*, No. 11, Feb. 1938, and No. 76, 26 Nov. 1953.
895	'Engine Drivers' Examinations', *Barrier Miner*, 16 Mar. 1922, 'Engine Drivers' Certificates', *Barrier Miner*, 12 May 1925, and BHP records, courtesy of Jenny Camilleri, Broken Hill Family History Group.
896	'RSA Debating Society', *Barrier Miner*, 1 July 1922. His boarding with the Returned Soldiers is a puzzle. According to family sources, Ryan disliked the Returned Sailors' and Soldiers' Imperial League of Australia (RSSILA – the forerunner of today's RSL). Many ex-soldiers shied away from the RSSILA, with that word 'Imperial' so prominent in its name. By 1924, fewer than one in ten returned men were members. Perhaps the holdouts could smell the officers' club atmosphere at the top. In Broken Hill, the RSSILA became especially controversial because of its anti-union agitation. Sarah Gregson, 'Foot Soldiers for Capital: The influence of RSL racism on interwar industrial relations in Kalgoorlie and Broken Hill', unpublished PhD thesis (UNSW, 2003), esp. chs 6 and 7, and on membership of the RSSILA see Appendix A.
897	'W.E.A. Meeting', Barrier Miner, 12 Apr. 1923, 'W.E.A.', *Barrier Miner*, 28 Apr. 1925.
898	'Rechabitism', *Barrier Miner*, 27 Apr. 1926.
899	The birth certificate lists her as 'Mary Cameron McDonald', born at 'Talgarpna', probably Talgarno, Victoria, in 1894. VIC BDM 24747/1894.
900	'ATNA Examination Results', *Sydney Morning Herald*, 19 June 1920.
901	'Level Crossing Smash', *Barrier Miner*, 9 Apr. 1925.
902	'Sarah McDonald', *Narrandera Argus and Riverina Advertiser*, 6 May 1949, 'Alexander MacPherson', *Narrandera Argus and Riverina Advertiser*, 29 Nov. 1951.
903	'Presentation to Mr. E. Ryan', *Barrier Miner*, 6 Sept. 1926, and 'Personal', *Barrier Miner*, 18 Sept. 1926, and Gregson, 'Foot Soldiers', 236-237.
904	NSW BDM Marriage Certificate 14160/1926.
905	Interviews with Beth Sutton.
906	Advert for special meeting of Lindfield Branch ALP, *Labor Daily*, 30 Sept. 1936, '"Inner Group" Assailed by Union', *Workers' Weekly*, 16 Oct. 1936, 'Busy Time Ahead for Branches', *Labor Daily*, 14 Nov. 1936, 'As A Worker Sees It', *Workers' Weekly*, 11 Dec. 1936.
907	Interviews with Beth Sutton, and sound recording of interviews with Ken Tribe by Terry Colhoun, transcript of session 3, 1997, obj-206222048, ORAL TRC 3590 (National Library of Australia).
908	See her letter to the editor, 'Disease', *Daily Telegraph* [Sydney], 29 Mar. 1943.
909	NSW Death Certificate 27542/1943, and 'Cyclist's Death', *Sydney Morning Herald*, 11 Nov. 1943.
910	NSW Deceased Estate files 60873.
911	George Eliot, *Felix Holt, the Radical* (Oxford, 1991, originally published 1866), 11.
912	Private Thomas Lawrence Talty, interviewed by Peter Rubinstein, 26 June 1998, Sound item S03426 (AWM).
913	Manning, *Middle Parts of Fortune*, 34.
914	Max Hastings, *Catastrophe 1914: Europe Goes to War* (London, 2013), 552.

915 Among studies that are optimistic about the chances of peace see Ralph H. Lutz, introduction to Ebba Dahlin, *French and German Public Opinion and War Aims 1914-1918* (Stanford, 1933), Kent Forster, *Failures of Peace: The Search for a Negotiated Peace during the First World War* (Philadelphia, 1941), Gerda Richards Crosby, *Disarmament and Peace in British Politics 1914-1919* (Cambridge, Mass., 1957), Laurence Martin, *"Peace Without Victory": Woodrow Wilson and the British Liberals* (New Haven, 1958), David Woodward, 'Great Britain and President Wilson's Efforts to End World War 1 in 1916', *Maryland Historian*, I (Spring, 1970), 45-58, Z.A.B. Zeman, *A Diplomatic History of the First World War* (London, 1971), Sterling J. Kernek, 'Distractions of Peace During War: the Lloyd George Government's Reaction to Woodrow Wilson, December 1916-November 1918', *Transactions of the American Philosophical Society*, 65, 2 (1975), Arno J. Mayer, *The Political Origins of the New Diplomacy 1917-1918* (New York, 1979), Jo Vellacott, *Bertrand Russell and the Pacifists in the First World War* (Brighton, 1980), Michael Graham Fry, 'Why Wars Do Not End: Some Observations on the First World War', in his *Power, Personalities and Policies: Essays in Honour of Donald Cameron Watt* (London, 1992), 53-82, Thomas Knock, *To End All Wars: Woodrow Wilson and the Quest for a New World Order* (1992), W.H. van der Linden, *The International Peace Movement during the First World War* (Almere, 2006), David S. Patterson, *The Search for a Negotiated Peace: Women's Activism and Citizen Diplomacy in World War I* (New York, 2008), Adam Hochschild, *To End All Wars: A Story of Loyalty and Rebellion, 1914-1918* (New York, 2011), Neil Hollander, *Elusive Dove: The Search for Peace During World War I* (Jefferson, 2014), and Michael Kazin, *War Against War: The American Fight for Peace, 1914-1918* (New York, 2017).

916 Keith Jeffery, *1916: A Global History* (London, 2015), 369.

917 Hollander, *Elusive Dove*, 257.

918 Balfour memorandum, 6 Oct. 1917, reproduced in Wolfgang Steglich (ed), *Der Friedensappell Papst Benedikts XV vom 1 August 1917 und die Mittelmächte* (Wiesbaden, 1970), 558-9.

919 For a nuanced discussion of this, see John Kramer, *Dynamic of Destruction: Culture and Mass Killing in the First World War* (Oxford, 2007), Ch. 4. Kramer concludes that 'It would be quite incorrect to speak of a German singularity of destructiveness.'

920 Israel Zangwill, *The War for the World* (London, 1916), 196.

921 The best studies of the origins of the war, and its persistence, feature comparative perspectives. For example, Richard F. Hamilton and Holger H. Herwig (eds), *The Origins of World War I* (Cambridge, 2003), Holger Afflerbach and David Stevenson (eds), *An Improbable War: The Outbreak of World War I and European Political Culture before 1914* (New York, 2007), Richard F. Hamilton and Holger H. Herwig (eds), *War Planning 1914* (Cambridge, 2010), Holger Afflerbach (ed), *The Purpose of the First World War: War Aims and Military Strategies* (Oldenbourg, 2015), and Andreas Gestrich, Hartmut Pogge von Strandmann (eds), *Bid For World Power? New Research on the Outbreak of the First World War* (Oxford, 2017).

922 On the deep divisions inside Germany, see Gatzke, *Germany's Drive to the West*, Gerhard Ritter, *The Sword and the Scepter: The Problem of Militarism in Germany*, 4 Vols. (Coral Gables, Florida, 1973), Konrad Jarausch, *The Enigmatic Chancellor: Bethmann Hollweg and the Hubris of Imperial Germany* (New Haven, 1973), Welch, *Germany, Propaganda and Total War*, and Watson, *Ring of Steel*. For the clashes over policy and diplomacy, see E. Matthias, and R. Morsey (eds), *Der Interfraktionelle Ausschus* (Dusseldorf, 1959), Wilhelm Ribhegge, *Frieden für Europa: Die Politik der Deutschen Reichstagsmehrheit 1917-1918* (Essen, 1988), Petronilla Ehrenpreis, *Kriegs- und Friedensziele im Diskurs: Regierung und deutschsprachige Öffentlichkeit Österreich-Ungarns während des Ersten Weltkriegs* (Innsbruck, 2005), W.E. Winterhager (ed), *Mission für den Frieden* (Stuttgart, 1984), Wolfgang Steglich (ed), *Die Friedenspolitik der Mittelmächte 1917-1918* (Wiesbaden, 1964), Wolfgang Steglich (ed), *Der Friedensappell Papst Benedikts XV vom 1 August 1917 und die Mittelmächte* (Wiesbaden, 1970), Wolfgang Steglich (ed), *Die Verhandlungen des 2. Unterausschusses des Parliamentarischen Untersuchungsausschusses über die päpstliche Friedensaktion von 1917* (Wiesbaden, 1974), and Wolfgang Steglich (ed), *Die Friedensversuche der kriegführenden Mächte im Sommer und Herbst 1917* (Stuttgart, 1984).

923 Lothar Höbelt, 'Mourir pour Liège? World War I War Aims in a Long-Term Perspective', in Afflerbach, *Purpose of the First World War*, 151.
924 Ambassador Gerard to House, 15 Feb. 1915, Seymour, *Intimate Papers I*, 382.
925 Erzberger, from the *Kölnischer Volkszeitung*, 28 July 1917, quoted in Epstein, *Erzberger*, 215.
926 Baron von Romberg's evidence, *Official German Documents*, 180. Romberg also suggested that both the Kaiser and Bethmann Hollweg counted on the beginning of negotiation to hobble the annextionist hardliners.
927 Roger Chickering, 'Strategy, Politics, and the Quest for a Negotiated Peace', in Afflerbach, *Purpose of the First World War*, 115.
928 Holger Afflerbach, '... eine Internationale der Kriegsverschärfung und die Kriegsverlängerung ... War Aims and the Chances for a Compromise Peace during the First World War', in Afflerbach, *Purpose of the First World War*, especially 252-254.
929 Wilhelm Ernst Winterhager (ed), *Mission für den Frieden* (Stuttgart, 1984).
930 Höbelt, 'Mourir pour Liège?', 149, and Afflerbach, '... eine Internationale der Kriegsverschärfung ...', 243.
931 See Watson, *Ring of Steel*, Chs 11-13.
932 Lord Selborne to Bobby, 6 Aug. 1915, in George Boyce (ed), *The Crisis of British Unionism* (London, 1987), 142.
933 HC Deb 31 October 1916 vol 86 c1676; HC Deb 07 November 1916 vol 87 cc148; R.C. Lambert to Noel Buxton, 3 Nov. 1916, Buxton Papers (McGill University, Montreal).
934 Curzon to Cecil, 1 June 1917, Cecil Papers, TNA: FO 800/198.
935 Haig to Robertson, 13 Aug. 1917, William Robertson Papers, I/23/44 (King's College London).
936 Murdoch to 'Pompey' Elliott, 9 May 1918, Murdoch Papers, MS2823/34 (National Library).
937 War Cabinet Minutes, 10 Oct. 1917, TNA: CAB 23/13.
938 See Brock Millman, *Pessimism and British War Policy, 1916-1918* (London, 2001).
939 Lansing to Wilson, 6 Aug. 1915, quoted in van der Linden, *International Peace Movement*, 327.
940 Quoted by Seán Hemingway, 'Introduction', to *Hemingway on War* (London, 2014), xxiii.
941 Blunden, 'Third Ypres', *Undertones of War*, 259.
942 Ernest Hemingway, 'A Natural History of the Dead', in *Hemingway on War*, 48.
943 Private Thomas Lawrence Talty, interviewed by Peter Rubinstein, 26 June 1998, Sound item S03426 (AWM).
944 Thomas Louch, quoted in Westerman, 'Soldiers and Gentlemen', 274-275.
945 Lieutenant William Smith, quoted in Westerman, 'Soldiers and Gentlemen', 274.
946 Garstang, 'Crime and Punishment', 27-8. Glenister, 'Desertion Without Execution', in his Appendix C, finds a total of at least 20,000. Studies of discipline and courts martial in the AIF by Ashley Ekins, James Waddell, Graham Wilson, and Kay De Bellis have given different estimates of the total number of courts martial in the AIF, but none below 20,000. The latest research of courts martial in the AIF is based on 22,000 courts martial records. See Mark Finnane and Yorick Smaal, 'Character, Discipline, Law: Courts Martial in World War I', *Australian Historical Studies*, 51, 3 (Aug. 2020), 324-40.
947 Glenister, 'Desertion Without Execution', 25. Glenister estimates that AIF convictions for desertion included 266 men convicted for deserting twice, and 16 men convicted for deserting three times.
948 Ekins, 'Australians at the end of the Great War', 164.
949 A.D. Ellis, *The Story of the Fifth Australian Division* (London, 1919), 362-3, quoted by Glenister, 'Desertion Without Execution', 60-61.
950 Aldington, *Death of a Hero*, 332.
951 George Horan to his father, 23 Feb. 1917, George Horan Papers, MLMSS 1468/Item 2 (Mitchell Library).
952 George Baron Hay, interview, 11 Nov. 1976, OH4103/3 (State Library of Western Australia).
953 Bonhoeffer, 'After Ten Years', in Eberhard Bethge (ed), *Prisoner for God: Letters and Papers from Prison* (London, 1953), 15.
954 See Higgins and Kirwan, *CPD*, 23 July 1903, 2535.
955 Francisco de Vitoria, in *De Iure Belli (On the Law of War)*, epigraph to the Introduction, 'Sometime they'll give a war and nobody will come', in Andrea Ellner, Paul Robinson, and

	David Whetham (eds), *When Soldiers Say No: Selective Conscientious Objection in the Modern Military* (London, 2014).
956	Brian Imiola, 'The Duty of Diligence: Knowledge, Responsibility, and Selective Conscientious Objection', in *When Soldiers Say No*, Ch. 1.
957	H. Gordon Carter to his parents, 11 Nov. 1916, AWM: 1DRL/092.
958	Private Ernest Morton, Service Number 439, NAA: B2455, and Ernest Morton, interviewed by Alistair Thomson, 21 June 1985, Sound item S01322 (AWM). Perhaps this was in July 1918, for his service papers record that at that point he reverted to the rank of Private 'at [his] own request'.
959	Arthur Graeme West, Diary, 24 Sept. 1916, in Nigel Jones (ed), *Diary of a Dead Officer: Being the Posthumous Papers of Arthur Graeme West* (London, 2007), 110, 111 and 113.
960	Barwick, Diary, 29 Dec. 1918, MLMSS 1493/Box 3/Item 16.
961	Charlie Mance, AIF veteran, interviewed by Peter Rubinstein, 23 Oct. 1998, Sound item S03456 (AWM).
962	Lucy Masterman, wife of the Cabinet Minister Charles Masterman, preserved in her diary an incident from 1912 when she and her husband became convinced that Asquith 'is not fond of Labour at any time' and that Lloyd George's sympathies 'are not really entirely Labour'. See Lucy Masterman, *C.F.G. Masterman: A Biography* (London, 1968), 233-234.
963	Frances Stevenson, Diary, 1 Feb. 1916, *Lloyd George: A Diary*, 93.
964	Jack Lockett, interviewed 11 Jan. 2000, Australians at War Film Archive, Archive number: 2539. UNSW.
965	Jack Lockett, interviewed by Peter Rubinstein, 22 Jan. 1997, Sound item S03435 (AWM).
966	Private Thomas Lawrence Talty, interviewed 26 June 1998, Sound item S03426 (AWM).
967	'General Birdwood: to the Prime Minister', *Sydney Morning Herald*, 27 Oct. 1916.
968	Item A, court martial papers, Ryan, E.J. (Private), 12 Sept. 1917, NAA: A471, 10237. Underlining in original.

INDEX

Page numbers in *italics* refer to photographs.

A

Abraham, Eric 41, 111, 118, 121, 153, 247
absent without leave *see* Australian Imperial Force
Acre 96
Addams, Jane 76, *76–77*
Afflerbach, Holger 283
Africa, German colonies in 96–97
Aiseau 264
Albert 116
Aldington, Richard 111, 138, 287–288
Alexandretta (Iskenderun) 53
Alexandria 87–88, 99
aliens, internment of 70
All Quiet on the Western Front (Remarque) 246
Allsop, W.J. 257
Alsace-Lorraine 168, 172, 217–218, 231, 234
Amalgamated Miners' Association 25
Amalgamated Miners' Association Band 33, 39, 44
Amery, Leo 72
Angel, Harry 262
Anglican Church 233
Anglo-Egyptian War 87
Anglo-Persian Oil Company 52, 60
Anglo-Russian Convention (1907) 51
Anti-German Union 102
anti-war movement 38–39, 128, 137–138, 140, 166–167, 188, 220–223
Anzac Bulletin 114, 152, 160, 191–192, 197, 222, 243
Anzac Cove 17–18, 55
Anzac Police 90, 92
'Anzac spirit' 292
Arabs 69
Arbroath 166–167
Armand, Abel 231
arms trade 173

Army Act 1881 (UK) 7–8, 15, 174–175, 180, 183, 201, 210–211, 214
Army (Suspension of Sentences) Act 1915 237
artillery 105–106, 111–112, 119–120, 193
Asquith, Herbert Henry
　agrees to conscription 69–71
　appoints Hughes to Economic Conference 102–103
　claims to be fighting for democracy 284
　criticised by Ryan in letter to MacDonald 5, 145
　criticised for neglecting naval defence 30
　criticises British landings at Suvla 62
　dodges questions on aim of war 104
　increases pro-war rhetoric 143
　jokes about scheme for taking German colonies 47, 52
　lack of sympathy for working class 291–292
　outlines Britain's reasons for going to war 37, 46
　portrait of *30*
　postpones landings at Gallipoli 59
　prepares for Britain's intervention in war 34–35
　replaced by Lloyd George 157, 184
Asquith, Raymond 102–103, 143
Association for Peace Through Law 78
Auckland 278
Australia 26, 35–36, 241
Australian Army *see* Australian Imperial Force
Australian Consolidated Industries 279
Australian Imperial Force (AIF)
　1st Anzac Corps Reinforcement Camp 219
　1st Battalion 67, 111, 246, 259
　1st Division 144
　1st Field Ambulance 114
　2nd Division 144
　3rd Australian Field Ambulance 111
　3rd Training Battalion 91–92

4th Australian Divisional Artillery 209
4th Division 92, 99, 180, 187, 199, 201, 209, 250, 252, 260–261
5th Division 261, 287
6th Battalion 111, 258
6th Brigade *135*, 144
6th Division 243
7th Training Battalion 91
9th Field Ambulance 112, 131
11th Battalion 17–18, 36, 46, 56–57, 60, 68, 89, 116, 175, 276
13th Battalion 16, 36, 45, 51, 55, 60, 251
13th Infantry Brigade 92, 94, 199, 249, 252–253
15th Brigade 261
16th Battalion 250
22nd Battalion 291
24th Battalion 251
49th Battalion 92, 264
50th Battalion 92, 253, 264
51st Battalion xviii, 1, 36, 67, 89, 91–94, 99, 101, 105–106, 110–111, 116, 122, 187, 192, 194, 209, 220, 238, 245, 249–250, 253, 261, 263, 286
52nd Battalion 92
54th Battalion 286
59th Battalion 261–262
Australian Corps Punishment Compounds 257–258, 263
Australian Provost Corps 90
    Catholics in 62–63
    charged with protecting Egypt 88
    as a defence force 15
    desire of troops for peace 162
    disaffection among troops 258–261
    instances of absent without leave (AWOL) 123, 151–153, 166, 170, 175, 177, 179, 183–187, 204, 210, 212–213, 253–255, 259, 261–262, 287
    instances of desertion 123, 179–184, 193–194, 210–212, 219–221, 249–251, 259–262, 287
    legal position of Australian soldiers 15
    majority of soldiers vote for conscription 149
    mutiny of troops 259
    No. 1 Australian Command Depot 1–3, 129, 131
    No. 3 Depot Battalion 66
    payment of soldiers 41, 181–182
    recruitment numbers dwindle 243
    resistance to military discipline 185–186, 259
    rise in anti-war sentiment among troops 223
    soldiers' attitudes towards deserters 250–251
    soldiers kill prisoners 246
    troops moved to Belgium 263
Australian Labor Party 24, 38, 142, 191, 206, 241, 278
Australian Worker 161
Australian Workers Union 14
Austria-Hungary 34, 59, 68, 102, 191, 231–233
autocracy 284
AWOL *see* Australian Imperial Force (AIF)
Ayr 128

B

Balfour, Arthur 84, *85*, 162, 217, 222, 232–234, 245, 282
Balfour-Moton Agreement 172
Balkans 58
Banning, S.T. 175
Barber, James 106–107, 111
Barrier Daily Truth 22, 24, 29, 37–40, 121, 137–138, 141, 161, 178, 191, 240
Barrier Labour Federation 31
Barrier Miner 39, 91, 116, 121–122, 166
Barwick, Archie 67, 106–107, 111, 120, 162, 213, 223, 290–291
basic wage 22
Basra 48, 61
bayonet sticking 66–67
Bean, Charles 62, 114
Beaulieu 226
Beaverbrook, Lord 222
Bedlam trenches 2
Belgium 34–37, 46, 49, 68, 108, 229, 231, 234, 238, 263
Benckendorff, Count Alexander 49, *50*
Benedict XV, Pope 58, *58*, 60, 63, 195, 238
Benson, A.C. 45
Bernstorff, Johann Heinrich von 159
Bertie, Lord 157
Bethmann Hollweg, Theobald von 109, *110*, 154–155, 157, 189, 283
Birdwood, Sir William 6, 114, 141–142, 146, 209, 212, 220, 293
Blackboy Hill training camp 17, 45–46, 51, 65–68
Bleakdown Red Cross Hospital 125
Blunden, Edmund 92, 112, 187, 193, 223
Blytheswood Auxiliary Hospital 125
Boer War 107
Bolshevik Revolution 154, 177–178, 220, 228, 238, 243–244, 284
Bonar Law, Andrew 61, *62*, 103, 158
Bond, George 175
Bonhoeffer, Dietrich 288
Bottomley, Horatio 140
Bougainville 54
Boulogne 113, 115

Bovelles 252–253
Bown, William 42, 131
Bowra, Harry 254
Bradford, James 180
Brailsford, Henry 222
Brest-Litovsk 228, 235
Brest-Litovsk Treaty 243–245, 283
Briand, Aristide 155–156, 168, *169*, 216, 231
Bridger, James Richard 253
Bright, John 39
Brissenden, Edwin 209–210
Britain
  attempts to bribe Ottomans 233
  attempts to isolate Germany in negotiations 232–233
  captures German colonies 47, 54, 168, 172
  considers German peace offer 215–218
  considers US offer to mediate peace 83–84
  contemplates spoils of war 53–54, 311–313
  declares war on Germany 32, 35
  dismisses Russian peace negotiations 189
  divides up Middle East with France 95
  doubts about victory in the War Cabinet 285–286
  economic aims in Great War 101–103, 168, 238, 242, 244–245
  escalates war 47
  ignores Pope's peace offer 197
  keen to placate Russia 50–52
  keen to take Ottoman Empire territories 49
  National War Aims Committee 242
  opposes peace initiatives of Austria and Germany 231–234
  propaganda for the war 68–69
  rejects German and American Peace Notes 157–160, 162, 165, 167–168
  rejects peace negotiations 230, 282–283
  rejects Wilson's idea of Peace Without Victory 169–170
  releases Versailles Declaration 230
  rise of anti-war sentiment 220–223
  rivalry with France for Egypt and Sudan 87–88
  secret diplomacy of xviii, 52, 60–61, 69, 95–96, 104, 126, 140, 152, 168–169, 172, 188, 228, 232, 238–242, 244, 271, 304–305, 314–326
  seeks to crush Germany 47, 53, 101–103, 158–159
  self-righteousness of 37–38
  strikes deal with Italy 57–60
  superiority in tanks 246–247
  supports Japanese invasion of Russia 244
  Territorial Changes Committee 168
  War Cabinet plans colonial swaps and annexations 188
British Army
  1st Convalescent Hospital 113
  4th London General Hospital 118, 125
  8th Sherwood Foresters 250
  13th Stationary Hospital 113
  brutal treatment of military prisoners 226–227
  executes deserters 213, 219
  Indian Expeditionary Force 48
  Kitchener's New Army 2
British Council for Promoting an International Christian Meeting 233
British Empire Union 102
British Expeditionary Force 89, 114
British Mine sawmill 277
British Solomons 54
British Territorial Force 68
Brittain, Vera 163
Broken Hill
  anti-war sentiment 137, 165
  labour movement 23–31, 38, 82–83, 132–133, 165, 206
  as a mining town 9
  Mudie works for Council 20, 22–23
  Ottoman sympathisers ambush train 17
  rally against conscription 134
  Ryan returns to after war 274, 277–278
  typhoid fever outbreak 11
  unemployment in 39–40
  votes against conscription 149
  war supporters wreck Socialist Hall 39
Brooker, R.L.C. 174
Brookfield, Percy ('Jack') 132, *133*, 137, 165, 191
Browning, Robert Humphrey 175, 179
Buchanan, Donald Duncan 175
Buchanan, Sir George 50
Bucharest Conventions 126
Bulgaria 126, 252
Bulla, SS 63
Burrows, John 41
Burrows, Mary Ann 41
Byfleet 125–126

C

Caëstre 101, 219–220
Caillaux, Joseph 191
Cairo 56, 90–92, 275–276
Cambon, Paul 95, 168
Cameroons 54, 96–97
capital punishment 208–215, 219–221, 259

Carter, Gordon 290
Cass, Walter 286
casualties 105, 113–116, 122, 148, 218, 250, 285
see also shell shock
Catholic Centre Party (Germany) 189
Catholics 62–63, 195–196, 238
Catts, James 241–242
Caucasus 96, 238
Caux, Marcel 41, 120
Cave, Sir George 233–234
Cecil, Robert 284
censorship 70, 121–122, 141, 195, 239–242, 258
Central Organisation for a Durable Peace 78
Chamberlain, Austen 47, 188
Charlton, James Ross 278
Château de Bomy 197, 199, 201, 207
Château de Bovelles 247, 252–253
Chickering, Roger 283
Chinese labourers, from Qingdao 252
Christie, Bob 246
Christie, Robert 245, 255
Churchill-Smith, James 252–254
Churchill, Winston 47, 62
City of Exeter (ship) 274
City of London Royal Fusiliers 68
civilian casualties 102
Clemenceau, Georges 231, *267*, 268, *271*
Clémentel, Étienne 103
Clyde Workers' Committee 128
Cobden, Richard 39
Cock, Seymour 240
Cohen, Ben 73–74, 272–273
Colombo 81–82
concentration camps 107
conscience, and duty 289–292
conscientious objectors 211, 225–226
conscription
    Australian referendums on 6, 44, 133–134, 137, 141–142, 149, 165, 205–206, 213, 239–240, 293
    in Britain 69–70
    in the United States 173
Considine, Michael ('Mick') 40, 132, *132*, 137, 165, 242
Constantinople 49–50, 104, 152, 156
The Constantinople Agreement *see* Straits and Persia Agreement
Cook, Joseph 35
Corboy, Edwin 214–215
Corsican, HMT 89
Couch, Henry 12–13
Couch, James 11
Couch, Jane (née Pearce) 11, *11*

Couch, Thomas 12
Courland 244
Courtney, Lord 79–80, 222
courts martial 173–177, 199–205, 207–215, 287
Cox, Sir Herbert Vaughan 92
Crewe, Lord 103
Croly, Arthur England Johnson 175
Curzon, Lord 47, 158, 188, *285*
Cyprus 49, 88

D

Dahomey 54
Daily Herald (UK) 226–227
Daily Mail (UK) 70, 130, *134–135*, 144–145, 152
Daily News (UK) 269
Daily Telegraph (UK) 220, 222, 327–329
D'Arcy, William Knox 52, 60
Dardanelles 48, 57, 61, 238
Dark, Eric 112
Davies, David 162, 234
De Bunsen, Maurice 60–61
Deakin, Alfred 26, 31
Defence Act 1903 (Australia) 15, 210–211, 213–214, 289
Defence of the Realm Act 1914 (DORA) (UK) 8, 141
democracy 284–285
Derby, Lord 188
desertion *see* Australian Imperial Force (AIF)
Devonport 272
Dibbs, Sir George 25
Dickinson, Goldie 222
Dinant 264
Djibouti 54
Dock Strike (1889) 24
Domain, Sydney 206
Dos Passos, John 107, 115, 193, 197
Doumergue Agreement 172, 228
Doumergue, Gaston 172
Downing, Jimmy 247
dreadnoughts 30–31
Drummond, Eric 162–163
du Pan Mallet, Sir Louis 168, 188
Dunkirk 225
Dunn, Sergeant Major 66–67
Durban 273
duty, and conscience 289–292

E

Ebdon, Arthur 121
The Economist 103, 222
Edward, Prince of Wales 94, 98, 263, 265
Edwards, Eb 223
Egypt 45, 49, 56, 82, 87–94, 271
Egyptian Labour Corps 56
Einstein, Albert 78, *79*
Eliot, George 280
Elliott, 'Pompey' 261, 284
Ellis, Alex 287
Entente Cordiale 88, 147, 271
Entente Powers
　consider German and American peace notes 162
　economic blockade of Germany 103
　keen to take Ottoman Empire territories 48–49, 96
　lure Italy into war 58–59
　refuse to grant visas to socialists 43, 191
　secret deals negotiated by 104
　shun mediation 285
　squash Papal peace initiative 196
　war aims of xvii–xviii, 47, 167–168
　Wilson opposes views of 173
　see also Britain; France; Russia
Eritrea 54
Erzberger, Matthias 189, *190*, 282–283
Esher, Viscount 188
Esmerelda (ship) 57
Espionage Act (US) 173
Estonia 244
Étaples 113, 116, 252
Evans, Eric 251
Eveleigh Railway Workshops 206
Evening News (UK) 70
Evening Post (US) 228

F

Falkenhayn, Erich von 283
Ferguson, Justice 209
Ferguson, William 26
Finland 244
First World War *see* Great War
Fisher, Andrew 30–31, 38, *38*, 70, 211
Fitzgerald, Michael 179–180
Flannery, Jack 121
Fleurbaix 1, 101, 105, 110
Flixecourt 257
Florennes 263

Ford, Henry 80
Forster, Henry 227
Fortescue, Charles 203, 208
Forward (UK) 128, 166, 239
Foster, George 103
Fowke, Sir George 214, 259
France
　Britain promises naval support to 34
　considers German peace offer 215–218
　disaffection among troops 190–191
　Harcourt's territorial goals for 53–54
　ignores Pope's peace offer 197
　keen to take Ottoman Empire territories 48, 87–88
　Masterman's territorial goals for 68
　peace activists in 78
　prevents delegates from attending peace conference 76
　rejects German Peace Note 155–156
　rejects peace negotiations 230, 283
　releases Versailles Declaration 230
　ruling class opposes peace 75
　secret diplomacy of 244, 271
　signs Treaty of London 59
　Straits and Persia Agreement 152
　superiority in tanks 246–247
　Sykes-Picot Agreement 95–97
　war aims of 168, 172, 238, 242
Francis, Bob 276
Francis, Les 276
Franz Josef, Emperor 231
Fremantle 73, 273
Fribourg 231
Friedrich, General 189
Fromelles 2, 110, 113, 286

G

Gallipoli 17–18, 41, 49, 52, 55–63, 89, 220, 228, 238, 242
Garran, Robert 211
Garstang, Edward 287
'Gassed' (painting) 243
Gebel Habieta 94
Geddes, Clifford 251
George V, King 49, 180, 234
Georges-Picot, François 95–96
Gerard, James 282
Germany
　after the armistice 265–269
　Allied plans for 68–69
　applies for armistice 252

Britain attempts to isolate 232–233
Britain's criticisms of 36–37
civilian deaths after armistice 270
declares war on Russia 34
divisions within 282
economic blockade of 266, 270
imposes Brest-Litovsk Treaty upon Russia 243–245
invades Belgium 34–35
majority press for peace resolution in Reichstag 189–190, 282–283
militarism of 282
naval blockade of 101–102
peace offers by 49, 153–157, *155*, 215–218, 233–235, 252, 283
plans spring offensive 230, 243
radicalisation of politics in 189–190
resumes submarine warfare 169
severity of conditions imposed upon 268–271
Social Democratic Party formed 189
socialist government shunned 266
soldiers ill-equipped and starving 247
at Stockholm conference 191
Giles, Arthur 182
Gillett, Walter 66–67, 74
Gilroy, Norman 63
Gissing, H.E. 251
Glasgow 128
Glasgow, William 92, 199, 209
Glover, Leonard 67–68
Godley, Sir Alexander 45, 212
Gough, Sir Hubert 212
Gray, Harry 31
Great Naval Scare (1909) 30
Great War
    aims of 101–103, 168, 229, 238, 242, 244–245, 284–286, 304–305, 327–329
    armistice signed 257, 263, 265–268
    Britain contemplates spoils of war 53–54, 311–313
    economic pressure to enlist 40–41
    escalates on eastern front 126
    events leading up to 34–36
    initial enthusiasm of Australians for 36–39, 42, 46
    military stalemate in xix
    objections to xviii, 3
    Pope suggests Christmas Truce 60
    propaganda for 68–69, *134–135*, 141–142, 144–145, 149, 196, 240, 242–243
    soldiers' recollections of 106–107, 112–113, 291–293

trench warfare 2, 56–57, 106, 110–111
US entry into 170, 172–173, 178, 205
Versailles Treaty 268–272
see also anti-war movement; peace activism; peace negotiations
Grey, Sir Edward 49–50, 52, 55, 62, 75, 83–84, 95, 104, *104*, 109–110, 138, 140, 143, 157, 163
Guignemicourt 250, 253

H

Haifa 96
Haig, Sir Douglas 86, 114, *115*, 123, 192, 212, 234, 258–259, 284–285
Hall, William James 203, 208
Hamilton, Sir Ian 62
Hampson, Alfred 160
Hankey, Maurice 245
Hansard 241–242
Harburn, Billy 246
Harcourt, Lewis *53*, 53–54, 311–313
Hardie, Keir 27, *28*, *38*, 128
Hardinge, J.J. 225–227
Hardinge, Lord 48, *48*, 232
Harford, David 74–75, 82, 87, 91, 119–120
Hargicourt 259
Harvester Judgment (1907) 22
Hay, George Baron 67, 288
Hayden, Alfred George 237, 246
Hearst, William Randolph 239
Heliopolis 82, 89, 91
Henderson, Arthur 195, 197
Higgins, Henry Bournes 289
Higgs, William 161, 241
Hindenburg, Paul von 155, 230
Hirst, Francis 222–223
Hobbs, Talbot 261
Hobhouse, Emily 107–110, *108*
Hobson, John 222
Holman, William 83
Holmes, Sir Charles 209
Horan, George 129, 149, 288
Hororata, HMAT 17–18, 60
Hôtel Beau-Rivage 231
Hôtel du Chateau 231
Houlihan, John Vincent 180
House, Edward 75–76, 80, 83–84, *84*, 157, 159, 269, 282
Howard, Roy 129
Hugenberg, Alfred 190
Hughes, William Morris 'Billy'
    abuses MacDonald in public speeches 140

anti-German tirades by 70–72
appointed to Economic Conference 102–103
argues for death penalty 211
attacks Wilson's Peace Without Victory speech 192
becomes prime minister 70
criticised by *Barrier Daily Truth* 137–138
criticises opponents of war 146
criticises striking miners 83
departs for London 70
helps plan Paris Peace Conference 266
holds first referendum on conscription 6, 44, 133–134, 141–142, 146, 149, 205–206, 293
holds second referendum on conscription 239–240
imposes heavy censorship 239–241
keeps Australians in the dark re war aims 238–241
leaves ALP after referendum defeat 206
Montagu criticises hypocrisy of 267
pleads for more volunteers 61
portrait of 7
pressured to allow death penalty 211–212
promotes trade war 192
racism of 134
rails against Brest-Litovsk Treaty 244
rails against Lansdowne's peace proposal 222
rails against peace 191–192
reject German Peace Note 160–161
scolded in Parliament 152
stifles anti-war dissent 207, 239–242
vindictiveness towards Germany 269–272
visits 13th Infantry Brigade 253
wins 1917 election 191, 211
Hungary 126
Hurdcott Camp 265, 272
Hyde, Captain 260
Hyman, Arthur 210

I

Illger, Fred 250, 254
Imbros 51
Imperiali, Guglielmo 57
imperialism xix, 24, 29, 47, 52–54, 60, 87–88, 102, 173, 188, 195, 228, 238, 272, 282
Independent Labour Party (UK) 78, 128, 138, 140, 166
Independent Socialist Party of Germany (USPD) 207
India 60, 82

Industrial Workers of the World 207
influenza pandemic 252, 270
Inter-Allied Economic Conference 102–103
International Congress of Women 76, *77–78*
internationalism 29, 42, 173, 178, 195, 240
Iraq 48–49
Irish Easter Rising 71
Irish Home Rule 27
Irwin, Lieutenant 260
Italy 54, 57–60, 68, 96, 104, 156–157, 230–231, 238, 242
Ivernia, HMT 99–100

J

Jagow, Gottlieb von 108–109, *109*, 110
Japan 54, 172, 242, 244
Jeffery, Keith 281–282
John Bull 140
Jordan 96

K

Karl I, Emperor 231, *232*
Keighley by-election 223
Kelly, Fred 113
Kempton Park 184
Kerr, Philip 233
Kienthal 84, 86
King, George 100
King's Regulations and Orders for the Army (UK) 8, 128, 174–175, 183
Kipling, Rudyard 65
Kitchener's Army 2
Knight, Cecil Tribe 179
Königin Luise (ship) 272
Kornilov, Lavr 212
Kühlmann, Richard von 215, *216*, 217–218, 234, 282
Kut 71

L

Labor's Volunteer Army for Home Defence 133–134, 137
Labour Leader (UK) 128, 166, 239
labour movement 23–31, 38, 44, 82–83, 132, 137, 161, 165, 205–207
Labour Party (UK) 3, 26–27, 71–72, 138, 166, 195, 242

Lade, Raymond F. 253
Lane, Fredrick William 180
Lane, Zebina 10, 25
Lang, Jack 278
Lansdowne, Lord 147–149, *148*, 220–223, 323–329
Lansing Note 270
Lansing, Robert 285
Latvia 244
Lauder, Harry 291
Lausanne-Ouchy 231
Lawson, Henry 183
Le Barque 276
Le Havre 194–195, 198, 204, 264–265
Le Roux 264
lead poisoning 25
League for a New Fatherland (Germany) 78
League for the Rights of Man 78
League of Nations 78, 86, 155, 159, 168, 222, 230, 268, 270
League to Enforce Peace (US) 86
Leeds Convention 207
Lees Smith, Bert 147
Left Bank of the Rhine Agreement 172, 228
Leipnik, Ferdinand 232
Lemnos 55
Lenin, Vladimir 42, 86, 220, 228
Les Attaques 225–227, 245
Lewis, Athol 201, 235, 260
Liberal Party (UK) 30
Liebknecht, Karl 240
Linton, Albert 105
Lithgow 33, 36
Lithuania 244
Livonia 244
Lloyd George, David
　abandons Lord Lansdowne 222
　accused of neglecting naval defence 30
　attends Paris Peace Conference 267, 271
　challenged by Lord Lansdowne 148–149
　challenged by US entry into war 178
　claims war is a fight for democracy 284
　criticised by Ryan in letter to MacDonald 5–6, 145–146
　discusses peace offer with French 216
　exploits victory by calling election 266, 270
　keen for victory at any cost 233–234
　lack of sympathy for working class 291–292
　'Make-the-Germans-Pay' campaign 266
　negotiates with Karl I 231
　portrait of 5
　promises not to seek indemnity from Germany 269–270
　proposes keeping Germany's peace offer secret 215
　publicly denounced by Hughes 269
　rebadges himself as a moderate 229
　rejects American Peace Note 157–159, 162–163, 165
　rejects German Peace Note 157, 165
　rejects House's peace offer 84
　rejects mediation in interview 129–130, 142–143
　replaces Asquith as prime minister 184–185
　resumes hard line on war aims 230
　sacks Henderson 195, 197
　scolded by Ryan at court martial 204–205
　sends telegram to Hughes 160–161
　shouted down by angry workers 128
　sings at Welsh Eisteddfod 146
　spurns Wilson's offer to mediate 5–6, 129
　takes assent of Australia for granted 161
Lockett, Jack 120–121, 149, 292
London 127
Loreburn, Lord 79, 222
Ludendorff, Erich 154–155, 230
Ludgershall 131
Lusitania (ship) 76

M

MacDonald, David 138, 192
MacDonald, James Ramsay 1, 3–4, *4*, 6, 13, 26–27, 104, 128, 138–141, 143–144, 147, 240
MacDonald, Margaret 26–27, 138
Maclean, John 128
Magna Carta 174
malnutrition 102, 270
Mance, Charlie 291
Manchester Guardian (UK) 228, 238–239, 242
Manchester Unity Independent Order of Odd Fellows (IOOF) 17, 23
Mann, Leonard 65
Mann, Tom 28–31
Manning, Frederick 112, 179, 281
The Manual of Military Law (UK) 8, 174–175, 183
March, B.C. 204
March Revolution, Russia 170–172, 188–189, 192, 195, 205, 207
Maria Christina, Queen 231
Marling, Sir Charles 52
Marne, battle of the 108

Marseille 99–100
Mason, Robert 223
Massingham, Henry 159
Masterman, Charles 68–69
Mathews, James 160
Matringhem 199
Max, Prince of Baden 252, 266
McCay, James Whiteside 182, 186
McDonald, Murdoch 277
McDonald, Sarah (née MacPherson) 277
McMahon-Hussein Correspondence 69
Meaney, Neville 161
Mediterranean Expeditionary Force 89
Mensdorff, Count Albert von 233
Menzies, James Anthony 253
Mercer, Henry 46
Meterin 101
Michaelis, Georg 189
Middle East 47–48
Miliades, HMAT 74–75, 89, 91
Militarism and Anti-Militarism (Liebknecht) 240
military law 174–175
Milner, Lord 72, 158, *158*, 188
Mine Managers' Association 25, 277
mining industry, Broken Hill 25–31, 39–40
Molony, Frank 114, 199, 219, 235, 250–251, 275
Monash, John 201, 212, 235, 259
Mond, Henry 265
Montagu, Edwin 266–267
Montreuil 212
Moonta Mines 10–12
Moray Golf Club 143
Morocco 88, 191, 271
Morrow, Edgar 113, 129, 152
Morton, Ernest 249, 290
Mosul 60–61, 245
Mottram, R.H. 106, 194
Moulden, Arnold Meredith 253, 261
Mouquet Farm 2, 122
Mudie, Beatrice *20*
Mudie, Edward 21
Mudie, Elizabeth Martin 21
Mudie, James Ramsay 13, 17, 19–23, *20*, 31, 40–41, 91, 116, *117*, 121, 126, 166, 274
Mudie, Margaret Nicholas (née Couch) *11*, 12–13, *20*, 21–23, *117*
Mudie, Ruby *20*
Mudros 57
Murdoch, Keith 70, 284
Murray, Sir Archibald 94
Murray, Gilbert 222
Musica Viva 279

N

Namur 264
Nationalist Party (Australia) 191, 206, 239, 242
Neutral Conference for Continuous Mediation 81, *81*
Neuve-Chapelle, battle of 105
New Army 2
New Hebrides 54
New South Wales State Parliament 26, 29
New York Times 228, 239
New Zealand 54
Newhaven (ship) 116
Newton, Lord 189, 233–234
Nicholas II, Tsar 49, 170–171, *171*
Nixon, Stan 250
Northcliffe, Lord 70, 71, 102, 129–130, 143–144, 222

O

O'Dowd, Bernard 24
oil 52–53, 60–62, 245
Oliphant, Lancelot 96
Operation Michael 230
Opium War 289
Orlando, Vittorio 267
Oscar II (ship) 80–81
Ottoman Empire xix, 17, 47–50, 59–60, 71, 87–88, 95–96, 159, 232–233, 238, 244
Outhwaite, Len 80, 151

P

pacifists 207
Paget, Sir Ralph 231–232
Paget, Lady Walburga 231–232
Painlevé, Paul 21, 216
Palestine 53, 96
Palmer, Jesse 73
Pankhurst, Sylvia 222
Papal Note 195–197, 207
Paris Economic Conference 103
Paris Peace Conference 266, 270
Paris Resolutions 103–104, 168, 229
Parkes, Sir Henry 10
partition 232–233
Passchendaele 114, 192, 197, 218, 222, 235, 285
peace activism 75–81, *77–78, 81*, 107–108, 140, 241
peace negotiations
    America offers Peace Note 154, 157–160, 162–163, 165

between Britain and Austria 232–233
British Anglicans hold aloof from 233
Caillaux presses for 191
Central Organisation for a Durable Peace 78
feasibility of a negotiated peace 281–284
between France and Germany 231–232
German Catholic Centre Party proposes 189–190
Germany applies for armistice 252
Germany makes second peace offer 215–218
Germany offers Peace Note 154–157, 162–163, 165
House-Grey Memorandum 83–84
Hughes rails against 191–192
International Congress of Women 76–78, 77–78
Lansdowne urges Lloyd George to consider 148–149, 323–326
Pope Benedict issues Vatican Note 195–197
Russia proposes 188–189, 228
the Sixtus affair 231
Stockholm peace conference 191–192, 195, 208
summary of lost opportunities for 306–307
Union of Democratic Control (UK) 78, 140, 157, 240
willingness of Germany to negotiate 234–235
Wilson issues Fourteen Points 229–230
Wilson offers to mediate 83
Peace Ship 80–81
Pearce, George 209, 211–212, 239–241, 262
Penna, Reuben, P. 257
Perham Down 1–3, 6, 91, 129–131, 138, 141, 153, 166, 170, 177, 182, 184–186
Persia 51–53
Perth 14–15, 36, 41–42
Petrograd 170–172
Picquigny 250
Plumer, Sir Hubert 212
Pokrovsky, Nikolai 156
Poland 229, 244
Police Gazette 186
Ponsonby, Arthur 80, *80*
Port Pirie 31
Portugal 54
Pozières 2, 4, 113, 116, *134*, 144–145, 286
Price, Robert 226
Primitive Methodist Church 11, 13, 22
prisoners of war 189, 226–227, 233–234, 246, 291
Progressive People's Party (Germany) 189

propaganda 68–69, *134–135*, 141–142, 144–145, 149, 196, 240, 242–243
protectionism 102–103, 168, 173, 229
Provence 100
PTSD *see* shell shock
Purvis, William James 67

Q

Qingdao 252

R

racism 24, 29, 134, 253
Ralstoon, W.A. 212
Randwick Tramsheds 206
Rawlinson, Henry Seymour 212
referendums, on conscription 6, 44, 133–134, 137, 141–142, 149, 165, 205–206, 213, 239–240, 293
Reichstag *155*
Remarque, Erich Maria 246
Resch, Emil 277
Returned Soldiers' League 277
Reverta, Nikolaus 231
Rhineland 168, 172, 238
Ribot, Alexander 216, *217*, 231
Richardson, Bill 263
Ridley, John 187, 209
Rigby, Lieutenant Colonel 237
Riter, Beatrice Mary ('Beatie') 11–13
Riter, Frederick 11–12
River Somme 250
Rivery 254
Robertson, Sir William 217, 284
Romania 126, 154
Romanov regime 170–171
Romberg, Baron von 283
Rosenthal, Sir Charles 209, 212
Rosières-en-Santerre 245
Ross, Arthur M. 92, 100, 116, 122, 187, 286
Royal Australian Navy 31
Royal Dutch Shell 60
Royal Navy 101–102
Royal Prince Alfred Hospital, Sydney 277
Runciman, Walter 102
Russell, Bertrand 222
Russia
  approves Sykes-Picot Agreement 95
  Bolshevik Revolution 177–178, 220, 238, 243–244, 284

keen to take Ottoman Empire territories 48–53, 96, 104
Left Bank of the Rhine Agreement 172, 228
March Revolution 170–172, 188–189, 192, 195, 205, 207
mobilises against Austria-Hungary and Germany 34
objectives in Great War 238, 242
publishes secret agreements 228
rejects German Peace Note 156
secret diplomacy of 244
shut off from world oil markets 60
signs armistice with Central Powers 228
signs Treaty of London 59
at Stockholm conference 191, 196
Straits and Persia Agreement 51–52, 61, 104, 152, 228, 238, 242, 308–310
vision of a Greater Serbia 58
Ryan, Annie Kathleen 41
Ryan, Edward James ('Ted')
  birth and childhood 12–13, 19–21, *21*, 23
  charged with AWL 123, 152, 166, 170, 184–185, 254–255, 286
  charged with desertion 123, 179–184, 198–199, 286
  combative spirit 19
  condemns war xvii
  convalesces at Byfleet 125–126
  courts martial of xvii, xviii, 170, 173–177, 179–183, 199–205, *202–203*, 207–210, 252–256, 286, 300, 302–303
  death 279–280
  declines offer to join military police 90, 92
  deserts for second time 249–250
  enlists in army 13–16, 18, 41–42
  experience of the war 275
  faces battle for first time 110–111
  goes AWOL from Perham Down 151–153
  has death sentence commuted 219–220
  has prison sentence suspended 237, 245
  held in detention for six weeks 170
  imprisoned after court martial 219–220
  life after the war 277–280
  marries Marie McDonald 277–278
  member of trade union band 33
  moral conundrum faced by 288
  in No. 7 Military Prison, Les Attaques 225–228
  in No. 10 Military Prison, Dunkirk 225, 227
  outlines objections to war at court martial *202–203*, 204–205
  payment of as a soldier 41, 153, 177, 181–182, 184, 220, 245, 254–256, 265, 274
  portraits of vi, xx, *18*, 97–98
  punishment of 257–258
  receives letters from home 137, 185
  refuses order from officer 67–68
  released from Punishment Compound 264
  returns to Australia 265, 272–274
  returns to battalion after peace declared 264–265
  returns to front after being wounded 116
  returns to front after suspended sentence 238, 245–246
  returns to Perham Down after convalescence 129–131, 151
  sent back to France to fight 187, 192–193
  sentenced to death 208–210, 213–215
  suffers shell shock 119, 121–123, 151, 286
  summary of service record 301–303
  trains at Blackboy Hill camp 65–68
  trains in Egypt 7, 83, 88–94, 97–98
  trains near Sailly-sur-la-Lys 101
  transferred to 13th Infantry Draft at Perham 153
  travels from Marseille to the front 100–101
  travels to Scotland and London on leave 126–129
  voyage from Fremantle to Suez 73–75, 81–82
  voyage to Marseille 99–100
  walks away from post at Ypres 193–194, 197
  wounded for a second time 116–117, 286
  wounded near Fleurbaix 1, 111–113, 286
  writes letter to MacDonald denouncing war 3–8, 13, 137, *139*, 141, 143–147, 165, 265, 288, 297–299
  writes statement to his court martial 288, 300
  writes to uncle re bombardment 122
Ryan, Edward James Snr 9–10, *10*, 12–13, 26
Ryan, Elizabeth Margaret ('Beth') 278–280
Ryan, Elizabeth Martin (née Couch, née Riter) 10–13, *11*
Ryan, Ellen (née King) ('Nell') 276
Ryan, Elsie 276
Ryan, Ernest 276
Ryan, Helen 276, 279
Ryan, Henry Martin ('Harry')
  arrives in Egypt with 13th Battalion 45
  birth and childhood 12, *18*, 20
  death 276
  enlists in army 16, *16*, 36, 41
  experience of the war 275–276
  at Gallipoli 55–56
  marries Rose in Cairo 90

masquerades as brother to enlist 16, 276
moves to Lithgow 33
as an NCO in Cairo 56
returns to Australia 276
serves in military police 90, 92
spends Christmas at sea 75
visits Adelaide in 1939 276
Ryan, Jack 276
Ryan, Mary 276, 279
Ryan, Mary Cameron (née McDonald) ('Marie') 277, 279–280
Ryan, Rose 90, 275–276, 280
Ryan, Ross Marlen 278–279
Ryan, Ruby Elizabeth 90, 275–276
Ryan, Thomas Pearce Couch ('Tom')
  in the 11th Battalion 68
  awarded Military Medal 276–277
  birth and childhood 12–13, *18*, 20
  convalesces in London 89
  death 276–277
  in Egypt 89
  enlists in army 17, *18*, 36, 41, 45–46
  evacuated on hospital ship 57
  experience of the war 275–277
  at Gallipoli 56–57, 60
  goes AWOL 276
  leaves Egypt for France 89
  life after the war 276–277, 279
  moves to Perth 33
  trains at Blackboy Hill camp 66
  wounded and evacuated to England 116, 131, 276
Ryan, T.J. 211

S

Saarland 168, 172
Sailly-sur-la-Lys 101
Salandra, Antonio 58
Samoa 54
Sargent, John Singer 243
Sassoon, Siegfried 147
Sazonov, Sergei 50, *51*
Scotland 126–128, 166–167
Scott, Roy Alexander 180
Scullin, James 26
The Secret Treaties (Cock) 240
the 'secret war' xviii
Sedition Act (US) 173
Selborne, Lord 284
Sender, Toni 269
Sennett, Harry 225–226

Serapeum 89, 92, 94, 99
Serbia 58, 68–69, 231
Shaw, Harry E. 153
shell shock 1, 3, 116, 118–123, 151, 193, 253, 261–262, 274
Simon, Sir John 222
Sinclair-Maclagan, Ewen 175–176, 209
Sixtus affair 231
Sixtus, Prince of Bourbon-Parma 231
Smout, Ted 121
Smuts, Jan 233–234
social class 291–292
social democracy 25–26
Social Democratic Party (Germany) 79, 189
Social Democratic Party (Sweden) 191
socialism 27, 42, 79, 84–85, 191, 195, 228
Söderblom, Nathan 233
Somaliland 54
Somme, battle of 2, 86, 101, 105, 107, 110–111, 113, 122–123
Sonnino, Baron Sidney 57–58, 156, *156*
South Africa 54
South, F. 170
'spheres of interest' 52
Sri Lanka 81–82
St Jean de Maurienne 231
Stalinism 154
Standard Oil 60
Stanley, Venetia 47
Steenwerck 235
Stevenson, Frances 292
Stockholm 81, 191
Stockholm Conference 191–192, 195, 208
Straits and Persia Agreement 51–52, 61, 104, 152, 228, 238, 242, 308–310
strikes 24–25, 28, 31, 83, 178, 206–207
Sudan 87
Suez 82, 87, 89, 91
Suez Canal 94
suffragettes 237
Supreme War Council 230
Suvla 62
Swanwick, Helena 222
Switzerland 42
Sykes, Sir Mark 95–97
Sykes-Picot Agreement 95–97, 104
Syria 53, 96
Széchényi, Count Ludwig 232

T

Talty, Thomas 99, 281, 286, 292–293
Tardieu, André 196
Tarrant, Jack 149, 240
Taylorism 207
Teheran 53
Tel-el-Kebir 91–92
Tereshchenko, Mikhail 188–189
The Hague 76, 81, 189, 232–234
theatre 127
Thomas, Arthur 111, 162, 165, 223, 258
Thomas, Dylan 51
Thomas, Josiah 26
Tidworth 170, 186
Tillett, Ben 24, 28
The Times 70, 130
tinnitus 193
Togoland 54
Tomlinson, H.M. 105
Town, Charles 204
Townley, Sir Walter 232
trade unions 19, 23–31, 38, 82–83, 132, 207
Trades and Labour Council, Sydney 241
train hijack, Broken Hill 17
Transylvania 126
Treaty of London 57, 59–61, 104, 196, 228, 231, 238, 314–322
Treaty of Versailles 244, 268–272, *271*
trench warfare 2, 56–57, 106, 110–111
Trepov, Alexander 152
Trevalyan, Charles v, 80, *80*
Tribe, Ken Wilberforce 279
Trotsky, Leon 42, *43*, 228, 240
Turkey 47–49, 52, 68, 88, 96, 232, 252
Turkish Petroleum Company 60

U

Ukraine 244
Ulysses, HMAT 45, 75
unemployment 39–42, 73
Union of Democratic Control (UK) 78, 140, 157, 240
United Kingdom *see* Britain
United States
 enters the Great War 170, 172–173, 178, 205, 283
 introduces conscription 173
 issues Peace Note 157–160, 162–163, 167–168
 lends money to Entente Powers 173
 offers to mediate in war 35, 49, 83–84, 86, 129, 157–161, 167–170
 refuses to allow socialists to attend conference 191
 refuses to support peace initiatives 196, 208
 remains neutral 5
 Senate inquiry into military justice 237
 supports Japanese invasion of Russia 244
 Wilson's Fourteen Points 191, 229–230, 241, 243, 252, 269, 271
Unlawful Associations Act 1916 207
Uppsala 233
Urabi, Ahmed 91

V

van der Lancken, Oscar 231
Vendroux 225–227
Verdun 86, 197
Versailles 230
Versailles Declaration 230
Versailles Treaty 244, 268–272, *271*
Vitoria, Franciso de 289
Vladivostok 244

W

Wadwe, Sir Charles 29
Wahroonga 278
Walker, H.B 212
Walker, John J.A. 175
Walpole, Hugh 114
War Precautions Act 1914-1916 (Australia) 70, 207, 211, 239
Waterhouse, Jabez 153, 182
Watt, William 213
Weatherhead, Frank 106, 114, 193, 251
Weatherhead, Sister Hope 121
Weaver, Charles 14, 65
Webster, Sir Francis 166–167
Weimar Republic 268
West, Arthur Graeme 290
Western Australia 33
Western Front 99
Weston, Philip 203, 208
Wheen, Arthur 106, 119, 193, 246
White Australia policy 24, 29, 134, 253, 272
White Rocks 17
Whitham, John 255
Wilson, Woodrow
 attends Paris Peace Conference 266, *267*, *271*
 British oppose progressive ideals of 267
 criticises Berlin 196–197

    declares US entry into war 172–173
    exchanges cables with Prince Max 252
    gains agreement to set up League of
        Nations 268
    gives Peace Without Victory speech
        169–170, 192, 208
    House negotiates on behalf of 83, *84*
    issues Peace Note 157–163, 167–168
    offers to mediate 5, 35, 49, 86
    plans for peace 270
    preference for 'lone-wolf' diplomacy 80
    proposes Fourteen Points 191, 229–230, 241,
        243, 252, 269, 271
    puts forward internationalist ideals 178
    refuses to support peace initiatives 196
Wiltshire, Aubrey 220, 246, 251
Wisdom, E.A. 212
Wobblies 207
Wolseley, Lord 91
working class 291–292
World War I *see* Great War
Wright, Jabez 26

Y

YMCA 3
Ypres, 3rd battle for 114, 192, 197, 215, 218, 235

Z

Zaharoff, Basil 233
Zangwill, Israel 243
Zeman, Z.A.B. 157
Zimmerwald Manifesto 42–43
Zinoviev, Gregory 86
Zita, Empress 231

Lightning Source UK Ltd.
Milton Keynes UK
UKHW051654130721
387098UK00006B/1208